the psychology of human learning, the measurement of individual differences in mental ability and the genetic and environmental causes of group differences in intelligence. In the areas of his research interest he has published over 50 articles, papers, and books. His most recent books were: *Twins: Black and White* (1980) and *Human Variation: The Biopsychology of Age, Race, and Sex* which was co-edited with Clyde Noble and Nathaniel Weyl and published by Academic Press (1978).

Dr. Frank C. J. McGurk became interested in racial differences in intelligence in 1938 when, among other things, he noticed that a very large percentage of black children who were passing through the Richmond (Va.) juvenile courts were mentally retarded when they were evaluated on the published test norms. His first publication on black-white mental test differences appeared in 1943. He followed this experience with service in a black Special Training Unit of the Army, and through subsequent graduate training. His doctoral dissertation became the first objective test of the so-called Culture Hypothesis of Racial Differences in Intelligence. He has published some fifteen papers in the same field.

Dr. McGurk's training was done at the University of Pennsylvania in Philadelphia, and at the Catholic University of America, in Washington, D.C. He was School Psychologist in Pennsylvania, Approved Mental Examiner in Virginia, and a Licensed Psychologist in Alabama.

After forty years of clinical practice and college teaching (Lehigh University, the U.S. Military Academy at West Point, Villanova University, and the University of Montevallo) he is now retired, and lives in Sun City Center, Florida.

The Testing
of
Negro Intelligence

The Testing
of
Negro Intelligence

Edited by

R. Travis Osborne
and
Frank C. J. McGurk

VOLUME 2

The Foundation for Human Understanding
Athens, Georgia

International Standard Book Number 0–936396–02–4.

To the memory of Audrey M. Shuey

Contents

List of Tables. ix

List of Figures xi

Preface. xiii

I   Introduction 1
    R. Travis Osborne

II   Preschool Children. 5
    Frank C. J. McGurk

III   School Children 31
    Frank C. J. McGurk

IV   High School Students 100
    Frank C. J. McGurk

V   College Students. 109
    R. Travis Osborne

VI   Adults not in College 126
    R. Travis Osborne

VII   Delinquents 139
    R. Travis Osborne

VIII   Special Populations. 150
    R. Travis Osborne

IX   Race of Examiner Effects and the Validity of Intelligence
    Tests 158
    W. G. Graziano, P. E. Varca, and J. Levy

    X Doctoral Dissertations. 189
          R. Travis Osborne

   XI National Longitudinal Study of the High School Class of
       1972: An Analysis of Sub-population Differences. . . . 249
          R. Travis Osborne

  XII College Admissions: A 21-year Analysis of CEEB
       Scholastic Aptitude Test 277
          R. Travis Osborne

 XIII Summary and Conclusions 290
          R. Travis Osborne and Frank C. J. McGurk

       Appendixes 298
       References. 323
       Annotated Bibliography 349
       Author Index. 385
       Subject Index. 393

List of Tables

X–A   Dissertations Involving Preschool Pupils   191
X–B   Dissertations Involving School Children   193
X–C   Dissertations Involving High School Students   197
X–D   Dissertations Involving College Students   198
X–E   Dissertations Involving Adults not in College   199
X–F   Dissertations Involving Delinquents or Criminals   200
XI–A   States within each Region and Corresponding Percentages of Blacks and Whites   252
XI–B   Distribution of U.S. White Population   253
XI–C   Distribution of U.S. Black Population   253
XI–D   Analysis of Variance: The Effects of Race, Sex, Socioeconomic Status, and Geographic Region on Means of Various Ability and Achievement Measures   256
XI–E   Means and Standard Deviations of Measures of Ability and Achievement: For Total Group and By Sex   257
XI–F   Means and Standard Deviations of Measures of Ability and Achievement: By Race   260
XI–G   Means and Standard Deviations of Measures of Ability and Achievement: By Race and Socioeconomic Level   262
XI–H   Differences in Black and White Pupils in Ability and Achievement Scores by Socioeconomic Levels   263
XI–I   Means and Standard Deviations of Measures of Ability and Achievement: By Race and Geographic Region of the United States   266

XI–J   Differences Between Black and White Pupils in Ability
        and Achievement Scores by Geographic Region of the
        United States   268
XI–K   Correlations between Various Measures of Ability and
        Achievement and Certain Indexes of Degree of Pupil and
        Teacher Integration   269
XI–L   Means and Standard Deviations of Various Ability and
        Achievement Tests Administered at Twelfth-Grade Level:
        By Race and Degree of Teacher Integration in High
        School   270
XI–M   Differences Between Black and White Pupils on Ability
        and Achievement Tests Administered at Twelfth-Grade
        Level: By Degree of Teacher Integration in High School   272
XI–N   Means and Standard Deviations of Various Ability and
        Achievement Tests Administered at Twelfth-Grade Level:
        By Race and Degree of Pupil Integration in Twelfth Grade   273
XI–O   Differences Between Black and White Pupils on Ability
        and Achievement Tests Administered at Twelfth-Grade
        Level: By Degree of Pupil Integration in Twelfth Grade   274
XII–A   University System of Georgia Minority and Total
        Enrollments   281
XII–B   Rank Order Correlations between SAT Scores and
        Percent Blacks for Four Groups   288

List of Figures

XI–1   Distribution of White-Black score differences (in standard
        deviation equivalents) for sixteen subgroups on each of
        ten tests of ability or achievement.   275

XII–1   Mean SAT Verbal scores for white and black students
        of the University System of Georgia, 1957–1977.   282

XII–2   Mean SAT Mathematics scores for white and black
        students of the University System of Georgia, 1957–1977.   284

XII–3   Mean SAT Verbal scores for students of Georgia Institute
        of Technology and the University of Georgia, 1957–1977.   285

XII–4   Mean SAT Mathematics scores for students of Georgia
        Institute of Technology and the University of Georgia,
        1957–1977.   286

XII–5   Mean SAT scores (national norms), 1957–1977.   287

Preface

Because *The Testing of Negro Intelligence* has proved to be so controversial and because it is probably one of the most universally cited references on testing Negro intelligence and because it is now out of print, we believe the series, begun by Professor Audrey Shuey in 1958, should be continued. Graduate students and investigators planning research, school authorities evaluating test batteries, and industrial psychologists selecting employment tests will find in Volume II the most comprehensive review of the relevant studies of testing Negro intelligence.

The most hostile critics of the previous editions found the tables of numbers objectionable, saying only the New York telephone book contains more numbers than Shuey's survey. The implication is that numbers bear bad news and should be exorcised. In Volume II, tables have been reduced to the essential minimum. However, measures of central tendency, variability, and confidence levels have been retained and incorporated into the text.

The critic who likened the 2nd Edition to the telephone directory also complained that because of Dr. Shuey's vast system of distribution, her writings had great influence on the thinking and value systems of thousands who teach; who select and edit the news; and who play major roles in shaping public policy. This is simply not the case. Professor Shuey had no system for vast distribution of her book. In fact, it was rejected by name publishers, printed privately, and distributed personally by the author. The critic is right about Professor Shuey's influence; *The Testing of Negro Intelligence* is recognized for its thoroughness and scholarship.

Despite the silent treatment of Dr. Shuey's work by reviewers, after 15 years, according to one authority, it remains the most comprehensive review of relevant studies. To continue Dr. Shuey's important work is our purpose in preparing this book.

I

Introduction

R. Travis Osborne

After completing a monograph on "Own-race preference and self-esteem in young Negroid and Caucasoid children" in late 1977, Audrey Shuey returned to work on Volume 2 of *The Testing of Negro Intelligence*. As one of several friends who encouraged her to undertake the task, I agreed to assist her in any way I could. Because I had access to a large library, she frequently asked me to locate articles and unpublished dissertations. Once, after she received a long list of articles I had found for her, she called to express her appreciation. Just before she said goodbye, she asked me if I would finish Volume 2 if something were to prevent her from completing the task. I knew Audrey had been ill the previous winter, but recently she seemed to have fully recovered and was back at work. I had no reason to suspect that anything would happen to her; certainly nothing in our conversation led me to believe that Audrey Shuey would be dead within a few days of our talk.

Before her death, Audrey had told the executor of her estate of our conversation. Accordingly she left instructions that her notes, articles, and files be given to me. After examining the voluminous material she had gathered over the past thirteen years, I realized I was going to need help to finish Audrey's work. I thought of Frank McGurk, one of Audrey's old friends who, a decade before Jensen's 1969 *Harvard Educational Review* article, had published an article with essentially the same conclusions as "How Much Can We Boost IQ and Scholastic Achievement?" Frank needed little persuasion to co-edit the new book with me.

An examination of Audrey's files on testing Negro intelligence published since 1966, the date of the 2nd Edition, and our own personal files produced twice the number of articles in the 2nd Edition. Also, there were several large comprehensive investigations involving more subjects than appeared in all of the studies of the 1966 Edition combined.

It was obvious the project would be unmanageable if we attempted to follow the same format of the first two editions. Our overall goal,

1

however, has remained the same as stated in Chapter I of Dr. Shuey's pioneering work.

It is not the purpose of this book to prove that Negroes are socially, morally, or intellectually inferior to whites; nor is its purpose to demonstrate that Negroes are the equal of or are superior to whites in these several characteristics. Rather, it is the intention of the writer to convey with some degree of clarity and order the results of many years of research on one aspect of Negro behavior and to assess objectively the ever-growing literature on this subject.

A meaningful review of research, obviously, requires not only some evaluation and interpretation of individual studies but an organization of them into various significant categories and a presentation of conclusions—tentative or final. In the area of group comparisons, such as those between Negroes and whites, the interpretations and conclusions of the author are often of great importance to the reader as he relates them to himself, his family, and to larger groups with whom he identifies. If they are found to support his previously-formed attitudes on the subject the book and author are immediately given his approval. If they are in opposition to his attitudes he may reject the book by reading no further; however, if he does continue with it he frequently becomes depressed, annoyed, or outraged, the quality and intensity of the emotion varying, among other things, in proportion to the amount of research presented and the recognized logic of the analyses.

The author, like the reader, is often deeply concerned with the outcome of his research, and would generally find it all to the good if he could knock the props from under old prejudices. But at the same time he is aware that as a scientist he must proceed without wishful thinking, without undue concern for his theoretical interpretations, and without awe of prevalent opinion—whether it be found in the courts, in the pulpit, or in the press. Aware of his responsibilities, he must exercise his freedom to interpret research in fields where he presumes himself to be expert and assume that the reader can bear with him the burden of such interpretation. . . .

This book might properly be called *A Comparative Study of the Intelligence of American Negroes and Whites,* since there are continuous references to the scores earned by white groups throughout. Wherever experimenters tested both Negroes and whites comparable statistics have been included; where only Negro groups were examined, there are references to norms that have been derived mainly from standardization on white groups. But because specific studies made on whites alone have not been included, as they were when

Negroes were tested, the writer has preferred to place the emphasis upon *Negro* intelligence in the title.

We have employed the terms *Negro* and *colored* interchangeably and have occasionally used the expression *race* or *racial group* when referring to the Negro subjects examined. Probably all social psychologists have been alerted to the fact that the American Negro does not represent a pure racial group but rather one with a predominance of African ancestry yet they frequently allude to American Negroes and whites as races. The justification for this lies, no doubt, in the fact that except for small groups of transitional types, the American Negro constitutes a recognizable and clearly defined group, the criterion of membership in which group being that of more-or-less African ancestry.

Our continuation of Professor Shuey's work is called *The Testing of Negro Intelligence,* Volume 2. Unlike a revised text book or manual, it contains only new material published between January, 1966, and December, 1979, plus some references inadvertently omitted from the 2nd Edition and a few from the 1980's.

Tests referred to throughout this book are listed by name in Appendix A and identified by Buros Edition and page number. New and original tests are identified by author and publisher.

Volume 2 follows the effective pattern set by Shuey except for a few minor changes. Developmental studies involving only scales, such as the Yale or Gesell schedules, normally administered to young children before age two, are not reviewed in Volume 2 since these scales are somewhat unreliable as measures of intelligence. If a developmental scale is used in conjunction with the Binet or other intelligence tests that are standardized down to age two, results of both tests will be reported in Chapter II, "Preschool Children."

Studies published between 1966 and 1980 that involve primary and elementary school children are reviewed in Chapter III; high school students, Chapter IV; and college students, Chapter V. Shuey combined high school and college students into one chapter, but we believe there is enough new material for separate chapters.

The chapters, "The Armed Forces" and "Veterans and Other Civilians," were omitted from Volume 2 and combined into Chapter VI, "Adults not in College." Shuey's chapters entitled "Deviates" and "Delinquents and Criminals" have been replaced by our Chapter VII, "Delinquents." Miscellaneous articles not elsewhere classified were placed in Chapter VIII, "Special Populations." Chapter IX is called "Race of Examiner Effects and the Validity of Intelligence Tests." Chapter X reviews 89 doctoral dissertations concerned with the testing of Negro intelligence. All dissertations on the subject written between 1966 and 1979–80 were not reviewed. It was decided to omit those with fewer than 20 subjects and those using only the Bender, Rorschach and other tests known to be of limited validity for measuring mental ability. Condensed dissertation reviews follow the general pattern of the first two editions. In some few cases, e.g. Chapter IX, reviewed dissertations may be cited elsewhere in the book. Two original monographs were prepared especially for Volume 2. The first, Chapter XI, is a comprehensive analysis by race, SES, geographic region and degree of school integration of the mental test scores of participants of the Class of 1972 in the National Longitudinal Study (Levinsohn, 1976). The second, Chapter XII, is a 21-year longitudinal analysis of the SAT scores for the 33 units of the University System of Georgia.

Following the pattern set by Audrey Shuey, we have attempted to assemble and review critically the research in the field of Negro intelligence as determined by psychometric tests. Chapter XIII is our summary and conclusions regarding new research published since publication of the 2nd Edition of *The Testing of Negro Intelligence.*

In addition to the usual list of references cited or reviewed, an annotated bibliography of theoretical, conjectural and speculative papers, monographs, and books in the field of testing Negro intelligence has been added to this edition. Since entries in the bibliography are theoretical or speculative rather than experimental, they may not have been reviewed elsewhere in Volume 2. Cited are articles supporting both the environmental and hereditary positions. The supplemental Annotated Bibliography combined with the several hundred references and reviews in this book provide a comprehensive inventory of all significant U.S. research in the field of testing Negro intelligence published between 1965 and 1979–80.

II

Preschool Children

Frank C. J. McGurk

In an attempt to improve the Peabody Picture Vocabulary Test (PPVT) for use with black children, Ali and Costello (1971) modified the PPVT by administering each of the first 70 plates, arranged in random order, to 56 black 4- and 5-year old Chicago East Side Head Start and Day Care Center children, and attempted to motivate the children by praising their responses regardless of the correctness of those responses. The PPVT was administered under standard procedures to 52 black preschool children. The method of selecting the children was not given, but all were of low SES. The authors found a 7.00-point difference in raw score between the standard PPVT scores and the modified PPVT (MPPVT) scores, and concluded that MPPVT was the better test to use with black children. The variability of MPPVT was much smaller than that of PPVT (the SDs were 7.1 and 11.4, respectively). On the same page (p. 89), the authors concluded that the mean difference was the result of their modifications but, at the same time, that it could have occurred by chance. (See also Costello and Ali, 1971.)

In a sample of only 22 white and 28 black 5-year olds, Barclay and Yater (1968) attempted to validate the Wechsler Preschool and Primary Scale of Intelligence (WPPSI) for use with Head Start children. White and black subjects (from St. Louis, Missouri) were matched for sex, residence, and perhaps for Stanford-Binet (S-B) IQ. The mean S-B IQ was 100.90 for each sample. The SD of the white sample was 8.50; of the black sample, 14.80. The white sample was hardly representative of whites. The Full Scale IQ of the WPPSI (SDs in parentheses) was 93.80 (9.30) for whites, and 93.00 (13.00) for blacks. The authors concluded that WPPSI was less suited to black children than S-B because mean S-B IQ was the higher (See Fagan, et al., 1969; Sewell, 1977).

Three studies made use of the same set of black children and are better understood if described together. In two of the studies, the purpose was to show that differences in IQ were social class differences. The first of these studies (Golden and Birns, 1968) described the subjects as 11- to 25-month-old volunteers who were separated into three age groups (Ns in parentheses): a 12 month (66), an 18-month (60), and a 24-month (66) group. Within each age group the children (all black) were described as lowest SES (Group A), middle SES (Group B), and highest SES (Group C). The Cattell Infant Intelligence Scale (CIIS) was administered along with a modification of the Piaget Object Scale (POS). The mean CIIS IQ for the entire set of 192 children was 106.3 (reviewer's computation). No significant differences were found between any pairs of SES groups in any age sample. The authors gave a number of speculative explanations for their failure to find social-class differences between the groups.

In the second study (Golden, Birns, Bridger, and Moss, 1971) 89 of the 18- and 24-month groups from the first article were studied as a new sample. The children, now 3 and 4 years of age, were given the S-B. The specific purpose was to discover when social-class differences (that had not appeared in the first study) did appear. The children were still divided into the same SES groups as before and, in addition, the Hollingshead Index of Social Status was applied to each child. The pattern of findings was thought to support the authors' idea that *racial* differences were social-class differences, although N for some of the Hollingshead classes was as small as 5, and none was greater than 23. Mean S-B IQ for the entire 89 children was 104.37 (reviewer's computation). The authors concluded that social-class differences in IQ did not appear until the age of 3. A number of environmentally-oriented explanations were given.

In the final study of this trilogy (Birns and Golden, 1972), the authors attempted to demonstrate that, while no continuity in mental growth could be shown for IQ, continuity could be shown for personality traits. The authors restudied the data of some of the children of the former 18- and 24-month groups, but about this the authors were very hazy. Much of the present article repeated Golden, Birns, Bridger, and Moss, 1971. It was not clear when the Personality Rating Scale (PRS) had been given to some of the children, but correlation coefficients between PRS and CIIS, and PRS and S-B were reported. N was not clearly stated, but it was not greater than 35. How the children were selected was also unclear. The reported coefficients for the 18-month group ranged from −.09 to .33 for CIIS vs. PRS, and between −.11 and .29 for the S-B vs. PRS. For the 24-month group, the CIIS vs. PRS correlations ranged between −.29 and .52, and the range of the S-B vs. PRS coefficients was −.26 to .53. The authors concluded that continuity of intellectual growth with age could be predicted from the amount of pleasure a child obtained from taking a test.

The purpose of the Blatt and Garfunkel study (1967) was to demonstrate that school intervention programs would reduce the likelihood of mental retardation among disadvantaged children. Apparently, it was originally planned to select only children who had at least one mentally-retarded parent and a school-retarded sibling, but the authors finally decided on 60 black children who lived in a deprived, high-delinquency area not otherwise identified. Children with central nervous pathology were eliminated. The authors finally described their subjects as ordinary Head Start children. The sample was divided ". . . by stratified random assignment . . ." (p. 602) into 2 experimental groups and a control group. Stratification seems to have meant equating the groups for IQ on S-B, age, and sex. Whether there were 20 children in each group was not given. Between May, 1962, and May, 1965, the S-B, the PPVT, the Illinois Test of Psycholinguistic Ability (ITPA) and the Vineland Social Maturity Scale (VSMS) were administered to the experimental groups, but on no stated schedule. What happened to the control group was not stated, and neither was the treatment program. Oddly, the authors claimed that ". . . although execution was imperfect, an experimental design was maintained" (p. 603). No data were given. There were several different restatements of the experimental hypothesis. When the authors obtained disappointing findings, they explained that the tests were poor, child growth created unstable environments, the intervention program was either inadequate or tried at the wrong time in the lives of the children, and the sample was intellectually too high grade.

Bradley, Caldwell, and Elardo (1977) were interested in showing that "environmental process measures" were more predictive of IQ than the usual SES measures. "Environmental process" was defined by a specially-constructed Home Inventory (HOME) which was administered to the parents of 37 white and 68 black children when the children were 24 months of age. The S-B was administered to the children when they were age 3. Four SES variables were obtained for each child, also. How the children were selected, and when and where the study was done, were not given. The mean S-B IQ for the white children, according to this reviewer's computations, was (SDs in parentheses) 104.3 (14.5); for the black children 82.7 (15.1). Multiple correlations among IQ and SES and HOME scores were given and these led the authors to conclude that HOME was a better predictor of IQ than was SES. The authors made the erroneous claim that their findings agreed with the conclusions of Scarr and Weinberg that black children, when adopted by white families, scored as highly on IQ tests as adopted white children (see Scarr and Weinberg, 1976, p. 81).

In order to study the importance of play material in the mental growth of young black children, Busse, Ree, Gutride, Alexander, and Powell (1972) studied 123 blacks, aged 3 to 5 years, and enrolled in Head Start programs in Philadelphia, Pennsylvania. Sixty-two of the children became the enriched experimental group, and the other 61 became the control group. The S-B, 5 performance tests from the WPPSI, and 4 subtests of the ITPA were administered pre- and post-treatment to all children. Treatment was, a period of "enrichment" for the experimental children. Nothing was given about the selection of the subjects except that they were from the same residential district. The IQs of the enriched subjects, pre-treatment and post-treatment, were 94.56 and 102.15 for S-B; and 91.65 and 95.48 for WPPSI. The IQs of the control subjects, pre- and post-treatment, were 94.75 and 100.72 for S-B; and 88.97 and 96.59 for WPPSI. For the S-B, the enriched children gained 7.59 points, and the control children gained 5.97 points. The difference was called insignificant. For the WPPSI, the enriched group increased 3.83 points; the control group increased 7.62 points. The change was in the wrong direction. For the ITPA, 3 of the subtests changed in favor of the controls (wrong direction) and only Visual Sequential Memory showed a gain in favor of the enriched group—2.80 points (called significant). No t-statistics were published. The authors concluded that these unexpected findings resulted from teacher-shortcomings, but they did comment that "There can be too much of a good thing" (p. 21).

To evaluate the changes in learning aptitude among average, slow-learning, and mentally-retarded children, Cawley (1968) selected 142 4- to 5-year-old children (90% black) from 3 Head Start centers in a large eastern city. There was no control group. The Detroit Tests of Learning Aptitudes (DTLA) were administered pre- and post-treatment, and the S-B was given pre-treatment. The mean S-B IQ for all children, pre-treatment, was 88.68. Treatment was not described, and no post-treatment data were given. Cawley concluded cautiously that preschool education benefited young children.

Chovan and Hathaway (1970) sought to study the operation of cultural differences in the measurement of intelligence by the deliberate selection of two sets of children, one of which was low SES (blacks), and one of which was called a random sample of middle-class whites. Each set contained 15 children; both groups averaged 69.1 months of age, and all were in public kindergarten in the suburbs of a large North Carolina metropolitan area. The Kahn Intelligence Test (KIT) was given to all the children. The mean IQ for blacks was (SDs in parentheses) 95 (11.1); and for whites, 113 (10.6). The authors concluded that the learning problems of the black child were only partly environmental.

Costello (1970) studied the effects of pre-test, race of examiner, and familiarity of examiner on test scores. Sixty-two black children (49 to 60 months old) from a research nursery school in West Side Chicago, in 1966–7, were randomly assigned to a Pre-test Group or a No Pre-test Group. The S-B, PPVT, and tests of school skills were given to the 38 children in the Pre-test Group. To the 24 children in the No Pre-test Group (controls) only school skills tests were given. The PPVT was given to all children 4 months later, and the S-B, nine months later. With the PPVT, two black examiners tested 29 children, and two white examiners tested 28 children. The examiners were relative strangers to the children. A white psychologist, a complete stranger to the children, tested 27 of them (not identified), and 29 unidentified children were tested by their classroom teachers. No significant effects were found for pre-testing, race of examiner or familiarity of examiner. The author commented that it was "highly probable" that significant effects would have been found had she used another sample of subjects. No reasons for this were given.

Costello and Ali (1971) were interested in the investigation of the reliability and validity of the PPVT, and the reliability only of the Modified Peabody Picture Vocabulary Test (MPPVT). For the reliability study, the PPVT was given twice to 31 black Head Start children with a 2-week interval between tests, and the MPPVT was given twice to 36 black research school children and 31 Head Start children from Chicago West Side. All subjects were 4 to 5½ years old. Test-retest correlation for PPVT was .77; for MPPVT, .86. The authors thought both tests to be stable. For the validity study, the subjects were 60 children who had attended research preschool the preceding year (date not given). Nothing was given about their selection. Validity was defined as the correlation between PPVT and teachers' ratings on speech, scores on the ITPA, the Kohn Competence Scale (KCS), and psychiatric ratings. Mean IQs for the 60 children were given as 84.28 for PPVT and 99.56 for S-B. Validity coefficients ranged from .19 to .43, and the PPVT was called of modest validity. Data for MPPVT were not given (see also Ali and Costello, 1971). The authors concluded that PPVT had adequate stability ". . . over a brief time . . ." (p. 759). The modification of the PPVT (MPPVT) increased the score slightly.

In an article, the purpose of which seemed to be the comparison of the Leiter International Performance Scale (LIPS) with the S-B, Costello and Dickie (1970) reported on 17 of 22 black Head Start children who finished both the S-B and the LIPS. Mean age was 57 months. The mean S-B IQ was 89; the mean LIPS IQ was 83 (the difference was not significant). Correlation between the tests was .79 for mental ages, and .68 for IQs (N was 17 in each case). There were no sex differences. The authors concluded that LIPS had no advantage over the S-B, but that the reverse might be true.

D'Angelo, Walsh, and Lomangino (1971) examined 255 black Head Start children (New York City) to determine whether the Vane Kindergarten Test (VKT) was useful with such children. How the sample was selected was not given, and Ns in 2 tables in the article differ. Mean IQs and SDs were given for every six-month period from 48 to 71 months. Full Scale mean IQs (SDs in parentheses) for 119 males was 95.1 (11.6);

for 117 females, 98.6 (12.9). The authors concluded that the use of VKT for children under 54 months of age was "questionable" and that more study of VKT was needed.

Denmark and Guttentag (1969) described four experimental intervention programs ". . . for the cognitively deprived child" (pp. 375–6), and tested subjects in each program against a control group. There were 63 experimental children and 17 controls. All subjects were black, of low SES, with a mean age of 4.2 years. The method of their selection was not given. The children were pretested with the Reading Prognostic Test (RPT) and LIPS, and then placed in one of the intervention programs or the control group. The mean mental age for the LIPS was, for all 80 children, 3.77. There were no pretest differences among the 4 programs. N in no group exceeded 17. Significant pre- post-test increases (within any one program) appeared for the experimental, but not for the control, children. For LIPS, t-statistics were presented for pretest differences. The net changes computed by this reviewer varied from 0.61 to 0.93 years of mental age. Data for testing their significance were not available. The authors thought that intervention programs were ". . . effective compensatory spurs to the growth of specific cognitive and perceptual skills . . ." (p. 379) but none of their programs showed this. The authors commented that they presented their findings to keep ". . . the field in healthy agitation . . ." (p. 379), and they questioned whether it was profitable to such children (a) to expose them to children with higher capabilities, or (b) to give them special training in cognitive skills.

Fagan, Broughton, Allen, Clark, and Emerson (1969) compared the S-B and WPPSI IQs to determine which test was the better for low SES children (see also Barclay and Yater, 1968; Sewell, 1977). The authors selected 16 black and 16 white 4- to 5-year-olds who were attending day care centers for working mothers who lived in housing projects. The tests were given 1 to 5 days apart, and the order of administration was alternated. The mean S-B IQs were (SDs in parentheses) 92.3 (9.8) for blacks, and 98.1 (15.4) for whites. The Full Scale WPPSI IQs were 86.2 (11.7) for blacks; 87.9 (14.2) for whites. Correlations between the two tests were also given. The S-B was preferred because it is easier for low SES children.

Flick's study (1966) was to learn the relationship between eye and hand dominance and perceptual-motor functioning. Subjects were 216 male and 237 female black children whose average age was 48.17 months, selected at the Collaborative Child Development Program at Charity Hospital, New Orleans. Perceptual-motor functioning was tested by form copying and by Mazes III and IV of Porteus. Hand dominance was the preferred used in copying the forms and on the first trial of the Wallin Pegboard. Eye dominance was tested by a shoe box with a hole in one end and an object just inside the other end, which end was removed to allow light to enter. For intelligence, a short form of S-B was used. The mean S-B IQs (SDs in parentheses) were 85.96 (13.08) for males, 87.50 (13.06) for females, and 86.76 (13.09) for the entire set of black children. The author concluded that those subjects who were both left-handed and left-eyed were "overall deficient" in perceptual-motor functioning and in intelligence. Children with other combinations of handedness and eyedness were not statistically different in intelligence.

Fredrickson's (1977) article was ". . . an attempt to interpret the findings accrued within the context of the traditional nature-nurture controversy as it relates to race [differences] . . . among preschool children" (p. 96). The author talked of 25 black and 38 white subjects for the racial comparisons, but the discussion was not clear. Apparently, between 1969 and 1972, the WPPSI was administered to 63 children, but this is also unclear. The mean age of the children was 5–2 for blacks and 5–4 for whites. All children were from the Linn County (Iowa) Day Care Center and, apparently, were matched on the occupation of the family breadwinner, family income, and education of the parents. The mean WPPSI IQs were 101.40 for blacks; 104.03 for whites. The difference was called not significant. The author concluded that the lack of racial difference was because there were no cultural differences between the racial samples. He did not consider that matching for factors related to intelligence also matches for intelligence in some degree.

In order to compare the Wechsler Intelligence Scale for Children (WISC) and PPVT scores of young children, Hatch and Covin (1977) described 3 heterogeneous subject groups. The authors did not describe their selection techniques, but they presented a sample of 37 black Head Start children, 15 black children from an inner-city kindergarten, and 15 white children from a university study center. For the Head Start sample, the mean PPVT IQ was 63.59 and the mean WISC Full Scale IQ was 70.40. For the inner-city children, these data were 69.20 and 75.20, respectively. For all black children (N—52) mean PPVT IQ was 65.21; mean WISC Full Scale IQ was 71.78. For the white children, the respective mean IQs were 113.20 and 119.47. The authors concluded that PPVT-WISC difference was the same for children of poverty as it was for children of non-poverty status, and that this contradicted the literature. The authors warned about the smallness of their samples.

A paper presented at the APA Convention in 1972 was published by Kaufman in 1973. The purpose of the study was to compare the intellectual abilities of whites and blacks who were matched for a number of traits other than race. The samples were taken from Wechsler's standardization sample of the WPPSI; 132 whites were matched to 132 blacks in age, sex, geographic residence, father's or mother's occupation, and urban-rural residency. The age range was 4 to 6½ years. The Full Scale IQs were (SDs in parentheses) 98.9 (14.7) for whites; 87.2 (13.6) for blacks. Data were given for the Verbal and Performance IQs, also. All racial differences were called significant. Kaufman concluded that the findings were consistent with the literature. He also concluded that the "cumulative deficit" hypothesis was not confirmed.

The complex study of Kinnie and Sternlof (1971) involved the influence of three non-intellectual factors on intelligence test scores: (a) middle-class children are more comfortable with the usual test examiner than are lower-class children; (b) differences in familiarity with the language and test materials will influence test scores; and (c) differences in familiarity with the testing situation will influence test scores. The subjects were 123 children from Oklahoma City, 4 to 5 years old. In the middle class group were 42 white children from 3 private nursery schools. Two lower-class groups were (a) 41 black Head Start children, and (b) 40 white Head Start children. The method of selection was not given. The WPPSI was given to all children twice—9 weeks apart. The mean WPPSI Full Scale IQ of the middle-class whites was 116.57; that for the 40 low SES whites, 89.73; and that of the low SES blacks, 89.46. The children in the Examiner Familiarization Group (EFG) met with 3 different adults for 6 meetings (one week apart) of 30 minutes each. The adults talked to, read to, and played with the children. The children in the Test Familiarization Group were divided into 2 sections: TFG-1 was given exercises to increase their familiarity with the questions used in WPPSI, and the children were assisted in answering these questions by the adults. TFG-2 was like TFG-1 except that the language and materials used in TFG-2 were related to the S-B instead of to WPPSI. How often this training was given was not discussed. The authors presented an inclusive set of data showing the pre-treatment and post-treatment scores on WPPSI for the control group and the treatment group for each of the 3 samples of subjects, separately. The authors' conclusions, based on these data, were ambiguous, and when this reviewer compared the pre- and post-treatment changes for the treatment groups with like changes for the appropriate control group, in no case were the changes in the treatment groups significantly different from the changes in the control groups.

In an investigation of the factors basic to the ITPA, Leventhal and Stedman (1970) administered the ITPA to 285 whites and 55 blacks, all from Head Start programs in North Carolina. Mean age was 6–4. Blacks were lower than whites in SES. The authors described three modifications which they made in the test directions, and they presented means and SDs for all subtests of ITPA, along with subtest correlations. From these, the authors concluded that, except for Visual-Motor Sequential, Visual-Motor Association, and Auditory Vocal Sequential, whites were significantly superior to blacks. Boys were superior to girls on the Motor

Encoding subtest. The authors also concluded that there was little support for the factorial specificity of the ITPA subtests.

In Long Branch, California, from September 1969 to June 1970, 14 black 4-year-olds were enrolled in an intervention program which Marshall and Bentler (1971) called "innovative." Based on "internalized learning," the program involved an ". . . eclectic approach to promote independent thinking . . ." (p. 805). The authors' purpose was to evaluate this program. On 21 October 1969 (Test 1), and again on 17 June 1970 (Test 2), the PPVT was given to 11 of the 14 children. The mean IQ (SDs in parentheses) for Test 1 was 83.9 (14.1) and for Test 2, 107.5 (9.9); the difference was called significant. There was no control group. The details of the intervention program were not given, and nothing was said about the selection of the subjects. However, SD at Test 2 was so markedly smaller than the SD at Test 1 that the question of coaching must be raised.

McNamara, Porterfield, and Miller (1969) studied relationships among the WPPSI, the Bender-Gestalt (B-G), and Raven's Progressive Matrices (RPM). The subjects were 42 low SES black Head Start children from Dade County, Florida, between 4.8 and 6.6 years of age. All had had 4 to 10 months of preschool training before they were tested in the summer and fall of 1967. WPPSI Verbal IQ (SDs in parentheses) was 83.86 (11.57), Performance IQ was 86.98 (16.03), and Full Scale IQ was 83.88 (13.43). Mean raw score on RPM was 12.29 (2.36). Mean raw score for B-G was 16.60 (4.05). Correlations were given for all tests. The authors concluded that B-G was a better substitute for WPPSI than was RPM.

Fifty-nine low SES black children, all within 3 months of their third birthdates in the Spring of 1964, were chosen by Milgram (1971) for a study of IQ constancy. Subjects who missed one examination were dropped. The location of the study and the method of selecting the children were not given. The S-B had been given annually (1964 through 1969); the PPVT had been given in each of those years except 1966; part of the ITPA had been given in 1964 and 1965; Draw-A-Man Test (DAM) had been given in 1967 and 1968. The initial IQs of the 59 children were: for S-B, 85.49; for PPVT, 73.26; and for DAM, 86.36. Considerable other data were presented in the article and, from these, the authors concluded that children not exposed to enrichment do not show a decline in IQ betwen the ages of 3 and 4; after age 8, the decline is clear. PPVT scores actually rose between 3 and 7 years without enrichment. The "Culture Deficit Hypothesis" was rejected even though environmentally-oriented explanations were given for the findings.

Milgram and Ozer (1967) did not state a clear purpose for their paper, but it may have been to compare the performances of black children on the S-B and the PPVT. Two samples of low SES black children were studied: Group A (65 children, aged 4½ to 6 years) was given S-B once, and PPVT twice during a 6-week Head Start project, and Group B (51 children of the same age) was given S-B and PPVT at the age of 3 (August, 1964), and again at the age of 4 (June, 1965). Examiners were graduate students in psychology. In both groups, and for both tests, the mental ages of the children were below the normative MAs, and the PPVT MAs were lower than the S-B MAs. No IQs were given. The authors explained their findings as the result of "environmental impoverishment" and, while they presented much supporting argument, they presented no objective supportive evidence.

Using a sample of 40 males and 20 females, all black, all Head Start, and all between 47 and 76 months of age, Moore (1978) sought to demonstrate the relationship between intelligence test scores and racial preference of young blacks. Three white and 3 black examiners administered the WPPSI and a modification of Clark's Doll Test (Clark and Clark, 1947) to these children. Each child was shown 6 photographs (three of black and three of white female adults) in a line on a table and was asked to point to (a) a nice teacher, (b) a mean teacher, (c) the teacher you would like to have next year. The hypotheses to be tested were (i) "There is no difference between the IQs of children with a positive or negative attitude toward a black model or white model," and (ii) "There is no difference between the IQs of children who preferred a black model or white model" (p. 40). The data were presented in percentage form and, of his data, the author commented that ". . . children with higher IQs tended to perceive the black models more positively than the white models" (p. 42). He also commented that "The percentages suggested the majority of children preferred the black model, but concomitantly had a negative perception of the black model" (p. 42). When this reviewer reduced the author's percentages to frequencies, the total distributions for none of the three questions differed significantly from a chance distribution, and any "tendency" that appeared in the data was for these black children to regard a black model teacher as "mean." The author did not say what he did about his two hypotheses which, as they were stated, sounded very much alike.

Moore and Retish (1974) studied the effects of race of examiner on test scores of black children. They administered the WPPSI to 42 black Head Start and Day Care children, aged 47 to 69 months, in a midwestern industrialized area. The method of selection of these children (all low SES) was not given. The examiners were 3 white and 3 black inexperienced undergraduates of the University of Iowa. The administrators also scored the tests, but an experienced psychologist reviewed some of the scoring by random selection. The WPPSI was so given that if a black examiner tested a random half of the subjects on the first testing, a white gave the second test, and vice versa. For the WPPSI Full Scale IQs, the mean initial IQ for 42 black children was 89.17. When first and second tests were combined, the mean for those tested by white examiners (SDs in parentheses) was 87.74 (12.00), and the mean for children tested by black examiners was 93.22 (15.31). The authors concluded that examiner's race did influence the children's test scores. When this reviewer checked the authors' data, he was unable to verify the authors' conclusions. The mean difference in WPPSI Full Scale IQ between those tested first by a black then by a white was 2.85; its SE was 4.74; t was 0.60; and the significance level was .60. The mean difference in IQ for those tested first by a white then by a black was 8.10; its SE was 4.07; its t was 1.99; and the significance level was .10. For all children, IQs obtained by black examiners differed from those obtained by white examiners by 5.48 points; the SE was 3.00; t was 1.82; and the probability level was .10.

The validity of the WPPSI was the interest of Oakland, King, White, and Eckman (1971). In Part 1, the WPPSI, the WISC, and the S-B were administered to 24 black children, mean age of 6–2, who were enrolled in two Head Start classrooms selected at random from 12 available classrooms in a community of 250,000. All were low SES. In Part 2, the same tests were given to 24 white kindergarten children, mean age of 6–0, randomly selected from a total white kindergarten population of a community of 14,000. The sequence of testing varied from child to child. For blacks, WPPSI mean Full Scale IQ was (SDs in parentheses) 80.3 (8.5); the WISC mean Full Scale IQ was 84.1 (10.5); and the S-B IQ was 83.8 (7.2). For the whites, these data were 109.0 (10.2), 106.3 (10.7), and 112.8 (10.4), respectively. The authors concluded that blacks of low SES perform below the white mean of the WISC, but failed to note that the black-white difference was even greater on WPPSI and S-B. The authors noted also that their black sample did not represent blacks in general. The authors had thought that the WPPSI was more appropriate for black children because blacks were included in the normative sample of WPPSI. However, they concluded that WISC and S-B were better for blacks of low SES because black IQs were higher on the latter two tests.

The purpose of the Olivier and Barclay study (1967) was to describe the performance of black and white Head Start children on S-B and DAM. The samples were 148 black and 40 white Head Start children in programs in St. Louis, Missouri, and they were called representative of such children who were enrolled in summer Head Start programs in that area. The black and white children may have been matched for S-B IQ. The results of this study were not clear. From Table 1, the S-B mean IQ (SDs in parentheses) was 92.4 (14.65) and it appears that this included both races. From Table 2, which is labeled S-B data, the mean DAM IQ was 91.25 (12.97) for blacks, and 97.52 (13.14) for whites. The racial difference was called significant at the .01 level. The authors concluded that, on DAM, whites were superior to blacks, and girls to boys. S-B and DAM IQs were reported as not highly correlated, even though the subjects may have been matched for S-B IQ.

Osborne (1964) was interested in the study of the factor structure of the WISC for normal black children from preschool through grade 5. By creating at least 2 variables for each subtest of WISC, the author was able to define 26 possible variables for the entire test. WISC was given to 111 blacks who were entering school in September, 1961. Certain SES variables were also included in the factor study. Mean age at first examination was 6–1. Mean Full Scale WISC IQ was 84 (SD 11.8). The author commented on each of the emergent factors.

Quay (1972) raised the question of whether administering S-B in Negro dialect would result in different IQs from those obtained by giving the S-B in standard English. To 50 black children, selected at random from five Head Start centers in a deteriorated Northeastern city, a black female administered S-B in dialect to a random half of the children and in standard English to the other half. The mean of the standard English group was 97.48 (SD 12.18); the mean of the dialect group 93.72 (SD 9.70). The difference was not significant. No sex differences appeared. The author (a) concluded that Negro dialect did not help in the taking of S-B; (b) questioned whether Negro dialect was ever useful in any circumstance; (c) concluded, for both dialect and standard English, that performance on some verbal items was superior to that for some manipulative items, and (d) concluded that language comprehension of young blacks is not as low as some writers think.

Both the DAM and the Columbia Mental Maturity Scale can be administered in a short time and, because of this, Ratusnik and Koenigsknecht (1975) studied their utility with preschool children (see also Sternlof, Parker, and McCoy, 1968). Both tests were administered to (a) nonintegrated blacks of low SES, (b) blacks of moderate SES, (c) whites of low SES, and (d) whites of moderate SES. In each group, there were 18 boys and 18 girls, aged 4 to 6 years, from Chicago and Glenview, Illinois. Methods of selection of the subjects were not given. Testing was done individually at preschool or day care centers in counterbalanced order by 6 white and 6 black examiners. The tests were scored "blind" by a speech pathologist. For blacks of low SES, the mean IQs (SDs in parentheses) for DAM and CMMS were 103.62 (15.21) and 98.16 (8.66), respectively. For blacks of moderate SES, the same data were 109.80 (16.51) and 104.36 (12.78). For whites of low SES, these data were 101.69 (12.06) and 100.33 (11.55), and for whites of moderate SES, the figures were 106.11 (13.73) and 108.75 (10.05). The authors concluded that girls outscored boys on DAM in all of the groups and on CMMS in 3 of the 4 groups. There were no racial differences, but the authors thought that IQs were depressed by low SES. The authors refer to this as a "normative" study even though the samples were both small and of questionable representativeness.

Rieber and Womack (1968) did not state clearly any purpose, but it might have been to demonstrate the efficacy of Head Start programs. Extraordinary efforts, by home visitations, were made to recruit 568 low SES children for the Head Start Project. How samples of 173 blacks and 65 whites were picked from this pool was not disclosed. It is also unclear why N in some comparison groups was as low as 14. The PPVT was administered by 5 "neighborhood" workers to all 568 children, probably during the second week of a summer Head Start program. Spanish was used for some Latins, but not for all. An approximately 25% sample (N = 131) of the 568 children was selected for readministration of the PPVT after 5 additional weeks of Head Start, and the selection of this sample was not described. The mean PPVT IQs, for 65 whites, 271 Latins, and 173 blacks were, respectively, 85.0, 50.3, and 69.0. Increases in PPVT IQs from first to second administrations were, for 64 Latins, 53 blacks, and 14 whites, 9.6, 7.0, and 6.0, respectively. Only the IQ gain for Latins was considered significant, but the authors extolled ". . . the experience offered by the Head Start Program . . ." (p. 613). The authors considered PPVT to be an adequate test of intelligence for these children, but it is unlikely that these samples represented whites, blacks, or Latins. There were no control groups; significant changes from first to second administrations of PPVT should be understood in that light. The authors gave no data to permit the verification of their published results.

Scott (1969) attempted to illustrate a relationship between Piagetian seriation and (a) social class and race and (b) Metropolitan Reading Readiness Test (MRRT) scores. He selected 136 black and 136 white kindergarten children from 4 public schools in Waterloo, Iowa, by matching schools for segregation, integration, low SES, and middle SES. The ages of the children were not given. A self-constructed, two-part (Operational and Trial-Error) Seriation Test (ST) was administered to the children. Score was the sum of the two subtests. ST was so constructed as to have a mental age range of 3½ to 7 years and was given to half a classroom at a time, with no emphasis on speed. Four weeks later, MRRT was given to the same children. ST total score correlated significantly with MRRT, but correlation was higher for the Operational subtest than the Trial-Error subtest. Total mean ST score (SDs in parentheses) was 84.90 (15.35) for whites and 62.54 (19.84) for blacks. The author concluded that Seriation scores were stable, significantly correlated with MRRT, and significantly higher for whites (vs. blacks). There were no social class differences.

The Scott and Sinclair study (1977) was designed to determine the existence of specific school-skill defects among black children so that more effective intervention programs could be developed. The authors claimed to have administered the Iowa Test of Preschool Development (ITPD) to 145 black and 282 white children ages 24 to 39 months, but data were presented only for the black children. Both the white and black samples were regarded as representative of both racial groups, nationally, but nothing was said about the method of selecting the samples other than that the black children were volunteers. The blacks came from a midwestern city of 80,000 and the whites were selected ". . . from various Iowa communities. . . ." Data for blacks were presented in 5 age groups from 24 through 27 months, to 37 through 39 months. Ns for blacks, for the age groups, varied from 21 to 36. Even though no data were given for the whites, the authors indicated that the Ns for white age groups varied between 36 and 74. The mean ITPD "IQs" for blacks, by age levels, varied between 91.1 and 94.3 and, at every age level, were significantly inferior to the white "IQs." The authors concluded that, in some "school readiness" areas, special help for black children was urgent.

Seidel, Barkley, and Stith (1967) listed several "specific objectives" for their paper, all of which objectives were so subjective as to be untestable hypotheses. The general statement of the purpose of the paper was ". . . to evaluate the success of the Project Head Start . . ." (p. 187) for the Rocky Mount and Tarboro-Princeville areas of North Carolina. Subjects were 115 pre-school black children (ages not given) from these geographic areas so selected as to be a random, stratified sample of the Head Start enrollment in each area. Raven's Colored Progressive Matrices (RPM) and the Chicago Nonverbal Examination (CNV), given before and after Head Start training, were the measuring instruments. For 65 children from Rocky Mount, the before and after mean raw scores were, for RPM, 13.24 and 14.00; for the same children, the CNV mean raw scores were 16.79 and 16.66. For the 50 Tarboro-Princeville children, the before and after mean RPM raw scores were 15.45 and 16.09; for the same children, the CNV raw scores were 11.48 and 14.22. No change was significant but the authors concluded, nevertheless, that the Head Start programs were "generally successful" (p. 193). The authors explained their failure to obtain significant changes in test scores in terms of test characteristics and the teaching program.

Sewell (1977) compared low SES blacks on WPPSI and S-B by selecting 35 black children from 3 kindergarten classes in one elementary school in Philadelphia, Pennsylvania. Mean age was 62.29 months. How the children were selected was not given. The tests were administered by 3 students, 2 white and 1 black, in counterbalanced order. For the total sample, the mean S-B IQ (SDs in parentheses) of 91.46 (13.78) was called significantly lower than (a) the mean WPPSI Verbal IQ of 96.14 (12.07), (b) the mean Performance IQ of 96.11 (13.07), and (c) the mean Full Scale IQ of 95.78 (12.32). This reviewer's estimates of the ts for these comparisons, made without knowledge of the correlations (these were correlated samples), were 1.5, 1.1, 1.3, respectively. For a subset of 21 younger children (aged 54 to 63 months), the mean S-B IQ of 94.24 was called significantly lower than the WPPSI mean Full Scale IQ of 99.24. For a subset of 14 older children (aged 64 to 70 months), the S-B mean IQ of 87.29 was called significantly different from the mean Full Scale WPPSI IQ of 90.57. The WPPSI mean Full Scale IQ of 99.24 for the younger subset was called significantly higher than the WPPSI mean Full Scale IQ of 90.57 for the older children. The author concluded that his findings did not agree with earlier findings (see Barclay and Yater, 1968; Fagan, et al., 1969). Sewell noted that the mean S-B IQ of his sample was far below the 1972 norm and questioned the representativeness, not of his sample of 35, but of the normative sample. No sex differences were found. Sewell also questioned the interchangeability of the S-B and WPPSI for low SES black children, commenting that WPPSI might be the better test for such children.

When Sigel and Perry (1968) tested 25 black Detroit nursery school children with ITPA, they were trying to emphasize that the term "culturally deprived" was both derogatory and psychologically inaccurate because much heterogeneity existed among such children. Eleven of the 3- to 6-year olds came from intact homes, and the remainder from various types of broken homes. The authors presented means and SDs for the subtests of ITPA. Except for two subtests, all of the authors' data were considerably lower than the norms for the test. The authors argued that variability characterized these children and stressed the dangers of stereotyping. The authors also warned that the use of "culturally deprived" could result in useless intervention programs.

A complex investigation by Sitkei and Meyers (1969) sought to test four hypotheses about racial differences in factor scores: (a) middle class children should have higher scores than lower class children in both races; (b) superiority of middle class children over lower class children should be greater for semantic factors than for figural or memory factors; (c) within each class, whites should exceed blacks; and (d) the racial differences between the lower classes should exceed the racial differences between the middle classes. PPVT and 22 factor tests were administered to 25 children in each of these SES classes: lower white, middle white, lower black, and middle black. The subjects came from the Los Angeles area and were from 42 to 54 months of age. The method of selection was not given. The data were factor analyzed and reported in detail. The mean PPVT IQ (SDs in parentheses) for whites was 100 (9.6), and for blacks, 85 (11.0). The authors concluded that hypothesis (a) was sustained for verbal comprehension only; hypotheses (b) and (c) were sustained for verbal comprehension and Factor G (unhypothesized) only, and hypothesis (d) was sustained for perceptual speed only. Sex differences favored girls and were almost entirely confined to blacks.

To study the cognitive traits of disadvantaged preschool children, Southern and Plant (1971) chose a sample of 370 children enrolled in a pre-kindergarten project during 1967–8 and a sample of 245 kindergarten children. All children were from San Jose, California, and all were low SES. The method of selection was not stated. Both samples were combined into 438 Chicano, 85 black, and 92 white children. Two subtests of WPPSI, Information (Info) and Comprehension (Comp), and two subtests of the ITPA, Vocal Encoding (V-E) and Auditory Vocal Automatic (A-V) were given. Info was said to measure the "what" of the environment, and Comp was to measure the "why" of the environment. V-E was called a measure of the child's vocalizing ability, and A-V was called a measure of the ". . . ability to predict English language structure and to speak it correctly" (p. 262). Three hypotheses were tested: (a) Info scores would be significantly higher than Comp scores; (b) V-E scores would be significantly higher than A-V scores; and (c) ethnic scores would differ significantly on all tests. Hypothesis (a) was not supported. Hypothesis (b) was supported tentatively because the data were mixed. Hypothesis (c) was supported because the authors found significant mean differences *among* the ethnic means, but when this reviewer computed the *t*s for the 12 possible mean comparisons, the only significant differences occurred between the 4 Chicano-white comparisons. Regardless of any hypothesis, the mean differences involved less than 1.5 points in score in all comparisons. Moreover, the hypotheses have meaning only if one were willing to accept the authors' designations of what the subtests measured. The authors concluded that disadvantaged children (a) are deficient in general intellectual and language abilities, and (b) display different patterns of intellectual and language abilities. The authors were not sure whether these differences were racial or cultural.

No special purpose for the study by Sternlof, Parker, and McCoy (1968) was stated other than to determine the relationship between DAM and Columbia Mental Maturity Scale (see also Ratusnik and Koenigsknecht, 1975). Sternlof et al. supervised the administration by school teachers of DAM and CMMS to 34 black and 54 white children (mean age, 73 months) who were enrolled in integrated Head Start programs in a small town in Oklahoma. How the children were selected was not given. Tests were scored by a qualified psychologist. The Vineland Social Maturity Scale (VSMS) was administered to the mothers of the children, presumably by Head Start teachers. The authors reported the mean scores and SDs for each of the two racial groups, separated by sex. When the sexes were combined by this reviewer, the following appeared: for whites, the CMMS, VSMS, and DAM IQs were, respectively, 74.54, 81.50, and 63.39; for blacks, these respective means were 61.23, 77.71, and 59.12. The authors reported data in terms of analysis of variance and concluded that racial differences in CMMS and DAM were significant, but not so for VSMS. The t-statistics for the racial differences, computed by this reviewer, showed that the CMMS difference was significant at .001, the VSMS significant almost at .05 (t was 1.76), and DAM was not significant (t was 1.69). The authors concluded (not on the basis of statistical validity) that CMMS was an especially poor test for blacks and cautioned about the use of performance tests for blacks.

Walsh, D'Angelo, and Lomangino (1971) sought to evaluate the performance of black and Puerto Rican Head Start children on the Vane Kindergarten Test (VKT). Subjects were 176 black and 225 Puerto Rican children (aged 4½ to 6 years) from New York City. How the subjects were chosen was not given. VKT was administered during the Head Start program. The authors reported that Puerto Rican children were low on vocabulary, but were significantly superior to the black children on perceptual-motor subtests and on the Man subtest. Discounting the vocabulary deficit of the Puerto Rican children, the authors thought that the latter might be superior to the general Head Start population. No data were given.

Over 1,200 reports of intervention programs aimed at disadvantaged children were reviewed by Wargo, Campeau, and Talmadge (1971). Only 10 of the 1,200 programs met the reviewing criteria and these were added to 31 studies identified earlier. Of the 41 studies identified, two (#5 and #6) contained statistical information.

Study #5, the Mother-Child Home Program (pp. 127–132), was a study of 2- and 3-year old "volunteer" black children from 3 housing projects in Freeport, N.Y., designed to show the effects of an intervention program on the IQs of such children. In the first year, there was one treatment group of 33 children (T_1) and two control groups, C_1 (9 children) and C_2 (11 children). The PPVT and either the S-B or the CIIS were given to all children (a) pre-treatment and (b) after 7 months of treatment. Treatment consisted of regular visits by social workers who showed the mothers how to "interact" with their children by the use of "Verbal Interaction Stimuli Materials" (VISM). VISM were, simply, books and toys. The control children (C_1) were given no VISM, but were visited by "a kindly adult figure"; C_2 children received nothing. In Year 2 (1968–9), 9 children from T_1 received further VISM, and 5 of the T_1 children received additional home visits from non-professionals who had now replaced the social workers. T_2 was formed of 8 children from C_1 and 27 new children (total N of T_2 was 35). The same testing schedule was followed. In Year 3 (1969–70), T_3 was formed (30 children), and C_3 (12 children) was added to receive VISM books only. The same testing schedule was followed for T_3. No information was given about the selection of subjects. The authors regarded CIIS as a downward extension of S-B, and did not distinguish between the IQs of the two tests. For 1967-8, data were given for CIIS/S-B and PPVT; the mean difference between the pre-treatment and post-treatment scores were, on CIIS/S-B, 17.0 for T_1, 1.0 for C_1, and 2.0 for C_2. For PPVT, the differences were 12.2 for T_1, -4.0 for C_1, and 4.7 for C_2.

The authors concluded that, in the first year, significant gains had been made by the treatment group for both tests—gains not matched by either control group. However, the remaining data were very unclear. Two new treatment groups were added in 1968-9, and they may have contained subjects from C_1 and C_2 groups of the previous year. The authors discussed significant differences for CIIS/S-B and PPVT scores for 1968-9, but it was unclear how they tested their data for significance. Followup data were given for 1968-9, but for the treatment groups only.

Project Breakthrough, Study #6 (pp. 143-152), planned to show that Edison Responsive Environment (ERE) and social work services could raise the IQs of disadvantaged children aged 3½ to 5½ years. The children were furnished by the Illinois Department of Public Aid. At the beginning, N was 136 children who were separated into four groups of 34 each: Group 1 received ERE and intensive social services (ISS); Group II received ISS but no ERE; Group III received ERE and regular social services (RSS) and Group IV received no ERE, but did receive RSS. ERE consisted of "the nursery experience," Talking Typewriters, and "transfer sessions." ISS and RSS were not identified. S-B, PPVT, and VSMS were given to these children. Assignment to a group was called random, but such that each group would be equal in S-B IQ. Only the pre- and post-treatment differences were given for S-B and VSMS, and then only for ERE vs. Controls (the latter not identified). PPVT was given only at the end of the program; these IQs were given in "adjusted IQs," and for ERE vs. Controls only. No group comparisons were attempted. The authors concluded that ERE could raise the IQs of these children, but not the social quotient (SQ) of the VSMS. The significance of the IQ change was questioned by the authors, but they speculated that a longer training period might have caused substantial increase in this difference. ISS had no effect on IQ or SQ, but it was speculated further that ERE had kept these children from retrogressing.

In order to investigage the language patterns of low SES black children, Weaver and Weaver (1967) reported on 43 experimental and 18 control children selected from Gray and Klaus (1965). The latter had classified these children as T_1, T_2, and T_3, the first two as treatment groups, and the third as control. Ns were 22, 21, and 18, respectively. S-B IQs were available from Gray and Klaus (1965). The ITPA had been given (Klaus and Gray, 1968) to the same children in 1964, 1965, and 1966; then abandoned. The children had received training in the earlier program (Gray and Klaus, 1965). Klaus and Gray (1968) had shown that, from 1964 to 1966, ITPA mean scores for their treatment groups (T_1 and T_2) had declined 7.37 and 8.14 points, respectively, while the control group showed a mean increase of 2.39 points. Weaver and Weaver mention no such comparison. They analysed the variances among the same three means (T_1, T_2, and T_3) and concluded that a significant difference for total ITPA score in favor of the treatment groups existed. They also concluded that the patterning of scores for their groups was remarkably similar to the patterning of scores for both educable and trainable mental retardates, implying that this was important in the planning of remedial programs for the disadvantaged.

Whiteman and Peisach (1970) investigated 4 hypotheses about Piagetian conservation. Since the authors studied grade 3 children as well as kindergarten children, this paper is only noted here and will be discussed in Chapter III.

Willerman, Naylor, and Myrianthopoulos (1970) examined the intelligence of offspring of interracial parents. All subjects, the 4-year old children of Negro and Caucasian parents, were collected in a study done under the Perinatal Research Branch, National Institute of Neurological Diseases and Strokes, Bethesda, Maryland. Of 186 children originally involved, only 88 had reached the age of 4 at which time psychological tests were given. These 88 were obtained from 10 of the 12 collaborating institutions throughout the country. No other subject characteristics were given. The test was a short form of S-B. The authors assumed that, if intelligence were the result of additive genes, the mother's race should not be related to the intelligence of the child any more than should the father's. If intelligence were the result of environmental factors, since the mother is the dominant socializing factor in the child's growth, there should be a relationship between the child's IQ and the mother's race. Data for 61 of the offspring of white mothers and black fathers resulted in a mean IQ (SD in parentheses) of 100.9 (16.8). For the 27 offspring of black mothers and white fathers, the mean IQ was 93.7 (16.9). The difference was called significant by the authors and they regarded their hypothesis as supported. This reviewer computed the significance of the differences from the authors' data; t was 1.85 which, at 80 df, was significant at the .10 level. No alternative hypotheses were considered and, in the body of the article, the findings were called tentative. No such caveat existed in the abstract of the article.

Yater, Boyd, and Barclay (1975) attempted to establish the validity of WPPSI and WISC for young black children, including those of school age. The authors treated their article as if it were a longitudinal study and, therefore, it will be discussed in the next chapter.

Summary

Purposes of the Researches

Of the 49 articles that concerned themselves with the intelligence of black children, 7 (14.3%) may be considered in a miscellaneous category. Flick (1966) was interested in the relationships among eyedness, handedness, and intelligence. Sigel and Perry (1968) wrote to show that the term "culturally deprived" was both inaccurate and derogatory. Sternlof et al. (1968) may have been interested in studying the performance of Head Start children on the Columbia Mental Maturity Scale (CMMS) but this was not clear from the article. The authors finally concluded that CMMS was a poor test for blacks. Walsh et al. (1971) compared the performances of Puerto Rican and native black children and concluded that, while they exhibited a language difficulty, Puerto Rican children could otherwise be superior to the usual Head Start child. Whiteman and Peisach (1970) and Yater et al. (1975) were interested in school-age children as well as preschool children, and their articles will be reviewed in Chapter III. Finally, Weaver and Weaver (1967) indicated that their interest was in black test score patterns.

Thirteen articles (26.5%) expressed the convictions of the authors that race differences in intelligence were, in fact, social differences or "social-class" differences. In 3 publications with which Birns and Golden were associated and which utilized parts of the same set of subjects, the interest in black-white differences in intelligence was expressed differently, but all three articles attempted to show that racial differences were, in fact, "social-class" differences. Golden and Birns (1968) described their study as an attempt to discover the age at which "social-class" differences appeared between blacks and whites. They concluded that, at age 18 to 24 months, there were no "social-class" differences. In Golden et al. (1971), the goal was to examine the subjects recovered from Golden and Birns (1968) to see whether "social-class" differences, which had not appeared at age 18 to 24 months, could have occurred by the age of 3 to 4 years. From this, the authors found what they considered support for their hypothesis. Birns and Golden (1972) restudied some of the 18- and 24-month old children from Golden and Birns (1968) to see whether "continuity" of mental growth could be shown, but the authors were not clear about their purpose. When they demonstrated that "continuity of mental growth" could be shown for personality traits, the authors concluded that IQ could be predicted from the amount of pleasure a child obtained from taking an intelligence test. Busse et al. (1972), who were intent upon showing that play material (a social factor) was important to the mental development of young black children, found more increased scores in their control group than in their experimental children. Chovan and Hathaway (1970) argued that cultural differences (social differences) were so involved in intelligence tests that such tests measured social experiences rather than intelligence, but they concluded that the black's learning problems were only partly environmental. Fredrickson's (1977) statement of his purpose was extraordinarily not clear, but it was assumed from his conclusions that he intended to show that racial differences in intelligence tests were cultural differences. Fredrickson forgot to mention that the insignificant racial differences which he reported could have resulted from the matching of his samples for SES factors. Kaufman (1973) published the same article twice, but his purpose was unitary: to compare whites and blacks who had been matched for SES. Kaufman reported significant racial differences, and thought that his data refuted the "culture deficit" hypothesis. Kinnie and Sternlof (1971) studied the influence of 3 non-intellectual factors on the IQs of whites and blacks, but reported ambiguous conclusions. When this reviewer computed the net change of his pre- and post-treatment groups, the significant post-treatment change reported by the authors to have been caused by the non-intellectual factors turned out to be not significant. Moore (1978) was uncertain of his findings about the racial preferences of young blacks, but his conclusion that blacks preferred the black doll (of the Clark and Clark, 1947, study) was not supported by his data. Scott (1969) sought to explain the relationship among Piagetian seriation and (a) social class and race, and (b) achievement scores and race. He found that Seriation Test scores correlated with achievement scores more highly for whites than for blacks. Sitkei and Meyers (1969) studied 4 hypotheses about the social nature of race differences in intelligence; their hypotheses were sustained for specific test scores only. Southern and Plant (1971) concentrated on the cognitive traits of low SES children. Three hypotheses were posed: one was not sustained, another was questionable, and the third was sustained because of differences *among* the means, but not supported by difference *between* the means. Southern and Plant concluded that low SES children were deficient in general language abilities. Finally, the unique article of Willerman et al. (1970) studied the intelligence of children of interracial parents, assuming that, when the mother was white, the IQ of the offspring would be higher than when the mother was black. The authors concluded that their hypothesis was sustained but, oddly, this was not supported by their data.

Twelve articles (24.5%) stated an interest in the efficacy of Head Start programs. While other articles may also have been interested in the utilitarian aspects of Head Start, they did not say so. Blatt and Garfunkel (1967) were interested in showing that mental retardation could be reduced by Head Start, but got themselves into such a complex sampling situation that they abandoned their original intention and ended up studying an ordinary sample of Head Start children. When they obtained disappointing findings, largely because they seemed not to have realized that they had abandoned their original hypothesis, the authors faulted the tests, the environment, and the age of the children. They gave no data. Cawley (1968) set out to evaluate the changes among average, slow, and mentally-retarded children from 3 Head Start groups, but failed to provide for a control group. His cautious conclusion that Head Start was beneficial was, therefore, gratuitous. Denmark ana Guttentag (1969) claimed significant findings for their study of low SES children in a program related to Head Start, but they finally admitted strong suspicion about the effectiveness of all such intervention programs. Marshall and Bentler (1971) expressed considerable excitement over an intervention program that showed almost none of the characteristics of scientific inquiry, but which was admirably designed for presentation on nationwide television. Milgram (1971) described the constancy (or lack of it) of the IQs of an unidentified set of black children enrolled in an intervention program, concluding that there was no decline in IQ between the ages of 3 and 4 for children who were *not* exposed to "enrichment." Milgram rejected the "culture deficit" hypothesis. Earlier, Milgram and Ozer (1967) stated no clear reason for comparing black children on the Stanford-Binet Scale of Intelligence (S-B) and the Peabody Picture Vocabulary Test (PPVT). When the MAs of their subjects were found to be below the published norms, the authors concluded that this was caused by "environmental impoverishment." Olivier and Barclay (1967) compared black and white Head Start children on S-B and the Draw-A-Man Test (DAM). They found significant differences between the racial groups, but the description of what they did was not clear. Rieber and Womack (1968) were also unclear in their stated purpose, but a great deal of energy appeared to have been expended in coming to the conclusion that the PPVT was an adequate test for low SES children. Scott and Sinclair (1977), who wished to devise intervention programs that would fit intellectual deficits in blacks, concluded that in "school readiness areas" blacks needed greatest help. Seidel et al. (1967) announced that they were studying certain subjective aspects of Head Start projects and, when they obtained the predictably nondescript results, they blamed the tests and the teachers. Wargo et al. (1971) reviewed over 1200 Head Start programs. Summaries of two such reviews were included here because they, alone of the 1200, presented objective data. Study #5, the Mother-Child Home Program (Wargo, et al., 1971, pp 127–132), sometimes confused experimental and control children over a 3-year period and presented very unclear results. Study #6, Project Breakthrough (Wargo, et al., 1971, pp 143–152), combined social service work with Head Start training and while no group comparisons were given, the authors expressed doubt about IQ changes as the result of Head Start experience.

Seven articles (14.3%) were concerned with "improving" tests for administration to young children, especially to young black children. Ali and Costello (1971) followed up on their earlier attempt to improve the PPVT (Costello and Ali, 1971) but their findings were unclear again. Barclay and Yater (1968) attempted to validate the WPPSI on Head Start children and concluded that, in spite of their small sample (22 whites and 28 blacks), the S-B was the better test for such children. Bradley et al. (1977) were interested in showing that "environmental process measures" were more valid in predicting IQ than were the usual SES measures, and confused their findings with some conclusions incorrectly attributed to Scarr and Weinberg (1976, p. 81). Costello and Ali (1971) published the first of two articles on the modification of the PPVT (see Ali and Costello, 1971), but their work was unconvincing. D'Angelo et al. (1971), in a somewhat confusing article, concluded that the use of the Vane Kindergarten Test on children under 45 months of age was "questionable." Conflicting conclusions about the relative utility (validity) of the WPPSI and S-B raised questions about the adequacy of the Oakland et al. (1971) study, and what Ratusnik and Koenigsknecht (1975) called a normative study of the DAM and Columbia Mental Maturity Scale (on 36 black children) raised the question of whether the authors were interested more in racial differences than in validating the tests.

Five studies (10.2%) involved the comparing of two tests on black children and, while some of these studies seemed to be validating studies, they were not handled as such. Costello and Dickie (1970), for example, correlated the scores on the Leiter International Performance Scale (LIPS) of 17 black Head Start children and concluded that LIPS had no advantage over S-B. Fagan et al. (1969) correlated scores on the S-B and WPPSI for 16, each, low SES black and white children and concluded that the S-B was better than WPPSI because the former was easier. Hatch and Covin (1977) reported that the PPVT-WISC difference was the same for poverty-status and non-poverty-status children, but also warned about their small sample (52 black and 15 white children). McNamara et al. (1969) reported correlations among the WPPSI, the Bender-Gestalt (B-G), and Raven's Progressive Matrices for 42 black children, but made no attempt at validation even though they expressed a preference for the B-G as the better substitute for the WPPSI. Finally, Sewell (1977) compared the WPPSI and the S-B scores of 35 black children against the published norms for these tests and, without validating data, pronounced the WPPSI the better test for use with blacks.

Three studies (6.1%) were concerned with the effects on the IQ scores of black children of (a) race of examiner, (b) familiarity of the examiner, (c) pretesting, and (d) dialect in which the test was administered. While Costello (1970) found no significant effects for (a), (b), and (c), she thought that she might have found such significant effects had she used another set of subjects. Moore and Retish (1974) studied (a) and, while they concluded that race of examiner did affect test scores of black children, their data showed no such evidence. Quay (1972) came to a number of conclusions from his experiment, all of which were related to the central finding that administering a test to blacks in Negro dialect was of no advantage to the blacks.

Two sets of authors (4.1%) were interested in test structure. Leventhal and Stedman (1970) factor analysed the ITPA and reported it to be factorially impure, and Osborne (1964) described a number of factors for the WISC.

Sample Size

Sample size was computed on the basis of the size of each of the groups compared in those 46 articles that included preschool children only. In some articles, there were as many as 7 independent comparison groups (Golden et al. 1971). Some authors reported males and females separately for each race, and these were counted as separate comparison units. In all, there were 79 black comparison units and 21 white comparison units. In addition, there were 2 Latin (Chicano) units and 1 Puerto Rican unit.

The median size of the 79 black comparison units was 34, and the modal size was 15. Fifteen percent of the units had 100 or more subjects. Other percentages were: below 50 subjects, 66%; below 25 subjects, 41%; and below 15 subjects, 14%. The median size of the 21 white comparison units was 37, and the modal size was 15. Fourteen percent of the white comparison units contained 100 or more subjects. The other percentages were: below 50 subjects, 71%; below 25 subjects, 28%; and below 15 subjects, 5%.

When the white and black comparison units were combined, the median number of subjects in the 100 comparison units was 34. Fifteen percent of the units contained 100 or more subjects. Sixty-seven percent of all units contained fewer than 50 subjects, 40% contained fewer than 25 subjects, and 12% contained fewer than 15 subjects.

Selection of the Subjects

Six general categories accommodated the authors' statements of how the subjects were selected in the 46 articles that included preschool children only: Unknown, 26 articles; All Available Children, 7 articles; Matched for Race, IQ, SES, etc., 6 articles; Volunteer Subjects, 2 articles; Children Who Completed the Tests, 2 articles; and Representative and Random Selection, 3 articles. Thus, 93% of the articles (43 of 46) selected subjects on an other than random basis. Four of the six categories (Unknown, Volunteer Subjects, All Available Children, and Completed All of the Tests) have in common that they probably involved all subjects available when the tests were given; these accounted for 80% of the articles (37 of 46). Considering that broad generalizations about racial differences or about the utility of Head Start were made in these 46 articles, it is apparent that such generalizations were made on exceedingly unrandom samples.

Tests Used

Because some of the authors administered more than one test, the total incidence of test usage was 79, while the number of articles reviewed remained at 46—the number that included preschool children only. The data are presented here (a) in relation to the incidence of test usage (i.e., 79), and (b) in relation to the number of articles included (i.e., 46).

The Stanford-Binet Intelligence Scale, in some form, was used in 21 articles which is 26.6% of test usage, and 46% of the total articles. The second most popular test was the Peabody Picture Vocabulary Test, which appeared in 14 articles (17.7% of test usage, and 30% of the articles). The Wechsler Preschool and Primary Scale of Intelligence, the third most popular test, appeared in 12 of the 46 articles (15.2% of the test usage, and 26% of the articles). These three tests accounted for 59.5% of all test usage. Aside from the Illinois Test of Psycholinguistic Abilities, which appeared in 7 articles (8.9% of test usage, and 15% of the articles), no other test was used in more than 4 articles although, in all, 18 tests were used in these 46 articles.

Scores

Measures of cognitive ability were not always given but, when given, they were generally IQs. Among the 46 publications that included pre-school children only, 77 separate authors made 66 estimates of black mean IQ, and 25 estimates of white mean IQ. The median estimated mean black IQ was 89; the median estimated mean white IQ was 109. If white standard deviation be taken as 15, this 20-point difference in median estimated mean IQ represents a black overlap of 9.17%. This is somewhat lower than the estimated overlap made by Shuey (1966) and this writer (McGurk, 1975).

Presence or Absence of Control Groups

In 12 of the 46 articles that dealt with preschool children, a control group was required by the design of the experiment; in 6 of the 12 articles, it was not employed. In some of the articles, it was not always clear whether the control groups, when used, were or were not subject to any of the treatments given to the experimental groups. Again, in spite of this lack, the authors of these articles felt no compunction about making sweeping generalizations about the efficacy of Head Start.

On the whole, there is nothing among these 46 articles on preschool children that would support the hypothesis that blacks and whites are equal in intelligence. There is no support for the hypothesis that the differences noted were caused largely by environmental factors, cultural factors, or economic factors, and there clearly is no support for the notion that special intervention programs have reduced racial differences in intelligence. Since the estimated overlap of these 46 articles was below 10%, there is surely no evidence that any of the improvements in the black's cultural conditions in the past 60 years has, as posited by the Cultural Hypothesis, incréased his intelligence.

III

School Children

Frank C. J. McGurk

Abramson (1969) examined the effects of race of examiner on the Peabody Picture Vocabulary Test scores of black and white children in kindergarten and grade 1 of the New York City public schools. Two white and two black examiners ("neighborhood women") tested 44 black and 69 white kindergarten children and 41 black and 47 white grade 1 children who had been assigned to them randomly. The original selection of the samples was not given. The data were treated by ANOVA, leading the author to conclude that ". . . main effects and their interaction were statistically significant for first grade and not . . . kindergarten . . ." (p. 244). When this reviewer combined the data for the examiners and computed ts for the author's data, the mean difference between 35 whites tested by whites vs. 34 whites tested by blacks was, for kindergarten children, 5.03 points; its standard error (SE) was 2.74 and t was 1.82, significant at .10 level but not at the .05 level. For the 44 black kindergarten children, the mean difference between those 22 tested by whites vs. those 22 tested by blacks was 1.18 points; its SE was 3.00 and t was 0.39, not significant at the .90 level. For the grade 1 children, the mean difference between 25 whites tested by whites vs. 22 whites tested by blacks was 2.76 points; its SE was 2.53 and t was 1.09, significant at .30 level. For the 20 grade 1 black children tested by whites vs. those 21 blacks tested by blacks the mean difference was 1.48 points; its SE was 2.25 and t was 0.66, significant at .50 level. The author tried to explain why he found significant differences at one grade level and not at the other; some of his reasons were interesting.

Although the Ames and August (1966) study was primarily a report on racial Rorschach differences, the authors presented IQs on Wechsler Intelligence Scale for Children (WISC) and Slosson Individual Intelligence Test (SIIT) for 217 black, New Haven, Connecticut, children who ranged in age from 5 to 10 years. How the children were chosen was not given. Mean WISC IQs ranged from 105.4 to 118 for three schools; SITT averaged 93 for one school. Conclusions were limited to Rorschach:

black responses were less "good" than white responses. Blacks were less productive, less creative, less emotionally responsive, and more restrictive than same-aged whites, but blacks were more accurate than whites. Blacks resembled whites most at age 5; thereafter, racial differences became increasingly large.

The Ames and Ilg (1967) paper contained the same data that was presented in Ames and August, 1966. This time, Ames and Ilg stated that the work was sponsored by the Ford Foundation (a) to identify black children of academic promise, and (b) to compare the appearance of behavior patterns in blacks and whites. In Ames and Ilg, N was given as 388 blacks from Lincoln School in New Haven, Connecticut, in 1964–5; in Ames and August, N was given as 217. Identical mean scores were reported in each paper. However, Ames and August noted that some of the reported IQs were WISC data; in Ames and Ilg, no such notation was made. The grade range in Ames and Ilg was kindergarten to grade 5. Apparently, grade 5 children took the Slosson Individual Intelligence Test only. For all grades, all whites were excluded as were all over-age blacks and all others showing no academic promise. In spite of this, Ames and Ilg presented tables showing the percent of children per grade who were considered academically promising—based on the total number of children in that grade. Rorschach data were given.

Asbury's (1973a) study was done ". . . to add to, strengthen, and clarify existing research relating cognitive factors to the discrepant school achievement of white and Black . . . first grade children" (p. 126). During the 1968–9 school year, PPVT, four subtests of Primary Mental Abilities Test (PMA), a preschool inventory, and a reading readiness test were given to a random sample of 225 (98 black and 127 white) children from a rural North Carolina county. Ages ranged from 5–11 to 6–8. The data were treated by analysis of variance, and no mean scores were given. The author concluded that over- and under-achievers were not significantly different on cognitive tests and that there were no sex differences. Except for PMA Perceptual Ability subtest, whites scored significantly higher than blacks.

Asbury (1973b) reported on the same subjects on which he reported in Asbury, 1973a, except that, in 1973b, the sample of 225 was described as a random stratified sample. A SES measure was added in 1973b. As in 1973a, no mean scores for PPVT or PMA were included in 1973b, but there were several tables of chi square results between achievement level and several SES factors, although the author never made clear why he used chi square. There were no clear-cut conclusions.

The purpose of the Baker and Owen (1969) article was to compare "personality related variables" of children who were attending integrated schools for the first time (W-N and B-N) with those of children who had attended integrated schools the previous year (W-O and B-O). Subjects were selected from grade 1 (25 white and 10 black) and grades 4 and 5 (30 white and 7 black). The method of selection was not given. Lorge-Thorndike Intelligence Test (L-T) scores were available (school records?); a personality test and SES measures were administered to those chosen. For grade 1, the mean L-T IQs were: W-O 110, W-N 119, B-O 105, and B-N 96; Ns were, respectively, 17, 8, 1, and 9. For grades 4 and 5 combined, the L-T mean IQs were: W-O 111, W-N 105, B-O 107, and B-N 88; the respective Ns were 22, 8, 1, and 6. The authors treated their data by ANOVA, concluding that the L-T racial differences were significant and that both sets of B-N children were lower than the other groups.

Barnebey (1973) reported that she found only partial support for the hypothesis that race of examiner affected the test scores of the 80 children (40 black and 40 white) to whom 20 nonprofessional examiners administered the PPVT and the WISC Coding Subtest. The children were randomly selected from two integrated neighborhood elementary schools in an otherwise undescribed area. Each child was examined by one white and one black examiner. The data were treated by ANOVA. No support for the hypothesis was obtained from the WISC Coding Subtest. On PPVT, black examiners showed a small gain for white children from first to second test, but this did not appear among black examiners for black subjects. White examiners showed a slight gain for black children from first to second test. No data were presented, but the author concluded that white experimenters did not have a negative effect on black test scores.

In order to study the internal structure of Raven's Progressive Matrices (RPM), Bartlett, Newbrough, and Tulkin (1972) re-analyzed data published earlier (Tulkin, 1968; Tulkin and Newbrough, 1968). No data appeared in the present published article, but in a supplement offered by the authors, data in some detail were given. Item difficulty and set difficulty were the same for both racial groups. The authors speculated that the poorer performance of low SES blacks, relative to low SES whites, may have resulted from "perceptual rigidity" rather than from lack of reasoning ability (no racial differences had been found between high SES blacks and whites). The authors also concluded that further study of the internal structure of RPM was needed.

Baughman and Dahlstrom's book (1968) was a discussion of 3 separate studies. In Study 1, designed to show racial differences, the S-B was administered to 542 black and 464 white children who were 6 to 15 years of age. How the sample was selected was not given other than that they were children who, in 1961–2, were in 2 white schools and 1 black school, plus 60% of the children in a second black school. A fictitious name, Millfield, was given to the location of the study. The mean S-B IQs were 97.8, SD = 14.4 for whites and 84.6, SD = 13.0

for blacks. The racial difference was called significant at .001. The authors claimed a significant black overlap of the white mean, arguing that, from a knowledge of a child's IQ, one could not predict the child's race. Black overlap, however, was 18%. The authors pointed out that children of both races earned IQs in the 50–59 range, but forgot to say that there were 7 times more blacks than whites in that range. It was said also that 3.6 times as many blacks than whites needed special school programs.

PMA had been administered to 437 white and 642 black children in Millfield, probably during the 1961–2 school year. The selection of the sample was not discussed. The mean total IQ was 94.6, SD = 14.2 for whites and 77.4, SD = 14.1 for blacks. Black overlap was 11%. The authors presented a detailed description of the racial differences for the PMA subtests, but generally ignored the differences in total IQ. The authors concluded (a) that black IQ was significantly lower than white IQ; (b) that black PMA IQs were lower than their S-B IQs; and (c) that PMA was not an appropriate test for blacks.

Study 2, designed to show changes in IQ over time, began in the Fall, 1964. The subjects were 57 black children (those remaining of a set of 73 originally tested with S-B in Grade 1 in 1961–2). The subjects were retested with S-B in 1964. Twenty-nine boys decreased in IQ from 83.5 to 81.6, and 28 girls increased in IQ from 84.0 to 84.8. The authors said little about the mean changes; instead, they pointed out that 30% had gained in IQ by 5 or more points, and that 35% had lost in IQ by the same amount. Of an original set of 68 white children, 58 were recovered in 1964 and retested with S-B. Their initial IQs had been 97.6, SD = 17.5 for 29 boys, and 94.6, SD = 13.3 for 29 girls. The 1964 IQs were 98.2, SD = 21.6 for boys, and 95.1, SD = 15.9 for girls. Twenty-six percent of these children gained 5 or more points, and 29% lost 5 or more points.

Study 3 was to show the effects of kindergarten attendance on IQ. For 3 consecutive school years, the S-B had been given to white and black children, first when they entered kindergarten in the Fall, and again the following Spring. Over 3 years (1962–5), 83 white children had attended kindergarten; their mean initial IQ was 97.8, and their second IQ was 105.1. For 73 controls (non-kindergarten children), the same change was from 100.3 to 102.2. Why the authors called this change significant at .001 was not clear; the net change was 5.4 IQ points, and its significance can be questioned. For 80 black children similarly trained and tested, the change was from 91.2 to 92.3. For 74 black control children, the change was from 88.7 to 88.5. The net change was 1.3 IQ points. The authors concluded that kindergarten helps the white child, but not the black child. Enrollment in kindergarten had been limited to 5-year-olds from 2 school districts, and to those children of parents who enrolled them voluntarily. Attendance was not compulsory. The control children were selected from other school districts by an unknown means.

The PMA had also been given to 84 white and 81 black children who, over the same period of time, had attended kindergarten. Whether these were the same children as those included in the S-B study was not clear. However, the white children gained (in raw score) from 55.6 in the Fall of their kindergarten year, to 77.4 in the following Spring. For 70 white control children, the change was from 56.2 to 73.8. The authors called this change significant at the .01 level even though the net change in raw score was only 4.2 points. This would have been a very small change in IQ terms. For the 81 black kindergarten children so treated, the change was from 35.3 to 58.8. The black control children changed from 33.1 to 44.6. The authors called this significant at .001 even though the net change was 12.0 raw score points, and the IQ equivalent was not given. Data for testing the net change were also missing. The authors concluded that (a) all children benefited some from kindergarten; and (b) the effects of kindergarten were greater for blacks than for whites. It should be pointed out that the results from the PMA were almost exactly opposite of those obtained from the S-B, and that both tests were given to a select sample of children according to directions which were unique to these studies.

The purpose of the Burnes (1970) article was to study differences between SES and racial groups of subjects, particularly for patterns of performance among these groups on the subtests of WISC. The subjects were normal 8-year-old boys selected from a large Catholic school district of a midwestern metropolitan area on the bases of age, race, and SES. Subjects were separated into upper-middle-class blacks (N1), upper-middle-class whites (W1), lower-class blacks (N7), and lower-class whites (W7). There were 20 in each group except N1 where only 18 children were found, even after requirements had been relaxed. All 12 subtests of WISC were given to all children. Data were treated by ANOVA, but no data were given. Pattern of scores was strikingly similar. Mean white and black subtest scores were so alike the children could have been matched on them.

Caldwell and Knight's (1970) study was done to investigate the effects of examiner's race on test scores of black children. Both white and black examiners administered both Form L and Form M of the 1937 revision of the Stanford-Binet to 15 grade 6 black males so selected from two elementary schools in "a Southern city" that the children were matched on score on California Test of Mental Maturity (CTMM). Subjects were randomized into three sets (A, B, and C) of subjects of five each. C was a control group. CTMM IQ for all subjects was 93.13. The authors treated their data by ANOVA and concluded that there were no significant differences between the IQs obtained by black and white examiners.

To study the nature of the intellectual deficits of blacks, Caldwell and Smith (1968) reported on a set of WISC records from tests that had been administered in the 1950s. While no mental defectives were accepted, six black boys and six black girls were selected at random from each of five southern states for seven age groups from 5–7 to 12–6 (N per state was 84). They were selected only from those communities where a black or a white college existed. All 12 subtests of WISC had been given to each child. The mean Verbal IQ was 90.6, SD = 11.6; the mean Performance IQ was 82.7, SD = 13.2; and the mean Full Scale IQ was 85.6, SD = 11.2. Verbal IQs were significantly higher than Performance IQs, and there were no sex differences. Mean scores for some states were higher than those of other states for various parts of the WISC.

Carver's (1968) article is a non-professional's excellent description of what he calls an experiment that failed. In brief, the experiment was an attempt to reduce the racial difference in intelligence by designing a test so suited to the social scientists' opinions of why there are test score differences that such differences would disappear. The outcome was a test recorded on tape and taken aurally so as to overcome the low reading level of blacks and their lack of enthusiasm for the usual test. (Both of these factors were advanced as the two real causes of racial differences.) The test was first given to 393 grade 8 blacks in Washington, D.C. The School and College Ability Test (SCAT) and the Listening and Reading subtests of the Sequential Tests of Educational Progress (STEP) were also given. Correlation between the new test and the verbal part of SCAT was .61, and between the new test and STEP Reading Test, .49. Later, the new test and part of STEP and SCAT II were administered to 182 low-income blacks, 132 middle-income blacks, 110 low-income whites, and 191 middle-income whites. The new test was called both valid and reliable. The racial difference with the new test was approximately the racial difference found generally—the black mean was, roughly, 1 SD below the white mean. In spite of these findings, the author continued the article, making the best possible case for a cultural explanation of race differences and, among other things, suggesting that a test for blacks, on video tape, be devised.

In order to describe the influence of adjustment status and age on Bender-Gestalt performance, Cerbus and Oziel (1971) examined 20 black children selected by their school as having learning or adjustment problems and 20 black control children chosen at random from a pool of children without such problems. Controls and problem children were matched for grade and sex; all were 6–7 to 11–7 years of age, and all were in grades 1 through 4. The only datum reported was the mean Full Scale WISC IQ of 97, SD = 12.4 for the control children.

In 1970, Cicirelli, Evans, and Schiller wrote a long reply to the criticism of the Westinghouse Learning Corporation/Ohio University evaluation of Head Start. They defended the Westinghouse report but did so without the publication of data. Therefore, this article is included herein for the record only.

Cicirelli, Granger, Schemmel, Cooper, and Holthouse (1971) presented an analysis of the data for ITPA from the Westinghouse/Ohio University (1969) evaluation of Head Start Summer Programs, but reported no data for the control subjects, and did not report total ITPA scores. This article was in response to criticism of Smith and Bissell (1970). The subjects were from 75 summer Head Start centers in 1966–7; 71 centers had "graduates" in grade 1, 68 in grade 2, and 49 in grade 3. Eight "graduates" were selected randomly from each center at each grade level. At grade 1, 276 were white, 193 were black, and 64 were Mexican-American. At grade 2, these Ns were 271, 186, and 67, respectively. At grade 3, the respective Ns were 199, 159, and 22. The tests were administered by trained examiners. Data were presented for 10 subtests of ITPA by grade and total sample, for whites, blacks, and Chicanos separately. The scores of the Head Start children were below, and more variable than, those of the normative group. Head Start children tended to be stronger in "visual channels" and manual expression, and weakest in "auditory channels" and language. The three racial groups were remarkably similar in all scores, and each racial group seemed to have a different test pattern which was consistent over grade. The authors commented that Head Start programs should be designed around the racial test patterns.

The Cole and Fowler (1974) publication was to show whether, for 54 black children from northeastern Georgia and South Carolina, reliable differences existed among the subtests of WISC. All subjects (mean age 9–8) had been referred for testing because of academic problems. There was no difference between verbal and performance abilities, but the authors presented scores for subtests only. Significant differences were found between Picture Arrangement and each of the following: Similarities, Picture Completion, and Comprehension; also between Information and the same three tests mentioned above.

What is now known as the Coleman Report (Coleman, 1966) was written (as directed by Sec. 402 of the Civil Rights Act of 1964) as a survey of educational opportunities for minorities. A nationwide random stratified sample of school children of grades 1, 3, 6, 9, and 12 was planned to include 900,000 children, half of whom were to be white, the other half minorities (pp. 550–4). The school was the sampling unit. Tests for grades 1 and 3 were the Picture Vocabulary subtest of the Inter-American Tests of General Ability (IATGA) for verbal intelligence and the Association and the Classification subtests of IATGA for nonverbal intelligence. For grades 6, 9, and 12, the Sentence Completion subtests and the Synonyms subtest of the School and College Abilities Test

(SCAT) were the verbal intelligence measures; the Classification and the Analogies subtests of IATGA were the nonverbal intelligence measures (Table 9.9.1, p. 576).

Data for the intelligence of blacks and whites were limited. There were no age data, and SDs were completely absent. Table 9 (p. 20) presented scores for black and white grade 1 *and* grade 12 children. There were also scores for college students (grades 13 *and* 16), probably scores on the National Teacher Examination (Tables 4.5.2 to 4.5.6, pp. 345–6). The main data (grades 1 through 12) were contained in a series of bar diagrams (Figures 3.11.1 through 3.11.23, pp. 221–243). From these, this reviewer made the following estimates of black and white test scores (data are T-scores):

Estimated Median Ability Test
Scores by Grade

	Verbal			Nonverbal			
Grade	Black	White	% Black Overlap	Black	White	% Black Overlap	Source
1	47	54	24	43	55	12	pp. 221–2
3	45	53	21	46	52	27	pp. 223–5
6	43	52	18	44	54	16	pp. 228–9
9	42	53	15	44	54	16	pp. 232–3
12	40	52	11	42	53	14	pp. 242–3

Tables 8.12.1 and 8.12.2 (pp. 492–3) contained data for a study of the effectiveness of Head Start. The tests from which the data were derived were not specified (except as "ability scores"), but they may have been subtests of IATGA. The data presented below are this reviewer's combination of the author's data for five metropolitan and three nonmetropolitan areas:

Mean Ability Scores, Entire Country
Grade 1 Children

	Verbal		Nonverbal		N	
	Black	White	Black	White	Black	White
Head Start Not Available (could not participate)	16.448	19.252	18.734	26.454	5,371	5,545
Head Start Available (did not participate)	15.564	18.702	16.348	24.379	2,716	2,294
Head Start Available (participated)	15.702	18.065	16.089	22.484	6,012	2,990
Total	15.960	18.808	17.147	24.918	14,099	10,829

Head Start was no boon either for blacks or for whites, and Coleman commented that participants in Head Start programs were ". . . almost universally below . . . children in areas where the Head Start program was not offered" (p. 493). He could have commented also that, in general, Head Start participants were lower than children who did not attend Head Start programs where such programs were offered.

Tables 8.13.2 and 8.13.3 (pp. 495–6) contained data showing the influence of both kindergarten attendance and Head Start participation on grade 1 ability scores. These data were presented for metropolitan and nonmetropolitan areas separately, and were combined by the reviewer. (See tabulation on pg. 40.)

Whether verbal or nonverbal scores were considered, those children, black or white, who did not attend Head Start programs but who did attend kindergarten, had higher mean ability scores than the other two categories of subjects. However, there were no SDs for the measure used in Tables 8.13.2 and 8.13.3, and it is impossible to estimate whether the changes were random or significantly systematic. Kindergarten attendance raised the mean verbal score of blacks by 1.5 points; of whites, 1.3 points. Black nonverbal score was raised 3.6 points by kindergarten attendance; white nonverbal score increased 4.1 points. These changes may or may not have been significant. Coleman, himself, was cautious about his comments (pp. 494–7).

The purpose of the Cooper, York, Daston, and Adams article (1967) was to show that the practice of committing blacks to institutions for the mentally retarded was incorrect, and to devise some measure that would distinguish between "academically disabled" and the truly mentally retarded. When the authors applied the Cooper Behavior Index (CBI) to 58 already-committed southern black adolescents, they found disagreement between scores on the commitment tests and the CBI scores. On the basis of CBI scores, the authors separated the 58 subjects into 29 behaviorally retarded (Group A) and 29 behaviorally non-retarded (Group B). The pre-commitment data and the CBI scores were in sharp disagreement. The Porteus Maze Test (PMT) and the Ammons Picture Vocabulary Test (APVT) were administered, the latter for a second time to some of the patients since APVT, along with WISC and Army Beta, had been used as precommitment tests. The reported precommitment score for WISC Full Scale IQ of 20 Group A patients was 56.0, SD = 9.3, and the mean Beta IQ for 9 of the Group A patients was 48.6, SD = 7.9. For the Group B subjects, the mean Full Scale WISC IQ of 22 subjects was 63.1, SD = 8.3, and the Beta IQ for 7 Group B subjects was 59.4, SD = 9.1. The post-commitment mean score of 29 Group A subjects was, for APVT, 40.6, SD = 21.9, and for PMT, 63.6, SD = 15.6. For Group B subjects, the post-commitment mean score on APVT was 45.4, SD = 17.0, and the mean PMT IQ was 121.7, SD = 9.3. The authors concluded that only the PMT permitted the

Mean Ability Scores, Entire Country for Grade 1 Children with and without Kindergarten

	Verbal				Nonverbal				N					
	Black		White		Black		White		Black		White		Total	
	NKᵃ	Kᵇ	NK	K	NK	K	NK	K	NK	K	NK	K	NK	K
Head Start not available (could not participate)	15.604	17.194	18.389	19.601	16.472	20.710	23.646	27.560	2,396	2,681	1,411	3,870	3,807	6,551
Head Start available (did not participate)	15.215	16.195	18.185	19.497	15.334	18.286	22.651	27.210	1,620	970	1,170	768	2,790	1,738
Head Start available (participated)	15.293	16.808	17.876	18.401	15.481	17.762	22.154	23.058	3,994	1,638	2,030	856	6,024	2,494
Total	15.370	16.891	18.111	19.399	15.748	19.352	22.736	26.810	8,010	5,289	4,611	5,494	12,621	10,783

a = Did not attend kindergarten
b = Attended kindergarten

proper discrimination between the retarded and the non-retarded, but the authors failed completely to mention the validation of their CBI.

Covin and Hatch (1977) sought to study age changes in IQ of white and black children. The Wechsler Intelligence Scale for Children, Revised (WISC-R) had been administered by a white examiner who was unknown to 343 black males, 174 black females, 258 white males, and 156 white females, aged 6 through 15 years. The children had been referred by teachers for psychometric evaluation because of poor school performance; all were low SES from rural and small-town areas. Data were given for each age (6 through 15) by race, along with racial differences and ts. The authors concluded that whites were higher than blacks, significantly so at every age except 6, 8, and 10. This reviewer's computation of the mean IQs of all children yielded a black mean of 66.54 and a white mean of 76.35. The IQs of blacks decreased from age 10 through 14, but there was no clear change in white IQs. Since WISC-R had included blacks in the standardization sample, the authors regarded their findings as important.

In what was called a follow-up longitudinal study of children who were subjected to pre-school intervention programs in the 1960s, Darlington, Royce, Snipper, Murray, and Lazar (1980) described the results of the school progress of as many of the original children from 11 earlier studies as could be found in 1976. The authors adopted the criterion that, between the pre-school programs of the 1960s and the time the child was "recovered" for later study, if a child had not been held back in grade or assigned to a special class (other than for speech), that child was evidence of the success of the pre-school program. Out of about 2,700 original subjects, 1,599 were recovered. They ranged in age from 9 to 19 years, were 94% black, and from semiskilled- or unskilled-worker homes. Although the authors commented that intelligence test scores had been collected from the 11 earlier studies, no such data appeared in their article. The question of attrition was solved by noting that attrition in one study was about like attrition in another study. The authors concluded finally that preschool-program children had fewer school failures, fewer assignments to special class, and fewer grade retentions than control children who had not attended the special pre-school program. They, the authors, made no comment on the scientific adequacy of the studies upon which they based their article, and while they talked of 12 studies, they showed data for 11 of them without explanation. Only one of these studies (Gray and Klaus, 1970) is reviewed in the present volume. There is some question about the adequacy of the authors' statistics. Whatever the authors concluded about school progress, they failed to make any comment about changes in intelligence of their subjects.

The Datta, Schaefer, and Davis (1968) study was interested in attitudes of white teachers toward black pupils. From a pool of 177 blacks and

805 "others," 100 blacks and 100 "others" were chosen by a table of random numbers from the seventh grades of the schools in a northern Virginia area. The California Mental Maturity Test IQs were available from the school records. The mean IQ of the blacks was 87.5; of the "others," 113.0. Racial intelligence was not a major interest of the authors and their comments dealt, appropriately, with their interests.

Dillon and Carlson's (1978) general purpose was to compare the performance of different racial groups and different age groups of children when "testing-the-limits" procedures were compared with standard test directions. The subjects were 189 middle-class whites, blacks, and Mexican-Americans. Each racial group was equally represented by 63 children. The children were classified under three age groups (5 to 6, 7 to 8, and 9 to 10) and were randomly assigned to three testing conditions: Condition (a), standard test directions; Condition (b), verbalizing during and after the solution to a problem; and Condition (c), the verbalizing of Condition (b) plus an explanation of principles of the solution given by the tester. No other information about the subjects was given. The data were treated by ANOVA in 3 × 3 × 3 randomized block design where cell N was seven children each. The tests were the Matrices and the Order of Appearance subtests of Winkleman's Piaget-type test battery and were described in the article. The authors concluded that Conditions (b) and (c) improved test performance over that of Condition (a), but the authors correctly warned that interpretations of their results must be cautious and that further research was needed. In order to evaluate such research as this, it is essential that what transpires between tester and testee in Conditions (b) and (c) be clearly known. It is easily foreseen that some types of "testing-the-limits" could destroy the validity of a test, compared with what validity prevailed under standard testing conditions. While "testing-the limits" procedures may eliminate racial test score differences, this might be done at the expense of a test's validity. The authors did not seem aware of this problem.

In a long and complex article, Farnham-Diggory (1970) investigated this problem: Granted racial differences in intelligence, what are the differences, and how can they be reduced? The author answered with three experiments, two of which contained three tasks, and the third experiment contained two tasks. The tasks were original Piagetian problems that were well described in the article. In each experiment, the subjects were given pre-training which they were to use in a novel recombination to accomplish the tasks. In experiment 1, 96 blacks and 96 whites (half low SES, half high SES), selected by their teachers from grades 1 through 4 (aged 6 to 9 years), performed a Verbal Task, a Maplike Task, and a Mathematical Task. No racial differences were found for the Verbal Task; race, age, and SES differences appeared for the Maplike Task; and race, age, and SES differences were found for the Mathematical Task. In experiment 2, 110 black inner-city children were given another set of Verbal, Maplike, and Mathematical Tasks in order to see how the synthesizing ability of blacks could be raised. The author's conclusions are not clear. In experiment 3, 70 blacks and 70 whites (grades K *and* 2), aged 5 through 7 years, were selected from "Milltown" schools and were subjected to two tasks under seven experimental conditions. For the Maplike Task, the black and white reaction patterns differed. For the Mathematical Task, neither race benefited from pre-training.

The author concluded that children of both races may have a wider variety of "systems" available for operational thinking than is known. Differences between sexes and races in the occurrences of these "systems" should not involve stigma. We should teach children in accordance with the available "systems" possessed.

Frerichs' article (1971) was more related to self-esteem than to black intelligence. The author separated 78 grade 6 black children (from the inner city of a large midwestern city) into highest, middle, and lowest thirds by IQ. The IQ range (test unspecified) of the highest third was 97 to 142 (mean of 108), the middle third ranged between 87 and 96 (mean not given), and the range of the lowest third was 61 to 86 (mean of 80). Grade point averages and reading scores were given, as were scores on a self-esteem scale. The author confined his comments to self-esteem.

Gerstein, Brodzinsky, and Reiskind (1976) sought to demonstrate that the Rorschach Test was a more valid test of black intelligence than the usual intelligence test. They reexamined the test batteries of 87 white and 86 black children who had been patients at a child guidance clinic in Philadelphia, Pennsylvania, dividing them first into three age-groups (7–8, 10–11, and 13–14) and then into two IQ groups according to Full Scale WISC IQ. Blacks and whites were equivalent in IQ, age, and SES, and the children were ". . . heterogeneous with respect to diagnostic category" (p. 761). Rorschach protocols were rescored so as to yield degrees of organization. The mean developmental level (Rorschach score) of blacks was higher than that for whites, and the authors concluded that the low IQ blacks appeared to have ". . . intellectual capacities that are not reflected on standard intelligence tests" (p. 763); however, ". . . the present study seems to raise as many questions as it answers" (p. 764).

The problem in the Goffeney, Henderson, and Butler (1971) article was the determination of the ability by which the Bayley Infant Scale (BIS), given at 8 months of age, could predict WISC and Bender-Gestalt (BG) scores at 7 years of age. As of May 31, 1969, 626 children (229 black and 397 white) from the Collaborative Study on Cerebral Palsy at the University of Oregon Medical School (see Myrianthropoulos and

French, 1968) were selected because they had completed the BIS and the WISC and BG. The mean BIS scores (items passed) were: Mental, 78.1 for blacks and 78.5 for whites; Fine Motor, 2.28 for both races; Gross Motor, 6.38 for blacks and 6.11 for whites. The WISC IQs were: Full Scale, 90.8 for blacks and 97.9 for whites; Verbal IQ, 89.3 for blacks and 96.6 for whites; Performance IQ, 94.2 for blacks and 99.8 for whites. The BG mean scores were 8.84 for blacks and 6.99 for whites. The validity coefficients for all blacks varied between .05 and .20; for all whites, between .14 and .24. Many coefficients were called significant, but the authors were cautious in their comments. (See also Henderson, Butler, and Goffeney, 1969).

Goldman and Hartig (1976) questioned whether WISC was a valid measure of minority intelligence. They selected 320 Chicanos, 201 blacks, and 430 white children, aged 6 to 11 years, from the Riverside, California, schools. The whites were selected randomly from 11 predominantly white schools, and the blacks and Chicanos were all the children who attended three *de facto* segregated schools. The SES of the sample approximated the SES of the entire Riverside population. The mean WISC IQs of whites, Chicanos, and blacks, respectively, were 107, 89, and 91. The validity coefficients for Academic GPA, Social GPA, and Teachers' Ratings for Competence were .25, .49, and .46 for whites; .12, .28, and .26 for Chicanos; and .14, .30, and .34 for blacks. The authors concluded that while differences in variances may have contributed to the validity coefficients, the WISC was a valid predictor for whites but not for Chicanos or blacks.

Goldstein and Peck (1971) raised the question of whether ". . . racial differences reported for the general population are present in a mental health clinic population" (p. 379). The authors searched the files of the outpatient department of the Division of Child and Adolescent Psychiatry, King's County Hospital Center, for all patients 8 to 16 years old, whose records contained both WISC IQs and scores on "human figure drawing" (HFD). Children with language barriers were excluded, and all subjects were low and very low SES. There were 35 black males, 22 white males, 17 black females, and 18 white females. Mean ages of the four groups ranged from 10.5 to 12.4 years. The mean WISC Full Scale IQs were: black males, 89.72, SD = 18.21; white males, 91.95, SD = 21.21; black females, 83.00, SD = 14.97; and white females, 91.82, SD = 18.30. The authors built their rejection of Jensen and Shuey around a set of t-statistics of racial differences that could not be verified by this reviewer. So many of the published t-values were questionable that one would do well to regard this article with caution.

Gordon's study (1976) was done to describe ". . . the socio-structural correlates of differences in scholastic achievement . . ." (p. 4) between blacks and whites. The author selected 1,102 children from grades 5 and 6, classified them by race, sex, and SES (middle- and working-class), and divided each classification into 7 IQ groups. Of whites, there were 169 middle-class boys, 204 middle-class girls, 74 working-class boys, and 76 working-class girls. Of blacks, there were 91 middle-class boys, 104 middle-class girls, 178 working-class boys, and 206 working-class girls. The mean IQs (test unidentified) were (a) for whites: 107.6, SD = 13.5 for middle-class boys, 110.1, SD = 15.2 for middle-class girls, 99.7, SD = 12.4 for working-class boys, and 104.4, SD = 13.4 for working-class girls; and (b) for blacks: for the same SES categories, in the same order, the mean IQs were 100.2, SD = 11.5, 103.5, SD = 11.8, 93.8, SD = 12.7, and 94.2, SD = 11.5. Achievement test data were available, apparently from the records of an earlier experiment (from which the subjects may have been taken), but this is not clearly stated. The achievement data were analysed by IQ groups, which led to the conclusion that racial differences in achievement existed in all IQ groups, and that the data were insufficient to reject or support Jensen's thesis of racial disparities in intelligence.

To study the effects of race of examiner on the test scores of adolescents, Gould and Klein (1971) studied 46 blacks and 38 whites who were high-potential pupils at the Summer High School at Yale University in 1967. Ages were not given. The subjects were divided into four groups; two groups, each, were examined by black and white examiners. The Verbal and Abstract Reasoning Scales of the Differential Aptitude Tests (DAT) plus some social desirability scales were used. On Verbal Reasoning, the white mean (34.97) was significantly higher than the black mean (30.33). On Abstract Reasoning, whites (Mn. 40.76) were significantly higher than blacks (Mn. 36.18). Neither black nor white intellectual performance was affected by the race of examiner.

In 1963, Gray and Klaus published the first in a series of reports on a complex intervention program for young black children in Murphrees-boro and Columbia, Tennessee. The program began in 1961, and by 1963 Gray and Klaus had written two unpublished interim papers which were reviewed by Shuey in 1966. Briefly, 61 black children, 3 to 4 years of age in 1962, were divided randomly into three groups of about 20 each. T_1 and T_2 were treatment groups; T_3 was the local control group. A distal control group (T_4) of 27 children from Columbia was added. The intervention program was a mixture of summer school, home visits by welfare workers, and attempts at parental education. The Stanford-Binet Intelligence Scale (S-B), the Peabody Picture Vocabulary Test (PPVT), the Wechsler Intelligence Scale for Children (WISC), the Illinois Test of Psycholinguistics (ITPA), and achievement tests were used as measuring instruments.

Since 1963, three reports have been published, two of which may also be regarded as interim reports (Gray & Klaus, 1965; Klaus & Gray,

1968). Since nothing further has been published, it may be assumed that Gray and Klaus (1970) was the final report. The important consideration was the mental ability of the subjects at the end of the program (at which time the children were 9 to 10 years of age and in grade 4) compared to the mental ability of the children in May, 1962. By the end of the program, S-B had been administered to all children 8 times, PPVT 10 times, and WISC and ITPA abandoned during the program.

For S-B, as of May, 1962, the mean IQ for the treatment groups (T_1 and T_2 combined) was 90.05, and the mean IQ of the control groups (T_3 and T_4 combined) was 86.13. In July, 1968, the means for these two groups were 88.45 and 80.86, respectively. The net change was a loss of 3.67 points. For the PPVT, in May, 1962, the mean IQ of the combined treatment groups was 69.80, and the mean of the combined control groups was 70.66. By July, 1968, these two means were 85.60 and 80.06, a net change of 6.40 points. There were not enough data given to determine the significance of these two net changes. While the authors expressed disappointment about the S-B data, they were encouraged by the PPVT data. The authors also commented that "All four groups have shown a decline in IQ after the first grade . . ." (p. 918) allegedly because of SES factors.

The Green and Morgan (1969) article was concerned with the intellectual damage done to the black children of Prince Edward County (Virginia) when their schools were closed (1959–63) to forestall integration. The article compared the children who had had some education with those who had had no education during the years in which the schools were closed. The Stanford-Binet, 1960 revision, had originally been given to 35 of the Some Education Group and 31 of the No Education Group, and that test was repeated in 1965. The gain in IQ for the Some Education Group varied with age between 4.0 and 6.0 IQ points. For the No Education Group, the gain was equally modest for the 9–11 age group; for the 12–14 age group, the gain was 18 points (regarded as a significant gain); and for the 15–17 age group there was a loss of 0.5 points. The Chicago Non-verbal Examination, a group test, had been given in May, 1964, to 177 of the Some Education Group and 351 of the No Education Group. The subjects ranged in age from 8 to 17, and the Some Education children and No Education children, at each age level, were compared. Except at ages 11, 16, and 17, the Some Education children were significantly superior to the No Education children. The authors concluded that the children had been damaged by the closing of the schools.

The Guinagh (1971) article was an attempt to refute Jensen's (1969a) argument. Guinagh hypothesized that if children with low IQ but high basic learning ability (BLA) improved in IQ after training in the principles underlying the IQ test, and if the children of low IQ and low BLA did not improve after the same training, Jensen would be refuted (p.

28). Guinagh identified BLA with digit span (DS) and IQ with Raven's Progressive Matrices (RPM). Evidently, both measures had been given to 105 black and 84 white children—all from the Gainesville, Florida, area, all in grade 3, and all low SES. A score of 20 or less on RPM marked the low IQ children for each race. From this group, the 20 lowest on DS (Low BLA) and the 20 highest on DS (High BLA) were selected for each race. Randomly, each group of 20 was separated into 10 experimentals, 5 Hawthorne controls, and 5 pure controls. The experimentals, the treatment groups, received training in concepts underlying the RPM for seven, one-half hour sessions. The Hawthorne controls received the same amount of training in word skills. The pure controls received nothing. The RPM was given post-treatment and again four weeks later (the retention measure). The Hawthorne controls and the pure controls were finally combined. There were significant RPM differences between the racial groups pre-treatment and post-treatment, but there were no racial differences for the third administration of RPM. The author was modest in his claims about having refuted Jensen. A comparison of the mean differences indicated that the experimental Low IQ-Low BLA blacks and the experimental Low IQ-Low BLA whites, who should have shown no significant increases in RPM, made significant gains of 6.3 and 14.1 points, respectively, over their controls. In the case of blacks, the gain over controls of the Low IQ-High BLA group was significantly greater (.01 level) than the gain over controls of the Low IQ-Low BLA; but in the case of whites, the gain of the experimental over control for Low IQ-Low BLA was not significantly different from the experimental gain over controls for the Low IQ-High BLA.

To test the relationship between attention span and IQ, Hall, Huppertz, and Levi (1977) selected (randomly) 40 white and 40 black children, aged 7 and 8 years and of unknown school grade, from a pool of 600 such-aged children who had been so collected for another study that no more than four children were selected from the same classroom. Half of each racial sample was low SES, half middle SES. The Peabody Picture Vocabulary Test (PPVT), Raven's Colored Progressive Matrices (RCPM), and achievement tests were given. Three observers, using agreed-upon behavior categories, watched the classroom behavior of these children for several days. Test data were reported in mean percentiles by SES. For white low SES children, the mean percentile of RCPM was 52, for PPVT it was 64. For middle SES white children, the RCPM mean percentile was 79, and for PPVT it was 83. For black low SES children, RCPM mean percentile was 46, and for PPVT it was 39. For the middle SES blacks, the RCPM was 60, the PPVT was 54. Racial differences were called significant for both tests. The middle SES child was described as being as disruptive in class as the low SES child, and blacks as disruptive as whites. There was no relationship between achievement level and attention level, but PPVT and RCPM scores were significantly related to achievement. The authors rejected the notion that such tests as PPVT and RCPM should not be used on "disadvantaged" children because of the children's lack of attention.

Halpin, Halpin, and Torrance (1973) administered activities 4, 5, 6, and 7 of the Torrance Tests of Creative Thinking, Verbal Form B, to 61 blind residential children in institutions in three southern states in order to study the influence of sex, age, and race on creative thinking. Ages were 6 through 12, and both whites and blacks were represented. The data were treated by ANOVA. The mean score for whites at age 11 to 12 was significantly higher than the mean score of other whites at other ages and higher than blacks at some ages. The authors concluded that ". . . creative thinking abilities of blind children do not vary significantly as a function of sex, race, or age" (pp. 389–90).

Harris and Lovinger's (1968) purpose was to cast some light on (a) the reality of the black's reported tendency to drop in IQ with increasing age, and (b) the suitability of some of the measuring instruments used to measure black intelligence. The subjects were 80 blacks from the Queens Borough, New York, schools who had complete testing records for grades 1, 3, 6, 7, 8, and 9, and who were, apparently, selected from 196 children when in grade 7. The sample was not random. In grade 1, the Pintner-Cunningham Primary Test IQ was 97.60, SD = 13.07. In grade 3, the Otis Alpha IQ was 93.91, SD = 11.66; in grade 6, the Otis Beta IQ was 88.34, SD = 11.41. In grade 7, the Wechsler Intelligence Scale for Children (WISC) Full Scale IQ was 93.10, SD = 11.57. At grade 8, the Pintner General Ability Test, Verbal IQ, was 92.15, SD = 16.02, and the Cattell Culture Fair IQ was 96.19, SD = 15.46. At grade 9, the Full Scale WISC IQ was 96.16, SD = 10.42. The authors concluded that these data did not support the notion that black IQ falls with advancing age, but it should be noted that there was a broad mixture of tests and a non-random sample. The idea that black children are handicapped by verbal test material also was not supported. The CCFIT was considered "a promising test" for use with black children. Tests where black IQ was low were considered not appropriate tests for blacks.

Hawkes and Furst (1971) replicated an earlier study (Hawkes and Koff, 1970) which dealt primarily with a comparison of the anxiety levels of whites and blacks of varying SES, and the effects of anxiety on school achievement. In the replication the authors administered an anxiety questionnaire of their own and collected IQ data, achievement scores, and teachers' ratings (when available) on a number of grades 5 and 6 children from a variety of schools. Of the 1,010 reported IQs, 33 were from Stanford-Binet Intelligence Scale, 1960 revision; 60, from Kuhlman-Anderson Intelligence Scale; 210, from the California Test of Mental Maturity; and 707, from the Lorge-Thorndike General Intelligence Tests.

The authors reported a single composite IQ for 416 whites of 108.68, SD = 15.44, a composite IQ for 595 blacks of 88.20, SD = 13.54, and a t-value for the mean difference of 22.02. The authors' comments dealt almost entirely with anxiety.

The Henderson, Butler, and Goffeney (1969) study was done to show how effectively the Wechsler Intelligence Scale for Children (WISC) and the Bender-Gestalt (BG) could predict arithmetic and reading achievement scores for whites and nonwhites. The subjects were 83 non-white (95% black) children and 120 white children, aged 6–9 to 7–3 years, and from the Cerebral Palsy Study of the University of Oregon Medical School. (See also Goffeney, Henderson, and Butler, 1971.) All children were low SES. The Wide Range Achievement Test (WRAT) was also given. For whites, the BG mean score was 5.98, SD = 3.00, the mean WISC IQ was 99.12, SD = 12.88, the mean Arithmetic score was 28.92, SD = 5.51, and the mean Reading score was 27.31, SD = 6.30. For non-whites, these same means, in the same order, were 8.06, SD = 3.36, 92.13, SD = 11.83, 27.07, SD = 5.54, and 27.06, SD = 5.08. The authors concluded that BG added nothing to the predictive efficiency of WISC.

Henderson, Fay, Lindemann, and Clarkson (1973) sought to answer four questions about the use of psychological tests on school children. Their subjects were 247 black and 462 white 8-year-olds selected from the University of Oregon Child Development Study. Those children who had not completed certain preliminary tests were not included. Along with the Wechsler Intelligence Scale for Children (WISC) and the Bender-Gestalt (BG), the Goodenough-Harris Draw-A-Man Test (DAM), the Illinois Test of Psycholinguistic Abilities (word association subtest) (ITPA), and the Wide Range Achievement Test (WRAT) were given. The following data were abstracted from Table 1, p. 348:

	Black		White	
	Mean	SD	Mean	SD
WISC				
Full Scale IQ	91.19	11.39	98.00	12.53
Verbal IQ	89.99	11.32	96.70	12.21
Performance IQ	94.37	12.70	99.88	13.96
BG	2.87	0.63	2.49	0.70
ITPA Word Assoc.	17.50	3.18	19.08	2.78
DAM	18.70	6.08	18.28	5.60

All racial differences were called significant. The authors concluded that: (1) the lower mean test scores did not necessarily produce lower predictive value for a test; (2) the test battery predicted more accurately for females than for males but not significantly differently for blacks and whites; (3) achievement tests generally predicted other achievements for 8-year-olds better than IQ tests; and (4) the Full Scale IQ of WISC predicted 8-year-old reading best for white males, but not significantly differently for white females, black females, and black males; and the Performance IQ was as good for black males as for any other group.

Herzog, Newcomb, and Cisin (1972) investigated whether a nursery school intervention program enhances later school achievement. The experimental group (EG) was 30 low SES black 3-year-olds who had attended a nursery school program (never described) at Howard University (Washington, D.C.) during 1964-9, and who were selected from a pool of names obtained by house-to-house solicitation in Washington, D.C. The children had to be mentally and physically healthy, and the parents had to speak English and agree to the participation of the child. The EG was drawn randomly from one Washington census tract, and a control group (CG) of 66 was drawn randomly from 3 other Washington census tracts. EG attended nursery school for two years (1964-6) and remained a coherent group through the next three years of school (grades K through 2). Nothing was said about CG except that they entered kindergarten and completed grades 1 and 2 when EG did. As of 1972, both groups were still being followed. In 1964, the IQ on Stanford-Binet Intelligence Scale (S-B) for EG was 81, SD = 11 and in 1969, it was 92, SD = 13. For CG, these data were 85, SD = 11, and 87, SD = 12. The net change of 9 points was significant at .02 level. The authors noted that EG and CG reached their highest IQ in 1967 and that both were on the way down in 1969 (which result the authors called disappointing), but that one should attend to patterns of scores rather than to sizes of scores.

Holowinsky and Pascale (1972) were interested (a) in whether girls achieved more on some subtests of Wechsler Intelligence Scale for Children (WISC) than boys, and vice versa, and (b) in whether white scores were higher than black scores on certain WISC subtests. Subjects were drawn from a single school district (culturally heterogeneous) and had been referred for psychological study because of poor school achievement. Markedly retarded children and those with emotional problems were excluded. Subjects were generally low to mid-low SES. Four verbal subtests of WISC were used. Total N was 134 (77 black and 57 white) children with an IQ range of 57 to 129. As computed by this reviewer, the mean IQ of the 57 whites was 83.08; that of the 77 blacks was 76.93. After analyzing their data in detail, even though the samples were representative of neither blacks nor whites, the authors generalized widely about subtest performance, sex, and race.

The Hughes and Lessler (1965) article was written to illustrate whether the Peabody Picture Vocabulary Test (PPVT) could be used as a substitute for the Wechsler Intelligence Scale for Children (WISC) on mentally retarded children. Subjects were 83 black and 54 white children from low SES rural North Carolina who were referred for evaluation by their schools. Ages ranged from 6 to 16 years, and grades were from 2 to 10. When the sexes were combined, this reviewer computed mean IQs for WISC. For blacks, the mean Verbal IQ was 69.44, Performance IQ 66.33, and Full Scale IQ 64.98. For whites, Verbal IQ was 79.85, Performance IQ 78.66, and Full Scale IQ 77.28. The mean PPVT IQs were: blacks, 66.34; whites, 79.44. Correlations, called significantly different from zero, for the three WISC IQs and PPVT varied between .58 and .66 for black males, .41 to .56 for black females, .21 to .43 for white males, and .42 to .56 for white females. The authors discussed error for individual prediction of one test score from the other—up to 11 points for blacks when predicting WISC Performance from PPVT, and up to 15 points for whites.

Isaac (1973) had three purposes in mind when she published her article: (a) Between high and low SES children at the grade 1 level, were there significant differences in perceptual-motor scores?; (b) Do such differences exist between blacks and whites?; and (c) Does familiarity with the Bender Motor Gestalt Test, or incentives, improve the perceptual-motor scores of low SES children more than the same scores of high SES children? Subjects were 60 whites from seven grade 1 classes of two elementary schools in a suburban white school district, and 60, each, black and white children of low SES from 13 grade 1 classes of four elementary schools in a large, urban school district. While subjects were selected by random numbers, those repeating kindergarten or grade 1, those referred for psychological problems, those with poor vision or neurological impairment, and those whose parents spoke no English were excluded. The Bender Motor Gestalt, Koppitz scoring (BG), and the Peabody Picture Vocabulary Test (PPVT) were given individually, in the child's school, by a white female. Ten, each, boys and girls from each SES-racial grouping were assigned at random to one of three conditions: one to assess the effects of familiarity with the BG on repeat BG scores, one to assess the effect of incentive on repeat BG scores, and a control group. Oddly, nothing further was said about the control group. PPVT IQs for the high SES whites were 111.33, SD = 11.13 for girls and 117.30, SD = 15.96 for boys. For the low SES whites, these values were 103.23, SD = 14.77 and 100.17, SD = 19.73 for girls and boys, respectively. For blacks, all low SES, the mean IQs were 90.77, SD = 9.52 and 91.33, SD = 10.86 for girls and boys, respectively. No significant BG differences between the white groups appeared, but both white groups were superior to the blacks. The author speculated that the low performance of the blacks may have been related to the white tester and cited Anastasi (1958) as the only evidence. Familiarization and incentive did not improve significantly the low SES group more than the high SES group. There was no significant correlation between BG and PPVT IQ. The author thought that the findings had educational implications.

Jensen's first paper (1971) in this series was done to test the hypothesis that public schools discriminated educationally against minority children. Using the classroom as the unit of random selection, the author obtained 2,453 whites, 2,263 Mexicans, and 1,853 blacks, grades K through 8, from 10 counties in the California Greater Bay Area. Half of the children were tested by special testers, half by their classroom teachers. When a difference between tester and teacher appeared, the tester's data were taken; otherwise, the data were combined. Lorge-Thorndike Intelligence Test was given to all children. The Figure Copying Test was given to grades K through 6, and the Standard Matrices were given in grades 7 and 8. A test of rote memory was given in grades 2 through 8. Motivational and personality questionnaires and a Home Index (SES) were also given. When racial differences were expressed in white sigma units, there was no evidence of discrimination against either blacks or Mexicans. The latter, although the lowest of the groups in SES, were closer in score to whites than were blacks. The author concluded that not only was there no support in his data for the notion that schools discriminated against either minority group, there was no support also for the "cumulative deficit" theory.

The purpose of Jensen's second study (1973b) was to determine if the same Level I and Level II relationships occurred in an agricultural sample as in a highly urbanized sample. The subjects were grades 4, 5, and 6 children, all from one California school district, so sampled (classroom the unit of sampling) as to be a stratified random sample of the area's white, black, and Mexican school populations. SES varied with the sample: whites were middle and lower-middle SES; blacks were lower-middle and lower-SES; and the Mexicans were clearly the lowest in SES. N varied with grade. For grades 4, 5, and 6, respectively, white Ns were 237, 242, and 219; black Ns were 189, 198, and 169; and Mexican Ns were 239, 211, and 218. Tests used were the Lorge-Thorndike Verbal and Nonverbal Tests (L-T), Raven's Colored and Standard Matrices (Raven), Memory for Numbers and Listening Attention Test (DS), an achievement test, and the Home Index (SES). All tests were given in the late fall, within a week's period for any given class except for the achievement tests. Half the samples were tested by special testers, half by the classroom teachers; if no differences appeared, the data were combined.

Results for L-T Verbal IQ for whites, blacks, and Mexicans, respectively, were: for grade 4, 100.85, SD = 14.60, 88.03, SD = 11.27, and 89.76, SD = 12.17; for grade 5, 101.83, SD = 13.87, 87.36, SD = 11.38, and 89.65, SD = 13.11; and for grade 6, 100.93, SD = 13.09, 90.35, SD = 12.58, and 90.44, SD = 13.79. For L-T Nonverbal IQ, in the same grade order, for whites, blacks, and Mexicans, respectively, the scores were: for grade 4, 108.61, SD = 16.05, 92.33, SD = 14.20, and 99.84, SD = 14.57; for grade 5, 110.07, SD = 14.93, 93.79, SD = 13.25, and 99.47, SD = 14.77; and for grade 6, 110.22, SD = 12.89, 97.99, SD = 14.64, and 101.87, SD = 14.63. Data (in raw score form) for the three grades were not combined for the factor analysis; each grade was considered an independent replication of the entire study. Age was partialled out of all intercorrelations. Three factors emerged: g_c (crystallized intelligence), g_f (fluid intelligence), and memory. The first two corresponded with Level II abilities, the last with Level I abilities. The author concluded that, by using a different methodology, he had confirmed earlier findings regarding mean racial differences in Level I and Level II abilities. Consistent and significant differences in correlations of Level I and Level II abilities with SES appeared for whites only; blacks and Mexicans showed uniformly low correlations for ability factors and SES, and the author suggested that this was less a racial difference than a matter of the differential validity of the SES measure.

Jensen's (1974a) article was written to investigate the "cumulative deficit hypothesis" which holds that the IQs of blacks decrease with age because of poor environmental inputs. After a thorough review of the literature, the author found no satisfactory empirical evidence to support this hypothesis, and he then discussed possible longitudinal and cross-sectional experimental approaches to the problem as an introduction to his own experiment. Seventeen schools of the Berkeley (California) Unified School District included some 4,000 white and 2,600 black children in grades K through 6 (aged 5½ to 12 years). For grades K and 1, the Lorge-Thorndike Intelligence Test, Level 1, Form B, Primary, Nonverbal form was used; for grades 2 and 3, Level 2, Form B, Primary, Nonverbal form of L-T; and for grades 4, 5, and 6, Level 3, Form B, Verbal and Nonverbal forms of L-T. The mean younger-older sibling IQ difference and the absolute younger-older sib difference, within each family, were averaged over all families in each racial group. The author concluded:

> A progressive age decrement in Negro IQ could exist. But it is noteworthy that the prevailing general acceptance of the cumulative deficit hypothesis as an explanation for the generally lower IQ of Negroes as compared with Whites remains unsupported by any methodologically sound evidence in the literature. The results of the present study, in addition to the lack of contradictory evidence in the previous research literature, suggest that the causes of the Negro IQ deficit, whatever they might be, are not reflected in age decrements beyond about age 5 but appear largely to involve factors whose influences are already established before school age (p. 1018).

After reviewing the literature on the effects of race of examiner on IQs of black and white children, Jensen (1974b) described the results of the testing of about 9,000 children (virtually the total population) in 17 California schools (grades K through 6) by 8 black and 12 white examiners. The purpose was to assess the effects of race of examiner on test scores. All examiners held degrees in psychology or education and were given special training in testing with the Lorge-Thorndike Intelligence Test (L-T), the Figure Copying Test (FCT), the Listening-Attention and Memory for Numbers Test (LAMT), and the Speed and Persistence Test (SPT). Regarding the L-T nonverbal part, white examiners tested 2,642 whites and 1,893 blacks, and black examiners tested 1,624 whites and 988 blacks. On the verbal part of L-T, whites tested 1,190 whites and 567 blacks, and blacks tested 534 whites and 553 blacks. On FCT, whites tested 1,776 whites and 1,327 blacks, and blacks tested 1,331 whites and 924 blacks. For SPT, whites tested 2,656 whites and 1,729 blacks, and blacks tested 1,114 whites and 914 blacks. For LAMT, whites tested 1,870 whites and 1,466 blacks, and blacks tested 1,025 whites and 534 blacks. The data were treated by ANOVA, and it was concluded that the unsystematic differences showed ". . . negligible effects of race of E (examiner) on the mental test scores of the white and black school children" (p. 12). Because of the large and representative samples used in this study, the findings were considered to have wide generality.

In another article, Jensen (1974c) attempted to answer this question:

> Does the pupil's ethnicity *per se* make any independent contribution to the prediction of achievement over the predictive power obtained by the multiple correlation of a number of psychometric, personality, and background variables, none of which can be regarded merely as substitute code names for the ethnic variable? (p. 659).

The author's sample consisted of white, black, and Mexican-American children, grades 1 through 8, in a California school district (probably those described in Jensen, 1974a). The tests were those used earlier: Lorge-Thorndike Intelligence Tests, Verbal and Nonverbal (L-T); Raven's Progressive Matrices (RPM); Figure Copying Test (FCT); Listening-Attention Test and Memory for Numbers (DS), and Speed and Persistence Test (SPT). The criteria of scholastic achievement were various subtests of the Stanford Achievement battery. Gough's Home Index measured SES, and the Junior Eysenck Personality Inventory (Extraversion and Neuroticism) was the personality measure. Not all tests were given to all subjects.

Data were given in correlation coefficients. The author concluded:

In brief, the contribution of pupils' ethnic group membership to the prediction of scholastic performance, independently of psychometric, personality, and status variables, is practically nil. This also means that there is no evidence in these data that any differentially discriminative forces in the school . . . differentially affect the scholastic performance of children according to their ethnic membership independently of the characteristics measured by the independent variables in this study (p. 668).

Jensen's (1974d) monograph was actually three separate, complex studies, all related to the hypothesis that racial differences in IQ are caused by culture bias in the tests. All three studies measured large samples of black, white, and Mexican children. The Peabody Picture Vocabulary Test (PPVT) was administered to all children. Raven's Colored Progressive Matrices (Raven) were given to children under grade 7, and the Standard Matrices (also designated here as Raven) were given to grades 7 and 8. In Study I, the sample included 638 whites, 381 blacks, and 644 Mexicans from Riverside, California, public schools. School grades ranged from K through 6, and there were, roughly, equal numbers from each grade. Study II was performed on a random sample of 24 children of each sex from each of grades K, 1, and 3 from one all-white and one all-black school in Contra Costa, California. Total N was 288. The average age of the whites was 6–11; of blacks, 7–2. There were no Mexican children in this study. Study III involved a large, representative sample of the three racial groups for grades 3 through 8. The subjects were from Kern County, California. Ns were 841 for whites, 687 for blacks, and 788 for Mexicans. Among the three studies, various statistical treatments were used and some 10 hypotheses were tested. The author summarized the monograph by saying that the present set of analyses, in general, suggested little support for culture bias in black scores for either PPVT or Raven. There was almost no evidence of culture bias for Mexicans on Raven, but there was some doubt about the Mexicans' performance on PPVT. There was no doubt about the performance of blacks on either test. The author continued that if the racial differences in performance on PPVT and Raven were the result of cultural differences, it should be possible to construct other tests which are biased in favor of the minority groups, but which show the same psychometric properties as the present PPVT and Raven. If such new tests could also be found to stand the kind of analyses to which PPVT and Raven have been subjected, such ". . . would be a strong challenge to any theory which holds that the average racial difference in IQ is not attributable to cultural bias in the tests." (p. 243)

In order to determine the validity of his Level I-Level II Theory of

Intelligence, Jensen (1974e) established three specific hypotheses for testing: (a) SES classes will differ less in Level I ability than in Level II ability, (b) correlation between Level I ability and Level II ability will be greater in the upper and middle SES levels than in the low SES level, and (c) the development of Level II ability will be dependent upon the development of Level I ability, but not the reverse. The sample was composed of 1,489 white and 1,123 black children from grades 4, 5, and 6 in 14 elementary schools in the Berkeley Unified School District of California, and they may have been part of the sample used in Jensen, 1974a. The whites came from better-than-average SES, and the blacks were lower-middle to low SES. Tests (Memory for Numbers Test (DS), and Level 3, Form B of the Lorge-Thorndike Intelligence Test (L-T)) were administered in the classrooms by three white and three black testers who were assigned to the classrooms at random. Level I tests (DS) and Level II (L-T) were always given by a different tester in different sessions. The mean IQs for L-T were: Verbal IQ, for whites, 118.4, SD = 15.7 and for blacks, 92.8, SD = 13.9; Nonverbal IQ, for whites 120.24, SD = 14.6 and for blacks, 95.4, SD = 15.5. The total mean scores for DS were: whites 74.48, SD = 15.58; blacks 62.45, SD = 16.82. Regarding Hypothesis (a), the racial difference on L-T (Level II) was more than twice as much as the racial difference on DS (Level I). Regarding Hypothesis (b), higher correlations existed between DS and L-T scores among whites (upper SES) than among blacks (low SES). Hypothesis (c) was supported by the Nonverbal IQs but not by the Verbal IQs; it was concluded that low or high scores in Level I ability were not incompatible with low or high scores in Level II ability.

Jensen had commented earlier (Jensen, 1974a, p. 1018) that a progressive age decrement in black IQ could exist but that, with a California sample of blacks, no compelling evidence in support of that hypothesis had appeared. He was now (Jensen, 1977b) testing the cumulative deficit hypothesis with a rural, southern sample of both blacks and whites. The California Test of Mental Maturity (CTMM) was administered to all of the white (N = 653) and black (N = 826) children in the public schools in a small, rural, southeastern Georgia town. The mean age for whites was 12–4; for blacks, 11–8. No children were accepted from families of less than two, or more than five, children. Blacks were of low SES; whites, of low to lower-middle SES. The mean total IQs were 102, SD = 16.7 for whites, and 71, SD = 15.1 for blacks. All data were collected by what Jensen called the sibling method (Jensen, 1974a), i.e., the difference between a younger and an older sibling (Y-O). Y-O was computed for IQ for each-sibling-and-the-next-oldest-sibling pairs for all family sizes from two to five children, and if the Y-O difference was positive, an age decrement in IQ was indicated. The author concluded that for rural Georgia children, a clear, significant, and substantial decrement in both verbal and nonverbal IQ was shown for blacks but not for whites. He commented, "The phenomenon predicted by the cumulative deficit hypothesis is thus demonstrated at a high level of significance" (p. 190). However, Jensen emphasized that such a conclusion supported neither an environmental nor a genetic explanation of the findings, and he suggested that both, together, could be the proper explanation. However, since he had found no such support for the culture deficit hypothesis among California black children (1974a), the present finding favored an environmental explanation.

Jensen and Figueroa (1975) sought to demonstrate the validity of the Jensen Two-Factor Theory of Intelligence by showing that new predictions about black and white IQ differences would be statistically significant. In the Main Study, five novel hypotheses were considered; in the Supplementary Studies, three old ones were tested. For the Main Study, one boy and one girl were selected randomly from each randomly selected grade (K through 6) in each of 98 randomly selected California school districts. Blacks and whites were sampled separately. Ages ranged from 5–0 to 11–12. N for whites was 669; for blacks, 622. The Wechsler Intelligence Scale for Children—Revised (WISC-R) was given by trained psychometrists. Forward Digit Span (FDS) and Backward Digit Span (BDS) were measured by the WISC-R digit span series, neither of which series entered the computation of WISC-R IQs. For FDS, 3 to 9 digits were given twice; score was 1 point for each correct series. For BDS, 2 to 8 digits were given twice, scored as for FDS. All raw scores were converted to standard scores (Mn $= 10$, SD $= 3$) for each 4-month age interval separately. Hypothesis 1 predicted that BDS (Level II ability) would be more highly correlated with IQ than would FDS (Level I ability). This prediction was clearly demonstrated for blacks but less so for whites. Hypothesis 2 stated that BDS would show a greater racial difference than would FDS. The data showed that the racial difference for BDS was twice the size of the FDS racial difference. Hypothesis 3 stated that FDS and BDS would so interact with age that the FDS-BDS difference would decrease with age. When these differences decreased from 2.71 to 1.77, the hypothesis was confirmed. For Hypothesis 4, the prediction was that blacks, relative to whites, would show less convergence for FDS-BDS as age increased. The differences among these mean differences showed no significant linear component, and the hypothesis was rejected. Hypothesis 5 predicted an overall Race × Age interaction, and this hypothesis was rejected also.

In the Supplementary Studies the Anxiety Hypothesis was considered first. The authors selected random samples of 1,852 white and 1,476 black children (grades 2 through 8) from District A schools and 2,615 white and 2,134 black children (grades 2 through 6) from District B schools. FDS was administered by tape replay, with and without delayed recall. All findings were opposite to the predictions from the Anxiety Hypothesis which was rejected. For the Task Difficulty Hypothesis, short FDS series (4, 5, and 6 digits) and long FDS series (7, 8, and 9 digits) were given to 100 black and 100 white children selected randomly from the 11- and 12-year-olds from District A. The racial difference for short FDS was .12; for long FDS, .13. There was no significant Race × Series Length interaction. To test the Race of Examiner Hypothesis, one black and one white psychometrist administered FDS with both immediate and delayed recall to 98 white and 80 black children randomly selected from grades 2 through 6 from District B schools. The Race of Examiner × Race of Subject interaction was not significant at any age level.

In order again to test the validity of Jensen's Two-Factor Theory of Intelligence, Jensen and Frederiksen (1973) selected an age-matched sample of 120 black and white grade 2 and grade 4 children from two public schools—one dominantly white and one dominantly black. With respect to SES, the sample was considered typical of both races; blacks were low SES, and whites were middle SES. Ten white and 10 black children of each grade were assigned at random to an uncategorized list (Study A), a random-categorized list (Study B), and a block-categorized list (Study C). In each study, on five separate occasions, the subjects were presented with a set of 20 familiar objects at a two-second interval and were told to remember them for later recall. After each presentation, the subjects were given 90 seconds to recite the names of all of the objects remembered. In Study A, the objects could not be grouped into categories; learning was considered rote learning (Level I). In Study B, designed to measure Level II ability, the objects could be grouped by the subjects into four categories—clothing, tableware, furniture, and animals—but the objects were presented in random order. In Study C, also designed to measure Level II ability, the objects were the same as in Study B, but they were presented in categorized order, i.e., first the furniture objects, then the tableware objects, etc.

In Study A, no racial differences in recall appeared for either grade 2 or grade 4. This supported the hypothesis that there was little racial difference in Level I ability. The performance difference between grades 2 and 4 was significant and was consistent with the hypothesis that Level I ability increases with age. For Study B, the racial difference was not significant at grade 2 but was significant at grade 4, and this agreed with the hypothesis that Level II ability is a larger source of racial variance than is Level I ability in older, rather than younger, children. Grade 4 performance was not significantly different from grade 2 performance, although the whites showed the hypothesized growth in Level II ability from grade 2 to grade 4. Blacks showed no such growth, and the authors found this lack of black growth not only difficult to explain but in contradiction of the literature. Regarding Study C, grades 2 and 4 differed significantly, as expected, but the racial groups did not differ significantly. This suggested that block-presentation of the lists had no effect on either racial group at grade 2 but had a facilitating effect on both racial groups at grade 4, more so on blacks than on whites. Using the "clustering" measure from another source, the authors demonstrated that both racial groups in Studies B and C clustered more than chance expectancy. When clustering was measured on Study B data, the authors concluded that there was no racial difference in grade 2 even though the difference was in the expected direction. In grade 4, however, the racial difference was significant, but there was no significant difference between grades 2 and 4 largely because grade 4 blacks showed no more clustering ability than grade 2 blacks. When clustering was measured in Study C, grades 2 and 4 were significantly different; and while whites showed more clustering than blacks, in both grades, the racial differences were not significant. Blocking had increased clustering in both racial groups in grade 4, but how much was the result of true clustering or the result of the order of presentation was not determinable. The authors found these data in support of the hypotheses that whites show stronger Level II processes than blacks and that Level II ability is more strongly shown in older than in younger children.

John's (1963) article was intended as a report on the linguistic and cognitive development of black children, but it ended as a validity study of the Lorge-Thorndike Intelligence Test (L-T). Other tests used in this study were the Peabody Picture Vocabulary Test (PPVT) to measure "receptive" vocabulary and the WISC Vocabulary subtest to measure "expressive" vocabulary. A word association test was also used. Three groups of black children were selected from a larger sample of New York City area children. The children were classified as low-low SES to middle SES; 69 subjects were in grade 1, and 105 were in grade 5. How the children were selected and how the tests were given were not stated. Unidentified scores were given for PPVT for both grades. This reviewer computed the L-T IQs at 98.9 for grade 1 and 95.7 for grade 5. SDs were estimated to be 13.4 for both grades. Grade 1 children had taken the L-T Level 1 test; grade 5, L-T Nonverbal Battery, Level 3. The author concluded that consistent class (SES) differences in language skills were shown, but nothing was done to show what part of these differences were the result of differences in intelligence. The article contains a great deal of speculative "interpretation" about the effects of "culture."

Johnson and Mihal (1973) described a scheme for comparing the usual paper-and-pencil administration of the School and College Ability Test (SCAT) with a computerized administration. Ten white and 10 black grades 7 and 8 subjects were obtained from a public school in Rochester, New York, and were paired for test administration. To one of the pairs the computerized SCAT, Form 3A, was given while the other of the pair took the paper SCAT, Form 3B. When each subject was finished, the procedure was reversed, and when the pair had finished, each had taken both forms of SCAT—one on paper and one on computer. No information about the selection of the subjects was given, and no scores were published. The data were reported by a series of ANOVAs. The authors commented that white scores exceeded black scores on the verbal paper part of SCAT as well as on the quantitative paper and quantitative computer parts. On the verbal computer, there was no racial difference. For whites, there were no differences in score between the methods of administration. Blacks, however, responded so much better on the computer than on the paper administration that ". . . there was no discernible difference between races" (p. 698) because of the black computer performance on the verbal part of SCAT. There was also evidence that the faster a question was answered, the more likely was the answer to be correct.

The authors discussed tester bias, motivation, and test anxiety as the major causes of race differences, but they had had no chance to read studies on these matters which were done on much larger samples (Jensen, 1974b, d; Jensen and Figueroa, 1975). There is also the problem of the number and selection of subjects. It is hard to be convinced that a sample of 10 subjects is randomly representative of either blacks or whites, yet the validity of ANOVA depends on randomness. One markedly deviant subject in 10 could leave his mark on ANOVA. The authors also seemed overenthusiastic in their comments about computerized testing (p. 698), even though they finally commented that repetition of their study was needed (p. 699). The study was novel and interesting, and it should be repeated with larger samples. In such future repetitions, it is hoped that the authors will publish the scores of their subjects.

To test the hypothesis that their special teaching program would raise the IQs of young black children, Johnson and Jacobson (1970) selected three samples of black children who were entering grade 1, or repeating grade 1 or 2., the following fall. All children were from Amelia County, Virginia, all black, all related to a Head Start program. Their mean ages were between 74.6 (grade K) and 104.6 (grade 2) months. There were 14 children classified grade K; 14, grade 1; and 15, grade 2. Although the samples were called random, how they were chosen was not stated, and certain "untestable" children were replaced by "more mature" children after the program began. The training program involved the home, field trips, and classroom work, and was held 3 morning hours a day, 5 days a week, for 5 weeks. The Peabody Picture Vocabulary Test (PPVT) and achievement tests were given pre- and post-treatment by "outside reading specialists." There were no control groups, and only those children who completed the program were reported. The authors claimed the following gains for PPVT: for grade K, 17.5 points; for grade 1, 19.3 points; and for grade 2, 8.3 points. The post-treatment IQs were: grade K, 85.9; grade 1, 84.8; and for grade 2, 79.7. The training program, then, may have raised the IQs of these children not quite to the level usually found for black children. There was no control group; therefore, net changes in IQ could not be tested. The participation as teachers of those who were involved in the design of the teaching program raised further questions about the objectivity of the study.

The purpose of Kaufman and Kaufman (1973) was to study the performance of matched groups of blacks and whites on the McCarthy Scales of Children's Abilities (MSCA), which is well described in the article. The children were taken from McCarthy's standardization sample of 1,032 children 2½ to 8½ years of age (McCarthy, 1972). A white child was chosen to match each possible black child on age, sex, geographic region, father's occupation, education of parents, and grade in school. Out of the 154 blacks in the McCarthy sample, 148 were matched (roughly, 13 to 17 children at each of 10 age levels). The age levels were combined to yield 43 pairs of children at ages 2½ to 3½; 60 pairs at ages 4 to 5½; and 45 pairs at ages 6½ to 8½. Blacks and whites were compared (a) on the McCarthy General Cognitive Indexes (GCI) where the mean was 100 and SD was 16; (b) on Verbal, Perceptual-Performance, Quantitative, Memory, and Motor Indexes (mean was 50, SD was 10 for each). The mean GCI for the 2½ to 3½ group was 103.3, SD = 17.0 for whites and 97.4, SD = 17.2 for blacks; for the 4 to 5½ group, the means were 96.1, SD = 15.7 and 94.6, SD = 15.1 for whites and blacks, respectively. For the oldest group, the data were 98.1, SD = 15.4 for whites and 88.6, SD = 14.1 for blacks. The racial differences were called significant only in the oldest group. The authors presented data for other psychological tests and compared their present data with WPPSI data from an earlier study (Kaufman, 1973; see Chapter II). The authors concluded that there were no race differences on MSCA until 5½ years of age, and they speculated further that racial equality would have existed without the "rigorous" matching. Black children were called better coordinated than white children even though no racial differences were found at the oldest and youngest age levels. ". . . black children were *not* systematically deficient in abstract reasoning" (p. 206). The authors did not mention that such "rigorous" matching for SES also matched for intelligence.

Kennedy's 1965 publication was a follow-up of the Kennedy, Van De Riet, and White (1963) study. Tests for the 1965 study were administered 4 years after the tests reported in the 1963 publication, allowing Kennedy to (a) compare children who were successful in academics with those who were not, (b) determine the best predictors of IQ constancy, and (c) find ". . . specific indicators of academic abilities which remain

high, low, or shift" (p. 5). The subjects were one-fifth of the original
sample of 1,800 which was representative of five southeastern states.
Since there were no significant differences among the means of the five
original states in the 1963 study, the author selected Florida, alone,
for the sample for the present study. Of the original 360 Florida children
who were tested in the original group, 316 were recovered for the present
sample, and they represented rural, urban, and metropolitan children
in school—not children in general. If the same tests that were given in
1960 (p. 4) were readministered (the Stanford-Binet, 1960 Revision
(S-B), the Goodenough Draw-A-Man (DAM), and the California
Achievement Test (Cal AT), only the S-B and Cal AT were reported
in the follow-up study.

In 1960, the mean S-B IQ of the 312 children was 78.9, SD = 12.6;
in 1965, 79.2, SD = 14.3. The rural mean S-B IQ was 78.5, SD = 12.8
in 1960; and in 1965, 78.3, SD = 15.7. The urban S-B IQ in 1960 was
74.4; in 1965, 75.2 (SDs not given). None of the time period differences
was significant. Data were also presented for a number of subdivisions
of the total data. The results of the Cal AT scores were presented in
considerable detail, and the same time comparisons were made. The
general indication was ". . . a gradual falling behind through the upward
movement of grades . . ." (p. 98) during the 4-year period covered by
the data. There was, generally, a 3-year difference between the actual
grade placement and the Cal AT grade placement. As in the case of
the IQ data, achievement scores were presented in a number of different
breakdowns.

The author showed that the best predictor of 1965 S-B IQ was the
1960 S-B IQ, followed in order by the 1960 DAM, the Cal AT Reading
Vocabulary score, and next the Cal AT Mechanics of English score.
Similar comparisons were made for the several subtests of Cal AT. The
author concluded that S-B was the most powerful single predictor of
either later IQ or achievement, pointing ". . . to the amazing stability
of the IQ over the intervening {4} years" (p. 167). Remedial programs
for blacks should be inaugurated at an early age. Improvements in the
schools between 1960 and 1965 had not helped the black child. The
author made clear that the cause of the racial differences in IQ lay in
the cultural differences between the two races, but he produced no evidence for this.

Using a test that, in content, was biased toward the culture of India
(Shah's Nonverbal Group Test of Intelligence), Knowles and Shah (1969)
attempted to study its effects on black and white subjects in this country.
Shah's test had been standardized on 6,037 school children, aged 8
through 14, in 79 schools in the Gujarat State. It contains six subtests:
similarities (geometric forms), classification (pictures of objects), analogies (pictures of objects that belong together), absurdities (pictures of

objects which contain erroneous parts), progressive series (ordering pictures), and substitution (similar to the coding of WISC). The Shah test was given to 35 inner-city blacks, 29 suburban whites (all in Detroit), and 17 University of Michigan Laboratory School pupils. IQs were: blacks 103.6, SD = 12.7; suburban Detroit whites, 126.2, SD = 8.9; and white Lab School pupils, 123.1, SD = 13.1. Blacks were not significantly different from the Indian norms (100, SD = 14.8), but whites and blacks in the United States differed significantly. The authors commented that the data were what one would expect from the use of a verbal group test of intelligence, but they commented no further about this.

Kresheck and Nicolosi (1973) noted that, as widely-used as was the Peabody Picture Vocabulary Test (PPVT), little had been done to demonstrate its validity on "subcultural" groups. The authors, oddly, defined validity as black-white differences in PPVT score, and so sought to demonstrate validity by comparing PPVT scores of 50, each, black and white children of low SES, matched for age (mean, each group, was 6.1 years) and grade (grade data not given). Form A of PPVT was administered by a school speech clinician. Scores for blacks ranged from 33 to 68 (mean of 48), and for whites, from 42 to 76 (mean of 59). The racial difference was called significant at .001. The authors discussed PPVT scores from two unpublished samples which roughly agreed with the black performance reported here. Since their definition of validity fitted their data, the authors concluded that the PPVT was of questionable validity for blacks.

In the Lesser, Fifer, and Clark (1965) monograph, four trained psychometricians administered a special adaptation of the Hunter Aptitude Scales (for Gifted Children) (HAS) to 80, each, Chinese, Puerto Rican, black, and Jewish children in grade 1 in various parts of New York City. HAS was described in detail in the monograph. The children, all of whom were middle and low SES, were matched for age, sex, and school grade. The purpose of the study was to ". . . examine the patterns among various mental abilities in young children from different social-class and cultural backgrounds" (p. 1). All children were tested in their native language. The authors presented a table of 18 factors which they thought affected test scores and indicated the extent to which they (the authors) controlled these factors. Six hypotheses were to be tested: (a) significant differences in score will exist between the SES groups; (b) significant differences will exist among the scores of the ethnic groups; (c) there will be a significant SES × Ethnicity interaction in level of scores for the four scales; (d) significant differences between SES classes will exist in score patterns for the four scales; (e) significant differences among the ethnic groups will exist in score patterns for the four scales; and (f) there will be a significant SES × Ethnicity interaction in the score patterns for the four scales.

The mean scores are reported here in the order of Jewish, black, Chinese, and Puerto Rican (Table 12, p. 48): Verbal scores were 90.35, SD = 11.70, 74.29, SD = 16.48, 71.09, SD = 14.57, 61.92, SD = 17.41; Reasoning scores were 25.21, SD = 6.67, 20.41, SD = 9.43, 25.94, SD = 7.12, 18.90, SD = 8.62; Numerical scores were 28.50, SD = 9.88, 18.39, SD = 10.20, 27.79, SD = 9.35, 19.13, SD = 9.71; Space scores were 39.71, SD = 9.21, 34.42, SD = 11.56, 42.51, SD = 10.09, 35.09, SD = 9.70. A number of tables were devoted to ANOVA results and racial difference values, and a number of figures illustrated racial test-score patterns. A section of the monograph was devoted to detailed interpretations of the findings, and the major findings appeared in the summary in condensed form. Hypotheses (a), (b), (c), and (e) were confirmed; hypotheses (d) and (f) were rejected. Other specific conclusions were given.

Lessing's (1969) purpose was ". . . to investigate racial differences in regard to two indices of adaptive ego functioning shown . . . to be related to academic achievement . . ." (p. 155). To do this, the author selected 182 white and 55 black grade 8 children and 288 white and 33 black grade 11 children, taking from their Chicago suburban school records only those whose IQs were between 70 and 129, who had at least grade 4 reading ability, and who had completed two 7-item "Personal Control" questionnaires. In addition, the occupation of the family wage earner had to be available. Subjects had been tested by school personnel between September, 1963, and January, 1964, apparently with several different types of intelligence tests. For grade 8, the mean IQs were 105.94 for whites and 95.87 for blacks. For grade 11, white mean IQ was 107.50; black mean, 91.00. Both race differences were significant at .01. The author concluded (a) that blacks had lower academic achievement than whites; and (b) "Sense of Personal Control" and "Willingness to Delay Gratification" were significantly lower for blacks than for whites and were related to academic achievement. The author used the results of ANOVA to mask the significance of the racial differences in intelligence. It should also be noted that, in limiting the IQ of the sample to a low of 70, the author eliminated the lowest 20% of all blacks and the lowest 3% of all whites. The administration of the tests and the knowledge that several different types of tests might have been used are further questionable characteristics of this article.

The purpose of the Little, Kenny, and Middleton report (1973) was to examine the effects of home stability, parental education, and sex on IQ changes in black children 4 to 7 years of age. The authors selected 54, each, male and female black children from the Memphis, Tennessee, sample of a National Institute for Neurological Diseases and Blindness research. The Stanford-Binet Intelligence Scale, Short Form (S-B), had been given to all children as they reached the age of 4 years, and at 7 years the Wechsler Intelligence Scale for Children (WISC) had been given. No child was accepted without a complete history, and all subjects had to be neurologically sound. Home stability was estimated for each child. All subjects were low SES. The mean S-B IQ at age 4 was 89.8, and the mean WISC at age 7 was 91.13. Children of parents with higher education changed little in IQ between 4 and 7, but children of parents with less education increased significantly in IQ from 4 to 7. At age 4, stable homes were more closely related to lower IQ children than were middle- or low-stability homes, but by age 7, children from stable homes had increased in IQ more than children from unstable homes (the latter had decreased in IQ). Children of moderate and higher stability homes had higher IQs at age 7 than children in other type homes. The authors argued for an "interactionistic" relationship between genetic and environmental factors. The authors also compared scores on two different tests not in terms of SD units but in terms of IQ units.

Loehlin, Vandenberg, and Osborne (1973) were interested in testing Shockley's hypothesis that, in blacks, IQ increases as the admixture of white genes increases (Shockley, 1972). Blood group genes were used as the marker for racial ancestry. The subjects were two sets of 40 and 44 black adolescents who had been tested in earlier studies by two of the authors. Each set of subjects was regarded as an independent replication of the other. Nineteen cognitive measures were given to these subjects, and while the authors' evidence did not sustain Shockley's hypothesis, the authors did comment that ". . . the results do, in our view, lend support to the position of Shockley, Jensen (1969b), and others that research on U.S. Negro-White differences using blood group techniques is both practical and instructive" (p. 267).

The Lowe and Karnes paper (1976) is, essentially, a note on the interchangeability of the Lorge-Thorndike Intelligence Test, Level 2, Form A (L-T), and the Wechsler Intelligence Scale for Children—Revised (WISC-R) as measures of the intelligence of young black children. Both tests were administered to 45 former Head Start children whose ages and grades were not given. Classroom teachers administered L-T, and trained graduate students gave the WISC-R. All testing was done in the schools, which were not identified. The mean L-T (nonverbal) IQ was 88.08, SD = 9.4, and the mean WISC-R Full Scale IQ was 79.66, SD = 11.46. The mean difference was significant at .01. The authors concluded that the two tests were not interchangeable.

Lunemann (1974) studied the value of the Lorge-Thorndike Intelligence Test (L-T) for the prediction of reading ability as measured by the Stanford Achievement Test (SAchT). Both tests were administered to all pupils in grades K, 1, and 2 in the Berkeley, California, school district in a year not specified. A year following, the SAchT was given to all grades 1, 2, and 3 children. Still another year following, the SAchT was given in grades 1, 2, and 3. Subjects were classified as white, black, Asian, and "others" (the latter mostly Spanish surnames), and all children were included in the study who had a L-T score and 2-year-apart SAchT scores. In presenting the data, the author combined grade groups for each of the ethnic groups. When L-T and SAchT were given one year apart, the validity coefficients for L-T ranged between .35 and .48 for 1,441 white children, .27 to .46 for 1,167 black children, .29 to .57 for 227 Asian children and .34 to .72 for 121 "other" children. For all 2,956 children, the range of validity çoefficients was .50 to .61. When L-T and SAchT had been given 2 years apart, the range in correlation between L-T and SAchT was .39 to .47 for 570 whites, .30 to .39 for 455 blacks, .36 to .59 for 108 Asians, and −.26 to .61 for 38 "others." For the 1,171 children in the 2-year-separation group, the range of validity coefficients was .54 to .57. The author concluded that L-T predicts SAchT scores as well for one ethnic group as for another, but he pointed out that the proportion of variability in achievement scores accounted for by L-T was not substantial for any group. Moreover, the validity coefficients found in the study for non-whites were much lower than those presented by the test publisher. While it was not possible to make a clear statement about the effects of desegregation on the validity of L-T, the author suggested that ". . . these data do seem to suggest that perhaps desegregation was not, of itself, a major influence on the results" (p. 267). The author listed some implications of his study: (a) There was no evidence that L-T, as a predictor of SAchT, was biased against any ethnic group; (b) Schools wishing to use L-T as a predictor of reading ability should ". . . determine *a priori* the predictive validity situation-specific rather than rely on the assumed or generally published predictive power of the measure" (p. 267); and (c) Use IQ tests "with extreme care" in predicting any given child's educational progress.

In order to study the Bender-Gestalt (B-G) performances of Puerto Rican children, Marmorale and Brown (1977) administered B-G to 74 Puerto Rican, 44 white, and 47 American Negro children from a public school in New York City. The specific aims of the study were (a) to compare B-G scores of "non-middle-class" Puerto Rican and American Negro children and middle-class white children on the Koppitz norms, and (b) to examine the changes in B-G scores as these children matured. The B-G was administered first while the children were in the first 3 months of grade 1 (mean ages 6–5 to 6–6) and later when the children were in the last 3 months of grade 3 (mean ages 8–10 to 8–11). The Puerto Rican children were tested in Spanish. B-G was scored by the Koppitz Developmental Bender Scoring System (Koppitz, 1964). In grade 1, the Puerto Rican mean score was equivalent to the 5 to 5½ year norms, white mean score was equivalent to the 6 to 6½ year norms, and American Negro mean score was equivalent to the 5½ year norms.

There were no sex differences. Whites performed at the expected level, but the other two groups did not. The means of the Puerto Rican and American Negro subjects were significantly lower than the mean of the whites. In grade 3, at mean ages 8–10 to 8–11, Puerto Rican mean was equivalent to the 7 to 7½ year norms, the white mean was equivalent to the 8 to 8½ year norms, and the American Negro mean was equivalent to the 6½ to 7 year norms. Again, there were no sex differences. All groups made significant gains over grade 1 scores. Whites and Puerto Ricans were no longer significantly different even though the latter were a year below the former, and the authors questioned the adequacy of the norms because of this. Negroes made the smallest gains and were again significantly below the whites.

In the course of an investigation of self-concept among racial groups, McDaniel (1967) presented IQs from the short form of the California Test of Mental Maturity (CTMM) for 13 whites, 81 blacks, and 86 Chicanos. The subjects were selected from 16 public schools in Austin, Texas, which were receiving support under the 1965 Elementary and Secondary Education Act. Thirty children from each of grades 1 through 6 were selected, apparently at random by the school counselor. All children were low SES. The mean CTMM IQs were: for 13 whites, 105.46 for language, 104.85 for non-language, and 106.08 total; for 81 blacks, 92.44 for language, 94.59 for non-language, and 92.72 total; for 86 Chicanos, 84.94 for language, 92.47 for non-language, and 87.76 total. Numerous data for correlations between self-concept and IQ and achievement scores were given. All conclusions dealt with self-concept.

The main purpose of the Meeker and Meeker (1973) article was a discussion of a scoring scheme for the Stanford-Binet Scale of Intelligence (S-B) devised by the authors from Guilford's Structure of Intellect Model. This reviewer gathered that the authors had classified all S-B items as Operations, Contents, or Products, referring to each as a Category. The subjects were all males, and all low SES. They were either 4 to 5 years of age, or 7 to 9 years of age. The sample was divided as follows: 37 Mexican children, aged 4 to 5, tested in Spanish, whose mean IQ was 90; 33 Mexican children, aged 4 to 5, tested in English, whose mean IQ was 95; 35 Mexican children, aged 7 to 9, tested in English, whose mean IQ was 101; 31 black children, aged 4 to 5, whose mean IQ was 100, tested by blacks; 24 black children, aged 7 to 9, whose mean IQ was 103, tested by blacks; 33 white children, aged 4 to 5, whose mean IQ was 101, tested by whites; and 64 white children, aged 7 to 9, whose mean IQ was 104, tested by whites. How the samples were chosen and where the study occurred were not given. Data were presented for each sample subgroup in terms of the ratio of S-B items passed/items failed for each criterion. Weakness in any Category could be identified for each sample subgroup, and this information would be used by school authorities to see that the learning process began where the child was strongest. The authors listed five suggestions for making their system work, but it is not clear how one moves from the group data to individual diagnosis. Minority-majority differences were not discussed, and it is not clear how, or if, the authors used the data from the 7- to 9-year-olds.

Miele's (1979) articles tested the hypothesis that the Wechsler Intelligence Scale for Children (WISC) was racially biased against the black child. He approached the problem from four points of view: (a) factor loadings of the first principal component, (b) rank order of item difficulty, (c) the ratio of Race × Item interaction variance to total variance, and (d) the simulation of racial differences by within-race age differences. The subjects were 111 black and 163 white children roughly 6 years old from rural and industrial Georgia, first tested in 1961 (preschool) and thereafter at grades 1, 3, and 5. From the data presented, this reviewer computed the preschool Full Scale IQs to be 103.00, SD = 13.4 for whites and 84.24, SD = 11.9 for blacks. The IQs for grade 1 were 110.10, SD = 11.8 for whites and 92.53, SD = 11.7 for blacks; for grade 3 they were 107.79; SD = 11.1 for whites and 90.48, SD = 10.9 for blacks; and for grade 5 they were 110.90, SD = 12.8 for whites and 90.21, SD = 12.9 for blacks. The black and white factor loadings were not significantly different. Item analysis indicated the same order of item difficulty for each race. The Race × Item interaction variance was, roughly, 5% of total variance, and this ratio fell to less than 1% when whites of a given grade were compared with blacks of the next higher grade. When Yule's Coefficient of Association was computed, there was no racial bias among the WISC items, and when black performance at one grade level was compared with black performance at the next higher grade level, those items that discriminated blacks from whites at the lower grade level were the same items that blacks answered correctly at the next higher grade level. For a subsample of 80 whites and 48 blacks, correlation between WISC scores of all four grade levels and grade point averages at graduation from high school was not significantly different between blacks and whites. The author concluded that racial differences in test scores were the result of differences in mental maturity between the races.

Because of the evidence in the literature that darkly-pigmented subjects had difficulty in perceiving shades of blue, Mitchell and Pollack (1974) wondered whether the block design subtest of the Wechsler Intelligence Scale for Children (WISC) was a test of spatial ability or whether a racial difference in the ability to perceive space existed. To two groups of 20 children (one white, one black) the WISC Block Design subtest was given in red and white. To two similar groups (one white, one black) the same subtest was given in blue and yellow. California Test of Mental

Maturity (CTMM) IQs were available from school records and only those children with IQs from 70 to 112 were accepted for the study. The mean CTMM IQ of the red-white condition was 104.3 for whites and 86.4 for blacks. The mean IQ for the blue-yellow condition was 105.6 for whites and 89.0 for blacks. The subjects were in grades 4 and 5, from two grammar schools in northeastern Georgia, and ranged in age from 8 to 11. By converting the raw scores of the Block Design test into standard scores, age, as a factor, was eliminated. It was hypothesized that the scores of whites would exceed those of blacks, but when age and IQ were controlled, this hypothesis was not supported for the red-white condition. While lightly pigmented children had no difficulty with the blue-yellow designs, the reverse was true for darkly pigmented children. The authors speculated that the cause for this may have been that the perception of yellow designs had fuzzy outlines, causing the designs to lose their boundaries. When they duplicated the experiment on a bright, sunny day on 20 other black children—half in the red-white condition, half in the blue-yellow condition—the authors found no differences between these black groups. The authors concluded that further study of this problem was needed.

The purpose of the unpublished master's thesis of Morse (1963) was to investigate the relationship between school learning and self-image of black and white children from the urban, industrialized Midwest. The subjects (114 black and 1,482 white children) were from grade 8 in schools in one school system. How the sample was chosen is not clear. All children accepted in the sample had to have been in the school system for at least 4 years (grades 4 to 8) and had to have had two sets of IQs available from the California Test of Mental Maturity (administered in grades 4 and 6 by the school system). Mean IQs were, for blacks, 95.23; for whites, 107.02. Total grade point averages for Mathematics, English, Social Studies, and Science were 1.72 for blacks and 2.23 for whites. Correlation coefficients among the data were given extensively. The author concluded that IQ was a better predictor of achievement among whites than among blacks and that this limited the value of intelligence tests among blacks. A higher degree of achievement motivation among blacks contrasted with their low levels of actual achievement. Throughout the article, it was clear that the author computed SDs incorrectly (e.g., SD = .134 for black IQ of 95.23) which thus invalidated all of the author's t-statistics.

Muzekari's article (1967) intended (a) to present the relationship between the Goodenough Draw-A-Man test (DAM) and the Stanford-Binet Intelligence Scale, Forms L and LM (S-B L, and S-B LM), and (b) to study the adequacy of the Revised DAM Norms for Negroes. Sixty-four white and 41 black children, all local school children aged 6 to 16 who had been referred to the Philadelphia State Hospital for evaluation, served as the sample. All were low SES and considered "probably retarded." The range of IQs for whites for S-B L and S-B LM was 47 to 94 (mean 74.32, SD = 10.33). For blacks, this range was 30 to 82 (mean 62.17, SD = 9.47). DAM IQs ranged from 39 to 100 (mean 73.93, SD = 15.35) for whites and 32 to 99 (mean 63.65, SD = 16.45) for blacks. Correlations of S-B L and S-B LM with DAM were, respectively, .55 and .53 for whites, and with the old scoring of DAM, .57 and .66, respectively, for blacks. With the Revised DAM Norms for Negroes, the coefficients for blacks were .54 and .61, respectively. Muzekari questioned the wisdom of the use of the Revised Norms with black children.

Neal's (1975) purpose was ". . . to reveal significant deviations from expected values in errors on the PPVT {Peabody Picture Vocabulary Test} . . ." (p. 265) when blacks and whites are compared. Form A of PPVT was given in a unique manner to 25, each, black boys, black girls, white boys, and white girls. Only plates 10 through 85 were used so as to force the subjects to respond to all words. It is unclear but it seems that only 88 children completed the study. From an analysis of variance, it was shown that race and sex differences were significant, but no interaction was significant. The author concluded that her study should be replicated, and that some PPVT stimulus words should be reevaluated. No other data were given.

Nichols and Anderson (1973) selected two large geographic samples from the Collaborative Perinatal Study (Berendes, 1966). One sample was from Boston and the other from the Philadelphia and Baltimore areas (the PB sample). Subjects were obtained among those whose mothers voluntarily sought medical attention at the Study's various cooperating hospitals. Each child received an SES value based on parental occupation, education, and income. The SES of the Boston sample was significantly higher than the SES of the PB sample, but there was no racial difference in SES within either sample. The Stanford-Binet Intelligence Scale, Short Form (S-B) was given as the children reached the age of 4, and when the children became 7, four verbal and three performance subtests of the Wechsler Intelligence Scale for Children (WISC) were given. In the Boston sample, the mean S-B IQs were 108.0, SD = 15.9 for 6,475 whites and 102.0, SD = 14.5 for 797 blacks. The mean Full Scale WISC IQ was 104.2, SD = 13.4 for 4,721 whites and 100.0, SD = 12.6 for 492 blacks. In the PB sample, the mean S-B IQs were 96.8, SD = 15.4 for 937 whites and 92.6, SD = 14.2 for 7,471 blacks. The mean Full Scale WISC IQs were 95.3, SD = 12.9 for 535 whites and 91.2, SD = 12.1 for 4,121 blacks. The authors pointed out that matching for SES reduced all racial differences and, on that basis, commented (a) that whites have had more chance to change upward in SES than have blacks, and (b) that the correlation between SES and IQ was higher among whites than among blacks. Also without supporting evidence, the authors commented that heritability of IQ was lower among blacks than among whites. The authors seemed to understand that matching blacks and whites for SES also matched them for an unknown amount of IQ, but the authors made no allowance for this in their various explanations of their data.

In order to compare scores on the Quick Test (QT) with scores on the Wechsler Intelligence Scale for Children—Revised (WISC-R), Nicholson (1977) administered the WISC-R and three forms of QT to 62 school children, aged 72 months to 195 months, who had been referred to the author because of poor school work. Fifty-two of the children were black; 10 were white. The author found significant correlations between all forms of QT and all WISC-R scores, including all WISC-R subtest scores. No racial data were given. QT was accepted as a valid test for quick estimates of intelligence.

The 15th annual report of the Oakland Public Schools (1967) was a transmittal of the results of the 1966–7 testing program to the Oakland Board of Education. The State of California required the administration of the Stanford Reading Test to grades 1, 2, 3, and 6, the Test of Academic Progress Reading Test to grade 10, and Lorge-Thorndike Intelligence Test to grades 6 and 10. The racial composition (Spanish surnames, other white, Negro, Oriental, and other non-white) and the median test scores were presented for each of 63 elementary schools and 6 senior high schools in terms of California norms, national norms, and local school norms. There were no data for whites or blacks, specifically.

As the title of the article states, Osborne (1966) was interested in changes in the factor structure of the Wechsler Intelligence Scale for Children (WISC) subtests over time. In September, 1961, just prior to their entrance into grade 1, the WISC was given to 56 male and 55 female black children whose ages at that time ranged from 5–6 to 6–8. The mean WISC Full Scale IQ was 84, SD = 11.8 for the combined sexes. In the last two weeks of grade 1, 103 of the original children were retested, and at that time mean Full Scale WISC IQ was 93, SD = 11.6. Nine factors, with insignificant variations, were extracted from both the preschool and grade 1 sample. The author concluded that mental factors could be found at the preschool level and at the grade 1 level and several common to both grade levels.

Osborne's (1970) purpose was to study the fertility rates for families of school children in a rural Georgia county where the white and black populations were roughly equal. The California Test of Mental Maturity and the corresponding reading and arithmetic tests had been given to 1,314 (640 white and 674 black) children during the winter of 1969. The county population was stable; the high SES group was largely white, the middle SES group was an equal mixture of blacks and whites, and the low SES group was largely black. When the races were combined, the correlation between IQ and family size was −.367; for whites alone, −.132, and for blacks alone, −.103. The family reproduction rate for children whose IQs were below 70 was 12 times as high for blacks as for whites. The author commented that Shockley's (1970) expressed fears of population pollution had not been answered properly in the psychological literature.

To answer the question of whether, considering fertility rate and IQ, the trend in Georgia was eugenic or dysgenic, Osborne (1975) compared the relationship between a number of demographic variables and psychological test scores of 250,000 children in grades 4, 8, and 12 in the public schools of the 159 counties in Georgia. The Cognitive Abilities Test and the Iowa Tests of Basic Skills had been given in grades 4 and 8; Cognitive Abilities Test and Tests of Academic Progress had been given in grade 12. Four demographic variables from the 1970 census, the educational expenditure per child, average daily attendance, and 12 test variables were intercorrelated. From this matrix, 48 separate regression analyses were computed in each of which one test score variable (Verbal IQ, Nonverbal IQ, Reading Score, or Arithmetic Score) was the criterion. Correlation between fertility ratio and mean IQ was significantly negative both for Verbal and Nonverbal IQ at all three grades (range was −.43 to −.54). The dysgenic trend occurred for fertility and achievement test scores at all three grades.

In Georgia, correlations between educational costs per child and test scores were negative for all three grades. The differences between the multiple correlations (R^2) for the four-predictor model (county population, percent population change since 1960, percent black population, and fertility ratio) and for the three-predictor model (the four-predictor model less fertility ratio) were significant (.005 level or less) for all four criteria (Reading, Arithmetic, Verbal IQ, and Nonverbal IQ) at grades 4 and 8, but significant at grade 12 for Arithmetic and Verbal IQ only (.025 level). Since the R^2 for the predictor model which included fertility ratio was the higher, predictions of the criteria were significantly enhanced when the fertility ratio was included. When percent nonwhite and fertility ratio, as the predictors, were compared with percent nonwhite alone, the R^2s resulting from each model were significantly different (.05 or less) for grades 4 and 8 and for all but Nonverbal IQ at grade 12. Again, the predictions from percent nonwhite and fertility ratio were the higher, and the significant importance of fertility ratio was shown again. The author concluded that the relationship between fertility and mental ability was a significantly negative one which did not agree with earlier studies because those earlier studies included no black children.

Osborne (1978) studied 427 pairs of twins, 123 pairs black and 304 pairs white, in a duplication of the earlier works of Vandenberg (1967), Osborne and Gregor (1967), and Osborne and Suddick (1971). All 427 pairs were same-sex twins ranging in age from 12 to 20. The same 12 psychological tests used in an earlier work (Osborne and Gregor, 1967) were used and described in some detail in the present study. When heritability ratios were computed for each of the 12 tests, the author commented that the wide range suggested ". . . that mental abilities represented by the 12 tests are not uniform in their genetic and environmental characteristics" (p. 157). No racial difference in heritability appeared when the 12 subtests were averaged into a composite score. Factor analysis of the 12 tests yielded a verbal factor, a spatial factor, and a perceptual speed factor; and while significant racial differences appeared in heritability of Verbal and Spatial IQs, there were no racial differences in the Perceptual Speed IQ or in the full Scale IQ. When the first principal component was determined for the three factor IQs, it was found that, by correlating own-race-determined factor scores with opposite-race-determined factor scores and with total-group (both races)-determined factor scores, ". . . whatever mental factor is measured in the Caucasoid group is the same as that measured in the Negroid group and in the total sample" (p. 162). A reliability study, done by obtaining the first principal component on random halves of each racial group and repeating the intercorrelations for own-within-race, opposite-within-race, and total-group, yielded three correlations above .99. The validity of the first principal component was established against Primary Mental Abilities test scores. For Caucasoids, the validity coefficient was .85 for both own-race and opposite-race; for Negroids, these coefficients were .82 and .81, respectively. The author commented: ". . . it is clear that the same general factor is being measured in each group separately and in the composite group when the . . . races are combined" (p. 164). Heritability ratios obtained for the nine factor scores derived from own-race, opposite-race, and total-group showed no significant racial differences among own-race heritability, opposite-race heritability, and total-group heritability. The author concluded:

> In whatever way all individual tests or subtests were pooled, by simply averaging the 12 standard scores, combining the factor IQs to get a full scale IQ, or by using weighted scores determined from the first principal component factor analysis of either race singly or both races combined, the results were the same. Heritability variance ratios for both Negroids and Caucasoids were significant at the .01 level. In no case was the difference between variance ratios of the races significant (p. 167).

The problem for Osborne and Gregor (1967) was the testing of the hypothesis that the American Negro is intellectually handicapped because of his environmental disadvantage. The subjects were 172 pairs of monozygotic twins (determined seriologically) and 112 pairs of dizygotic twins, all 13 to 18 years old, and all from southeastern United States. Among them were 43 pairs of black twins and 241 pairs of white twins. The psychological tests used were Cube Comparison, Surface Development, Object Aperture, Mazes, Paper Folding, Newcastle Spatial, and Identical Pictures. All tests were described in the article. Four heritability ratios were computed on all tests, and the authors commented:

> The remarkable agreement among four heritability ratios invites speculation that the mental abilities represented by the eight spatial tests are independently inherited, with as much as 78% of the within-family variance accounted for by hereditary factors. Heredity and environment produce significantly greater differences in fraternal twins on mental tests . . . than environmental influences alone produce in identical twins (p. 7).

The authors concluded: "It is clear . . . that only the Object Aperture Test yields consistently higher heritability ratios for white than for Negro children. On the basis of the data . . . the hypothesis of the differential rate of genetic or biological contributions for whites and Negroes on spatial test performance must be rejected" (p. 8).

Osborne and Suddick (1971) sought to use blood group gene frequencies to investigate the heritability of mental test performance. The sample comprised 54 whites and 42 blacks—all those from the Georgia study (Osborne and Gregor, 1967) whose seriological and psychological tests were complete. Ages ranged from 13 to 18 years. A battery of 19 psychological tests was given to measure, primarily, verbal, perceptual, and spatial abilities. Three factors resulted from the analysis of the test results: Verbal Comprehension, Perceptual Speed, and Spatial Relations. A three-factor Mental Ability Index was constructed of those tests having a loading of .40 or better. In the construction of a multiple correlation for the pooled subjects for the prediction of the Mental Ability Index from race and blood groups, race alone resulted in R^2 of .39. Sixteen additional steps beyond race increased R^2 by .12. When races were separated, the zero order correlations between Mental Ability Index factors and blood groups ranged from .29 to −.28 for whites; from .36 to −.41 for blacks. Correlations in the 30s and 40s were more frequent among blacks than among whites. The R^2 for the three factors in the Mental Ability Index were, for whites, .29, .20, .36, and .34 for Factors I, II, III, and Total, respectively; for blacks, these R^2 values were .60, .36, .57, and .58, respectively. Not all R^2s were significant.

In a comparison of sex differences of rural black children in performance on the Wechsler Intelligence Scale for Children (WISC), Pavlos (1961) selected, at random, 29 male and 29 female children. These children were selected from a group of 173 who had been selected from 904 rural black children (ages 11 to 15) of Holland, Ohio, by discarding all who were retarded in school by one or more grades. Thus, 731 of the 904 blacks were retarded by at least one grade and were, therefore, eliminated. The mean WISC IQs were: Verbal, 88.62, SD = 7.87 for girls, and 93.52, SD = 8.00 for boys; Performance, 98.28, SD = 9.59 for girls, and 98.45, SD = 26.56 for boys; Full Scale, 92.38, SD = 10.91 for girls, and 95.07, SD = 9.74 for boys. The author described his sample as random and concluded that sex differences among black subjects did not differ from sex differences among whites.

The purpose of the Perney, Hyde, and Machock (1977) article was to demonstrate the need for further research into the problem of black-white differences in intelligence. The subjects were the entire populations of grade 1 of the school years of 1973–4 (N= 540) and 1974–5 (N= 579) from six East Cleveland (Ohio) public schools. All were low SES and 98% of the sample was black. The seventh edition of the Kuhlman-Anderson Test of Intelligence, Form A, was given by the teacher in the child's classroom. The mean IQs were: school year 1973–4, 101.22, SD = 12.48; 1974–5, 102.44, SD = 11.35. Both means were significantly higher than the normative mean of 100, SD = 16.00. The authors used the F test to claim that the SDs of the samples were significantly smaller than the SD of the normative sample. In addition, the authors presented the IQ data by stanines, showing the proportion of each of the two samples, and the proportion of the normative population, at each stanine. They concluded that the Cleveland samples contained significantly fewer dull children and significantly more average children than the normative sample. The authors also showed that the IQ of blacks was not related to SES and entertained the idea that Head Start may have helped the Cleveland children. Since these findings are so at variance with all other large studies of racial differences in intelligence, the authors very correctly concluded that more study of racial differences in intelligence was needed.

After a review of the literature, Quay (1974) announced his purpose: ". . . to investigate the effects of the two dialects (standard and nonstandard {English} on the Binet IQ scores of black boys and girls of two age levels (third and sixth grade)" (p. 464). Subjects were 104 low SES blacks, randomly selected from the grades 3 and 6 classes from two Philadelphia public schools. Children from each grade and each sex, separately, were assigned at random to a treatment or control group, thus forming eight groups of 13 children each. Mean age for grade 3 was 8–6; for grade 6 it was 11–7. A nonstandard English translation of the Stanford-Binet Intelligence Scale (S-B) was used along with the standard English form; each was given to half of the children of each grade and sex by a black female. For standard English, the mean IQs were 87.77, SD = 11.13 for grade 3, 81.27, SD = 10.22 for grade 6, and

84.52, SD = 11.08 for the combined grades. For the non-standard dialect, the mean IQs were 88.19, SD = 10.71 for grade 3, 80.96, SD = 9.04 for grade 6, and 84.58, SD = 10.47 for the combined grades. Six out of 72 test items showed significant differences between the two dialects; three favored one dialect and three favored the other. The author regarded these as chance differences and concluded that these children comprehended both dialects equally well. Decreasing IQ with increasing age was confirmed.

In order to demonstrate the effectiveness of money and praise (as rewards) on psychological test performance, Quay (1975) studied 92 low SES blacks from two "high impact" schools in a large northeastern city. Ages ranged from 8–11 to 10–2. The subjects, randomly selected from all grade 4 classes in the two schools, were assigned either to a "money" or a "praise" group, and the 1960 revision of the Stanford-Binet Intelligence Scale (S-B) was administered to all the children by a black male. No significant differences in IQ appeared as the result of the type of reward. The author concluded that these two incentives did not influence the psychological test performance of lower-class black children.

The purpose of the Roach and Rosecrans (1971) article was to describe the relationship between hearing loss and (a) Verbal IQ and (b) Performance IQ, both as measured by the Wechsler Intelligence Scale for Children (WISC). The subjects were 18 black children, 6 to 13 years old, probably from Birmingham, Alabama, referred for hearing loss study to a local medical facility. The mean WISC IQs for children with high frequency loss were: Verbal, 80.2, SD = 13.1; Performance, 82.1, SD = 13.1. The mean WISC IQs for children with monaural loss were: Verbal, 91.3, SD = 24.0; Performance, 87.8, SD = 16.6. Ns for neither of these sets were given. The authors noted that the Verbal-Performance IQ differences were not significant; also, the differnces for both Verbal and Performance IQs between the groups were not significant. The authors computed product moment correlations for seven audiometric thresholds for Verbal and Performance IQs, each separately, and even though in these correlations Ns were never greater than 18, the authors gave significance to some of the correlations, arguing that ". . . the impact of impaired hearing is considerably more disturbing to the black student {than to the white student}." (p. 138). In spite of the general finding that blacks perform better on verbal parts of tests than on performance parts (McGurk, 1975; Jensen, 1980), the authors commented that "verbal-vocabulary" {tests may yield} a spuriously low IQ score {for blacks}." (p. 138). The authors also suggested that the "negatively social" activities of blacks may result from ". . . misunderstanding of content of oral communication . . ." (p. 139). On the other hand, the authors asked readers to regard their findings as tentative.

In the second report on the intellectual development of children, Roberts (1971) presented scores on the Vocabulary and Block Design subtests of the Wechsler Intelligence Scale for Children (WISC) plus 51 tables of detailed data. The study, begun in 1963 and completed in 1965, was done under the direction of the Health Examination Survey of the Public Health Services. The sample was presumed to represent 24 million non-institutionalized children aged 6 through 11 years and included 20,403 whites, 2,271 blacks, and 110 others. Data also were collected from the entire WISC, the Draw-A-Man Test, five cards from the Thematic Apperception Test, and achievement tests. Marked regional differences appeared: the Northeast, West, and Midwest were clearly higher in score than the South on both subtests, and whites consistently and significantly exceeded blacks on both subtests in all geographic regions. Moreover, for both subtests, the racial differences increased with age, as did absolute variability in raw scores—more rapidly on Block Design than on Vocabulary. Some sex differences were reported. A sizeable correlation between subtest scores and educational level of parents was reported. All racial differences were said to have been caused by SES differences, and emphasis was placed on the fact that WISC had been standardized on white children only.

Because lower-class children in middle-class high schools have better grades and are less delinquent than lower-class children in lower-class high schools, Robins, Jones, and Murphy (1966) concluded (and stated as the hypothesis of their paper) that "The more children having social characteristics associated with good school performance there are in a school, the better will be the performance of the remainder of the student body" (p. 428). They studied 528 black males entering 18 St. Louis, Missouri, public schools in 1937–8 (excluding those who had attended for less than 6 years). From school records, a number of demographic variables were obtained: SES, social mobility, family structure, intelligence, school performance, and school milieu. For the 132 children whose IQs were below 75, 96% had academic problems, and 70% had behavior problems. For the 125 whose IQs were 76 to 84, the respective percents were 85 and 49; for the 130 whose IQs were 85 to 95, the respective percents were 62 and 39; and for the 141 whose IQs were 96 and above, the respective percents were 33 and 25. IQ was considered the most powerful predictor of both types of problem. Freedom from school problems was associated with high IQ and high SES. Other relationships between school problems (or freedom from them) and demographic variables were described. The authors did not indicate acceptance or rejection of their hypothesis.

The purpose of the Rohwer, Ammon, Suzuki, and Levin (1971) article was to study the question of whether the discrepancy in school achievement between low SES black children and high SES white children was the result of a discrepancy in learning proficiency between these two groups, or whether some other process was involved. As possible measures of learning proficiency, the Peabody Picture Vocabulary Test (PPVT), Raven's Colored Progressive Matrices (RCPM), and a paired-associates test (described in the article) were administered individually to a representative sample of 288 children drawn equally from six populations—high SES whites in grades K, 1, and 3 and low SES blacks in the same grades. The geographical location of the subjects was not stated. The data indicated that, if PPVT and RCPM were the criteria of learning proficiency, the test scores supported the likelihood that the difference in school achievement of the two sample populations resulted from a learning proficiency difference. However, if the paired-associates were the criterion of learning proficiency, the results indicated that there was no learning proficiency difference. In order to resolve what seemed to be a dilemma, the authors discussed Jensen's Level I-Level II hypothesis (1969b), but they found that the correlational material of their present study contradicted Jensen's prediction that the correlation between Level I (paired-associates) and Level II (PPVT and RCPM) abilities would be higher among high SES subjects than among low SES subjects. An alternate explanation of the findings was ". . . that paired-associate tasks do not elicit the kinds of learning processes necessary for successful performance on school learning tasks or on IQ tests" (p. 13), and the authors noted that they were studying this explanation. Still another explanation was that if high SES children learn more than low SES children from any given learning task, tests that measure recall of such learning will show a difference between the two subject populations. The authors decided that, because of their data, this explanation had to be rejected.

The research bulletin of Rosenfeld and Hilton (1969) was based on scores of 316 blacks and 501 whites, presumed to have been selected randomly from 803 white and 648 black children selected from six high schools in two cities—one midwestern and one western, and who had attended school so consistently as to have taken the same battery of tests in grade 5 (in 1961) and in grades 7, 9, and 11. It was said that roughly 9,000 children had been tested originally (in 1961); thus the sample represented a selected fraction of the original sample. The test battery consisted of the School and College Ability Test (SCAT), the Sequential Tests of Educational Progress (STEP), and the Background and Experience Questionnaire. SES was measured by the sum of parental occupation, parental education, and the number of bathrooms in the home. The data were treated by a complex ANOVA about which results the authors cautioned care because the sample was not random. The authors concluded that racial differences were significant at all four grades for both SCAT and STEP. Racial differences increased with passage of time for some subtests—not for others. Those whose initial scores were high increased in score more than those whose initial scores were low.

At grade 5, blacks were a year behind whites on STEP Mathematics and on both Verbal and Quantitative scores of SCAT; at grade 11, the gap had widened to 2 to 4 years. The overall academic growth of blacks did not depend on the school curriculum.

The Scarr and Weinberg (1976) study was designed to show the beneficial effects on black children of their being adopted by white families. One hundred and one families were recruited by the Open Door Society, the Lutheran Social Service, the Children's Home Society, and the State of Minnesota Department of Public Welfare Adoption Unit. Among these families were 321 children aged 4 years or more; 145 were biological children, and 176 were adopted. Of the 176 adopted children, 130 were black or inter-racial, 25 white, and 21 were Asian/Indian. All families lived within a 150-mile radius of Minneapolis-St. Paul. All members of these families who were 4 years of age or over were tested by randomly-assigned graduate students. The Wechsler Adult Intelligence Scale (WAIS) was given to those over 16 years of age (including parents), the Wechsler Intelligence Scale for Children (WISC) for those 8 to 15 years of age, and the 1960 revision of the Stanford-Binet Intelligence Scale (S-B) for those 4 to 7 years of age. Adoptive parents were high in education, occupation, and IQ. Natural parents were above average in education. The mean IQ for 130 adopted black and inter-racial children was 106.3, SD = 13.9; for 25 adopted white children, 111.5, SD = 16.1; and for 21 Asian/Indian children, 99.9, SD = 13.3. IQs represented combined IQs from all three tests; the authors considered this appropriate (p. 731). The mean IQ of 29 black children who had two black parents was 96.8, SD = 12.8, and for 68 children with one black parent, the mean IQ was 109.0, SD = 11.5. The difference, significant at .001, was explained in terms of maternal education and preplacement history. Adopted children were above average on Vocabulary, Reading, and Mathematics (55th to 57th percentiles) but were below natural children (71st to 74th percentiles). Children of less well-educated natural mothers were placed for adoption later than those of better educated mothers, were adopted by lower SES families, and were mostly black, yet the authors denied selective placement of the children. They concluded that white environments increased the mean IQ of the adopted blacks because these adopted blacks ". . . scored as highly on IQ tests as did white adoptees in previous studies with large samples (Burks, 1928; Leahy, 1935)" (p. 737).

Schneider's (1968) article was a study on the conforming behavior of 96 black and 96 white grades 7 and 8 children who were matched for sex and grade into four experimental groups which were, otherwise, random. Stanine scores on the Test of General Ability (TGA) were obtained from school records. SES, based on fathers' or mothers' occupations, was not disclosed. According to this reviewer's tabulation, the mean TGA stanine values were 6.00 for whites and 3.81 for blacks. The difference was significant at .001 level. The author did not discuss racial intelligence.

Scott (1966) hypothesized that if the northern environment were able to increase the psychological test scores of black children, a comparison of the scores of the same black children at grades 1 and 9 would show a significantly higher score for the latter grade. In 1963, 65 grade 9 black children were chosen at random from the records of "a Chicago Negro public high school," taking only those whose grade 1 test scores were also available. At grade 1, the mean Kuhlman-Anderson Scale of Intelligence IQ was 93.06; at grade 9, the mean California Test of Mental Maturity IQ was 89.92. The loss was significant at the .05 level and was opposite to the hypothesized direction. The author commented that the loss might have resulted from very large losses on the part of a few children, but he made no conclusions about his work.

Three articles of Scott (1973, 1974, 1976) reported on the same sample on which the author was testing his "Home Start" intervention program. Home Start was initially composed of "Horizontal Home Start" (HHS) and "Vertical Home Start" (VHS), each of which involved low SES children in Waterloo, Iowa. In HHS, 20 black and 20 white 4-year-olds during each of the school years of 1968–9 and 1969–70 participated in a year of pre-kindergarten enrichment. VHS included 51 black and 38 white 2- to 5-year-olds for a 3-year period beginning in summer, 1968. VHS was a program of home visits by neighborhood "paraprofessionals" who then consulted with a committee of 8 professionals. In both types of programs, the effects of the treatment were measured by comparing the Primary Mental Abilities (PMA) IQs of the experimental children, taken at age 5, with the PMA IQs of their older siblings which latter had been taken earlier in grade 1 of the schools. For the children in HHS (actually 17 blacks and 23 whites), no significant differences appeared between them, after enrichment, and their unenriched, older sibs. For the VHS children (actually 30 blacks and 14 whites) significant differences were reported between the enriched experimental group and their unenriched, older sibs. While the author cautioned against generalizations (because of the small samples), he concluded that, particularly for VHS, his program had benefited low SES children.

When Scott published his first follow-up of these children (1974), he had abandoned the HHS program as ineffective. Nineteen months after the end of the initial program, the PMA was re-administered to the 30 black and 14 white children of the initial study, and these new IQs were compared with the old (original) grade 1 IQs of their older sibs. For the 30 blacks, mean total PMA IQ decreased from 100.9 to 99.3; since their older sibs remained at 93.5 (their grade 1 value) the difference (99.3 − 93.5) was called significant. For the 14 whites, mean total PMA

IQ decreased from 113.3 to 109.4. Since the mean IQ of their older sibs remained at 103.4 (the grade 1 value) the difference (113.3 − 103.4) was called not significant. After analyzing PMA sub-test IQ changes at some length, the author concluded that blacks, only, had profited from VHS. After another warning against generalization, the author wrote ". . . that promising educational results are feasible when black children are provided with very early preschool enrichment . . ." (p. 149).

In the 1976 article, Scott was able to recover only 22 black and 9 white VHS children. Sometime between the first paper of this triad and this last paper, the Iowa Tests of Basic Skills (ITBS) had been given to 25 of the children. For the remaining 6 children, it was necessary to obtain "adjusted" grade equivalent scores on ITBS because they had taken the test at times different from that at which the 25 children had been tested. Exactly how their older sibs were treated is completely unclear, but the author compared the grade equivalencies of the enriched group with the grade equivalencies of their older sibs for 15 educational areas by means of the Wilcoxon test, and concluded that while the 22 black children had improved significantly in school achievement, the whites had not. There were further cautions about generalizations and that the study should be replicated, but there was no caution about the use of older sibs as a control group, the pro-rating of test scores, or the non-random character of the original sample.

Sekyra and Arnoult (1968) described their paper as a test of the hypothesis that when the Stanford-Binet Scale of Intelligence (S-B), the Wechsler Intelligence Scale for Children (WISC), and the Columbia Mental Maturity Scale (CMMS) were administered to black children, no differences among the mean scores would be found unless the S-B was scored according to the black norms suggested by Kennedy, Van De Riet, and White (1961). The authors selected 10 children, each, from grades 2, 5, and 8 of the elementary schools in Starkville, Mississippi, (pop. 13,500) as their urban sample and a duplicate sample from the elementary schools of Crawford, Mississippi, (pop. 350) as their rural sample. Chronological age (CA) was limited to a 5-month span for each grade; CA range for grade 2 was 89 to 93 months, for grade 5, 125 to 129 months, and for grade 8, 161 to 165 months. This limitation eliminated the bright, if any, and the very dull children. WISC and CMMS were reported according to the test manuals; S-B IQs were reported (a) according to the scoring manual, and (b) according to black norms established by Kennedy et al. (1961). For the urban sample, the IQs for WISC, CMMS, and S-B (Caucasian norms) were, for grade 2, 80, 72, and 83, respectively; for grade 5, 83, 67, 82; and for grade 8, 84, 59, and 82. For the rural sample, the IQs for the same tests, same order, for grade 2 were 72, 73, and 74; for grade 5, 78, 56, and 76; and for grade 8, 69, 51, and

71. When the Kennedy, Van de Riet, and White correction factor was applied, the S-B IQs were increased markedly. The authors presented multiple correlations for the three tests, but it is not clear what was correlated. The authors concluded that neither WISC nor CMMS ". . . is giving an adequate indication of intellectual functioning for Negroes" (p. 568), and they recommended re-evaluation of these two tests.

Semler and Iscoe described their 1966 study as an extension of their earlier article (1963) which latter was reviewed by Shuey (1966). In the 1963 article, the authors showed that paired associate (PA) learning of southern white and black children did not differ significantly among 8- and 9-year-olds even though the Full Scale IQs of the Wechsler Intelligence Scale for Children (WISC) of the blacks were significantly lower than those of the whites. The subjects of the 1966 study were 134 black and 141 white children, aged 5 to 9 years, who were part of the authors' 1963 sample to whom WISC had been given earlier, and to whom Raven's Colored Progressive Matrices (RCPM) were administered for the 1966 article. After some undescribed, random discarding of subjects, both WISC and RCPM data were reported in the 1966 article. The authors concluded that the black-white differences were larger on WISC than on RCPM (there were no significant racial differences in RCPM scores at ages 8 and 9) and that this agreed with their hypothesis that WISC was more culturally-loaded than RCPM. However, for 7-year-olds, blacks were significantly lower than whites on both WISC and RCPM which, to the authors, indicated the effects of "experimental factors," or different instrument-demands, at age 7 which did not exist at ages 8 and 9. The authors likened the performance of the 8- and 9-year-olds on RCPM to their earlier performance (Semler and Iscoe, 1963) on PA learning. The authors found that, for RCPM, black and white subtest intercorrelations were so similar that they, the authors, concluded that the stages of cognitive development sampled by RCPM were much alike for the two races, but the authors also commented that more analysis was needed along this line of thinking. There was some suggestion that, for WISC, dissimilar intercorrelation patterns existed for the two racial groups which the authors related to dissimilar educational experiences.

Sewell and Severson (1975) described the predictive ability of the Wechsler Intelligence Scale for Children (WISC) for the academic progress of black children who were regularly placed in school. The subjects were 84 black children, 5–10 to 7–5 years of age, randomly selected from five grade 1 classes from a public elementary school in Milwaukee. Seven subtests of WISC, plus Word Reading and Arithmetic sections of the Stanford Achievement Test, were administered. The mean WISC Full Scale IQ was 86. Performance IQs were higher than Verbal IQs in 66% of the children. The correlations between IQ and achievement (otherwise not identified) were significant at .001 but were below those usually reported. The authors felt that the low WISC IQs obtained by the black children led to ". . . discriminatory social and educational practices . . ." (p. 112), but the authors presented no evidence for their statement. WISC ". . . individual subtests must be used with caution for diagnostic or predictive purposes." (p. 112) with such children.

Silverstein's (1973) purpose was to study the factorial structure of the Wechsler Intelligence Scale for Children (WISC) using 505 whites, 318 blacks, and 487 Chicanos, all originally selected by Jane R. Mercer (Mercer and Smith, 1972) and all between 6 and 11 years of age. Mean age of the whites and Chicanos was 8.5 years, and of the blacks, 8.4 years. The mean Full Scale IQs for the children were: whites, 105.2, SD = 14.88; blacks, 91.9, SD = 11.87; and Chicanos, 91.1, SD = 12.45. Out of the 11 WISC subtests, the author extracted two factors: Factor I (information, comprehension, arithmetic, similarities, and vocabulary, plus digit span for blacks only); and Factor II (block design and object assembly, plus picture completion and picture arrangement for blacks only). The author concluded that his findings did not imply that WISC was a fair and proper test for blacks or Chicanos; the findings ". . . simply suggest that the test measures the same abilities in Anglo, Black, and Chicano children" (p. 410).

In order to study the effect of race of examiner on children's test scores, Solkoff (1974) had two black and two white examiners administer the Wechsler Intelligence Scale for Children and the Sarason Test Anxiety Scale to 54 black and 54 white children from St. Louis, Missouri. SES for the children, based on father's education and occupation, was upper-lower and lower-middle class. All examiners, high school graduates without prior experience in testing, were trained by an experienced white female. The protocols were first scored by the examiners; however, a single experienced clinician, who knew neither the children nor the examiners, rescored them. Significant main effects for child's race were found for all subtests except Comprehension, Picture Arrangement, and Coding; blacks were consistently below whites. Higher scores were produced by black examiners on Comprehension and Digit Span and by white examiners on Vocabulary, and there was a significant interaction between Race of Subject and Race of Examiner on Similarities and Object Assembly (whites scored higher with black examiners, blacks lower with black examiners). Race was the only variable associated with the three IQs, and blacks were lower on all three. The WISC Full Scale IQs, with a black examiner, were 97.12, SD = 11.07 for black children and 109.39, SD = 10.50 for white children; with a white examiner, they were 98.46, SD = 9.11 for black children and 108.15, SD = 10.31 for white children. There were no significant interactions with the anxiety measure. The author felt that his St. Louis study confirmed his Buffalo findings (Solkoff, 1972), and he concluded that examiner's race had ". . . no appreciable effect on the intellectual performance of either black or white children" (p. 1066).

Solomon (1969) described the general factorial nature of academic achievement. The subjects were 73 black grade 5 children drawn from one low SES elementary school in Chicago. Children without two parents in the home were excluded; otherwise, the selection of the sample was not described. The Lorge-Thorndike Intelligence Test (L-T), not otherwise described, and the California Achievement Test (CalAT) were group-administered in the school. Academic and conduct ratings, each separately, for grades 3, 4, and 5 were converted into 3-year averages. In addition, each child was given a set of six tasks to accomplish, and each performance was rated on a 4-point scale. The L-T Verbal IQs were 92.00, SD = 9.57 for 35 girls and 82.08, SD = 13.05 for 38 boys. L-T Nonverbal IQs were 89.23, SD = 12.33 for girls and 85.74, SD = 12.58 for boys. Total CalAT scores were 46.46, SD = 8.51 for girls and 40.53, SD = 9.05 for boys. Considerable data on the factor analysis of L-T, CalAT, and the six tasks were presented, and six factor clusters were described. The author concluded that general academic achievement was "a unitary dimension" and was only moderately related to achievement behavior. Although achievement behavior seemed unrelated in different situations, as situations became more alike, the behaviors became more related. There was discussion of a "typology of achievement-related tasks" and three general dimensions of these tasks were described.

Starkman, Butkovich, and Murray (1976) sought to determine whether learning of low SES blacks was enhanced more by training in what Jensen (1969b) called Level I ability or by training in ". . . general cognitive development-enhancing experiences . . ." (p. 52). Three hypotheses were tested: (a) children who showed the highest school achievement at the end of grade 6 would also show the highest learning proficiency and/or cognitive development; (b) both learning and Piagetian tasks were composed of a common factor; and (c) if (b) were supported, a reciprocal relationship would exist between learning and Piagetian tasks. Subjects were 80 low SES grade 7 Chicago black children selected at random from 163 children in an "Upper Grade Center." Average age was 13.6 years. Mean IQ on the California Test of Mental Maturity was 93.74 for Verbal IQ, 97.82 for Quantitative IQ, and 95.84 for Total IQ. Wide Range Achievement Test grade equivalencies were 5.78 for Reading, 6.02 for Spelling, and 5.61 for Arithmetic. A series of individual tests (Linguistic Coding, Sentences, Reading, Bottles, Similarities, and Digit Span) were administered, and factor analysis was performed. Four factors were developed. Hypothesis (a) was not supported. Hypotheses (b) and (c) were supported. The authors commented that they were surprised at the poor performance of these children on the cognitive tasks (Bottles and Similarities), and they also challenged Jensen's (1969b) Two Factor Theory.

Stephenson and Gay (1972) investigated the psycholinguistic abilities of 80 black and 80 white children who ranged in SES from lower-lower to upper-middle class, apparently to see whether there was "language code continuum." All subjects had to be between 83 and 89 months of age, between 90 and 110 in IQ as determined by the Peabody Picture Vocabulary Test (PPVT), and of appropriate SES. The Illinois Test of Psycholinguistic Ability (ITPA) had also been given to these children, and the raw scores were converted to age equivalents. SES was found to be significantly related to ITPA scores of white children but much less so for black children. The authors concluded that SES was significantly related to ITPA—causally. For all children, Verbal Expression was low. There was no confirmation of the literature that held that the lower SES was visual-motor oriented, or that the middle class was auditory-vocal oriented.

Trotman (1977) argued that when black and white families were equated for SES on Warner's Index of Status Characteristics (ISC), racial differences in intellectual home environment (IHE) as measured by ". . . Wolf's (1964) measure of the home environment . . ." (p. 267) would still exist, thus indicating that IHE was the cause of racial IQ differences. Out of a middle SES suburban school system population of 225 white and 91 black grade 9 children, 71 whites and 75 blacks were selected by random serialization, and letters soliciting cooperation in the study were sent to the parents of these children. Telephone calls were made to those who did not respond to the letters until 50, each, black and white children were secured. The sample was further limited to those children whose school records contained scores for the Metropolitan Achievement Tests (MAT) and the Otis-Lennon Test of Mental Ability (O-L). The author sought to test three hypotheses: (a) when black and white families were equated for SES, IHE differences would still appear; (b) a significant correlation would exist between IHE and O-L IQ; and (c) the IHE of the family would predict the child's grade point average (GPA) as well as the child's IQ would. IHE and ISC were both administered and scored by the author. Hypothesis (a) was sustained; white IHE score was significantly higher than black IHE score. Thus, white homes were considered to be higher in intellectual development than black homes, and IHE was accepted as the causal factor in racial differences in intelligence. Since the IHE questionnaire had been validated against both MAT and IQ on the Henmon-Nelson Test of Mental Ability (H-N), this finding might just as easily have been regarded as evidence of a racial difference in the intelligence of the mothers who were interviewed. Hypothesis (b) was also sustained; the correlation between IHE and O-L IQ was .68 for blacks and .37 for whites. This racial discrepancy was strongly criticised by Wolff (1978). Once again, because of the validation of the IHE, a correlation of fair size between IHE and O-L IQ might have been expected. Hypothesis (c) was also sustained; the correlation between IHE and GPA was at least as high as the correlation between IQ and GPA. Again, considering the validation of IHE, one would have expected this. The author summarized her article by stressing the different cultures of the two racial groups, concluding that this cultural difference was the cause of racial differences in IQ. However, it might as well have been argued that IHE, validated as it was, was a good test of intelligence and that the IHE racial difference was another aspect of the racial difference in intelligence.

One should not read Trotman (1977) without reading Longstreth (1978a) and Wolff (1978). Longstreth regarded Trotman's work as ". . . seriously inaccurate and misleading" (p. 469), and he pointed out why he considered none of Trotman's conclusions as necessarily true. Longstreth stressed the lack of knowledge of what the IHE actually measured, arguing that content validity for it was lacking and that it could be measuring intelligence. Longstreth concluded that Trotman's paper emphasized ". . . that SES is a poor index of parental behavior in the home, and that other approaches might be better" (p. 471). Wolff's (1978) criticisms of Trotman supplemented, but deliberately did not duplicate, those of Longstreth. Wolff charged Trotman with experimenter bias because she administered both the IHE and the ISC measures, pointing out that Trotman's environmental bias could easily have led her to score the IHE, or ISC, or both, in a biased fashion, particularly since many of the items on IHE and ISC required subjectivity on the part of the scorer. Wolff then discussed six "anomalies" of Trotman's paper, concluding:

> If we accept at face value the various anomalies in Trotman's data . . . we are obliged to conclude that her sample is highly peculiar, and therefore, findings based on this sample lack external validity. If the sample is considered representative . . . serious doubts about the internal validity of her study are immediately raised by the several anomalies just considered. (p. 476)

In response to Longstreth, Trotman (1978) quoted her original findings (p. 479). In response to Wolff's criticisms, Trotman commented that "The six so-called anomalies listed by Wolff are basically his opinions and interpretations; the disputed data are not anomalous at all" (p. 480).

Tulkin (1968) intended to show the relationship between SES factors and racial differences in intelligence by showing that, as SES factors became more alike for the races, test-score differences were reduced.

His sample was composed of 137 high SES whites, 85 low SES whites, 52 high SES blacks, and 115 low SES blacks. How the sample was selected was not given, but all children were from grades 5 and 6 in a Maryland school system. Scores on L-T were obtained from school records. The mean Verbal IQs were: high SES whites 114.48, SD = 14.56, high SES blacks 109.15, SD = 12.88, low SES whites 92.67, SD = 12.84, and low SES blacks 90.04, SD = 12.08. The mean Nonverbal IQs were: high SES whites 112.10, SD = 12.20, high SES blacks 107.81, SD = 11.79, low SES whites 95.41, SD = 13.57, and low SES blacks 91.01, SD = 12.38. Measures of SES and cultural participation were administered either by the author or by the schools. The upper SES blacks and whites differed significantly on both Verbal and Performance IQs; the lower SES blacks and whites differed significantly on Performance IQ only. The author concluded that, when controlled for broken home, maternal employment, and crowdedness in the home, no racial differences appeared for the upper SES children. Nothing clear was stated about the lower SES children, and nothing could be said about racial differences in general because middle SES children were excluded from the study. The author failed to note that, in controlling for home factors, employment, and crowdedness, he was also controlling for intelligence in an unknown degree.

In order to determine the effects of "life experiences" upon Raven's Progressive Matrices (RPM) Tulkin and Newbrough (1968) administered the RPM and a culture measure to 203 white and 153 black grades 5 and 6 children from a suburban Maryland school system. The subjects may have been part of the sample reported in Tulkin, 1968. Nothing was given about the method of selection of the original 389 children (Tulkin, 1968) or the present sample. Data were available from school records for the L-T and the Iowa Test of Basic Skills (ITBS). SES was determined by the Hollingshead Index. The cultural measure contained a Cultural Participation Scale (CPS), a two-part Family Participation Scale (FPS), and a Family Structure (FS) measure. The entire cultural measure had been validated through judgments by ". . . 10 members of the professional staff of {a} Mental Health Study Center" (p. 401). Blacks and whites were equated for SES. The final sample then consisted of 128 high SES whites, 75 low SES whites, 50 high SES blacks, and 103 low SES blacks. When a three-way ANOVA revealed that there were main effects for SES and race, but not for interactions, the authors concluded that race and SES were confounded. A two-way ANOVA was then performed for the RPM scores of the two SES racial groups using only 4 items of FS as covariate controls. Racial differences for the high SES groups disappeared, but racial differences for the low SES groups remained significant. When this reviewer tested the significance of the mean racial differences by the t-statistic, high SES whites vs. high SES blacks produced a t of 1.92 when 1.96 was required for significance at the .05 level. Low SES blacks differed from low SES whites at the .001 level.

The authors concluded that whites, and the high SES groups, produced higher RPM scores, and that the finding that race was important in describing low SES racial differences only was contradicted by other reports in the literature. RPM was moderately related to L-T, but less so to achievement, and RPM was not closely related to cultural differences. Sex differences were evident, particularly among blacks. The authors did not consider the possibility that the controlling for cultural factors may also have matched for intelligence, or that the validation process of the culture measure (the staff of a Mental Health Study Center could be expected to have strong environmental bias) could have produced items that could have acted differently on high and low SES groups, or on blacks and whites. However, from the authors' Table 6 (p. 403) there was reason to suspect that CPS was also measuring intelligence.

The tenor of the Vance and Engin (1978) article was that the subtests of the Wechsler Intelligence Scale for Children, Revised, (WISC-R) do not measure black intelligence. Apparently, the authors' criterion of validity was the magnitude of the subtest score; those subtests wherein scores were high were valid measures of black intelligence, and vice versa. The WISC-R was administered to 154 black children, aged 6–1 to 15–11, most of whom lived in rural North Carolina or Virginia. Most of the subjects were low SES and ranged in school grade from 1 to 7. The sample contained no emotionally disturbed children or those visually or auditorially handicapped. In one place (p. 453) the Full Scale WISC-R IQ was given as 66.7, SD = 11.17, ranging from 41 to 113. In another place (p. 454), the Full Scale WISC-R IQ was given as 68.6, SD = 11.1, the Performance IQ as 70.2, SD = 11.4, and the Verbal IQ as 68.3, SD = 10.8. Blacks were said to have shown much unevenness among the WISC-R performance subtests, but nowhere is the black patterning of subtest scores linked to an objective criterion. The authors concluded that results obtained on the WISC-R are valid.

The purposes of the Vane, Weitzman, and Applebaum (1966) article were: (i) to study the existence of S-B subtest performance differences between (a) blacks and whites matched for S-B IQ, and (b) problem and nonproblem children also matched for S-B IQ; (ii) to determine if the mean S-B IQ of suburban whites (stratified by SES) would differ from the theoretical S-B mean IQ of 100; and (iii) to compare the S-B performance of black suburban children (stratified by SES) with normative data from Kennedy, Van De Reit, and White (1963). The sample for purpose (i) was obtained from the records of 110 white and 110 black children (matched for S-B IQ) selected from a suburban New York City school district. Children with behavior problems, the severely retarded, and brain damaged children were excluded. The age range of the children was not given. The comparison of problem and nonproblem children did not show a racial separation, and is here omitted. For purpose (ii), the authors selected a sample of 113 white children aged 6, 7, and 8 ("the Normative White Group"), so stratified by fathers' occupations as to match the frequency of fathers' occupations in the 1960 census for urban whites. The source of the sample was not given. A similar sample of 100 for purpose (iii) was selected for blacks ("the Normative Negro Group"), also from an undisclosed source, and also stratified so that fathers' occupations matched in frequency those in the 1960 census for urban blacks. The children were also 6, 7, and 8 years of age. The mean IQs of the children in sample (i) were 108.8 for whites and 107.5 for blacks. The mean S-B IQ of the "Normative White Group" was 112.7, and the mean S-B IQ of the "Normative Negro Group" was 103.3. The authors concluded that the pattern of S-B subtest performance was very similar for blacks and whites.

Warden and Prawat (1975) stated two purposes for their article: (a) to correct the literature which had confounded race and SES, and (b) to assess racial differences in mental ability other than those of divergent, or creative, mental ability. To their sample of 130 black children (96 low SES and 34 high SES) and 224 white children (70 low SES and 154 high SES) they administered Guilford's five tests of divergent-convergent thinking. Divergent thinking was measured by Word Fluency and Utility Test. Convergent thinking was measured by Naming Meaningful Trends, Letter Grouping, and Word Grouping. All of these tests were described in the article. All children were between the ages of 12–7 and 15–6 years, and all were in grade 8. All were found in a large Northeastern city, but the method of their selection was not given. SES was determined by the occupation of the head of the family.

Data were presented in one table (p. 717) and the results of ANOVA were given. Neither SES nor race was found to be a significant source of variance for the Divergent Thinking tests: no racial or SES differences were shown for Word Fluency or Utility. However, both race and SES were significant sources of variance in Convergent thinking. High SES children outperformed low SES children on Letter Grouping, Word Grouping, and Naming Meaningful Trends, and whites performed better than blacks on all three of the latter tests. There were no significant interactions. Relevant conclusions of Jensen (1969b) and Rohwer (1971) were compared with the authors' findings, and the authors concluded that ". . . ethnicity as well as social class must be taken into account in future attempts to specify patterns of abilities across various types of tasks" (p. 718).

To study the effects of examiner's race on test scores, Wellborn, Reid, and Reichard (1973) had three white and three black examiners administer the Wechsler Intelligence Scale for Children (WISC) to 48 black and

48 white children (half of each racial group was in grades 2 and 3, and half was in grades 7 and 8) in two rural public schools in Florida. Ten subtests of WISC were given by both a black and a white examiner to each child, with a 7-day period between tests. When the examiners were paired racially, each pair administered tests to eight black and eight white children at both grades 2 and 3 and grades 7 and 8. Each examiner tested equal numbers of blacks and whites first and second and at both grade levels. For the black children at grades 2 and 3, mean IQ was 87.291 with a black examiner and 85.583 with a white examiner. For white children at grades 2 and 3, the mean IQs were 103.791 and 103.166 for black and white examiners, respectively. For grades 7 and 8 black children, the mean IQs were 86.458 and 88.291 for black and white examiners, respectively. For grades 7 and 8 white children, these means were 101.541 and 99.700 for black and white examiners, respectively. None of the differences was significant. Race of children was the only significant main effect; there were no significant interactions between race of examiner and child's IQ. Retest scores, generally, were 8 points higher than original scores for all subjects, and the gain was called significant at .05 level. The authors concluded that, for Full Scale WISC IQ, race of examiner had no effect on either black or white children. The authors noted, however, that their findings concerned groups of black and white children only; they could say nothing about the effects of race of examiner on individual children.

The Westinghouse Learning Corporation-Ohio University Report (1969) (the "Report") was done at the request of the Office of Economic Opportunity to demonstrate the efficacy of Head Start programs nationwide. From the total listing of all Head Start centers in the United States (N = 12,927), a random sample of 300 centers was obtained. Each center represented a target area, and all children within any target area were part of the potential sample. The first 100 areas selected were asked to participate; if any refused, or if any did not meet the criteria established by the Report, a center from the 200 in reserve was selected randomly. The Report stated that 70% of the centers nationwide had summer programs only and that 30% had full-year programs; the sample was so chosen as to reflect these proportions. Eight (plus 2) experimental children were selected from each target area; all had participated in Head Start programs. In addition, 8 (plus 2) comparable children who had not participated in Head Start programs were selected from the same target area on the same basis as the experimental children. Selection was based on residential area, Head Start experience, sex, race, grade, and kindergarten experience. All children were in grades 1, 2, and 3 in 1968–69. Head Start centers with summer programs only were sampled independently of centers with full-year programs. The following tests were given to the children in both types of program: the Illinois Test of Psycholinguistic

Ability (ITPA) to all children in all grades; the Metropolitan Readiness Test (MRT) to children in grade 1 only; and the Stanford Achievement Test (StanAch) to children in grades 2 and 3 only. The data collected were extensive and are summarized in the following tabulation:

Grade and Race	Exp.	Scores Cont.	Diff.	p	Number of Centers	Subjects
Illinois Test of Psycholinguistic Ability*						
Summer Programs (p. 134)						
Grade 1: Mostly black	187.25	177.87	9.38	.12	11	176
Mostly white	190.54	198.42	−7.88	.05	19	304
Grade 2: Mostly black	208.41	206.87	1.54	.81	9	144
Mostly white	230.59	230.65	−0.06	.99	19	304
Grade 3: Mostly black	244.98	238.59	6.39	.20	11	176
Mostly white	263.41	261.94	1.47	.81	13	208
Full-Year Programs (p. 152)						
Grade 1: Mostly black	178.82	171.81	7.01	.19	11	176
Mostly white		No data				
Grade 2: Mostly black	208.85	198.80	10.05	.08	13	208
Mostly white		No data				
Metropolitan Readiness Test**						
Summer Programs (p. 136)						
Grade 1: Mostly black	45.77	45.69	0.08	.98	11	176
Mostly white	53.55	55.60	−2.05	.24	19	304
Full-Year Programs (p. 153)						
Grade 1: Mostly black	48.56	43.57	4.99	.11	11	176
Mostly white		No data				
Stanford Achievement Test***						
Summer Programs (pp. 138–9)						
Grade 2: Mostly black	1.48	1.45	0.03	.57	9	144
Mostly white	1.67	1.78	−0.11	.07	19	304
Grade 3: Mostly black	2.05	1.93	0.12	.05	11	176
Mostly white	2.44	2.48	−0.04	.54	13	208

* Mean total raw scores
** Mean readiness score
*** Median grade level

The conclusions of the Report were also extensive but are well summarized in this quotation:

In summary, when one looks at the observed effects of Head Start according to the test of practical relevance, it must be concluded that the effects found on standardized tests are indeed small in magnitude, with the exception of a few differences in subgroups of full-year centers on the ITPA, and do not meet the criterion of practical relevance. (p. 168)

In 1970, Smith and Bissell wrote a rejection of the Report, its methods, and its findings. Cicirelli, Evans, and Schiller (1970) replied to Smith and Bissell in the same issue of the *Harvard Educational Review*. Neither article added new testing data, but the arguments for and against the Report were noteworthy. Finally, Cicirelli, Granger, Schemmel, Cooper, and Holthouse (1971) published a re-analysis of the Report data confining themselves to the summer programs and the ITPA subtest scores; no total ITPA scores were published which makes the summarizing of them awkward.

Cicirelli et al. (1971) intended their article to be a set of norms for grades 1, 2, and 3, for black, white, and Mexican-American low SES children, noting that their data were below the norms for "middle-class whites" and that strong and weak points of low SES children could be derived from the comparison of their norms with middle-class white norms. Intercorrelations among ITPA, MRT, and StanAch were given. Two important questions were stated: (a) ". . . why is there such a contrast in the profiles of the whites, blacks, and Mexican-Americans in regard to the memory abilities?" (p. 246), and (b) could not a stronger intervention program be designed around the deficiencies of the low SES children? Answers were not given, but further research on these questions was recommended.

To investigate four hypotheses about Piaget's Principle of Conservation, Whiteman and Peisach (1970) examined 32 kindergarten and 31 grade 3 children, all low SES, all black, and all from New York City schools. The grade K children were all those in two classes of the same teacher who were able to pass a qualifying perception test. Their mean age was 5–10. The grade 3 children were also required to pass the same perception test, but in spite of this, the authors called their sample a random sample. S-B IQs were available for 19 grade K children (mean IQ was 94.05) and for 26 grade 3 children (mean IQ was 98.08). The same Conservation Test was given to all children. They were asked who had the more M&M candies when one set was placed before the child and another set before the examiner. Discussion and conclusions were confined to Piagetian principles.

Willard's (1968) purpose was to demonstrate whether ". . . so-called culture fair tests . . ." measure black intelligence any better than do ". . . tests which do not make allowance for cultural differences" (p. 584). The author defined intelligence in a series of verbal statements coming, finally, to the statistical definition that intelligence means school success. The subjects were 89 black children from three grade 6 classes of the New Haven, Connecticut, public schools, all low SES, all "deprived." Scores on the Academic Promise Test (APT) and the Cattell Culture Fair Intelligence Test (CCFIT), described in the paper, and on the Stanford-Binet Intelligence Scale (S-B) and the Stanford Achievement Test (StanAch) Reading and Arithmetic subtests were available from the school records. CCFIT was given, also, to 83 black children who were in classes for the mentally retarded in five New Haven schools. Instead of APT scores, the author presented IQs for the Wechsler Intelligence Scale for Children (WISC) as he estimated them from the APT scores. CCFIT IQs were presented as such. The mean estimated WISC IQ was 90.8, SD = 12.2 and the mean CCFIT IQ was 94.4, SD = 16.0 for the 89 grade 6 children. Correlations among the scores were given: APT score and (a) CCFIT IQ .49, (b) Reading .78, (c) Arithmetic .76; between estimated WISC IQ and (a) CCFIT IQ .55, (b) Reading .75, (c) Arithmetic .73; between CCFIT IQ and (a) Reading .57, and (b) Arithmetic .50. A value of 67.6 was shown as if it were the mean APT IQ, but this was not clear. The range of the 83 mentally retarded children on CCFIT was 98 to 57, and on S-B was 81 to 51. For the 83 children, mean IQ was 63.1 for S-B, and 70.0 for CCFIT. The author concluded that the black child is no more disadvantaged by APT or S-B than by CCFIT, commenting that "Non-verbal intelligence seems to be of no major advantage in the school situation" (p. 589).

The purpose of the Yando, Seitz, and Zigler study (1979) was not clearly stated. The paper involved two samples of children (a Matched Group and a Typical Group) who were required to take a battery of 16 performance tests and to undergo interviews. One purpose could have been to study the performances of both Groups on the same set of performance tests and interviews. What the authors called "subsidiary issues" (p. 9) were (a) to compare "economically disadvantaged" (low SES) children from 2-parent homes with low SES children from 1-parent homes, and (b) to compare low SES black children who had attended predominantly white schools with low SES black children who had attended predominantly black schools. In the Matched Group study, 48 "economically advantaged" (high SES), and 48 low SES children were drawn from grades 2 and 3 from 36 schools in urban Massachusetts. Children with gross physical or emotional defects, those whose IQs were below 85, and those who had failed a grade in school were omitted from the sample. Each group of 48 children was composed of 24 white and 24 black 8-year-olds. The Matched Group was not a representative sample of either blacks or whites. In the Typical Group sample, 80 high and 80 low SES children were matched for CA only. No child had any gross physical, intellectual, or emotional defect. In each SES group were 40 black and 40 white children, drawn from grades 2 and 3 from 29 schools in several urban Massachusetts areas. Selection, with respect to IQ and MA, was called random.

The 16 performance tests, specified as measuring Creativity, Self-confidence, Autonomy, Curiosity, Frustration Threshold, and Dependency, were administered to all of the subjects, and these data became the primary concern of the authors. The children were told that they were testing toys for a toy manufacturer, and no child was permitted to know that he failed at anything. Each child was tested for 1½ hours. None of the tests was validated against a criterion. IQs were reported for a number of subgroups of the samples. For the Typical Sample, IQs were 102 and 104 for high SES black subjects, and 89 and 93 for low SES black subjects. For white subjects in the Typical Sample, the IQs were 112 and 117 for high SES subjects, and 102 and 105 for the low SES subjects. The Reading grade equivalents reported were: for the Matched Group: high SES blacks 3.8, high SES whites 3.7, low SES blacks 2.7, low SES whites 3.4; for the Typical Group: high SES blacks 3.4, high SES whites 3.7, low SES blacks 2.8, low SES whites 2.8. The reported Arithmetic grade equivalents were: for Matched Group: high SES blacks 3.6, high SES whites 3.2, low SES blacks, 2.5, low SES whites 3.2; for the Typical Group: high SES blacks 3.6, high SES whites 3.5, low SES blacks 2.2, low SES whites 2.9.

Self-confidence was said to be higher among low SES black children attending predominantly white schools than among such black children attending predominantly black schools. The presence or absence of the father had little to do with the child's IQ—black or white. Little relationship was found among the tests thought to measure Creativity; a closer relationship was found among the tests designed to measure Self-confidence. There was "resonable" relationship among the tests thought to measure Dependency. No such comments were made about the tests of Autonomy, Curiosity, and Frustration Threshold. Extensive comments were made about the interview measures and the Teacher Rating Scale, none of which comments was related to IQ. All racial IQ differences were explained environmentally. The authors confined their conclusions largely to the racial performance test differences.

Yater, Boyd, and Barclay (1975) noted that in the standardization of the Wechsler Intelligence Scale for Children (WISC) no black children had been included. In the standardization of the Wechsler Preschool and Primary Scale of Intelligence (WPPSI), however, black children were included. The authors, therefore, sought to test the hypothesis that WISC is biased against black children by showing that blacks obtained higher IQs on WPPSI. Both tests were administered to 20 children from a Head Start (HS) project by 2 white males, 20 from a Follow-Through Kindergarten (FTK) and 20 from a Follow-Through First Grade (FTFG) project by 1 black female, 1 white male, and 2 white females. All testers were graduate students with experience. All subjects came from the same metropolitan area, and all FTK and FTFG children had had HS experience. The HS children were 60 to 68 months of age; those in FTK were 62 to 79 months; and those in FTFG were 73 to 95 months of age. How the subjects were selected and where the study was done were not given. Testing was done in an HS center close to the child's home. At the HS level, all WISC IQs were consistently higher than the WPPSI IQs—a contradiction of the authors' hypothesis. Only 2 of 9 possible comparisons (Verbal and Full Scale IQs at FTK) confirmed the authors' hypothesis. The authors concluded that no "cumulative deficit" appeared even though all IQs at FTFG were lower than those at HS, and for WISC, the differences were sizeable. In spite of the confused or contradictory evidence, or perhaps because of it, the authors concluded that ". . . cultural bias does not seem to be controlled by including cultural minorities in national standardization samples . . ." (p. 80). With such small samples of questionable representativeness, it is difficult to consider meaningful any conclusions of this study.

Yawkey and Jantz (1974) investigated ". . . the effects of each of the variables (e.g. intelligence, race, sex, and SES) within a specific population of sixth graders using a particular achievement measure" (p. 4). Two relevant hypotheses were presented for study: (a) there are no significant differences in mathematics performance between black and white grade 6 children, and (b) there are no significant differences in the gain (between grades 5 and 6) in mathematics performance of black and white grade 6 children. Subjects were all children who had attended grade 6 in a midwestern school district. Data were obtained from school records only for those children whose records contained information for sex, race, IQ, occupation of the head of the household, and grades 5 and 6 mathematics scores. Out of 3,536 children possible, 3,184 were accepted. The Iowa Test of Basic Skills (ITBS) and the Lorge-Thorndike Intelligence Test, Multilevel Edition (L-T) had been given at the ends of grades 4, 5, and 6. Hypothesis (a) was rejected; racial differences in mathematics scores were significant at .01 level. Hypothesis (b) was not rejected. The authors presented 3 related topics on which they thought further research was needed. No IQ data were given.

Summary

The number of school children tested in the 126 studies reviewed in Chapter III approaches 100,000 including blacks, whites, Mexican-Americans, Puerto Ricans, Chicanos, and Asians. An exact subject count by race is not possible because some investigators described their subject pool as "90% black," mostly white, or called all non-whites "others." On the whole, however, investigators using school children as subjects can not be faulted for small samples.

If test usage is determined by the number of investigators selecting a particular scale the Wechsler tests were most frequently administered. Almost ¼ of the identified tests were either the WISC or WISC-R. Next in order of popular usage were the Binet, Lorge-Thorndike, Peabody

Picture Vocabulary Test, California Test of Mental Maturity, the Raven, and the Bender-Gestalt. If, however, test usage is determined by the number of children taking a particular test then the scales selected for the large national or statewide summaries would be group paper and pencil tests such as the Educational Testing Service School and College Ability Test series rather than individual tests.

For the purpose of this summary the articles in Chapter III have been divided roughly into several broad categories representing the purpose of the study. Not all articles are reviewed again but typical and significant papers with sound designs and adequate samples are selected to represent the category.

1. Comparative Studies of Racial Differences in Intelligence.

Comparison of test scores by race was not the main purpose of the majority of Chapter III studies. Of the 35 articles that did report comparative test scores, two are especially significant. *Negro and White Children: A Psychological Study in the Rural South* was published by Baughman and Dahlstrom in 1968. The purpose of the study was to contribute to the development of a comparative behavioral map of children in the rural south. The Binet, Primary Mental Abilities Test and the Stanford Achievement Test comprised the test battery. Findings in general were unwelcome and difficult for the authors to rationalize. An analysis by race and sex shows that in general whites approximate the national norms in mental ability and school achievement. In every comparison, Negro boys are lowest in mental ability. Although in the earlier grades Negro girls do poorly on the ability tests, by age 14 their scores approach scores for white boys. The overlap of the mental ability scores was found to be 18%; that is, 18% of the black children reach or exceed the mean for whites.

In 1973 Jensen published a landmark paper, "Level I and Level II Abilities in Three Ethnic Groups." (Jensen, 1973b) A battery of seven tests including the Lorge-Thondike, Raven, and Stanford Achievement Test was administered to some 2,000 white, black and Mexican Americans. The children were typical of the general population of California. Mean L-T IQ was 105 for white, 92 for blacks and the Mexican-American mean was located somewhere between the means of blacks and whites.

Mean factor scores of the three groups differed significantly and showed interaction with ethnicity in accordance with Jensen's two-level theory of abilities. The white and black groups differed markedly on "gc" and "gf" but not in memory. The white and Mexican-Americans differed markedly in "gc" but less in "gf" and memory. Jensen concludes that this study supports the two level theory in so far as it demonstrates population differences, and it further substantiates the empirical findings of white-Negro interaction with Level I and Level II.

2. Reliability and Validity.

Although about ¼ of the 126 articles of Chapter III examine the persistent questions of test reliability and validity, one study stands out above the others because of its design and sample size, Kennedy (1965). This Kennedy study is a reassessment of a representative sample of a stratified random sample of 1,800 Negro elementary children tested with the Binet in 1960. Of the original sample 312 were located and tested again with the Binet and the California Achievement Test. Kennedy's results provide the opportunity to examine the stability (reliability) and the forecasting efficiency (validity) of the Binet for Negro school children. With regard to these two vital test characteristcs, the author concludes:

> The mean on the Stanford-Binet, Form L-M, for this portion of the sample in 1960 was 78.9; in 1965 it was 79.2, a nonsignificant change. The standard deviation in the sample increased from 12.6 in 1960 to 14.3 in 1965, and the range in scores increased slightly. (p. 165)
>
> The multiple analyses, which produced coefficients of correlation generally in the range of .70, all point to the fact that the Stanford-Binet IQ is quite probably the most powerful single variable in the prediction of either IQ variables or achievement variables, and again points to the amazing stability of the IQ over the intervening years. It is evident that the degree of modification in the environment, particularly the school environment, which has occurred in the past four years, has not been sufficient to make any major differences in the intelligence test performance of this sample. (p. 167)

3. Explanation of IQ Differences in Terms of Socioeconomic Status.
Despite the many critics of the Coleman Report (Coleman, 1966) this investigation remains the largest and perhaps the best study of the influence of a school's facilities on the verbal achievement (verbal ability) of its pupils. Coleman found that for each racial group most of the variation in verbal achievement (verbal ability) occurs *within* schools and less than 20% between schools. If variations were largely the result of school factors or community differences then school-to-school differences would increase over the grades in school. Several other large studies (Jensen and Figueroa, 1975; Osborne, 1975; Osborne, 1978) refute the environmentalists' claim that mental ability differences are explained on the basis of SES factors.

In defense of a contrary point of view, see "Race, IQ, and the Middle Class" (Trotman, 1977). The author defends with less than convincing *ad hoc* arguments that traditional intelligence tests function to deny societal rewards to those with other than white middle-class values and lifestyles.

4. Tests of Theories of Intervention and Compensatory Education.

Head Start Programs of the 1960's and 1970's are perhaps the best known educational programs designed to enhance school achievement of disadvantaged children. The Coleman Report, The Westinghouse Study, and a recent paper by Darlington, (Darlington et al., 1980) all address the question of the effectiveness of Head Start.

Head Start programs were generally planned for and attended by those children who had the most to gain: children from families of low socioeconomic status. The programs were offered in communities where they were most needed. Where Head Start programs were most effective they served pupils from the poorest families. Negroes were more likely to be helped by intervention programs than whites, and children from low SES families to benefit more than those from high SES.

Coleman says, "In general, Head Start participants of a given race did not perform as well on the verbal and nonverbal reasoning tests as nonparticipants. It is important to note that these pupils, from poor families, have not yet "caught up" to their classmates, even though they participated in the Head Start program." (p. 523)

In 1969 the Westinghouse Learning Corporation published an evaluation of the 12,927 Head Start programs based on a random sample of 300 programs on the OEO list of approved programs. Objective findings are not encouraging to supporters of the massive intervention programs: The Westinghouse Study concludes: "In summary, when one looks at the observed effects of Head Start according to the test of practical relevance, it must be concluded that the effects found on standardized tests are indeed small in magnitude, with the exception of a few differences found in subgroups of full-year centers on the *ITPA,* and do not meet the criterion of practical relevance." (p. 168) Despite the generally negative findings the authors point out: (a) "One possibility is that Head Start has actually been effective, but that the limitations of the present study design preclude the detection of the full effects of Head Start" (p. 245); (b) while the summer Head Start programs are so negative that it is doubtful that any change in design would reverse the findings, the somewhat positive results of the year long Head Start programs suggest that these programs should be encouraged and supported.

In a follow-up of the educational intervention programs of the 1960's, Darlington et al. (1980) summarized the results of 8 well-known projects, basing their evaluation of the programs on 3 criteria: (1) rate of meeting high school requirements, (2) frequency of being placed in special education programs, and (3) frequency of being retained in grade. According to these criteria Darlington et al. judged the Head Start programs they reviewed to be successful.

The authors report no follow-up test results but add this caveat: "Our findings replicated results on IQ reported by numerous previous investigators—large effects in tests given soon after the program, tapering down to smaller but statistically significant effects 3 or 4 years after preschool and vanishing thereafter. This finding has a positive aspect: if 1 year of enrichment still has effects 3 or 4 years later, then 12 years of enriched schooling might have lifelong effects. IQ's, however, are merely indirect predictors of school success; our most important analyses concerned the effect of preschool on direct measures of school success." (p. 203)

Studies not falling under one of the major headings in the summary make up a miscellaneous collection of articles not easily categorized. Most are unique in purpose or sample. Test findings, however, are in general no different from those of other reviewed studies of school children.

To compare black-white test results obtained from the summary of the articles reviewed in Chapter III with similar results obtained between 1921 and 1965, median IQs were calculated from all studies reporting test scores. Since some investigations were not comparative there were more articles reporting IQs for blacks than for whites, 195 for blacks, 89 for whites. The median value of the 195 IQs for blacks was 90; the corresponding value for the 89 IQs for whites was 103.

Scores from Shuey's analysis of test results of school children in the 2nd Edition and the corresponding scores from Chapter III of Volume 2 are tabulated below:

Differences in IQ of Black and White School Children 1921–1980

Source	Type of Test	Means				Medians	
		1921–44		1945–65		1965–80	
		W–B	Diff	W–B	Diff	W–B	Diff
Shuey 2nd Ed.	Individual	99–85	14	96–82	14	—	
Shuey 2nd Ed.	Group Non-Verbal	99–83	16	101–88	13	—	
Shuey 2nd Ed.	Group Verbal	98–85	13	99–83	16	—	
Osborne & McGurk Volume 2	All tests Individual & Group	—		—		103–90	13

In the two earlier surveys Shuey analyzed results by type of test as well as by date the test was given. In the later edition IQs from individual, group verbal, and group nonverbal tests are combined. The consistency of the black-white IQ differences for school children over a period of 6 decades is nothing less than remarkable.

IV

High School Students

Frank C. J. McGurk

Angoff and Ford (1973) were interested in studying the nature of racial test score differences by examining the relative item difficulty on the Preliminary Scholastic Aptitude Test (PSAT). Their 10 sets of subjects were obtained from a pool of Georgia high school pupils who had taken PSAT in 1970. Two random samples of Atlanta blacks (Sample 1, N = 300, and Sample 2, N = 340); a selected sample of 280 Atlanta blacks (Sample 3) matched for PSAT Verbal score to a sample of Atlanta whites; and (Sample 4) a selected sample of 275 Atlanta blacks matched to a white sample on PSAT Math score were taken. There were two mutually exclusive random samples of Atlanta whites of 300 subjects each (Samples 5 and 6); a sample of 280 Atlanta whites (Sample 7) matched on PSAT Verbal score with a sample of Atlanta blacks; and (Sample 8) 275 Atlanta whites matched on PSAT Math score with a sample of Atlanta blacks. Sample 9 was a random sample of 125 Savannah blacks, and Sample 10 was a random sample of 300 "Nonurban" blacks. Matching was done on a sample-to-sample basis so that the frequency of subjects at each score in one sample equalled the frequency of subjects at each score in the matched sample.

The mean Verbal scores for Samples 1 and 2 were 13.51, SD = 10.64 and 13.18, SD = 10.10, respectively; the mean Math scores were 8.88, SD = 8.00 and 8.07, SD = 7.58, respectively. The unselected white samples (Samples 5 and 6) produced mean Verbal scores of 28.32, SD = 12.17 and 28.45, SD = 12.58, respectively; their mean Math scores were 21.11, SD = 9.54 and 21.57, SD = 9.65, respectively. Blacks who were matched to whites on Verbal score (Sample 3) had a mean Math score of 9.09, SD = 7.67; and blacks matched to whites for Math score (Sample 4) produced a mean Verbal score of 14.45, SD = 10.15. Whites matched to blacks on Verbal score (Sample 7) had a mean Math score of 14.80, SD = 8.98; and whites matched to blacks on Math score (Sample 8) had a mean Verbal score of 18.75, SD = 9.94. The mean Verbal score of the Savannah blacks (Sample 9) was 13.00, SD = 9.48 and the mean

Math score was 7.74, SD = 8.00. The mean Verbal score of the "Non-urban" blacks was 8.36, SD = 8.07, and the mean Math score was 5.18, SD = 6.35.

Most of the authors' conclusions concerned the finding that, when blacks were matched to whites, black test performance was closer to white test performance than when unselected blacks and unselected whites were compared. The means for the unselected white samples on both sections of the PSAT are about 1 to 1⅓ standard deviations higher than the means for the unselected black samples. After matching on the alternate score, means for both sections of the PSAT come closer in line, the means for whites dropping and the means for blacks rising to a point where they are only one half to ⅔ standard deviation apart.

In his monograph, Bachman (1970) sought to emphasize the effects of environmental factors on human development. He described the random selection of 25 grade 10 boys from each of 87 schools—one school per county and metro area—an original sample of 2,213. He hoped to obtain a "bias free" sample of all 10th-grade boys in the United States. The Quick Test (QT), the General Aptitude Test Battery, Part J (GATB-J), and Raven's Progressive Matrices (RPM) were administered to varying numbers of children. For the QT, the author reported a mean raw score of 110.4, SD = 10.8 for 1,912 whites and a mean of 95.7, SD = 14.7 for 256 blacks (total N = 2,168). For GATB-J, comments appeared only in data tables and these were not separated by race. Reference to RPM in the text was limited, but a mean raw score of 23.3, SD = 5.0 was reported for 2,177 whites, and a mean of 16.0, SD = 7.2 for 291 blacks. Bachman commented that he had avoided all firm conclusions about racial differences except that they ". . . are primarily—if not exclusively—differences in cultural . . . opportunities" (p. 201).

In order to determine whether racial or SES groups showed patterning in their mental abilities, Backman (1972) selected 1,236 Jewish whites, 1,051 gentile whites, 488 blacks, and 150 Orientals from the Data Bank of Project Talent. Subjects were restricted to those who had answered a followup study done 5 years after high school graduation, and included only those subjects determined to be in the middle SES area. The data for 6 mental abilities were reported in what appeared to be standard score form, and patterns of test performance were determined by ANOVA. The author reported that sex differences in test patterning appeared and seemed to increase with age; moreover, the effects of SES on test patterning may have been obliterated by the bias in the sample. ". . . the average level of the pattern of mental abilities of the Negroes . . . was significantly lower (p < .01) than . . . the other ethnic groups." (p. 7)

Boney (1966) selected 118 girls and 104 boys (all black, all from grade 12, and all from Port Arthur, Texas) for a study of the validity of the

Differential Aptitude Tests (DAT), the California Mental Maturity Test (CMMT), and the Cooperative School Ability Test (CAT) as predictors of school progress. Grade point average was the criterion of school progress, and correlations between the criterion and the test scores, plus regression weights, were the only data given. The author concluded that these tests predict school progress for blacks as well as they do for whites.

The purpose of the Bonner and Belden (1970) study was the determination of whether, for black high school pupils, WAIS IQs could be predicted from PPVT IQs. The sample was a group of 16- and 17-year old black high school seniors, from rural and urban Oklahoma schools. All were of normal intelligence (others were systematically rejected from the sample). In spite of this bias in the sample, they were called representative of 16- and 17-year old blacks and were randomly selected from the black population of 3 high schools. Three samples of 20 pupils each, Samples A, B, and C, were originally selected and no significant differences among sample variances were found. A final sample (D) of 31 pupils was selected randomly from groups A, B, and C. Mean WAIS IQs were: Verbal, 100.77; Performance, 95.00; and Full Scale, 98.23. Mean PPVT IQ was 95.03. Correlation between PPVT and WAIS Verbal IQ was significantly different from zero, but not so the correlation between PPVT and WAIS Performance IQ. The conclusions of the authors seemed to have been predicated upon their having selected a random and representative sample of blacks.

Cardall and Coffman's (1964) article was published to develop and illustrate a method for comparing responses of different groups of subjects to a set of test items. Samples of 300 each were selected from the May, 1963, administration of the College Board Scholastic Aptitude Test (SAT) from three sources: sample (a) from testing centers in Illinois and Indiana within 50 miles of Chicago and Ft. Wayne; sample (b) from the Bronx, New York City; and sample (c) from centers in the southeast where only blacks were registered. Two ANOVA were performed for each sample, and data were presented in the usual ANOVA form. "There are highly significant group main effects indicating that the three groups differ in overall verbal and mathematical ability as measured by these particular samples of items . . . It is clear that the major difference is between Group 1 and 2 on the one hand and Group 3 on the other. The performance of Group 3 is clearly inferior to that of the other two groups." (p. 6) No test scores or mean data were presented.

Cleary and Hilton (1968) were interested in whether the Preliminary Scholastic Aptitude Test (PSAT) was biased against either blacks or SES groups. Their sample consisted of all of the black pupils in 7 integrated schools in 3 large metropolitan areas which had been selected out of a larger sample. Whites were selected randomly from the same sources. The 636 Group I pupils had taken PSAT in 1961; the 774

Group II pupils had taken it in 1963. In each Group, blacks and whites were equal in number. SES data were gathered from the House-Home Index, and Groups I and II took alternate forms of PSAT. The data were treated by ANOVA. The authors concluded that, while white scores were significantly higher than black scores, PSAT was not biased against blacks.

The purpose of the Dubin, Osburn, and Winick article (1969) was to determine whether extra practice, additional testing time, or both, would improve the test scores of blacks more than those of whites. The authors selected 235 black and 232 white high school pupils from the Galena Park (Texas) High School. Ages were not given. The subjects were divided into Groups S_1, S_2, P_1, and P_2. The S-groups were given speeded tests; the P-groups received power tests (triple time limits). Subjects were familiar with the tests which were Numerical Ability, Space Visualization, Numerical Reasoning, and Verbal Reasoning, subtests of the Employee Aptitude Survey (EAS). A SES questionnaire was also given. Test data were reported in raw scores. The authors concluded that whites were superior to blacks on each test condition; the hierarchy of test scores (high to low) was high SES whites, low SES whites, high SES blacks, and low SES blacks. For both races, test scores increased as testing time increased. The hypothesis that, with extra practice, black scores would improve more than white scores (Hypothesis 1) was rejected. Special pairing of subjects led to the rejection of the hypothesis that extra testing time would favor the blacks (Hypothesis 2). Using the same matching as for Hypothesis 2, Hypothesis 3 (that blacks would benefit the more from a combination of extra practice and extra time) was also rejected. Thus, the testing procedure was considered not to be a major factor in differences between blacks and whites.

Hennessy and Merrifield (1976) were interested in whether the Comparative Guidance and Placement Examination Program, a test battery from the College Entrance Examination Board (1970), had equal ". . . cross-ethnic construct validity . . ." (p. 754) for 431 blacks, 163 Hispanics, 573 Jewish and 1,818 Gentile-Caucasians, representing a wide range of SES. All subjects were high school seniors planning to enter the City University of New York, an open enrollment institution. How or when the subjects were chosen was not given. The Program consisted of 10 mental ability and achievement subtests. In addition, SES data were collected and partialled out of the factor analyses that were done on the test results. The authors concluded that there were no meaningful differences in factor structures among the four groups of subjects and that the Program ". . . has a high degree of cross-ethnic factorial validity . . ." (p. 759). "While there may be differences in level of performance on the various tests between different ethnic groups, they {the tests} seem to be measuring the same abilities across these groups." (p. 759)

The expressed purpose of the Kassinove, Rosenberg, and Trudeau article (1970) was to cross-validate and determine the general "adequacy" of Mathis' Environmental Participation Index (EPI) (Mathis, 1967). The subjects were 54 black, 13 white, and 29 Spanish-speaking high school pupils who were considered as having "potential for academic success" and who were enrolled in a summer remedial program at Hofstra University. Mean age was 16–11, and mean school grade was 10.6. In spite of the restrictions imposed by the sample selection, the authors called the sample of average intelligence. WAIS or WISC was given to each subject, and no IQ-distinction was made between the two tests. For the blacks, the Verbal, Performance, and Full Scale IQs were 100.8, 94.8, and 98.1, respectively; the corresponding scores for whites were 110.4, 107.8, and 109.8; for Spanish-speaking subjects, 99.0, 95.7, and 97.4. Correlations between EPI and IQ ranged between .40 and .49 for 47 blacks, and between −.50 and −.02 for 11 whites—a racial difference about which the authors made no comment. To the authors, the "adequacy" of the EPI was its ability to predict IQ. Thus, the authors concluded that, while EPI was highly reliable, it was of only slight value as a predictor of IQ or school achievement. "None of the relationships found had practical utility." (p. 376)

After a brief review of the literature on the nature of creativity, Kazelskis, Jenkins, and Lingle (1972) announced as their purpose the clarification of this topic. They selected a sample of 111 pupils in grades 10 and 11 in a ". . . rural, predominantly Negro (70 percent), high school in Mississippi" (p. 59). Whether the authors administered the Lorge-Thorndike Intelligence Test, Form 1, Level G (L-T) or obtained these data from school records was not clear and neither was the method of selecting the sample. However, the authors reported these mean L-T IQs: Verbal, 81.95, SD = 13.02; Nonverbal, 83.66, SD = 14.39 and concluded "These results . . . indicate that creativity . . . is substantially correlated with intelligence." (p. 61)

Powers, Drane, Close, Noonan, Wines, and Marshall (1971) presented a short synopsis of research on the self-perception of adolescents, noting particularly that the self-image of blacks has been shown to be higher than that of whites even when this seemed to be a contradiction of general expectation. The authors then announced their purpose: ". . . to determine differences in self-image and selected educational variables for Black, Jewish-white, and non-Jewish-white youths integrated in an inner suburban high school" (p. 666). Data were gathered by the use of 5 self-perception scales, teacher-comments, and school records of grade point average, absences, credits accumulated, tardiness, IQ, and length of time in the school system. The subjects were 49 black, 106 Jewish-white, and 60 gentile-white grade 10 pupils from a predominantly Jewish suburban section adjacent to a large metropolitan area. The sample was a random sample stratified according to the population of the three groups in the general population of the area. Mean IQs (tests not identified) were 103.38 for blacks, 116.37 for Jews, and 114.88 for non-Jewish-whites. Blacks were significantly lower than either of the white groups. Racial differences in a number of other variables were given. There was no evidence that blacks were lower than whites on any of the self-perception measures and, in self image, the blacks were higher than the non-Jewish-whites.

The purpose of the Resnick and Entin (1971) article was to investigate the validity of the Satz and Mogel (1962) method of abbreviating the WISC. Fifty-five black subjects were selected from outpatient clinics in Memphis, Tennessee, Richmond, Virginia, and Waterford, Connecticut, and 25 more black subjects were taken from the Richmond, Virginia, public schools. How the selecting was done was not stated, and the authors admitted that their sample was not representative of blacks in general. The WISC, which had been given in its full form to each child at the clinic of origin, was rescored into an abbreviated form according to the Satz and Mogel method. The mean full form Full Scale IQ was 76.19, SD = 14.62 and the mean abbreviated form Full Scale IQ was 78.76, SD = 15.67. The difference was called significant at .01. IQ and subtest correlations between the two forms of WISC were high (only Comprehension was under .80). The authors concluded that their data agreed with the literature that high correlation existed between the full form Full Scale and the abbreviated form of WISC and that this supported the conclusion that the abbreviated form was valid, but then the authors added: ". . . when the data are further examined by comparing the mean differences, new information is obtained that appears to contradict the validity implied by the correlations; that is, significant differences are found between the two forms for Verbal IQ and Full Scale IQ as well as for several subtests, with Performance IQ approaching significance" (p. 98). The authors also emphasized individual differences between the full form and the abbreviated form scores as further evidence of the lack of validity of the abbreviated form. The authors did not consider an external measure as a criterion of validity, and part of their rejection of the abbreviated form of WISC was based on their failure to understand that correlation between the two forms of WISC was independent of the relationship between their mean scores.

Samuel, Soto, Parks, Ngissah, and Jones (1976) reported 2 experimental situations designed to test the hypothesis that racial differences in test scores were the result of motivational factors which, in turn, resulted from the subjects' perceptions of the testing situation. Two testing atmospheres were arranged for the subjects: in the Evaluative Atmosphere, the subjects were told that the tests were to measure their intelligences and capacities; in the Gamelike Atmosphere, the subjects were told to relax and play games. In each Atmosphere, the experimenters created Expectations: in the High Expectation, the subjects were told that they were expected to do well; in the Low Expectation, the subjects were told the opposite. In each Expectation, each race of subjects (black or white) was tested by each race of tester (black or white). Males and females were tested separately.

In Experiment 1, 208 black and 208 white subjects were selected from among a set of high school pupils who, in 1972–3, had secured parental permission to participate. All subjects were 12 to 16 years of age, and all were paid for participating. IQ was estimated from 4 WISC Performance subtests. In addition, each subject completed a self-rating scale about his performance, described his testing attitude by means of an adjective check list, and completed an anxiety scale. SES was estimated from parental occupation and home value. Mean data were published on sets of 13 subjects (the size of the ANOVA cells). The mean black IQ for the entire sample of 208 was 109.45; for the 208 white subjects, the mean IQ was 111.13. There were no sex differences in mean IQ. IQs obtained by white testers were generally higher than those obtained by black testers even when the testees were black. At no Expectation did a black tester secure a significantly higher IQ than the white tester in the same Expectation. The authors speculated about the causes of their findings.

In Experiment 2, 104 white and 104 black junior high school pupils who, in 1973–4, were 12 to 16 years old, were treated as in Experiment 1, but only male subjects were used. There was no statement about how the subjects were selected. SES was added as a fifth variable, replacing sex. This "replication" of Experiment 1 yielded somewhat different results. In general, the authors considered that they had sustained their hypothesis, but they were somewhat unsure of themselves.

When this reviewer combined the sexes and computed t-statistics for the mean differences published in Experiment 1, no difference between the High and Low Expectations, for either Atmosphere and for either race, appeared at any level of significance higher than .10. The design of the study, however, was attractive, and it might be well to repeat it with larger samples.

Simpson's (1970) article was designed to study the validity of the WISC and WAIS as tests for mentally retarded subjects. Each test appeared to have served as the criterion for the other. All of the subtests of both tests were administered randomly to 40 whites, 40 Mexican-Americans, and 40 blacks. Subjects, all of whose IQs were below 90, came from 10 junior and senior high schools in Los Angeles and were within 3 months of their 16th birthdate. For the whites, WISC Verbal, Performance, and Full Scale IQs were, respectively, 82.55, SD = 12.52, 91.72, SD = 12.71, and 85.55, SD = 11.51. The same data, in the same order, for WAIS IQs were 90.47, SD = 10.96, 93.12, SD = 9.76, and 91.50, SD = 9.28. For the Mexicans, WISC IQs (same order as above) were 77.65, SD = 8.94, 88.25, SD = 14.23, and 81.02, SD = 10.61; their WAIS IQs (same order) were 83.92, SD = 8.05, 90.80, SD = 9.15, and 86.35, SD = 7.26. For blacks, the WISC IQs were (same order) 80.15, SD = 10.20, 85.57, SD = 14.53, and 81.00, SD = 11.01; their WAIS IQs were 89.10, SD = 8.09, 88.25, SD = 10.77, and 88.58, SD = 8.59. The overall variance among the Verbal IQs was called significant at .001; for Performance IQs, significant at .01; and for Full Scale IQs, significant at .001. Racial variance among the three IQ means was called significant at .05. There were no sex differences. The author presented a set of correlations among the various IQs (range .324 to .864) and concluded that the two tests were not comparable for retarded subjects. As their titles indicate the WISC and WAIS are not designed for the same age groups. The maximum tabled age in the WISC Manual is 15–11; the minimum tabled age in the WAIS Manual is 16.

In a short report designed to predict high school achievement from elementary school records, Solomon, Scheinfeld, Hirsch, and Jackson (1971) selected certain black pupils from 2 consecutive graduating classes from a large Chicago high school. Eighteen boys and 19 girls were selected as "High" achievers and an unstated number of pupils were selected as "Low" achievers. In addition, 29 boys and 18 girls were selected from school records as "Dropouts," but the school records were not identified as either elementary or high school records. Data on the relationships between school performance and high school achievement were given for a number of factors. IQs (at grade 6; test not identified) for "Highs," "Lows," and "Dropouts" were, for boys, 93.9, 93.1, and 91.0, respectively; for girls these data were 102.8, 92.9, and 86.6. The differences among the means for boys were not significant; those among the girls were significant at .05.

Wilson, Jensen, and Elliott (1966) authored an unpublished monograph the purpose of which was to describe the sociological characteristics of being "educationally disadvantaged." By way of describing the status of being disadvantaged, the authors reported on the Differential Aptitude Test scores of Richmond, California, black, Mexican, white, and Oriental secondary school pupils, but presented no IQ data, ages, or specific school grades. Sixty-two percent of 657 blacks and 38% of 66 Mexicans fell in the lowest third of scores; only 19% of 1,126 whites, and 14% of 41 Orientals did. Eight percent of blacks, 13% of Mexican-Americans, 41% of whites, and 41% of Orientals fell in the highest third. The selection of the sample was not discussed. The remainder of the article touched on various qualitative characteristics of the disadvantaged and the teaching practices that have characterized the remedial programs which have been devised to help the disadvantaged.

Summary

This chapter is an odd miscellanea of 17 articles having to do with the testing of high school students. The small number of studies is surprising when compared to the 55 located and reviewed in the 2nd Edition.

The number of subjects examined is substantial, over 16,000, including approximately 5,500 blacks, 8,000 whites, 2,000 Jewish, 300 Spanish-speaking Americans, and 200 Orientals. In one study, one sample was described as approximately 70% black.

Because of the variety of research designs, subject pools, and psychological tests employed, any effort to summarize the overall findings for Chapter IV would necessarily be a recapitulation of the individual article summaries. However, the following comments concerning Chapter IV, the testing of high school students, seem justified.

1. Six of the 17 Chapter IV articles were multi-racial. Where means were reported, significant black-white differences were found, with Spanish-speaking Americans sometimes above and sometimes below the means for blacks. With the exception of the large California study, mean scores for the other five groups seem to be elevated. One study of retardates, for example, reported mean IQs of 88.6 for white, 84.8 for black, and 83.7 for Spanish-speaking subjects. In terms of overlap on the Differential Aptitude Test, the ethnic groups are ranked Orientals 1st, whites 2nd, Mexican-Americans 3rd, and blacks a distant 4th.

2. To tease out the black-white differences, one investigator administered a mental ability test under standard conditions and also as a power test. The idea was to determine if additional time (three times as much) would attenuate black-white differences. The additional testing time did not favor blacks or reduce the black-white IQ difference.

3. To no one's surprise, the authors of one investigation reported that creativity is substantially correlated with intelligence.

4. Among the 17 articles reviewed for this chapter, there were fifteen estimates of IQ scores for blacks where the number was given for each estimate; 8 estimates were reported for IQs of white high school students. The median for blacks was 90; for whites, 108. Assuming the standard deviation for the white IQ was 15, the black overlap of the white mean was 12%, roughly the overlap reported by Yerkes (1921), Shuey (1966), and McGurk (1975), but considerably less than that found for school children (Chapter III), and considerably more than we will find in the next chapter, College Students.

V

College Students

R. Travis Osborne

Twenty-eight studies of college students involving over 16,000 blacks, almost 45,000 whites, 70 Asians, and 31 Mexican-Americans are reviewed in this chapter. In addition to the 28 journal articles, there is a recently released survey of the Graduate Record Examination scores for all students who took the GRE in 1978 and 1979 (Wild, 1980). The base group of 196,404 includes 13,025 blacks and Afro-Americans, 161,592 whites, 1,436 Latin-Americans, 2,923 Asian-Americans, 1,057 American Indians, 2,417 Mexican-Americans, 1,452 Puerto Ricans, 4,395 "other" ethnic groups, and 8,107 who did not indicate race.

The major thrust of the 28 journal articles was to examine the forecasting efficiency of psychological tests for black and white college students. Black-white comparisons comprise only about ¼ the total number of studies. The investigations were conducted in the late 60's and 70's except for 2 that were inadvertently omitted from the 2nd edition of *Testing Negro Intelligence.*

Twenty different standardized tests were used in the 28 articles; however, the College Entrance Examination Board Scholastic Aptitude Test was the test of choice in 15 of the 28 investigations. While most of the other tests such as the American College Testing Program, American Council on Education Psychological Examination, National Teachers Examinations, and the Graduate Record Examination are well known, some were special purpose tests, others were novel and unvalidated such as the Programmer Aptitude Test and the Black Intelligence Test.

Ninety-three black sophomores of Tennessee A & I State University were subjects for Atchison's (1968) investigation of achievement and intellectual factors related to anxiety as measured by the Taylor Manifest Anxiety Scale. Correlations between anxiety level and both non-intellectual and intellectual factors for both low and high anxiety groups were positive but insignificant for the high anxiety group. Otis IQs for both groups were within the normal range, High Anxiety $\overline{X} = 103$; Low Anxiety $\overline{X} = 99$. The difference was significant at .05 level.

A significant paper by Arthur L. Benson, Director of the National Teachers Examinations, was published in 1955. The paper is remarkable because it provides a bench mark against which present NTE data may be compared with those of a quarter century earlier. Benson's paper is even more remarkable because it was not cited in any of the earlier well known reviews of testing Negro intelligence, Shuey (1966), McGurk (1975), Miller and Dregor (1973).

Problems of Evaluating Test Scores of White and Negro Teachers (Benson, 1955) was an invited address presented in Louisville, Kentucky, December 2, 1954, to the Southern Association of Colleges and Secondary Schools. In his paper, Benson examines mental test results and many variables thought to be related to teacher and school administrator success, such as SES, sex, and geography. Here we will review only results of the 1953 National College Freshman Testing Program and the 1954 National Teacher Examinations. Both programs were in operation while there were still legally segregated colleges and secondary schools.

Subjects for Benson's study were selected from 9 colleges "located in states which require segregation of students by race" (p. 8). More than ⅓ of the students were planning to teach. Four of the colleges were white institutions which enrolled 698 freshmen; five were Negro institutions which enrolled 761 freshmen. "The average Total Raw Score on the American Council on Education Psychological Examination for the white freshmen was 92.2, and for the Negro freshmen 47.1. These average raw scores corresponded to percentile ranks of 35 and 5 for these two groups respectively. . . ." (p. 8). Approximately 50 percent of the Negro freshmen earned scores below those achieved by 95% of the white freshmen.

The second part of the Benson study involved the National Teacher Examinations. The subject sample included 1,429 seniors at 37 colleges located in 9 different states. There were 912 white seniors tested at 26 colleges in 7 states, and 517 Negro seniors tested at 11 colleges in 5 states. Both the Common Examination and the Optional Examinations of the NTE were administered. The Common Examination is composed of five tests covering knowledges and abilities which are generally considered to be desirable for all teachers regardless of specialization. The Optional tests are designed to measure knowledge of subject matter and teaching methods in the prospective teacher's field of specialization. "For the Weighted Common Examination Total Score, the mean achieved by white students was 580, and for Negro students was 434. These correspond to percentile ranks of about 49 and 4, respectively, for the normative group" (p. 11).

Benson says the figures are impressive for a number of reasons. "They are not based on prospective teachers tested at a single institution or even in a single state" (p. 11). They are not collected from a single type of institution, but include state teachers colleges, liberal arts colleges, and universities.

The NTE remains the preadmission test preferred by many colleges of graduate education.

Designed by Boone and Adesso (1974), the Black Intelligence Test contains concepts and phraseologies specific to the black environment and to the history of the black people. Comprehensive non-standard English is also part of the BIT.

The authors administered the BIT to 100 black and 100 white college students enrolled at the University of Wisconsin-Milwaukee. An item analysis revealed that 95% of the BIT items were more difficult for whites than for blacks. Correlations between scores of the BIT and those of the vocabulary section of the Shipley tests were insignificant. However, the white students performed better than blacks on this more conventional intelligence test. Boone and Adesso conclude that "While it is clear that the BIT may not be a valid measure of intelligence, it does demonstrate the broad cultural dichotomy found between black and white groups. In addition to the need for reliability data on the BIT, there is also the problem of demonstrating its relationship to traditional measures of intelligence" (p. 435). To which the reviewer would have to agree.

While Associate Director of Research, National Merit Scholarship Corporation, F. H. Borgen (1972) examined the validity of the National Merit Scholarship Qualifying Test for predicting college grades for black students attending five types of schools. The base group of 4288 black high school seniors was nominated by high school principals for participation in the program. In 1966, one year after graduation from high school, a questionnaire was mailed to all participants asking about their college progress and asking for other information concerning their colleges.

Because of the usual mail questionnaire problems, the usable sample was reduced to 477 men and 837 women, a number which is not unimpressive. Women respondents outnumbered men by about 2 to 1 because more principals recommended women than men and women returned the questionnaire in greater proportion than did men.

The five types of colleges were: predominantly black schools which were classified as either public or private and predominantly white colleges which were classified as highly selective, moderately selective, and of low selectivity.

Borgen found substantial differences among black students attending the five types of colleges, the most striking being the inverse relationship between average college grades and average National Merit Scholarship Qualifying Test scores. The obtained correlation between GPA and NMSQT scores for all black students was .03. However, when correlations were computed between test scores and GPA for each of the five types of colleges, the r's ranged from .02 to .54 with a median r of .27. $\overline{X}$

NMSQT scores for all five colleges were: males, 105.7, SD = 19.5; females, 100.0, SD = 20.1.

In September, 1968, the University of Illinois at Urbana admitted to its Special Educational Opportunity Program (Bowers, 1970) 515 freshmen, most of whom were black. The SEOP was not unlike programs in other universities designed to enable those students with no firm post-high school plans to attend college. Since SEOP students were recruited late in their senior year most had no pre-admission test scores. However, scores on the School and College Ability Test and the Cooperative Reading Comprehension Test were given during the freshman orientation program. Mean SCAT verbal scores for the SEOP men was 17, SD = 7; regular men students 32, SD = 9; SEOP women 17, SD = 7; regular women 34, SD = 9. Quantitative scores for SEOP men were 16, SD = 6; regular men 35, SD = 8; SEOP women 12, SD = 5; regular women 29, SD = 8.

Bowers concluded that different regression equations were necessary for predicting GPA of regular and SEOP students at the University of Illinois. High school percentile ranks and SCAT verbal scores were significant predictors of GPA for all groups. SCAT Q score was a significant predictor of GPA for regularly admitted men only.

In an attempt to isolate non-intellective correlates of academic achievement, Cameron (1968) administered two tests of the Michigan M-Scales (Word Rating List and Human Trait Inventory) to 58 Negro women enrolled in his educational psychology classes. School and College Ability Test scores were also available. The best single predictor of GPA was SCAT-Total, $r = .57$. When SCAT-Total was combined with the scores from the Word Rating List, $\overline{X} = 30$, SD = 8, and Human Trait Inventory, $\overline{X} = 18$, SD = 4, an R of .59 was obtained. The contribution of the Michigan M-Scales subtests to the validity coefficient was negligible.

A team of research psychologists from Educational Testing Service (Centra, Linn, and Parry, 1970) investigated the academic growth in predominantly black and predominantly white colleges. Seven white colleges were selected from 90 colleges that had recently used both the Scholastic Aptitude Test and the Graduate Record Examination area tests. They were chosen to be as comparable as possible to the seven black colleges that had also given both the SAT and GRE area tests. All but one of the 14 schools were located in the South and all were small, private, liberal arts colleges. Six of the seven in each group were church affiliated. From each school a sample of approximately 100 seniors who had completed a GRE area test was selected. For schools with fewer than 100 seniors, the entire class was chosen. Only those students whose SAT scores were on file were retained—327 from black colleges and 406 from white colleges. The resulting number of students from each college ranged from 31 to 69 for Negro colleges with a mean of 47, and from 32 to 82 for white colleges, with a mean of 58.

Students were grouped by major field of study to correspond to the three GRE area tests, Natural Science, Humanities, and Social Science. Because of the small number of students in some majors at some colleges, students in some schools were combined.

Despite efforts by the investigators to equate black and white colleges for mean SAT this goal was not reached. Scores from white colleges were 37 points above those from black colleges on the SAT-V and 49 points on the SAT-M. Both differences are significant. The usual mean black-white difference of approximately 1 standard deviation was, however, reduced to less than ½ standard deviation.

The SAT-V correlations with the GRE area tests are quite similar for Negroes and whites. With the exception of the natural science majors, the SAT-M correlations with the GRE area tests are also quite similar for blacks and whites. The subgroups of Negro and white colleges did not seem to differ in predictability of their GRE scores. There is considerable disparity in the academic effectiveness among both Negro and white colleges. There is no evidence that either type of college is more effective in fostering academic achievement measured by the GRE area tests.

Another significant study was conducted while the investigator was with the Educational Testing Service, Cleary (1968). Cleary examined test bias in predicting grades of Negro and white students in integrated colleges. Subjects were 273 blacks, 318 whites, matched for curriculum and class and, in one school, for sex; and a random sample of 2,808 white students. Two major difficulties were encountered: (1) it was difficult to find sufficient numbers of black and white students in the same colleges; (2) it was also difficult to identify students by race. This latter difficulty was perhaps the result of federal regulations that eliminated this bit of information from the application blank. Three schools were used in this study. For school 1 "The race of the students was identified by having two persons examine independently the standard identification pictures in the school files. Wherever there was disagreement, a third judge was used. If agreement could not be reached, the student was classified as white. Corroboration was obtained from a list of Negro students provided by the NAACP: five students not on the NAACP list had been classified as Negro, and one student on the NAACP list had been classified as white. The five students not on the NAACP list were retained as Negroes after further examination of the identification pictures. The race code of the one student who was on the NAACP list but who had not been classified as Negro was changed to Negro" (p. 116). For school 2 Negro students were identified by 2 persons who examined the school identification files. For school 3, race was identified by the school admissions officer. The three schools used in Cleary's study were (1) an eastern state-supported institution of approximately 5,000 male students; (2) an eastern state-supported institution of approximately 10,000 students; (3) a state-supported institution in the southwest with approximately 6,000 students.

School #1 must have been highly selective, especially for blacks whose mean SAT-V was 495, SD = 67, and SAT-M 525, SD = 74. The means are among the very highest reported for any group of black college students in this chapter. Mean SAT's for black students in the late 1960's were generally in the 350–450 range.

School #2 is also selective for blacks, $\overline{X}$ SAT-V = 486, SD = 67; $\overline{X}$ SAT-M = 468, SD = 68. For a random selection of whites in the same institution, the $\overline{X}$ SAT-V was 502, SD = 80; $\overline{X}$ SAT-M = 517, SD = 85.

Test score $\overline{X}$'s at school #3 were more in line with those of other state supported institutions. Means for blacks were SAT-V 338, SD = 71; SAT-M 371, SD = 66. For the random white group $\overline{X}$ SAT-V was 436, SD = 100; and SAT-M 461, SD = 101.

Despite the differences in the SAT $\overline{X}$'s among the 3 schools, the GPA's are remarkably similar for blacks: School 1 = 1.82, School 2 = 1.80, and School 3 = 1.81. For the three schools, random white GPA's are 2.18, 1.94, and 2.38, respectively.

Validity for school #1 should perhaps be discounted. For blacks SAT-V correlates with GPA .47, within the range usually found between college grades and SAT. However, the SAT-M scores yield a validity coefficient of .01. The correlation between SAT-V and SAT-M is only .12.

In School #2 none of the validities is impressive. For blacks the r's range from .02 to .26; for whites from .30 to .38.

For School #3 the similarities of validities for blacks and whites and for random whites are rather striking in view of the discrepancy among means and variances. All r's with GPA are high, ranging from .39 to .67.

Cleary concludes that in the 3 colleges studied there was little evidence that the SAT is biased as a predictor of college grades. In the 2 eastern schools, there were no significant differences in regression lines for Negro and white students. In the college in the southwest the regression lines for blacks and whites were significantly different. Negro scores were overpredicted by the use of the white regression lines.

A comparison of characteristics of Negro and white college freshman classmates was made at the University of Illinois by Davis, Loeb, and Robinson (1970). Subjects were 152 blacks and over 10,000 whites who entered the Urbana-Champaign campus fall 1966 or 1967.

Negro and non-Negro students were compared on the ACT and high school percentile rank. The Negro and non-Negro groups had essentially the same high school average but mean ACT scores differed by approximately 1 standard deviation.

The authors concluded that despite these differences, the prediction of GPA from high school grades and ACT scores is approximately as good for Negro students as for the total freshman class. Although both the 1966 and 1967 total groups showed significant correlations between HSPR and ACT, neither of the Negro groups did. In other words, high school performance as measured by the HSPR is not significantly correlated with an achievement test covering high school subject matter for Negro students. The significant correlation of ACT and GPA in both Negro groups supports the use of the ACT as a predictor of academic success among Negroes.

In a College Board Review article, Davis and Temp (1971) identified 27 traditionally white institutions with substantial numbers of black students. The authors were successful in obtaining data from 13 of the 27 schools. Data from 6 additional colleges were obtained from an agency in one southern state, making a total of 19 schools. Altogether there were 1,571 black and 2,373 white students. These institutions were used in an effort to determine if the SAT is biased against black students.

To Davis and Temp, if a test is biased against blacks it would mean that although there is a substantial relationship between SAT scores and grades for whites, a lower or no relationship exists for blacks. Or if given a similar relationship between SAT scores and grades for whites and blacks, bias would mean that blacks of a given score-level make higher grade averages than whites of the same score-level.

Validity coefficients were computed for blacks. The range was from .06 to .65 with a median value of .26; for white groups, the range was from .15 to .55 with a median of .38.

The authors summarize their findings thusly: (1) validity of the SAT for predicting grades varies from college to college; (2) in some institutions, the validity of the SAT is not significantly different for blacks and whites; (3) where black and white validities differ, there is a tendency for validities to be higher for whites than for blacks; (4) if predictions of grades from SAT scores are based upon equations drawn from experience with white students, then blacks are generally predicted to do better than they actually do.

This article by Davis and Temp and one by Temp (1971) apparently used the same data base. All 19 schools comprised the data base for the Davis and Temp article; 13 of the same schools are studied by Temp. Since both articles appeared at approximately the same time, and since neither article refers to the other, there is no way to determine which study was the original and which was the spin off. This research will be discussed more fully later in this chapter (see Temp, 1971).

While on the staff of IBM, Robert D. Dugan (1966) described some of the facts which illustrate problems industrial psychologists face in the new era of "equal opportunity." Dugan says that the evidence is overwhelming that test performance of Negroes trained in southern colleges is different from that of whites who are graduates of northern colleges.

The Dugan paper is reported in two parts. The first deals with test results obtained by an IBM recruiter who visited several southern segregated Negro colleges where he encouraged graduates to take a 5-part (unnamed) test as a preliminary step before being considered for employment. At the same time graduates of northern integrated colleges were also being recruited.

Five percent of the 374 blacks were found to be qualified for the second step of the employment program. Of approximately 3,400 white graduates, 50% passed the first level of testing.

The second part of Dugan's study involves the IBM Programmer Aptitude Test administered to 104 graduates of southern, predominantly Negro colleges. To obtain the 104 prospects, 425 interviews were made. Of the 104, 20 were invited to visit one of the company's locations; 11 were offered positions; 7 accepted. The mean PAT score of the Negro group that was offered positions was at the 82nd percentile of Negroes tested. The same score was at the 24th percentile of applicants from integrated colleges.

The study by Epps, Perry, Katz, and Runyon (1971) is a two-part replication of an earlier study by Katz, Epps, and Axelson (1964). Their purpose was to examine the effect of racial variation of a peer comparison group on cognitive performance of 305 Negro male college students. Samples were drawn from one southern and one northern Negro college. Students tested by Negro examiners at both colleges performed better on tests of scrambled words, arithmetic, and digit symbol substitution when the comparison group was white rather than Negro.

The primary finding by the authors is that when relatively simple cognitive tasks (the tests were not further identified) are presented by Negro examiners, both northern and southern Negro male college students will respond favorably to an intellectual comparison with white peers.

Farver, Sedlacek, and Brooks (1975) examined the long-range prediction of university grades for blacks and whites. Their idea was that if differential variables are affecting education for blacks and whites, it may be that predictions of freshman grades would yield different results than those of other years. This longitudinal study was attempted in spite of the fact that it has been shown repeatedly that first quarter GPA is a better predictor of subsequent college marks than any battery of preadmission test scores.

Black students from the entering classes at the University of Maryland in 1968 (n = 126) and 1969 (n = 133) were selected for study. Samples of whites were randomly drawn for comparison. Mean SAT for neither group was reported but it was acknowledged that means were lowest for black males and highest for white females. Standard deviations were reported to be smaller for blacks than whites but no values were given. Attrition was similar for both groups.

Multiple correlations for 1968 entrants ranged from .60's for freshman end-of-year grades to .30's and .40's for senior year grades. Multiple R's for 1968 were generally low.

Generally, SAT-V was the most consistent predictor for all groups and tended to be best for black males. The SAT-V tended to carry relatively little weight for white females who entered in 1969. The authors conclude that because of the uniqueness of the results for black males and white females their research strongly supports the use of separate race/sex subgroups for any academic predictions.

In 1959, J. R. Hills, Director of Testing and Guidance for the University System of Georgia, began a series of studies reporting the forecasting efficiency of college grades by the SAT. The first two articles were reviewed in the 2nd edition of Shuey. Hills' 1964 paper summarizes validity for all 19 Georgia state-supported colleges. The data were obtained from official records for approximately 30,000 students over the five year period 1958–1962 inclusive. Correlations and multiple correlations between SAT scores and fall quarter average grades are given for all schools for each of the five years of the study.

The average multiple correlation for five years was .71 for females and .60 for males. For the sexes combined, the average r between HSA and FQG was .55; the average multiple correlation adding SAT-V&M was .66.

The SAT means and standard deviations by school are not shown but are available in Chapter 12. For all units of the university system, the five year average was SAT-V 401, SD = 106; SAT-M 436, SD = 111.

To demonstrate that means and SD's in the data have little consistent effects on sizes of correlations, Hills points out that the three predominantly black colleges, with SAT means for males of 270 verbal and 305 math, yield average multiple correlations for the five years of .57.

Hills concludes that the mean level of correlations remains quite stable from year to year when all freshmen in a state's institutions of public higher education are included in the data and that grades for females are markedly more predictable than for males.

In a paper which appeared in 1968, Hills and Gladney examined the possibility of predicting college grades from chance-level test scores. The subjects were drawn from the same three predominantly Negro schools studied in the previous paper, but they were selected for a different year, 1964. Six hundred sixty-seven black students were involved; mean

SAT-V = 274, SD = 57; mean SAT-M = 305, SD = 53. Hills and Gladney concluded that chance-level test scores are not significantly different in their predictions of the practical criterion (college grades) from above-chance test scores. There would seem to be no special need to be concerned about the validity of making decisions on the basis of low scores if the selection instrument is generally valid and if the regression is as rectilinear as was the case in these data.

Hills (1964) found the SAT to be a dependable predictor of first quarter marks at three Negro colleges. In another paper Hills and Stanley (1970) suggest that an easier test, the School and College Ability Test (SCAT), Level 4, might be more appropriate for predicting first quarter marks in the three Negro colleges studied by Hills in 1964 and Stanley and Porter (1967). Stanley and Porter report average multiple correlations of college grades with SAT scores and high school averages as .60 for black men and .63 for black women.

Hills and Stanley reported a mean R based on SAT scores and high school grades of .59 and a mean multiple R based on SCAT scores and high school grades of .65, a difference of .06 in favor of SCAT-4.

The authors favored the explanation that the easier test yields the higher multiple R. However, they point out that there are other possible reasons for the high validities. All 997 black students took the SCAT at the same time. The test was administered by examiners of their own race after students had been accepted for admission and only shortly before first quarter grades were reported. In addition, there was only one form of the SCAT-4 but there were several forms of the SAT. All of these factors, believe Hills and Stanley, may have enhanced the SCAT multiple correlations.

Subjects for Lane's (1973) study were 22 black graduates of Ohio universities. Selected for this study were students who met the following criteria: (1) birth date between 1929 and 1946, (2) must have attended one of 9 Cleveland, Ohio, elementary schools and have taken tests routinely given in grades 2 (Kuhlmann-Anderson), 6 (Cleveland Classification Test), and 8 (Terman-McNemar).

When in the second grade the selected children averaged near the medians for their elementary schools which were below average for the city.

In the 6th grade the selected students still showed rather ordinary performance for future college students, $\overline{X}$ IQ = 97.

The commonplace test performance of the selected subjects during elementary school changed dramatically in the 8th grade when they showed an average increase of 8 IQ points over 2nd grade scores. Lane attributes the gain to lack of validity of earlier IQ tests for poverty blacks.

She suggests also that the fact that 6 of the 22 subjects were still scoring below IQ 100 in the 8th grade casts some doubt on the accuracy of the 8th grade tests.

To locate 22 college graduates with poverty backgrounds it was necessary to search through the files of hundreds of graduates. The question may be raised: Were the other 90 to 95% of graduates not selected from non-poverty backgrounds? Even so, 22 misses or false negatives from "many hundreds" would be well within the standard error of estimate for most paper and pencil tests.

Longstreth (1978b) explored the interaction between racial membership and type of test in academic achievement of college students. Jensen's hypothesis of Level-I and Level-II abilities is applied for the first time to college-age students. Three hundred twenty-five students from introductory courses were subjects; there were 172 white, 70 Asian, 52 black, and 31 Mexican-American.

The Cognitive Abilities Test, Nonverbal Battery, was selected to reflect Level-II ability ("g") and the Forward Digit Span, Level-I ability.

Longstreth concludes that his studies seem to indicate rather clearly that Jensen's Level-I—Level-II theory has implications for an important real-life situation: performance on college examinations.

McKelpin's 1965 study appeared while the 2nd edition of Shuey was in press. The paper was read at the annual meeting of the National Council on Measurement in Education in February, 1964, but was not published until 1965. North Carolina College at Durham, a predominantly black school, began using the SAT in 1961. McKelpin's paper is a three-year study of the North Carolina College preadmission testing program involving 830 students.

Mean SAT scores are much like those for predominantly black colleges reported elsewhere in this chapter, $\overline{X}$ SAT-V = 303; $\overline{X}$ SAT-M = 324. Despite the restricted range, McKelpin found the predictive validities as high as those reported for other college freshmen. Multiple correlations between the SAT-V, SAT-M, and HSA (high school average) for both males and females are above .60. Furthermore, SAT scores account for almost 60% of the variation in grades explained by the preadmission data. McKelpin concludes that SAT scores do give a fair appraisal of what is expected of these North Carolina College students. ". . . while the abilities measured by the SAT have not been developed to any great extent in the students tested, the extent to which the abilities have been developed is reliably measured" (p. 163).

While Munday (1965) was on the staff of the American College Testing Program, he obtained a list of predominantly Negro colleges which was checked against a list of ACT Research Service participating schools. Data were obtained from five schools involving 1,658 students in four different states. In general, the mean ACT scores for the five selected schools are 1.4 to 1.95 standard deviations below the national norms for the ACT. However, grades at the five schools were as predictable as grades at any typical college participating in the ACT Research Service Program. Most multiple R's were in the .50 to .60 range.

A short paper by Pandey (1974) examines the intellectual characteristics of successful, drop out, and probationary black and white college students. Three subtests of the Guilford-Zimmerman Aptitude Survey were administered to 219 white and 131 black students of Lincoln University, Jefferson City, Missouri. There were no significant main effects due to academic status for any of the three subtests but a significant interaction of race by status was found on the Verbal Comprehension subtest. Means and standard deviations for the Verbal Comprehension subtest for the six subgroups are given. All means are negative except for the white probationary students. Pandey says negative means occurred because the score is the number right minus the number wrong. This would seem to indicate that most scores are at chance level or below.

Pandey found white students in good standing and white probationary students performed better than blacks on the Verbal Comprehension subtest. Among drop outs there were no apparent racial differences.

The findings of this study would seem to be of limited reliability because of the chance-level scores on the Guilford-Zimmerman.

Pentacoste and Lowe (1977) administered the Quick Test and the SAT to 42 black entering freshmen at a midwestern university. Mean SAT-V = 318, SD = 79; mean SAT-M = 339, SD = 74. Means from the several forms of the Quick Test ranged from 94 to 96. Correlations between the GPA and the Quick Test were all above .70; GPA and high school rank = .36, GPA and SAT-V = .28, and GPA and SAT-M = .14.

The authors conclude that the traditional predictive measures, high school rank and SAT scores, are inadequate for black freshmen and suggest a combination of the Quick Test, SAT, and high school rank for preadmission data. They conclude that further work obviously needs to be done in this area. The reviewer would agree.

At the University of Maryland, Pfeifer (1976) studied the relationship between scholastic aptitude, perception of university climate, and college success for black and white students. The subjects were 138 black and 550 white college students. Tests included an original scale to measure five factors of university climate and the Scholastic Aptitude Test. The grade point average was the criterion. Although mean black-white SAT scores differed by as much as one standard deviation unit, there was no difference in SAT correlations with the GPA. Pfeifer concluded that the SAT is a valid predictor of GPA for both blacks and whites. The jury is still out on the validity of the university climate scales. Correlations with GPA are mostly negative and insignificant for whites; mostly positive but insignificant for blacks.

In a University of Maryland study Pfeifer and Sedlacek (1971) compared the forecasting efficiency of several predictors of college grade point average of 126 black and 178 white students. Both parts of the SAT and high school GPA were predictors. The criterion was the Maryland grade point average.

Mean SAT-V scores ranged from 419 for black females to 511 for white females. In standard deviation units the black-white difference for males was .612 on the V-scale and 1.028 for females on the same scale. For the M-scale black-white differences in sigma units were .927 for males and 1.134 for females. Needless to say, all the differences are significant.

The predictive average index was derived from a random sample of the entire student population. Both black samples were overpredicted when the Predictive Index weights were used to predict Maryland GPA. The PI predicted a mean of 1.89 for black males and 1.98 for black females. The actual grades were 1.64 and 1.75 respectively. White males were overpredicted but not significantly (less than .05).

Based on their findings the authors emphasize the importance of separate prediction equations for race-sex groupings.

At Fisk University performance on the SAT and the GRE Aptitude Test were compared by Roberts, Horton and Roberts (1969). Subjects were 349 students enrolled in a predominantly Negro liberal arts college. As freshmen the students took the SAT and as seniors, the GRE.

The total group was divided into subgroups by sex, major field of study, and region, yielding in some cases samples of 1, 14, and 19 subjects. Looking only at the total group of scores by sex it is seen that mean scores on both SAT and GRE are not much different from those of other blacks in liberal arts colleges. For male students mean SAT-V = 408, SD = 87; SAT-M = 437, SD = 84; GRE-V = 398, SD = 77; GRE-Q = 451, SD = 102. For female students the figures are: 409, 86; 391, 90; 419, 92; and 382, 85.

The authors expected to find "a relative increase in test score performance" between the initial testing in 1965 and the later testing in 1968; that is, they apparently expected the GRE to reflect educational growth from freshman to senior years in college. Appropriate GRE advanced tests or other achievement tests perhaps would have given a better indication of educational growth since both SAT and GRE Aptitude are aptitude tests.

The University System of Georgia provided test data for at least four of the 28 studies in this chapter. In no other state have precollege admission tests been as systematically administered and the results as carefully preserved. Since fall 1958 the College Board SAT has been required of all students attending any branch of the University System. The Norms Manual, published each year by the Board of Regents, is the source of raw data for the comparative investigation of the validity of the SAT for white and black college students by Stanley and Porter (1967).

Mean SAT scores for blacks which have been reported elsewhere in this chapter are of no concern to the authors of this validity study. Their main interest is the forecasting efficiency of the SAT for black college students. Mean SAT-V score for the 1,097 black students in three predominantly black schools is 270; SAT-M, 305. Average multiple R's for the six years covered by the Stanley and Porter study are: WF,.72; NF,.63; NM,.60; and WM,.60.

Stanley and Porter conclude that the Georgia data and several related studies suggest that SAT-type test scores are about as valid for Negroes competing with Negroes and taught chiefly by Negroes as they are for non-Negroes competing with non-Negroes and taught chiefly by non-Negroes.

Tatham and Tatham (1974) investigated academic prediction of 73 black college students. SAT scores of successful (graduates or students with GPA of C or above) and unsuccessful students were compared. A subgroup of 7 subjects makes generalization hazardous especially since the 7 unsuccessful college women had a mean verbal SAT of 447 while the successful women students had a mean verbal SAT of 402.

The authors conclude that tests such as the SAT should not be the only means used in selecting black students for college. Other measures such as motivation or SES need to be explored. The results of this study suggest that the variable of sex must be controlled.

It was mentioned earlier in this chapter that Davis and Temp (1971) and Temp (1971) used essentially the same data base to investigate the differential prediction of college marks for 1,246 blacks and 1,298 whites. Of the 19 schools analyzed in Davis and Temp, 13 are reexamined by Temp. The most remarkable finding of the Temp study is the unusually high mean SAT's in both types of subjects in integrated schools. Median SAT's for the 13 schools are verbal 604 and math 616 for white students. Blacks are also about one standard deviation higher than generally reported in the literature for black students. For the thirteen selected schools the median V-score is 473; median M-score is 489.

Despite the highly selective nature of the thirteen schools in the Temp study, he concludes that when prediction of GPA is based on SAT scores, regression equations suitable for white students predict black students to do about as well or better than they actually do. There are some exceptions because validity coefficients vary widely from institution to institution for both blacks and whites. The author recommends that institutions routinely conduct their own validity studies.

Educational Testing Service has, since 1975–76, asked Graduate Record Examinations test takers a series of "background questions." In an E.T.S. publication, Wild (1980) offers the first opportunity to examine GRE scores by ethnic, sex, and other background information.

Short of the federal government, only an agency the size of E.T.S. would attempt to or could administer, score, and analyze tests for 218,682 prospective graduate students.

Wild points out that care should be taken in drawing conclusions beyond those obvious on the face of the data. For example, some schools do not require the GRE. Others may require applicants to submit scores, but do not use the results as part of the admissions procedure. Students also change their minds about graduate majors between the time they take the test and the time they actually enroll for classes. These and other limitations that may occur to the reader pale into insignificance when the sample size is considered. Virtually all liberal arts students who planned to attend graduate school, with the exceptions of those entering professional schools such as law, medicine, education, pharmacy, and veterinary medicine, are represented in the 1978–79 GRE summary by Wild.

The interested reader is referred to the original study of over 100 pages which includes 68 tables. In this review an analysis of the total columns from three tables will suffice. On the background questionnaire students indicated their ethnic group membership. Included in the sample of U.S. citizens in sufficient numbers to make meaningful interpretations were: American Indian, black or Afro-American, Mexican-American, Asian-American, Puerto Rican, Latin-American, white, other, and finally "no response." The tabulation on page 124 is condensed from Wild's Tables 56, 57, and 58.

Little can be added to this summary. Rank order of mean GRE scores for the various ethnic groups corresponds almost perfectly to that of other studies of college students and school children where ethnicity has been known.

Thirty-six percent of the American Indian graduate students reach or exceed the GRE-V national norm while only 10% of black Afro-Americans earn scores that high. Forty-five percent of the graduate students of Oriental or Asian background earn GRE-V scores above 500; however, on the GRE-Q 71% reach or exceed that score. Sixteen percent of the Puerto Ricans and 38% of other students of Latin-American descent score above the national norm on the GRE-V scale. Other ethnic groups correspond almost exactly to other ethnicity studies reviewed in this chapter. In every case the black Afro-Americans earn the lowest among all groups on all three GRE tests. The black-white difference, for example, reaches or exceeds 1 standard deviation unit on the verbal, quantitative, and analytical tests of the GRE.

About 4% of the test takers chose not to respond to the question concerning ethnicity. The "no response" group is much like the base group on the GRE scales. Forty-six percent equal or exceed the national mean on the GRE-V scale; 45% on the Q-scale.

Four thousand three hundred ninety-five or 2% of the total group

Means and Standard Deviations of GRE Tests by Ethnic Group

	American Indian	Black Afro-American	Mexican American	Asian American	Puerto Rican	Latin American	White	Other	No Response	Tot. N.
	(N = 1057)	(N=13025)	(N=2417)	(N=2923)	(N=1452)	(N=1436)	(N=161592)	(N=4395)	(N=8107)	(N=196404)
GRE-V										
Mean	459	363	419	480	389	465	511	532	513	499
SD	114	99	110	120	105	113	111	123	126	118
GRE-Q										
Mean	457	358	422	566	418	468	525	532	519	512
SD	123	107	122	129	120	126	122	129	135	130
GRE-A										
Mean	457	352	412	510	385	460	529	531	517	513
SD	120	106	117	124	112	125	111	120	126	121

were not members of any of the 7 ethnic groups mentioned above. These students were lumped under the heading "other." This group earned the highest mean scores on both GRE-V and GRE-A tests. Since the response sheet provides no space for subjects of European extraction, it must be assumed that "Other" graduate students are from Europe or of European extraction.

Summary

The primary purpose of the majority of studies reviewed in this chapter was to examine the forecasting efficiency of preadmission college aptitude tests for blacks. In addition, the data presented provide opportunity to compare scholastic aptitude test performance of blacks with other United States minority groups and with whites, and to examine the effectiveness of less conventional and novel intelligence tests designed especially for blacks.

The major findings of this chapter are summarized here: (1) Despite the fact that blacks score, on the average, one standard deviation below the mean of whites on the SAT and ACT, there is little evidence that these tests are biased against blacks. (2) If predictions of college marks are based upon equations drawn from experience with white students, then blacks are predicted to do better than they actually do; that is, blacks are overpredicted with the white regression equations. (3) Both the SAT and ACT are significant predictors of academic success for black college students. (4) The mean level of correlations between SAT and GPA (.55) for black and white college students remains quite stable from year to year when all freshmen are included in the data. (5) Chance-level SAT scores are not significantly different from above-chance scores in their predictions of college grades for black students. (6) The consistency of the black-white test overlap, the percent of blacks reaching or exceeding the mean of the whites, is remarkable. Average overlap of 6 to 10 percent was recorded as early as 1954 and as late as 1980. (7) New intelligence tests designed especially to reflect knowledge of the black environment and the comprehension of non-standard English are poor substitutes for the more conventional tests of scholastic aptitude. Black Intelligence Test (BIT) scores correlate insignificantly with the vocabulary section of a traditional intelligence test and are otherwise unvalidated. (8) When United States minority groups are compared on a test of scholastic aptitude, such as the GRE, all groups including American Indian, Mexican-American, Asian-American, Puerto Rican, and Latin-American earn mean scores above those of blacks.

VI

Adults Not in College

R. Travis Osborne

The 21 studies in this chapter appear at first to represent a miscellaneous assortment of unrelated papers not elsewhere classified. Upon closer examination, it is seen that this group of studies is much more homogeneous than those in some other chapters. With few exceptions all subjects are adults entering the military or seeking civilian employment. The authors are primarily concerned with determining whether differential validity of employment tests is established and recommended for U.S. blacks, whites, and Spanish speaking Americans. The findings are convincing and in most cases the authors can not be faulted for inappropriate research design or small samples.

In 1972 Boehm summarized the research evidence for Negro-white differences in the validity of employment selection procedures. Altogether there were 13 studies involving 2,557 whites and 1,311 blacks. Six published papers examined by Boehm are reviewed elsewhere in this chapter.

The range of occupations studied in the Boehm review is broad, ranging from administrative personnel to welders. Only two of the 13 studies examined validity coefficients of the same occupations.

One hundred of the 160 validity coefficients computed in the thirteen studies did not yield significant correlations for either ethnic group. When the investigator was able to exert control of the hiring process and include in the base group substantial numbers of blacks and whites who did not meet hiring standards, validity coefficients were enhanced.

In the Boehm review there were 60 instances where the predictor showed significant criterion related validity for either one or both ethnic groups. To determine whether differential or single validity would yield better prediction, Boehm examined the 60 validity coefficients by race. The coefficients rarely differed in degree of validity for Negroes and whites with significant differences being found in only seven instances. Boehm concludes "The combination of ethnic groups yields lower validity than for either group separately on only 3 out of the 120 instances. Overall, there is very little evidence of differential validity . . ." (p. 33)

A two page study by Cole and Williams (1967) examines the intellectual ability of patients and attendants in a Negro ward at a state hospital. Subjects were 41 attendants and 53 patients. The patients and attendants were given the Quick Test. Calculating IQs from the existing manual showed IQs of 87 for the attendants who attended high school, 81 for those that did not attend high school, and 61 for the patients. With the revised norms, the scores became 102, 96, and 76, respectively. The reason for the discrepancy in the two sets of norms was not explained. These data would seem to have limited value outside the hospital where the study was conducted.

Deitz and Purkey (1969) examined teacher expectations of performance based on race of the student. One hundred forty-seven teachers were asked to estimate future academic performance of a student described by the investigators. The teachers were given identical paragraphs except half described the subject as a "boy"; the other half as a "Negro boy." Group differences and student expectations were not significant. The author questions the commonly held assumption that teachers enter the classroom with differential expectations for students of different races.

"How good are our schools?" by DeNeufville and Conner appeared in *American Education* October, 1966. The purpose of the study was to examine "failure in the schools." This was done by regional, ethnic, and draft rejection rates on the Armed Forces Qualification Test (AFQT).

From the Surgeon General's office, the authors report that: (1) failure rates on the AFQT and related tests range from a low of 6% in the state of Washington to a high of 55% in the District of Columbia (the national average was 25%); (2) the rejection rates based on mental tests were lowest in the western and midwestern states, highest in the south. An unpublished supplement to the study showing detail by race revealed that: (1) southern whites are behind whites in all other regions of the country and southern Negroes are behind Negroes in all other regions of the country; (2) in every state, test performance is significantly higher for whites than for Negroes. Nationally, only 19% of the whites failed the mental tests, compared to a failure rate of 68% for Negroes.

The same regional and ethnic differences show up in the draftee failure rate:

Draftee failure rate (by percent) FY 1966

Army Area	All	White	Negro
III (South) Ala., Fla., Ga., Miss., N.C., S.C., Tenn.	31	18	68
IV (South Central) Ark., La., N. Mex., Okla., Texas	20	12	57

Army Area	All	White	Negro
I, II (Northeast)			
Conn., Maine, Mass., N.H., N.J.,			
N.Y., R.I., Vt., Del., D.C., Ky.,			
Md., Ohio, Pa., Va., W. Va.	15	12	45
V, VI (Midwest and West)			
Colo., Ill., Ind., Iowa, Kans.,			
Mich., Minn., Nebr., N. Dak.,			
S. Dak., Wis., Wyo., Ariz., Calif.,			
Idaho., Mont., Nev., Oreg.,			
Utah, Wash.	10	8	37

By way of explanation, DeNeufville and Conner find "The extreme variations in regional performance clearly suggest that schools have not erased inequality based on accidents of geography;—the extreme racial variations make it clear that the schools have yet to overcome the environmental handicaps of the Nation's Negro students. It is unlikely that the talent pool in any one State is substantially different than the talent pool in any other State." (p. 6)

Despite claims by DeNeufville and Conner, two explanations for subpopulation differences are not true: (1) The authors say, "usually greater than majority-minority differences, however, are the regional differences." (p. 6) Their own data refute this claim. Whether measured by differences in draftee rejection rates or differences in mean test scores, regional differences do not approach the difference of one standard deviation unit found between blacks and whites on the AFQT and other similar tests. (2) The authors also say, "Since it is as axiomatically true in education as elsewhere that you get what you pay for . . ." (p. 6). The implication here is that increased expenditure per child in education would enhance achievement and perhaps reduce draftee rejection rate. Again from their own data, it is seen that school expenditure per pupil is no certain predictor of literacy or guarantee of the reduction in the draftee rejection rate.

Gael, Grant, and Ritchie published two similar papers simultaneously in the *Journal of Applied Psychology*. Both studies examined empirical test validities for minority and non-minority telephone employees.

The first study (1975a) includes 1,091 applicants for three Bell System telephone operator jobs. There were 501 young blacks, 126 Spanish surnamed, and 464 whites who took 10 specially devised tests for Bell System operator jobs. Operator proficiency was evaluated during a standardized one hour job simulation.

Data were combined across jobs because the authors found the jobs to be similar and the patterns of validity coefficients with the composite proficiency index also were similar for each operator job.

All ten test differences between black and white sample means, except the filing test, were significant, favoring whites. Only one difference between black and Spanish surnamed groups was not significant. In every case the Spanish surnamed group attained the higher mean. Four white-Spanish surnamed comparisons on the ten tests are statistically different. Three of the four favor the Spanish sample.

On the basis of their research, the authors believe the Bell System proficiency measures are unbiased against minority group members and "Whatever reasons underlie the fact that minority job applicants score lower on the average on tests and on job proficiency criteria than their non minority counterparts, the use of aptitude and ability tests that are valid for minority job applicants certainly does not contribute to, but may alleviate, some of the problems associated with discriminatory employment practices." (p. 419).

The second study by Gael, Grant, and Ritchie (1975b) is of the same design and purpose as the first, the only differences being the sample and criteria. Subjects were 143 black, 74 Spanish surnamed, and 185 white, newly hired Bell System clerical employees. Predictors were the same 10 intelligence tests used in the previous study by Gael, Grant, and Ritchie (1975a). Criteria were work samples developed to represent clerical activities required by the Bell System such as dialing, posting, checking, and coding.

Practically all, 19 of 21, differences between black and white predictors and criteria means were statistically significant. The higher mean in each case was obtained by the white sample. Many (14 of 21) of the white-Spanish surnamed differences were statistically significant. Each significant difference favored the white sample. In one third of the black-Spanish surnamed comparisons significant differences were obtained, with the Spanish surnamed group obtaining the higher means. Based on their research, the authors recommend the composite predictor for minority and non-minority clerical applicants. The total sample regression equation does not underpredict prospective proficiency levels of minority clerks.

In *Mankind Quarterly,* 1967, Garrett examined the same data base used by DeNeufville and Conner and arrived at diametrically opposite conclusions. Garrett's view that native differences in ability to think abstractly play a major role in black-white differences in mental test scores is not the view held by the Office of Education.

"In its booklet, *American Education,* we find the following: 'It is a demonstrable fact that the talent pool in any ethnic group is substantially the same as that in any other ethnic group.' No demonstration is provided of the truth of this glittering generality—because there is none. Curt

Stern, a distinguished geneticist, has remarked that 'Such statements lack a factual basis.' " (p. 78)

The Department of Labor, in a report on the Negro family (Moynihan, 1965), offers this flat assertion: "There is absolutely no question of any genetic differential . . . Intelligence potential is distributed among Negro infants in the same proportions and patterns as among Icelanders or Chinese or any other group." Regarding this statement, we quote from Arnold Gesell (1943), well-known child psychologist and for many years director of the Institute of Child Development at Yale University: "Every child is born with a *naturel* which colors his structures and experiences . . . He has constitutional traits and tendencies largely inborn, which determine *how, what* and to some extent *when* he will learn. These traits are both racial and familial."

Gordon, Arvey, Daffron, and Umberger (1974) compared test performance of whites and blacks before, during, and after exposure to a federally sponsored Manpower Development Project for the unemployed and underemployed. They investigated the impact of mathematics instruction on numerical competence (measured by the California Achievement Test, Junior High Level) of a class of 80 black and 83 white trainees.

Significant main effects for the administrations suggested that both races profited from the training. However, the whites clearly derived greater benefit than did blacks. The authors conclude that racial differences in mathematical competency are not reduced by training, but may, in fact, be increased.

Greene (1962) was published before 1965 but not reviewed in the 2nd edition of Shuey. Data for this study were obtained from a 1956 dissertation by E. C. Phillips, Jr., written under the direction of Greene. The study compares 542 white and 313 Negro teachers on 43 variables thought to be related to teacher competency. In this review we will only mention breifly the results of the analysis of "A Standardized Test of Teaching Competency" which can only be one of the versions of the National Teacher Examinations. $\bar{X}$ scores for the NTE subtests are reported for both black and white teachers. Differences are highly significant with only 6% of the black teachers reaching or exceeding the mean for whites.

Heilbrun and Jordan (1968) examine the demographic and intellectual correlates of successful Vocational Rehabilitation participants. Subjects were 185 rehabilitation clients; 62% were black and 38% white. Women outnumbered men by almost 2 to 1. The mean age for males was 29.4 with a range from age 16 to 64; for females, 30.2 with a range from 16 to 61.

There were two criteria of vocational rehabilitation success. Successful outcome required that the client complete the program, obtain employment, and remain on the job for 6 months. An unsuccessful client may have completed the program but did not find or did not take a job during the 6-month follow-up period. Fifty-three clients who failed to complete the program were also designated unsuccessful.

Findings with respect to age and education were interesting. Contrary to earlier studies, the authors found no relationship between educational level and vocational rehabilitation outcome. Age was positively correlated with successful completion of the program, which was also contrary to previous follow-up studies of rehabilitation clients.

Significant findings reported by Heilbrun and Jordan were: (1) Successful rehabilitation clients, as a group, were brighter than unsuccessful ones. (2) IQ was more clearly related to outcomes for women than for men. (3) Whites consistently obtained higher total IQs than blacks. (4) Fifty percent of the white successful clients improved their employment level upon completion of the program. The figure was 68% for blacks.

Three years before *Bias in Mental Testing* (Jensen, 1980) was published Jensen examined the cultural bias in the Wonderlic Personnel Test (Jensen, 1977a). The reader interested in any aspect of cultural bias in psychological tests is encouraged to obtain a copy of Jensen's (1980) book which covers all aspects of test bias from ability grouping to z-scores. For our purpose, it will suffice to report that whatever abilities or aptitudes the Wonderlic measures, they are measured by items that are internally consistent within both black ($N = 548$) and white ($N = 548$) samples.

"The present analyses yield no consistent or strong evidence that the Wonderlic is reacted to differently by Blacks and Whites, except in overall level of performance, in which the normative populations differ by about one standard deviation." (p. 64)

Encouraged by fallout from the Motorola case (French, 1965) and the Equal Employment Opportunities Commission (EEOC, 1966) the Ford Foundation sponsored a massive research program to obtain and evaluate evidence regarding possible unfair discrimination in industrial selection. The final report was prepared by a team of psychologists from New York University, Kirkpatrick, Ewen, Barrett, and Katzell (1967). Altogether there were five studies involving 1,208 subjects, 795 white, 325 black, and 88 Spanish speaking, 6 job situations, 26 different tests, a variety of indicators of cultural deprivation and socioeconomic status. The general approach was to study the validity of selection tests, taking ethnic and cultural factors into account.

Sponsored by the Ford Foundation, this series of studies is only one of a spate of such reports that appeared in the late 1960's. Most of the findings offered by Kirkpatrick et al. in their concluding statement have since 1967 been refuted by new, more convincing evidence.

The authors make 6 claims in their concluding statements: (1) Tests valid for one ethnic group are not necessarily valid for the other. Of course, the statement is self evident, except that it tells us nothing about blacks and whites in the United States. Other studies in this chapter conducted in the United States support single group predictions (see Boehm 1972, Gael et al. 1975a and Gael et al. 1975b). (2) Tests may operate unfairly against certain ethnic groups. The statement simply is untrue for the ethnic groups studied by Kirkpatrick et al. (see Jensen, 1980). (3) The moderated prediction technique may be useful in improving predictions. Moderator variables may be useful in prediction, but their value was not demonstrated convincingly by Kirkpatrick et al. (4) Training may increase predictor scores for all ethnic groups. Training did not reduce mean test score differences between white, Spanish speaking, and black subjects in the Ford Foundation studies. (5) Factor analysis is a useful approach to the measure of "cultural deprivation." Factor analysis is also useful to demonstrate lack of bias in mental tests (see Jensen, 1980, p. 446 ff). (6) Non-verbal tests do not necessarily improve prediction. This should come as no surprise to readers familiar with Jensen (1980, p. 465 ff).

In a study published in 1966, Levinson compared northern and southern homeless Negro men. Twenty-four pairs of northern and southern Skid Row men were matched for full scale WAIS IQ, mean 84.8; SD 13.5. Levinson believed that IQs were depressed due to inadequate acculturation brought about by poor schooling and poor economic opportunities.

The unfavorable subcultural forces, instead of permanently depressing the intellectual potential of these men, merely froze it, permitting it later to grow. "Apparently, the Skid Row has a differential effect on its denizens. . . . While for most men, living on the Skid Row means a descent in standard of living, for many Negroes it meant maintenance of previous standards, and possibly even an ascent to a higher level." (p. 150)

The establishment of a new position of Female Toll Collector by the New York Port Authority provided Lopez (1966) the opportunity to validate a battery of tests and rating scales on a large number of job applicants over a relatively short time. Applicants were first interviewed and then referred for two tests. Of 2,000 applicants, 865 were tested, 300 were placed on the eligible list and 182 were employed (102 Negro and 80 white).

According to Lopez the program judged by subjective opinion of patrons, supervisors, and employees was a success from the very beginning.

To get more empirical evidence the author obtained (1) absentee rates, (2) tolls accuracy rates, (3) records of continuous employment for 6 months, and (4) supervisors' ratings which were correlated with scores from the DAT Clerical Test, a custom-designed written mental ability test, and the Interviewer's Check List.

Lopez found that Negro appointees achieved scores significantly lower than whites on the mental ability test and on the Interviewer's Check List despite the fact that there was no difference in job performance criteria by the two groups. The author concluded that the marked differences in predictor performance were not indicative of differences in job performance.

The patterns of association for white and Negro groups are quite dissimilar. For the Negro group, high scores on the predictors are unfavorably associated with continual employment, but favorably associated with tolls accuracy. For the white group, high scores on the predictors are unfavorably associated with tolls accuracy and with continual employment, but a high score on the written test only is associated unfavorably with attendance. If only supervisory ratings are considered, high scores on the two paper-and-pencil tests are associated with job success for the white but not the black toll collector. For blacks the interview is a good predictor of job success but not for whites. Based on his research, Lopez concluded ". . . we are not only justified in using different standards for different subcultural groups, but we are obliged to do so . . ." (p. 18)

The Black Intelligence Test of Cultural Homogeneity (BITCH) was developed under a grant of $153,000 from the NIMH to Robert Williams. In 1977, Matarazzo and Wiens made the first independent attempt to validate this novel, culture specific "intelligence" test.

Black and white police applicants (17 black, 66 white) were given both the WAIS and the BITCH. Age range of the subjects was in the 20's; mean educational level was 2½ years of college. The mean WAIS IQ for white applicants was 117; for blacks, 105.

According to armchair speculations by Williams, the BITCH has the advantage of dealing with material with which the black is familiar. One question on the vocabulary section, for example, asks the subject the meaning of "The Bump." According to Williams, a combination of dialect specific and culture specific tests would certainly enhance the possibility of measuring accurately what is inside the black's head. Matarazzo and Wiens describe the BITCH as covering a wide range of "street wise" knowledge familiar to blacks. In a personal communication to the authors of this article, Williams pointed out:

". . . that 'Ebonics' is a more appropriate term for what the test samples than is 'street wise.' Ebonics may be defined as 'the linguistic and paralinguistic features which on a concentric continuum represents the communicative competence of the West African, Carribean, and the United States slave descendants of African origin. It includes the various idioms, patois, argots, idealects, and social dialects of black people.' " (p. 58)

BITCH scores show no significant correlations with intelligence as measured by the WAIS or with education as measured by years in school.

To (a) develop an Environmental Participation Index (EPI) that would measure exposure to American middle-class environment, (b) to validate it against the U.S. Department of Labor General Aptitude Test Battery (GATB), and (c) to examine racial differences on GATB in terms of EPI were the purposes of the Mathis (1968) article. An EPI checklist was constructed of 26 household possessions and 48 (or more) activities. It and the GATB were administered to 136 white and 123 black walk-in applicants at a Chicago, Illinois, Youth Center (YC). All subjects were 18 to 25 years of age. All nine black GATB subtest scores were significantly lower than corresponding white subtest scores, but the sizes of the differences were said to decline as one went from "verbal-intellec-tual" to "non-verbal-dexterity" subtests. When the EPI was administered to a sample of 75 white and 5 black college students, a hierarchy of scores was established from black YC applicants, to black college stu-dents, to white YC applicants, to white college students. Correlations between EPI and GATB scores were higher than correlations between education and GATB scores. Age was not related to EPI. For an ANOVA study, 15 pairs of white and black subjects were obtained for each of three EPI levels (high, middle, and low). Among the paired subjects, racial differences were markedly reduced in all GATB areas, and in two dexterity subtests blacks exceeded whites, but not significantly so. The author did not consider, however, that matching for age and educa-tion also matched for intelligence. Correlations between GATB subtests and EPI scores ranged from .31 to .67. Because of these findings, the author considered the EPI to have demonstrated "construct validity" with GATB scores by assuming that GATB scores were caused by envi-ronmental stimulation.

McClelland (1974) examined the effects of interviewer-respondent race interactions on cross-section samples of Detroit's population between the ages of 18 and 49. There were 188 black and 177 white subjects and 8 white and 6 black interviewers. Interviewers were balanced by race and respondents by sex within each race group. The tests used were Digit Span Test (Wechsler, 1955), Sentence Completion (Lorge and Thorndike, 1954), Raven Progressive Matrices (Raven, 1956), Digit Symbol Test (Wechsler, 1955), Quick Vocabulary Test (Ammons and Ammons, 1962), Information Test (Wechsler, 1955) and Picture Order Test (Hagen, 1967). Not all subjects took all tests.

Analysis of variance on the seven intelligence tests showed whites significantly higher than blacks, and black interviewers eliciting signifi-cantly higher scores on four of the seven tests. There were no interactions.

The author concluded that because white interviewers obtained lower refusal rates they may have been perceived as more demanding or authoritative than black interviewers by both black and white respondents. In general, the white interviewer may have presented a more dominating presence.

To determine whether the Revised Beta Examination would be useful for the assessment of general intellectual functioning of indigent Negroes, Rochester and Bodwell (1970) compared Beta scores with those of the WAIS. Subjects were 50 male and 50 female Negro adults selected from an evaluation and training center in a metropolitan area. No other restrictions were imposed except participants had to be (1) 16 to 60 years of age, (2) illiterate, and (3) unemployed or have a gross annual income of $3,000 or less.

The Beta, a non-verbal test, correlates with the WAIS Performance at .70 or above. With the WAIS Verbal, Beta r's are significant but considerably lower: .59 for the males; .29 for the females.

For both sexes, the average Beta IQ was in the 80's; the average WAIS IQ's were 2 to 6 points lower. Except for the Beta-WAIS Performance difference for females of 2 IQ points, all other differences were significant. Based on their research, Rochester and Bodwell conclude that as a group or individual testing instrument for making screening decisions regarding selection, classification, or identification, the Revised Beta received their support. The user, however, is cautioned not to compare directly WAIS and Beta IQs.

Ruda and Albright (1968) examined racial differences on the Wonderlic Personnel Test and scores on a weighted application blank for job applicants in an attempt to predict job performance and to reduce job turnover. Of the 1,034 applicants, 327 were employed, 707 were rejected.

Test results were available for 484 white applicants, 304 of whom were rejected. Ninety-seven of the 159 black applicants were rejected. Black-white differences on the Wonderlic were highly significant in favor of whites regardless of whether the applicant was rejected or hired. When racial groups were combined, on the average those hired had higher Wonderlic scores than rejectees, despite the fact that a high Wonderlic score carried a negative weighting on the application blank.

The relationship between job turnover and Wonderlic scores is interesting. For whites, there is a clear and significant negative relationship between test scores and survival. For blacks, the trend is neither significant nor consistent. The most striking finding for blacks is the high proportion remaining on the job regardless of test scores.

The author concludes that, "The Wonderlic, although valid for the white majority of the sample, was not valid for the Negroes. . . . It appears, therefore, that the Wonderlic (and similar instruments) represents the different measurement standard for the two racial groups and it would be unrealistic to require the same passing score of both." (p. 40)

The purpose of the study by Thumin and Goldman (1968) was to compare test performance of Negro and white women who were competing in the same employment market. The sample consisted of 299 women between the ages of 17 and 45 who had applied for secretarial positions on the Washington University campus. There were 61 black and 238 white applicants. The mean ages and educational levels of the two groups were quite similar.

All subjects took the Wonderlic Personnel Test, the Short Employment Tests, and the Guilford-Martin Personnel Inventory as part of the application process. Mean black-white differences on the ability tests were highly significant, with the differences on the Wonderlic reaching 1.23 standard deviation units in favor of the white sample. To determine whether personality factors on the Guilford were related to differences in intelligence, the authors selected from the pool of 299 subjects 44 blacks and 44 whites, matched for total raw score on the Wonderlic. With intelligence controlled, the smaller groups no longer differed as much on the personality factors. Significant differences on two personality scales were eliminated altogether; differences on one, cooperativeness, was reduced but still remained significant. The authors interpret this to mean that brighter subjects were able to select the more socially desirable items on the Guilford-Martin and thus gain higher personality scores.

In a 1969 study, Wysocki & Wysocki set out to show the cultural differences reflected in the adult Wechsler. Wechsler-Bellevue II was administered to 247 veteran participants. There were 137 whites ranging in age from 17 to 42 and 100 blacks from 21 to 26 years of age. The age differences were not significant, but preservice education differed by .75 years, which was significant.

All subtests of the Wechsler-Bellevue II were administered except the vocabulary subtest ". . . on the assumption (made by the director of rehabilitation program) that the items based on Vocabulary would handicap those with lower educational levels." (p. 96)

All black-white differences on the W-B II subtests were significant in favor of the whites except Digit Span which favored the blacks. This reversal is not remarkable when examined in terms of the Spearman-Jensen hypothesis (Jensen, 1980, p. 585).

Black-white IQs differed by at least 1 standard deviation unit. The direction of the verbal-performance difference is consistent with McGurk, Shuey, and Jensen. On Wechsler type tests, blacks perform better on verbal than they do on performance items. This, of course, is contrary to the prediction made by the investigator who eliminated the vocabulary test from the present experiment because he believed blacks, of limited formal education, would be expected to do poorly on this and perhaps other subtests of the Wechsler because:

The Wechsler-Bellevue intelligence test is standardized on a white population as are other intelligence tests. Thus, the tests are white-oriented and do not take into consideration cultural and environmental characteristics of non-white American populations. As the present writers elsewhere remarked, "Until really 'culture free' intelligence tests are developed—free of education, culture and socio-economic status influences—any comparisons of national groups based solely on intelligence tests scores should be treated with caution." (Wysocki & Cankardes, 1957). This is also true with regard to the comparison of racial groups. (p. 100)

The choice of the Wechsler-Bellevue II for a 1969 study by Wysocki & Wysocki is puzzling, especially since the authors fault the test because it "is standardized on a white population as are other intelligence tests." First published in 1946, the W-B II did not include non-whites in the normative data. However, the WAIS, first published in 1955, fourteen years before the study by Wysocki & Wysocki, did include in the standardization non-whites, "pro rated according to the 1950 U.S. census." For a study conducted in 1969, the authors seem to have gone out of their way to find an adult test that did not include non-whites in the normative sample.

Summary

The 21 studies reviewed in this chapter include patients and attendants at a mental hospital, public school teachers, military draftees, prospective telephone operators, vocational rehabilitation clients, homeless men, police applicants, and toll collectors for the New York Port Authority. The subjects are adults and senior citizens of both sexes, about 60% are white, 38% black, and 2% Spanish speaking Americans. The number of subjects per study varies from less than 50 to several hundred thousand. The two studies which analyze the same basic data from the AFQT are not included in percentage breakdown reported above.

Authors were not so much interested in examining racial differences in test performance as they were in determining whether differential validity of employment tests is established and recommended for U.S. blacks, whites, and Spanish speaking Americans. The variety of tests employed was wide, including an original battery designed for Bell System job applicants, Revised Beta Exam, WAIS, Wonderlic Personnel Classification Test, a novel test called the Black Intelligence Test of Cultural Homogeneity (BITCH), among others. Where racial comparisons of test performance were made, the usual pattern of differences was found: whites > Spanish speaking Americans > Blacks. Where scores or normative data were given, white-black differences ranged from .75 to more than 1 SD. Mean test scores for Spanish speaking Americans were usually between the other two groups.

While there is almost unanimous agreement among the authors that racial differences in mean scores on the Wonderlic, AFQT, WAIS, and the other mental tests are significant there is no consensus that these tests can be used with equal effectiveness for job selection of applicants from different ethnic groups. The case made for differential validity by Kirkpatrick et al. (1967), Lopez (1966), and Ruda and Albright (1968) is in no way as sound and as convincing as those who argue for single group prediction, Boehm (1972), Gael et al. (1975a), Gael et al. (1975b), and Jensen (1977a).

VII

Delinquents

R. Travis Osborne

In this chapter we use the term delinquent to apply to a broad range of individuals who have been convicted of violation of state or federal laws and are serving prison sentences. In addition to the hardened criminal, our definition of delinquents includes those groups designated delinquent by the investigators including drug addicts, truants, and first time felons.

An exact breakdown of subjects by race is not possible since blacks and Mexican-Americans were combined in 2 of the 16 studies reviewed.

In all, there were over 7,000 subjects, approximately 3,000 whites, 3,000 blacks, and 1,000 Latin-Americans. Under the Latin-Americans were grouped Mexican-Americans, Puerto Ricans and Chicanos and the minority called "Latins" by one investigator. Of the 7,000 subjects, only 492 were identified as females; 8 studies reported all males. In 4 studies the sex of the subjects, who were burglars, forgers, rapers, and murderers, was not given. I think it is safe to assume participants in all but 3 of the 16 studies were all male; that is, only about ½ of 1% of all delinquents studied were female. The age range of the groups studied was from 10 to mature adult.

The type of crime committed by participating subjects was spelled out in only 2 or 3 papers. Other writers did not refer to the nature of the crime other than to say inmates of a minimum security prison, a rehabilitation center, or similar institution for delinquents.

A short paper by Christensen, Leunes, and Wilkerson (1975) was designed to examine the effectiveness of the Otis Quick Scoring Mental Ability Test, Form Beta, to differentiate an inmate sample. Subjects were 168 public offenders serving sentences in the Texas Department of Corrections; 91 were white, 28 Latin-American, and 49 Negro. The group included burglars, forgers, narcotics offenders, robbers, murderers, and other felons.

Test scores were analyzed to determine whether significant differences existed between race, type of offense, or between the first offender-recidivist classification. Only the breakdown by race yielded a significant difference. Mean IQ for whites was 95.8, Latin-Americans 85.3, and blacks 88.5.

The authors conclude that their results indicate that the Otis Beta differentiates across racial lines, but not with respect to type of offense or whether the subject was a first offender or a recidivist.

Condit, Lewandowski, and Saccuzzo (1976) used the Peabody Picture Vocabulary Test to estimate WISC scores for a delinquent population. In previous studies by the authors, mostly of retardates, the WISC and PPVT were found not to be interchangeable.

Subjects were 106 juveniles tested at the Center for the Study of Crime, Law Enforcement and Corrections. All were male; the age range was from 13 to 16. Participants were described as being of low SES but it is not clear how SES was determined. Sixty-six subjects were black; 40 were white.

Direct WISC and PPVT comparisons by race were not reported. Mean black and white WISC IQs estimated by the reviewer from the authors' data differed by less than two points, which is only a fraction of the differences reported in the literature.

Condit et al. conclude that the WISC and PPVT IQ's are not interchangeable and the PPVT is of limited value in estimating WISC IQ's in a delinquent group.

Diener & Maroney (1974) examined the relationship between the Quick Test and the WAIS for black adolescent underachievers. Subjects were 72 young males sent to an institution designed to rehabilitate juvenile offenders. Median grade level of the group was 8; however, the boys were reading and performing arithmetical computations at below the 6th grade level.

The three forms of the Quick Test and the WAIS were given to all participants. Multiple regression coefficients were computed to determine optimal predictability of the WAIS from QT IQs. Results indicate that using more than one form of the Quick Test added very little to the predictability of WAIS IQs. From the regression equation the following WAIS IQ's were associated with five representative Quick Test IQ's: QT 55, WAIS 79; 65, 83; 75, 88; 85, 93; and 95, 97. It is apparent that QT scores approximate WAIS IQ's quite well in the mid-range of the sample. The Quick Test overestimated the WAIS IQ at the upper end of the distribution. No Quick Test scores were above 100 and only 12.5% of the sample fell within the average range of intelligence. With the limited range of scores in the present sample, the authors recommend that local norms be prepared and classification not be made on the basis of the QT alone.

Fisher (1967) studied the relationship between type of criminal offense, race, intelligence, educational level, age, and social desirability as measured by the Marlowe-Crowne Social Desirability Scale (M-C). In comparison with other studies of delinquents, the sample was impressive, consisting of 492 white, 108 Mexican American, and 182 Negro male prisoners being processed at Southern California Reception-Guidance Center at the Department of Corrections.

Criminal offenses were described as: white collar (embezzlement and forgery), N = 127; assault, N = 208; burglary, N = 267; rape, N = 8; sex perversion, N = 59; drug (possession and sales), N = 104; and involuntary manslaughter, N = 9.

While other variables are examined, the primary thrust of this study is the investigation of the relationship of the M-C Scale to age, race, IQ, and type of crime.

Neither age nor type of criminal offense was related to social desirability scores. However, IQ, education, and race were significantly correlated with the M-C. Since IQ was significantly correlated with M-C, the authors thought that the difference in the M-C scores by race might be an artifact of IQ differences. Group IQ's were calculated: white M 108, SD 13.8; Mexican-American M 97.2, SD 13.7; Negro M 95.4, SD, 9.5. Differences between whites and the other two groups were significant; Mexican-Americans and Negroes did not differ significantly, $t = 1.11$.

After the racial groups were adjusted for IQ differences, they were still found to differ on the M-C. Interpreting the Marlowe-Crowne score as a measure of defensiveness, Fisher found criminals to be more defensive than non criminals; Negro and Mexican-American criminals are equally defensive and more defensive than white criminals. Fisher did not report the relationship of IQ and type of criminal offense which would have been interesting for such a large group of prisoners representing such a wide range of offenses.

The same year Jensen published "How Much Can We Boost IQ" (Jensen, 1969a), Flanagan and Lewis (1969) published a short paper in the *Journal of Social Psychology*. Their purpose was to compare scores of lower class Negro and white men on the GATB and the MMPI. Subjects were 93 Negro and 103 white men sentenced to the Cook County Jail, Chicago, for minor offenses. The groups were similar with respect to education and SES. The authors see advantages of using inmates rather than high school or college students. The prison group is similar with respect to certain environmental and motivational factors that are hard to control outside a correctional setting.

Mean scores were not reported but Flanagan and Lewis found Negro-white GATB differences significant at the .05 level on all tests except the motor coordination. When an attempt was made to match Negro and white subjects on SES, personality differences were attenuated. However, aptitude differences remained after the groups were matched for SES.

Wechsler Verbal-Performance IQ differences for delinquents were reported by Henning and Levy (1967). A survey of 24 independent delinquency studies suggested a Wechsler pattern of Performance IQ > Verbal IQ. The authors felt this pattern might reflect learning disability which is not peculiar to delinquents.

First admission male delinquents assigned to the Illinois Youth Commission Reception and Diagnostic Center were given the WISC and the WAIS. The sample of 2,361 was divided into four groups by race and by test. The test groups were further divided by age at time of testing. Because of age differences, the groups were not evenly divided by test. Six hundred ninety-seven whites took the WISC, 725 blacks; 553 whites took the WAIS, 386 blacks.

To investigate the possible Verbal-Performance discrepancies at each age level the mean subtest scores were ranked. Rankings were compared with rankings of two other studies, one of delinquent unsuccessful readers and one of non-delinquent mentally retarded readers.

In addition to the usual W-B differences of approximately one SD for both WAIS and WISC tests, the WISC sample produced Performance IQs > Verbal IQs more often than did the WAIS. White Ss earned higher Performance IQs in relation to Verbal than did Negroes.

When subtest patterns were compared with delinquent poor readers and non-delinquent poor readers on both tests the white subjects showed significant correlations with poor reading patterns while black subjects lacked this relationship. This was interpreted by Henning and Levy as support for the idea that a reading disability pattern rather than sociopathic personality is what is being seen in the intra-subtest Wechsler patterns of white male delinquents.

The 1962 study published by Laskowitz was not reviewed in Shuey's 2nd edition. Since it is one of the limited number of attempts to relate drug addiction to race and IQ, it is reviewed here. Protocols of 497 Wechsler-Bellevue forms were randomly selected from the Psychology Department at Riverside Hospital. The sample was representative of the total first admission population with regard to race and sex; 220 were black, 146 Puerto Rican, and 131 white.

Male and female addicts within the three ethnic groups do not form homogeneous groups with respect to specific W-B I subtest scores. When Full Scale IQs are ranked by race, the order is white, Negro, and Puerto Rican. Whites are significantly higher than the other two groups but the differences between black and Puerto Rican females was not significant on the W-B Full Scale IQ. When female addicts were compared with a comparable group of female non-addicts, there was no significant difference on 8 of the 10 W-B I subtests.

White male addicts generally perform better than their Negro or Puerto Rican counterparts. For males, Negroes' and Puerto Ricans' performances were quite similar except on the Verbal Scale where the Negro addicts earned higher IQ scores.

In each of 6 addict groups, Performance IQ > Verbal IQ except for white females. Also in the 6 groups Picture Arrangement + Object Assembly > Block Design + Picture Completion. Arithmetic score was lowest for all groups and Comprehension was highest.

Levi and Seborg (1972) studied intelligence and school achievement differences of a multi racial group of drug addicts, the entire population of the California Rehabilitation Center Women's Unit located at Patton, California. The base group consisted of 200 white, 67 Mexican-American, and 68 black female drug addicts. In addition, there were 79 who could hardly read and write who were called illiterate. Of the latter group, 14 were white, 28 black and 37 Mexican-American. The base group was given the Army Alpha, Raven, and the California Achievement Test. The revised Beta was substituted for the Alpha in the illiterate group.

Data are not tabled but the authors offer to provide a complete analysis including scattergrams. Means are given in the summary but no measure of variability is shown. Reported IQs are on the whole much higher than would be expected of a total prison population. For whites the mean Alpha IQ was 112; blacks 97; and Mexican-Americans 107. Raven IQs also seemed to be elevated for delinquents: white 111; Mexican-American 104; and black 101. On the California Achievement Test scores were: white 10.8; black 10.5; and Mexican-American 9.8.

The authors conclude their "findings indicate very clearly that the results of the usual group verbal I.Q. tests administered to members of minority groups are very misleading, i.e., they did not reflect the real intellectual capacity of the testees." (p. 584) It should be pointed out that the Army Alpha, designed for use in World War I, is not the "usual" test administered to adults in the early 1970's. No other investigation reviewed in this chapter chose the Army Alpha Examination. For group testing of delinquent populations, the Wonderlic, Army General Classification Test (AGCT), the General Aptitude Test Battery (GATB), and the Wechsler Scales are the preferred tests. Despite the claims by Levi and Seborg that the Army Alpha does not reflect true capacity of the subjects studied, the mean IQs for whites compare favorably with national norms for college freshmen in the 1970's. The reviewer would have to agree with Levi and Seborg that the group verbal test they used does not reflect the true intellectual capacity of the subjects. For an entire prison population, the mean scores reported are at least ¾ to 1σ too high.

Five years after the study of women drug addicts was published by Levi & Seborg (1972) a team of psychologists, Levi, Tanner, Wirth, Lawson, and Sheetz (1977), examined a multiracial group of male drug addicts for the purpose of comparing their scholastic achievement and intellectual ability. The Army Alpha, used in the earlier study, was omitted from the study of male addicts. In its place was the Comprehensive Tests of Basic Skills. The Raven was retained for the study with men. Subjects were 129 whites, 129 Mexicans, and 106 blacks, most of whom were committed for the first time to the California Rehabilitation Center.

On the common mental ability test, Raven, mean scores for men were 2 to 6 points below those for women reported in the previous study. Mean Raven IQs were: white 107, σ 17; Mexican 98, σ 17; black 99, σ 13. White-black and white-Mexican-American IQ differences were significant. The blacks were significantly above the Mexican-Americans on the arithmetic subtest.

The relationship between IQ and scholastic scores is higher for whites, which, according to the authors ". . . indicates that other factors besides intelligence, as measured by the Raven IQ test, are responsible for learning of minority groups: possibly lower quality of education, less encouragement at home, perceived less rewards for academic success, etc. In spite of the significant correlations obtained, the Raven does not appear to be a reliable indicator of academic success for all the groups." (pp. 456–7) The authors conclude: "The question arises as to why drug addicts are more intelligent than the average population. At this point the answer could only be speculative, but the fact remains that our population have the capability to perform well in society *when and if they want to.*" (p. 456) A more parsimonious explanation may occur to the reader.

Long (1970) studied the relationship of personality and social variables in conforming judgment for 109 inmates of a Florida minimum security prison. Fifty-five subjects were Negro and 54 white. It is assumed all subjects were male since the sex was not specified. The age range was not given.

The experimental procedure involved testing for differences in conforming judgment according to social structure of the groups. Subjects were assigned to one of 4 experimental groups. Members of group 1 were black and were tested individually with 3 white confederates. Members of group 2 were black and were tested individually with 3 black confederates. This procedure was repeated for groups 3 and 4 composed of white subjects.

Four measures or scales were given to each inmate: (1) California Capacity Questionnaire, (2) Agreement Response Set Scale, (3) Form E of the Dogmatism Scale, and (4) Vertical Line Test.

Long found subjects in each group to have similar agreement response set and dogmatism traits but to differ significantly in IQ and conforming behavior. A *t* test revealed significant intelligence differences between black and white subjects when they were tested with a black or white confederate.

Long says, "It would be easy to arrive at the conclusion that the major difference among the independent variables among the four groups was in their IQ scores." (p. 179) He then offers an *ad hoc* explanation for his findings. The reviewer is inclined to accept the parsimonious explanation.

In a study conducted at the Youth Development Center, Milledgeville, Georgia, McCandless, Persons, and Roberts (1972) selected from a base group of about 500, 177 young delinquents age 15 to 17. The boys were of low SES with IQ's ranging from the high 40's to the high 130's. Many were retarded and at least 20 percent were non-readers; 119 were black, 58 white.

Subjects were given a series of short answer questionnaires concerning delinquent behavior. Physical measurements were taken in an attempt to relate mesomorphy to delinquency. A rating of attractiveness was also made by independent raters. Unfortunately, WAIS test results were available for only 74 subjects.

The authors found the questionnaire to report unreasonably rosy protocols, especially when taking into account the given background of the boys. Low reliability of a questionnaire given to this group of subjects, some of whom had IQs below 50, should not have been unexpected. Mean WAIS IQ was 75, for blacks 72, for whites 89.

The data provided no support for the hypothesis that links mesomorphy to delinquency. Nor was there support for the idea that age and race of the investigator affected response of a bi-racial delinquent group.

The attractiveness variable, surprisingly reliable and remarkably independent of differences between body build and race of subjects and race and age of the raters, entered into no relationship with any other variable.

The largest sample of delinquents reviewed for this chapter is reported by Murray, Waites, Veldman, and Heatly (1973) who examined the WAIS-WISC patterns of 2,498 delinquent boys from different ethnic groups. The subjects were from Gatesville State School for boys where they had been placed for various types of delinquent behavior. The age range was from 10 to 19 years with a mean age of 14.7. The ethnic breakdown was 1,007 Anglo, 808 black, and 663 Chicano.

The purpose of the Murray et al study was to examine WAIS and WISC subtest patterns of a large multi-racial group of delinquent boys. Boys 15 years or younger took the WISC; those older than 15 took the WAIS.

The main idea was to examine the Performance > Verbal subscale difference reported in other studies of delinquents. Results were as expected from previous research, with Anglos scoring substantially higher than subjects from the other 2 groups. WISC IQ's were lower than those of the WAIS for all ethnic groups.

Verbal-Performance IQ differences were consistent with the Wechsler manual except the WISC P>V differences were twice as great as the differences on the WAIS.

Murray and his colleagues suggest the WAIS-WISC difference in IQ could be the "result of test item characteristics." No claim is made by Wechsler that the WAIS and WISC are perfectly articulated. The tests were designed for slightly overlapping ages but the norm groups were quite different and the two tests were published 6 years apart. For the results of two different intelligence tests not to differ by a few I.Q. points in a cross sectional study would be the exception.

Fifty young male inmates of the State Correctional Institute at Camp Hill, Pennsylvania, were subjects for a comparative study of the Kahn Intelligence Test and the WAIS by Ream (1978). Thirty subjects were black, 20 white, with an age range of 16 to 21. Eliminated from the sample were subjects who were non-English speaking and those with physical or emotional handicaps.

Since the purpose of Ream's study was to compare group scores on the KIT with those of the WAIS, IQ's were not reported by race. On the Kahn Intelligence Test, the combined mean IQ was 76, σ 8. WAIS Full Scale IQ was 92, σ 11. The two tests correlated .71.

"The Truant Before the Court" by Reinemann (1948) was not cited by Shuey in either previous edition. It deserves review in this chapter on delinquents because, according to the author, the Director of Probation of the Municipal Court of Philadelphia, in practically all juvenile court laws the term "delinquency" is defined so as to include truancy.

The main purpose of this study was to "spot" potential delinquents at the earliest possible stage and to make suggestions to implement cooperations between school and court.

The subjects for study were 163 boys (113 white, 50 non-white) and 57 girls (40 white, 17 non-white) who had been referred to the court exclusively for truancy. The truant group comprised only about 10% of the delinquents referred to the court. The exact breakdown by age was not given. Two thirds of the group were ages 14 and 15; only 9% were over 16. Data were analyzed under 3 major headings: (1) environment, (2) school history, and (3) court history. Aspects of environment were examined in terms of (a) family size, (b) marital status of parents, (c) home conditions, (d) neighborhood, and (e) employment of mother. School history was studied by type of school and by grade. Court history was analyzed by: (a) previous court referral, (b) sibling delinquency, (c) physical status, and (d) intelligence.

With regard to environment, the major conclusions were: (1) Truants, as a group, were from large families. (2) Two thirds of the cases were from broken homes. This was a larger percentage than found in the total delinquent group. (3) About one third of home and neighborhood conditions were rated "poor."

From the school history the authors concluded: (1) One fourth of the truants were in special classes or schools. (2) One half were retarded.

An analysis of the court history indicated: (1) Siblings of the truants had been referred to the court for delinquency in 61% of the cases. (2) Only in about one fourth of the truant population were the physical examinations negative. (3) There were fewer children with low IQs in the truant group than in the total delinquent group; 44% had IQs of 85 and below. Since all non-white subjects were lumped together, it was not possible to make a direct black-white comparison. The median IQ for whites was found by the reviewer to be 89; for non-whites 80.

Cattell's Culture Fair Intelligence Test (CCFIT) and the WISC-R IQ's for 51 delinquents were compared by Smith, Hays, and Solway (1977). Their purpose was to locate an intelligence screening device for juvenile courts that would have "as little cultural bias as possible." Subjects were 51 male and female referrals to the Harris County Juvenile Probation Department (Houston Area); 24 were white and 27 black or Mexican-American. The age range was from 11 to 17, mean 14.9. No effort was made to control for SES or for type of offense. Scores for blacks were combined with those of Mexican-Americans for analysis. This group was called "minorities."

Mean IQs for "minorities" was 84 on the CCFIT and 76 for the WISC-R; for whites the CCFIT mean was 95 and the WISC-R 94. Because of the larger difference on the WISC-R than on the CCFIT, the authors conclude that the CCFIT "is a better measure of intelligence for minority groups than is the WISC-R, since it eliminates at least some of the bias in the WISC-R . . . and presents a more accurate picture of their intellectual capacity." (p. 181) It would, of course, be equally accurate to say that the WISC-R and CCFIT are equally good measures of intelligence because both tests yield approximately the same IQ's for whites and, furthermore, the white-minority differences are comparable with the important literature on bias in mental testing.

Wenk, Rozynko, Sarbin, and Robison (1971) investigated the effect of different incentives upon the GATB scores of white and black inmates at a California Reception Guidance Center. This study grew out of a similar one conducted previously by two of the present authors who found results contrary to their predictions ". . . that differences on non-verbal tests would be less than differences on verbal tests and that minority groups would 'catch up'. Although the Mexican-American sample tended to follow the prediction of the experimenters, the Negro sample did not." (p. 54)

A plausible new hypothesis was advanced:

That motivational factors were important in test performance, that blacks were earning lower scores because of a sub-cultural de-emphasis on intellectual competition.

Subjects were 220 (121 white, 99 black) inmates assigned to 1 of 6 sub-samples which ranged in size from 28 to 42. Age range was not reported; neither was sex given. It is assumed that all participants were male.

Inmates were tested on 4 non-verbal tests of the GATB under one control and 2 experimental conditions for each race. For one experimental condition, subjects were given a "ducat" redeemable for canteen goods. The second experimental condition involved verbal encouragement to the inmates to improve their scores. The control group was simply re-tested.

The hypothesis that an effective incentive (material reward) would operate to narrow the gap between whites and Negroes was not upheld. Whites widened the initial advantage over Negroes under material incentive on all scales except K, on which Negroes had an initial lead and extended that lead upon retest.

The idea that score gain for whites and blacks would be greatest under the material incentive and least under no incentive was not confirmed.

The authors conclude that material reward provided some incentive for test score elevation but the efforts were slight and unrelated to ethnic status.

Summary

Despite over-crowded prisons and youth detention and classification centers and the massive federal funds available for prison study in recent years, only 14 studies published since Shuey's 2nd edition, and 2 inadvertently omitted from her survey, were located that attempted to relate psychological test results to criminal behavior of different racial groups. Authors of one paper, Flanagan and Lewis (1969), suggest that prison inmates comprise a more homogeneous group than school children and college students and thus should be a better group to study because all are usually similar in education, SES and mental ability.

Between 1966 and 1980 investigations of prison populations were selective with regard to female delinquents. Only about ½ of 1% of the 7,000 subjects studied were not male. The small number of women examined could be a function of careless reporting. In several studies, subjects were not identified by sex. With such a small proportion of the total population women, present findings can only apply to males.

One paper comprised only of women drug addicts, Levi and Seborg (1972), deserves special mention. The authors tested an entire female prison population and reported a mean Army Alpha IQ of 112 for whites, almost equal to the average of college freshmen in the 1970's and almost 1σ above the national adult norm for whites. Scores for female blacks and Mexican-Americans also seem to be elevated in the Levi and Seborg study.

While there is no general consensus among the authors of studies reviewed in this chapter, there are some interesting findings that may be gleaned from their data:

(1) Mental test scores are not significantly related to type of criminal offense or to whether the inmate is a "first timer" or a recidivist.
(2) There was no support for the idea that links mesomorphy to delinquency.
(3) The Wechsler pattern of PIQ > VIQ among delinquents is given modest support.
(4) Among truants, it was found that siblings of truants had been referred to juvenile court in 61% of the cases.
(5) The idea that effective incentive (material reward) would operate to narrow the gap between test scores of whites and blacks was not supported.

One general finding of this chapter that is supported almost without exception by data, if not by ideology, is that white-black-Spanish-American IQ differences found in public schools, colleges and industries also obtain in prison. Whereas the general population mean IQ is 100 for whites and 85 for blacks, the inmate average is more like 95 and 80 or in some cases 90 and 75. Means for Spanish speaking Americans usually fall between those of whites and blacks. These differences are found regardless of test employed, the age of the sample, the SES of the subjects or the race of the examiner.

VIII

Special Populations

R. Travis Osborne

Special Populations, a miscellaneous collection of 13 articles not elsewhere classified, involves fewer than 3,000 subjects, of which 1,127 are found in one study. One study examines test performance of indigent pregnant Negro girls; the largest in terms of numbers of subjects is the standardization sample of the WAIS in Puerto Rico. In 8 studies subjects are described as being mentally retarded. Some subjects of the remaining studies are undoubtedly mentally retarded but the reason for being selected for study was not their retardation.

Because almost one half the studies in this chapter are one-of-a-kind involving unique groups of subjects or novel tests, no attempt will be made to tabulate the overall findings or summarize the results.

Retardate intelligence and adaptive behavior were studied by Adams, McIntosh, and Weade (1973) because ". . . there seems to be little information available concerning the effects of ethnic background on measured intelligence or on adaptive behavior scores." (p.1)

The 109 subjects were patients at a metropolitan state research and training facility for mentally retarded children. The age range was from 4 to 17 with a mean just over 8. There were 56 boys (26 black, 30 white) and 53 girls (24 black, 29 white).

To compare the retardate adaptive behavior measured by the Vineland Social Maturity Scale with IQ was the main purpose of the study. A 2×2 analysis of variance showed only the main effect for IQ by race significant. There was no effect of sex and no race-sex interaction for IQ.

The same analysis of the Deviation Social Quotient (DSQ) showed no significant race or sex differences.

The authors conclude that their study of retardates supports many previous studies with these and other types of children, indicating poorer performance on IQ tests for blacks than for whites. They suggest, however, that the two groups are comparable on a simple measure of adaptive behavior and the discrepancy between IQs and adaptive behavior scores is significantly greater for blacks than for whites. They also suggest that it is possible that the lower IQs of blacks are accurate reflections of the likelihood of their success in conventional schools, while adaptive behavior scores may more accurately represent success in social and vocational undertakings.

A validity study of the Slosson Drawing Coordination Test was conducted by Alcorn and Nicholson (1972) of North Carolina Central University at Durham. Subjects were 114 boys and 77 girls (135 black and 56 white) ranging in age from 14 to 19. Subjects were Vocational Rehabilitation clients with IQs below 90 and were enrolled in classes for mentally retarded in central North Carolina. All or selected parts of the following tests were given: WAIS or WISC, Benton Visual Retention Test, Slosson, and the Raven Progressive Matrices.

Slosson scores were correlated with results from other scales by race and sex. Most r's were considerably lower than generally found between the Wechsler scales and other intelligence tests.

Mean scores were remarkably consistent by race and by sex. Wechsler Full Scale IQ for blacks was 70.55, for whites 71.12. Mean Slosson scores were 28.25 for blacks and 29.07 for whites.

It appears that by restricting the range of the sample (no subjects had an IQ above 89) Alcorn and Nicholson attenuated their Slosson validity coefficients and at the same time equated mean scores by race and sex on other psychological tests.

A study by Alley and Snider (1970) deserves special mention because it is one of the very few studies reporting perceptual motor test performance of blacks to be significantly above that of whites. Participants (32 whites, 18 blacks, ranging in age from 7 years-5 months to 9 years-10 months) were drawn from an elementary school for educable mentally retarded in Davenport, Iowa. The two groups did not differ significantly in age or in IQ.

The test battery was broad including: (a) the Lincoln-Oseretsky Motor Development Scale, (b) Purdue Perceptual-Motor Survey, (c) Balance and Posture Area, (d) Body Image and Differentiation Area, (e) Benton Visual Retention Test, (f) Kuhlmann-Finch Tests, (g) Marianne Frostig Developmental Test of Visual Perception and (h) a concept-formation measure.

The primary hypotheses were: Between the Negro mentally retarded population and the white mentally retarded population there is no difference in: (1) sensory motor performance, (2) visual perception, and (3) concept-formation performance.

On the Lincoln-Oseretsky test of sensory motor performance the black group obtained higher mean scores on 41 of the 53 tasks. On thirteen tasks, the differences were significant. Some of the items on which blacks excelled were: winding a thread, cutting a circle, jumping over a rope, catching a ball, jumping in the air and making an about face, standing on one foot with eyes closed, throwing a ball, and balancing on tip toe. On the basis of the Lincoln-Oseretsky findings, hypothesis #1 was rejected.

Tests of Visual Perception indicated no significant differences between whites and blacks. Hypothesis #2 was retained.

There were also no significant differences between the two groups on concept-formation (ITPA) performance. This is not unexpected since the groups were of equal IQ at the beginning of the experiment ($\bar{X}$ black IQ = 67.94; white, 65.75). The examination used to match or equate the groups is not named. If it is the ITPA or a similar paper and pencil test the insignificant group differences at the second testing would not be remarkable.

The authors *ad hoc* conclusions are:

1. Negro children are stimulated toward physical interaction by their mothers and become "physically oriented" toward their environment. Geber and Dean (1957) stated that African Negro children are afforded more physical contact during the nurturing period by the mother. Because the mentally retarded is slow in his developmental patterns, the Negro mother may overcompensate by offering more physical contact and thereby further stimulating the mother-child physical interaction.

2. Negro children may be motivated toward sensory motor performance as an avenue of success. This motivation may be overtly and/or covertly encouraged or verbally reinforced, by example, by parents, siblings, peers and/or "hero" images. The Negro mentally retarded child may realize by internal or external feedback that academic and intellectual goals are inaccessible to him. He, therefore, compensates by motivation and strivings with heightened zeal toward sensory motor activities.

3. Negro and white groups used in the present investigation, as well as previous research in this area, have not been specifically controlled for such variables as measures of physical growth, previous experiential training, and attitudes toward perceptual motor development. (p. 113)

Anderson, Kern, and Cook (1968) examined the effects of race, sex and brain damage on Raven Coloured Progressive Matrices scores. Adult Vocational Rehabilitation clients of the Georgia Rehabilitation Center were subjects. The 147 subjects, ranging in age from 16 to 65, were divided into 8 groups by type of brain damage, sex and race. With only 20 blacks altogether, black subjects in all cells were in short supply; i.e., 2, 4 and 7 subjects. Added to the small number of blacks was the fact that both groups were labeled *brain damaged.* In other words, it was not possible to determine from the table which subjects were brain damaged and which were not brain damaged. The significant differences found for some of the tests should perhaps be discounted because of the very small numbers and because the direction of the differences was not clear from Table 1.

Blue and Vergason (1973) investigated the echoic language behavior of culturally deprived black (60) and white (60) children from the Atlanta public school system. Since the possible influence of school integration was of interest to the authors, the subjects were taken from schools with at least a 5 year history of stability and equality of racial composition.

The Rystrom Dialect Test was administered via tape recorder. An analysis of variance was computed which indicated main effects of race (black $\bar{X}$ 13.5; white 17.2) and grade to be significant (p < .01). There was no significant interaction. Blue and Vergason conclude that black children do not perform at as high a level as white children in the oral repetition of standard English phrases. This finding supports an earlier study by Rystrom (1969).

Although the age-race interaction was not significant, there is slight evidence of a reduction in the performance gap with increasing grade level.

The investigators were initially concerned about limited short term memory or inattention of children in the lower grades but found no evidence of decreased short term memory in this study. Children of both groups were alert and responded to 99% of the taped sentences.

In a one page paper, Clegg and White (1966) report the results of their examination with the Leiter International Performance Scale of 108 black children from a public residential school for the deaf. Subjects ranged in age from 6 to 14, median 11. There were 63 boys and 44 girls (sic). The group mean IQ was 73.3; 70.9 for boys and 76.9 for girls. The sex difference was not significant.

Covin (1976) investigated the suitability of using the Peabody Picture Vocabulary Test, Form B, instead of the WISC for classifying children participating in a black Head Start program. Subjects were 37 black children (22 boys, 15 girls) who were suspected by their teachers of being mentally retarded. The mean age was 64.3 months, σ 1.6 months.

The mean PPVT Form B IQ for girls was 63.1, σ 11.3; for WISC Full Scale, IQ = 71.6, σ = 7.8. For boys the mean PPVT was 64.0, σ = 11.3; for WISC Full Scale IQ, 70.0, σ = 10.7. For both boys and girls the WISC verbal, performance and full scale IQs were consistently .75σ or more above those of the PPVT.

This 1973 article by Goldfarb, Basen, and Kersey is perhaps misclassified but after considering other options it was decided to review the study of pregnant indigent Negro adolescents in this chapter.

The purpose of the study was to determine the level of mental functioning by age and to compare the scores with published Quick Test (QT) norms. Subjects were 323 pregnant indigent Negro adolescents at Jefferson Davis Hospital, City of Houston, Harris County, Texas. The age range was 13 through 18.

Means and σ's were computed for each age group and compared with those of the QT provisional manual (Ammons and Ammons, 1962). Analysis of variance of IQ at the various age levels indicated significant black-white differences, ranging from 11.3 to 14.2 IQ points.

The authors offer the following explanations for their findings:

> The background experience [sic] of the two samples were different in that ours was strictly a Southern Negro population, while the Ammons' white sample came from Louisville, Kentucky . . .
>
> . . . educational experiences were not the only factors that could contribute to the present discrepancy. The QT is a verbal-perceptual test of intelligence . . . The simple verbal recognition skills required for the QT may not have developed in our sample as highly as in the standardization sample . . .
>
> . . . Whether pregnancy was influential is unknown for this sample. How such biological changes affect motivation is not fully understood. (p. 542)

"On the correlation between IQ and amount of 'white blood' " was the title of a paper by Green (1972) presented at the 80th Annual American Psychological Convention. Subjects for the study were members of a stratified random sample, ages 16 to 64, who participated as the standardization sample of the project to translate and adapt into the Spanish language the WAIS in Puerto Rico. The 1960 U.S. census was used to obtain what Green calls ". . . the most representative sample of a well-defined total population that has been obtained for any similar study." (p. 285)

In order to study "racial" differences, the sample (N = 1,127) was divided into five color groups. Group 1 consisted of 260 apparently pure white individuals and Group 5 (N = 38) consisted of the darkest and almost certainly the most purely Negro individuals in the sample.

Test administrators were carefully trained on ratings of color. Green notes that the examiners were Puerto Rican and represented the first four color groups.

A breakdown of results is given by color group, age, education and other test variables. A one way analysis of variance was not significant. However, when Group 5 was contrasted with a pool of the other 4 groups, differences were significant. No statistically reliable differences existed between any of Groups 1, 2 and 3 on any test variable. Group

4 tended to be significantly lower than groups 1 and 2 on the Verbal scores and on the Full Scale scores. By way of explanation of his findings Green says:

> . . . the Puerto Rican does not regard the Color Groups 2 and 3 as defined in this study as "Negro." They are Puerto Rican. Color Group 4 may or may not be considered to be "Negro" depending on presence or absence of other traits such as hair texture or eye color. Color Group 5 is very likely to be considered to be "Negro." From the results reported here, it can reasonably be concluded that there are some residual cognitive test differences between individuals in Puerto Rico who are regarded as being Negro and those who are not regarded as being Negro. Among color groups who are not regarded as being Negro, reliable differences in IQ do not occur.
>
> The Puerto Rican result shows very clearly that changes in mental ability scores tend to follow the prejudice line much more closely than the genetic line, if it follows the latter at all. (p. 286)

Using Green's 5 Puerto Rican color groups, it appears that changes in mental ability scores also tend to follow the color line.

In a validity study of the Black Intelligence Test of Cultural Homogeneity (BITCH) Long and Anthony (1974) correlated scores on the WISC with those on the BITCH. The number of subjects was small, only 30 EMR black students, 16 girls and 14 boys. The age range was not given but, with a median age of 16, it is reasonable to assume a significant portion of the group was older than the ceiling age of the WISC.

For the administration of the BITCH, the subjects were divided into two groups. Subjects in Group I read the test items; subjects in Group II heard the items read by the examiner. Group II scores were slightly but significantly above those of Group I. Girls were also slightly better than boys on the BITCH.

The correlation coefficient between the BITCH and the WISC for all subjects was .319, which is significant (.05).

The authors conclude that "The low positive correlation between the BITCH and WISC scores suggests that there is no significant difference between the scores obtained by Black EMR students on these tests." (p. 311)

The Arrow-Dot test is a perceptual motor task on which the subject is required to draw the shortest line from the point of the arrow to a dot. An ego score (E) results when the subject draws the shortest possible line, a super ego score (S) results when an overly long route to the dot is taken, and an impulsiveness score (I) results when the subject ignores directions and crosses the line. McCormick, Schnobrich, and Footlik (1966) studied Arrow-Dot performance of 72 (28 boys and 44 girls)

Negro adolescents of lower (below 80) IQ in their investigation of reading skills. Mean age of the group was 15–9. The mean Kuhlmann-Anderson IQ was 66.48.

There were no sex differences on the impulsiveness scale. Girls were significantly lower on the ego scale; higher on the super ego scale. The authors conclude test differences can not be attributed to IQ or SES differences since sexes were equated for IQ. It is suggested, however, that "socialization experiences" may be specific for Negro females with low IQ.

Arrow-Dot scores were not correlated with the Kuhlmann-Anderson IQs.

The Nalven, Hofmann and Bierbryer (1969) paper is not a study of intelligence tests results of blacks and whites, but a study of psychologists' estimates of a subject's "True IQ" from the same WISC protocols variously labeled black or white; CA 8 or CA 14; male or female; and low or middle SES. Altogether there were 16 background information categories assigned to the same WISC protocol.

Six hundred fifty members of the Clinical Psychology and School Psychology sections of the 1967 American Psychological Association were randomly selected to respond to the one item question (What is the "True IQ" of the child described on the protocol?). The first 20 usable replies for each category were selected for the experiment.

The authors found considerable variation among the "True IQ" estimates. The highest mean was 104.7 assigned to a 14 year-old lower class Negro girl; the lowest was 91.1, assigned to a 14 year-old white middle class boy.

The four subject variables were correlated with "True IQ" ratings. Race and SES were significantly related to True IQ; age and sex were not.

The authors conclude:

> A child's age or sex evidently does not influence psychologists' judgments as to whether his obtained WISC Full Scale IQ score represents an accurate estimate of his true potential. In contrast, a child's social class background, to a great extent, and his race, to a lesser extent, significantly shape psychologists' judgments as to whether his obtained IQ scores are representative. The results point to the fact that psychologists assume that lower class and Negro children's obtained WISC IQ scores represent significant underestimates of their true intellectual capacities. (p. 274)

Smith and Caldwell (1969) examined the patterns of WISC score differences for black and white mental retardates. One hundred ninety-nine subjects with WISC Full Scale IQs below 69 comprised the base group.

There were 78 black males, 37 white males, 56 black females, and 28 white females. Both blacks and whites were of rural, low SES background.

A cross validity group of 141 was selected in the same manner as the base group. In this group there were 55 black males, 20 white males, 52 black females, and 14 white females.

The hypothesis that mean test values were the same for both retarded racial groups was rejected for both sexes. The black-white difference was especially noticeable in the performance section of the WISC.

Classification of retardates of both sexes on the basis of the WISC scores was moderately successful. The error in the base group was 27 percent and for the cross validation group, 39 percent for boys and 35 percent for girls.

The major black-white difference was in the performance tests scores. A performance test, Coding, had the largest weight on the discriminant functions for males. Black males scored near the whites on all WISC verbal tests except Digit Span. For girls, the performance tests were also the bases for classifying subjects into racial groups.

On the basis of this and other studies, the authors conclude that Southern Negro mental defectives may not be typical retardates, and since Negroes do not have the same pattern of abilities as white mental defectives, perhaps they should be diagnosed and instructed by different procedures.

IX

Race of Examiner Effects
and the
Validity of Intelligence Tests

W. G. Graziano, P. E. Varca, and J. Levy

The nomological network surrounding the construct of intelligence has been intensively and extensively investigated for many years. Despite the magnitude of research effort, important questions about intelligence have not been answered unequivocally. It is the purpose of this chapter to review, organize, and evaluate the most recent evidence relevant to one such question: Is an examinee's performance on intelligence tests systematically biased by examiners of different races? The term "race" is used here merely for ease of exposition. It is used solely to refer to self-identified sub-populations within the larger human population (cf. Jensen, 1980). The literature reviewed covers the period from 1966 through 1980, although references to earlier work will be made where necessary. The journals exhaustively reviewed were: *Child Development, Developmental Psychology, Journal of Negro Education, Journal of Applied Psychology, Journal of Consulting and Clinical Psychology, Journal of Educational Measurement, Journal of Educational Psychology, Journal of Personality and Social Psychology, Perceptual and Motor Skills,* and *Psychological Bulletin.* Where relevant, articles from other journals are cited. In addition, unpublished doctoral dissertation research was reviewed when it was available.

The issue of examiner bias is important because many issues of validity are related to it. First, if examiners systematically bias scores against examinees of a race different from themselves, then examinees of the

---

[1] This chapter constitutes the major portion of a paper to be published elsewhere by professors W. G. Graziano, P. E. Varca, and J. Levy. The editors, needless to say, are most indebted to the authors for their generosity in allowing this important paper to be incorporated in a book that is not their own.

same race as the examiner should obtain higher scores on such tests than should examinees of a race different from the examiner. Second, if such bias can be demonstrated, and if we assume more minority children are assessed by non-minority than minority examiners, then these social processes may account for the mean differences found between black and white intelligence test scores. Third, if racial bias of examiners can be demonstrated, then the predictive validity of intelligence test scores as a whole would be lessened. Fourth, if such bias can be demonstrated, then the predictive value and practical utility of intelligence test scores for ethnic minority examinees assessed by non-minority examiners would be greatly diminished, and less biasing assessment procedures must be developed.

Methodological Considerations

Many methodological pitfalls await the researcher interested in investigating race of examiner effects. To facilitate the evaluation of the relevant literature, some of the major pitfalls will be examined in this section. First, the design of an examiner effect study must be such that race of examiner effects are not confounded with some other aspect of the study (see Jensen, 1980, p. 596). There are several different ways such confounding can occur. Any study that uses only one examiner, or only one examiner for each ethnic group, has confounded race with other characteristics of the examiner (e.g., the black examiner may also be taller, more physically attractive, or of a different gender than the white examiner). In such studies, differences in examinee scores for examiners of different races could be due to any confounded attribute, or combination of attributes. Another methodological problem occurs when examinees are not randomly assigned to examiners. For example, if one examiner, or group of examiners, assess only children expected to have some special problem, then there is a confounding of characteristics of the child with characteristics of examiner.

Second, when outcomes of race of examiner effects are evaluated statistically, the power of the statistical tests must be sufficiently large to detect any effects if they are in fact present. That is, power should be sufficiently large to reject a null hypothesis with reasonable probability. For relatively large effects, a small sample size will yield power sufficient to detect the effect. For relatively smaller effects, however, larger samples are needed to reject the null hypothesis and detect the effect (Cohen, 1977). For example, imagine an examiner effects study involving only ten white and ten black examinees that reports no evidence of bias. In this case, it is possible that the sample size is too small to detect even a relatively large bias effect. It should be noted, however, that power is a two-edged sword. First, if a very large sample is collected, even trivially small effects can be detected. In such cases, the theoretical and practical implications of such small effects need to be carefully considered. Second, if the null hypothesis cannot be rejected with relatively large samples, it is possible the effect is trivial (i.e., too small to be detected). In such cases, even null results may be informative in evaluating the impact or practical importance of examiner effects (cf. Greenwald, 1975).

Third, the ideal examiner effect study should be designed to detect race of examiner × race of examinee *interactions,* and not designed to detect race of examiner main effects. Following Jensen (1980, p. 597), we shall call the former "complete designs," and the latter "incomplete designs." In general, incomplete designs are vulnerable to more alternative explanations for examiner effects than are complete designs. For example, an examiner using an incomplete design finds children obtain higher intelligence test scores from a black examiner than a white examiner. Such an outcome yields a race of examiner main effect. One explanation is that the white examiner is biased. Other explanations are that the black examiner is more motivating, more attractive, more novel, more lenient, etc. This interpretative problem is aggravated when a study uses examiners of only one race. Evidence for a race of examiner effect would be less equivocal if the study had been designed to detect black children obtaining higher scores from black examiners than from white examiners *and* white children obtaining higher scores from white examiners than from black examiners. This latter study was designed to detect an interaction of race of examiner × race of examinee. There are other less pervasive methodological problems that arise in the literature, but these shall be discussed within the context of specific studies. In all cases, the examiner bias interpretation of studies will be evaluated in terms of its plausibility relative to other interpretations of the data.

For ease of exposition, studies reviewed in this chapter are presented in chronological order, and classified in a four-fold scheme as being: (1) "adequate" or "inadequate," and (2) "complete" or "incomplete" (cf. Jensen, 1980, p. 596). To be classified as *adequate,* a study must meet two minimal conditions: (a) there are at least two (but ideally, several) examiners of each race, and (b) there are no systematic biases in the assignment of examinees or examiners. This can usually be accomplished through random assignment of examinee to examiner. The *inadequate* classification is used for those studies that do not meet these two minimal requirements. The classification of a study as "adequate" is not intended to imply the study is necessarily valid or free of any methodological flaws. Independent of their classification on the adequate vs. inadequate dimension, studies were classified as "complete" or "incomplete." To be classified as *complete,* examinees must be sampled from two or more racial groups. The *incomplete* classification is used for those studies that sample examinees of only one racial sub-group.

Inadequate Designs

Incomplete Sampling

Caldwell and Knight (1970) examined the performance of 15 sixth grade black pupils on Forms L & M of the Stanford-Binet. Subjects were students in the elementary school system of a southern city (75,000 population) and matched on grade and similarity of scores on the California Test of Mental Maturity.

Students were randomly divided into three groups. Group A took Form L of the Stanford-Binet from a black female examiner and then within a week Form M from a white male examiner. The procedure was reversed for Group B. Group C was given both forms by the white examiner. All tests were given in the same room. Both examiners had graduate training on individual testing and rechecked each other's scoring. However, interjudge reliability was not given.

The authors reported no significant differences among test scores due to the form of the test or examiner's race. It should be noted that based on the text and data presentation it appears the statistical procedures (a two-way analysis of variance) did not employ a repeated measures design. Thus, the results are suspect and difficult to interpret.

Carringer and Wilson (1974) investigated the effects of type of reinforcement (giving praise versus giving correctness/incorrectness feedback), subject sex, socioeconomic status (SES) and race of experimenter on a puzzle task. Subjects were 48 first grade black students in the Savannah, Georgia, school system equally divided for sex and SES level. (Note: SES determined by father's occupation resulted in a low and middle SES grouping.) The task involved dropping a blue square or a yellow cylinder-shaped puzzle piece into its appropriate place. Although this is not a formal test of mental ability the task does resemble in content the form- and block-matching tasks of the Stanford-Binet scale. Procedurally the study entailed instructing subjects individually and allowing them to work at the task under conditions of praise or correctness reinforcement. Two male experimenters—one black and one white—were employed to conduct the sessions. Both examiners were graduate students at the University of Georgia.

The project was treated as two separate studies with the white examiner examining all 48 students first and then the black examiner following identical procedures for the same students two months later. Similarly, data from the two studies were analyzed separately with a $2 \times 2 \times 2$ (sex $\times$ reinforcement $\times$ SES) ANOVA design. Both analyses resulted in a significant SES main effect ($p < .01$) with the middle SES group performing best and a significant sex $\times$ reinforcement $\times$ SES ($p < .01$) interaction. Group means were not presented.

In order to test for differences between the black and white examiners, data from the two studies were combined and t tests were performed comparing all possible group means. This procedure resulted in 23 comparisons of which seven were significant at the .01 level and five at the .05 level. In all cases differences were in the direction of better performance with the black examiner. Again, group means were not presented.

Several methodological flaws confound these results and make interpretation difficult. The overall project was a repeated measures design. However, treatment order (black/white examiner) was not counterbalanced. The black examiner followed the white examiner in all cases. Thus, learning and experience are alternative explanations for students doing better with the black examiner. In addition, inappropriate statistical procedures were employed. The use of separate ANOVA procedures followed by direct difference t tests for all possible comparisons inflated the probability of Type I errors. Correct analyses would have involved a repeated measures ANOVA followed by group mean comparisons in the event of significant interactions. Also, the authors failed to use the correlated t-test method rather than the direct difference method.

Summary of Inadequate-Incomplete Studies

The two studies in this section provide little support for the contention that race of examiner affects scores on intellectual tasks. One study (Caldwell & Knight, 1970) reported no significant results while the other study (Carringer & Wilson, 1974) reporting significant race of examiner effects was flawed methodologically.

Complete Sampling

Scott, Hartson, and Cunningham (1976) examined the effects of race on the preschool test performance of 28 black and 37 white children (ages 2–3½ years) in a medium sized midwestern city. The sample was not described in terms of sex composition. Subjects were from homes in integrated but low SES neighborhoods and participants in the Home Start, Title III ESEA project.

Level I of the Iowa Test of Preschool Development (see Scott, 1975) was used in the testing situation. This test is designed for children from two to five years and consists of eight dimensions (receptive language, expressive language, large motor, small motor-A, small motor-B, visual memory, auditory memory, and concepts).

The examiners were six females described as "paraprofessionals" with 25 hours of training on the Iowa Test and experience as a mother with school-age children. Five examiners were white and one black. A majority of the testing (85%) occurred in the children's homes with the remainder occurring at relatives' or babysitters' homes or day care centers. The project employed a repeated measures design with children being tested by both black and white examiners at a six month interval. It is not possible to determine from the text if order of treatment was completely counter-balanced.

The authors describe their statistical procedure as a "2 (race of subjects) × 2 (race of examiners) × 2 (race of subjects × race of examiners) × 9 (skill areas and total score) analysis of variance (unweighted means) with repeated measures on the last factor." This is incorrect. It appears from the summary table in the text that data were analyzed using 2 × 2 (race of subject × race of examiner) ANOVAS on the eight subtest scores and the total test score. Also, it appears from the summary table that race of examiner was not analyzed as a repeated treatment variable.

Results yielded significant main effects for examiner's race on expressive language ($p < .05$), visual memory ($p < .05$) and concepts ($p < .01$). The black examiner produced higher scores on the concepts subtest and the white examiners higher scores on the other two dimensions. There were significant main effects for children's race on visual memory ($p < .01$), auditory memory ($p < .05$) and concepts ($p < .01$) with blacks doing best on auditory memory and whites best on visual memory and concepts. Finally, there was a significant examiner's race × child's race interaction ($p < .01$) on the large motor subtest with white children doing best with the black examiner and black children doing best with the white examiner. These data, although apparently analyzed improperly, provide no evidence of white examiners systematically deflating the scores of black children on the Iowa Preschool Test.

Samuel, Soto, Parks, Ngissah, and Jones (1976) published a paper containing two studies using junior high and high school students. This study and the next one by Samuel are inadequate. Although two examiners were used from each race, only one examiner conducted the testing. Thus, race of examiner effects were limited to one person. Study I employed 208 black and 208 white students equally divided by sex and ranging from 12–16 years of age in the Sacramento, California, school system. In addition to race of examiner and race of subject, test atmosphere and expectation were investigated.

Atmosphere was manipulated by telling students their scores would be evaluated against norms—the evaluative condition—or by asking them to relax since no one would be compared or evaluated—the gamelike condition. Also, the examiner wore a coat and tie and used a conspicuously placed timer in the evaluative sessions. Expectation was manipulated by informing students that academic records had been reviewed and based on their class grades they should expect either an easy time (high expectation condition) or a difficult time (low expectation condition) with the tests.

Sessions were conducted by two pairs of examiners—both examiners in one pair were black, while both examiners in the other pair were white. The examiners were in their twenties but no history of testing or training experience was given. Sessions were divided into two parts with the first examiner manipulating test atmosphere and expectation and administering the Object Assembly subtest of the WISC. Next the second examiner, blind to previous manipulations, was introduced, the first examiner left and students were administered the Picture Arrangement, Picture Completion, Block Design and Coding subtests. Both pairs of examiners assessed white and black students.

Data were analyzed using a $2 \times 2 \times 2 \times 2 \times 2$ (race of examiner $\times$ race of student $\times$ sex $\times$ atmosphere $\times$ expectation) analysis of variance procedure. Since results are complex, only findings pertinent to the current topic are discussed. There was a significant main effect ($p < .001$) for student race with white students' IQ scores (M = 111.13) higher than black students' scores (M = 96.67). There was a significant main effect ($p < .01$) for examiner race with students of both races scoring higher with the white examiner (M = 106.76) than the black examiner (M = 101.04). Also, there was a significant atmosphere $\times$ expectation interaction ($p < .02$) with high expectations yielding high scores in the evaluative atmosphere and low expectations yielding high scores in the gamelike atmosphere.

Finally, there was a complex, marginally significant ($p < .10$) race of examiner $\times$ sex of student $\times$ atmosphere $\times$ expectation interaction. The authors suggest that this four-way interaction resulted largely from black males and white females outperforming their counterparts when given low expectations by the white examiner in the evaluative atmosphere. There were no other significant examiner race $\times$ subject race interactions.

Samuel et al. (1976) replicated Study I using 104 black male and 104 white male students from the same school system and age groupings. That is, data from Studies I and II were combined in a $2 \times 2 \times 2 \times 2 \times 2$ factorial design (race of examiner $\times$ race of student $\times$ atmosphere $\times$ expectation $\times$ replication) to test for significant interactions involving the replication factor (i.e., Study I vs Study II). In general, results of the earlier study were replicated. The main effects for race of examiner and race of subject and the atmosphere $\times$ expectation interaction were again significant and consistent with the previous pattern of scores.

The authors noted that IQ scores were somewhat higher in Study II than Study I and attributed this difference to a higher level of socioeconomic status (SES) among Study II students. For this reason, the male data from both studies were combined and partitioned by SES based on previously gathered demographics (parent occupation and home values in student neighborhoods). A $2 \times 2 \times 2 \times 2 \times 2$ factorial design (race of examiner $\times$ race of student $\times$ SES $\times$ atmosphere $\times$ expectation) resulted in a significant SES main effect ($p < .01$). The high SES group

(M = 109.52) scored approximately seven points above the low SES group (M = 102.72). Also, there was a significant examiner race × student race × SES × atmosphere interaction ($p < .01$) which was somewhat attributable to high SES blacks performing well in the evaluative condition with the white examiner. Again, there were no significant two-way interactions involving examiner and student race.

In 1977, Samuel reported a complex study that investigated background and contextual influences on adolescents' performance of intelligence tests. A total of 416 female adolescent students under 16 years of age (208 black, 208 white) participated in the study. All adolescents completed the performance subtests of the Weschler Intelligence Scale for Children (WISC). The contextual and background variables investigated in the study were: (1) test atmosphere (evaluative or game-like), (2) tester expectation (high or low), (3) race of the tester (black or white), (4) gender of the tester (male or female), (5) race of the adolescent (black or white), and (6) socioeconomic status of the adolescent's background (above or below the group median). Because this study is large and complex, it will be necessary to restrict our focus to those variables crucial to the present review.

When the adolescent arrived at the office provided by the student's school for testing, he/she encountered either one of two male examiners, or one of two female examiners. There were four teams of examiners: two male teams (both examiners black, both examiners white), and two female teams (both examiners black, both examiners white). All examiners were graduate students or advanced undergraduate students in psychology. The first examiner manipulated experimental atmosphere and the adolescent's expectations about his/her performance on the tests, and administered the Object Assembly subtest of the WISC. The second examiner, who was blind to the adolescent's previous treatment, administered the remaining WISC performance subscales.

Results of statistical analyses were complex, and only the most relevant outcomes will be summarized. First, there were statistically significant main effects for (a) gender of examiner (female examiners elicited higher scores than did male examiners), (b) SES background of adolescent (higher SES adolescents obtained higher scores than lower SES adolescents), and (c) race of adolescent (white adolescents obtained higher scores than did black adolescents). Second, there was no statistically reliable effect for race of examiner. There was, however, a significant gender of examiner × race of examiner interaction. The adolescents exhibited higher achievement with the female examiners than with the male examiners, but this effect was more pronounced when the examiners were black (i.e., the black female examiners elicited the highest WISC scores from the adolescents). Third, there was no statistically reliable race of adolescent × race of examiner interaction.

Summary of Inadequate-Complete Studies

The three studies reviewed in this section included both races and examined a number of variables (i.e., SES, atmosphere, expectation) in addition to race of examiner. One study (Samuel et al., 1976) found a significant but complex four-way interaction involving examiner race, examinee race, SES, and atmosphere. Another study (Samuel, 1977) reported an examiner race × examiner gender interaction. The only study (Scott, et al., 1976) with a significant two-way race of examiner × race of subject interaction found that white children performed best with a black examiner and black children best with a white examiner. Viewed as a group, these studies do not provide strong or consistent support for the hypothesis that examiner's race systematically affects intelligence test performance.

Other Studies

Quay (1971; 1972; 1974) conducted a series of studies focusing on the impact of using standard English and non-standard English (Negro) dialects when administering the Stanford-Binet. In all cases, only black children were examined and only black examiners were employed. Thus, these studies did not test race of examiner effects. However, the findings may have implications for the race of examiner literature.

In her first study (1971), Quay examined the Stanford-Binet performance of 100 (55 males and 45 females) children, aged 3–8 to 5–3, who were enrolled in a Philadelphia Head Start Program. Two black male examiners administered the Stanford-Binet varying the type of reinforcement (verbal praise and candy) and the dialect used (standard or non-standard English). An analysis of variance found no significant group differences and no significant interactions.

In her second study (1972), Quay worked with a "severely deprived" group of children (25 males and 25 females) enrolled in a Head Start Program in a northeastern city. The children ranged from 3–11 to 5–3 years, with a mean of 4–7 years. A black female, proficient in English and Negro dialect, examined the children in one of the two dialect conditions. Again, there were no significant group differences in Stanford-Binet scores.

Finally, Quay (1974) examined 104 lower class black children of both sexes attending the third and sixth grades in a Philadelphia grammar school (Note: Based on the text it appears an equal number of males and females were examined.) A black female examiner administered the Stanford Binet in one of two dialects—English or Negro. ANOVA procedures produced a significant main effect for age ($p < .01$) with younger children scoring highest. No other significant effects were found. In sum, Quay's studies do not support the hypothesis that dialectical differences are a major factor suppressing black IQ scores.

Research by Hall, Reder, and Cole (1975) appears to contradict Quay's findings. Hall et al. (1975) tested the story recall of New York City children using standard and non-standard English dialects. Thirty-two children (16 white and 16 black) approximately 4.5 years old listened to stories supplemented with pictures (cf., E. J. Bartlett, 1971). The 16 black children were part of a Head Start Project in central Harlem and the 16 white children were from a Manhattan nursery school.

Children participated in two sessions—one with a white experimenter and one with a black experimenter. They listened to two stories in each session—one in each dialect. Stories were assigned using a Latin Squares design such that story presentation was counterbalanced within each cell. Results indicated that whites performed better than blacks in standard English vernacular ($p < .05$) and blacks performed better than whites in non-standard English vernacular ($p < .05$). The authors concluded that dialectical variations are most influential when new material must be assimilated and recalled. It should be pointed out also that the Hall et al. (1975) study differs from the Quay (1971; 1972; 1974) studies methodologically. Possibly, dialectical differences have greater impact in informal social situations, for example, story telling, than in more formal situations such as test administration.

Adequate Designs

Incomplete Sampling

Smith and May (1967) reported a study of examiner effects in which race of examiner was considered. A total of 96 white children, all enrolled in an "Operation Head Start" project in a metropolitan area in the southeastern United States, participated. Their mean age was 72 months. (Note: Details of this study were incorrectly reported in Jensen's (1980) review.) All children completed, in the school setting, the Stanford-Binet (Form L-M) and the Illinois Text of Psycholinguistic Abilities (ITPA). These tests were administered by six examiners (two black: one female, one male; four white: two females, two males) who were either guidance counselors or psychology graduate students. All six examiners were given two weeks of training on the administration of the tests used in the study. The study does not report how children were assigned to examiners. The results indicated that children's performance was affected by different individual examiners on both tests, but there were no reliable effects for race of examiner. For example, the black female examiner elicited higher scores on the Stanford-Binet than did one of the white males, but did not differ from the other white male examiner, or any other examiner. Different examiners may elicit different performance, but this study offers no reliable evidence for systematic race of examiner effects.

In an unpublished doctoral dissertation, Pelosi (1968) investigated race and sex of examiner effects on the intellectual performance of 96 adult black males, enrolled in anti-poverty work experience. All participants took a test battery consisting of (a) six subtests from the Wechsler Adult Intelligence Scale (WAIS): Information, Comprehension, Vocabulary, Digit-Symbol, Block Design, Picture Arrangement; (b) the Purdue Pegboard, and (c) the IPAT Culture Fair Intelligence Test. Pelosi varied warmth, gender, and race of examiner. There were three examiners within each race-gender category. The study does not report how examinees were assigned to examiners.

Pelosi found no evidence that race of examiner significantly influenced examinees' performance. On all but one subtest, examinees tested by white examiners received slightly higher scores than examinees tested by black examiners, but these differences were small and non-significant. It is likely, however, that the relatively small number of subjects per cell led to statistical tests of very low power.

Goldsmith (1969), in an unpublished dissertation, examined the digit symbol (WAIS subtest) performance of 120 male and 120 female black students (ages 17–19) enrolled as freshmen or sophomores in a New York City community college. Students were part of the College Discovery Program (an aid program for economically and culturally disadvantaged students). They were contacted by mail and asked to participate. Upon agreeing, they were randomly assigned to a black or white examiner. Four examiners were used—a black male, a black female, a white male, and a white female. Examiner training was not addressed.

During testing, students were subjected to one of three incentive conditions—praise, criticism, or control. Analysis of variance procedures indicated that students performed significantly better when tested by a same-sexed examiner. Also, students did best in the praise condition. There was no significant effect due to race of examiner.

Costello (1970) investigated the influence of race of examiner, pretest sensitization, and an examiner's knowledge of previous test outcomes on black children's performance on the Peabody Picture Vocabulary Test (PPVT). A total of 62 black preschool children (30 females, 32 males) from the west side of Chicago, Illinois, participated in the pretest sensitization phase. Children were randomly assigned to a pretest or a no-pretest condition. The randomness of the assignment, however, is questionable, given that 38 children received the pretest treatment but only 24 children received the no-pretest treatment. In the pretest condition, children were given both the Stanford Binet (SB) and the PPVT, while in the no-pretest condition, children were given tests of preschool skills. All children were given the PPVT four months later, and the SB nine months later.

Twenty-nine children were tested by two black examiners, while 28 children were tested by two white examiners. All examiners were teachers from the children's school, but no examiner tested children from his/her own classroom (Gender of examiners was not reported). Four months later, children were retested either by a white psychologist or by white teachers from their own classrooms. There were no statistically significant effects for any of the variables investigated.

Turner (1971) examined the impact of mixed-race situations on CVC trigram learning. Subjects were 80 white males (ages: 13–15 years) in the ninth grade class of an all male parochial school (presumably in New York City). The school faculty was all male and all white. Students were classified as belonging to the three lowest SES groups according to the Warner, Meeker, and Eells (1949) parental occupation classification system.

Eight experimenters (ages: 20–25 years), unaware of the hypothesis, conducted the testing—two black males, two black females, two white males, and two white females. The procedure involved presentation of a list of eight CVC trigrams (three-letter nonsense syllables) on a memory drum. Subjects saw the list nine times after initial presentation and received positive feedback ("You are doing very well") after the first, third, and fifth trials.

Analysis of variance procedures revealed a significant main effect for race of tester ($p < .05$). Students remembered more trigrams with the white tester ($M = 39.07$) than the black tester ($M = 36.35$). There were no significant effects due to sex of tester or tester race $\times$ tester sex interaction. The authors conclude that same race testers are more likely to motivate their subjects. This conclusion is not fully justified, however, since only white male parochial school children participated in the study.

In an unpublished doctoral dissertation, Dill (1971) investigated the effects of the race of examiner and kinds of reinforcements (positive, neutral, negative) delivered to children during the course of test administration. A total of 120 black second grade children enrolled in four public schools in the Harlem area of New York City participated. Six undergraduate male students (3 black, 3 white) administered the Torrance Test of Creative Thinking (Form A, verbal and figural activities) and the Lorge-Thorndike Test (Form A, primary level). Children were randomly assigned to reinforcement conditions and examiners. Results indicated that positive reinforcement led to significantly higher scores on certain creativity subscales, that there was a significant positive correlation between the composite creativity score and the intelligence score, but that race of examiner did not have a significant effect on children's performance on the creativity test. Results for the Lorge-Thorndike test were not reported.

Moore and Retish (1974) investigated the effect of examiner's race on black children's performance on the Wechsler Preschool and Primary Scale of Intelligence (WPPSI). A total of 42 children (28 black males,

14 black females), all enrolled in "Head Start" or a day care program in an industrialized area in the midwestern United States, participated. Their mean age was 60.37 months. All children took the WPPSI twice over a two-week period. For a random half of the boys and a random half of the girls, a black examiner administered the first test and a white examiner administered the second test. For the other half of the sample, a white examiner administered the first test and a black examiner administered the second test. A total of six inexperienced female examiners (3 black, 3 white) were given a 13-hour training program on test administration. When the verbal scale was analyzed, three statistically significant effects were found: (1) an "administration" main effect—children performed better at the second testing than at the first, (2) an "administration" × sex interaction—females gained more in the second testing than did males, and (3) race of examiner main effect—black examiners elicited higher mean verbal scores than did white examiners. When the performance scale and full scale scores were analyzed, only the main effect for examiner race was significant. In the full scale in particular, the black examiners elicited higher mean scores ($M = 93.21$) from black children than did white examiners ($M = 87.74$).

Summary of Adequate-Incomplete Studies

When a study uses several examiners of two races, but uses subjects of only one race, it is not possible to obtain a race of examiner × race of subject interaction. When a researcher using such a study can reject a null hypothesis, he/she can only conclude that examiners of one race or another elicit different levels of responses from the particular children in the sample. Of the seven studies reviewed in this section, two studies found statistically reliable race of examiner effects. One study, Turner (1971) found that white children remembered more trigrams when tested by a white examiner than by a black examiner. Whether black children would have remembered more from the white examiner also, or whether these trigram memory effects can be generalized to intelligence testing contexts is not known. In the second study, Moore and Retish (1974), black examiners elicited higher performance from black children than did white examiners on an intelligence test. Again, it is unclear whether black examiners would have elicited higher performance from white students also, due to the incomplete nature of the design. Taken as a whole, these seven studies can provide at best only mixed support for the hypothesis that an examiner's race has a systematic influence on intelligence test takers' performance.

Complete Sampling

Abramson (1969) investigated the influence of race of examiner on children's performance on the Peabody Picture Vocabulary Test (PPVT).

A total of 201 children (88 white, 113 black) kindergarten and first-grade children from New York City schools participated. Mean age of the children was not reported. The examinees were two white and two black neighborhood women who were working in the school as paraprofessionals. These women were selected from a larger pool of women, based on a supervisor's recommendation that they worked well with children. All examiners were trained in the use of the PPVT. There was simple random assignment of children to examiners.

Abramson reported significant main effects for race of examiner, race of child, and a significant race of examiner × race of child interaction, but observed that the effects were too small to be of much "practical" significance. It should be noted, however, that Abramson used the wrong error term in computing his analyses of variance. Since he did present a full summary table, it is possible to analyze the results correctly. When the correct analyses are performed, the significant main effects and interactions disappear. In sum, when the correct analyses are performed, Abramson found no evidence for an examiner's race influencing children's performance on the PPVT, in either first grade or kindergarten.

In an unpublished doctoral dissertation, Dyer (1970) examined several sources of "unwanted variance" in the test performance of black and white college students. Race of examiner was considered one potential source of "unwanted variance." Examinees were paid volunteers attending predominantly black or predominantly white colleges in the southern United States. The tests used were standardized measures of logical reasoning ability, widely used as selection tests by industry. All students were tested three times at two-week intervals, to assess practice effects. Half the students were tested by a black administrator, while the other half were tested by a white administrator. The study does not report how students were assigned to test administrators.

Dyer reports that both black and white college students obtained slightly higher scores from black administrators than from white administrators. Differences attributable to race of student were two standard deviations. Differences attributable to the potential "unwanted" sources were approximately ¼ of a standard deviation.

Gould and Klein (1971) investigated the effects of race of tester on the intellectual performance of economically disadvantaged adolescents. The adolescents (46 black, 38 white) attended a special demonstration program at Yale University during the summer of 1967. All students were administered the verbal and abstract reasoning scales of the Differential Aptitude Tests (DAT), the Marlowe-Crowne Social Desirability Scale, and the Edwards Social Desirability Scale. In addition, self- and other ratings were completed. The four examiners (presumably 2 blacks and 2 whites) were of approximately the same age and educational background (all had a minimum of a master's degree).

The DAT was given in a counterbalanced order by the race of the tester. One white and one black examiner administered the verbal reasoning test under timed conditions (30 minutes), and then the abstract reasoning test under untimed conditions. The other white and black examiners administered the abstract reasoning test first under timed conditions, and the verbal reasoning under untimed conditions. Apparently, black and white examiners were "yoked" into pairs.

Gould and Klein found no statistically reliable effect for race of examiner, nor did race of examiner interact with timed versus untimed conditions for the two DAT measures. There were, however, significant main effects for race of adolescent on both verbal reasoning and abstract reasoning. The white adolescents scored higher on both verbal reasoning ($M = 34.97$) and abstract reasoning ($M = 40.76$) than did the black adolescents ($M = 30.33$, and $M = 36.18$, for verbal and abstract, respectively). There was no main effect for race of examiner on the non-intellectual measures, although black adolescents scored higher than white adolescents on need for approval.

There were significant race of examiner $\times$ race of adolescent interactions, but these appeared on non-intellectual attitudinal measures only. For example, all students tended to rate all ethnic groups more positively in the presence of an examiner of another race.

Yando, Zigler, and Gates (1971) investigated the hypothesis that attributes of teachers influence the scholastic performance of lower-class children. The two teacher attributes investigated in this study were rated effectiveness of the teacher and race of the teacher. A total of 12 female elementary school teachers (6 black, 6 white), all from the same school system as the children who participated in the study, were rated by a white school psychologist as being "effective" or "ineffective" in working with children. The psychologist was familiar with the teachers' performance and had access to ratings and judgments made by the teachers' principals. Of the 12 teachers, 6 were judged highly effective (3 black, 3 white) and 6 were judged non-effective (3 black, 3 white). Each teacher was assigned 12 children (6 black, 6 white), "roughly matched" on the basis of gender, MA, and IQ, with whom she was not personally acquainted.

A total of 144 second-grade children (72 black, 72 white), drawn from integrated neighborhood schools in the midwestern United States, participated. All children were judged to be members of lower socioeconomic class families, based on the occupational status of head of household. No child had a previously tested IQ of 85 or lower, nor any gross physical handicaps. An equal number of girls and boys participated.

All participants completed the Peabody Picture Vocabulary Test (PPVT). The examining teacher administered the PPVT, but did not score it. This was done later by the investigators. In addition, measures of interpersonal distance and expected classroom behaviors were collected. Each child's actual classroom behavior, as rated by the child's own teacher, was compared with the examining teachers' expectation of that child's behavior.

Yando et al. (1971) found no evidence that race of examiner influenced children's performance on the PPVT. There were no main effects or interactions associated with race of examiner. There was, however, a main effect for examiner quality: Children obtained higher MA scores when tested by an effective teacher ($M = 7.32$) than by a non-effective teacher ($M = 6.92$). There was also a child's race × child's gender interaction, in which white male children obtained significantly higher scores than the other children. The non-scholastic measures show several main effects and interactions, but their interpretation is complex. For example, white examiners rated all children as significantly more attention-seeking than black examiners, but white children were rated as more attention-seeking than black children. Furthermore, a significant examiner quality × examiner race interaction reflects the fact that examiner race differences appeared only among the effective teachers. In summary, although the results of this study are complex, it is clear that attributes of teacher/examiners may influence children's performance on scholastic tasks, but there is no evidence in this study that the teacher/examiners' race is one of these attributes, when other background attributes of teachers and children are carefully controlled.

Solkoff (1972) investigated the effects of race of examiner on children's performance on intelligence and anxiety scales. A total of 224 children (112 black, 112 white) between the ages of 8 and 11 years, participated. There were an equal number of boys and girls in each group. The black and white children were drawn from different neighborhoods in an unspecified city (presumably Buffalo, N.Y.), but all children fell within the upper-lower to lower-middle class range, based on father's education and occupation. A total of eight inexperienced female examiners (4 black, 4 white) were given intensive training in the administration of the Wechsler Intelligence Scale for Children (WISC), and ran six practice trials with 3 black and 3 white children. Finally, each examiner was observed administering the test twice by the author.

Each child was picked up at his/her home by the same black woman, and transported to the examiner's university office. Each examiner tested 28 children, 14 black and 14 white, with an equal number of boys and girls in each group. Each child provided biographical information, a score for the Sarason Test Anxiety Scale for Children, and a complete WISC, with only the mazes sub-test eliminated. One half of the 224 WISC protocols were scored by three experienced clinical psychologists, all of whom were blind to the race of the child, race of the examiner, or purpose of the study. Because there was "extremely high" interscorer reliability, the remaining 112 protocols were scored by only one psychologist. As a further check on examiner bias, each examiner's administrations were sporadically tape recorded to check on such gross potential sources of bias as suggesting correct solutions or misreading instructions.

In analyzing the results, Solkoff first checked for differences between examiners within race. Since there were no statistically significant differences, further analyses collapsed across examiner within race, producing a 2 × 2 × 2 factorial (race of child × race of examiner × gender of child). There were significant main effects for child's race on all the WISC subscales, except Comprehension, Arithmetic, and Coding. In all instances, the black children scored lower than the white children. There were significant main effects for examiner's race for the Comprehension and Picture Completion subtests. The white examiner elicited lower comprehension and lower levels of picture completion performance than did black examiners. The race of child × race of examiner interaction was significant only on the Information subtest (the interaction was ordinal). Both black and white children received higher scores from the black examiner than from the white examiner. There were no significant main effects or interactions on the anxiety measure.

Solkoff (1974) attempted to replicate his earlier study in another city (St. Louis, Missouri). In the second study, a total of 108 children (54 blacks, 54 whites) participated. The mean age for the black children was 10.12 years, while for the white it was 9.65 years. Four inexperienced female examiners (2 black, 2 white) received a training program on the use of the WISC, using procedures similar to the first study. Each examiner tested both black and white children, and the obtained WISC performances were scored by an experienced clinical pscyhologist who was blind to the race of the child, race of the examiner, or purpose of the study.

As in the previous study, results were analyzed in a 2 × 2 × 2 factorial design (race of child × race of examiner × gender of child). There were significant main effects for children's race on all of the WISC subscales, except Comprehension, Picture Arrangement, and Coding. In all instances, the black children scored lower than white children. There were significant main effects for examiner's race for Comprehension, Digit Span, and Vocabulary. The black examiners elicited higher scores on Comprehension and Digit Span, but the white examiners elicited higher scores on Vocabulary. The race of child × race of examiner interaction was significant on the Similarities and Object Assembly. In both cases, the white children received the higher score with the black examiners, but the black children received the lower score with the black examiners. As in the previous study, there were no significant main effects or interactions on the anxiety measure.

The two studies conducted by Solkoff (1972, 1974) were carefully executed and methodologically sound. Taken together, these studies provide little support for the claim that white examiners systematically depress the intellectual performance of black children or elicit greater test anxiety than do black examiners. There are, nonetheless, inconsistencies between the two studies that make generalizations dangerous. For example, Solkoff (1972) found a significant race of child × race of examiner interaction on the Information subtest only, and indicated both black and white children obtained higher scores with black examiners. But Solkoff (1974) did not find the same interaction for the Information subtest; instead only the Similarities and Object Assembly subtests showed a significant race of child × race of examiner interaction, indicating children obtained higher scores with examiners of another race. Perhaps differences are due to different locations of testing, minor procedural differences, or sampling fluctuations attributable to relatively small sample sizes.

In an unpublished doctoral dissertation, Savage (1971; see also Savage & Bowers, 1972) investigated the effects of race of examiner on children's performance of the Digit Span and Block Design subtests of the Wechsler Intelligence Scale for Children (WISC). A total of 240 children were randomly drawn from either a monoracial black, monoracial white, or multiracial school at each of three grade levels (1, 3, and 5). The children were randomly assigned to one of 20 female examiners (10 black, 10 white). White children scored significantly higher than black children on both tasks, but black children scored significantly higher on the Block Design task (and not Digit Span) with a same-race examiner. There were no interactions with grade level or type of school.

In an unpublished doctoral dissertation, Barnebey (1972) investigated the influence of examiner's race on children's performance on intelligence and behavioral rating scales. A total of 80 third grade children (40 black, 40 white) from two integrated elementary schools were assessed by 20 examiners (10 black, 10 white). Each child was administered the Peabody Picture Vocabulary Test (PPVT), the Coding B subtest of the WISC, and a behavioral rating scale, on two occasions (test-retest). How children were assigned to examiners was not reported. Results were analyzed in a series of 2 × 2 × 2 factorial analyses of variance (race of examiner × race of child × time of test administration). There was a significant effect for time of testing on the coding measure: Children obtained higher scores on the second testing. There was also a significant examiner race × race of child × time of testing interaction, which indicated black examiners elicited higher scores from white children on the second testing. There was no evidence, however, that black children received lower scores from white examiners than from black examiners.

France (1973) investigated the effects of "white" and "black" examiners' voices on children's performance of the Peabody Picture Vocabulary Test (PPVT). Recordings were made of eight male undergraduate students (4 black, 4 white) reading the instructions and questions to the PPVT. Segments from these recordings were then rated by 50 undergraduate students, who perceived 87.5% of the black voices as having "black accents," and 96% of the white voices as having "white accents." These tapes were then used to administer the PPVT to a total of 252 elementary school children (124 black, 128 white). Children were separated from the experimenter by a partition and were unable to see him. The tests were administered solely through the tapes. The author reports a significant race of child × race of voice interaction on the PPVT: White children's scores were affected by the race of the examiner's voice, but black children's scores were not. It should be noted, however, that neither the design nor analysis format are clearly stated in the report, and there appear to be errors in the analysis (e.g., the race of voice × race of child interaction was tested with one and six degrees of freedom).

Wellborn, Reid, and Reichard (1973) investigated the effects of race of examiner of children's performance on the Wechsler Intelligence Scale for Children (WISC). A total of 96 elementary school students (48 black, 48 white) from two rural Florida public schools participated in the study. Six female examiners (3 black, 3 white), all of whom had at least one graduate level course in the administration of individual intelligence tests, assessed the children on the WISC. Each examiner tested an equal number of black and white students. Furthermore, each child was tested by both a black and a white examiner, with a 7-day interval between test administrations. There was a significant main effect for race of child, with black children scoring lower than white children. There was no effect for race of examiner, although children did earn significantly higher scores in the second testing session. Wellborn et al. speculate that these students had been in integrated schools for some time, and exposure to black and white teachers may have reduced the importance of the examiner's race.

Marwit and Neumann (1974) investigated the hypothesis that black and white children may differ in their comprehension of standard English, and this difference may affect children's performance on standardized tests when administered by black and white examiners. A total of 113 second grade children (60 black, 53 white) from St. Louis County (Missouri) public school system participated. Four male undergraduate examiners (2 black, 2 white) administered the test materials. There were two formats for the test materials, standard English and non-standard English forms of the Reading Comprehension section of the California Reading Test for first- and second-graders. The non-standard English form was prepared by asking two St. Louis-born blacks to translate all test materials, including instructions, into the language of the black St. Louis school child. Inter-interpreter agreement was "uniformly high." Children were randomly assigned within race to conditions in a $2 \times 2 \times 2$ design (race of child $\times$ race of examiner $\times$ test format).

There were three significant effects. First, there was a main effect for race of child, with white children receiving higher comprehension scores than black children. Second, there was a main effect for format, with children obtaining higher scores with the standard English format than with the non-standard format. Third, there was a significant three-factor interaction. Black children obtained the highest scores with standard English when tested by the white examiner. There were no comparable differences for the white children. In general, this study offers no support for the hypothesis that black children's performance on standardized tests is attenuated by white examiners, or by the use of standard English testing formats.

Pryzwansky, Nicholson, and Uhl (1974b) investigated the hypothesis that the urban or rural background of children would influence their reaction to examiners of different races. A total of 70 second grade girls from the North Carolina public school system participated. There were 27 black girls (16 from rural neighborhoods, 11 from urban neighborhoods), and 43 white girls (24 from rural neighborhoods, 19 from urban neighborhoods). The mean age was 97.9 and 96.3 months for the black and white girls, respectively. Eight master's level school psychology students (4 black, 4 white) administered the Slosson Intelligence Test to the children. All examiners received a two-hour training session in which test administration and scoring was reviewed. Children were randomly assigned to either a black or white examiner.

Results were analyzed using $2 \times 2 \times 2$ analyses of variance (type of neighborhood $\times$ race of child $\times$ race of examiner). The only significant effect was race of child, with black children scoring significantly lower than white children. There were no significant main effects or interactions with either race of examiner or type of neighborhood background. The authors do report a "trend" for the black examiners to elicit higher scores from black children from urban backgrounds, but this effect is not present for black children of rural backgrounds. In any case, this "trend" was not even marginally significant statistically. Several limitations of the present study should be noted, however. The authors offer no evidence that their samples are representative of children from urban and rural background. Furthermore, the relatively small sample size limits the power of the statistical tests to detect a genuine effect of neighborhood or examiner, had such effects actually been present.

In an effort to overcome the problems of small sample sizes and low statistical power that limited previous research, Jensen (1974) examined the influence of race of examiner on children's test performance using a sample of approximately 9,000 children. The sample consisted of the total white and black elementary school (grades kindergarten through six) population of the Berkeley, California, Unified School District. All classes in 17 schools were tested, but the 11% of the school population who were Oriental or other ethnic minorities were excluded from the analyses. The total school population involved in the study was 60% white and 40% black. The child's ethnicity was determined from the child's school records, which included the parent's statement of the child's race.

A total of 20 examiners, all of whom had at least a bachelor's degree in psychology or education, administered the tests. There were 12 white (10 women, 2 men) and 8 black (6 women, 2 men) examiners. All examiners were given manuals of instructions for test administration to study prior to three all-day training sessions on the use of individual tests. The training sessions were intensive, and the importance of strict adherence to standard instructions and time limits were stressed. The assignment of examiners to schools and classes was random within race of examiner. Random assignments were made on a day-to-day basis, to assure that all examiners had an equal chance of testing in all schools. Every school received both black and white examiners.

All children completed the following measures: (1) the Verbal IQ and Non-verbal IQ from the Lorge-Thorndike Intelligence Test, (2) the Figure Copying Test (Ilg & Ames, 1964), (3) the Listening-Attention Test, (4) Memory for Numbers Test, and (5) Speed and Persistence Test. A wide variety of tests were used because it was possible that different kinds of tests were sensitive to examiner effects in different degrees. It is possible, for example, that the race of the examiner is more likely to influence a child's motivation and persistence that his/her short-term memory.

Results were analyzed in a series of separate 2×2 analyses of variance, with race of examiner nested within race of child. The main effects for race of examiner were based on unweighted means. To facilitate comparisons across grades and across tests, all differences were expressed in sigma units. In every case, the sigma unit was the standard deviation of test scores within the particular grade and particular test; variance due to race of examiner, race of child, and their interaction was excluded.

Analyses of the Lorge-Thorndike Intelligence test revealed several significant effects. First, there was a statistically significant main effect for race of examiner on Non-verbal IQ, but only in grades one and two. For children in these two grades, white children scored significantly higher with white examiners and black children scored significantly higher with black examiners. The race of examiner effect was not significant (i.e., less than $\frac{1}{5}$ of a standard deviation), and the direction of the effect is not consistent from grade to grade. Second, there was a statistically significant race of examiner main effect on Verbal IQ, with both black and white children performing significantly better with white examiners than with black examiners. Again, the effects are not consistent from one grade level to another. Third, there was a significant main effect for race of child, with black children consistently scoring lower than white children at all grade levels.

Analyses of the Figure Copying Test revealed a small, but significant, effect for race of examiner. The effect was not systematic or consistent from grade to grade (e.g., white examiners elicit higher performance from white children at grades three and four, but black children show no comparable effect). The main effect for race of child was consistently significant at all grade levels.

Analyses of the Speed and Persistence tests revealed the largest race of examiner effects in the present study, with differences amounting to half a standard deviation or more. The white examiners consistently elicited higher scores than did black examiners at all grade levels.

Analyses of the Listening/Attention and Memory for Numbers tests revealed the smallest race of examiner effect. This was anticipated because the examiner served only to proctor the administration of tape recorded instructions. Again, the race of examiner effect was small and non-systematic. The race of child effect was consistent and significant at all grade levels, with white children receiving higher scores than black children.

Based on his data, Jensen (1974b) reached several conclusions. First, the magnitude of the race of examiner effect on cognitive tests is small and unsystematic, relative to other factors. The slight race of examiner effect did not consistently favor children of one race or the other. Second, the race of examiner effects have more influence on measures of motivation than on measures of cognitive ability. For example, the race of examiner had considerable influence on children's performance on the persistence task, but a much smaller influence on the Lorge-Thorndike test. Third, the results of the present study are consistent with most other studies in the literature that have failed to find significant, systematic race of examiner effects on cognitive ability tests. In sum, the present study provides no support for the hypothesis that children's performance on standardized intelligence tests are systematically influenced by the race of the examiner administering the test.

In an unpublished doctoral dissertation, Abercrombie (1975) investigated the hypothesis that contextual factors influence preschool children's task performance. A total of 80 five-year-old boys (40 black, 40 white) participated. Four male college students (2 black, 2 white) served as examiners. The contextual factors examined were examiner's race and examiner's use of social reinforcement. All children completed a matching to sample task, and productivity, accuracy, and time at task were measured. There is no description of how children were assigned to examiners. Results revealed a significant race of examiner × race of child interaction on the productivity measure. Black children completed more pages of the task than did white children when the examiner was white. There was also a social reinforcement × race of examiner interaction, which indicated that children spent less time on task when praised by a black examiner than when praised by a white examiner.

Ratusnik and Koenigsknecht (1977) investigated the hypothesis that children's performance on intelligence tests was influenced by the child's family socioeconomic class level and by the race of the examiner. A total of 144 preschool children (72 blacks, 72 whites) ranging in age from four years three months to five years ten months participated in the study. Children within each racial group were classified as being in either the lower- or middle-socioeconomic group, based on the Warner, Meeker, and Eells' (1949) Social Status Index. The children were drawn from geographically separate and racially homogeneous areas of metropolitan Chicago, Illinois. All children completed the Goodenough Drawing Test (1926) as the index of intelligence as one part of a preschool day care screening activity. Six graduate speech and language clinicians (3 black, 3 white) were trained in the administration of the drawing test, and then examined an equal number of children from each of the four groups (black-lower SES, black-middle SES, white-lower SES, and white-middle SES). The authors report that the order in which the children were tested was randomized. Once the data had been collected, identifying information was removed and the drawings were coded by a speech clinician who was blind to the child's group membership.

The authors analyzed the results for black children and white children in two separate 2 × 2 analyses of variance (socioeconomic group × race of clinician). The authors report that black children received significantly higher scores from black clinicians than from white clinicians, but there was no interaction with the child's socioeconomic status background. The authors report no comparable statistically significant effect for white children. It should be noted, however, that the authors seem to have analyzed their data incorrectly. Since the authors report means and standard deviations for each group on Table 1 (Ratusnik & Koenigsknecht, 1977, p. 11), it is possible to recompute analyses. Consider the means and standard deviations for the lower SES black children examined by both groups of clinicians: For the black clinicians, $M = 108.63$, $SD = 15.80$, while for the white clinicians, $M = 98.61$, $SD = 13.17$. Assuming the design was between-subjects, the resulting t-value is 1.43, which is not statistically significant even with a one-tailed test. When a similar analysis is performed on the middle-SES black children, we again find a non-significant t-value for black versus white clinician. Thus, the means reported by Ratusnik and Koenigsknecht (1977) do *not* support their interpretation that black children obtain significantly higher scores on intelligence tests from black examiners. In previous reviews of this article, the mismatch between the reported data and interpretation was overlooked (e.g., Jensen, 1980, p. 602).

Summary of Adequate-Complete Studies. The fifteen studies reviewed in this section investigated the potential influence of race of examiners, as well as many other ancillary variables, by using subjects of two races, examiners of two races, and two or more examiners within each race. Of the fifteen studies in this section, only seven found statistically reliable evidence for a race of examiner × race of subject interaction. In these seven, no systematic pattern emerged: One found evidence of the examiner effect on personality measures but not on intellectual measures (Gould & Klein, 1971); one found that both black and white children received higher scores from a black examiner, but only on one subscale (Solkoff, 1972); one found black examiners elicit higher performance from white children but not black children, but only on two subscales (Solkoff, 1974); one found black children perform the block design, but not digit span, at higher levels with a black examiner (Savage, 1971); one found white children were influenced by an examiner's voice, but black children were not (France, 1973); one found that black children obtain higher intelligence scores from a white examiner using standard English than a black or white examiner who uses non-standard English (Marwit & Neumann, 1974); and finally, one found statistically significant but very small race of subject × race of examiner interactions, but these were more pronounced on motivational measures and only at certain grade levels, (Jensen, 1974b).

Taken as a whole, these studies do not show a consistent, systematic relationship between the race of examiner and person's performance on intelligence tests. This becomes particularly apparent in the large studies (e.g., Jensen, 1974b) in which several factors are investigated simultaneously. In the Jensen study, for example, the race of examiner influenced children in one pattern at one age, but in a different pattern at another age. Furthermore, the magnitude of the examiner effect was small, relative to other effects. In sum, these studies offer almost no evidence that an examiner's race systematically alters performance on intelligence tests.

Other studies. The following empirical studies do not directly investigate the hypothesis that an examiner's race influences performance on intelligence tests, yet they are relevant to the general issue of race of examiner effects. Several of these studies were reviewed in Shuey (1966), but are reported here for the sake of completeness.

Kennedy and Vega (1965) investigated the effects of race of examiner, school grade level, intelligence level, and type of social reinforcement (praise, blame, control) on black children's performance on an oddity discrimination task. A total of 324 black children in grades 2, 6, and 10 from a rural area in Florida participated. Six male psychology graduate students (3 black, 3 white) served as experimenters. Results revealed a significant race of examiner × child's grade level × type of social reinforcement interaction. Blame from white examiners had a more detrimental effect on black children's performance than did blame from black examiners. At the sixth grade level, however, the white examiner's blame had a less pronounced effect.

Katz, Roberts, and Robinson (1965) investigated the hypothesis that black students may find a white examiner more drive-arousing than a black examiner. Deriving predictions from the Yerkes-Dodson Law, they predicted that when a digit symbol task is described to black subjects as nonintellectual the presence of a white tester will facilitate performance more than will the presence of a black tester on a relatively easy version of the task. On medium and hard versions, however, this relationship will be reversed. Furthermore, Katz et al. predicted that on the version of the task that showed the greatest advantage to the white tester relative to the black tester, describing the task as an intelligence test would lower the score obtained from the white tester and raise the score obtained from the black tester.

A total of 184 black male undergraduates from Fisk University were paid volunteers. Subjects were assigned to either a white or a black adult male experimenter based on a complex pre-test matching procedure in order to produce equivalent groups. It is not clear from the report how many examiners of each race were employed.

Results were generally not consistent with predictions. First, there was a statistically significant task difficulty × race of examiner interaction. Black and white examiners elicited equivalent performance, except for the hardest task, at which the white examiner elicited higher performance than did the black examiner. Second, when the task was described as an intelligence test, subjects tested by a white examiner performed less well than when the task was described as a motor test. However, the intelligence test description did not significantly facilitate the performance of subjects tested by the black examiners. The authors note that the net effect of describing a task as an intelligence test is to eliminate differences attributable to race of tester. Finally, there were no statistically significant differences between subjects tested by black and white examiners on self-rated stress, or concern about doing well.

Baratz (1967) investigated the effects of race of examiner, type of instructions, and type of social comparison on self-reported anxiety. A total of 120 black Howard University undergraduates (67 females, 53 males) were tested in classroom groups. One white male and one black male psychology graduate student served as experimenters. Subjects were randomly assigned to conditions in a 2 × 2 × 2 design (race of examiner × instruction: intelligence test vs. attitude test × social comparison: predominantly black colleges vs. predominantly white colleges). In the intelligence test conditions, the subjects' intelligence was made salient, while in the attitude conditions, subject's feelings were made salient. In the social comparison conditions, subjects in the predominantly black colleges condition were told their responses would be compared with students at Fisk, Morgan State, and Howard, while in the predominantly white college conditions subjects were told their responses would be compared with students at Harvard, Yale, and Princeton. In fact, all subjects were asked to complete the Test Anxiety Questionnaire (TAQ) developed by Mandler and Sarason (1952).

An analysis of variance revealed two significant effects. First, there was a race of examiner main effect, with black students reporting greater anxiety when tested by the white examiner ($M = 34.08$) than by the black examiner ($M = 30.48$). Second, there was a marginal instruction $\times$ social comparison interaction, which the author does not discuss. The reliability of Baratz's results, however, may be questioned on at least three grounds: (a) there was only one examiner of each race, confounding race with acquaintanceship, teaching history, etc., (b) Katz, Roberts, and Robinson (1965) did not find a comparable examiner effect in self-rated anxiety in their larger study, and (c) the absolute magnitude of the difference is quite small.

Katz, Henchy, and Allen (1968) investigated race of examiner effects in terms of social approval seeking and stereotypes about black and white adults. A total of 148 black males ranging in age from 7 to 10 from low-income neighborhoods in a large northern city participated in the study. Four adult males (2 black, 2 white) examined the children in several community centers where the children were enrolled in summer programs.

Groups of children of about equal size and matched on age were assigned to various testers. Each child was asked seven questions from a specially adapted version of the Marlowe-Crowne Social Desirability Scale (Crandall, 1966), and was then administered a 10-item paired associates task. The task was presented to each child eleven times in differential serial orders, and the child was instructed to call out the name of the present object as it was shown. Half of each tester's children received approval ("You're doing very good. I'm pleased with how good you're doing") or disapproval ("You're doing very poorly. I'm very disappointed with how bad you're doing.") The feedback was given at the end of the third and fifth trials.

Results were analyzed in a $2 \times 2 \times 2 \times 3$ design (approval feedback $\times$ need for approval $\times$ race of tester $\times$ blocks upon performance scores). First, there were two statistically significant main effects: (a) approval feedback-performance was generally better with approval than with disapproval and (b) black examiners elicited higher performance than did white examiners. Second, there was a significant approval feedback $\times$ need for approval $\times$ race of examiner interaction. Children with high need for approval perform less well when receiving disapproval from a white examiner than when receiving approval from a black examiner. Children with low need for approval perform poorly in all conditions except in the black examiner-approval condition. Third, there was a significant race of tester × trial blocks interaction, reflecting that the black children learned at a faster rate from black examiners than from white.

Sherwood and Nataupsky (1968) took an approach considerably different from previous researchers who investigated the race of examiner issue. The authors collected biographical background data from 82 researchers who had collected data on comparative studies of black and white intelligence. Sherwood and Nataupsky found 7 biographical variables that differentiated researchers who reported no difference between blacks and whites in intelligence, relative to researchers who reported differences. These variables were: age when research was published, birth order, whether the researcher's grandparents were American or foreign born, mother's educational level, father's educational level, childhood in urban or rural setting, and undergraduate scholastic standing. Some of these outcomes are intuitively reasonable (e.g., relatively few researchers whose grandparents were foreign-born reported data implying blacks were "innately inferior"), while others are very difficult to interpret (e.g., researchers who report blacks are "innately inferior" have well-educated mothers). While the results of this study are interesting, they shed little light on the race of examiner effect as it pertains to the assessment of individual persons.

Summary and Conclusion

The importance of examiner bias as an issue related to the validity of intelligence tests was noted at the beginning of this paper. As previously mentioned race of examiner has been viewed as a source of error adding imprecision to the measurement of intelligence. Moreover, it has been hypothesized that race of examiner is one factor contributing to the mean differences found between black and white intelligence test scores.

The present paper reviewed the empirical literature relevant to race of examiner effects in intelligence testing. Specifically, evidence was reviewed concerning the hypothesis that white examiners systematically elicit lower intelligence test scores from black examinees than do black examiners. The tabulation on pages 186 and 187 provides a summary of the 28 studies conducted since 1966 related to this hypothesis. The second column of the tabulation indicates whether a significant race of examiner main effect (for incomplete designs) or race of examiner × race of subject interaction (for complete designs) was found, and whether the results were consistent with the hypothesis. Results that were significant but opposite to the hypothesis are so indicated. Significant higher-order interactions are not summarized. Of the 28 studies, 11 reported statistically significant race of examiner main effects or race of examiner × race of subject interactions. However, seven of these 11 studies have methodological inadequacies, have apparently analyzed their data incorrectly, or report outcomes contrary to the hypothesis (Abercrombie, 1975; Carringer & Wilson, 1974; Moore & Retish, 1974; Ratusnik & Koenigsknecht, 1977; Scott et al., 1976; Solkoff, 1974; Turner, 1971).

Taken as a whole, these studies provide no consistent or strong evidence that examiners of different races systematically elicit different performance in black and white examinees. On the other hand, these studies do not lay to rest the issue of examiner's race. The finding that in some cases same race examiners enhance test performance while at other times suppress performance and a number of higher-order interactions involving other variables such as expectations or SES produce more questions than answers. If examiner's race affects performance under what circumstances does the effect consistently occur? And will the effect be positive or negative? In sum, the empirical literature does not support the hypothesis that race of examiner is a factor contributing to mean differences in black and white intelligence scores. However, the issue is too complex to be resolved by testing this simple hypothesis.

One source of confusion stems from the quality of the research in the area. It is difficult to draw firm conclusions about the work that has been already done, due to serious methodological shortcomings. As previously noted, inadequate designs and adequate designs with incomplete sampling leave many alternative explanations. Furthermore, lack of appropriate control groups, instances of unbalanced treatment presentations, possible non-random assignment of examinees to treatment conditions, and inappropriate data analysis all make unequivocal interpretation of the literature difficult.

Beyond the issues noted above, the narrow conceptualization of the race-of-examiner problem has resulted in oversimplified research questions and a disjointed, often contradictory, body of literature. Previous work has generally been atheoretical, or loosely derived for some vague hypothesis. Some rigorous theoretical work is sorely needed if research in the area is to progress.

This review points to several areas in need of conceptual clarification. If examiner's race is a factor influencing test performance, precisely what aspect of the examiner's race is the causal agent presumed to influence examinees? Is the critical variable prejudice, status difference, evaluation apprehension, familiarity with persons similar to the examiner, dialect differences, empathy, or some combination of these? Historically, examin-

Study	Race of Examiner Effect	Sample	Test
Adequate Incomplete			
Smith and May (1967)	No	White children n = 96	Stanford-Binet (S-B) and Illinois Psycholinguistic
Pelosi (1968)	No	Black adult males n = 96	WAIS subtests, Purdue Pegboard and Culture Fair
Goldsmith (1969)	No	College students male and female n = 240	WAIS subtest
Costello (1970)	No	Black children male and female n = 62	Peabody Picture Vocabulary Test (PPVT) and S-B
Turner (1971)	Yes	White adolescent males n = 80	CVC trigrams
Dill (1971)	No	Black children n = 120	Creative Thinking and Lorge-Thorndike
Moore and Retish (1974)	Yes	Black children male and female n = 42	WPPSI
Adequate Complete (Note: samples in this section include both races)			
Abramson (1969)	No	Children pre-school and grammar school n = 201	PPVT
Dyer (1970)	No	College students n = ?	Reasoning ability
Gould and Klein (1971)	No	Adolescents n = 84	Differential Aptitude Test
Savage (1971)	Yes	Children grammar school n = 240	WISC
Yando, Zigler, and Gates (1971)	No	Children grammar school n = 144	PPVT
Barnebey (1972)	No	Children grammar school n = 80	PPVT and WISC
Solkoff (1972)	Yes	Children 8–11 yrs male and female n = 224	WISC
France (1973)	Yes	Children n = 252	PPVT
Wellborn, Reid, and Reichard (1973)	No	Children grammar school n = 96	WISC

Study	Race of Examiner Effect	Sample	Test
Jensen (1974)	Yes	Children pre-school and grammar school n = 9000	Lorge-Thorndike Figure Copying Listening-Attention Number Memory Speed and Persistence
Marwit and Neumann (1974)	No	Children grammar school n = 113	California Reading Test: (English and Non-English standard versions)
Pryzwansky, Nicholson and Uhl (1974)	No	Children grammar school females only n = 70	Slosson IQ Test
Solkoff (1974)	Yes opposite	Children age and sex composition similar to 1972 n = 108	WISC
Abercrombie (1975)	Yes opposite	Children pre-school males only n = 80	Experimental task
Ratusnik and Koenigsknecht	Yes (No, with re-analysis)	Children pre-school n = 144	Goodenough Drawing Test
Inadequate Incomplete Caldwell and Knight (1970)	No	Black children grammar school n = 15	S-B
Carringer and Wilson (1974)	Yes	Black children male and female grammar school n = 48	Puzzle task
Inadequate Complete (Note: samples in this section include both races) Samuel, Soto, Parks, Ngissah and Jones (1976) a—Study I	No	Junior high and high school students n = 416	WISC subtests
b—Study II	No	Junior high and high school students n = 208	WISC subtests
Scott, Hartson and Cunningham (1976)	Yes	Preschool children n = 65	Iowa Preschool Development
Samuel (1977)	No	Adolescents females only n = 416	WISC

er's race has been treated as a "macro-variable," with all white examiners seen as interchangeable and all black examiners seen as interchangeable. Future research must be more analytic.

Similarly, race of subject has been viewed as a singular construct. However, previous research has indicated that examinee's age is one factor moderating the race of examiner effect (e.g.: Jensen, 1974b). It is likely that other examinee characteristics such as testing experience also mediate the race of examiner effect.

To some extent research in the area has been correlational in nature. That is, same-race situations were hypothesized to be associated with good test performance and cross-race situations with poor test performance. It may be more fruitful to focus on the processes involved in same-race and cross-race situations, and the subtle social process variables mediating any race-of-examiner effects (e.g., self-fulfilling prophecy processes).

Another area in need of conceptual clarification revolves around the nature of the assessment task itself. Researchers have used a wide variety of tests (e.g., WISC, PPVT, marble dropping). It would be naive to assume these tests all measure the same cognitive ability to the same extent. Also, it is probable that the test itself will affect examiner-examinee interactions. Some tests require an apparatus; others are paper and pencil; and others largely oral. Some are highly structured and others projective in nature. Are some kinds of tasks more likely to elicit race-of-examiner effects than are other kinds of tasks? At present, there is no clear answer.

Previous research suggests that test format will moderate the race of examiner effect (e.g., Marwit & Neumann, 1974). However, most research in the area has not asked precisely what intellectual ability is being measured, how it is being measured, or how race of examiner might confound the measurement process. It seems that a taxonomy of tests susceptible to race of examiner effects is needed before any generalizations can be made.

Perhaps the best orientation race of examiner research can take is not to be concerned with race of examiner, per se. Rather, the concern should be more generally placed on the social psychology of the testing situation. This orientation provides a broader conceptual framework and emphasizes the interactive nature of examiner characteristics, examinee characteristics, and contextual situations. Even if no studies found race of examiner effects, it would be unwise to conclude that race of either examiner or examinee are inert in the testing situation, or that in some situations, or at some times, white examiners cannot suppress the scores of black examinees. The critical issue is the precise specification of those circumstances in which such suppression might occur.

X

Doctoral Dissertations

R. Travis Osborne

In previous compilations of studies of testing Negro intelligence doctoral dissertations have been reviewed along with published articles and books. Because of the almost countless number of doctoral degrees awarded between 1964 and 1978, we decided to devote an entire chapter to the review of dissertations reporting the results of testing Negro intelligence. In addition to being listed in this chapter, a very limited number of dissertations are reviewed elsewhere.

More than 400 unpublished dissertations thought to involve the testing of Negro intelligence were examined for this chapter. Those that were speculative or conjectural without test data were not included. Since the dissertations were not published and are not readily available, findings of each study are summarized and pertinent comments of the authors are quoted.

The reader will find some research conducted under less than optimal conditions. To be included the study had to report the age, race, sex of the subjects, the names of the tests administered, and the means and standard deviations of relevant test scores. When on a few occasions the reviewer thought the study of sufficient interest and relevance, one or more of these criteria were waived. For example, one doctoral candidate investigated the response time in computerized psychological tests. Ages were not given nor was the racial background of subjects. This study was included in our review.

The 89 dissertations reviewed were conducted at 49 different institutions, most of which are in the East and South.[1] However, Colorado and Utah chipped in with one study each. Three were written in California, one each at Stanford, University of California at Los Angeles, and the California School of Professional Psychology. Forty dissertations were

---

[1] Following Shuey's system we have classified as Southern the 11 states of Alabama, Arkansas, Florida, Georgia, Louisiana, Mississippi, North Carolina, South Carolina, Tennessee, Texas, and Virginia.

written in 15 southern universities. Most of the remainder were conducted in the East or Midwest. Only one school, Florida State University, contributed more than five studies. Three universities, Michigan, Georgia, and Mississippi State, all shared second honors contributing five dissertations each.

To pinpoint the geographic origin of participating subjects was not as easy as locating the university where the study was conducted. Our best guess is that subjects of 36 dissertations were from the South. In addition, there were eight southern probables. In at least two cases subjects from more than one region were participants in a single study. For example, one candidate compared Dearborn Heights, Michigan, blacks with an equal number of Mound Bayou, Mississippi, blacks on the Peabody Picture Vocabulary Test.

Altogether over 50 different psychological tests were included in the test batteries. This number does not include projective tests, school achievement tests, personality scales, and original tests administered along with the tests of mental ability, which are our primary concern. In the list of 50 tests the several forms of the Wechsler Scales are counted as separate tests. However, alternate forms of the same tests are counted as only one test. Because of the wide age range of subjects and the variety of tests used in the dissertations, no effort will be made to combine or compare results of two or more studies. In some cases only raw scores were reported, in some cases IQs, and in other cases z-scores were given or confidence levels were shown. If the confidence levels were reported in the study, they will be the basis of comparison. If confidence levels were not given, the differences will be converted to sigma units; that is, the difference divided by standard deviation.

For easy reference, dissertations are listed alphabetically by author and are numbered from 1 to 89. In the summary they are referred to by number or by author. For discussion the dissertations are grouped as the published articles were: preschool, school children, high school, and so forth.

Preschool

Seventeen dissertations reviewed involved 2,130 black and 466 white preschool children who were tested with one or more of 20 psychological tests (Table X–A). Participating preschoolers were drawn from kindergartens, anti-poverty programs, Head Start programs, and clinics. Children of two studies were in the first grade at the time of the investigation, but they had previously attended a Head Start program.

If there is a general theme running through the preschool research, it is the evaluation of Head Start programs. There were four such studies. Findings for Head Start enthusiasts are not encouraging. One study

Table X–A
Dissertations Involving Preschool Pupils

Diss. No.	University	Region	Diss. No.	University	Region
2	Miss. State	S	47	Michigan	N
13	Fla. State	S	59	Florida	S
17	Fla. State	S	63	Virginia	S
22	Alabama	S	69	Georgia	S
32	Houston	S	71	Kent State	N
33	Tennessee	S	80	St. John's	N
41	UCLA	N	83	Florida	S
42	Georgia	S	88	Catholic U. of Am.	N
43	Fordham	N			

(diss. #2) reported gains for blacks who attended Head Start but attributed the significant black-white differences in scores on the Illinois Test of Psycholinguistic Abilities to possible cultural bias of the ITPA. A multi-racial Head Start study by Hutton reported insignificant overall differences for Anglos, blacks, and Mexican-Americans on the Slosson.

Carpenter suggested that the Head Start program is not long enough to prepare disadvantaged children to read. In a longitudinal study Emanuel found Head Start attenders achieving above non-attenders in the second grade but not in the first or third.

The remaining dissertations have little in common except the subjects were black and white preschool children. Many dissertations have novel designs and interesting explanations for the findings. One doctoral candidate (diss. #17) administered the WPPSI in "standard English" and in "black English." Neither the race of the examiner nor the language of presentation attenuated the black-white score differences. Another experimenter (diss. #69) designed a "naturalistic" test from schoolroom and playground material. On the "naturalistic" test the author reported that black students consistently scored one standard deviation below white students.

When material reward was tried on lower SES pupils, it did not decrease black-white differences. The author (diss. #63) said, "White subjects under both reward conditions showed a mean IQ increase of 9.95, whereas Negro subjects under both reward conditions showed a mean IQ increase of 5.18" (p. 66).

Asymptomatic lead poisoning was investigated by one doctoral candidate (diss. #43) who suggested that school performance may be affected by an undetected, asymptomatic, increased blood lead burden.

In a multi-racial study of blacks, whites, and Lumbee Indians, Yen found no significant differences between the races, but Lumbee Indian boys outscored both black and white boys. The difference was only a fraction of a point, but the direction of the difference is unique. There were no Indian girls in the study.

Regional differences in mental test performance were investigated by McAdoo who compared Dearborn Heights, Michigan, blacks with a similar group from Mound Bayou, Mississippi. A significant difference was found favoring Michigan blacks.

School Children

Over 60,000 public school children were subjects for 43 doctoral dissertations. The research was not concentrated in any one region or single university. There were 17 dissertations written in 11 southern universities; 26 in 19 northern schools. Thirty different institutions were represented; the University of Michigan, New York University, and Mississippi State University contributed three dissertations each to this section (Table X–B).

Questions under investigation concerned many of the school-related problems of the 1960's and 1970's. The 43 studies fall into six broad areas. Six dissertations examined some aspect of the effect of racial segregation on mental ability and school achievement. Four were multiracial studies; and four investigated the race of the examiner as it related to student test performance. Two doctoral candidates were concerned with achievement and intelligence of children from broken homes. Eight candidates found nonsignificant black-white mental ability differences or found that black test means were equal to the national norms. The remaining 19 dissertations in general supported the published findings of Shuey (1966), Jensen (1969a), McGurk (1975), and Osborne (1980). All reported significant black-white differences or reported that blacks scored approximately .75 standard deviation below national norms. All 19 studies are reviewed in this section, but only one, that of Strauch, will be discussed.

The zeal of six candidates who investigated the effects of different aspects of segregation on IQ and achievement is only matched by the paucity of positive findings. One investigator (diss. #66) said unequivocably that "The interpretation of this analysis is that I.Q. need no longer be regarded as a variable in achievement" (p. 24). Another candidate (diss. #73) found a significant increase in IQ in racially mixed schools but added this disclaimer: "This study, because of its non-experimental nature, leaves itself open to criticism of its internal validity. One factor which may be operating here is regression" (p. 55). Altogether these six studies will bring little comfort to those who believe that black children perform better in school and earn higher IQs if they attend predominantly white schools.

Findings from the four multi-racial studies (diss. #4, 45, 67, and 74) are ambivalent. One reported Hispanics to be highest in intelligence but not significantly so. Three found that Anglo-Americans outperformed both blacks and Spanish surnamed groups. Blacks were outscored by

Table X–B
Dissertations Involving School Children

Effects of Segregation on Mental Ability and School Achievement			Multi-Racial Studies of Test Performance		
Diss. #	University	Region	Diss. #	University	Region
1	Michigan	N	4	Texas	S
11	Wayne State	N	45	NYU	N
24	N. Texas State	S	67	Cal. Sch. of Prof. Psy.	N
51	Miss. State	S	74	Houston	S
66	So. Miss.	S			
73	S. Florida	S			

Race of Examiner and Test Performance			Black Test Performance Equal to White or Equal to National Norms		
Diss. #	University	Region	Diss. #	University	Region
19	NYU	N	8	Florida	S
20	Michigan	N	12	Washington	N
77	Georgia	S	16	Fordham	N
78	Florida State	S	21	Fordham	N
			31	Florida	S
			58	Miss. State	S
			61	Michigan	N
			75	Penn. State	N

White Test Performance Significantly Above Blacks or Blacks .75 SD Below National Norms			Mental Ability and School Achievement of Children from Broken Homes		
Diss. #	University	Region	Diss. #	University	Region
14	Alabama	S	18	Catholic U. of Am.	N
15	Indiana	N	57	Minnesota	N
23	Ohio State	N			
25	N. Texas State	S		Race × Sex × Ability Interaction		
27	N. Carolina	S				
28	Columbia	N	Diss. #	University	Region
34	Colorado State	N	68	Penn. State	N
39	Columbia	N			
46	Stanford	N			
48	George Washing.	N			
50	St. John's	N			
54	Temple	N			
62	Miss. State	S			
70	Wisconsin	N			
79	NYU	N			
84	Georgia	S			
86	Kentucky	N			
87	N. Carolina	S			

the other two groups in three of the four dissertations. These findings came as no surprise to Sternberg who said, ". . . no other results can be expected when the bulk of the sample upon which the test was standardized was composed of Caucasians" (p. 39).

The effect of parental deprivation on the intelligence and achievement of black school children was the primary purpose of two dissertations. The jury is still out. Deutch found at each age there was no difference in measured intelligence between father-deprived and non-deprived boys, and the same finding occurred irrespective of the intelligence test used. Phillips reported:

> The results of the present study support the assumption that father-absence is a salient determinant of the responsiveness of young Negro boys to the race of adult reinforcing agents and the type of social reinforcer dispensed in a task situation. (p. 66)

Among the 89 dissertations reviewed, there are at least seven in which the race of examiner was one of the primary variables studied. Only four will be mentioned here because the others involved a different age-group or the race of examiner was of secondary interest to the investigator. In dissertations #19, 20, and 77, the experimenter's race was not found to significantly influence students' test performance. However, Vega reported that response differences elicited as a function of the examiner variable were due to the anxiety generated in the Negro children by the close interpersonal contact with the white examiners in the experimental situation.

To examine the race, sex, ability interaction, Strauch obtained test results for over 50,000 students from three separate data banks: Project Talent, Pennsylvania State Department of Education, and the WISC-R standardization data. Strauch said,

> The main conclusion of the investigation was that the sex × race interaction is not a real phenomenon, insofar as mental ability is concerned. The inconsistency of the findings, along with the failure of most analyses to demonstrate a significant interaction, led to the conclusion that chance was probably the main determinant of the ability interaction. (p. ix)

His failure to find a significant sex-race interaction led Strauch to suggest,

> The fact that the interaction occurs in the settings of college attendance and occupational status suggests that these occurrences are due not to an ability interaction but to environmental attributes. Among those suggested were racial prejudice and a history of greater

achievement motivation in the black female than the black male. (p. ix)

While racial prejudice may be a factor in the insignificant race-sex interaction, it would be difficult to ascribe to racial prejudice the consistent 1 SD differences in black-white ability for both sexes on all three tests. Both the magnitude and direction of the black-white difference is nothing less than remarkable when it is considered that more subjects were involved in this one dissertation than in all the other 88 combined, and the three projects consolidated by Strauch were conducted independently over a period of almost two decades by a state, a federal, and a private agency.

Not all candidates found the black-white differences reported by Strauch. Some reported insignificant racial differences while others investigated possible environmental causes for the black shortfall on mental ability tests. In a study conducted at Fordham in 1969, Collins found that many of the negative traits attributed to Negro youth were not found to apply to the sample group. The groups were more alike than different in intelligence scores; median IQ for the total group was 101. She concluded, "the Negro parochial school children of the study sample were not typical of the Negro children described in the literature" (p. 168).

In another Fordham dissertation Duva studied the effects of asymptomatic lead poisoning and psychological functioning of school-age urban children. "Results indicated that there were significant differences between groups on the variables of verbal and performance IQ, test hyperkinesis, and educational levels of both the mother and the father" (p. 80). Although significant IQ differences were found between the normal and elevated lead groups, the difference was not found in school achievement, leading Duva to suggest

that the lack of significance for variables of academic achievement and classroom performance may have been due to the confounding effects of compensatory reading and mathematics programs in the Newark Public Schools, raising academic skills of most children to similar grade levels. (p. 81)

In a 1973 dissertation written at the University of Florida, Hutson found young black children to perform slightly above the national average on the WISC Similarities test. By way of explanation, he suggested that disadvantaged Negro children are in general more adept at the kind of thinking required on the Similarities subtest, but he could not adequately test this hypothesis.

Raggio, writing a dissertation supervised at Mississippi State, found test taking stimulation (practice) on WISC Performance subtests enhanced disadvantaged blacks by about 14 IQ points, from an IQ of 75 to 89. Practice increased advantaged whites by only 2 IQ points, from 107 to 109.

J. S. Ryan, in a 1975 dissertation supervised at the University of Michigan, selected 49 black school children from a pool of 987. Twenty-five of the 49 children tested were intellectually superior. Thirty-eight of the 49 children were above average intelligence.

Comparing pre- and post-test scores on the Pictorial Test of Intelligence for 65 Title IX black children, Tillery found a mean post-test IQ of 97. Between testings the gain on the Binet was 6 points; pretest IQ = 86; post-test, 92.

Black and white children in two Florida Special Education Centers were studied by Bowles at the University of Florida in 1968. The WISC was given first in 1965 and then again 20 months later. Bowles' findings are spectacular, especially if his 1968 study can be replicated. He reported:

> All of the Negro subjects had scored in the retarded range prior to being assigned to special education. Many of these subjects scored in the range of normal on the retest, leading to the conclusion that the test instrument was not as valid for identifying retardation in the Negro subjects as it was in identifying retardation in the white subjects. (p. 40)

Burnes, studying at Washington University, investigated the relationship between WISC scores and non-intellective factors for children of two SES groups and two races. He reported important differences for Full Scale IQ, Verbal IQ, and Performance IQ for the SES groups, but he found no significant racial differences.

High School

High-school students were subjects for 13 dissertations. Participants were 1,500 blacks, 500 whites, and 100 with Spanish surnames. Seven studies involved only blacks; one was multi-racial (Table X–C).

The effect of desegregation on school achievement and IQ was the concern of four candidates. The findings were contradictory. Klein, in a dissertation written at the University of South Carolina, found it both ways. "The integrated school setting is neither educationally deleterious nor educationally beneficial for Negro students . . ." (p. 49). Elsewhere he wrote:

1. The academic achievement of matched groups of integrated and segregated Negroes did not differ significantly.
2. The academic achievement of matched groups of integrated white and integrated Negro students did not differ significantly.
3. The academic achievement of matched groups of segregated Negro students and integrated white students did not differ significantly.
4. The academic achievement of Negroes attending an integrated school was significantly greater in specific subject areas than that of an unmatched group of Negroes attending a segregated all-Negro school. (pp. 49–50)

Robertson found that attending a segregated junior high school negatively affects grades of both Negro and white students who subsequently attend an integrated high school. However, he found no differences in objective measures of achievement that could be ascribed to segregation.

In terms of number of subjects and design, a study by James is probably the best in this group. James examined three levels of desegregation. One group of students remained in predominantly Negro schools, one group was forced by court order to move to a predominantly white school, and the third group voluntarily transferred to white schools. After one year James found no significant differences in self-concept or in mean IQ between the groups.

Finding self-concept lower for the experimental (integrated) group than for the control (segregated), Bienvenu suggested:

It is, perhaps, the belief of many Negro youth and their families that the advantages of transferring into a white school are questiona-

Table X–C
Dissertations Involving High School
Students

Diss. #	University	Region
5	Florida State	S
6	Florida State	S
7	Texas	S
10	N. Carolina	S
26	Ball State	N
29	Pennsylvania	N
35	So. Mississippi	S
38	S. Carolina	S
44	Oklahoma	N
49	Houston	S
60	Michigan	N
76	Columbia	N
82	Columbia	N

ble when one is confronted with unacceptance, social isolation, re-
buffs, stiff academic competition and loss of status with one's own
racial peer group. (pp. 73–74)

Two investigators found mental test performance of black high-school
students to be within the normal range. Manning reported a mean Binet
of 91.5 for 50 black tenth-graders. Trotman found 50 blacks to have a
mean Otis-Lennon IQ of 100.2; whites earned 112.2 on the same test.
Trotman concluded,

> The results cannot provide definitive or conclusive evidence in support
> of any of the major interpretations of the IQ difference between
> the races; they are, however, pertinent to any attempt to disentangle
> the variables involved in the IQ controversy. (pp. 48–49)

The seven remaining dissertations involving high school students all
showed black-white differences with whites consistently scoring 10 to
15 IQ points above blacks on the same test.

College

College students were subjects for nine dissertations. With two exceptions, all found black-white differences to approximate 1 SD regardless
of whether the test was the American College Test, the Scholastic Aptitude Test, or the Primary Mental Abilities Test. At the college level
the differences appear to be more convincing than in grade or high school
(Table X–D).

There were two studies in this section that reported insignificant racial
differences. O'Leary, in a dissertation supervised at the University of
Maryland, found little difference in learning ability of white and Negro
students on a relatively simple learning task such as paired associates.

Table X–D
Dissertations Involving College Students

Diss. #	University	Region
9	Tennessee	S
30	Georgia State	S
36	Miss. State	S
52	Utah	N
53	Maryland	N
56	Maryland	N
64	Pittsburgh	N
72	Oklahoma	N
89	Connecticut	N

O'Leary's finding would seem to support the Jensen hypothesis of attenuated black-white differences on Level I tasks.

Comparing white students from Oklahoma State with blacks from Oakwood College, Huntsville, Alabama, Tate found the black sample of over 250 scored higher than whites on the Henmon-Nelson intelligence test. Tate also reported that Negroes in Social-Status Index I and II achieved as well as their white counterparts.

Adults Not In College

Among the 89 dissertations there were only four that involved adult subjects not in college. One (diss. #3) examined core city black illiterates. A second (diss. #37) compared black and white homeless men found in welfare shelters in New York City (Table X–E).

The two remaining studies of adults investigated the effect of race or color of the examiner on test performance. Pelosi found insignificant differences for both race and sex of examiner. Pelosi concluded that the direction of the difference clearly contradicts the proposition that white examiners have a deleterious effect on test performance of Negro subjects.

In a Florida State University dissertation Winokur was interested in verbal reinforcement and color of examiner on concept formation. No examiner difference was found.

Delinquents or Criminals

Delinquents and criminals were subjects for three dissertations. The number of subjects involved was small, only 348 altogether. Results were not remarkable and were well summarized by Worthington's comments in dissertation #85. Worthington found results to be in agreement with previous studies of delinquents who scored below their non-delinquent contemporaries on IQ tests (Table X–F).

Following, listed in alphabetical and numerical order, are summaries of the 89 dissertations reviewed in this chapter. The information common

Table X–E
Dissertations Involving Adults not in College

Diss. #	University	Region
3	SUNY—Buffalo	N
37	Yeshiva	N
55	Syracuse	N
81	Fla. State	S

Table X–F
Dissertations Involving Delinquents or
Criminals

Diss. #	University	Region
40	Ill. Inst. of Tech.	N
65	Missouri	N
85	Georgia	S

to most studies include: number, age, and race of the subjects; location of the study; names of tests used; results; and comments of the author. Tests are given by name or acronym. All tests are identified in Appendix A where the reader will find the MMY volume and page reference for each standard test. The primary source for a new or original test is also cited in Appendix A.

#1   Aberdeen, F. D. *Adjustment to desegregation: A description of some differences among Negro elementary school pupils.* The University of Michigan, 1969.
      SUBJECTS AND METHOD OF SELECTION: Ss were 40 Negro school children who were bussed from black to predominantly white schools. They were in grades K–3 in 1965 in Ann Arbor, Michigan.
      TEST: Lorge-Thorndike Intelligence Test.

RESULTS:	N	Mn	SD
Boys	17	94.9	11.6
Girls	23	100.4	13.8

      COMMENT OF AUTHOR: For the segregated Negro child, intelligence as measured by current standardized instruments does not provide valid information on which to base educational decisions for the child.

#2   Arnoult III, J. F. *A comparison of the psycholinguistic abilities of selected groups of first grade children.* Mississippi State University, 1972.
      SUBJECTS AND METHOD OF SELECTION: From a base of 2,300 first-grade children of Jefferson Parish, Louisiana, 60 Ss who had attended the Head Start program and 60 Ss who had not attended the program were selected. Only children with WISC or Binet IQs between 95 and 105 were selected for the experiment.
      TESTS: Stanford-Binet Intelligence Scale (L-M), Wechsler Intelligence Scale for Children (WISC), and Illinois Test of Psycholinguistic Abilities, Revised, 1968.

RESULTS: Illinois Test of
Psycholinguistic Abilities
Age-Scores

	N	Mn	SD
Black Ss in Head Start	30	66.5	5.6
Black Ss not in Head Start	30	57.2	7.8
White Ss in Head Start	30	75.3	4.9
White Ss not in Head Start	30	69.1	9.2

COMMENT OF AUTHOR: Improvement in the psycholinguistic age-scores for first-grade Negro children was associated
with their attending the Head Start program.

#3   Berke, N. D. *An investigation of adult Negro illiteracy: Prediction
of reading achievement and description of educational characteristics of a sample of city core adult Negro illiterates.* State University
of New York at Buffalo, 1967.
SUBJECTS AND METHOD OF SELECTION: Ss were 10
black men and 32 black women, classified as illiterate (score
of less than 1.9 grade equivalent), from adult education classes.
Their ages ranged from 22 to 66 with a median age of 46.
TESTS: Wechsler Adult Intelligence Scale, Leiter Adult Intelligence Scale, Davis-Eells Games, and Experience Inventory constructed by the author.
RESULTS: WAIS Full Scale IQ: Mn, 67.9; SD, 9.7.
COMMENT OF AUTHOR: None of the Wechsler Adult Intelligence Scale subtests, or the Leiter Adult Intelligence Scale
subtests, correlated significantly with the criterion variable,
reading gain.

#4   Bernal Jr., E. M. *Concept learning among Anglo, black, and Mexi-
can-American children using facilitation strategies and bilingual
techniques.* The University of Texas at Austin, 1971.
SUBJECTS AND METHOD OF SELECTION: Ss were 192
eighth-grade children from eight schools. There were two
groups of 96, one experimental and one control. Four ethnic
groups were represented: (a) Anglo-American, (b) Blacks, (c)
Mexican-Americans who speak no Spanish, and (d) Mexican-
American bilinguals. Each ethnic group was further broken
down by SES—Upper Middle, Working, and Lower class.
TESTS: Spatial Relations Test from Primary Mental Abilities,
Letters Sets Test (LST), and Numbers Sets Test (NST).
RESULTS: While the author said there were no substantial
differences in IQ scores across treatment groups and no reliable
differences across ethnic groups, the following mean IQs were

reported: control group, Mexican-American (monolingual), 100.5; Mexican-American (bilingual), 100.1; Anglo-American, 106.8; Black, 96.7. For the experimental group the average ethnic IQs were 101.8, 95.6, 101.9, and 96.1, respectively.

COMMENT OF AUTHOR: The unusual pattern of IQ scores across SES may have been caused by some SES misclassification of Ss in this group.

#5 Bienvenu Sr., M. J. *Effects of school integration on the self concept and anxiety of lower-class, Negro adolescent males.* The Florida State University, 1968.

SUBJECTS AND METHOD OF SELECTION: All Ss were from lower SES ninth, tenth, and eleventh grades. The age range was from 13.9 to 18.3. Forty blacks in the experimental group were recent transfers from black to white schools in north Florida. The control group had always attended an all-black school and had remained in the same school.

TEST: California Test of Mental Maturity.

RESULTS: Experimental group mean CTMM IQ = 80; control group mean = 78.

#6 Blair, G. E. *The relationship of selected ego functions and the academic achievement of Negro students.* Florida State University, 1967.

SUBJECTS AND METHOD OF SELECTION: Ss were 462 black students in the ninth grade in Gadsden County, Florida. There were 232 males and 230 females.

TESTS: Cattell Culture Fair Intelligence Test, Metropolitan Achievement Test, Junior-Senior High School Personality Questionnaire, and Index of Adjustment and Values.

RESULTS: Mean CCFIT IQ was 77.5; SD, 19.9.

COMMENTS OF AUTHOR: When statistics were compared with the normal mean of 100, it was obvious that the group was lower in the ability measured by the test. There was hope that this nonverbal test might contribute substantially to the understanding of Negro potential. The principal differences in the findings of the present study and the findings of similar studies using white samples were in the low level of achievement and measured intelligence in the Negro sample.

#7 Boney, J. D. *A study of the use of intelligence, aptitude, and mental ability measures in predicting the academic achievement of Negro students in secondary school.* The University of Texas, 1964.

SUBJECTS AND METHOD OF SELECTION: Random samples of 50 males and 50 females were drawn from each of the tenth and twelfth grades. Ss all came from one Negro school in Port Arthur, Texas. Ninety-seven percent of the Ss had "laboring class" parents.

TEST: California Test of Mental Maturity.

RESULTS:

	CTMM IQ	
	Mn	%ile
10th grade boys	84.2	20
10th grade girls	81.9	10
12th grade boys	83.9	20
12th grade girls	81.4	10

COMMENTS OF AUTHOR: A significant finding of this study was the manner in which the instruments consistently yielded substantial correlations with GPA and with achievement variables of the STEP. Although many of the scores were quite low, the correlations were impressively high.

#8   Bowles, F. L. *Sub-test score changes over twenty months on the Wechsler Intelligence Scale for Children for white and Negro special education students.* University of Florida, 1968.

SUBJECTS AND METHOD OF SELECTION: Ss were 52 Negro and 48 white children from St. Petersburg, Florida, (Special Education Center) and Pinellas Park, Florida, (Special Education Center). The average age of the white children was 11+ years, and the average of the Negro children was 9 years. There were 38 black and 31 white males and 14 black and 17 white females.

TEST: The Wechsler Intelligence Scale for Children was administered in 1965 and again 20 months later.

RESULTS: Race as a single predictor produced significant interactions in which the Negro subjects gained more than did the white subjects in each instance.

#9   Bradley Jr., N. E. *The Negro undergraduate student: Factors relative to performance in predominantly white state colleges and universities in Tennessee.* The University of Tennessee, 1966.

SUBJECTS AND METHOD OF SELECTION: Students were Negro undergraduates attending seven formerly all-white colleges in Tennessee. Of the base group of 583, only 275 had ACT scores on file from fall of 1963 to spring of 1965.

TEST: American College Test (ACT).

RESULTS:

	Mn	ACT %ile Norms 1963–64
Composite	15.1	20.1
English	15.6	19.4
Mathematics	13.6	19.5
Social Studies	15.5	20.3
Natural Science	15.4	20.5

COMMENT OF AUTHOR: Even though their mean performance on the ACT was below the twentieth percentile for national college-bound students, about half of the regularly enrolled Negro undergraduates made satisfactory progress toward baccalaureate degree attainment.

#10 Bridgette, R. E. *Self-esteem in Negro and white southern adolescents.* University of North Carolina at Chapel Hill, 1970.

SUBJECTS AND METHOD OF SELECTION: Ss were from rural segregated schools in North Carolina. A small number of blacks attended white schools with special permission. Tests were administered in three sessions. Although school enrollment remained constant during the experiment, the number of students participating fluctuated. From the subject pool of 350 children, 156 attended all three sessions.

TEST: Otis Quick Scoring Test of Mental Ability (Form Gamma).

COMMENTS OF AUTHOR: The Otis IQ test was administered by the school guidance teachers (one Negro and one white). Racial differences in IQ scores were significant at .001 level. White Ss tended to score above national mean, while Negro Ss scored almost 1 SD below national average. Race of the examiner had no appreciable effect on IQ score. IQ measures did not differ across sex. The single item assessing attitude toward school integration was answered in a pro-integration manner by most of the black Ss, but a few did check pro-segregation responses. White Ss responded to either the mildly or pro-segregation categories.

#11 Burke, B. P. *An exploratory study of the relationships among third grade Negro children's self-concept, creativity, and intelligence and teachers' perceptions of those realtionships.* Wayne State University, 1968.

SUBJECTS AND METHOD OF SELECTION: Ss were 65 third-grade black children enrolled in a de facto segregated Detroit public school. There were 40 females and 25 males

whose parents were primarily middle and upper-middle class.
TEST: California Test of Mental Maturity, Short Form.
RESULTS: This study attempted to assess relationships between intelligence and a number of factors including self-concept and creativity. There was no correlation between intelligence (total, language, or nonverbal) and creativity. Correlation
was very high between teachers' perceptions of creativity and
intelligence. There was no correlation between self-concept and
intelligence. The reviewer found an overall mean IQ of 93.6.
COMMENT OF AUTHOR: Undue reliance on the intelligence
test score alone may result in denying to certain children whose
creative abilities may not be completely revealed by these tests
the opportunity of fully realizing their maximum potential.

#12   Burnes, D. K. S. *A study of relationships between measured intelli-
gence and non-intellective factors for children of two socioeconomic
groups and races.* Washington University, 1968.
SUBJECTS AND METHOD OF SELECTION: Ss were drawn
primarily from children in a large parochial school in a metropolitan area of the midwest. There were 40 white and 38 black
children in grades 1–4 with ages ranging from 8–0 to 8–11.
TEST: Wechsler Intelligence Scale for Children (WISC).
RESULTS: Mean Full Scale IQ for 40 white Ss was 97.8; for
38 blacks the mean was 95.2.
COMMENTS OF AUTHOR: The most basic conclusion one
could make from the comparison of the groups' test scores
was that differences were generally related to a child's socioeconomic status and not his race. In fact, racial differences were
very slight on the subtest scores, and when comparing sums
of scores such as the Full Scale IQ and Verbal IQ, these differences were negligible. On Performance IQ, white Ss were about
5 points higher.

#13   Carpenter, F. A. *A study of the reading achievement of Negro
"Head Start" first-grade students compared with Negro "Non-Head
Start" first-grade students.* The Florida State University, 1967.
SUBJECTS AND METHOD OF SELECTION: The 361 black
Ss in the study were drawn from three elementary schools in
Brevard County, Florida. The experimental group consisted
of all first-grade pupils in the designated schools who had been
in the eight-week Head Start program. The control group was
made up of first-grade pupils who had not been in Head Start.
TESTS: Metropolitan Reading Readiness Test (Form R) and
Stanford Achievement Test (Primary 1 Battery).

RESULTS:		MRR Test		S Ach Test	
	N	Mn	SD	Mn	SD
Experimental Group	193	37.3	12.2	13.9	2.1
Control Group	168	34.8	13.2	13.9	1.9

COMMENTS OF AUTHOR: An 8-week Head Start Readiness program may not have been long enough to adequately prepare disadvantaged children for learning to read. While the Head Start program was of some benefit to the experimental Ss, the planned program during the school year may not have been of a nature to maintain the benefit.

#14   Carroll, I. V. *A comparison of the intelligence quotients of sixth grade children of Negro and Caucasian educators and non-educators.* University of Alabama, 1970.

SUBJECTS AND METHOD OF SELECTION: Group I consisted of seventh-grade students with at least one parent employed as an educator with Mobile, Alabama, School System. There were 28 black males, 18 black females, 28 white males, and 27 white females for a total of 101 black and white students in Group I. Group II consisted of seventh-graders whose parents were not educators but who were in the same school system as Group I. There were 28 black males, 18 black females, 28 white males, and 27 white females for a total of 101 black and white students in Group II. All students must have attended the same school system (Mobile, Alabama) in grade 6. The average age was 11.7 years.

TEST: California Short Form Test of Mental Maturity (administered in Grade 6).

RESULTS: Comparing all children of black educators with all children of white educators on language, non-language, and total IQ, significant differences were found in all comparisons. These differences were in favor of children of Caucasian educators. The group means for language, non-language, and total IQ were 10 to 13 points higher than those of children of Negro educators.

#15   Carwise, J. L. *Aspirations and attitudes toward education of over- and under-achieving Negro junior high school students.* Indiana University, 1967.

SUBJECTS AND METHOD OF SELECTION: Of a total of 439 black junior high-school students at Pinellas High School, Clearwater, Florida, IQ and grade point average data were obtained on 395. There were 154 seventh-graders, 125 eighth-graders, and 116 ninth-graders. It appears this was an all-black school. The students were described as coming from "low socio-economic" or "impoverished backgrounds."

TEST: Pintner General Abilities Test (language series).

RESULTS: Mean IQ, 85.7.

COMMENT OF AUTHOR: High ability students were more favorable than low ability students in answering certain questions about educational aspirations.

#16 Collins, Sister M. A. *Achievement, intelligence, personality and selected school-related variables in Negro children from intact and broken families attending parochial schools in central Harlem.* Fordham University, 1969.

SUBJECTS AND METHOD OF SELECTION: Ss were fourth, sixth, and eighth graders from five parochial schools in central Harlem. Schools in the study were staffed by a religious order founded specifically to educate American Indians and Negroes. Three hundred Ss, 150 boys and 150 girls, all black, were chosen from the three grade levels on the basis of intactness of family.

TEST: SRA Primary Mental Abilities Test.

RESULTS: The results of the study did not support many theories advanced to explain the underachievement of disadvantaged children. Few differences were found between the intact and broken family groups. Many of the negative traits attributed to Negro youth were not found to apply to the sample group. The groups were more alike than different in intelligence scores.

COMMENT OF AUTHOR: The Negro parochial school children of the study sample were not typical of the Negro children described in the literature.

#17 Crown, P. J. *The effects of race of examiner and standard vs. dialect administration of the Wechsler Preschool and Primary Scale of Intelligence on the performance of Negro and white children.* The Florida State University, 1970.

SUBJECTS AND METHOD OF SELECTION: Ss were 56 kindergarten-age children, randomly drawn from "a Negro school" and a "predominantly white school" in Wakulla County, Florida. There were 28 white children and 28 black children.

TEST: Wechsler Preschool and Primary Scale of Intelligence.

RESULTS: Negro children continue to score lower than white children. Negro children did better on verbal subtests than on performance measures. The author found no significant effect of presentation language (standard English vs. black dialect) or race of examiner for either black or white children. Blacks scored significantly below whites. Since both white and black children's performances were below norms (both races were below national average in SES), it was suggested that SES differences, not race differences, were causal. Deprivation must begin before 5 years of age.

COMMENTS OF REVIEWER: This is an important study indicating that race of examiner or language of presentation does not attenuate black-white IQ differences. Race difference appeared even though both groups were alleged to be below national average in SES. There were no individual SES data reported, but the county had per capital income less than $3,700 and was designated by the Federal Government as "totally disadvantaged."

#18 Deutch, J. A. *Paternal deprivation: Some effects upon eight and nine year old Negro boys.* The Catholic University of America, 1969.

SUBJECTS AND METHOD OF SELECTION: The population of this study was comprised of 56 8- and 9-year-old Negro boys selected from those children who participated in round 4 of the Johns Hopkins Study of Prematures.

TESTS: Stanford-Binet, Gesell Development Schedule, and Wechsler Intelligence Scale for Children.

RESULTS:

	Father-Absent Boys			Father-Present Boys		
	N	Mn	SD	N	Mn	SD
Gesell (Age 3–4)	22	91	11.5	23	97	14.8
Stanford-Binet (Age 6–7)	28	89	10.6	28	90	9.1
WISC (Age 8–9)	28	86	11.0	28	87	12.0

COMMENTS OF AUTHOR: At each age there was no difference in measured intelligence between father-deprived and nondeprived boys. The same finding occurred irrespective of the intelligence test used. It is suggested that lower-class Negro fathers do not serve as verbal intellectual resources for their sons.

#19 Dill, J. R. *A study of the influence of race of the experimenter and verbal reinforcement on creativity test performance of lower socioeconomic status black children.* New York University, 1971.

SUBJECTS AND METHOD OF SELECTION: The Ss were 120 black second-grade children enrolled in four public schools in Harlem, New York City. Reinforcement conditions consisted of positive, negative, and neutral statements by the examiner. TESTS: Torrance Test of Creative Thinking and Lorge-Thorndike Intelligence Test, Form A, primary level. RESULTS: 1. Positive reinforcement led to significantly higher scores on the following creativity measures: verbal fluency, verbal flexibility, and verbal total scores. In some cases, scores obtained under the positive reinforcement condition were not greater than scores obtained under the neutral condition. 2. Race of the experimenter, per se, did not have a significant effect on creativity test performance. 3. The interaction of black experimenters and positive reinforcement led to significantly higher scores only for the verbal total creativity measure.

#20 Dukes, P. E. *Effects of race of experimenter, self-concept and racial attitudes in the performance of black junior high school students.* The University of Michigan, 1975.

SUBJECTS AND METHOD OF SELECTION: The Ss, 144 eighth-grade black males, were selected on the basis of their responses to the scales used to assess level of self-concept and racial attitudes.

TESTS: Four tests varying in test requirements were administered—Code, Anagrams, Verbal Recall, and Digit Span.

RESULTS: For the first hypothesis, the experimenters' race was not found to significantly influence students' performance. The second hypothesis was partially supported. Significant F ratios were observed for three of the four tests. However, it was only on the Code test that students' performance was in the predicted direction. On the Code test, Ss with a high self-esteem performed better with black experimenters than Ss with a low self-esteem, while on the other tests, Ss with a low self-esteem performed better with black experimenters.

#21 Duva, N. A. *Effects of asymptomatic lead poisoning on psychoneurological functioning of school-age urban children: A follow-up study.* Fordham University, 1977.

SUBJECTS AND METHOD OF SELECTION: Subjects were 60 black school-age children ranging in age from 5 to 7. They lived in an area of Newark, New Jersey, habituated primarily by low-income, disadvantaged Negro families. The subjects were selected from children attending Martland Medical Center Lead Clinic in Newark, New Jersey. There were 30 children with elevated Pb (lead) levels with a mean age of 79 months and 30 children with a normal serum Pb with a mean age of 78 months.

TESTS: Wechsler Preschool and Primary Scale of Intelligence (subjects 5–6 years) and Wechsler Intelligence Scale for Children—Revised (subjects of 7 years).

RESULTS:

	Lead Level			
	Normal		Elevated	
	Mn	SD	Mn	SD
Age (months)	77.5	9.0	79.1	10.1
School Grade	1.3	.4	1.4	.5
Verbal IQ	91.7	12.1	84.6	12.0
Performance IQ	91.3	11.4	81.1	12.3
Full Scale IQ	89.0	16.1	81.4	12.4

COMMENTS OF AUTHOR: These findings indicated that asymptomatic lead poisoning did adversely affect performance on a standardized intelligence test to a significant degree. These children also showed significantly more hyperkinetic behaviorisms than did normal lead level children. It was suggested that the lack of significance for variables of academic achievement and classroom performance may have been due to the confounding effects of compensatory reading and mathematics programs in the Newark public schools, raising academic skills of most children to similar grade levels. Furthermore, results indicated that parental educational level, rather than socioeconomic status, is the most significant indicator of a child's probability to ingest lead.

#22   Emanuel, J. M. *The intelligence, achievement, and progress scores of children who attended summer Head Start programs in 1967, 1968, and 1969.* University of Alabama, 1970.

SUBJECTS AND METHOD OF SELECTION: Ss were 559 children who completed Cattell Culture Fair Intelligence Test. They were drawn from "two Negro elementary schools."

TEST: Cattell Culture Fair Intelligence Test.

RESULTS: There was no significant difference between Head Start attendees (HSA) and non-attendees (HSN) at grade 1. HSA scored significantly above HSN at grade 2 but not at grade 3.

#23   Emmons, C. A. *A comparison of selected gross-motor activities of the Getman-Kane and the Kephart perceptual-motor training programs and their effects upon certain readiness skills of first-grade Negro children.* The Ohio State University, 1968.

SUBJECTS AND METHOD OF SELECTION: Ss were 121 black male and female first-graders from a Texas elementary school. A control group and two experimental groups (physical exercise-training and motor training) were formed.

TESTS: California Short-Form Test of Mental Maturity (Pre-Primary, K–1) and Metropolitan Readiness Test (Form A) scores taken from school records.

COMMENT OF AUTHOR: It would appear that the changes that took place were due only to chance, and neither the Kephart nor the Getman-Kane training program in gross motor skills was of significant value to increase certain mental processes as measured by the California Test of Mental Maturity and the Metropolitan Readiness Test.

#24 Evans, C. L. *The immediate effects of classroom integration on the academic progress, self-concept, and racial attitude of Negro elementary children.* North Texas State University, 1969.

SUBJECTS AND METHOD OF SELECTION: The Ss were 99 black children drawn from grades 4, 5, and 6 from "a large urban school district." Their distribution was as follows: 28, grade 4; 44, grade 5; 27, grade 6.

TESTS: Pooled results of the Primary Mental Abilities Tests and the Kuhlmann-Anderson Test.

RESULTS: Integrated Ss: Mn IQ = 90.0; SD, 11.5. De facto segregated Ss: Mn IQ = 90.2; SD, 10.4.

COMMENT OF AUTHOR: Direct comparison with normative groups is not necessarily valid; that is, a disadvantaged child with an IQ of 86 is not the equivalent in ability of an advantaged child with similar scores.

#25 Gay, C. J. *Academic achievement and intelligence among Negro eighth grade students as a function of the self concept.* North Texas State University, 1966.

SUBJECTS AND METHOD OF SELECTION: Ss were 207 Negro children, ages 12–15, in the eighth grade. There were 105 boys and 102 girls. Ss attended a segregated junior high school located in a medium-sized metropolitan city. Ss lived predominantly in low-rent housing.

TEST: Otis Quick Scoring Mental Abilities Test—Beta Test, Form A.

RESULTS:

	MN	SD
IQ of Males	86	14
IQ of Females	90	12
IQ of Combined group	88	13

COMMENTS OF AUTHOR: Subjects' intelligence contributed more highly to the subjects' scores on an achievement test than it did to their grade point averages. Speculation might be that the Otis Quick Scoring Tests of Mental Ability do not test adequately the experiences most common to culturally disadvantaged minority groups, while teachers generally adapt subject matter content and teaching methods to experiences and levels of understanding of their students.

#26 Georgi, N. J. *The relationship of self-concept in high school Negro students in Muncie, Indiana to intelligence, achievement, and grade point average.* Ball State University, 1971.
SUBJECTS AND METHOD OF SELECTION: The Ss were drawn from 278 Negro students enrolled in grades 10 and 11 in Muncie, Indiana. One-third of the total population was selected for this study. There were 45 boys and 47 girls.
TEST: Lorge-Thorndike Intelligence Test.
RESULTS: Intelligence test means for males and females were 91.2, SD 13.3, and 92.1, SD 10.2.
COMMENT OF AUTHOR: Self-concepts of Negro students, both male and female, were inter-related with intelligence, with reading achievement, and with grade point average.

#27 Harris, G. R. *A study of the academic achievement of selected Negro and white fifth-grade pupils when educational ability is held constant.* The University of North Carolina at Chapel Hill, 1967.
SUBJECTS AND METHOD OF SELECTION: The Ss were 1,161 fifth-grade pupils, 591 Negro and 570 white, drawn from 18 elementary schools in central North Carolina. The students were placed in one of five IQ levels: 70 and below, 71–85, 86–100, 101–115, and above 115.
TEST: SRA Tests of Educational Ability.
RESULTS: The mean IQ of the total group was 97.8, of the Negroes, 91.6, and of the whites, 104.2.
COMMENTS OF AUTHOR: The white pupils performed significantly better on the SRA Tests of Educational Ability than the Negro pupils. White pupils generally performed better on the achievement tests even when educational ability was held constant. At lower levels of educational ability the achievement of Negro and white pupils was approximately the same. There was a pattern of increasing difference in achievement between Negro and white pupils in each higher level of educational ability.

#28 Harris, H. *The development of moral attitudes in white and Negro boys.* Columbia University, 1967.

SUBJECTS AND METHOD OF SELECTION: The Ss were 100 white and 100 black boys in grades 4–6, ranging in age from 9½ to 11½ with an average of 11 for both groups. They were drawn from six public schools in the New York City area.

TEST: Wechsler Intelligence Scale for Children—Vocabulary.

RESULTS: Level of maturity of moral attitudes was related to race, social class, and intelligence. Negro children in the study were found to be less intelligent than the white children.

COMMENT OF AUTHOR: Generally, children who gave more mature responses on all five subtests of moral attitudes were likely to be more intelligent than children who did not.

#29 Herskovitz, F. S. *The effects of an educational-vocational rehabilitation program upon the self-concepts of disadvantaged youth.* University of Pennsylvania, 1969.

SUBJECTS AND METHOD OF SELECTION: Ss were selected by Philadelphia school counselors and vice-principals for evaluation by the school psychologist. The IQ range for the 88 blacks was 56 to 109 (median, 80), and ages ranged from 15–10 to 18–5. The group had a high incidence of delinquency, gang activity, and mental retardation.

TEST: Wechsler Adult Intelligence Scale.

COMMENTS OF AUTHOR: The overall level of self-esteem did not covary with scores on the WAIS. A modest association was found between scores on the WAIS and reading and arithmetic tests in both pre- and post-test. The relationships of WAIS scores to production earnings and ratings by staff were of lower order; that is, brighter students did not perform work tasks more efficiently and did not get higher ratings for attitude and performance from supervisors. Arithmetic scores were positively associated with both earnings and ratings.

#30 Howell Jr., G. C. *An investigation of response time in computerized psychological tests.* Georgia State University, 1977.

SUBJECTS AND METHOD OF SELECTION: Ss were 98 graduate and undergraduate volunteers from various classes of business administration at Georgia State University. Ages and the number of whites and blacks were not given.

TEST: Primary Mental Abilities Test—Adult Form—Automated Presentation.

COMMENTS OF AUTHOR: Although the coefficients were of only moderate strength, the data indicated a tendency for white Ss to excel over black Ss on each of the six subtests. The poorer performance of black Ss relative to white Ss in this test battery was due to incorrect answers, not speed of performances.

COMMENTS OF REVIEWER: The primary purpose of the study was to investigate response time to a computerized administration of psychological tests. Because of the otherwise weak design, one reviewer suggested that only minimum notice should be made of this study.

#31   Hutson, B. A. M. *Conservation and the comprehension of syntax in economically disadvantaged seven-year-old Negro children.* The University of Florida, 1973.

SUBJECTS AND METHOD OF SELECTION: The Ss were 25 black boys and 25 black girls eligible for free lunches at a public school in a medium-sized southern city. The age range was from 7.0 to 8.8.

TEST: Wechsler Intelligence Test for Children. Vocabulary, Block Designs, and Similarities subtests only. IQs were prorated from these three tests.

RESULTS:

	Mn IQ	SD
Boys	95.4	10.9
Girls	94.5	9.5

COMMENTS OF AUTHOR: Vocabulary and Block Design were both below the national average, but Similarities was slightly above the average. The difference in means would seem to be more likely due either to the type of response required on the test, to specific differences in experiences relevant to each of the tests, or to the pattern of mental abilities in this group of children.

#32   Hutton, J. B. *Relationships between preschool screening test data and first grade academic performance for Head Start children.* University of Houston, 1970.

SUBJECTS AND METHOD OF SELECTION: Ss were 108 children enrolled in a 1967 Head Start program in Harris County, Texas. All Ss were eligible for first-grade enrollment in fall of 1967. There were 20 white, 52 black, and 36 Hispanic children. Their mean age was 75.9 months, standard deviation, 3.9.

TESTS: Slosson Intelligence Test, Sprigle School Readiness Screening Test, and Screening Test of Academic Readiness.

RESULTS: Slosson Intelligence Test

	N	IQ(Mn)	SD
Whites	20	71.3	10.4
Blacks	52	68.2	12.3
Hispanics	36	64.3	9.7

COMMENTS OF AUTHOR: The three ethnic groups did not differ significantly on mean scores when an overall F test was applied. However, the groups did differ on the individually administered tests.

#33   Ilardi, R. L. *Family disorganization and intelligence in Negro preschool children.* The University of Tennessee, 1966.

SUBJECTS AND METHOD OF SELECTION: Ss, chosen from the Child Development Program, were born to a random sample of mothers who applied for prenatal care at John Gaston Hospital, Memphis, Tennessee. Children must have gone through the 4-year program and have had complete records. All Ss were within 3 months of their fourth birthdays. Stable and unstable groups were matched for race, age, and SES.

TEST: Stanford-Binet, 1960 Revision.

RESULTS:

Group	N	Mn IQ	SD
Stable	224	91.7	9.6
Unstable	189	87.5	10.4
Organic	37	81.3	9.8
Total	450	88.8	12.2

COMMENT OF AUTHOR: Large significant differences were found in the IQ scores obtained by the several examiners who administered the tests.

COMMENTS OF REVIEWER: After administration of the Stanford-Binet, Ilardi found that mean IQ of the unstable group was significantly lower than the mean IQ of the stable group. Since the only variable altered was that of family organization, Ilardi concluded that family disorganization affects intelligence test performance, producing a lower IQ score. In addition, this deficit was greater for girls than boys, the reason for this being that in Negro homes the amount of parental interaction for Negro boys is the same in stable and unstable homes. Quality rather than quantity of child-parent verbal interaction was seen as the key here by the author.

#34   Jackson, A. M. *Differential characteristics of reasoning ability in Negroes and whites.* Colorado State University, 1967.

SUBJECTS AND METHOD OF SELECTION: From a base group of 296 junior high-school children from Denver, Colorado, 240 were selected for this study. There were 60 black boys, 60 black girls, 60 white boys, and 60 white girls.

TEST: Otis Intelligence Test.

RESULTS:

	Middle SES		Lower SES	
	Mn	SD	Mn	SD
White	110.0	13.3	101.8	11.4
Black	98.6	11.7	95.5	11.7

COMMENTS OF AUTHOR: The present research was based on the premise that convergent and divergent thinking, as postulated by Guilford (1959), were different cognitive factors and may be directly related to race, sex, and socioeconomic level. Race accounted for more of the variance than the other two factors of SES and sex. White Ss scored significantly higher on the Symbolic Divergent Test and also received significantly higher mean scores when the three tests of divergent thinking were combined. White Ss achieved significantly higher scores on all tests of convergent thinking.

#35   James, D. H. *The effect of desegregation on the self-concept of Negro high school students.* University of Southern Mississippi, 1970.

SUBJECTS AND METHOD OF SELECTION: Ss were 221 black students from nine predominantly Negro high schools in the Mobile, Alabama, area. The students were divided into three groups: A—those remaining in predominantly Negro schools; B—those voluntarily moving to predominantly white schools; and C—those forced by federal judges to move to predominantly white schools. (For post-tests, only 136 students were available.)

TESTS: Otis Beta (pre-test) and Otis Gamma (post-test).

RESULTS:

	Pre-test		Post-test	
	N	Mn	N	Mn
Group A	171	81	96	81
Group B	22	81	15	82
Group C	28	82	25	83

COMMENTS OF REVIEWER: The author found no significant difference at or beyond the .05 level of significance in self-concept among any of the groups for a period of one year. No significant difference was found in mean IQ scores for any of the groups in post-test or pre-test. The highest significant levels were found in areas of Self-Criticism, Family Self, and Personality Integration.

#36   Johnson, G. A. *A study of the relative academic success of Negro junior college graduates who transferred to Negro senior colleges in Mississippi in 1964.* Mississippi State University, 1970.

SUBJECTS AND METHOD OF SELECTION: Ss were 1,013 native students and 412 transfer students from Mississippi Negro junior colleges who were classified as juniors at Mississippi senior colleges in fall term, 1964. Six senior colleges and ten junior colleges were represented.

TEST: American College Test.

RESULTS: ACT scores

	Mn	SD	N	Range
Transfer	10.8	4.0	412	01–22
Native	10.6	4.7	1013	01–31

Note. Entrance scores were mainly ACT; when ACT was not used, SAT, CTMM, or CQT scores were converted to ACT equivalents.

COMMENT OF AUTHOR: No statistically significant differences were found between transfer and native students when factors of ACT scores, academic probation, and academic dropout were employed.

#37   Kean, G. G. *A comparative study of Negro and white homeless men.* Yeshiva University, 1965.

SUBJECTS AND METHOD OF SELECTION: Three groups of 30 Ss each were selected as follows: (a) The Ss for Group N-1 were homeless native American Negro men (mean IQ 88), selected from the Men's Shelter of New York City Department of Welfare. (b) Group N-1 was matched with Group W-1 which was composed of native American white homeless men (mean IQ 88). (c) Group N-1 was matched with Group N-2 which was composed of native American Negro men (mean IQ 94) who had permanent residence and regular employment.

TEST: Information, Comprehension, and Picture Completion subtests of the Wechsler Adult Intelligence Scale.

COMMENTS OF AUTHOR: There were minimal statistical differences among groups; the presence of sociopathological and psychopathological forces were detected to be responsible for homelessness in N-1 and W-1. Sociopathological forces had a more significant role for N-1, psychopathological forces were more predominant causal factors in W-1. Ss had limited intellectual potential and revealed limited abilities in areas requiring a general knowledge of facts and practical judgment.

#38   Klein, R. S. *A comparative study of the academic achievement of Negro 10th grade high school students attending segregated and recently integrated schools in a metropolitan area of the South.* University of South Carolina, 1967.

SUBJECTS AND METHOD OF SELECTION: There were five major groups of tenth-grade Ss: 38 integrated blacks; 38 integrated whites; 38 segregated blacks; 38 segregated whites; and a randomly selected group of 38 segregated black students. Ss were matched for IQ; the group mean IQ was 93. Schools were located in a metropolitan area of South Carolina.

TESTS: Otis Intelligence Test, Cooperative English, Biology, Arithmetic, Algebra I, Algebra II, and Plane Geometry.

COMMENT OF AUTHOR: The integrated school setting is neither educationally deleterious nor educationally beneficial for Negro students, at least over an 8-month period.

#39   Laryea, E. B. *Race, self-concept and achievement.* Columbia University, 1972.

SUBJECTS AND METHOD OF SELECTION: Ss were sixth graders selected from public school districts in New Jersey. District #1 was middle SES with 43 black males, 38 black females, 108 white males, and 120 white females. District #2 was lower SES with 78 black males, 99 black females, 34 white males, and 32 white females.

TESTS: Lorge-Thorndike Intelligence Test (District #1) and short form Test of Academic Aptitude (District #2).

RESULTS:

IQs—Dist. 1	N	Mn	SD
Black boys	43	94.9	14.7
White boys	108	110.3	14.6
Black girls	38	99.7	11.5
White girls	120	110.1	13.1

IQs—Dist. 2	N	Mn	SD
Black boys	78	86.7	13.0
White boys	34	99.1	15.0
Black girls	99	84.5	10.5
White girls	32	94.2	16.2

COMMENT OF AUTHOR: The purpose of the study was not to compare IQ but to extend the research on the relationship between self-concept and achievement to black students in sixth grade and to determine if the relations observed for white students also held for blacks.

#40 Levine, B. L. *Psychometric and demographic comparisons of Negro and white delinquents.* Illinois Institute of Technology, 1969.

SUBJECTS AND METHOD OF SELECTION: The Ss were 165 black and white male delinquents between the ages of 10 and 17 housed at the Illinois Youth Commission, Reception and Diagnostic Center (R & D), Joliet, Illinois. There were 97 black and 68 white Ss. Only first admissions were selected for study. No effort was made to match Ss for education, SES, etc.

TESTS: R & D battery was made up of Lorge-Thorndike Intelligence Test, Stanford Achievement Test, SRA Non-verbal Test, Revised Beta Examination, Wechsler Intelligence Scale for Children, and Stanford-Binet, Form L-M. All subjects did not take all tests of the battery. The Occupational Aptitude Test Battery (OAT), developed by Phil and Harriet Shurrager, was made up of six subtests: (a) Learning Figures, (b) Learning Reversals, (c) Learning Accuracy, (d) Learning Number Accuracy, (e) General Ability, and (f) Shop Tools.

COMMENTS OF AUTHOR: The purpose of the study was to determine whether or not Negro and white male delinquent adolescents would show comparable test performance on the Reception & Diagnostic Center Test Battery and the Occupational Aptitude Test Battery. Results showed that the two racial groups differed significantly on all seven tests. While both groups did poorly overall, the whites did significantly better than the Negro delinquents.

#41 Levinson, F. V. D. K. *Early identification of educationally high risk and high potential pupils: Influences of sex and socio-cultural status on screening techniques.* University of California, Los Angeles, 1976.

SUBJECTS AND METHOD OF SELECTION: Ss were 209 kindergarten children from four Los Angeles public schools. There were 75 Anglo, 39 black, and 95 Spanish-speaking children. Ages ranged from 60 to 81 months, mean was 71 months, SD 4.0.

TESTS: Sprigle School Readiness Test, Peabody Picture Vocabulary Test, Wechsler Preschool and Primary Scale of Intelligence, ABC Inventory, and Bender-Gestalt.

RESULTS: Multivariate analyses showed that for the majority of subtests, Anglo Ss scored higher than black and Spanish-speaking Ss, and that black Ss scored higher than Spanish-speaking Ss. The mean Peabody Picture Vocabulary Test total scores were 59.2 for Anglo Ss; 47.2 for the black Ss; and 27.6 for Spanish-speaking Ss.

#42 Long, M. L. *The influence of sex, race, and type of preschool experience on scores on the McCarthy Scales of Children's Abilities.* University of Georgia, 1976.
SUBJECTS AND METHOD OF SELECTION: Ss had participated in preschool (pilot program to aid children not ready for formal grade 1). All Ss were from the Dublin, Georgia, area. The names of all children enrolled in kindergartens (and non-kindergarten children) were obtained by contacting churches, day-care centers, nursery schools, and via newspaper ads. Parents were contacted by phone for permission to use their children as Ss. For post-test, there were 138 Ss, 35 black and 103 white.
TESTS: McCarthy Scales of Children's Ability and Kaufman Short-form of MSCA.
RESULTS: In comparing the mean raw scores of black children with the mean raw scores of white children on all the MSCA scales, a consistent difference in favor of white children was found on all scales. The differences on the MSCA Verbal, General Cognitive, and Kaufman Short-form MSCA were of such a magnitude as to be deemed significant at the .05 level of significance.

#43 Mac Isaac, D. S. *Learning and behavioral functioning of low income, black preschoolers with asymptomatic lead poisoning.* Fordham University, 1976.
SUBJECTS AND METHOD OF SELECTION: The Ss were 80 black preschool children attending the lead clinic at Martland Medical Center in Newark, New Jersey, between April and August, 1975. The mean age was 65 months.
TESTS: Wechsler Preschool and Primary Scale of Intelligence, Beery-Developmental Test of Visual-Motor Integration, and memory subtests of the McCarthy Scales of Children's Abilities.
COMMENT OF AUTHOR: These findings suggest the possibility that some urban school children, exhibiting patterns of hyperkinetic behavior and impaired school performance and consequently labeled "learning disabled" or "MBD," may in fact be affected by an undetected, asymptomatic, increased blood lead burden.

#44   Manning, E. J. *Intelligence and reading achievement of black disadvantaged tenth grade students.* The University of Oklahoma, 1977.
      SUBJECTS AND METHOD OF SELECTION: Ss were 25 males and 25 females randomly selected from 515 black students in participating school systems with predominantly black populations. The Ss were from the tenth grade with lower socioeconomic status.
      TESTS: Henmon-Nelson Test of Mental Ability (Form A) and Stanford-Binet (Form L-M).
      RESULTS:

	Mn IQ	SD
Henmon-Nelson	89.2	11.1
Stanford-Binet	91.5	14.7

      COMMENTS OF AUTHOR: The mean intelligence scores of the total student population were within normal range on the Stanford-Binet Intelligence Scale and the Henmon-Nelson Test of Mental Ability. However, the mean score was slightly below the mean score for the general population, consistent with research findings for the lower socioeconomic level as a group.

#45   Marsh, L. K. *Self-esteem, achievement responsibility, and reading achievement of lower-class black, white, and Hispanic seventh-grade boys.* New York University, 1974.
      SUBJECTS AND METHOD OF SELECTION: Ss were 303 seventh-graders from New York junior high schools in lower SES areas. Eliminated were those children in slow track classes and those with physical or emotional problems. Also eliminated were youngsters in bilingual classes and those with IQ below 75. There were 101 Ss in each group (black, white, Hispanic).
      TESTS: Goodenough-Harris Measure of Intellectual Maturity and Metropolitan Achievement Test.
      RESULTS:

	IQ		Reading	
	Mn	SD	Mn	SD
White	97.9	14.5	7.3	2.3
Black	96.5	16.5	6.1	2.0
Hispanic	99.7	13.5	5.5	2.1

      COMMENT OF AUTHOR: A significant finding was that intellectual maturity correlated significantly with achievement in the black and white samples but not in the Hispanic sample.
      COMMENT OF REVIEWER: There was no comment on equivalence of IQ scores in black, white, and Hispanic Ss except that the author noted that Anastasi and de Jesus found no

significant differences among black, white, and Puerto Rican preschool Ss on Goodenough Test.

#46   Matzen, S. P. *The relationship between racial composition and scholastic achievement in elementary school classrooms.* Stanford University, 1965.
       SUBJECTS AND METHOD OF SELECTION: Ss were selected from several large school districts in the San Francisco Bay area.
       TEST: California Test of Mental Maturity.
       RESULTS:

		N	Mn IQ	SD
	Black	294	93.6	6.1
5th grade—				
	White	258	109.8	10.2
	Black	259	91.3	7.9
7th grade—				
	White	252	106.3	10.5

       COMMENTS OF AUTHOR: When means were computed separately for Negro and non-Negro students, the fifth-grade data showed marked racial differences in achievement, SES, and intellectual ability. Class averages for seventh-grade non-Negroes were higher than the comparable averages for Negroes, but the differences were not as large as those in grade 5.

#47   McAdoo, H. A. P. *Racial attitudes and self concepts of black preschool children.* The University of Michigan, 1970.
       SUBJECTS AND METHOD OF SELECTION: Ss were 78 black preschool children with a median age of 5.8 years. There were 43 children from Mound Bayou, Mississippi, and 35 from Dearborn Heights, Michigan.
       TESTS: Peabody Picture Vocabulary Test and Williams and Roberson Measure of Racial Attitudes.
       RESULTS:

	N	Mn IQ	SD
Southern	43	86.7	14.8
Northern	35	96.9	11.3

       COMMENTS OF AUTHOR: The findings were: (a) No correlation was found between racial attitudes and self-concept. (b) Children in the all-black southern rural community were significantly higher in self-concept, while no difference was found in their racial attitudes. (c) No correlation between IQ and the two main variables was found, and the Northern sample was significantly higher than the Southern one in IQ scores. (d) No significant difference was found between children from

intact and those from nonintact homes on the two main variables. However, the nonintact children were consistently higher
on all self-concept scores and subscores, and they had a nonsignificantly more positive attitude towards blacks. (e) Boys were
significantly higher than girls on self-concept, while no statistically significant sex difference was found on the racial attitude
scores. With modified scoring of the self-concept test, boys were
nonsignificantly higher than girls.

#48 McClary, G. O. *Cognitive and affective responses by Negro and
white children to pictorial stimuli.* The George Washington University, 1969.
   SUBJECTS AND METHOD OF SELECTION: The Ss were
   four groups of boys and four groups of girls, each from the
   first- and fifth-grade levels in regular public elementary schools
   in Richmond, Virginia. All Ss attended racially segregated
   classes. At each grade level there were two separate groups
   of 22 Negro males, Negro females, white males, and white females.
   TESTS: Metropolitan Reading Readiness Test, Lorge-Thorndike Intelligence Test, and Peabody Picture Vocabulary Test.
   RESULTS: Peabody Picture Vocabulary Test IQs:

	N	Grade 1	N	Grade 5
Black (M & F) Modified	44	92.7	44	91.2
Black (M & F) Regular	44	93.7	44	92.4
White (M & F) Modified	44	99.2	44	103.8
White (M & F) Regular	44	100.0	44	109.5

   COMMENTS OF AUTHOR: All children, both Negro and
   white at the first- and fifth-grade levels, had significantly more
   errors on PPVT items with human content than on items with
   all non-human content. At both levels white children had significantly higher IQ scores on the PPVT than Negro children.
   The finding regarding preferences of pictures of white or black
   Ss on PPVT—modified by author—tended to confirm theoretical positions and previous research which indicate that, at both
   levels, both Negroes and whites show low identification with
   pictures of Negroes and high identification with pictures of
   white humans.

#49 Miller, M. D. *Patterns of relationships of fluid and crystallized
   mental abilities to achievement in different ethnic groups.* University of Houston, 1972.
   SUBJECTS AND METHOD OF SELECTION: The Ss were
   from the same geographical region (Aldine, Texas) and of the

same SES level. All subjects were from lower to middle SES. There were 85 Mexican-Americans, 95 whites, and 90 blacks. The age range was from 16 to 20 years.

TESTS: Cattell Culture Fair Intelligence Test and Primary Mental Abilities Test. Scores on both were converted to standard scores with mean 0 and standard deviation 1.00.

RESULTS: The hypothesis that group means were derived from a single population was rejected. The three ethnic groups represent three distinct populations. White-black difference was about 1 SD on "gc" tests and about .5 SD on "gf."

COMMENT OF AUTHOR: From the study there were basically two conclusions; the first was that ethnic groups can be differentiated in terms of intellectual abilities when these are defined under Cattell's theoretical classification into fluid and crystallized modes of functioning, and the second was that different ethnic groups utilized their fluid and crystallized intellectual components in different manners to attain educational achievement.

#50   Misa, K. F. *Cognitive, personality, and familial correlates of children's occupational preferences.* St. John's University, 1966.

SUBJECTS AND METHOD OF SELECTION: The Ss were 255 black and white students from the fourth, fifth, and sixth grades in suburban New York City with an age range of 9 to 13. There were 88 from the fourth grade, 95 from the fifth, and 72 from the sixth. There were 115 black Ss and 140 white. The Ss were selected from those who shared an interest in one of four occupational categories.

TEST: Otis Quick-Scoring Mental Ability Test, Beta Form.

RESULTS:

	N	Mn	SD
Black males	58	103.3	10.4
White males	66	115.9	10.0
Black females	57	101.8	9.1
White females	74	114.7	12.9

Note. Black-white differences were significant at the .001 level.

COMMENTS OF AUTHOR: Every comparison resulted in Caucasian boys obtaining significantly higher mean scores than Negro boys. Caucasian girls obtained significantly higher mean scores than Negro girls.

#51   Moorehead, N. F. *The effects of school integration on intelligence test scores of Negro children.* Mississippi State University, 1972.

SUBJECTS AND METHOD OF SELECTION: The Ss were black children enrolled in integrated classes from the time of their entry into school. The groups consisted of 30 Ss from each of the first three grades. Children from special education classes for EMRs were also included. The age ranges were 6–4 to 7–3 for first-graders, 7–4 to 8–3 for second-graders, and 8–4 to 9–3 for third-graders.

TEST: Wechsler Intelligence Test for Children.

RESULTS:

	Grade 1		Grade 2		Grade 3	
	Mn	N	Mn	N	Mn	N
Verbal IQ	82.1	30	87.1	30	88.9	30
Performance IQ	80.9	30	83.2	30	88.7	30
Full Scale IQ	79.9	30	83.8	30	87.8	30

COMMENT OF REVIEWER: Significant increases in Verbal, Performance, and Full Scale scores were found between the first- and third-graders but not between first- and second-graders nor between second- and third-graders.

#52 Needham, W. E. *Intellectual, personality, and biographical characteristics of southern Negro and white college students.* University of Utah, 1966.

SUBJECTS AND METHOD OF SELECTION: The Ss were 175 college students consisting of the following: 31 whites from Tulane University; 79 whites from Louisiana State University at New Orleans; and 65 blacks from Dillard University.

TEST: Guilford-Zimmerman Aptitude Survey Verbal Comprehension.

RESULTS:

	N	Mn	SD
Tulane	31	37.3	13.1
LSU-NO	70	28.8	11.3
Dillard	58	16.4	9.2

COMMENTS OF AUTHOR: The findings indicated Negro Ss scored significantly lower on the majority of the intellectual tests than did white Ss. It was consistently found that there were no significant differences between white and Negro groups in terms of Word Fluency, a symbolic, divergent thinking intellectual trait. Comparing personality, there were no consistent racial differences in Manifest Anxiety, and this appeared more a function of class standing and age than race. Negro Ss as a group also placed less value on Support and Recognition than white Ss of essentially the same age and class standing.

#53   O'Leary, B. S. *Learning measures as predictors of task performance in two ethnic groups.* University of Maryland, 1972.

SUBJECTS AND METHOD OF SELECTION: The Ss were 46 white and 48 Negro freshmen and sophomores from the University of Maryland.

TESTS: Wonderlic Personnel Test, French's Wide Range Vocabulary and Arithmetic Tests, and a digit span test.

RESULTS: Results indicated there was little difference in the learning ability of white and Negro students on relatively simple learning tasks such as the paired-associate task. However, performance on this relatively simple task did not predict performance on the programmed instruction criterion. With more complex learning tasks such as the concept and principle learning tasks, white students obtained higher levels of achievement and also exhibited a larger gain-in-proficiency than their Negro counterparts even though there were no significant pretest differences between the two groups. Thus, it is unlikely that the use of such measures as predictors will eliminate mean differences in predictor performance for white and Negro Ss.

COMMENTS OF AUTHOR: The results suggested that learning measures may be less biased as compared to traditional psychological tests. Learning measures exhibited biased relationships in 25% of the predictor-criterion comparisons as opposed to 67% for the traditional tests. However, in over half the biased relationships observed, criterion performance was over-predicted for Negroes, indicating that a reduction of bias might result in fewer Negroes being selected.

#54   Olshin, D. *The relationship of race and social class to intelligence and reading achievement at grades one and five.* Temple University, 1971.

SUBJECTS AND METHOD OF SELECTION: Ss were 160 children from elementary schools of the Baltimore City Arch-Diocesan school system. There were 80 from the first grade: 20 lower SES black, 20 lower SES white, 20 middle SES black, and 20 middle SES white. There were 80 children from the fifth grade with the same SES distributions as shown for the first grade.

TESTS: Wechsler Preschool and Primary Scale of Intelligence and Wechsler Intelligence Scale for Children.

COMMENTS OF AUTHOR: Racial membership was highly related to performance on the Full Scale IQ for the groups at grades 1 and 5. Racial membership was moderately related to performance on the Verbal IQ for the groups at grade 1. For the groups at grade 5, racial membership was moderately related to performance on the Performance IQ for the groups when tested at grade 1. For the groups at grade 5, racial membership was highly related to performance on the Performance IQ. The cumulative deficit hypothesis of decrease in IQ from the first to the fifth grade groups was not quantitatively supported. However, differences in the results for the WISC-fifth grade groups were more accentuated than for the first grade groups. There was a tendency toward greater differences in the results for the lower-class than the middle-class groups at the fifth grade than at the first grade. There was also a tendency toward greater differences in the results for the Negro than the Caucasian groups at the fifth grade than at the first grade.

#55   Pelosi, J. W. *A study of the effects of examiner race, sex, and style on test responses of Negro examinees.* Syracuse University, 1968.

SUBJECTS AND METHOD OF SELECTION: Ss were 96 black males with an age range of 16 to 25, mean 18.2 years. Ss were selected from 200 enrollees in a Neighborhood Youth Corps summer work project in Syracuse, New York. Each S received $5 for participating.

TESTS: Wechsler Adult Intelligence Scale (six subtests) and Cattell Culture Fair Intelligence Test.

RESULTS: Mean WAIS verbal IQ was 94.0, SD 13.0. Black-white examiner differences were not significant. Style of examiner, warm-cold, was not significant. Sex differences of examiners were not significant.

COMMENTS OF AUTHOR: The direction of the trend for examiner race and examiner style is an interesting one. None of the mean differences were statistically significant, of course, but the overall direction of the difference clearly contradicted the proposition that white examiners have deleterious effects on test performance of Negro Ss.

#56   Pfeifer Jr., C. M. *Academic ability and university climate in biracial academic prediction.* University of Maryland, 1972.

SUBJECTS AND METHOD OF SELECTION: Ss were 168 college students at the University of Maryland. There were 108 whites and 60 blacks.

TEST: Scholastic Aptitude Test.

RESULTS: Mean SAT Scores

	Mn	SD	N
White freshmen—verbal	498.6	89.1	50
White upper classmen—verbal	508.2	77.3	58
White freshmen—math	536.1	102.2	50
White upper classmen—math	548.0	94.1	58
Black freshmen—verbal	392.1	69.6	25
Black upper classmen—verbal	439.3	92.1	35
Black freshmen—math	409.8	91.3	25
Black upper classmen—math	420.3	81.8	35

SUMMARY: This study was not designed to compare black-white SAT scores. The purpose was to study academic ability and university climate in biracial predictions.

#57   Phillips, J. *Performance of father-present and father-absent southern Negro boys on a simple operant task as a function of the race and sex of the experimenter and the type of social reinforcement.* University of Minnesota, 1966.

SUBJECTS AND METHOD OF SELECTION: Ss were drawn from five all-black elementary schools serving predominantly disadvantaged lower-class areas in a mid-southern city. One-half of the Ss were from a home with a father figure, and one-half were from a home without a father figure. Their ages ranged from 9.0 to 10.11 years.

TESTS: Otis Quick Scoring Mental Abilities Test (IQ) and Metropolitan Achievement Test (ACH).

RESULTS:	Father Present			Father Absent		
	N	Mn	SD	N	Mn	SD
IQ	114	84.3	13.4	113	81.4	13.2
ACH	119	3.7	1.7	117	3.6	1.6

COMMENTS OF AUTHOR: Overall responsiveness and changes in rate of responding after the onset of one of three conditions of social reinforcement (praise, silence, or criticism) were related to the race and sex of the adult reinforcing agent by means of a Type III analysis of variance design. As predicted, Ss responded more to Negro than white experimenters, and father-absent Ss were more responsive than father-present Ss. The expectation that father-absent Ss, assumed to be lacking in identification with the noncompetitive Negro male sex-role, would be more responsive to white experimenters and less responsive to Negro experimenters than father-present Ss was supported by results obtained when Ss were criticized for their performance. The results of the study supported the assumption that father-absence is a salient determinant of the responsiveness of young Negro boys to the race of adult reinforcing agents and the type of social reinforcer dispensed in a task situation.

#58 Raggio, D. J. *Effect of test taking experience simulation on the scores of black, disadvantaged and white, non-disadvantaged children on selected subtests of the WISC performance scale.* Mississippi State University, 1974.

SUBJECTS AND METHOD OF SELECTION: Ss were disadvantaged black children from a rural county in Mississippi of lower SES. The nondisadvantaged white children were from a metro area of Mississippi with a family income greater than $10,000 a year. There were 32 children in each group, all in grade 2, with a mean age of 8 years.

TEST: Wechsler Intelligence Scale for Children (Performance section).

RESULTS:

	Test Simulation Absent		Test Simulation Present	
	Mn	SD	Mn	SD
Black—disadvantaged	74.8	12.0	88.6	7.3
White—nondisadvantaged	106.6	16.0	108.7	16.3

COMMENT OF AUTHOR: The difference in mean IQ scores that occurred between the black disadvantaged groups as a result of the TTES was much greater than the difference that occurred between the white nondisadvantaged groups as a result of the TTES.

#59 Resnick, M. B. *Language ability and intellectual and behavioral functioning in economically disadvantaged children.* University of Florida, 1972.

SUBJECTS AND METHOD OF SELECTION: Ss were 135 black children of indigent mothers from Alachua County, Florida. All children were delivered normally in local hospitals.

TESTS: Bayley Scales of Infant Development, Stanford-Binet, Arthur's Adaptation of Leiter International Scale, and Peabody Picture Vocabulary Test.

RESULTS:

	N	Mn	SD
Bayley Scale (IQ)	128	84.9	13.1
Stanford-Binet (IQ)	135	90.9	11.9
Leiter Scale (scores)	130	2.9	2.7
Peabody (IQ)	129	79.6	13.0

COMMENTS OF AUTHOR: This research indicated that the Bayley Scales of Infant Development at 2 years of age and the Stanford-Binet at 3 years of age were mainly composed of a language component which was highly correlated to intellectual measurement derived from these tests. Kagan stated that IQ scores become stable after 2 years of age. This research indicated that at 2 years of age language competence had become a major factor in intellectual performance.

#60   Robertson, W. J. *The effects of junior high school segregation experience on the achievement, behavior and academic motivation of integrated tenth grade high school students.* The University of Michigan, 1967.

SUBJECTS AND METHOD OF SELECTION: Ss were 120 tenth-grade students from Pontiac, Michigan, public schools. No special education or mentally handicapped students were included. The major independent variable was the average Negro-white ratio at the students' junior high schools during their attendance. The three levels were called High Segregation, Moderate Integration, and High Integration.

TESTS: Cattell Culture Fair Intelligence Tests and Otis Quick Scoring Intelligence Test, Gamma.

RESULTS:

	Cattell (Raw Scores) Mn	Otis (Raw Scores) Mn
Black	42.7	32.2
White	49.7	44.2

Black-white differences were significant at .001.

COMMENTS OF AUTHOR: The results of this study suggested that attendance at a segregated junior high school negatively affects the grades of both Negro and white students who subsequently attend an integrated high school. There were no systematic differences in objectively measured achievement, behavior ratings, or academic motivation that could be ascribed to the segregation experience variable. The Negro-white differences on objective achievement and grades could be ascribed to differences in the abilities measured by the Otis test.

#61   Ryan, J. S. *Early identification of intellectually superior black children.* The University of Michigan, 1975.

SUBJECTS AND METHOD OF SELECTION: Ss were 21 children selected from 417 black kindergarten pupils and 28 selected from 570 black third-graders.

TESTS: Goodenough-Harris Draw-A-Man Test, Stanford-Binet, and Leiter Intelligence Performance Scale.

RESULTS: Intellectual superiority was defined as an IQ of 120 and above. Achievement data obtained from the Wide Range Achievement Test revealed none of the third-grade children identified as intellectually superior were functioning up to their ability in arithmetic. Identification was more difficult at kindergarten than at third grade. The Draw-A-Man was found to be ineffectual in identifying superior black children.

#62   Ryan, L. E. *An investigation of the relationship between the scores earned by selected Negro and white children on the Wechsler Intelligence Scale for Children and the Wide Range Achievement Test.* Mississippi State University, 1973.

SUBJECTS AND METHOD OF SELECTION: The Ss had been tested within a 3-year period on WISC and WRAT for special education classes. The age range was from 6–5 to 15–11. Their IQ range was from 46 to 85. Ss with severe physical handicaps were not included.

TESTS: Wechsler Intelligence Scale for Children and Wide Range Achievement Test.

RESULTS:

		WISC Full-Scale IQ	
	N	Mn	SD
White boys	119	72.3	8.9
White girls	64	68.6	9.1
Black boys	271	65.1	9.3
Black girls	158	63.6	9.0

COMMENTS OF AUTHOR: Knowledge of race, sex, age, and IQ as measured by the WISC significantly increased the predictability of WRAT scores. The preponderance of the evidence shows that the WISC is not a valid test for southern Negroes.

#63   Sandy, C. A. *The effects of material reward, sex, race, and socioeconomic strata on the Pintner-Cunningham Primary Test scores of kindergarten students.* University of Virginia, 1970.

SUBJECTS AND METHOD OF SELECTION: The Ss were 187 (129 black; 58 white) kindergarten children from 12 public school classes in Richmond, Virginia. Ss were matched as to SES and occupation of the family head.

TEST: Pintner-Cunningham Primary Test.

COMMENTS OF AUTHOR: The major hypotheses of this study were based on the assumption that material reward provided to lower socioeconomic strata Ss would serve as a motivator to improve measured intelligence. Based on the assumption that the discrepancy was due primarily to poor motivation for cognitive tasks rather than to intellectual inferiority, it was hypothesized that lower socioeconomic strata kindergarten Ss receiving material reward would "catch up" with their middle socioeconomic strata counterparts in terms of measured intelligence. Largely as predicted, middle socioeconomic strata Ss did have higher mean pre-test IQs than lower socioeconomic strata Ss. However, on post-testing, with material reward introduced, the hypothesized IQ increases of lower socioeconomic strata rewarded Ss, in excess of IQ increases of the other groups, were not found. Other analyses of data indicated that, by themselves, the major variables of socioeconomic strata, reward condition, and sex did not contribute significantly to the predictability of IQ change; however, knowledge of race did contribute significantly ($p < .01$) to the predictability of IQ change.

#64   Smith, W. R. B. *The relationship between self-concept of academic ability, locus of control of the environment, and academic achievement of black students specially admitted to the University of Pittsburgh.* University of Pittsburgh, 1972.

SUBJECTS AND METHOD OF SELECTION: Ss were 147 black freshman volunteers enrolled in the University of Pittsburgh Community Education Program for minority and poor students admitted under special conditions.

TEST: Scholastic Aptitude Test (total score).

RESULTS:

	Mn	SD	N
1970–71	709.3	124.7	74%[a]
1971–72	808.6	143.5	82%[b]

[a]58 of 80Ss
[b]55 of 67 Ss

COMMENTS OF AUTHOR: There was no significant relationship between SAT scores and academic achievement for either sample. There was no significant relationship between self-concept of academic achievement and SAT scores for the 1970–71 sample, but there was a significant relationship in the 1971–72 sample.

COMMENT OF REVIEWER: Smith's findings suggested that the higher the self-concept of academic ability, the higher the academic achievement.

#65   Soltz, W. H. *Comparative study of Negro-white differences on the MMPI and PAS.* University of Missouri, 1970.

SUBJECTS AND METHOD OF SELECTION: Ss were convicted female felons serving prison terms at Tipton, Missouri, State Penitentiary. There were 52 whites and 24 blacks. The age range was 17 to 53, mean of 27.6.

TESTS: Wechsler Adult Intelligence Scale (the vocabulary test was not given); the WAIS was used as the assessment measure for the Personality Assessment System (PAS).

RESULTS:	White Mean	Black Mean	Difference
Performance IQ	95.2	87.5	7.7
Verbal IQ	96.4	89.0	7.4
Full Scale IQ	95.6	88.1	7.5

COMMENTS OF REVIEWER: Soltz's results indicated that the factor scales of Harrison and Kass were supported by the data. Personality description of Negro-white differences was found to be similar to some past research. Trends were indicated in PAS data not in the expected direction. Soltz suggested that greater significance had to be placed on sex variables in future PAS research.

#66   Starnes, T. A. *An analysis of the academic achievement of Negro students in the predominantly white schools of a selected Florida county.* University of Southern Mississippi, 1968.

SUBJECTS AND METHOD OF SELECTION: The Ss for the investigation were fourth, sixth, and eighth grade Negro students who were enrolled in the public schools of an urban, northwest Florida county during the 1966–67 school year. The schools and classes from which the Ss were drawn were randomly selected. The Ss from the predominately white schools were assigned to Group A, and the Ss from the predominately Negro schools were assigned to Group B. The number of students in Groups A and B was not given.

TEST: California Test of Mental Maturity.

RESULTS: Results tended to substantiate the basic hypothesis of the study, namely, Negro students in predominately white schools make greater achievement gains than those that attend predominately Negro schools. These findings were also consistent with the findings of the U.S. Department of Health, Education, and Welfare which also indicated that a positive relationship exists between achievement of Negro students and the environment of predominately white schools. (The .25 confidence level was adopted.)

COMMENTS OF AUTHOR: In summary, the intercorrelation analysis further substantiated the basic hypothesis of this study that Negro students in predominately white schools would make greater achievement gains than Negro students in predominately Negro schools. The achievement-IQ ratio for the predominately Negro school group was .380. That ratio indicates that IQ accounted for 14.4 percent of the variance in the achivement gain of that group. On the other hand, the achievement-IQ ratio for the predominately white school group was only .054, and it was not significant. The correlation ratio indicates that IQ accounted for less than 1 percent of the variance in the achievement of the predominately white school group. Since IQ and achievement were correlated in the predominately Negro school group, but not in the predominately white school group, the superior achievement gain of the latter group must be attributed to factors other than native ability, namely, those elements of the predominately white schools which distinguish them from the predominately Negro schools.

#67   Sternberg, R. I. *The relation between total and partial IQ's on the 1960 Stanford-Binet: A cross-ethnic comparison.* California School of Professional Psychology, Fresno, 1976.

SUBJECTS AND METHOD OF SELECTION: Ss were students referred for testing in New York City schools for admission selection purposes, periodic evaluation, and special evaluation for state aid. All were normal evaluative referrals (excluding referrals for behavioral problems or intellectual deficiencies) who had not been previously tested with Stanford-Binet. There were 52 white, 36 black, and 18 Puerto Rican Ss. The age range was 5.8 to 16.0, mean of 10.2 years.

TEST: Stanford-Binet Intelligence Scale, Form L-M, 1960 Revision.

RESULTS:

	Mean IQs	
	Full Test	Vocabulary Test
White	115.8	115.8
Black	100.7	96.9
Puerto Rican	106.5	94.3

COMMENT OF AUTHOR: This study indicated that whites score up to one standard deviation above other ethnic groups on measures of intelligence.

#68   Strauch, A. B. *An investigation into the sex × race × ability interaction.* The Pennsylvania State University, 1975.

SUBJECTS AND METHOD OF SELECTION: Ss were made available from three large data sources: (a) the standardization sample of the WISC-R in which there were 2,200 children ranging in age from 6 to 16; (b) Pennsylvania Department of Education results of 153,000 children in grades 5, 8, and 11, who were tested in 1974; and (c) data from Project Talent tests which were taken by 400,000 high-school students in 1960.

TESTS: Wechsler Intelligence Scale for Children—R, Educational Quality Assessment (EQA), verbal and math subtests, and Project Talent Test of Cognitive Ability.

RESULTS: Cognitive Ability

		N	Mn	SD
White	Male	1,693	150.9	47.9
	Female	1,678	156.3	45.8
Black	Male	97	90.5	38.9
	Female	111	92.0	37.9

WISC Verbal IQ

		N	Mn	SD
White	Male	945	103.3	14.7
	Female	925	100.7	14.3
Black	Male	143	87.6	12.5
	Female	162	88.0	13.7

Educational Quality Assessment—Grade 5

Verbal		N	Mn	SD
White	Male	21,124	17.8	5.6
	Female	20,544	19.0	5.4
Black	Male	1,216	13.7	4.9
	Female	1,249	14.2	4.7

Math		N	Mn	SD
White	Male	21,104	19.3	4.8
	Female	20,539	19.5	4.4
Black	Male	1,213	15.0	4.5
	Female	1,244	15.1	4.4

COMMENT OF AUTHOR: Although the literature supports the notion of a female superiority to resist stress at young ages, the failure to discern an interaction led to questions regarding the application of this phenomenon to explain race and/or sex differences in mental ability.

#69 Summerford, J. D. *Study of the basic concepts of disadvantaged kindergarten children in artificial and naturalistic contexts.* University of Georgia, 1977.

SUBJECTS AND METHOD OF SELECTION: Ss were 22 white and 25 black kindergarten children from a rural northeast Georgia county. The pupils had been assigned to classes through stratified random selection to balance classes by race and sex. Ss were also placed in one of four experimental groups by random selection. The mean age was 71 months, SD 5 months. TESTS: Boehm Test of Basic Concepts and "Naturalistic Tests" devised by Summerford.

RESULTS:

Test	Black		White	
	Mn	SD	Mn	SD
Individual Boehm	18.8	5.0	24.0	3.4
Group Boehm	18.4	5.7	23.9	3.3
Classroom	19.3	5.9	24.2	3.4
Playground	19.3	5.2	24.8	2.9
	N = 25		N = 22	

COMMENT OF AUTHOR: Black students consistently score approximately one standard deviation below white students on concept tests (Boehm Test and Naturalistic Tests).

COMMENTS OF REVIEWER: Summerford utilized Boehm Test of Basic Concepts and "Naturalistic Tests" which he devised. These naturalistic tests consisted of 30 concepts from the Boehm Test "restructured to provide naturalistic measures of children's knowledge of basic concepts." The two forms are the *Classroom Test* (requiring students to manipulate familiar objects found in classrooms) and the *Playground Test* (having pupils actively position their bodies in relation to playground apparatus). "Basic Concepts" is *never* fully defined; however, they are supposed to represent "the four context categories of space, quantity, time and miscellaneous."

#70   Sweet, R. C. *Variations in the intelligence test performance of lower-class children as a function of feedback or monetary reinforcement.* The University of Wisconsin, 1969.

SUBJECTS AND METHOD OF SELECTION: Ss were 204 children from Milwaukee city schools with an age range of 6 to 13. Of these, 156 had been referred for psychological evaluations; 72 were middle-class whites, 48 were lower-class whites, 36 were lower-class blacks. The remaining 48 had never been referred for testing.

TEST: Wechsler Intelligence Scale for Children given under three conditions: Treatment C, standard procedures; Treatment K, subject was told when responses were correct; Treatment M, following a correct response, subject was given a monetary reward.

RESULTS:		C	K	M
Middle-class white	PF IQ	105.7	104.3	105.0
	V IQ	107.4	104.3	109.3
Lower-class white	PF IQ	92.0	91.2	94.1
	V IQ	88.6	99.4	103.8
Lower-class black	PF IQ	92.7	91.9	90.9
	V IQ	89.2	91.6	92.7
Never referred	PF IQ	—	—	—
	V IQ	105.9	102.4	111.7

COMMENTS OF AUTHOR: The main findings of this study were as follows:
1. As predicted, MCWs did not differ in performance across treatments.
2. LCWs performed as predicted, except for the unexpected improvement of LCWs tested under feedback conditions (K).
3. LCNs tested under conditions of monetary reward (M) did not differ from LCNs tested under standardized (C) or feedback (K) conditions. These results were not predicted. However, there were no differences between LCWs and LCNs tested under standardized procedures. This last finding was in line with previous data which indicated that there were no differences between LCWs and LCNs in their previous Full Scale WISC IQs.
4. Comparisons between Group R and NR verified the prediction regarding the lack of a significant Referral Status × Treatment interaction. However, there was an unexpected Referral Status main effect, due most likely to a Group R sampling artifact.
5. There were no significant Examiner or Examiner × Treatment effects.

#71 Takacs, C. P. *Comparison of mental abilities between lower socio-economic status five-year-old Negro and white children on individual intelligence measures.* Kent State University, 1971.
SUBJECTS AND METHOD OF SELECTION: Ss were 60 black and 60 white children from selected counties of Ohio. The children were 5 and 6 years of age, from lower SES families, and were enrolled in the Head Start program.
TESTS: Wechsler Preschool and Primary Scale of Intelligence and Merrill Palmer Developmental Test.
COMMENTS OF REVIEWER: Takacs' results showed a quantitative difference in intellectual performance on some of the subtests with black children performing less well than white children; however, there were only negligible qualitative differ-

ences in the intellectual processes. In contrast, while quantitative performance levels for the two sexes were similar, there appeared rather large differences in the intellectual processing of various tasks. The major hypothesis of race differences in mental abilities was supported for Spatial Organization and Verbal Comprehension, and was rejected for Ideational Fluency, Language Problem Solving, and Originality. The hypothesis of deficiency of black children on spatial tasks was supported.

#72   Tate, D. T. *A study of the relationship of socio-economic status and intelligence and achievement scores of white and Negro groups.* Oklahoma State University, 1967.
      SUBJECTS AND METHOD OF SELECTION: Ss were 257 Negroes from Oakwood College, Huntsville, Alabama, and 277 whites from Oklahoma State University, Stillwater, Oklahoma.
      TESTS: Henmon-Nelson Test of Mental Ability, ACT battery, and Hollingshead's Two-Factor Index of Social Position.
      RESULTS: The F ratios derived from the undifferentiated groups, except by race, showed the Negro sample consistently significantly higher on the intelligence measures. The achievement variables showed F ratios significantly higher for the white sample, prior to controlling for socioeconomic status.

#73   Taylor, D. R. *A longitudinal comparison of intellectual development of black and white students from segregated to desegregated settings.* University of South Florida, 1974.
      SUBJECTS AND METHOD OF SELECTION: All Ss had attended segregated schools for grades 1–3, then enrolled in desegregated schools for grade 4. The schools were in Hillsborough County, Florida. There were 220 black Ss and 780 white Ss, randomly selected to yield appropriate "proportional percentage" from each school. Subjects' SES was assessed.
      TEST: Otis-Lennon Mental Ability Test, Elementary II Level.
      RESULTS: Black increase in deviation IQ $= 6.5$, $t = 7.0$. White increase in deviation IQ $= 4.2$, $t = 12.9$.
      COMMENTS OF AUTHOR:
      1. The black students in this study significantly increased their mental ability scores by an average of about 6.5 (DIQ) points. Thus, for most black children, entry into the racially mixed public schools had a positive effect on their intellectual development.
      2. Black students from the lower socioeconomic status group benefited slightly more than those from the middle socioeco-

nomic group in terms of intellectual development. However, both groups showed significant gains.

3. The white students in this study significantly increased their mental ability scores by an average of about 4.2 (DIQ) points. Thus, for most white students, entry into the racially mixed public schools had no deleterious effect on their intellectual development. They did, in fact, make significant gains.

4. White students from the lower socioeconomic status group showed more of a gain in intellectual development than did the whites from either the middle or the upper socioeconomic status groups. The whites from the middle group also experienced significant gains. However, while the white upper group experienced some gains, these were not found to be significant.

#74   Thorne, J. H. *An analysis of the WISC and ITPA and their relationships to school achievement, socio-economic status, and ethnicity.* University of Houston, 1974.

SUBJECTS AND METHOD OF SELECTION: The population of this study was 417 students, 202 normals and 215 referred or specially placed students. There were 322 students classified as "Other", who were primarily Anglo with four Oriental-surnamed students. Forty-seven were black and 48 were Spanish-surnamed. The study was conducted in Aldine, Texas. All were between 6.0 and 10.0 to remain within the overlapping age range of the ITPA and WISC. Ethnicity was determined from school records and examiner's observations at the time of testing. A Spanish surname was the basis for determining Mexican-American ethnic groups.

TESTS: Illinois Test of Psycholinguistic Abilities, Wechsler Intelligence Scale for Children, and Wide Range Achievement Test.

COMMENTS OF AUTHOR: The evidence clearly indicated that while there were ethnic patterns, these patterns each correlated significantly with school achievement as measured by the WRAT. The WRAT indicated that all three ethnic groups followed the same general curve, but the "Other" group was consistently higher and the Spanish-surnamed group was consistently lower than the black group.

#75   Tillery, W. L. *A comparison of the Pictorial Test of Intelligence (PTI) and Stanford-Binet (S-B) with disadvantaged children.* The Pennsylvania State University, 1972.

SUBJECTS AND METHOD OF SELECTION: Ss were 65 black children from Title IX schools in the Philadelphia, Pennsylvania, area. At the time of the study, the Ss were in the second grade with a mean age of 84.9 months. Of the nine examiners used, four were female and three were black.

TESTS: Stanford-Binet, Form L-M, Pictorial Test of Intelligence, and Wide Range Achievement Test.

RESULTS:

	N	Pretest Mn	SD	Post-test Mn	SD
PTI	65	90.6	15.3	96.7	14.2
Binet	65	85.7	13.2	91.5	15.6

COMMENT OF REVIEWER: The purpose of Tillery's investigation was to compare the PTI and S-B in terms of test-retest reliability and predictive validity.

#76   Trotman, F. K. *Race, IQ, and the middle-class.* Columbia University, 1976.

SUBJECTS AND METHOD OF SELECTION: Ss were ninth-grade girls from Teaneck, New Jersey, public schools. Those who did not have one or more of the selected tests were eliminated. The number eliminated was only 4%. Invitations offering $5 an hour were extended to the mothers of the Ss to conduct interviews in their homes. One hundred mothers were interviewed and gave their permission to use the IQs and school records of their children.

TESTS: Otis-Lennon Mental Ability Test and Metropolitan Achievement Test.

RESULTS:

	Black N	Mn	SD	White N	Mn	SD
Otis-Lennon	50	100.2	12.7	50	112.2	13.3
Metropolitan	50	76.8	20.8	50	91.4	12.6

COMMENTS OF AUTHOR: The results provided little or no support for the genetically-deficient interpretation of the relatively poor intelligence test performance of black Americans. Neither could the data provide fuel for either side of the debate over cultural deficiency versus cultural difference.

#77   Tufano, L. G. *The effect of effort and performance reinforcement on WISC-R/IQ scores of black and white EMR boys.* University of Georgia, 1975.

SUBJECTS AND METHOD OF SELECTION: Ss were 60 boys from Oglethorpe County, Georgia, public schools. There were 30 blacks and 30 whites; the age range was from 10 to 14 years.

TESTS: Wechsler Intelligence Scale for Children—R and Iowa Test of Basic Skills.

RESULTS: Ss were randomly assigned to treatment groups: reinforcement for effort vs. for performance. Mode of treatment did not differentially affect WISC-R scores. Examiner-race interaction was insignificant.

COMMENT OF AUTHOR: Black and white students' ITBS scores clearly indicated the two groups differed intellectually.

#78 Vega, M. *The performance of Negro children on an oddity discrimination task as a function of the race of the examiner and the type of verbal incentive used by the examiner.* The Florida State University, 1964.

SUBJECTS AND METHOD OF SELECTION: Ss were 324 Negro school children, grades 2, 6, and 10, from a southern rural area. White examiners tested one-half of the Ss, and the other half were tested by Negro examiners. The children were tested under three reward conditions: praise, blame, and no incentive. Oddity problems were presented twice to elicit two series of responses. Between presentations, Ss were told they had done well or done poorly or told nothing about their performance.

TEST: California Test of Mental Maturity.

RESULTS: For the total sample, Negro examiners elicited decreased trial two mean reaction time, while white examiners elicited increased trial two mean reaction time. Ss tested by Negro examiners reduced trial two mean reaction time under all incentive conditions; those tested by white examiners showed decreased trial two mean reaction time under praise and no incentive but demonstrated a marked increase under reproof.

#79 Whipple, D. W. *A study of the relationships among ethnic-social class, intelligence, achievement motivation and delay of gratification.* New York University, 1972.

SUBJECTS AND METHOD OF SELECTION: Ss were 189 seventh-grade students attending Catholic parochial schools in Newark, New Jersey.

TESTS: Lorge-Thorndike Nonverbal Group Intelligence Test. Achievement motivation was measured by Thematic Apperception Test as revised by McClelland.

COMMENTS OF AUTHOR: It was found that of the three independent variables studied, intelligence accounted for by far the largest proportion of variation in delay of gratification, in fact, twice as much as achievement motivation and three times as much as ethnic-social class. This has contradicted the basic assumption taken beforehand in this study, that delay of gratification is primarily determined by social class, i.e., is a function of the white middle-class value system. The results showed that when intelligence and achievement motivation are taken into account (partialled out), ethnic-social class and delay of gratification are not significantly related. When comparing the two ethnic-social class sub-samples, the main difference appeared to be in the much greater predictive importance of intelligence in the black lower-class group. It can be tentatively concluded that at lower levels of intelligence, delay of gratification ability is greatly affected by intelligence. As a group achieves a higher mean intelligence and a higher average social class, other factors, such as achievement motivation and social class, contribute relatively more to the ability to delay gratification.

#80   Williams, D. E. *Self-concept and verbal mental ability in Negro pre-school children.* St. John's University, 1968.
SUBJECTS AND METHOD OF SELECTION: Ss were black children enrolled in preschool programs in New York City. From a master list of applications on file at anti-poverty programs, the first 50 boys and 50 girls were chosen. There were also 81 children enrolled in an integrated preschool program. Of the total 181 Ss, there were 98 boys and 83 girls. The Ss were divided into six groups as follows:
   Group 1—De Facto, boys (father present),
   Group 2—De Facto, girls (father present),
   Group 3—De Facto, boys (father absent),
   Group 4—De Facto, girls (father absent),
   Group 5—Pre-K girls (father present),
   Group 6—Pre-K boys (father present).
TESTS: Van Alstyne Picture Vocabulary Test and U-Scale Test.
RESULTS: Mental Age Scores

	N	MN	SD	IQ Equivalent
Group 1	26	52	10.7	96
Group 2	24	50	10.0	90
Group 3	24	51	7.1	94
Group 4	26	48	8.4	88
Group 5	33	54	9.5	101
Group 6	48	51	7.4	96

COMMENTS OF AUTHOR: Negro girls enrolled in a suburban integrated preschool program were significantly superior in mental ability to Negro girls enrolled in an urban de facto segregated preschool program. Negro boys enrolled in a suburban integrated preschool program were not superior in verbal mental ability to boys enrolled in a de facto segregation program.

#81 Winokur, D. J. *The effects of verbal reinforcement combinations and color of examiner on shifts in concept formation.* The Florida State University, 1964.

SUBJECTS AND METHOD OF SELECTION: Ss were 80 adult Negro patients from South Carolina State Hospital. The IQ range was from 70 to 110, with a mean of 80. There were 44 males and 36 females with a mean age of 32. Patients who were receiving shock treatment or those otherwise judged to be confused or out of contact were not included in the study.

TEST: Wechsler Adult Intelligence Scale (only the Comprehension, Digit Symbol, and Block Design subtests).

COMMENTS OF AUTHOR: The primary focus of investigation was the comparison of the Nothing-Wrong with the Right-Nothing verbal reinforcement combination in a conceptual learning task. Acquisition of a simple color concept and subsequent relearning of a simple shape concept under the two conditions were studied. The concept shift was a nonreversal one as the shift was made to a different dimension. The conclusion was that the NW combination was seen to be superior to the RN combination only in the case of a shift both in concept and in reinforcement condition. It was also found that more Ss failed to learn the first concept under the RN than under the NW condition. Half of the Ss were run by a white and half by a Negro examiner. No examiner differences in learning performance were found. The variable of race of examiner was not, apparently, a significant one in this study.

#82 Winter, G. D. *Intelligence, interest, and personality characteristics of a selected group of students: A description and comparison of white and Negro students in a vocational rehabilitation administration program in Bassick and Harding high schools, Bridgeport, Connecticut.* Columbia University, 1967.

SUBJECTS AND METHOD OF SELECTION: There were 80 Ss from a list of candidates for the Vocational Rehabilitation Administration Pilot Project at Bassick and Harding high schools. The first 20 candidates who met race and sex requirements were chosen. Ss were assigned to four groups: WM, BM, WF, and BF.

TEST: Wechsler Adult Intelligence Scale.

RESULTS: On the Performance section of the Wechsler Adult Intelligence Scale whites scored significantly higher, at the .01 level, than the Negroes. This reflected the higher mean score of the white male (96.9) over both the white female (91.3) and Negro male (91.35) and the comparatively low mean score (84.5) for the Negro female. The difference between the elevated white male mean score and the depressed Negro female mean score accounted for the significance of the difference. The mean scores for the white males, white females, and Negro males were all in the average range while the mean score for the Negro females was in the dull normal range.

COMMENTS OF AUTHOR: The results of the Wechsler Adult Intelligence Scale would tend to lead the counselor to the conclusion that his group of Negroes is capable of producing on the level of his white counselees in the area of verbal tasks. He must, however, take into consideration that their production in the area of nonverbal tasks is lower than had been expected. It had been commonly held that occupations in the field of mechanics or other manipulative industrial arts would be appropriate fields for Negroes. The results of the study with the Negro group being significantly lower in the area of Performance IQ would tend to contra-indicate the choice of non-verbally oriented occupations. This would be particularly true for the Negro female who often was chosen for assembly line production, since her scores on Performance IQ were exceptionally low for the group.

#83   Wolfe, B. E. *A comparison of the impact of two kindergarten programs on the creative performance of disadvantaged Negro children.* University of Florida, 1970.

SUBJECTS AND METHOD OF SELECTION: Ss for the study were 40 black 5-year-olds from Jacksonville, Florida. The group was split into groups and matched on SES, cultural background, age, sex, and school readiness.

TEST: Stanford-Binet.

RESULTS: Pre- and Post-treatment mean IQs

		Pre		Post	
	N	Mn	SD	Mn	SD
Learning to Learn	20	90.0	9.7	99.2	11.1
Public Kindergarten	20	89.5	8.4	88.3	12.8

COMMENT OF AUTHOR: The Learning to Learn program appeared to be more effective in enhancing the intellectual performance of its participants than in augmenting their creative performance.

#84 Woodall, F. E. *Relationships between social adaptability and below average intelligence test performance for black and white elementary school children.* University of Georgia, 1975.

SUBJECTS AND METHOD OF SELECTION: Ss were 101 mentally retarded children. There were 48 blacks and 53 whites whose ages ranged from 6 to 13 years with a mean of 8.7 years. They were selected for inclusion only if they obtained a FSIQ between 52 and 84. There were two groups into which they were divided: retarded (FSIQ, 52–69) and low average (FSIQ, 70–84).

TESTS: Wechsler Intelligence Scale for Children-R and Young Educable Mentally Retarded Performance Profile (YEMR).

RESULTS: Blacks and whites scored significantly different on the Comprehension subtest and the Picture Arrangement subtest. The analyses by race of the Verbal, Performance, Full Scale IQ, and Habile Index were not significant.

COMMENTS OF AUTHOR: There appears to be little difference in the scoring patterns of black and white southern children on the WISC-R. This conclusion contradicts some previous research on the WISC, the predecessor to the WISC-R. There may be some variation in scoring patterns of southern black and white children but not within the IQ range in this study.

#85 Worthington, C. F. *An analysis of WISC-R score patterns of black adolescent male delinquents.* University of Georgia, 1977.

SUBJECTS AND METHOD OF SELECTION: Ss were 105 black males ranging in age from 12 to 15, of lower SES, and divided into two groups, delinquents and nondelinquents. The nondelinquent group was from public school, grades 7 and 8, who participated in free or reduced lunch program (low SES). There were 45 nondelinquents. There were 60 delinquents divided into two groups of 30, aggressive and nonaggressive. This classification was based on types of delinquent acts and "diagnosis" of two professionals. The delinquents were from a local juvenile detention home group facility for delinquents and a residential center for delinquents. All delinquents had to have been incarcerated twice or more on delinquency charges.

TEST: Wechsler Intelligence Scale for Children-R.

RESULTS: Mean Full Scale IQs

	N	Mn	SD
Control Group	45	84.2	13.1
E-1 Aggressive	30	68.5	12.3
E-2 Nonaggressive	30	73.4	10.4

COMMENTS OF AUTHOR: These findings are in agreement with results of previous research in which delinquent Ss scored lower than their nondelinquent contemporaries on IQ tests. In the present study all three IQ scores, Full Scale, Verbal, and Performance, were in the borderline retardation group or lower for the delinquent Ss. The black adolescent male from lower SES is most likely to become a delinquent and educational failure is one of the most consistent characteristics. Implications for school personnel are for the early identification for these high risk students. Identification of the poorest readers in the primary grades is a logical beginning. If so identified, they should then be examined with a number of evaluative instruments.

#86   Wyatt, M. A. *A study of the interaction between personality traits, IQ, and achievement in Negro and white fourth grade children.* University of Kentucky, 1972.
SUBJECTS AND METHOD OF SELECTION: Ss were 109 fourth-grade children from two elementary schools of a large urban community. Both schools were completely integrated, and both had recently begun a new method of teaching. One group was from a diverse but depressed neighborhood. The other group was from an integrated government housing project with an average yearly income of $4,000. There were 37 white boys, 35 white girls, 19 black boys, and 18 black girls.
TEST: Lorge-Thorndike Intelligence Test—Level B.
RESULTS: No significant difference was found between the Negro and white children's ability. There was no significant interaction between sex and school, nor between sex and race.
COMMENTS OF AUTHOR: It is of interest to note that although no differences in ability were found between the races, a difference was found in achievement. This points out that factors, other than intelligence as measured by an IQ test, are operating in the way a child performs in school.

#87   Yates, L. G. *Comparative intelligence of Negro and white children from a rural-southern culture.* The University of North Carolina at Chapel Hill, 1967.
SUBJECTS AND METHOD OF SELECTION: Ss were 731 children in grades 2–8 from a rural, southern, segregated mill community. Children were selected at random from two Negro elementary schools and two white schools.
TESTS: Stanford-Binet, Form L-M, Primary Mental Abilities, and Stanford Achievement Test.

RESULTS: Stanford-Binet IQs were computed by reviewer from mental ages given in Table 12:

	White		Black	
Grade	N	Mn	N	Mn
2	56	109	45	88
3	52	106	68	93
4	50	107	51	94
5	39	105	62	89
6	51	104	52	87
7	55	102	55	88
8	52	101	43	86

COMMENTS OF AUTHOR: Results indicated that significant race differences in these Negro and white children, who were significantly different in mean mental age, were all in favor of the white children. These differences were found at every grade level and on every variable except spelling at grades 5 and 8 and number at grade 6. The variables which were significant varied with grade level in a pattern which seemed to be influenced by the changes in test form which occurred at grades 3, 5, and 7. It was hypothesized that this test effect was related to a slower rate of development in the Negro than in the white children of the skills and knowledge necessary for the new test forms. As the Negro gained the necessary skills, the number of variables involved in race differences decreased only to increase again when a more advanced test form was introduced. If this hypothesis is correct, a factor which may have contributed to this slowness is schooling. The schooling of Negro and white children of the community may not have been of equal quality, and many of the variables which appeared only at grades 3, 5, and 7 are influenced by school curriculum.

#88   Yen, S. M. Y. *A comparative study of test variability with Peabody Picture Vocabulary Test, Goodenough's Draw-A-Man Test, and Stanford-Binet Intelligence Scale as intellectual measurement with a group of urban low socio-economic status pre-school pupils.* Catholic University of America, 1969.

SUBJECTS AND METHOD OF SELECTION: Ss were 100 preschool children from the inner city area of Baltimore. The age range was from 4.0 to 4.11. There were 20 white boys; 20 white girls; 20 black boys; 20 black girls; and 20 American Indians (Lumbee), 17 boys and 3 girls. All the children were free from physical handicaps and lived in environments of low SES. Family structures were different.

TESTS: Draw-A-Man (DAM), Peabody Picture Vocabulary Test (PPVT), and Stanford-Binet (S-B).

RESULTS:	White Boys	White Girls	Black Boys	Black Girls	Indian Total
DAM MN	88.0	94.5	87.2	101.4	89.3
SD	17.9	15.2	13.3	13.6	11.0
PPVT MN	87.1	91.3	83.8	93.6	88.8
SD	15.6	16.1	18.1	16.8	22.6
S-B MN	99.9	101.6	94.5	99.2	100.6
SD	10.4	10.8	11.8	13.0	13.6

COMMENTS OF AUTHOR: These findings differ from most of the previous studies of a similar nature in which children from poverty areas with low SES have been found to obtain rather low IQ scores. There was moderate to high correlation between PPVT and S-B but moderate to poor correlation between DAM and PPVT and between the DAM and S-B scale. There were no significant differences in reference to attributable variables, such as inherent racial abilities and family differences.

#89   Zagarow, H. W. *The prediction of academic success for black and white college students.* The University of Connecticut, 1973.
SUBJECTS AND METHOD OF SELECTION: Ss were 558 college freshmen (279 white, 279 black) admitted to the main campus of the University of Connecticut, September, 1970, and September, 1971. Ss were matched on the basis of sex. All were resident students admitted by the regular admissions procedure.
TEST: College Entrance Examination Board (Scholastic Aptitude Test).
RESULTS: Scholastic Aptitude Test

	N	Verbal		Quantitative	
		Mn	SD	Mn	SD
Black	279	417	109	425	97
White	279	546	78	582	72

COMMENT OF AUTHOR: The results of this study indicated that the predictive efficiency of the optimum established batteries (HS Avg., SAT-V, SAT-M, sex, age, mother's occupation, father's occupation) for both the black and white samples was not significantly increased by the addition of new noncognitive predictor variables to those batteries.

XI

National Longitudinal Study of the High School Class of 1972: An Analysis of Subpopulation Differences

R. Travis Osborne

Introduction

This original monograph was prepared especially for Volume 2 of *The Testing of Negro Intelligence.* Although the National Longitudinal Study (Levinsohn, Lewis, Riccobono, and Moore, 1976) tapes are available to all investigators through the Freedom of Information Act and numerous studies based on the NLS data have been published, none has analyzed the unique subpopulation differences reported here. Presented first will be new evidence from the NLS regarding race, sex, and SES differences in intelligence and achievement. Next, test scores from a stratified random sample of school children from all 50 states and the District of Columbia will be analyzed by geographic region and degree of pupil integration.

The National Longitudinal Study (NLS) of the High School class of 1972 was designed to:

> provide statistics on a national sample of students as they move out of the American high school system into the critical years of early adulthood. . . . The primary purpose of NLS is the observation of the educational and vocational activities, plans, aspirations, and attitudes of young people after they leave high school and the investigation of the relationships of this information to their prior educa-

tional experiences, personal, and biographical characteristics (Levinsohn et al., 1976, pp. iii; 1).

The study was supported by the National Center for Education Statistics,
Office of the Assistant Secretary for Education in the Department of
Health, Education, and Welfare. The base year (1972) survey data, with
which this report is concerned, were collected by the Educational Testing
Service.

The population from which the sample was drawn consisted of all
twelfth-grade students enrolled in 1972 in all public, private, and church-
affiliated high schools in the 50 states and the District of Columbia.

The sample design was a deeply stratified two-stage probability sample
with schools, as first-stage sampling units, selected from files maintained
by USOE and by the National Catholic Education Association. Schools
were sampled based on the following variables: type of control, geographic
region, grade 12 enrollment, proximity to institutions of higher learning,
percentage of minority group enrollment, income level of the community,
and degree of urbanization. Schools located in low-income areas and
schools with a high percentage of minority students were sampled at
about twice the sampling rate of other schools so the number of disadvantaged students might be increased.

Students, as second-stage units, were sampled from each school at
the rate of about 18 per school with 5 additional students being selected
from each school as alternates.

Data were collected on 22,532 students from 1,318 schools. For a
more complete description of the sampling procedure, the reader is referred to *NLS Data File Users Manual* (Levinsohn et al., 1976).

Although the NLS base group numbered 22,532, all students did not
complete every instrument. Only 16,683 completed the Base Year Questionnaire, 15,860 submitted usable test books, but 21,625 filled out the
Student Record Information Form. This monograph is primarily concerned with the 15,860 participants who completed the psychological
test battery, a number which must be further reduced in some cases
because a small number of students who completed the test battery failed
to provide information for proper SES or other classification. Nonetheless,
the size of the NLS base test group we will analyze is still substantial—
over 14,000 high school students, with males and females about equally
represented: 7041 and 7172, respectively.

The socioeconomic status of each student was determined according
to: (a) father's education, (b) mother's education, (c) parents' income,
(d) father's occupation, (e) household items which are indicative of personal wealth. After factor analysis had revealed a common factor with
approximately equal weights for each component, the components were
then standardized, and the sum of these five standard scores yielded

the SES raw scores which ranged from −2.3930 to 2.4540. The SES raw scores were then divided into quartiles: the upper quartile ranged from 0.4410 to 2.4540; the two middle quartiles from .4409 to −.4975; and the lower quartile from −.4976 to −2.3930. Participants whose SES raw scores were in the lower quartile were assigned a code of 1; in the middle two quartiles, a code of 2; and in the upper quartile range, a code of 3. The final breakdown of the total sample:

National Longitudinal Study
SES Classification

	High SES	Medium SES	Low SES
Black	104	591	1,243
White	3,422	6,337	2,516

The 50 states and the District of Columbia were divided into four regions: North East; North Central; South; and West. The rationale for the classification by states is not made clear in the *NLS Data File Users Manual* (Levinsohn et al., 1976). The states within each NLS region are listed in Table XI–A.

In several NLS publications the regional divisions were merely South or North, with the states listed under South in Table XI–A being one group, and all other states being called North. Consequently, the terms *North* and *South* applied to the NLS regions have next to nothing to do with latitude.

The distribution of the NLS white population by region follows fairly closely the U.S. Census estimate for 1977, Table XI–B.

Approximately 29.1% of the U.S. white population is found in the 16 "southern" states and the District of Columbia; 29.83% of the NLS white sample is found in these states. Because of the arbitrary decision to place Delaware, Maryland, West Virginia, the District of Columbia, Oklahoma, and Texas in the South, black population distribution is skewed and does not reflect the region's true ratio of blacks, Table XI–C. The NLS sample of blacks further dilutes the proportion of blacks outside the South. The South, as defined in the NLS, reported 50.55% of the total U.S. black population in 1977. The NLS assigned 66.9% of all NLS blacks to this region. The District of Columbia alone has more blacks than the total number of blacks in 11 of the 13 states in the NLS Western region. The six states gratuitously assigned to the South by NLS are homes for more blacks than the total number of blacks who live in 8 of the 9 states of the North East. The NLS geographic regions do not correspond to the nine WWI Army Service Commands nor to the six Army Areas nor any combination of Areas and Commands. For example, Delaware is in II Area along with Pennsylvania and Ohio.

Table XI-A

States within Each Region and Corresponding Percentages of Blacks and Whites[a]

North East			North Central			South			West		
State	W%	B%	State	W%	B%	State	W%	B%	State	W%	B%
CT	93.4	6.1	IL	85.3	13.7	AL	74.2	25.4	AK	78.8	<1.0
ME	99.3	<1.0	IN	92.4	7.3	AR	81.6	16.9	AZ	90.7	3.0
MA	95.7	3.6	IA	98.4	1.4	DE	84.8	14.7	CA	88.0	7.6
NH	99.3	<1.0	KS	94.4	4.7	FL	85.1	14.2	CO	95.3	3.4
NJ	87.2	11.9	MI	87.5	11.9	GA	73.5	26.1	HI	36.5	<1.0
NY	85.4	13.2	MN	98.0	1.0	KY	92.5	7.2	ID	98.2	<1.0
PA	90.6	8.8	MO	88.8	10.6	LA	69.8	29.8	MT	95.2	<1.0
RI	96.3	3.0	NB	96.2	3.0	MD	78.9	20.1	NV	91.7	6.0
VT	99.2	<1.0	ND	96.7	<1.0	MS	63.6	35.9	NM	90.2	<1.0
			OH	89.9	9.6	NC	76.9	21.9	OR	97.0	1.3
			SD	93.9	<1.0	OK	88.7	7.1	UT	97.5	<1.0
			WI	96.1	3.1	SC	68.8	30.8	WA	94.9	2.3
						TN	84.1	15.6	WY	96.9	<1.0
						TX	86.9	12.5			
						VA	80.5	18.7			
						WV	96.1	3.6			
						DC[b]	25.9	74.1			

[a] Source: U.S. Bureau of the Census (estimated July 1, 1977)
[b] Source: U.S. Bureau of the Census (estimated July 1, 1975)

252

Table XI–B
Distribution of U.S. White Population

Total White Population by Region. U.S. Census Estimate, 1977		Total White Population in NLS Sample by Region	
	%	N	%
Northeast	25.54	2895	23.58
North Central	27.16	3700	30.14
South	29.10	3662	29.83
West	18.19	2018	16.43

Table XI–C
Distribution of U.S. Black Population

Total Black Population by Region. U.S. Census Estimate, 1977		Total Black Population in NLS Sample by Region	
	%	N	%
Northeast	21.66	264	13.62
North Central	19.89	202	10.42
South	50.55	1298	66.97
West	7.88	174	8.97

New Mexico, Oklahoma, Texas, Arkansas, and Louisiana comprise the IV Area. Thus, the South as defined by the NLS was grossly overrepresented by blacks. For the types of analyses reported by NLS the assignment of states to a region made little difference in the outcome. NLS investigators seemed to be interested in attendance in black colleges, college survival rates, and reasons for "failure of desegregation in the South to raise achievement test scores . . ." (Crain and Mahard, 1978, p. 58).

Here we are primarily interested in tests of Negro intelligence as they relate to SES and geographic region. Since this is our primary concern, and since we are quite aware of the attenuating effect of blacks on total mean mental ability scores, we plan to follow the NLS geographic classifications, but shall make analyses for blacks and whites separately. Our subpopulation definitions—race, SES, and geographic region—are those of the NLS.

The sample on which our analyses will be based and which we will refer to as the total group includes the NLS sample of white and black students who took the psychological tests. Other races have been excluded. Since seven of the nine race classifications comprise only 10% of the total sample, only the two largest groups—whites and blacks—are examined in our sample.

The NLS Test Battery

A 69-minute test battery administered to each student provided measures of both verbal and non-verbal ability. The battery consisted of six tests described in the preliminary *NLS Data File Users Manual* as follows:

1. *Vocabulary.* A brief test using synonym format. The items were selected to avoid academic or collegiate bias and to be of an appropriate level of difficulty for the twelfth grade population. (15 items, 5 minutes)
2. *Picture Number.* A test of associative memory consisting of a series of drawings of familiar objects, each paired with a number. The student, after studying the picture number pairs, is asked to recall the number associated with each object. (30 items, 10 minutes)
3. *Reading.* A test based on short passages (100–200 words) with several related questions concerning a variety of reading skills (analysis, interpretation) but focused on straight-forward comprehension. In combination with the vocabulary test, it provides a means to derive a verbal score which can allow links to the normative data available for SAT. (20 items, 15 minutes)
4. *Letter Groups.* A test of inductive reasoning requiring the student to draw general concepts from sets of data or to form and try out hypotheses in a nonverbal context. The items consist of five groups of letters among which four groups share a common characteristic while the fifth group is different. The student indicates which group differs from the others. (25 items, 15 minutes)
5. *Mathematics.* Quantitative comparisons in which the student indicates which of two quantities is greater, or asserts their equality or the lack of sufficient data to determine which quantity is greater. This type of item is relatively quickly answered and provides measurement of basic competence in mathematics. (25 items, 15 minutes)
6. *Mosaic Comparisons.* A test which measures perceptual speed and accuracy through items which require that small differences be detected between pairs of otherwise identical mosaics or tile-like patterns. A deliberately speeded test, it has three separately timed sections consisting of increasingly more complex mosaic patterns. (116 items, 9 minutes) (pp. 22–23)

The test battery data consisted of 11 subtotal and total scores in all—one score each for Vocabulary, Reading, Letter Groups, and Mathematics; two subscores and a total for Picture Number; and three subscores and a total for Mosaic Comparisons. All tests were scored with the formula: $R-W/(C-1)$ where R = number of right responses, W = number of wrong responses, and C = number of responses per item. The formula scores were then standardized with a mean of 50 and a standard deviation of 10, with scores ranging from 1 to 99. Our analyses of the NLS battery will include the total scores of each test and an ability index which is the sum of the standard scores earned on the Reading, Mathematics, Vocabulary, and Letter Groups tests.

Data pertaining to the students' scores on standardized tests (College Board Scholastic Aptitude Test and American College Testing Program) were obtained from a Student's School Record Information Form.

Although the term *subpopulation* is widely used and generally understood, Jensen's (1973a) definition, which follows, will be used in our analysis of the NLS data.

> *Subpopultaion* has the advantage of being a theoretically neutral term. Unlike such terms as *social class* and *race,* a subpopulation does not connote more than its bare operational definition. Thus, the term *subpopulation* does not beg any questions. It can help to prevent us from mixing up the questions with the answers. And it can help to forestall fallacious thinking about social classes and races as Platonic categories. A subpopulation is simply any particular subdivision of the population which an investigator chooses to select for whatever purpose he may have. The only requirement is operational definition, that is to say, clearly specified objective criteria for the inclusion (and exclusion) of individuals. The reliability of the classification procedure is strictly an empirical question and not a matter of semantic debate. It can be answered in terms of reliability coefficient, which can take any value from 0 (no reliability whatsoever) to 1 (perfect reliability). A subpopulation can consist of redheads, or females, or owners of a Rolls Royce, or persons with incomes under $4000 per annum, or whatever criteria one may choose. All other questions follow, their relevance depending on the purposes of the investigator (p. 28).

Based on this definition of subpopulation, it is believed that race, sex, socioeconomic status, and geographic region are all classifications which may be used legitimately to assign members of the NLS sample to various subpopulations. These classifications have all been discussed in the section dealing with a description of the sample. The first point of the analysis will deal principally with subpopulation differences in ability and achievement levels of the students in the base year of the study, when all of the students were in grade 12.

To determine the effects of race, sex, socioeconomic status (SES), and geographic region on measures of ability and achievement, an analysis

Table XI–D

Analysis of Variance: The Effects of Race, Sex, Socio-economic Status, and
Geographic Region on Means of Various Ability and Achievement Measures

Test	Main Effects				Interactions				
	Race	Sex	SES	Region	Race × Sex	Race × SES	Sex × SES	Sex × Region	Sex × SES × Region
Vocabulary	**	**	**	**			**		*
Picture Number	**	**	**		**				
Reading	**	*	**	**					
Letter Groups	**	**	**	**					
Mathematics	**	**	**	**					
Mosaic Comparisons	**	**	**		**	*			
SAT-Verbal	**		**	**					
SAT-Math	**	**	**			*		*	
ACT Total	**		**	**		*			
Ability Index[a]	**		**	**					

Note. All possible interactions were computed but only those significant at the .05 level are shown.

[a] Vocabulary + Reading + Mathematics + Letter Groups.

* $p < .05$.

** $p < .01$.

of variance, using the principle of least squares to fit a fixed-effects linear
model to our data, was computed with the SAS program for the general
linear model (Barr, Goodnight, Sall, and Helwig, 1976, pp. 127–144).
The results of this analysis of variance are given in Table XI–D. Both
race and socioeconomic status show significant main effects on each of
the 10 measures of ability or achievement. Sex shows significant main
effects on the six tests of the NLS battery (but not the ability index)
and SAT math. The region in which the high school was located had
a significant effect on all variables except Picture Number, Mosaic Comparisons, and SAT math. There are relatively few significant interactions
among the four classifications (only 8 of a possible 110).

Sex Differences in Ability and Achievement

Since tests of the NLS battery vary in length, content, and difficulty,
tabled results are shown in T-scores for the NLS tests, in the customary
scoring system of the ACT and SAT, and also in standard deviation
units. This procedure does not convert all scores to Wechsler-type scaled
scores, but it does make it possible to compare at a glance mean group
differences even though the tests may differ widely in score range and
means. The advantages of the system are illustrated in Table XI–E when

Table XI–E
Means and Standard Deviations of Measures of Ability and Achievement: For Total Group and By Sex

Test	Total			Males			Females			Sex Diff. F–M	Diff. ÷ SD
	No.	Mn	SD	No.	Mn	SD	No.	Mn	SD		
Vocabulary	14213	50.7	10.0	7041	50.5	9.9	7172	50.9	10.0	0.4	.04
Picture Number	14213	50.3	9.9	7041	49.0	9.8	7172	51.5	9.9	2.5	.25
Reading	14213	50.6	9.9	7041	50.4	9.9	7172	50.8	9.8	0.4	.04
Letter Groups	14213	50.5	9.8	7041	49.5	10.1	7172	51.5	9.3	2.0	.20
Mathematics	14213	50.5	9.9	7041	51.8	9.9	7172	49.3	9.7	-2.5	.25
Mosaic Comparisons	14213	50.3	9.8	7041	49.2	9.8	7172	51.3	9.7	2.1	.21
SAT-Verbal	5404	451.9	110.5	2737	454.7	109.0	2667	449.0	112.0	-5.7	.05
SAT-Math	5384	484.3	115.9	2729	506.4	116.3	2655	461.5	111.0	-44.9	.39
ACT Total	3979	19.7	5.5	1957	20.2	5.7	2022	19.2	5.4	-1.0	.18
Ability Index[a]	14213	202.4	33.1	7041	202.2	33.6	7172	202.5	32.7	0.3	.01

[a] Vocabulary + Reading + Mathematics + Letter Groups.

comparing sex differences on the NLS vocabulary test and the SAT verbal section. Means show a difference of .4 points favoring girls on the vocabulary test and 5.7 points favoring boys on the SAT verbal. The difference divided by the standard deviation method shows the first test to favor girls by a .04 SD which is significant. The other comparison yields a .05 SD insignificant difference favoring boys. Of course a .4 point test score difference is of little practical importance. In the remainder of this monograph, wherever possible, group differences are shown in SD units as well as in the more conventional systems.

Some sex differences in psychological tests are fairly well established. The direction of the difference is convincing, but its magnitude is of little predictive or useful importance. In their seminal work, Maccoby and Jacklin (1974) found that girls' verbal abilities mature somewhat more rapidly than boys'. After about age 11, female superiority on verbal tasks becomes increasingly apparent. Girls score better on higher-level verbal tasks as well as on tests of word fluency. The differences reported by Maccoby and Jacklin amounted to about .25 SD. Converted to IQ equivalents, this would mean that girls outperformed boys on the verbal scales of mental tests by about 4 IQ points. The SE_m of the verbal IQ of the WISC is 3 at age 13.5.

Maccoby and Jacklin (1974) found that boys are better on both visual-spatial and mathematical abilities. The spatial differences are not present in early childhood but show up in adolescence. The same is true for mathematical ability when differences become apparent in the teens. In terms of IQ points, test differences favoring boys approach the SE_m. However, when the verbal and mathematical sections are combined, as they are in the Wechsler scale and the SAT, differences are offsetting, resulting in only a fraction of a SD difference, as we shall see in the next section.

Table XI–E lists, by sex, means and standard deviations for the NLS ability and achievement measures. Although the analysis of variance indicates that 7 of the 10 are significant, the real differences are in fact quite small. Significant differences follow the pattern reported by Maccoby and Jacklin (1974) and many others. At the high-school level girls are better on verbal-reading tasks; boys are better in mathematics. The two largest differences in Table XI–E favor boys and are found on the math sections of the SAT and NLS. On the five reading and verbal tests of the NLS, girls were the high scorers.

The observed sex differences range from a score difference equivalent to .01 SD to a difference of .39 SD, with the average SD equivalent for the 10 tests of .16 SD. In terms of IQ equivalents, the mean difference is equal to only 2 IQ points. This gives us the right to assume that practically there are no differences in mean scores earned by males and females on the NLS measures; as a consequence, we shall not make any further analysis by sex.

Racial Differences in Ability and Achievement

Table XI–F lists the mean scores earned by white and black students on the 10 measures of ability and achievement. On each of the six tests of the NLS battery and the composite ability index whites exceeded blacks, with score differences ranging from .64 to 1.16 SD equivalents. The tests measure all aspects of ability and achievement including vocabulary, associative memory, reading, inductive reasoning, mathematics, and perceptual speed and accuracy. On the College Board Scholastic Aptitude Tests, which measure verbal and mathematical aptitudes, and on the ACT, which measures achievement in four subject areas, white students exceeded black students by differences equivalent to more than a full standard deviation.

Racial Differences in Ability and Achievement by Socioeconomic Status

Despite the convincing arguments of Tyler (1965), Shuey (1966), and Jensen (1973a; 1980) that the relationship of measured intelligence to socioeconomic status is one of the best documented findings in mental test history, we shall examine again with new data the SES—mental ability association. In summarizing her findings on the SES—IQ correlation in *The Testing of Negro Intelligence* (2nd edition), Shuey wrote:

> Where Negro pupils have been compared with whites of the same occupational or socioeconomic class and where children from two or more classes have served as subjects, a greater difference has been found between the racial samples at the upper than at the lower level. McGurk and Sperrazzo and Wilkins, for example, have reported large differences between the means of their Negro and white Ss identified as belonging to the *high* socioeconomic group and smaller differences between the means of their samples belonging to the *low* socioeconomic group (p. 519).

Dr. Shuey's remarks are no less appropriate today than when they were written in 1966. Fifteen years of unlimited funds, the most sophisticated experimental techniques, and massive government intervention have made no detectable change in the SES—IQ correlation.

In the NLS base groups there were three SES levels; high, medium, and low. When the data were analyzed by race and SES, some cells were found to have fewer than 30 subjects. In our analysis of the NLS data, high and medium SES classifications were collapsed making our

Table XI-F
Means and Standard Deviations of Measures of Ability and Achievement: By Race

Test	Blacks			Whites			Diff. W-B	Diff. ÷ SD
	No.	Mn	SD	No.	Mn	SD		
Vocabulary	1,938	42.6	7.6	12,275	52.0	9.7	9.4	.94
Picture Number	1,938	44.8	9.6	12,275	51.1	9.7	6.3	.64
Reading	1,938	42.6	8.7	12,275	51.9	9.4	9.3	.94
Letter Groups	1,938	42.2	10.4	12,275	51.8	9.0	9.6	.98
Mathematics	1,938	41.7	8.0	12,275	51.9	9.5	10.2	1.03
Mosaic Comparisons	1,938	42.8	10.6	12,275	51.4	9.2	8.6	.88
SAT-Verbal	554	344.3	89.4	4,850	464.2	105.9	119.9	1.09
SAT-Math	544	365.8	91.4	4,840	497.6	110.7	131.8	1.14
ACT Total	331	12.9	4.5	3,648	20.3	5.2	7.4	1.35
Ability Index[a]	1,938	169.1	27.7	12,275	207.6	30.8	38.5	1.16

[a] Vocabulary + Reading + Mathematics + Letter Groups.

final grouping (a) high-medium SES, and (b) low SES, rather than high, medium, and low. The breakdown was as follows:

Collapsed Socioeconomic
Classification

	High-Medium SES	Low SES
Black	695	1,243
White	9,759	2,516

From Table XI–D it was seen that for students in the National Longitudinal Study SES had a significant effect on tests of mental ability and school achievement. Table XI–G shows means and SDs for the 10 NLS measures by SES for the total group and for each race. Again it was seen that test means vary in the expected direction, high-medium > low SES. The relationship holds for the highly verbal tests such as Reading and Vocabulary and the verbal section of the SAT as well as for the "culture fair" tests, Picture Number and Mosaic Comparisons. SES differences for the latter tests are somewhat less than those for verbal tests, but all differences are significant even for the smallest groups.

The within-race differences between the two SES groups are the same for white and black students. That is, SES affects test performance of both racial groups about the same. When the two races are grouped separately by SES, whites outscore blacks on each NLS measure with the average black-white difference approximately the same in high-medium and low SES groups.

In the high-medium SES groups the average between-race difference was equivalent to .92 SD and .82 SD in the lower SES group (Table XI–H). If converted to IQ equivalents, the differences would represent approximately 14 IQ points for the high-medium SES and 12 IQ points for the low. These IQ differences follow a pattern described by Shuey in 1966, but they are not quite as large, especially for the high-medium SES pupils. Shuey reported black-white differences of 20 IQ points at the high end of the SES scale and 12 points at the low. However, considering only the longer, more reliable measures, our findings are very similar to Shuey's. Both the verbal and mathematics SAT scales yield black-white differences of about 1 SD for the two SES groups. The ACT, which is thought to be more achievement oriented than some of the NLS battery, produced the highest SES differences, about 1.25 SDs.

The consistency of the findings is remarkable when it is considered that Shuey's results are based on the analysis of 32 different studies conducted in the 1950's and 1960's, while our findings are based on one, large, nationwide study of 14,000 high-school graduates a decade later.

Table XI–G

Means and Standard Deviations of Measures of Ability and Achievement: By Race and Socioeconomic Level

Test	High-Medium SES			Low SES		
	No.	Mn	SD	No.	Mn	SD
Vocabulary						
Black	695	44.7	8.5	1243	41.4	6.8
White	9759	53.0	9.7	2516	48.0	9.1
Total	10454	52.5	9.5	3759	45.8	8.9
Picture Number						
Black	695	45.7	9.3	1243	44.4	9.7
White	9759	51.6	9.8	2516	49.3	9.8
Total	10454	51.2	9.9	3759	47.6	10.1
Reading						
Black	695	45.0	9.2	1243	41.2	8.2
White	9759	52.7	9.4	2516	48.4	9.5
Total	10454	52.2	9.5	3759	46.0	9.7
Letter Groups						
Black	695	44.3	10.5	1243	41.0	10.3
White	9759	52.6	8.7	2516	48.9	9.6
Total	10454	52.1	8.8	3759	46.3	10.5
Mathematics						
Black	695	43.6	8.4	1243	40.7	7.6
White	9759	52.9	9.3	2516	48.1	9.3
Total	10454	52.3	9.5	3759	45.7	9.5
Mosaic Comparisons						
Black	695	44.0	9.9	1243	42.1	10.9
White	9759	51.9	9.2	2516	49.6	9.6
Total	10454	51.4	9.3	3759	47.1	10.6
SAT-Verbal						
Black	324	354.8	96.2	230	329.6	76.9
White	4452	467.2	105.9	398	430.4	98.9
Total	4776	459.5	109.3	628	393.5	103.5
SAT-Math						
Black	318	373.6	97.5	226	354.8	81.4
White	4446	500.3	110.9	394	466.1	105.1
Total	4764	491.9	114.3	620	425.5	110.9
ACT Total						
Black	139	13.6	5.1	192	12.3	4.0
White	3240	20.5	4.9	408	19.1	5.3
Total	3379	20.2	5.2	600	16.9	5.9
Ability Index[a]						
Black	695	177.7	28.9	1243	164.4	25.7
White	9759	211.3	29.7	2516	193.4	30.4
Total	10454	209.1	30.6	3759	183.8	32.0

[a] Vocabulary + Reading + Mathematics + Letter Groups.

Regional Differences in Achievement and Ability

Since Hippocrates tried to explain the differences in character and personality between the populations of Asia and Europe, men have been interested in the geography of intellect. Until fairly recently philosophers and psychologists lacked tools to measure observable differences, relying for the most part on generalizations and descriptions. The development

Table XI–H

Differences in Black and White Pupils in Ability and Achievement Scores by Socioeconomic Levels

Test	High-Medium SES		Low SES	
	White-Black	Diff. ÷ SD	White-Black	Diff. ÷ SD
Vocabulary	8.3	.83	6.6	.66
Picture Number	5.9	.60	4.9	.49
Reading	7.7	.78	7.2	.73
Letter Groups	8.3	.85	7.9	.81
Mathematics	9.3	.94	7.4	.75
Mosaic Comparisons	7.9	.81	7.5	.77
SAT-Verbal	112.4	1.02	100.8	.91
SAT-Math	126.7	1.09	111.3	.96
ACT Total	6.9	1.25	6.8	1.24
Ability Index[a]	33.6	1.02	29.0	.88
Average		.92		.82

[a] Vocabulary + Reading + Mathematics + Letter Groups.

by Robert M. Yerkes (1921) during WWI of a system of mental measurement opened up to psychologists the first opportunity to examine on a large-scale basis individual and regional differences in intelligence. With WWI recruits as a data base, Yerkes reported regional differences in the Army Alpha and Beta test scores that usually favored soldiers from the North and East over the South. Also apparent were urban-rural differences, which generally favored the recruits from the cities.

Perhaps the best-known, although certainly not the best, studies derived from WWI data were those of Klineberg (1935; 1944) who selected from Yerkes' Tables 200 and 262 the four southern states where the white Alpha medians were *lowest* and the four northern states where the black Alpha medians were *highest*. Klineberg tabulated the medians of these eight groups and observed that northern Negroes were superior to the white groups from a number of southern states. Of course, as Garrett (1960) and many others pointed out, Klineberg not only selected the states by test scores, but failed to include scores on the Beta Examination, the test given to most Negro recruits. If the Canadian psychologist had reported the results of both WWI tests, the false impression that race made no difference would have been avoided.

WWII mental test data were usually analyzed by Army Command and AGCT Grade rather than by state and mental age level.

A comparison of the AGCT Grade distribution of the whites in the all Southern Command (IV) with the Grade distribution of the Negroes in the particular Northern Command (I) *where their scores were best* shows that proportionally, five times as many Southern whites as Northern Negroes were in Grade I, and proportionally, two times as many Southern whites as Northern Negroes were in Grade II; at the lower end of the scale, there were relatively fewer Negroes than whites in Grade V but more Negroes in Grade IV. Combining Grades I and II, and similarly Grades IV and V, it appears that about *21 percent* of the Southern whites and *9 percent* of the Negroes of the best Northern Command scored in the two highest Grades, and about *51 percent* of the Southern whites as opposed to *59 percent* of these Northern Negroes scored in the two lowest Grades of the Army test (Shuey, p. 352).

In Table XI–D it was shown that on 7 of the 10 NLS measures there were significant regional differences in test performance. The two culture fair scales, Picture Number and Mosaic Comparisons, and SAT-math test showed insignificant regional differences. The pattern of regional test score differences was not as clear for the NLS battery (Table XI–I) as it was for the Alpha, Beta, and AGCT. Both black and white students in the North East tended to be the highest scorers on the NLS test while those students from the West were best on the SAT and ACT. If only the combined black-white means are considered, the South was lowest on all but one test. With two-thirds of all NLS blacks assigned to the Southern region, this finding is not unexpected. When scores in Table XI–I are examined by region and race rather than combined group, regional differences are attenuated. The largest regional differences divided by the standard deviations for each of the 10 measures range from .09 to .48. The average greatest difference for blacks is .24 SD; for whites, .21 SD; and for the total group, .34 SD. Converted to IQ equivalents these differences would be equal to 3 IQ points for whites, 4 for blacks, and 5 for the combined group. This is not to say students of both races living in the South do not lag behind students of other regions, especially those of the North East and West. On some tests, however, blacks and whites scored higher than students from other regions. The differences were not significant, but the direction of the differences is surprising. On the SAT math section southern blacks scored higher than blacks from the East. On the NLS math tests, southern whites were higher than whites from the West. Looking at mean scores of the races separately, there were reversals of the general trend, South < North East. However, all differences are small and are perhaps the result of sampling accidents.

We shall now determine if black-white differences in scores vary among the four geographic regions. Table XI–J shows the differences in mean scores earned on the various measures of ability and achievement by white and black students and the standard deviation equivalents of these differences. Note how similar the differences are across regions, with the mean differences for the four regions being equivalent to 1.00, .97,

.98, and .98 standard deviations. We conclude that, regardless of the geographical area from which subsamples are drawn, whites exceed blacks in mean scores by a difference equivalent to approximately 1 SD.

From the above analysis it is clear that the student's geographical region has apparently the same effect on scores earned by both black and white students. High scores are generally from the North East, and low scores of both races are from the southern region. On no NLS test did blacks of one region equal or exceed the whites from their own or any other region.

Effect of Integration on Black-White NLS Score Differences

It has been observed that the average difference between blacks and whites on the NLS measures of mental ability and school achievement is equivalent to 1.02 standard deviations. When blacks and whites are grouped by geographic region, the average black-white score difference is also equal to about 1 SD in each of the four regional groups (Table XI–J). The average black-white score differences in the two SES groups are .92 SD and .82 SD (Table XI–H). From this evidence we must conclude that, although socioeconomic status, and to a lesser degree geographic region, have significant effects on test scores of both black and white students, these two variables do not explain score variances between the two races. We must look elsewhere for factors which may be related to differential mental test performance of black and white school children.

For many years, and certainly since the Supreme Court handed down the Brown vs. Board of Education ruling in 1954, conventional wisdom has had it that blacks perform less well in segregated classes than in classes with whites; that "separate but equal" educational opportunities cannot, in fact, be equal. The NLS survey provides data which can help determine the extent to which black-white differences in ability and achievement scores can be attributed to segregation. Students in the NLS sample were asked to indicate the percent of white students in their classes and to respond to the question, "When you were in high school, about how many of your *teachers* were white or Caucasian?" The breakdown which the students used to indicate the percentage of white students at each of the four grade levels was as follows: None = 0; 1–10% = 1; 11–25% = 2; 26–50% = 3; 51–75% = 4; 76–90% = 5; 91–99% = 6; and all (100%) = 7. The possible responses to the question relative to the number of white teachers in the student's high school were: None = 0; Some = 1; About half = 2; Most = 3; and All =4.

The first step in the analysis of the effects of school integration on achievement and ability scores was to correlate these measures with self-reported indexes of degree of school integration. These indexes (percentage of white students in grade 12 and proportion of white teachers in

Table XI-I

Means and Standard Deviations of Measures of Ability and Achievement: By Race and Geographic Region of the United States

Test	North East			North Central			South			West		
	No.	Mn	SD	No.	Mn	SD	No.	Mn	SD	No.	Mn	SD
Vocabulary												
Black	264	44.3	9.0	202	43.6	8.1	1298	41.9	7.1	174	44.1	7.4
White	2895	53.9	9.7	3700	51.6	9.6	3662	50.6	9.6	2018	52.8	9.6
Total	3159	53.1	10.0	3902	51.2	9.7	4960	48.3	9.8	2192	52.1	9.7
Picture Number												
Black	264	44.8	8.9	202	44.0	8.5	1298	45.1	9.8	174	44.2	10.2
White	2895	51.5	9.7	3700	51.2	9.7	3662	51.4	9.8	2018	50.1	9.7
Total	3159	51.0	9.9	3902	50.8	9.7	4960	49.7	10.1	2192	49.6	9.9
Reading												
Black	264	44.7	8.9	202	43.7	8.7	1298	41.8	8.5	174	43.8	8.5
White	2895	52.8	9.3	3700	51.5	9.4	3662	51.4	9.4	2018	52.0	9.6
Total	3159	52.1	9.5	3902	51.1	9.5	4960	48.9	10.1	2192	51.4	9.7
Letter Groups												
Black	264	44.4	10.2	202	42.8	10.8	1298	41.6	10.4	174	42.4	10.0
White	2895	52.9	8.6	3700	52.1	8.9	3662	50.9	9.1	2018	51.6	9.1
Total	3159	52.2	9.1	3902	51.6	9.2	4960	48.5	10.3	2192	50.8	9.5
Mathematics												
Black	264	42.9	8.4	202	42.6	8.1	1298	41.2	7.8	174	42.5	8.4
White	2895	52.9	9.4	3700	52.0	9.4	3662	51.4	9.4	2018	51.1	9.6
Total	3159	52.0	9.7	3902	51.5	9.6	4960	48.8	10.1	2192	50.5	9.8

	N	Mean	SD	N	Mean	SD	N	Mean	SD	N	Mean	SD
Mosaic Comparisons												
Black	264	43.9	10.3	202	43.7	9.6	1298	42.4	11.0	174	43.0	8.3
White	2895	51.2	8.4	3700	51.4	8.5	3662	51.3	9.8	2018	52.1	10.2
Total	3159	50.6	8.8	3902	51.0	8.8	4960	49.0	10.8	2192	51.4	10.4
SAT-Verbal												
Black	158	349.9	96.9	42	364.8	97.5	302	337.5	86.9	52	350.3	69.6
White	2058	460.0	104.1	925	473.8	107.7	1299	454.9	106.1	568	484.7	105.5
Total	2216	452.1	107.4	967	469.0	109.5	1601	432.8	112.6	620	473.4	109.5
SAT-Math												
Black	157	358.7	89.5	42	374.0	88.0	293	366.7	95.7	52	375.6	74.3
White	2055	490.6	111.7	922	513.5	110.0	1298	490.4	107.6	565	513.2	110.8
Total	2212	481.3	115.4	964	507.5	112.7	1591	467.6	115.9	617	501.6	114.7
ACT Total												
Black	4	11.0	7.4	81	13.2	4.9	233	12.8	4.3	13	13.1	3.9
White	111	20.0	6.0	1640	21.0	5.1	1360	19.4	5.1	537	20.3	5.3
Total	115	19.7	6.2	1721	20.6	5.4	1593	18.5	5.5	550	20.1	5.4
Ability Index[a]												
Black	264	176.4	30.1	202	172.8	28.4	1298	166.6	26.8	174	172.8	26.8
White	2895	212.4	30.4	3700	207.2	30.4	3662	204.3	30.9	2018	207.5	31.1
Total	3159	209.4	32.0	3902	205.4	31.2	4960	194.5	34.2	2192	204.8	32.2

[a] Vocabulary + Reading + Mathematics + Letter Groups.

Table XI-J

Differences Between Black and White Pupils in Ability and Achievement Scores by Geographic Region of the United States

Test	North East		North Central		South		West	
	Diff. W-B	Diff. ÷ SD	Diff. W-B	Diff. ÷ SD	Diff. W-B	Diff. ÷ SD	Diff. W-B	Diff. ÷ SD
Vocabulary	9.6	.96	8.0	.80	8.7	.87	8.7	.87
Picture Number	6.7	.68	7.2	.73	6.3	.64	5.9	.60
Reading	8.1	.82	7.8	.79	9.6	.97	8.2	.83
Letter Groups	8.5	.87	9.3	.95	9.3	.95	9.2	.94
Mathematics	10.0	1.01	9.4	.95	10.2	1.03	8.6	.87
Mosaic Comparisons	7.3	.74	7.7	.79	8.9	.91	9.1	.93
SAT-Verbal	110.1	1.00	109.0	.99	117.4	1.06	134.4	1.22
SAT-Math	131.9	1.14	139.5	1.20	123.7	1.07	137.6	1.19
ACT-Total	9.0	1.64	7.8	1.42	6.6	1.20	7.2	1.31
Ability Index[a]	36.0	1.09	34.4	1.04	37.7	1.14	34.7	1.05
Average		1.00		.97		.98		.98

[a] Vocabulary + Reading + Mathematics + Letter Groups.

Table XI–K

Correlations between Various Measures of Ability and Achievement and Certain Indexes of Degree of Pupil and Teacher Integration

Test	Percent White Students— Grade 12		Proportion of White Teachers in High School	
	Black	White	Black	White
Vocabulary	.04	.03	.10	.08
Picture Number	−.02	.05	.03	.07
Reading	.02	.04	.13	.07
Letter Groups	.00	.07	.11	.09
Mathematics	.07	.06	.14	.09
Mosaic Comparisons	−.11	.03	.04	.04
SAT-Verbal	.14	.06	.15	.08
SAT-Math	.13	.07	.15	.06
ACT Total	.07	.09	.11	.10
Ability Index[a]	.04	.06	.15	.10

[a] Vocabulary + Reading + Mathematics + Letter Groups.

high school) are not available as continuous variables but are reported as mentioned above on an eight-point scale for percent of white students and on a five-point scale for proportion of white teachers. Table XI–K shows the results of this analysis. For both blacks and whites all r's between indexes of school integration and test scores show negligible relationships (r's of .15 or less). Neither racial composition of the senior class nor the racial composition of the high school teachers of a school is significantly related to test performance of the senior class.

To maximize achievement, perhaps there is an optimum white-non-white ratio of class and teacher composition which may or may not be the same for black and white students. In order to examine the observed test scores earned by black and white students in schools with varying proportions of white high-school teachers, Table XI–L was prepared. On 8 of the 10 ability measures, the within-race differences between the highest and the lowest means of the five teacher-integration groups were equivalent to about .5 standard deviation or less for both the black and white students. A few other observations from the table will be made. On the ACT, black students who attended high schools with all white teachers earned a mean score equivalent to a full standard deviation higher than blacks who attended high schools with no white teachers. On the Reading test scores of the NLS battery those blacks who attended schools where most of the high-school teachers were white exceeded those blacks who attended schools which had no white high-school teachers by a difference equivalent to .79 standard deviation. The mean standard deviation equivalent difference between highest and lowest integration groups for the 10 ability measures was .46 for blacks and .43 for whites. It is apparent from Table XI–L that, for both blacks and whites,

Table XI-L

Means and Standard Deviations of Various Ability and Achievement Tests Administered at Twelfth-Grade Level: By Race and Degree of Teacher Integration in High School

| | Proportion of High School Teachers Who Were White | | | | | | | | | | | | | | | | |
| Test | None | | | Some | | | About Half | | | Most | | | All | | | Largest Diff. | Diff. ÷ SD |
	No.	Mn	SD	No.	Mn	SD	No.	Mn	SD	No.	Mn	SD	No.	Mn	SD		
Vocabulary																	
Black	14	41.9	7.3	318	41.8	6.3	433	41.8	7.1	689	43.9	8.2	179	43.1	8.4	2.1	.21
White	74	50.4	10.3	333	49.2	8.8	335	48.2	9.1	3933	52.6	9.5	6145	52.8	9.7	4.6	.46
Picture Number																	
Black	14	44.8	7.5	318	44.5	9.8	433	44.9	9.7	689	45.3	9.4	179	45.4	9.1	.9	.09
White	74	48.8	10.7	333	49.1	9.4	335	48.7	9.5	3933	51.3	9.6	6145	51.9	9.7	3.2	.32
Reading																	
Black	14	36.4	7.4	318	41.5	8.2	433	41.6	8.3	689	44.2	9.0	179	43.4	8.7	7.8	.79
White	74	48.5	10.0	333	48.6	8.8	335	48.8	9.4	3933	52.6	9.1	6145	52.5	9.4	4.1	.41
Letter Groups																	
Black	14	41.6	9.4	318	40.4	9.6	433	41.1	10.4	689	44.1	10.4	179	41.8	9.9	3.7	.38
White	74	48.8	9.6	333	49.5	9.2	335	48.3	10.2	3933	52.2	8.6	6145	52.7	8.7	4.4	.45
Mathematics																	
Black	14	38.6	5.1	318	39.8	6.7	433	40.9	7.4	689	43.2	8.5	179	41.7	8.3	4.6	.46
White	74	48.4	10.9	333	48.6	9.3	335	47.9	8.9	3933	52.6	9.2	6145	52.6	9.4	4.7	.47
Mosaic Comparisons																	
Black	14	44.1	8.2	318	42.6	11.2	433	42.1	11.5	689	43.3	9.7	179	43.7	10.6	2.0	.20
White	74	51.0	10.8	333	51.1	9.8	335	50.2	11.6	3933	51.5	8.9	6145	52.0	8.8	1.8	.18
SAT-Verbal																	
Black	10	334.0	90.3	79	334.2	90.9	102	319.1	72.5	233	356.0	87.7	58	369.5	103.9	50.4	.46
White	26	463.1	98.3	115	418.2	96.8	78	429.1	105.9	1751	464.4	107.2	2484	471.0	103.8	52.8	.48
SAT-Math																	
Black	10	317.0	75.3	74	348.4	93.9	101	350.9	85.9	229	378.4	93.8	58	378.6	92.5	61.6	.53
White	26	475.4	126.5	114	453.2	98.8	78	460.8	116.6	1744	501.7	111.7	2483	502.8	108.2	49.6	.43
ACT Total																	
Black	7	8.4	2.6	41	13.2	3.3	75	12.5	4.4	126	13.1	4.7	43	13.9	5.4	5.5	1.00
White	27	18.0	6.5	86	19.0	5.1	64	17.9	5.1	1211	20.1	5.2	1910	20.8	5.1	2.9	.53
Ability Index[a]																	
Black	14	158.5	18.1	318	163.4	23.5	433	165.5	26.6	689	175.4	29.2	179	170.0	29.0	16.9	.51
White	74	196.1	34.8	333	195.9	29.6	335	193.2	31.0	3933	210.1	29.6	6145	210.5	30.3	17.3	.52

[a] Vocabulary + Reading + Mathematics + Letter Groups.

students attending schools where most or all of the high-school teachers were white scored higher than did students who attended high schools where less than 50% of the teachers were white. The observed score differences are equivalent to about .5 standard deviation. Converted to IQ equivalents, these differences would represent approximately 8 IQ points.

We shall now compare the differences between black and white students who attended schools that had approximately the same proportion of white high-school teachers. Table XI–M shows the black-white score differences on each of the 10 ability and achievement measures for each of the five teacher-integration groups. It is interesting that the average black-white difference in schools where all high-school teachers were white is about the same as in schools where none of the high school teachers were white (differences equivalent to about 1 SD). The least black-white differences occurred for students attending schools where about one-half the high-school teachers were white. The averages of the differences for the five integration groups is about .92 standard deviation.

Although statistically the degree of pupil integration affects ability and achievement scores, especially for whites, the actual observed differences for both white and black students are quite small. When grouped according to 12th-grade integration ratios, the maximum score difference for blacks ranged from a standard deviation equivalent of .04 (Picture Number) to .36 (SAT-math) with a mean difference of .18; for whites it ranged from .12 (Mosaic Comparisons) to .31 (ACT) with a mean of .22. It should be noted that the greatest differences between any two integration groups tend to occur in ACT or SAT variables, subsamples which are composed primarily of students planning to enter college (Table XI–N).

Our next step was to compare mean NLS scores of 12th-grade blacks and whites within each of the four integration groupings. Although the number of blacks and whites who attended 12th-grade classes in which pupil enrollment was 0–25% white was approximately the same, the mean scores of the whites exceeded those of blacks on the average by .95 SD (Table XI–O). In classes where whites are in the minority (0–25%) or where blacks are in the minority (76–100% white students) or where blacks and whites are almost evenly represented (26–50% and 51–75% whites), whites consistently exceed blacks on NLS tests by a difference of approximately 1 SD.

To summarize the effects of integration on test performance of white and black students:

1. The relationships between each of 10 measures of ability and achievement with indexes of pupil and teacher integration were negligible. (All correlation coefficients were .15 or below.)

Table XI-M

Differences Between Black and White Pupils on Ability and Achievement Tests Administered at Twelfth-Grade Level: By Degree of Teacher Integration in High School

| | Proportion of High School Teachers Who Were White | | | | | | | | | |
| | None | | Some | | About Half | | Most | | All | |
Test	Mn Diff. W-B	Diff. ÷ SD	Mn Diff. W-B	Diff. ÷ SD	Mn Diff. W-B	Diff. ÷ SD	Mn Diff. W-B	Diff. ÷ SD	Mn Diff. W-B	Diff. ÷ SD
Vocabulary	8.5	.85	7.4	.74	6.4	.64	8.7	.87	9.7	.97
Picture Number	4.0	.40	4.6	.46	3.8	.38	6.0	.61	6.5	.66
Reading	12.1	1.22	7.1	.72	7.2	.73	8.4	.85	9.1	.92
Letter Groups	7.2	.73	9.1	.93	7.2	.73	8.1	.83	10.9	1.11
Mathematics	9.8	.99	8.8	.89	7.0	.71	9.4	.95	10.9	1.10
Mosaic Comparisons	6.9	.70	8.5	.87	8.1	.83	8.2	.84	8.3	.85
SAT-Verbal	129.1	1.17	84.0	.76	110.0	1.00	108.4	.98	101.5	.92
SAT-Math	158.4	1.37	104.8	.90	109.9	.95	123.3	1.06	124.2	1.07
ACT Total	9.6	1.75	5.8	1.05	5.4	.98	7.0	1.27	6.9	1.25
Ability Index[a]	37.6	1.14	32.5	.98	27.7	.84	34.7	1.05	40.5	1.22
Average		1.03		.83		.78		.93		1.01

[a] Vocabulary + Reading + Mathematics + Letter Groups.

272

Table XI-N

Means and Standard Deviations of Various Ability and Achievement Tests Administered at Twelfth-Grade Level: By Race and Degree of Pupil Integration in Twelfth Grade

							Percent White Pupils					
	0–25			26–50			51–75			76–100		
Test	No.	Mn	SD	No.	Mn	SD	No.	Mn	SD	No.	Mn	SD
Vocabulary												
Black	629	42.6	7.1	318	42.5	7.5	326	42.9	7.8	363	43.4	8.5
White	685	51.4	9.6	858	51.0	9.5	1628	51.9	9.8	7588	52.8	9.6
Picture Number												
Black	629	45.1	9.4	318	44.9	9.7	326	44.8	9.5	363	45.2	9.7
White	685	50.9	9.9	858	50.0	9.3	1628	50.8	9.7	7588	51.9	9.7
Reading												
Black	629	42.7	8.3	318	42.5	9.1	326	43.1	8.6	363	43.1	9.2
White	685	51.0	9.8	858	50.7	9.3	1628	52.0	9.2	7588	52.6	9.3
Letter Groups												
Black	629	42.3	10.0	318	41.6	10.7	326	43.4	10.4	363	42.0	10.3
White	685	50.5	9.3	858	50.4	9.5	1628	51.8	8.6	7588	52.8	8.6
Mathematics												
Black	629	41.0	7.2	318	41.9	8.3	326	42.5	8.2	363	42.2	8.8
White	685	51.0	9.7	858	50.3	9.4	1628	51.8	9.4	7588	52.8	9.3
Mosaic Comparisons												
Black	629	44.2	11.2	318	41.8	11.2	326	42.3	9.4	363	41.9	9.4
White	685	51.0	9.1	858	50.8	9.3	1628	51.1	8.8	7588	52.0	9.0
SAT-Verbal												
Black	192	332.8	82.8	87	335.8	84.1	90	350.7	83.3	115	371.5	99.4
White	277	458.1	106.8	296	449.4	108.1	674	453.2	105.6	3196	471.4	104.6
SAT-Math												
Black	183	355.5	93.0	87	351.1	84.6	89	372.0	90.9	115	392.5	94.6
White	275	485.3	103.6	295	479.4	110.5	672	487.9	109.0	3192	506.3	110.0
ACT Total												
Black	104	12.7	4.0	50	12.2	4.2	65	13.3	4.7	72	13.5	5.3
White	198	20.0	5.7	232	19.0	5.1	482	19.9	5.2	2375	20.7	5.1
Ability Index[a]												
Black	629	168.7	25.4	318	168.3	29.0	326	171.9	28.3	363	170.7	30.3
White	685	204.0	32.0	858	202.5	30.8	1628	207.5	30.1	7588	211.0	30.0

[a] Vocabulary + Reading + Mathematics + Letter Groups.

273

Table XI-O

Differences Between Black and White Pupils on Ability and Achievement Tests Administered at Twelfth-Grade Level: By Degree of Pupil Integration in Twelfth Grade

| | Percent of White Pupils in Grade 12 | | | | | | | |
| | 0–25 | | 26–50 | | 51–75 | | 76–100 | |
Test	Mn Diff. W-B	Diff. ÷ SD	Mn Diff. W-B	Diff. ÷ SD	Mn Diff. W-B	Diff. ÷ SD	Mn Diff. W-B	Diff. ÷ SD
Vocabulary	8.8	.88	8.5	.85	9.0	.90	9.4	.94
Picture Number	5.8	.59	5.1	.52	6.0	.61	6.7	.68
Reading	8.3	.84	8.2	.83	8.9	.90	9.5	.96
Letter Groups	8.2	.84	8.8	.90	8.4	.86	10.8	1.10
Mathematics	10.0	1.01	8.4	.85	9.3	.94	10.6	1.07
Mosaic Comparisons	6.8	.69	9.0	.92	8.8	.90	10.1	1.03
SAT-Verbal	125.3	1.13	113.6	1.03	102.5	.93	99.9	.90
SAT-Math	129.8	1.12	128.3	1.11	115.9	1.00	113.8	.98
ACT Total	7.3	1.33	6.8	1.24	6.6	1.20	7.2	1.31
Ability Index[a]	35.3	1.07	34.2	1.03	35.6	1.08	40.3	1.22
Average		.95		.93		.93		1.02

[a] Vocabulary + Reading + Mathematics + Letter Groups.

2. Within each of four pupil-integration groups at the 12th-grade level, whites exceeded blacks on ability and achievement scores by an average amount equivalent to .96 SD.

3. When white and black students were grouped according to the proportion of their high-school teachers who were white, it was found that the average of the greatest group difference on each of the 10 measures was equivalent to about .5 SD for both blacks and whites while the average white-black difference within the five teacher-integration groups was equivalent to .92 SD.

4. The effect of degree of teacher or pupil integration on scores earned by each race was considerably less than the black-white differences within each integration group.

In order to bring together the various score differences which have been presented in tabular form, Figure XI–1 was prepared. The figure displays the range and means of black-white differences in standard deviation equivalents for each of the 10 ability and achievement measures as well as for an average of these measures. In the analysis for Figure 1 black and white pupils were divided into the 16 subgroups discussed previously. Score differences were computed for each group for each of

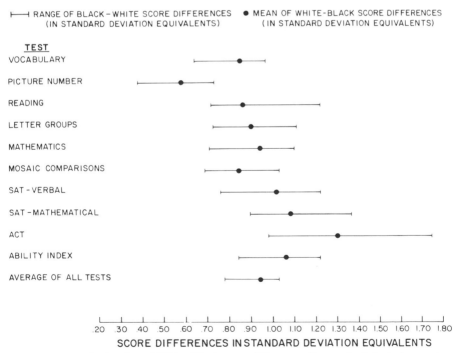

Figure XI–1. Distribution of White-Black score differences (in standard deviation equivalents) for sixteen subgroups on each of ten tests of ability or achievement.

10 test variables. Differences ranged from a standard deviation equivalent of .38 to 1.75.

In Figure 1 the averages of the differences for the 10 tests in the NLS battery on each of the 16 subpopulations are also plotted. Differences in SD units range from .58 to 1.30, with a mean difference equivalent to .94 SD.

Concluding Remarks

It has been found universally since the seminal work of Robert M. Yerkes (1921) during WWI that there is a significant mean difference in mental test performance between U.S. blacks and whites. The racial difference that has appeared most consistently and which has attracted most attention from researchers is the 15 IQ points or 1 standard deviation discrepancy in the mean mental test scores of blacks and whites. The NLS data are no exception to this established law. The finding stands up regardless of the nature of the mental task, the degree of pupil and teacher integration, the geographic region of residence, or the socioeconomic status.

XII

College Admissions: A 21-year Analysis of CEEB Scholastic Aptitude Test

R. Travis Osborne

This is the second of two monographs prepared especially for Volume 2 of *The Testing of Negro Intelligence*. The University System of Georgia is one of the select few state-wide systems of higher education that has kept and published admissions test data for all branches of the System for over 20 years. Test results for the 21-year period provide exceptional opportunity to examine subpopulation score differences during two decades of greatly expanding facilities and radically changing educational practices. During the period covered by this study, 1957–1977 inclusive, over 300,000 freshmen entered the various branches of the University System; all were required to take the College Board Scholastic Aptitude Test. Results were summarized and published each year for use by admissions officers and high school counselors. The purpose of the test was outlined in the first Normative Data Manual:

In 1957, the Board of Regents of the University System of Georgia required that all entering freshmen in any of the 16 undergraduate units of the University System submit, prior to admission, the scores on the College Board Scholastic Aptitude Test. This requirement was enacted to permit a searching analysis of measures which might prove effective for guidance purposes, or for identifying, against the time when the number of applicants may far exceed facilities, those most likely to succeed in each unit of the System. It was also felt that a period of intensive search for factors related to success in the different colleges, and the establishment of pilot programs, might identify the issues which must be taken into account in any sensible, selective admissions program. The Director of Testing and Guidance is charged with supervising and conducting such research as may be necessary to establish the meaning and appropriate use of such measures by each individual unit.

The Scholastic Aptitude Test of the College Board provides two measures of academic aptitude or general intelligence, relatively unaffected by training. The verbal score reflects ability to handle ideas expressed as language, while the mathematical score reflects ability to work with ideas expressed in numbers or mathematical concepts. In varied research over the country, this test has generally proved to be a useful predictor of academic performance in college (1958, p. vi).

In 1957 the 16 units of the University System admitted 5,190 freshmen. In 1977 there were 33 units in the System admitting 23,101 freshmen. Thus, between 1957 and 1977 the number of freshmen accepted to the University System of Georgia colleges increased over 300%, and the number of colleges to accommodate them doubled.

The year to year variations and the composition of the classes entering the System are duly recorded in an official publication of the University System Board of Regents, Normative Data Manuals, which are summarized and reported in Appendix B of this monograph. In 1957, there were no black students attending any one of the 13 "predominantly" white institutions. Three colleges in the System were "predominantly" or all black. In fact, for the first 11 years of the Regents' admissions testing program, test results were listed separately for the races. Beginning in 1968, scores for the races were combined, but test scores for individual units of the System continued to be summarized as before.

For three years, 1967, 1968, and 1969, the verbal and mathematics scores of the SAT were summed, and only the total scores were reported. Tapes and records of the part scores were destroyed. In the tables in Appendix B, verbal and mathematics scores for the years 1967, 1968, and 1969 were prorated from the reported total scores. That is, the total scores are correct as shown in the norms tables, but the part scores are estimated. There is no satisfactory way to arrive at a good estimate of the standard deviations for the prorated scores. With this minor exception, tables in Appendix B are summaries by college and by year for data contained in the Normative Data Manuals. In the norms tables, high school achievement and college achievement data are also published. Since we are primarily concerned with psychological test scores, achievement measures will not be directly considered nor discussed.

One reason for selecting the SAT in the first place was that it was designed to yield consistent and reliable scores from year to year. This is accomplished by the psychometric professionals at Educational Testing

Service working under contract with the College Entrance Examination Board.

Test form equating has been a paramount concern in all College Board tests since 1941. Equating successive test forms is not performed by some statistical legerdemain, but by simply adding test sections that are identical across test administrations and across testing years. By retaining identical items in the test forms in a systematic way, all forms can be reported on the same score scale.

Until fairly recently, the experts were successful in maintaining a steady mean of 500 and a standard deviation of 100 year after year. However, in the mid and late 60's, changes in scores became apparent to test users and test makers alike. Changes were not limited to the College Board tests. The other large, national testing agency, the American College Testing Program, reported similar declines beginning about the same time.

Explanations for the SAT and the ACT declines ranged from the ludicrous to the unthinkable. Fred Hechinger (Hechinger, 1974) invoked the "Yogi Bear" hypothesis to explain the declining SAT scores. About the same time Nobel Laureate William Shockley suggested the problem could be related to dysgenics.

Because score declines were observed in so many different groups and so many different areas and for both major testing programs, the College Board staff concluded that the decline was real and not the result of some fluke sampling accident.

Many causes for the decline have been investigated by Educational Testing Service; among them, changes in user colleges, changes in test taking populations, increasing number of SAT repeaters, and increasing number of low SES students. Public schools have been cited as accountability factors in the score decline. It is claimed by some that high schools are graduating less capable students than in previous years. Trends for promoting and graduating students who have not mastered essential skills and reduction in course requirements are usually the focus of explanations pointing to the schools.

Only recently has the question of differential performance by blacks and whites been acknowledged by the College Board. In January, 1976, Breland, writing in a publication jointly sponsored by College Board and the Educational Testing Service, stated, "However, in relation to college enrollments as a whole, the increase in minority enrollment is such a small proportion that it is unlikely that a significant part of the score decline could be attributed to this increase. . . . Such a small proportional increase in minorities could have only minimal impact on these scores" (Breland, 1976, p. 19).

However, testifying before the U.S. House of Representatives Sub-

Committee on Civil Service, May 15, 1979, W. H. Manning, Vice President of Educational Testing Service, said, "While scores for whites and disadvantaged minority groups overlap, a typical result is to find that only 10–20% of disadvantaged minority groups score above a point that is average for whites."

A mean majority-minority difference equal to the standard deviation of the combined group is not insignificant even if the minority group accounts for only 10% of the total SAT test takers. This, of course, is contrary to Breland's 1976 statement, but in a letter to *Saturday Review,* April 4, 1974, Osborne said, "The amount of decline can be predicted by anyone familiar with Jensen's 1969 HER article . . . an increase of 1% in black enrollment is accompanied by a decline in mean total SAT's by four or five points" (pp. 8–12).

Data in this monograph cover a period of history of the University System of Georgia which reflects the change in mean SAT scores as the System moved from a completely segregated system through a period of token integration, to a fully integrated program. In 1957 there were 16 units in the University System. Thirteen were all white, three all black. In mid 1961, two black students transferred from black schools in the Atlanta area to the University of Georgia in Athens. Within three to five years, all units of the University System had some black students enrolled. Whites in significant numbers did not seek admission to the black schools until the early 70's.

In the late 60's and early 70's, there was no accurate way of determining the race of University System applicants. For several years, the Department of Health, Education and Welfare eliminated that bit of information from all University System applications. The question was restored by the agency in the 70's to assist in determining University compliance with HEW guidelines.

From 1957 through 1967 the System SAT norms tables reported annual summary information for each school in the System and a composite table for blacks and whites separately (Appendix B). For reasons not clear, beginning Fall 1968, the System composite table lumped together blacks and whites. Since a student's race could not be obtained by the admissions office, there was no accurate method for determining the racial composition of students attending various units of the System between 1968 and 1972. In 1972, under court order, the System registrars were required to obtain race or national origin of enrolled students. A summary of minority and total enrollments for the University System was published in the *System Summary,* September, 1977 (Table XII–A). This table not only gives the number of minority students attending majority schools between 1972 and 1976 inclusive, but it also shows the number of majority students attending minority branches of the System. From Appendix B, Table XII–A, and national trends published

Table XII–A
University System of Georgia Minority* and Total Enrollments

	Enrollments at Predominantly White Institutions					
	Black Students In Fall Quarters of Years Shown					All Students Fall Quarter
	1972	1973	1974	1975	1976	1976
Universities						
Georgia Institute of Technology	155	168	249	351	407	9,496
Southern Technical Institute	31	67	66	94	110	1,993
Georgia State University	1,785	2,052	2,284	2,920	3,003	20,283
Medical College of Georgia	136	143	220	237	198	2,602
University of Georgia	896	536	634	732	753	21,238
Subtotals, Universities	3,003	2,966	3,453	4,334	4,471	55,612
Senior Colleges						
Armstrong State College	153	292	479	466	435	3,276
Augusta College	337	278	369	438	447	3,647
Columbus College	302	564	763	937	1,013	5,277
Georgia College	210	350	474	534	540	3,510
Georgia Southern College	270	192	351	368	377	6,114
Georgia Southwestern College	181	241	383	431	452	2,409
North Georgia College	34	39	43	42	58	1,857
Valdosta State College	433	391	550	576	659	5,011
West Georgia College	375	368	421	558	581	5,366
Subtotals, Senior Colleges	2,295	2,715	3,833	4,350	4,562	36,467
Junior Colleges						
Abraham Baldwin Agric. College	89	124	148	261	251	2,577
Albany Junior College	166	211	208	406	475	2,040
Bainbridge Junior College	—	41	75	99	88	538
Brunswick Junior College	166	189	237	274	251	1,167
Clayton Junior College	72	115	92	117	96	3,107
Dalton Junior College	49	44	55	92	71	1,599
Emanuel County Junior College	—	34	70	70	114	391
Floyd Junior College	105	111	117	196	197	1,558
Gainesville Junior College	47	48	59	91	66	1,556
Gordon Junior College	55	92	90	105	152	1,203
Kennesaw Junior College	88	134	56	59	50	3,211
Macon Junior College	134	144	183	337	352	2,506
Middle Georgia College	90	61	124	194	199	1,695
South Georgia College	175	200	238	284	297	1,263
Waycross Junior College	—	—	—	—	45	341
Subtotals, Junior Colleges	1,236	1,548	1,752	2,585	2,704	24,752
Totals	6,534	7,229	9,038	11,269	11,737	116,831

	Enrollments at Predominantly Black Institutions					
	White Students In Fall Quarters of Years Shown					All Students Fall Quarter
	1972	1973	1974	1975	1976	1976
Senior Colleges						
Albany State College	44	63	70	122	93	2,228
Fort Valley State College	11	44	117	229	198	1,870
Savannah State College	103	275	292	421	385	2,656
Subtotals, Senior Colleges	158	382	479	772	676	6,754
Junior Colleges						
Atlanta Junior College	—	—	63	84	67	1,684
Subtotals, Junior College	—	—	63	84	67	1,684
Totals	158	382	542	856	743	8,438
GRAND TOTALS	6,692	7,611	9,580	12,125	12,480	125,269

* Black students at predominantly white institutions, white students at predominantly black institutions

by the College Board (Breland, 1976), it was possible to estimate with a high degree of accuracy the number of minority students attending majority schools during five additional years. We now have a record for the racial composition of freshman students enrolled in the University System for 10 consecutive years, which, when combined with the 11 preintegration years, 1957–67, gives the 21 years covered by the study.

Figure XII–1 traces the rise and the decline of verbal SAT for the University System of Georgia. For the first 10 years, beginning in 1957, there was a steady increase in mean scores for students attending white segregated state supported colleges in Georgia. For black schools of the System, the trend was also positive from 1961–67.

Beginning in 1968, black and white test scores for the System were combined, making it impossible to determine exactly the number of minority students attending majority schools. Combined black-white means were reported in the norms tables and are plotted on Figure XII–1. The drop in mean verbal scores for the combined group between 1969 and 1975 is clear and steady.

To compare patterns of score change for minority and majority groups, means for the predominantly white and predominantly black units were

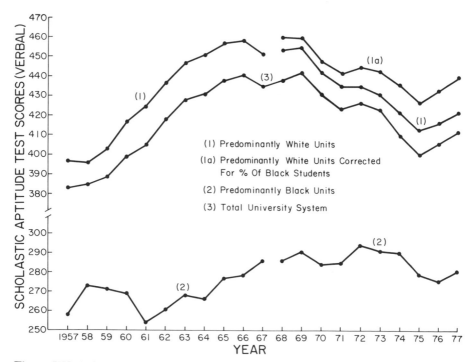

Figure XII–1. Mean SAT Verbal scores for white and black students of the University System of Georgia, 1957–1977.

computed from the data in Appendix B. After 1966, not all students attending predominantly white schools were majority members. Thus, the differences observed are under-estimates of the majority-minority differences as per the Manning report and the *System Summary,* both mentioned earlier. This is seen in Figure XII–1 where a graph of the SAT verbal means of the University System, combined black and white, are shown as well as a graph representing mean scores for the predominantly white institutions. In the same figure is a graph of the means for the predominantly black schools. The difference between the University System mean and the mean for the predominantly white schools is approximately 10 SAT points for any year beginning in 1968. These differences are consistent over the 10-year period and are statistically significant.

The decline in scores is attenuated when only predominantly white institutions are considered (Figure XII–1). From a high in 1969 of 442 on the verbal scale to the low point of 400 in 1975, the University System suffered a loss on the verbal scale of 10%. For the predominantly white schools, the loss was 9%. However, during this same period, black institutions showed a net loss of only 4% on the verbal scale. In fact, the average of the minority schools showed a steady but modest *increase* in verbal SAT scores from 1961 to 1972.

To examine in a different way the effect on the overall mean of combining blacks and whites into one composite score, another graph was prepared and is shown in Figure XII–1. From the University *System Summary,* it is possible to determine accurately the number of blacks attending majority units in the System. From Appendix B it is possible to determine the mean SAT scores for the predominantly white and predominantly black schools. It is assumed that black students in the various predominantly white units of the University System are not unlike the black students in predominantly black units of the System. With this information, mean scores for white students attending predominantly white units were estimated. The result is seen in Figure XII–1. The loss for white students in predominantly white schools from 1966–75 is now 31 SAT points. Thus, almost one-third of the decline in mean, verbal SAT scores of predominantly white units is directly attributable to the combining of black and white test scores. As we shall see later, national norms are also attenuated because of the increasing number of black students added to the data base.

The above procedure was applied to the SAT math scores with the results shown in Figure XII–2. 1965 was the high point in performance of the SAT math sections for majority schools of the System. The low point after 1965 was 1975. The loss for the combined groups was 50 points or 11%. For the predominantly white units the loss was 10%; and for the adjusted or corrected means for predominantly white institu-

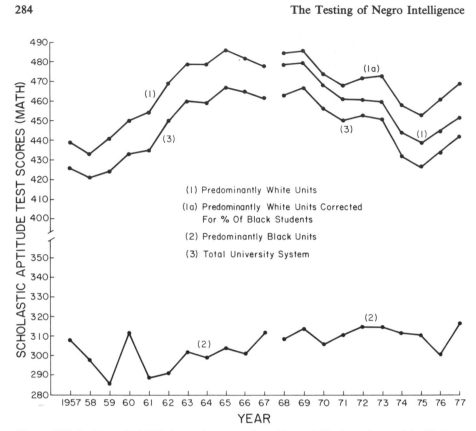

Figure XII–2. Mean SAT Mathematics scores for white and black students of the University System of Georgia, 1957–1977.

tions, the loss was 7% between 1965 and 1975. Although math scores tended to be higher than verbal by approximately 25 SAT points for both minority and majority students, the percent loss between 1965 and 1975 was almost the same as on the verbal section. It is interesting to note on Figure XII–2 that there was no significant decline in math scores for predominantly black schools between 1965 and 1975. In fact, there was a net gain of 7 SAT points during the period the System-wide white schools were in decline. The gain for black schools was only 2%, but nevertheless, it bucked the national trend of declining SAT scores. Thus, the decline in SAT performance in the University System seemed to be selective for predominantly white schools. Those schools with the largest percentage of blacks seemed to show the largest decline.

The next step was to examine SAT scores for two large universities in the University System by methods applied to the entire system. Results are much the same as for the entire System except in the case of Georgia Institute of Technology where native minority students in some years constituted less than 1% of the total freshman class. The overall changes at Tech are small but still apparent in Figures XII–3 and XII–4.

The University of Georgia mean SAT scores loss is similar to the whole University System, or as we shall see later, to the decline in the national average. Increasing black enrollment is accompanied by declining means for verbal and math SAT scores at the University of Georgia. Graphically, the trend is clear. Statistically, the differences are significant.

Are these trends unique to Georgia where until 1961 there were two separate but equal systems of higher education, or are the trends national? A report published jointly by the College Board and Educational Testing Service gives a summary of SAT verbal and math means for all students who took the test between 1957 and 1974 (Breland, 1976). The same report also gives the total minority college enrollment for nine years, 1964–1972. Additional information in the report enables a reader to estimate fairly accurately the number and percentage of minorities enrolled nationally in 1962, 1963 and also 1973 and 1974. With this information we now have data for 13 years, 1962 through 1974, during which time SAT scores peaked and began what appeared to be a dramatic

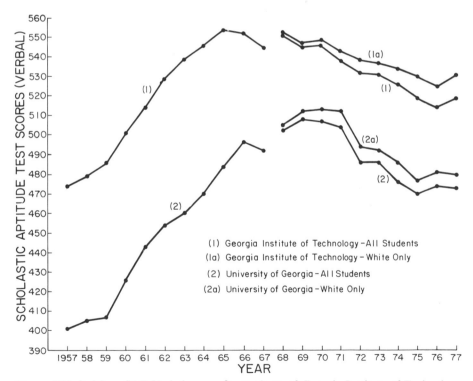

Figure XII–3. Mean SAT Verbal scores for students of Georgia Institute of Technology and the University of Georgia, 1957–1977.

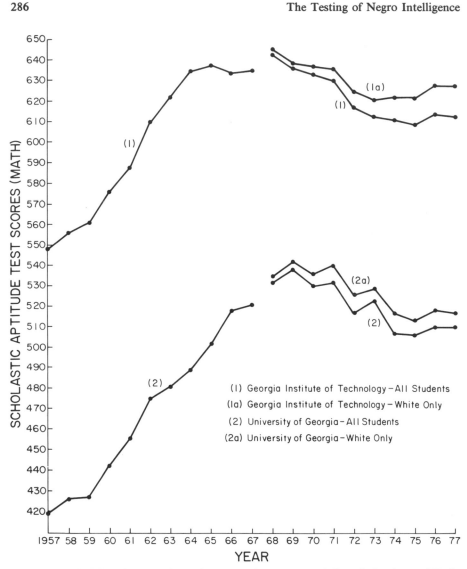

Figure XII–4. Mean SAT Mathematics scores for students of Georgia Institute of Technology and the University of Georgia, 1957–1977.

nation-wide decline. Since the SAT test takers are fairly representative of the more than five million college freshmen who take entrance examinations each year, it is assumed that SAT results can be generalized nationally. The assumption is not unreasonable because the same declining trends we have observed for SAT are also seen in the American College Testing program. Together the two programs serve over 90% of the colleges and universities requiring preadmission tests.

In this section of the study, national means from Breland (1976) were plotted for the verbal and math sections of the SAT (Figure XII–5). Breland also gives the total minority college enrollment for 1964–72.

Figure XII–5 shows a monotonic decline of both verbal and math College Board scores beginning in 1962 and extending through 1974. Although the math scores are higher by about 25 points than those for the verbal section, the slopes of the two graphs are not too different. From a peak of 478 in 1962 to the low point in 1974, the loss on the verbal scale was 8.57%. For the same period, the math decline was 29 points or 5.78%. The two curves represent means for all College Board scores *reported* between 1957 and 1974. These means differ insignificantly from the means of students *enrolled* in college.

Data in the Manning report and data from the College Board files (Breland, 1976) give national means and standard deviations for both blacks and whites for the five year period, 1972–1976. Manning shows in 1972 whites had a mean verbal scale score of 462; blacks, 342. The combined verbal score reported for 1972 by Breland was 443. In 1972 minorities made up 8.7% of the total freshman enrollment. Thus, for each percentage point of minority enrollment in the total subject pool, mean verbal scores declined approximately 2.18 points. From the University System norms tables where the number of blacks and whites are well documented, the SAT point loss for 1% of minority enrollment ranges from 1.4 to 1.9 points. Two and eighteen hundredths SAT points decline for 1% black enrollment is not too far off the results found in Georgia. A second curve was generated by joining the estimated white verbal means for each year.

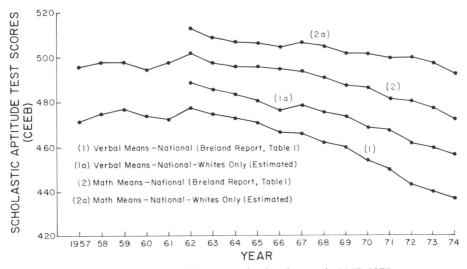

Figure XII–5. Mean SAT scores (national norms), 1957–1977.

These estimates are larger by 4 to 8 points than those that would have been obtained by the method used for the University System and the two universities reported in Figures XII–1 through XII–4. The Breland-Manning derived curves are based on national College Board data involving reports of several million students. The national curve is perhaps a good estimate of what happens to the SAT means when the subject pool is changed significantly.

In Figure XII–5 it is seen that the SAT score decline is attenuated when means are adjusted for the percentage of blacks in the total group. For the 13 years for which data are available, score loss for the verbal scale for the total group is 8.6%, for the white group, 6.5%. As was found in the Georgia data, math scores hold up much better than verbal (Figure XII–5). In fact, the estimated national math scores for whites were at or above the theoretical mean of 500 for 11 of 13 years. The two years that it was below were two years the percentage of blacks were estimated. The 25 point math-verbal difference found in the Georgia data is confirmed on the national level by data from Breland (1976) (Figure XII–5).

To examine the declining SAT scores in another way, correlations were computed between the mean of combined black-white scores and the percentage of minority enrollment. Data for the computations were obtained from Appendix B, Table XII–A, Breland (1976) and Manning (1979). Correlations for two universities, the University System of Georgia, and the national average are shown in Table XII–B. All correlations are negative. The University of Georgia correlations are −.45 for verbal scores and −.58 for math scores. The University System, Georgia Tech, and the national norms yield high negative correlations between mean SAT scores and percent of black enrollment for both verbal and math scores, with r's ranging from −.87 to −.97.

Beginning the first year for which percent minority college enrollments and mean SAT scores are available, verbal test scores have been in decline. On the national scale the loss between 1962 and 1974 was 8.6%; for the white mean, 6.5%. This compares with a 5.8% loss on the national

Table XII–B

Rank Order Correlations between SAT Scores and Percent Blacks for Four Groups

	Years included in Sample	SAT Verbal vs. percent Blacks	SAT Math vs. percent Blacks
Georgia Institute of Technology	1968–77	−.93	−.88
University of Georgia	1968–77	−.45	−.58
University System of Georgia	1968–77	−.89	−.87
National population[1]	1962–74	−.97	−.96

[1] All scores reported by Educational Testing Service, 1962–1974.

scale for the math test and a 3.9% loss on the white scale. During this same time, black schools of the University System of Georgia enjoyed an 11.5% increase in verbal scores. At first glance it would appear that national norms should be enhanced by the addition of even a small number of improving blacks. The reason for the paradox is that the mean for the blacks is consistently 1.20 standard deviations below the white mean. Additionally, blacks make up less than 10% of the total test reports. In 1962 the white mean was 513 on the math scale; in 1972 it was 500, the theoretical mean for the SAT; and in 1974 it was 493.

Summary

From the early 1940's to the early 1960's College Entrance Examination Board SAT scores remained stable around a mean of 500 and a standard deviation of 100. In the early and mid 60's, despite the built-in controls, scores began to decline. A number of variables, external to the students taking the test, were hypothesized to influence test performance and result in the score decline.

Published articles, educational research reports, and doctoral dissertations suggest that SAT score decline is the result of a) a greater number of lower SES students attending college; b) high schools graduating less capable students; c) societal factors such as drug usage, alcoholism, and television watching. The evidence is ambiguous or negative. The parsimonious explanation, the addition of an increasing number of blacks to the subject pool, was rejected out of hand because "such a small proportional increase in minorities could only have a minimal impact on mean scores" (Breland, 1976, p. 19). This monograph has offered evidence from a 21-year longitudinal study of the University System of Georgia of higher education and the results from national norming data that the recent SAT score decline is related in a significant way to the number of blacks in the data base.

Between 1962 and 1974, on national norms, math scores for whites declined insignificantly from a mean of 513 to 493 or 3.9% in 13 years. The white decline on math scores is from 513, which is 13 points above the theoretical mean of 500. For this period the loss of whites on the verbal scale was 6.54% or about one-half of 1% per year. In the University System of Georgia, scores for blacks on both College Board tests actually increased between 1962 and 1974. The paradox is explained by the fact that the means for blacks on both scales of the SAT are consistently 1.20 standard deviations below those of whites tested the same year. The test score declining trend becomes increasingly apparent and significant when blacks are added to the subject pool.

XIII

Summary and Conclusions

R. Travis Osborne and Frank C. J. McGurk

The 1st and 2nd editions of Audrey Shuey's *The Testing of Negro Intelligence* examined over 380 studies involving testing Negro intelligence. Her surveys, covering a span of more than 50 years, reviewed every significant study on the subject published between World War I and 1966.

Volume 2 follows the general plan of the first two editions, but, with few exceptions, it contains entirely new research published after 1965 and before 1980. Considered are test results of some 3,000,000 children and adults (black, white, Mexican-American, Spanish-speaking American, Chicano, Puerto Rican, and Asian), who were examined with one or more of over 100 different psychological tests. With rare exceptions, all subjects are U.S. citizens.

Volume 2 comprises 13 chapters which carry basically the same headings as the earlier editions. Shuey's 2nd edition on high school and college students was divided into two chapters, one covering high-school, the other college students. Chapter V, "The Armed Forces," and Chapter VI, "Veterans and other Civilians," were combined in Volume 2 and titled "Adults Not in College," and a new chapter was added, "Race of Examiner and Mental Test Performance." Shuey's chapters on "Selective Migration" (X) and "Racial Hybrids" (IX) have been dropped from Volume 2.

Eighty-nine dissertations containing research in the field of Negro intelligence as determined by psychometric tests are reviewed in Chapter X. Dissertation reviews follow the general outline and pattern of Shuey's 2nd Edition. Chapters XI and XII are original monographs prepared especially for this new book.

Preschool Children

Forty-nine studies were reviewed in Chapter II. Altogether, there were, roughly, 5,000 children including 3,700 blacks, 1,000 whites, 400 Chicanos, and 200 Puerto Ricans; these numbers, however, should be considered approximations because some authors used the same children in more than one study.

The 49 articles were grouped into 7 categories, including a miscellaneous category of 7 articles (14.3%). The largest category discussed race differences as SES differences (13 articles, 26.5%), and included a "longitudinal" series of reports by Golden and Birns (1968), Golden et al. (1971), and Birns and Golden (1972).

Twelve other articles (24.5%) sought to describe the effects of Head Start programs on black and white children, the most comprehensive of which was Wargo, et al. (1971). Seven articles (14.3%) were interested in problems related to the validity of tests for black children, and all of these were characterized either by small samples or by oddly-chosen samples. Five articles (10.2%) compared the scores of black children on 2 or more tests, but were not validity studies. Another category of 3 articles (6.1%) studied the effects of race of examiner, test familiarity, pretesting, and the dialect in which the test was administered, and a further set of 2 studies (4.1%) were concerned with the comparison of the factorial structure of psychological tests for blacks and whites.

The Stanford-Binet Intelligence Scale was the most frequently used test; the Peabody Picture Vocabulary Test was second, and the Wechsler Preschool and Primary Scale of Intelligence was third.

Among the 49 studies, median sample size was 34 for blacks and 37 for whites. The modal sample size was 15 for both racial groups. In 26 of the articles (53%) the method of selecting the subjects was not given. Seventy-seven authors made 66 estimates of black mean IQ and 25 estimates of white mean IQ. The median of the black mean IQ estimates was 89; that for whites was 109. Taking 15 as the SD of the white scores, black overlap was 9%. This was lower than the estimates of Yerkes (1921), Shuey (1966), and McGurk (1975).

School Children

Considering the number of authors, the variety of tests, and the range of hypotheses investigated, Chapter III was by far the largest in Volume 2. Altogether, 126 articles were reviewed including upwards of 100,000 black, white, Chicano, Puerto Rican, and Asian children. These numbers must also be regarded as approximations for the same reason given for Chapter II.

The articles reviewed were classified by authors' purposes into 8 categories. A group of 35 articles (27.8%) discussed racial differences, *per se,* and some of these, particularly Jensen's (e.g., 1971) involved large samples of children. A further group of 25 articles (19.8%) described the validity of intelligence tests for blacks and whites, and included Kennedy's (1965) follow up of a large sample from an earlier study (Kennedy, Van De Riet, and White, 1963).

Fourteen articles (11.1%) dealt with the effects of SES on racial IQ differences. Here was included the large and famous Coleman Report (1966). In 13 other articles (10.3%), the authors' purposes were direct discussions of the effects of school intervention programs, and this category was distinguished by four sets of longitudinal studies: Darlington, et al. 1980; the Gray and Klaus (or Klaus and Gray) series (1965, 1968, and 1970); the Scott series (1973, 1974, and 1976); and the Westinghouse Learning Corporation, Ohio University Report (1969). In none of these articles was there any clear indication that such programs improved the test scores of blacks.

Aside from the miscellaneous category of 16 articles (12.7%), no other category equalled or exceeded 10% of the total number of articles reviewed.

Some form of the Wechsler Intelligence Scale for Children was the most popular test. The Stanford-Binet Intelligence Scale was second, and the Lorge-Thorndike Intelligence Scale was third.

Among the 126 articles, mean sample size was 35 for blacks and 64 for whites. In 44 studies (35%) the method of selecting the samples was not given. One hundred and ninety-three (193) authors made 179 estimates of black mean IQ, and 88 estimates of white mean IQ. The number of children had been given for these estimates, but there were other estimates of mean IQ for which Ns were not given. The median of the mean IQ estimates was 89 for blacks, and 103 for whites. Assuming the SD of the white scores to be 15, black overlap was 16% when all estimates were used, but only 13% when only those studies with random samples or all-available-children samples were used. The latter overlap agrees closely with the estimates of Yerkes (1921), Shuey (1966), and McGurk (1975).

High School Students

The small number of studies involving high school students (17) was surprising when compared to the 55 studies located by Shuey in her 2nd Edition. However, among the present 17 studies, the number of subjects was substantial (over 16,000), but an exact tally was not possible because, in one study, the sample was described as 70% black.

Six articles (35.3%) concerned racial differences, and 7 other articles (41.2%) described test validity in some aspect. The remaining 4 articles (23.5%) discussed racial differences as SES differences, self-perception, and the factorial nature of creativity.

Median sample size for 15 samples of blacks was 50; for 8 samples of whites, it was 40. The median IQ of the black estimates was 90, and that for the white estimates was 108 (N had been given for each estimate). Assuming, again, a SD of 15 for the white distribution of scores, black overlap was 12% for all 15 estimates, but dropped to 5% when only the studies with random samples or all-available-subject samples were considered. The latter overlap estimate was based on a very small number of estimates; the former figure of 12% is in keeping with the estimates of Yerkes (1921), Shuey (1966), and McGurk (1975).

College Students

Test scores of more than 2,000,000 college students are represented in the 28 studies and one monograph reviewed in Chapter V. To a greater extent than in previous chapters, the subject pool has an international background.

The major purpose of the majority of the studies was to examine the forecasting efficiency of preadmission tests for blacks. The significant findings are:

1. Blacks score, on the average, at least 1σ below whites on the College Board Scholastic Aptitude Test and on the American College Test.
2. Blacks are predicted by tests to do better than they actually do in college classrooms.
3. The mean correlation between the Scholastic Aptitude Test and the Grade Point Average (.55) for black college students remains stable from year to year.
4. Black-white mental test overlap of 6 to 10% is constant from year to year.
5. Novel tests designed especially to reflect knowledge of the black environment correlate insignificantly with traditional tests such as the Scholastic Aptitude Test and the American College Test and are unvalidated.
6. When U.S. minority groups are compared on a test of scholastic aptitude, such as the Graduate Record Examination, all groups, including American Indians, Mexican-Americans, Asian-Americans, and Puerto Ricans earn scores above those of blacks.

Adults not in College

Authors of 21 studies reviewed in Chapter VI were not so much interested in racial differences in test performance as they were in determining whether differential validity of employment tests is established and recommended for U.S. blacks and Spanish-speaking Americans.

The subjects in Chapter VI range in age from young adults to senior citizens. About 60% are white, 38% black, 2% Spanish-speaking Americans. The variety of tests is wide, ranging from an original battery designed for the Bell System to a novel test called the Black Intelligence Test of Cultural Homogeneity (BITCH).

Racial comparisons of test performances revealed the usual scale of difference: whites > Spanish-speaking Americans > blacks. Where scores or normative data are given, white-black differences range from .75 to more than 1 SD equivalent. While there is almost unanimous agreement among the authors that racial differences in mean test scores on such tests as the Wonderlic, AFQT, and the WAIS are significant, there is no consensus that the tests can be used with equal effectiveness for job selection of applicants from different ethnic groups. The case made for differential validity is in no way as sound and convincing as the case of those who argue for single-group prediction.

Delinquents

Among the studies reviewed for Volume 2 of *The Testing of Negro Intelligence,* only 16 attempt to relate psychological test results to criminal behavior of different racial groups, despite the fact authors of one paper suggest that prison inmates comprise a more homogeneous group than school and college students and consequently should be easier to study, since they are usually similar in education, SES, and mental ability.

While there is no consensus among the authors, these general observations are made from their data:

1. Mental test scores are not significantly related to type of criminal offense or to whether the inmate is a "first timer" or a recidivist.
2. There was no support for the idea that links mesomorphy to delinquency.
3. Among truants, it was found that siblings of truants had been referred to juvenile court in 61% of the cases.
4. The idea that effective incentive (material reward) would operate to narrow the gap between test scores of white and black inmates was not supported.

One general finding of this chapter supported almost without exception by the data is that the ethnic IQ differences found in public schools, colleges and industries show up in prison. Whereas the general population mean IQ is 100 for whites and 85 for blacks, the inmate average is closer to 95 for whites and 80 for blacks or in some cases 90 for whites and 75 for blacks. Means for Spanish-speaking Americans usually fall between those of whites and blacks. These differences are found regardless of the test employed, the age of the sample, the SES of the subjects or the race of the examiner.

Special Populations

There were only 13 studies dealing with special populations not elsewhere classified. Results of eight studies differed insignificantly from the majority of those reviewed in previous sections, with blacks scoring significantly below whites or in single group studies significantly below published norms. The five remaining studies support a contradictory view: black-white test score differences are small or the means vary insignificantly. In the case of perceptual motor tasks, blacks were found to excel whites. In regard to the relationship of skin color to mean mental ability, one investigator found differences "tend to follow the prejudice line rather than the genetic line."

Race of Examiner

Race of examiner has been viewed as a source of error adding imprecision to the measurement of intelligence. It has also been hypothesized that the race of the examiner is one factor contributing to the mean difference found between black and white intelligence test scores.

Reviewed in Chapter IX are 28 related experiments involving over 12,000 subjects. Evidence was examined concerning the hypothesis that white examiners systematically elicit lower intelligence test scores from black examinees than do black examiners.

Of the 28 studies, 11 reported significant race of examiner main effects or race of examiner × race of subject interaction. However, 7 of the 11 studies have methodological inadequacies, apparently analyzed their data incorrectly, or report outcomes contrary to the hypothesis.

Taken as a whole, the empirical literature does not support the hypothesis that race of examiner is a factor contributing to the mean differences in black-white intelligence tests score differences.

The issue of the relationship of the race of examiner to differences in test scores may be too complex to be resolved by testing the simple hypothesis that race of examiner is a factor contributing to mean differences in black-white intelligence scores. Inadequate research designs with incomplete sampling leave many alternative explanations, all of which need conceptual clarification. For example, what aspect of the examiner's race is the causal agent present to influence examinees' test scores? Are some tests more likely to influence race of examiner effects than others?

Geographic Region

Black-white differences in ability and achievement are quite similar across regions of the U.S. with the mean differences for the four main regions being equivalent to 1.00, .97, .98, and .98 standard deviation units. Regardless of the region from which such samples are drawn whites exceed blacks in mean scores by a difference equal to approximately 1 SD.

It is clear that a student's region has the same effect on scores earned by students from both ethnic groups. High scores are generally found in the North East, and low scores of both races are from the southern region. In no test of the National Longitudinal Study did blacks of one region equal or exceed whites from their own or any other region.

Effects of Integration

The most comprehensive study of the effects of integration was the National Longitudinal Study. Results of this survey may be summarized as:

1. A negligible relationship exists between each of the 10 N.L.S. tests of ability and achievement with indexes of pupil and teacher integration.

2. Within each of four integration groups at 12th-grade level, whites exceed blacks on ability and achievement scores by an average amount equal to .96 SD.

3. When white and black students are grouped according to the proportion of their high-school teachers who were white, it was found the average of the greatest group difference on each of the 10 N.L.S. scores is equivalent to about .5 SD for both blacks and whites. The average white-black ability-achievement difference within the 5 teacher-integration groups is equivalent to .92 SD.

4. The effect of teacher or pupil integration on scores earned by each race is considerably less than the black-white difference within each integration group.

Declining SAT Scores

A 21-year longitudinal study of a state university system of higher education and the results of national norming data demonstrated that the recent SAT score decline is related in a significant way to the number of blacks in the data base.

Between 1962 and 1974, on national norms, SAT math scores for whites declined insignificantly from a mean score of 513 to 493 in 13 years. For this period the loss of whites on the verbal scale was 6.54% or about ½ of 1% per year. In the University System of Georgia, scores for blacks on both SAT tests actually increased between 1962 and 1974. The paradox is explained by the fact that the mean for blacks on both scales of the SAT are consistently 1.20 standard deviation units below whites tested the same year. The SAT declining trend becomes increasingly apparent when blacks are added to the subject pool.

Concluding Remarks

The remarkable consistency in test results, whether they pertain to school or preschool children, to children between Ages 6 to 9 or 10 to 12, to children in Grades 1 to 3 or 4 to 7, to high-school or college students, to enlisted men or officers in training in the Armed Forces— in World War I, World War II, or the Post-Korean period—to veterans of the Armed Forces, to homeless men or transients, to gifted or mentally deficient, to delinquent or criminal; the fact that differences between colored and white are present not only in the rural and urban South, but in the Border and Northern states; the fact that the colored preschool, school, and high school pupils living in Northern cities tested as far below the Southern urban white children as they did below the whites in Northern cities; . . . the tendency toward greater variability among whites; the tendency for racial hybrids to score higher than those groups described as, or inferred to be, unmixed Negro; the evidence that the mean overlap is between 7 and 13%; the evidence that the tested differences appear to be greater for logical analysis, abstract reasoning, and perceptual-motor tasks than for practical and concrete problems; the evidence that the tested differences may be a little less on verbal than on nonverbal tasks; the indication that the colored elementary or high-school pupil has not been adversely affected in his tested performance by the presence of a white examiner; . . . the unproved and probably erroneous assumption that Negroes have been less well motivated on tests than whites; the fact that differences were reported in practically all of the studies in which the cultural environment of the whites appeared to be similar in richness and complexity to that of the Negroes; the fact that in many comparisons, including those in which the colored have appeared to best advantage, Negro subjects have been either more representative of their racial group or more highly selected than the comparable whites; all taken together, inevitably point to the presence of native differences between Negroes and whites as determined by intelligence tests.

This remarkable statement becomes all the more remarkable when it is recognized as Audrey Shuey's concluding words in her 2nd Edition. Volume 2's documentation of racial differences in mental ability is even more convincing.

Appendix A

List of Tests

This list identifies all mental tests for which test scores are reported in Volume 2 of *The Testing of Negro Intelligence*. Tests are listed in alphabetical order by title and in some cases also by acronym. For tests reviewed in the Buros Mental Measurement Yearbooks or in *Tests in Print,* the MMY or TIP volume and test reference are shown in the list. For new or original tests and tests out of print, the author's source or the journal reference is cited. In some cases the publisher is given.

Our procedure for identifying tests cited in Volume 2 differs from that of the 2nd Edition, where tests were reviewed in detail by Professor Shuey. Since the Buros Yearbooks are readily available and provide impartial reviews of published tests, we decided not to duplicate test reviews found in the 2nd Edition or in standard reference works.

The list does not show projective tests, occupational rating scales, or personality inventories that are not usually classified as intelligence tests. Tests listed here are also included in the subject index.

ABC Inventory to Determine Kindergarten and School Readiness, 7th MMY, 739.
Academic Promise Tests, 7th MMY, 672
ACE, 6th MMY, 438.
ACT, 7th MMY, 330.
AFQT, see Armed Forces Qualification Test.
AGCT, 6th MMY, 441.
American College Test, 7th MMY, 330.
American Council on Education Psychological Examination, 6th MMY, 438.
Ammons Full-Range Picture Vocabulary Test, 6th MMY, 521.
Arithmetic Test, Mukherhee, B. N. Simple arithmetic test. Unpublished Ph.D. thesis, University of North Carolina, 1963.
Armed Forces Qualifications Test, Anastasi, Anne, *Psychological Testing.* London: The Macmillan Company, 1968, 229–230.
Army Alpha, TIP I, 726.

Army Beta, 6th MMY, 494.
Army General Classification Test, 6th MMY, 441.
Army Group Examination, Alpha, TIP I, 726.
Arrow-Dot Test, 6th MMY, 220a.
Bayley Scales of Infant Development, 7th MMY, 402.
Bell System Qualification Test I, Gael, S., Grant, D. L., & Ritchie, R. J. "Test validation for minority and non-minority clerks with work sample criteria." *Journal of Applied Psychology,* August, 1975, 60(4).
Bender-Gestalt Test, 7th MMY, 161.
Benton Visual Retention Scale, 6th MMY, 543.
BIT, see Black Intelligence Test.
BITCH, TIP II, 343.
Black Intelligence Test, Boone, J. A., & Adesso, V. J. "Racial differences on a black intelligence test." *Journal of Negro Education,* 1974, *43,* 429–436.
Black Intelligence Test of Cultural Homogeneity, TIP II, 343.
Boehm Test of Basic Concepts, 7th MMY, 335.
Calendar Test, Remondino, C. *Revue de Psychologie Applique,* 1962, *12,* 62–81.
California Achievement Tests, 7th MMY, 5.
California Capacity Questionnaire, TIP I, 730.
California Mathematics Test, 7th MMY, 455.
California Reading Test, 7th MMY, 683.
California Short-Form Test of Mental Maturity, 7th MMY, 337.
California Test of Mental Maturity, 7th MMY, 338.
Cancellation Test, "A twin study of spatial ability." by Steven S. Vandenberg, University of Louisville School of Medicine, Report No. 26, April, 1967.
Card Rotations Test, 6th MMY, 551.
Cattell Culture Fair Intelligence Test, 6th MMY, 453b.
Cattell Infant Intelligence Scale, 6th MMY, 515.
CCFIT, 6th MMY, 453b.
Chicago Non-Verbal Examination, TIP I, 735.
Clark's Doll Test, Clark, K., & Clark, M. Racial identification and preference in Negro children. In T. Newcomb and E. Hartley (Eds.). *Readings in Social Psychology.* New York: Holt, 1947.
Cognitive Abilities Test, 7th MMY, 343.
Columbia Mental Maturity Scale, 6th MMY, 517.
Comprehensive Tests of Basic Skills, 7th MMY, 9.
Cooperative English Tests, 6th MMY, 256.
Cooperative Guidance and Placement Program-Form SP6, 1970. College Entrance Examination Board. Educational Testing Service. Princeton, N.J., 1970.
Cooperative Reading Comprehension Test, 7th MMY, 16 and 17.
Cooperative School Ability Test, 7th MMY, 347.
CTMM, 7th MMY, 337.
CTMM, S-F, 7th MMY, 337.
Cube Comparisons Test, 6th MMY, 551.
DAT, 7th MMY, 673.
Davis-Eells Test of General Intelligence, 5th MMY, 326.

Detroit Tests of Learning Aptitude, 7th MMY, 406.

Developmental Test of Visual-Motor Integration, 7th MMY, 867.

Deviation Social Quotient, Silverstein, A. B. Deviation social quotients for the Vineland Social Maturity Scale, *American Journal of Mental Deficiency,* 1971, *76,* 348–351.

Differential Aptitude Tests, 7th MMY, 673.

Digit Span Test, Original test devised by author, see Jensen, A. R., "Interaction of Level I and Level II abilities with race and socioeconomic status." *Journal of Educational Psychology,* 1974, *66,* 99–111.

Drawing A Man, by F. L. Goodenough. Goodenough, F. L. *The measurement of intelligence by drawings.* Yonkers: World Book Company, 1926.

Educational Quality Assessment, Pennsylvania Department of Education. *Manual for interpreting elementary school reports.* Harrisburg, PA: Division of Educational Quality Assessment, 1974.

Edwards Social Desirability Scale, Solomon, L. F., & Klein, E. B. The relationship between agreeing response set and social desirability. *Journal of Abnormal and Social Psychology,* 1963, *66,* 176–179.

Employee Aptitude Survey, 6th MMY, 769.

Environmental Participation Index, 7th MMY, 660.

Figure Copying Test, Jensen, A. R. Do schools cheat minority children? *Educational Research,* 1971, *14,* 3–28.

Form Board Test, 6th MMY, 551.

French's Wide Range Arithmetic Test, 6th MMY, 551.

French's Wide Range Vocabulary Test, 6th MMY, 551.

GATB, 7th MMY, 676.

Gates Reading Survey, 7th MMY, 689.

General Ability Tests, 6th MMY, 768b.

General Aptitude Test Battery, 7th MMY, 676.

Gesell Developmental Schedules, 6th MMY, 522.

Goodenough Drawing Test, Goodenough, F. Measurement of intelligence by drawings. New York: Harcourt Brace, and World, 1926.

Goodenough-Harris Drawing Test, 7th MMY, 352.

Graduate Record Examination Aptitude Test, 7th MMY, 353.

Guilford-Martin Personnel Inventory, 6th MMY, 109.

Guilford's Five Tests of Divergent-Covergent Thinking, Guilford, J. P. *The nature of human intelligence.* New York: McGraw Hill, 1967.

Guilford-Zimmerman Aptitude Survey, 6th MMY, 772.

Harris-Goodenough Drawing Test, 7th MMY, 352.

Heim Self-Judging Vocabulary, Heim, A. W. Self-judging vocabulary test. *Journal of Genetic Psychology,* 1965, *72,* 285–294.

Henmon-Nelson Test of Mental Ability, 6th MMY, 462.

Hunter College Aptitude Scale for Gifted Children, in Lesser, G., Fifer, G., & Clark, D. H. Mental abilities of children from different social classes and culture groups. Monographs of the Society for Research in Child Development, Serial No. 102, 1965, Vol. 30, No. 4.

Identical Pictures Test, 6th MMY, 551.

Illinois Test of Psycholinguistic Abilities, 7th MMY, 442.

Impulsiveness-Ego-Superego Test, 6th MMY, 220.

Inference Test, 6th MMY, 551.
Inter-American Test of General Ability: Picture Vocabulary, Coleman, J. S. "Equality of educational opportunity," U.S. Government Office, 1966.
Iowa Test of Pre-School Development, Scott R. Iowa Test of Pre-School Development. Cedar Falls, Iowa: Go Mo Industries Press, 1975.
Iowa Tests of Basic Skills, 6th MMY, 13.
ITBS, 6th MMY, 13.
ITPA, 7th MMY, 442.
Jr.-Sr. High School Personality Questionnaire, 7th MMY, 97.
Junior Eysenck Personality Inventory, 7th MMY, 96.
Kahn Intelligence Test, 7th MMY, 411.
Kuhlmann-Anderson Intelligence Tests, 6th MMY, 466.
Kuhlmann-Finch Tests, TIP, I, 785.
Leiter Adult Intelligence Scale, 6th MMY, 525.
Leiter International Performance Scale, 6th MMY, 526.
Letters Sets Test, 6th MMY, 551.
Lincoln-Oseretsky Motor Development Scale, TIP I, 1669.
Listening-Attention Test, Jensen, A. R. Do schools cheat minority children? *Educational Research,* 1971, *14,* 3–28.
Logical Reasoning Test, 6th MMY, 551.
Lorge-Thorndike Intelligence Tests, 7th MMY, 359–360.
L-T, 7th MMY, 359–360.
Marianne Frostig Developmental Test of Visual Perception, 7th MMY, 871.
Marlowe-Crown Social Desirability Scale, Crown, D. P. & Marlowe, D. A new scale of social desirability independent of psychopathology. *Journal of Consulting Psychology,* 1960, *24,* 349–354.
Mazes Test, "A twin study of spatial ability." Vandenberg, S. S., University of Louisville School of Medicine, Report No. 26, April, 1967.
McCarthy General Cognitive Indexes, McCarthy, D. *Manual of the McCarthy scales of children's abilities.* New York: The Psychological Corporation, 1972.
McCarthy Scales of Children's Abilities, TIP II, 506.
Mechanics of Expression, 6th MMY, 258.
Memory For Numbers, Jensen, A. R. Do schools cheat minority children? *Educational Research,* 1971, *14,* 3–28.
Merrill-Palmer Developmental Test, 6th MMY, 527.
Metropolitan Achievement Tests, 7th MMY, 14.
Metropolitan Readiness Test, 7th MMY, 757.
Metropolitan Reading Readiness Test, TIP I, 1500.
Michigan M-Scales, Cameron, H. K. *Journal of Negro Education,* 1968, *37,* 252–257.
Monroe Standardized Silent Reading Test, 6th MMY, 798.
National College Freshman Testing, see American Council on Education Psychological Examination.
National Longitudinal Study Test Battery, Data File Users Manual. Levinsohn, J., Lewis, L., Riccobono, J., and Moore, R. Center for Educational Research and Evaluation, Research Triangle Institute, Research Triangle Park, North Carolina, 27709, 1976.

National Merit Scholarship Qualifying Test, 7th MMY, 670.
National Teacher Examinations, 7th MMY, 582.
Newcastle Spatial Test, Smith, I. M., & Lawes, J. S. *Newcastle Spatial Test.* Bedford, England: Newnes Educational Publishing, 1959.
NMSQT, 7th MMY, 670.
NTE, 7th MMY, 582.
Object-Aperture Test, Dubois, P. H., & Gleser, G. Object-Aperture Test. *American Psychologist,* 1948, *3,* 363.
Otis Alpha, 6th MMY, 481a.
Otis Gamma Tests of Mental Abilities, 6th MMY, 481c.
Otis-Lennon Mental Ability Test, 7th MMY, 370.
Otis Quick-Scoring Mental Ability Test, 6th MMY, 481.
Otis Quick-Scoring Mental Ability Test, Beta Test, Form A, 6th MMY, 481b.
Paper Folding Test, 6th MMY, 551.
Peabody Picture Vocabulary Test, 7th MMY, 417.
Personality Assessment System, Gittinger, J. W. *Personality Assessment System,* Volume I: The E Series; Volume II: The I Series. New York: Human Ecology Fund, 1964.
Personality Rating Scale, 6th MMY, 158.
Pictorial Test of Intelligence, 7th MMY, 418.
Picture Order Test, Hagen, J. W. The effect of distraction on selective attention. *Child Development,* 1967, *38,* 685–694.
Pintner-Cunningham Primary Test, TIP I, 827a.
Pintner General Abilities Test—Verbal Series, TIP I, 827.
PMA, 7th MMY, 680.
Porteus Maze Test, 7th MMY, 419.
PPVT, 7th MMY, 417.
Preliminary Scholastic Aptitude Test, 7th MMY, 375.
Pre-Nursing and Guidance Examination, 6th MMY, 1162.
Preschool Inventory Test, 7th MMY, 404.
Primary Mental Abilities, 7th MMY, 680.
Programmer Aptitude Test, 7th MMY, 1089.
Project Talent Test of Cognitive Ability, 6th MMY, 764.
PSAT, 7th MMY, 375.
Purdue Pegboard, 6th MMY, 1081.
Purdue Perceptual-Motor Survey, 7th MMY, 874.
Quick Test, 7th MMY, 422.
Raven's Coloured Progressive Matrices, 7th MMY, 376b.
Raven's Progressive Matrices, 7th MMY, 376.
Reading Progress Test, TIP II, 1589.
Revised Beta Examination, 6th MMY, 494.
Revised Visual Retention Test, 6th MMY, 543.
Rystrom Dialect Test, Rystrom, R. C. Testing Negro-standard English dialect differences. *Reading Research Quarterly,* 1969, *4,* 500–511.
Sarason Test Anxiety Scale, Sarason, S. B., Davidson, K., Lighthull, F., and Waite, R. A. A test anxiety scale for children. *Child Development,* 1958, *29,* 105–113.
SAT, 7th MMY, 344.

S-B, (Forms L and M), 5th MMY, 413.
S-B Form L-M, 7th MMY, 425.
SCAT, 7th MMY, 347.
Scholastic Aptitude Test, College Board, 7th MMY, 344.
School and College Ability Tests, 7th MMY, 347.
Screening Test of Academic Readiness, 7th MMY, 765.
Self-Judging Vocabulary Test, Heim, A. S. Self-judging vocabulary test. *Journal of Genetic Psychology,* 1965, *72,* 285–294.
Sequential Tests of Educational Progress, 6th MMY, 25.
SET, 6th MMY, 1045.
Shah's Nonverbal Group Test, Original test devised by author; Shah, Gunvant B. "Construction and standardization of a nonverbal group test of intelligence with special reference for the Gujarat State. Unpublished doctoral dissertation, University of Baroda, 1964.
Ship Destination Test, 6th MMY, 500, 551.
Shipley—Institute of Living Scale for Measuring Intellectual Impairment, 7th MMY, 138.
Short Employment Tests, 6th MMY, 1045.
SIT, 7th MMY, 424.
Slosson Drawing Coordination Test, 7th MMY, 140.
Slosson Intelligence Test, 7th MMY, 424.
Social Perception, Whiteman, M. The performance of schizophrenics on social concepts. *Journal of Abnormal and Social Psychology,* 1954, *49,* 266–271.
Spatial Relations Test, TIP I, 1930.
Speed and Persistence Test, Jensen, A. R. Do schools cheat minority children? *Educational Research,* 1971, *14,* 3–28.
Sprigle School Readiness Screening Test, 7th MMY, 766.
SRA Non-Verbal Test, TIP I, 840.
SRA Primary Mental Abilities, 7th MMY, 680.
SRA Tests of Educational Ability, 6th MMY, 495.
Stanford Achievement Test—Reading, 7th MMY, 708.
Stanford-Binet Intelligence Scale, Forms L and M, 5th MMY, 413.
Stanford-Binet Intelligence Scale (L-M), 7th MMY, 425.
Stenquist Test of Mechanical Ability, Stenquist, J. L. Yonkers: World Book Company, 1921
STEP, 6th MMY, 25.
Surface Development Test, 6th MMY, 551.
Terman-McNemar Test of Mental Ability, TIP I, 860.
Test Anxiety Questionnaire, Mandler, G., & Sarason, S. B. A study of anxiety and learning. *Journal of Abnormal and Social Psychology,* 1952, *47,* 166–173.
Test of Academic Aptitude (Short Form), 7th MMY, 387.
Tests of Academic Progress, 7th MMY, 31.
Torrance Tests of Creative Thinking, 7th MMY, 448.
U-Scale, Clark, E. T. *Preliminary manual for the U-Scale.* Department of Psychology, St. John's University, 1966.
Utility Test, 6th MMY, 551.
Van Alstyne Picture Vocabulary Test, 6th MMY, 537.

Vane Kindergarten Test, 7th MMY, 428.

Vineland Social Maturity Scale, 6th MMY, 194.

WAIS, 7th MMY, 429.

Wallin Pegboard B, Stutsman, R. Mental measurement of preschool children. Tarrytown-on-Hudson, N.Y.: World Book Company, 1931.

W-B I, 6th MMY, 539.

W-B II, 6th MMY, 539.

Wechsler Adult Intelligence Scale, 7th MMY, 429.

Wechsler-Bellevue Intelligence Scale—Form I, 6th MMY, 539.

Wechsler-Bellevue Intelligence Scale—Form II, 6th MMY, 539.

Wechsler Intelligence Scale for Children, 7th MMY, 431.

Wechsler Intelligence Scale for Children—Revised, *Manual for the Wechsler Intelligence Scale for Children—Revised.* New York: The Psychological Corporation, 1974.

Wechsler Preschool and Primary Scale of Intelligence, 7th MMY, 434.

Wide Range Achievement Test, 7th MMY, 36.

Wide Range Vocabulary Test, 6th MMY, 551.

Williams and Roberson Measure of Racial Attitudes, Williams, J., & Roberson, K. A method for assessing racial attitudes in preschool children. *Educational and Psychological Measurement,* 1967, *27,* 671–689.

WISC, 7th MMY, 431.

Wonderlic Personnel Test, 7th MMY, 401.

Woody-McCall Mixed Fundamentals in Arithmetic, 4th MMY, 421.

Word Fluency, 6th MMY, 562.

WPPSI, 7th MMY, 434.

WRAT, 7th MMY, 36.

Appendix B

UNIVERSITY SYSTEM OF GEORGIA
ENTERING FRESHMEN 1957 - 1977
COLLEGE BOARD SCHOLASTIC APTITUDE SCORES

| YEAR | UNIVERSITY SYSTEM (WHITE) | | | | | UNIVERSITY SYSTEM (BLACK) | | | | | UNIVERSITY SYSTEM (TOTAL) | | | | |
	NO.	VERBAL MEAN	S.D.	MATH MEAN	S.D.	NO.	VERBAL MEAN	S.D.	MATH MEAN	S.D.	NO.	VERBAL MEAN	S.D.	MATH MEAN	S.D.
1957	4677	397	108	439	92	513	258	39	308	31	·	·	·	·	·
1958	6081	396	97	433	103	611	273	37	298	38	·	·	·	·	·
1959	5829	403	97	441	103	699	271	38	286	44	·	·	·	·	·
1960	6682	417	102	450	104	918	269	44	312	41	·	·	·	·	·
1961	6655	425	97	454	102	874	254	47	289	44	·	·	·	·	·
1962	6598	437	97	469	104	796	260	49	291	45	·	·	·	·	·
1963	7135	447	98	479	104	845	268	51	302	48	·	·	·	·	·
1964	9017	451	97	479	104	1097	266	53	299	50	·	·	·	·	·
1965	10567	457	96	486	104	1255	277	53	304	53	·	·	·	·	·
1966	11507	458	96	482	104	1175	279	54	301	55	·	·	·	·	·
1967	12996	451	·	478	103	1370	286	·	312	·	·	·	·	·	·
1968	·	·	·	·	·	·	·	·	·	·	14234	438	·	463	·
1969	·	·	·	·	·	·	·	·	·	·	18621	442	·	467	·
1970	·	·	·	·	·	·	·	·	·	·	20858	431	106	456	112
1971	·	·	·	·	·	·	·	·	·	·	22175	424	105	450	111
1972	·	·	·	·	·	·	·	·	·	·	20254	427	103	453	110
1973	·	·	·	·	·	·	·	·	·	·	19256	423	103	451	110
1974	·	·	·	·	·	·	·	·	·	·	20968	410	104	432	111
1975	·	·	·	·	·	·	·	·	·	·	25727	400	108	427	111
1976	·	·	·	·	·	·	·	·	·	·	25101	406	107	434	114
1977	·	·	·	·	·	·	·	·	·	·	23101	412	107	442	114

UNIVERSITY SYSTEM OF GEORGIA
ENTERING FRESHMEN 1957 - 1977
COLLEGE BOARD SCHOLASTIC APTITUDE SCORES

YEAR	ALBANY STATE					ARMSTRONG STATE				
		VERBAL		MATH			VERBAL		MATH	
	NO.	MEAN	S.D.	MEAN	S.D.	NO.	MEAN	S.D.	MEAN	S.D.
1957	122	252	31	301	31	•	•	•	•	•
1958	152	268	32	289	28	186	379	85	400	89
1959	241	270	34	286	39	189	404	89	416	87
1960	221	257	37	313	41	239	405	87	407	83
1961	254	253	46	289	40	226	429	94	428	94
1962	234	253	43	281	43	209	428	79	436	81
1963	238	261	52	297	42	245	450	82	457	87
1964	321	260	49	297	48	359	456	87	468	88
1965	415	271	50	300	50	265	453	86	471	93
1966	337	277	47	295	50	300	456	85	460	90
1967	458	293	•	312	•	407	429	•	442	•
1968	346	298	•	319	•	378	431	•	445	•
1969	397	305	•	326	•	380	428	•	441	•
1970	328	293	55	314	56	471	427	99	440	92
1971	391	295	62	319	64	613	421	102	432	101
1972	340	296	61	318	59	622	434	94	449	102
1973	405	291	58	317	62	576	422	92	440	96
1974	497	281	61	312	60	621	414	96	429	104
1975	681	269	62	306	57	734	408	97	427	99
1976	586	262	64	287	65	563	413	89	431	96
1977	474	275	65	313	64	635	423	85	431	96

UNIVERSITY SYSTEM OF GEORGIA
ENTERING FRESHMEN 1957 - 1977
COLLEGE BOARD SCHOLASTIC APTITUDE SCORES

| | AUGUSTA COLLEGE | | | | | COLUMBUS COLLEGE | | | | |
| | | VERBAL | | MATH | | | VERBAL | | MATH | |
YEAR	NO.	MEAN	S.D.	MEAN	S.D.	NO.	MEAN	S.D.	MEAN	S.D.
1957	.	.	.	.	.	.	.	.	.	.
1958	242	378	102	397	89	138	377	87	390	89
1959	266	381	89	419	91	160	416	89	438	85
1960	266	396	94	431	89	238	404	89	422	88
1961	236	410	92	439	85	245	417	87	431	90
1962	228	412	93	447	84	282	413	87	430	92
1963	245	427	90	466	86	267	422	90	436	85
1964	376	423	83	451	87	329	433	89	438	83
1965	368	445	84	467	85	506	431	82	441	83
1966	407	431	93	447	84	435	433	81	444	84
1967	443	438	.	458	.	378	437	.	448	.
1968	353	448	.	469	.	437	431	.	441	.
1969	444	445	.	465	.	471	441	.	452	.
1970	573	444	92	468	87	876	421	92	429	89
1971	711	445	96	459	94	993	412	88	423	90
1972	632	453	88	464	90	902	417	89	428	89
1973	589	468	79	480	81	870	405	90	414	90
1974	717	426	97	440	92	1085	397	101	405	95
1975	861	413	99	434	95	1275	383	100	398	96
1976	1662	408	102	431	98	1075	387	100	402	96
1977	843	412	95	430	95	977	387	99	400	92

UNIVERSITY SYSTEM OF GEORGIA
ENTERING FRESHMEN 1957 - 1977
COLLEGE BOARD SCHOLASTIC APTITUDE SCORES

| | FT. VALLEY STATE | | | | | GA. MEDICAL COLLEGE | | | | |
| | | VERBAL | | MATH | | | VERBAL | | MATH | |
YEAR	NO.	MEAN	S.D.	MEAN	S.D.	NO.	MEAN	S.D.	MEAN	S.D.
1957	191	259	40	306	41	•	•	•	•	•
1958	206	271	36	308	40	•	•	•	•	•
1959	221	271	38	283	44	•	•	•	•	•
1960	286	275	40	313	38	•	•	•	•	•
1961	299	254	47	291	47	•	•	•	•	•
1962	259	262	54	298	47	•	•	•	•	•
1963	321	265	49	301	49	•	•	•	•	•
1964	384	263	49	294	45	•	•	•	•	•
1965	426	270	49	300	46	32	528	73	498	80
1966	395	275	53	301	54	42	502	59	485	75
1967	484	280	•	306	•	39	469	•	456	•
1968	505	277	•	303	•	39	496	•	481	•
1969	580	278	•	305	•	23	536	•	520	•
1970	633	274	47	301	52	23	488	112	476	92
1971	635	276	47	303	50	52	450	91	460	93
1972	381	281	57	308	55	92	447	94	453	90
1973	310	279	52	310	60	74	433	76	460	88
1974	399	279	55	311	60	104	422	81	446	66
1975	459	270	66	305	61	104	420	75	439	73
1976	441	262	57	293	54	28	383	70	412	57
1977	449	265	61	308	57	30	446	81	435	77

UNIVERSITY SYSTEM OF GEORGIA
ENTERING FRESHMEN 1957 - 1977
COLLEGE BOARD SCHOLASTIC APTITUDE SCORES

| | GEORGIA COLLEGE | | | | | GEORGIA SOUTHERN | | | | |
| | | VERBAL | | MATH | | | VERBAL | | MATH | |
YEAR	NO.	MEAN	S.D.	MEAN	S.D.	NO.	MEAN	S.D.	MEAN	S.D.
1957	205	393	91	395	75	158	358	84	383	73
1958	180	390	85	389	74	245	355	78	383	79
1959	277	397	90	401	80	210	358	81	391	82
1960	297	408	95	400	78	304	373	84	389	78
1961	321	420	90	411	88	353	399	79	412	84
1962	295	422	82	415	82	402	400	76	412	79
1963	300	417	84	414	80	439	421	80	427	78
1964	330	433	89	433	82	659	429	80	438	86
1965	377	443	84	437	79	923	433	84	445	83
1966	303	445	88	438	81	959	438	79	447	80
1967	392	427	•	439	•	1003	438	•	454	•
1968	321	443	•	455	•	942	438	•	454	•
1969	375	437	•	449	•	1172	441	•	457	•
1970	394	446	92	459	91	1310	437	83	462	80
1971	533	399	95	418	97	1375	435	81	466	80
1972	516	394	89	416	90	1263	413	83	465	81
1973	589	398	96	416	99	1009	425	78	457	83
1974	433	394	88	418	91	1004	424	80	457	86
1975	453	387	91	414	93	1187	412	83	446	89
1976	415	386	88	411	90	1255	411	86	441	87
1977	514	383	92	407	92	1345	413	82	440	87

UNIVERSITY SYSTEM OF GEORGIA
ENTERING FRESHMEN 1957 – 1977
COLLEGE BOARD SCHOLASTIC APTITUDE SCORES

| YEAR | GEORGIA TECH | | | | | GA. SOUTHWESTERN | | | | |
	NO.	VERBAL MEAN	VERBAL S.D.	MATH MEAN	MATH S.D.	NO.	VERBAL MEAN	VERBAL S.D.	MATH MEAN	MATH S.D.
1957	1105	474	76	548	65	176	353	81	404	85
1958	1172	479	91	556	83	225	344	76	377	75
1959	1118	486	85	561	80	217	349	80	380	76
1960	1299	501	89	576	80	219	351	82	383	83
1961	1067	514	86	588	74	182	366	82	387	88
1962	1022	529	86	610	72	169	399	82	410	90
1963	1160	539	85	622	73	140	397	82	422	67
1964	1144	546	83	635	70	303	395	76	421	76
1965	1412	554	80	638	73	426	398	74	418	76
1966	1379	552	81	634	69	375	394	72	406	74
1967	1445	545	•	635	•	554	398	•	414	•
1968	1331	551	•	643	•	453	396	•	412	•
1969	1817	545	•	636	•	607	398	•	413	•
1970	1682	546	83	633	72	590	392	82	411	79
1971	1419	538	81	630	72	589	385	82	410	86
1972	1443	532	87	617	79	575	390	86	415	88
1973	1446	531	85	613	78	418	393	89	419	94
1974	1625	526	93	611	83	386	388	85	406	88
1975	1829	519	94	609	85	405	363	96	394	96
1976	2124	514	95	614	86	385	373	86	399	90
1977	2205	519	94	613	80	417	381	88	397	91

UNIVERSITY SYSTEM OF GEORGIA
ENTERING FRESHMEN 1957 - 1977
COLLEGE BOARD SCHOLASTIC APTITUDE SCORES

YEAR	GEORGIA STATE					KENNESAW JR.				
	NO.	VERBAL MEAN	VERBAL S.D.	MATH MEAN	MATH S.D.	NO.	VERBAL MEAN	VERBAL S.D.	MATH MEAN	MATH S.D.
1957	544	378	95	395	78	•	•	•	•	•
1958	713	386	87	398	77	•	•	•	•	•
1959	261	414	79	432	78	•	•	•	•	•
1960	303	449	87	448	82	•	•	•	•	•
1961	212	464	77	465	77	•	•	•	•	•
1962	397	456	79	460	79	•	•	•	•	•
1963	467	474	84	472	84	•	•	•	•	•
1964	704	473	88	476	81	•	•	•	•	•
1965	952	464	87	473	85	•	•	•	•	•
1966	832	475	85	479	84	364	425	81	426	78
1967	998	466	•	481	•	332	441	•	449	•
1968	745	466	•	482	•	367	436	•	445	•
1969	1272	462	•	477	•	525	433	•	442	•
1970	1539	463	92	474	88	585	435	84	446	83
1971	1366	476	92	490	90	832	421	90	428	93
1972	1158	474	90	484	88	690	434	94	443	93
1973	999	463	96	477	94	703	425	92	437	92
1974	1183	452	92	458	94	846	423	95	428	94
1975	1299	450	94	457	93	1156	409	91	418	87
1976	1361	445	87	455	92	1089	417	90	427	91
1977	921	466	84	480	85	844	413	87	428	89

UNIVERSITY SYSTEM OF GEORGIA
ENTERING FRESHMEN 1957 - 1977
COLLEGE BOARD SCHOLASTIC APTITUDE SCORES

	NORTH GEORGIA					SAVANNAH STATE				
		VERBAL		MATH			VERBAL		MATH	
YEAR	NO.	MEAN	S.D.	MEAN	S.D.	NO.	MEAN	S.D.	MEAN	S.D.
1957	304	435	83	.	85	200	260	44	311	43
1958	326	393	84	422	74	253	278	40	299	41
1959	311	404	75	444	80	237	270	40	288	47
1960	347	420	90	443	86	411	269	49	310	43
1961	442	410	86	443	80	321	256	47	287	44
1962	338	435	85	467	83	303	264	50	294	44
1963	368	434	85	462	80	286	278	52	306	50
1964	350	459	83	483	81	392	274	58	306	56
1965	396	450	85	480	78	414	290	59	313	60
1966	512	454	84	483	79	445	285	59	307	58
1967	389	469	.	483	.	428	292	.	311	.
1968	345	471	.	486	.	505	288	.	307	.
1969	351	480	.	494	.	495	294	.	314	.
1970	394	464	86	483	76	553	291	60	308	57
1971	394	454	85	482	77	529	287	54	314	57
1972	307	463	82	486	82	402	305	67	318	60
1973	296	446	85	474	85	431	300	66	318	60
1974	353	411	90	431	91	508	290	60	310	61
1975	367	413	95	435	93	619	287	67	315	65
1976	400	410	89	430	97	430	284	65	309	62
1977	387	407	95	427	93	544	278	62	311	60

UNIVERSITY SYSTEM OF GEORGIA
ENTERING FRESHMEN 1957 - 1977
COLLEGE BOARD SCHOLASTIC APTITUDE SCORES

| | | SOUTHERN TECH | | | | | VALDOSTA STATE | | | |
| | | VERBAL | | MATH | | | VERBAL | | MATH | |
YEAR	NO.	MEAN	S.D.	MEAN	S.D.	NO.	MEAN	S.D.	MEAN	S.D.
1957	248	355	77	421	81	185	377	86	387	85
1958	283	354	71	426	75	187	370	87	386	81
1959	224	365	78	428	77	194	380	94	392	79
1960	269	355	80	426	77	211	379	93	398	73
1961	304	369	75	433	73	252	401	84	417	81
1962	284	377	75	446	77	224	408	85	425	81
1963	292	376	64	448	64	263	418	85	432	80
1964	307	398	74	471	74	356	428	88	433	81
1965	387	404	79	474	74	532	436	86	449	83
1966	304	397	77	464	70	533	441	79	447	82
1967	307	401	•	464	•	642	435	•	446	•
1968	143	414	•	480	•	521	443	•	454	•
1969	234	407	•	472	•	613	434	•	444	•
1970	321	408	79	469	81	810	425	93	440	94
1971	355	406	74	484	76	798	428	89	447	92
1972	164	435	69	512	67	813	438	91	449	94
1973	159	419	70	491	56	805	409	91	434	91
1974	307	403	83	457	82	901	405	89	429	90
1975	353	396	85	465	79	1018	397	91	412	93
1976	307	392	84	465	80	866	392	95	414	95
1977	302	394	82	465	86	813	403	93	418	94

UNIVERSITY SYSTEM OF GEORGIA
ENTERING FRESHMEN 1957 - 1977
COLLEGE BOARD SCHOLASTIC APTITUDE SCORES

| | UNIVERSITY OF GA. | | | | | WEST GEORGIA | | | | |
| | | VERBAL | | MATH | | | VERBAL | | MATH | |
YEAR	NO.	MEAN	S.D.	MEAN	S.D.	NO.	MEAN	S.D.	MEAN	S.D.
1957	864	401	94	419	85	260	355	82	404	82
1958	1145	405	90	426	83	306	352	72	386	86
1959	1256	407	92	427	86	327	351	75	389	75
1960	1511	426	92	442	85	309	370	83	394	78
1961	1493	443	88	456	83	421	377	77	403	80
1962	1673	454	86	475	84	269	410	76	440	77
1963	1803	460	90	481	82	329	418	76	437	70
1964	2089	470	87	489	81	505	424	79	444	77
1965	1995	484	88	502	84	589	439	80	458	78
1966	2313	496	83	518	77	642	438	79	456	75
1967	2342	492	•	521	•	730	435	•	457	•
1968	2599	502	•	532	•	914	425	•	447	•
1969	3268	508	•	538	•	1293	426	•	447	•
1970	2712	507	88	530	82	1469	413	84	437	84
1971	2636	504	87	5??	80	1282	417	84	443	82
1972	2953	486	94	51?	??	1069	412	78	428	84
1973	2588	486	87	523	84	824	405	83	419	87
1974	1740	476	88	507	88	975	406	91	412	92
1975	2999	470	90	506	91	964	379	96	394	89
1976	2923	474	87	510	89	1036	384	96	398	93
1977	3161	473	89	510	91	1170	378	97	389	91

UNIVERSITY SYSTEM OF GEORGIA
ENTERING FRESHMEN 1957 - 1977
COLLEGE BOARD SCHOLASTIC APTITUDE SCORES

| | A. B. A. C. | | | | | ALBANY JR. | | | | |
| | | VERBAL | | MATH | | | VERBAL | | MATH | |
YEAR	NO.	MEAN	S.D.	MEAN	S.D.	NO.	MEAN	S.D.	MEAN	S.D.
1957	182	332	72	398	75	•	•	•	•	•
1958	208	337	75	383	79	•	•	•	•	•
1959	294	335	82	378	75	•	•	•	•	•
1960	271	334	73	383	75	•	•	•	•	•
1961	247	358	76	391	74	•	•	•	•	•
1962	307	346	81	389	78	•	•	•	•	•
1963	241	367	82	405	77	•	•	•	•	•
1964	332	364	87	404	77	•	•	•	•	•
1965	433	380	86	419	72	•	•	•	•	•
1966	275	381	81	413	71	324	407	93	423	94
1967	649	385	•	415	•	264	406	•	421	•
1968	487	398	•	430	•	316	412	•	426	•
1969	654	399	•	431	•	460	406	•	420	•
1970	805	387	83	416	87	585	395	102	408	105
1971	907	384	81	416	86	700	400	102	406	101
1972	931	368	84	396	88	516	412	104	423	105
1973	885	367	87	399	89	650	403	103	421	108
1974	938	367	89	389	89	663	395	98	411	106
1975	1136	355	92	383	89	786	378	108	399	103
1976	1102	361	90	391	91	555	380	102	405	101
1977	786	361	84	392	89	585	389	102	410	101

315

UNIVERSITY SYSTEM OF GEORGIA
ENTERING FRESHMEN 1957 - 1977
COLLEGE BOARD SCHOLASTIC APTITUDE SCORES

YEAR	ATLANTA JR. NO.	VERBAL MEAN	S.D.	MATH MEAN	S.D.	BAINBRIDGE JR. NO.	VERBAL MEAN	S.D.	MATH MEAN	S.D.
1957	•	•	•	•	•	•	•	•	•	•
1958	•	•	•	•	•	•	•	•	•	•
1959	•	•	•	•	•	•	•	•	•	•
1960	•	•	•	•	•	•	•	•	•	•
1961	•	•	•	•	•	•	•	•	•	•
1962	•	•	•	•	•	•	•	•	•	•
1963	•	•	•	•	•	•	•	•	•	•
1964	•	•	•	•	•	•	•	•	•	•
1965	•	•	•	•	•	•	•	•	•	•
1966	•	•	•	•	•	•	•	•	•	•
1967	•	•	•	•	•	•	•	•	•	•
1968	•	•	•	•	•	•	•	•	•	•
1969	•	•	•	•	•	•	•	•	•	•
1970	•	•	•	•	•	•	•	•	•	•
1971	•	•	•	•	•	•	•	•	•	•
1972	•	•	•	•	•	•	•	•	•	•
1973	•	•	•	•	•	143	366	110	378	96
1974	434	309	71	316	58	165	372	90	387	97
1975	733	286	71	315	64	221	376	100	392	90
1976	467	299	69	320	60	226	364	90	383	91
1977	231	332	95	354	84	175	373	101	388	93

UNIVERSITY SYSTEM OF GEORGIA
ENTERING FRESHMEN 1957 - 1977
COLLEGE BOARD SCHOLASTIC APTITUDE SCORES

| | BRUNSWICK JR. | | | | | CLAYTON JR. | | | | |
| | | VERBAL | | MATH | | | VERBAL | | MATH | |
YEAR	NO.	MEAN	S.D.	MEAN	S.D.	NO.	MEAN	S.D.	MEAN	S.D.
1957	•	•	•	•	•	•	•	•	•	•
1958	•	•	•	•	•	•	•	•	•	•
1959	•	•	•	•	•	•	•	•	•	•
1960	•	•	•	•	•	•	•	•	•	•
1961	•	•	•	•	•	•	•	•	•	•
1962	•	•	•	•	•	•	•	•	•	•
1963	•	•	•	•	•	•	•	•	•	•
1964	146	399	87	422	90	•	•	•	•	•
1965	128	432	94	447	94	•	•	•	•	•
1966	214	393	97	409	102	•	•	•	•	•
1967	259	396	•	406	•	•	•	•	•	•
1968	198	397	•	406	•	•	•	•	•	•
1969	252	408	•	418	•	386	418	•	427	•
1970	332	403	96	405	94	661	424	83	433	81
1971	373	408	96	407	88	864	425	85	435	84
1972	342	399	98	401	100	647	438	86	442	82
1973	365	399	100	414	104	902	434	78	442	79
1974	408	386	98	394	98	990	423	87	418	83
1975	451	374	101	385	98	1359	410	94	412	86
1976	439	373	99	387	96	1170	407	94	413	86
1977	319	398	98	410	99	853	429	80	446	80

UNIVERSITY SYSTEM OF GEORGIA
ENTERING FRESHMEN 1957 - 1977
COLLEGE BOARD SCHOLASTIC APTITUDE SCORES

	DALTON JR.					EMANUEL JR.				
		VERBAL		MATH			VERBAL		MATH	
YEAR	NO.	MEAN	S.D.	MEAN	S.D.	NO.	MEAN	S.D.	MEAN	S.D.
1957	.	.	.	.	.	.	.	.	.	.
1958	.	.	.	.	.	.	.	.	.	.
1959	.	.	.	.	.	.	.	.	.	.
1960	.	.	.	.	.	.	.	.	.	.
1961	.	.	.	.	.	.	.	.	.	.
1962	.	.	.	.	.	.	.	.	.	.
1963	.	.	.	.	.	.	.	.	.	.
1964	.	.	.	.	.	.	.	.	.	.
1965	.	.	.	.	.	.	.	.	.	.
1966	.	.	.	.	.	.	.	.	.	.
1967	327	370	.	375	.	.	.	.	.	.
1968	309	384	.	389	.	.	.	.	.	.
1969	400	374	.	380	.	.	.	.	.	.
1970	273	388	96	392	90	.	.	.	.	.
1971	559	377	91	386	83	.	.	.	.	.
1972	537	388	91	402	91	.	.	.	.	.
1973	396	404	95	411	93	68	394	85	408	74
1974	471	401	89	400	85	139	382	93	401	94
1975	625	390	92	400	86	136	355	98	376	93
1976	481	398	94	409	93	138	382	107	401	107
1977	530	398	91	416	94	165	360	94	393	98

UNIVERSITY SYSTEM OF GEORGIA
ENTERING FRESHMEN 1957 - 1977
COLLEGE BOARD SCHOLASTIC APTITUDE SCORES

YEAR	FLOYD JR.					GAINESVILLE JR.				
		VERBAL		MATH			VERBAL		MATH	
	NO.	MEAN	S.D.	MEAN	S.D.	NO.	MEAN	S.D.	MEAN	S.D.
1957	•	•	•	•	•	•	•	•	•	•
1958	•	•	•	•	•	•	•	•	•	•
1959	•	•	•	•	•	•	•	•	•	•
1960	•	•	•	•	•	•	•	•	•	•
1961	•	•	•	•	•	•	•	•	•	•
1962	•	•	•	•	•	•	•	•	•	•
1963	•	•	•	•	•	•	•	•	•	•
1964	•	•	•	•	•	•	•	•	•	•
1965	•	•	•	•	•	•	•	•	•	•
1966	•	•	•	•	•	228	354	87	376	80
1967	•	•	•	•	•	246	366	•	393	•
1968	•	•	•	•	•	241	385	•	413	•
1969	•	•	•	•	•	301	390	•	418	•
1970	318	365	79	382	89	303	386	87	417	97
1971	443	378	96	387	91	432	391	79	410	85
1972	372	379	89	386	89	453	384	90	406	90
1973	350	392	96	410	95	386	397	93	413	88
1974	411	387	91	396	87	438	393	94	401	87
1975	478	373	94	384	91	596	376	90	392	87
1976	451	392	95	397	92	510	385	86	400	89
1977	565	393	92	402	92	465	397	88	405	88

UNIVERSITY SYSTEM OF GEORGIA
ENTERING FRESHMEN 1957 - 1977
COLLEGE BOARD SCHOLASTIC APTITUDE SCORES

YEAR	GORDON JR. VERBAL NO.	MEAN	S.D.	GORDON JR. MATH MEAN	S.D.	MACON JR. VERBAL NO.	MEAN	S.D.	MACON JR. MATH MEAN	S.D.
1957	·	·	·	·	·	·	·	·	·	·
1958	·	·	·	·	·	·	·	·	·	·
1959	·	·	·	·	·	·	·	·	·	·
1960	·	·	·	·	·	·	·	·	·	·
1961	·	·	·	·	·	·	·	·	·	·
1962	·	·	·	·	·	·	·	·	·	·
1963	·	·	·	·	·	·	·	·	·	·
1964	·	·	·	·	·	·	·	·	·	·
1965	·	·	·	·	·	·	·	·	·	·
1966	·	·	·	·	·	·	·	·	·	·
1967	·	·	·	·	·	519	382	·	391	·
1968	·	·	·	·	·	405	429	·	435	·
1969	·	·	·	·	·	777	421	89	416	88
1970	·	·	·	·	·	704	404	91	416	92
1971	·	·	·	·	·	580	404	91	415	92
1972	214	379	100	392	94	728	404	93	422	88
1973	224	368	93	394	94	669	410	86	414	86
1974	400	392	96	398	94	744	403	92	412	92
1975	401	394	99	413	100	788	404	97	407	90
1976	433	390	100	410	97	714	412	96	415	91
1977	494	383	94	408	94					

UNIVERSITY SYSTEM OF GEORGIA
ENTERING FRESHMEN 1957 - 1977
COLLEGE BOARD SCHOLASTIC APTITUDE SCORES

MIDDLE GEORGIA JR.

YEAR	NO.	VERBAL MEAN	VERBAL S.D.	MATH MEAN	MATH S.D.
1957	213	344	69	408	81
1958	276	351	85	404	89
1959	267	352	77	402	90
1960	301	367	81	422	80
1961	284	371	83	426	85
1962	210	383	88	445	84
1963	301	384	79	433	85
1964	356	416	86	455	86
1965	478	418	80	457	88
1966	359	422	82	453	88
1967	464	416	•	454	•
1968	551	406	•	444	•
1969	1041	402	•	440	•
1970	1145	391	82	430	91
1971	858	402	92	442	92
1972	851	398	86	436	92
1973	705	389	83	429	92
1974	747	381	88	414	90
1975	839	368	90	402	95
1976	826	369	92	405	96
1977	665	369	92	407	94

SOUTH GEORGIA

YEAR	NO.	VERBAL MEAN	VERBAL S.D.	MATH MEAN	MATH S.D.
1957	233	339	78	385	72
1958	249	340	73	379	80
1959	258	343	74	385	78
1960	298	353	88	387	78
1961	370	357	79	391	80
1962	289	364	80	394	79
1963	275	354	73	388	77
1964	372	373	77	394	78
1965	368	396	77	410	75
1966	409	399	68	413	81
1967	386	401	•	410	•
1968	381	390	•	399	•
1969	405	389	•	398	•
1970	396	387	81	402	86
1971	832	364	92	388	96
1972	489	367	85	387	89
1973	363	367	91	389	91
1974	411	357	88	374	89
1975	459	344	95	367	85
1976	405	345	96	370	94
1977	373	348	99	366	84

UNIVERSITY SYSTEM OF GEORGIA
ENTERING FRESHMEN 1957 - 1977
COLLEGE BOARD SCHOLASTIC APTITUDE SCORES

WAYCROSS JR.

YEAR	NO.	VERBAL MEAN	S.D.	MATH MEAN	S.D.
1957	.	.	.	.	.
1958	.	.	.	.	.
1959	.	.	.	.	.
1960	.	.	.	.	.
1961	.	.	.	.	.
1962	.	.	.	.	.
1963	.	.	.	.	.
1964	.	.	.	.	.
1965	.	.	.	.	.
1966	.	.	.	.	.
1967	.	.	.	.	.
1968	.	.	.	.	.
1969	.	.	.	.	.
1970	.	.	.	.	.
1971	.	.	.	.	.
1972	.	.	.	.	.
1973	.	.	.	.	.
1974	.	.	.	.	.
1975	.	.	.	.	.
1976	164	395	86	407	94
1977	150	430	85	420	95

References

Abercrombie, D. H. Performance of black and white five year old children as a function of the race of the examiner and the praise and no praise conditions. (Doctoral dissertation, Hofstra University, 1975). *Dissertation Abstracts International*, 1975, *36*, 1468 B. (Order No. 75-15,003).

Aberdeen, F. D. *Adjustment to desegregation: A description of some differences among Negro elementary school pupils.* (Doctoral dissertation, University of Michigan, 1969).

Abramson, T. The influence of examiner race on first grade and kindergarten subjects' Peabody Picture Vocabulary Test scores. *Journal of Educational Measurement*, 1969, *6*(4), 241–246.

Adams, J., McIntosh, E. I., & Weade, B. L. Ethnic background, measured intelligence, and adaptive behavior scores in mentally retarded children. *American Journal of Mental Deficiency*, 1973, *78*(1), 1–6.

Alcorn, C. L., & Nicholson, C. L. Validity of the Slosson Drawing Coordination Test with adolescents of below-average ability. *Perceptual and Motor Skills*, 1972, *34*, 261–262.

Ali, F., & Costello, J. Modification of the Peabody Picture Vocabulary Test. *Development Psychology*, 1971, *5*(1), 86–91.

Alley, G. R., & Snider, B. Comparative perceptual motor performance of Negro and white young mental retardates. *Developmental Psychology*, 1970, *2*(1), 110–114.

Ames, L. B., & August, J. Rorschach responses of Negro and white 5- to 10-year-olds. *Journal of Genetic Psychology*, 1966, *109*, 297–309.

Ames, L. B., & Ilg, F. L. Search for children showing academic promise in a predominantly Negro school. *Journal of Genetic Psychology*, 1967, *110*, 217–231.

Ammons, R. B., & Ammons, C. H. *The Quick Test (QT): provisional manual.* Missoula, Mont.: Psychological Test Specialists, 1962.

Anderson, H. E., Kern, F. E., Cook, C. Sex, brain damage, and race effects in the Progressive Matrices with retarded populations. *Journal of Social Psychology*, 1968, *76*, 207–211.

Angoff, W. H., & Ford, S. F. Item-Race interaction on a test of scholastic aptitude. *Journal of Educational Measurement,* 1973, *10*(2), 95–106.

Arnoult, J. F. *A comparison of the psycholinguistic abilities of selected groups of first grade children.* Dissertation, 1972, Mississippi State University.

Asbury, C. A. Cognitive correlates of discrepant achievement in reading. *Journal of Negro Education,* 1973, *42*(2), 123–133. (a)

Asbury, C. A. Sociological factors related to discrepant achievement of white and black first graders. *Journal of Experimental Education,* 1973, *42*(1), 6–10. (b)

Atchison, C. O. Relationships between some intellectual and non-intellectual factors of high anxiety and low anxiety Negro college students. *Journal of Negro Education,* 1968, *37,* 174–178.

Bachman, J. G. *Youth in transition,* Volume II. Ann Arbor, Michigan: The University of Michigan, 1970.

Backman, M. E. Patterns of mental abilities: Ethnic, socioeconomic, and sex differences. *American Educational Research Journal,* 1972, *9*(1), 1–12.

Baker, E. A., & Owen, D. R. Negro-white personality differences in integrated classrooms. *Proceedings,* 77th Annual APA Convention, 1969, 539–540.

Baratz, S. Effect of race of experimenter, instructions, and comparison population upon level of reported anxiety in Negro subjects. *Journal of Personality and Social Psychology,* 1967, *7,* 194–196.

Barclay, A., & Yater, A. A comparative study of the Wechsler Preschool and Primary Scale of Intelligence and the Stanford-Binet, form L-M, among culturally deprived children. Paper read at 1968 Midwestern Psychological Association Convention, Chicago, Illinois.

Barnebey, N. S. Effect of race of examiner on test performance of Negro and white children. *Proceedings,* 81st Annual Convention, APA, 1973, 647–648.

Barr, A. J. Goodnight, J. H., Sall, J. P., & Helwig, J. T. *A user's guide to SAS 76.* Raleigh, NC: SAS Institute Inc., 1976.

Bartlett, D. P., Newbrough, J. R., & Tulkin, S. R. Raven Progressive Matrices: An item and set analysis of subjects grouped by race, sex, and social class. *Journal of Consulting and Clinical Psychology,* 1972, *38*(1), 154.

Bartlett, E. J. *Adventures in living: A preschool program.* New York: Western Publishing Co., 1971.

Baughman, E. E., & Dahlstrom, W. G. *Negro and white children.* New York: Academic Press, 1968.

Benson, A. L. Problems of evaluating test scores of white and Negro teachers. *Quarterly Review of Higher Education Among Negroes,* 1955, *23,* 5–15.

Berendes, H. W. The structure and scope of the Collaborative Project on Cerebral Palsy, Mental Retardation, and Other Neurological and Sensory Disorders of Infancy and Childhood. In S. S. Chipman, A. M. Lilienfeld, B. G. Greenberg, and J. F. Donnelly (eds.), Research methodology and needs in perinatal studies, 1966. Charles C. Thomas, Springfield, Illinois.

Berke, N. D. *An investigation of adult Negro illiteracy: Prediction of reading achievement and description of educational characteristics of a sample of city core adult Negro illiterates.* Doctoral dissertation, State University of New York at Buffalo, 1967.

Bernal Jr., E. M. *Concept learning among Anglo, black, and Mexican-American children using facilitation strategies and bilingual techniques.* Doctoral dissertation, University of Texas at Austin, 1971.

Bienvenu Sr., M. J. *Effects of school integration on the self-concept and anxiety of lower-class Negro adolescent males.* Dissertation, The Florida State University, 1968.

Birns, B., & Golden, M. Prediction of intellectual performance at 3 years from infant tests and personality measures. *Merrill-Palmer Quarterly,* 1972, *18,* 53–58.

Blair, G. E. *The relationship of selected ego functions and the academic achievement of Negro students.* Doctoral dissertation, Florida State University, 1967.

Blatt, B., & Garfunkel, F. Educating intelligence: Determinants of school behavior of disadvantaged children. *Exceptional Children,* 1967, *33,* 601–608.

Blue, C. M., & Vergason, G. A. Echoic responses of standard English features by culturally deprived black and white children. *Perceptual and Motor Skills,* 1973, *37,* 575–581.

Boehm, V. R. Negro-white differences in validity of employment and training selection procedures: Summary of research evidence. *Journal of Applied Psychology,* 1972, *56,* 33–39.

Boney, J. D. *A study of the use of intelligence, aptitude, and mental ability measures in predicting the academic achievement of Negro students in secondary school.* Doctoral dissertation, The University of Texas, 1964.

Boney, J. D. Predicting the academic achievement of secondary school Negro students. *The Personnel and Guidance Journal,* 1966, *44,* 700–703.

Bonner, M. W., & Belden, B. R. A comparative study of the performance of Negro seniors of Oklahoma City high schools on the Wechsler Adult Intelligence Scale and the Peabody Picture Vocabulary Test. *Journal of Negro Education,* 1970, *39*(4), 354–358.

Boone, J. A., & Adesso, V. J. Racial differences on a black intelligence test. *Journal of Negro Education,* 1974, *43,* 429–436.

Borgen, F. H. Differential expectations? Predicting grades for black students in five types of colleges. *Measurement and Evaluation in Guidance,* 1972, January, *4*(4), 206–212.

Bowers, J. The comparison of GPA regression equations for regularly admitted and disadvantaged freshmen at the University of Illinois. *Journal of Educational Measurement,* Winter, 1970, *7*(4), 219–225.

Bowles, F. L. *Sub-test score changes over twenty months on the Wechsler Intelligence Scale for Children for white and Negro special education students.* Doctoral dissertation, University of Florida, 1968.

Bradley Jr., N. E. *The Negro undergraduate student: Factors relative to performance in predominantly white state colleges and universities in Tennessee.* Doctoral dissertation, The University of Tennessee, 1966.

Bradley, R. H., Caldwell, B. M., & Elardo, R. Home environment, social status, and mental test performance. *Journal of Educational Psychology,* 1977, *69*(6), 697–701.

Breland, H. M. The SAT score decline: A summary of related research. Prepared for the Advisory Panel on the Scholastic Aptitude Test Score Decline, jointly sponsored by the College Board and Educational Testing Service. Princeton, N.J. January, 1976.

Bridgette, R. E. *Self-esteem in Negro and white southern adolescents.* Doctoral dissertation, University of North Carolina at Chapel Hill, 1970.

Burke, B. P. *An exploratory study of the relationships among third grade Negro children's self-concept, creativity, and intelligence and teachers' perceptions of those relationships.* Doctoral dissertation, Wayne State University, 1968.

Burks, B. S. The relative influence of nature and nurture upon mental development; a comparative study of foster parent-foster child resemblance and true parent-true child resemblance. *Yearbook of the National Society for the Study of Education,* 1928, *27,* 219–316.

Burnes, D. K. S. *A study of relationships between measured intelligence and non-intellective factors for children of two socioeconomic groups and races.* Doctoral dissertation, Washington University, 1968.

Burnes, K. Patterns of WISC scores for children of two socioeconomic classes and races. *Child Development,* 1970, *41,* 493–499.

Buros, O. K. (Ed.). *Mental measurements yearbook* (7 vols.). Highland Park, N.J: Gryphon Press, 1938–1972.

Buros, O. K. (Ed.). *Tests in print* (2 vols.). Highland Park, N.J.: Gryphon Press, 1961; 1974.

Busse, T. V., Ree, M., Gutride, M., Alexander, T., & Powell, L. S. Environmentally enriched classrooms and the cognitive and perceptual development of Negro preschool children. *Journal of Educational Psychology,* 1972, *63*(1), 15–21.

Caldwell, M. B., & Knight, D. The effect of Negro and white examiners on Negro intelligence test performance. *Journal of Negro Education,* 1970, *39,* 177–179.

Caldwell, M. B., & Smith, T. A. Intellectual structure of southern Negro children. *Psychological Reports,* 1968, *23,* 63–71.

Cameron, H. K. Nonintellectual correlates of academic achievement. *Journal of Negro Education,* 1968, *37*(3), 252–257.

Cardall, C., & Coffman, W. E. A method for comparing the performance of different groups on the items in a test. College Entrance Examination Board. Research and Development Reports. RDR-64-5, No. 9, 1964.

Carpenter, F. A. *A study of the reading achievement of Negro "Head Start" first-grade students compared with Negro "Non-Head Start" first-grade students.* Doctoral dissertation, The Florida State University, 1967.

Carringer, D., & Wilson, C. S. The effects of sex, socioeconomic class, experimenter race, and kind of verbal reinforcement on the performance of black children. *Journal of Negro Education,* 1974, *43,* 212–218.

Carroll, I. V. *A comparison of the intelligence quotients of sixth grade children of Negro and Caucasian educators and non-educators.* Doctoral dissertation, University of Alabama, 1970.

Carver, R. P. An experiment that failed: Designing an aural aptitude test for Negroes. *College Board Review,* 1968–69, No. 70, 10–14.

Carwise, J. L. *Aspirations and attitudes toward education of over- and under-achieving Negro junior high school students.* Doctoral dissertation, Indiana University, 1967.

Cawley, J. F. Learning aptitudes among preschool children of different intellectual levels. *Journal of Negro Education,* 1968, *37,* 179–185.

Centra, J., Linn, R., & Parry, M. Academic growth in predominantly Negro and predominantly white colleges. *American Educational Research Journal,* January, 1970, *7*(1), 83–98.

Cerbus, G., & Oziel, L. J. Correlation of the Bender-Gestalt and WISC for Negro children. *Perceptual and Motor Skills,* 1971, *32,* 276.

Chovan, W. L., & Hathaway, M. L. The performance of two culturally divergent groups of children on a culture-free test. *Journal of School Psychology,* 1970, *8,* 66.

Christensen, L., Leunes, A, & Wilkerson, D. The effectiveness of Otis Quick-Scoring Mental Ability Test to differentiate an inmate sample. *Journal of Clinical Psychology,* 1975, *31,* 694–695.

Cicirelli, V. G., Evans, J. W., & Schiller, J. S. The impact of Head Start: A reply to the report analysis. *Harvard Educational Review,* 1970, *40*(1), 105–129.

Cicirelli, V. G., Granger, R., Schemmel, D., Cooper, W., & Holthouse, N. Performance of disadvantaged primary-grade children on the revised Illinois Test of Psycholinguistic Abilities. *Psychology in the Schools,* 1971, *8,* 240–246.

Clark, K., & Clark, M. Racial identification and preference in Negro children. In T. Newcomb and E. Hartley (Eds.), *Readings in Social Psychology.* New York: Holt, 1947.

Cleary, T. A. Test bias: Prediction of grades of Negro and white students in integrated colleges. *Journal of Educational Measurement,* 1968, Summer, *5*(2), 115–124.

Cleary, T. A., & Hilton, T. L. An investigation of item bias. *Educational and Psychological Measurement,* 1968, *28,* 61–75.

Clegg, S. J., & White, W. F. Assessment of general intelligence of Negro deaf children in a public residential school for the deaf. *Journal of Clinical Psychology,* 1966, *22,* 93–94.

Cohen, J. *Statistical power analysis for the behavioral sciences* (Rev. ed.). New York: Academic Press, 1977.

Cole, N. S., & Fowler, W. R. Pattern analysis of WISC scores achieved by culturally disadvantaged southern blacks. *Psychological Reports,* 1974, *36,* 305–306.

Cole, S., & Williams, R. The Quick Test as an index of intellectual ability on a Negro admission ward. *Psychological Reports,* 1967, *20,* 581–582.

Coleman, J. S. et al. *Equality of Educational Opportunity.* Washington, D.C.: U.S. Office of Education, 1966.

College Entrance Examination Board. *Comparative Guidance and Placement Program, Form SP6, 1970.* Princeton, N.J.: Educational Testing Service, 1970.

Collins, Sister M. A. *Achievement, intelligence, personality and selected school-related variables in Negro children from intact and broken families attending parochial schools in central Harlem.* Doctoral dissertation, Fordham University, 1969.

Condit, J. E., Lewandowski, D. G., & Saccuzzo, D. P. Efficiency of the Peabody

Picture Vocabulary in estimating WISC scores for delinquents. *Psychological Reports,* 1976, *38,* 359–362.

Cooper, G. D., York, M. W., Daston, P. G., & Adams, H. B. The Porteus Test and various measures of intelligence with southern Negro adolescents. *American Journal of Mental Deficiency,* 1967, *71,* 787–792.

Costello, J. Effects of pretesting and examiner characteristics on test performance of young disadvantaged children. Proceedings, 78th Annual Convention, APA, 1970, *5,* (Pt. 1), 309–310.

Costello, J., & Ali, F. Reliability and validity of Peabody Picture Vocabulary Test scores of disadvantaged preschool children. *Psychological Reports,* 1971, *28,* 755–760.

Costello, J., & Dickie, J. Leiter and Stanford-Binet IQ's of preschool disadvantaged children. *Developmental Psychology,* 1970, *2*(2), 314.

Covin, T. M. Comparability of the Peabody and WISC scores among black five-year-olds. *Psychological Reports,* 1976, *38,* 1346.

Covin, T. M., & Hatch, G. L. WISC-R Full Scale mean IQs for both black and white children, aged 6 through 15 and having difficulty in school. *Psychological Reports,* 1977, *41,* 1201–1202.

Crain, R. L., & Mahard, R. E. *National longitudinal study: The influence of high school racial composition on black college attendance and test performance.* Prepared for National Center for Education Statistics, U.S. Department of Health, Education, and Welfare, by Rand Corporation, Santa Monica, CA, 1978.

Crandall, V. C. Personality characteristics and social and achievement behaviors associated with children's social desirability response tendencies. *Journal of Personality and Social Psychology,* 1966, *4,* 477–486.

Crown, P. J. *The effects of race of examiner and standard vs. dialect administration of the Wechsler Preschool and Primary Scale of Intelligence on the performance of Negro and white children.* The Florida State University, 1970.

D'Angelo, R., Walsh, J., & Lomangino, L. IQs of Negro Head Start children on the Vane Kindergarten Test. *Journal of Clinical Psychology,* 1971, *27,* 82–83.

Darlington, R. B., Royce, J. M., Snipper, A. S., Murray, H. W., & Lazar, I. Preschool programs and later school competence of children from low-income families. *Science,* 1980, *208,* 202–204.

Datta, L.-E., Schaefer, E., & Davis, M. Sex and scholastic aptitude as variables in teachers' ratings of the adjustment and classroom behavior of Negro and other seventh-grade students. *Journal of Educational Psychology,* 1968, *59*(2), 94–101.

Davis, J., & Temp, G. Is the SAT biased against black students? *College Board Review,* 1971, Fall, No. 81, 4–9.

Davis, S. C., Loeb, J. W., & Robinson, L. F. A comparison of characteristics of Negro and white college freshman classmates. *Journal of Negro Education,* 1970, *39,* 359–366.

Deitz, S., & Purkey, W. Teacher expectation of performance based on race of student. *Psychological Reports,* 1969, *24,* 694.

DeNeufville, R., & Conner, C. How good are our schools? *American Education,* 1966, *2,* 1–9.

Denmark, F. L., & Guttentag, M. Effect of integrated and non-integrated programs on cognitive change in preschool children. *Perceptual and Motor Skills,* 1969, *29,* 375–380.

Deutch, J. A. *Paternal deprivation: Some effects upon eight and nine year old Negro boys.* Doctoral dissertation, The Catholic University of America, 1969.

Diener, R. G., & Maroney, R. J. Relationship between Quick Test and WAIS for black male adolescent underachievers. *Psychological Reports,* 1974, *34,* 1232–1234.

Dill, J. R. *A study of the influence of race of the experimenter and verbal reinforcement on creativity test performance of lower socioeconomic status black children.* Doctoral dissertation, New York University, 1971.

Dillon, R., & Carlson, J. S. Testing for competence in three ethnic groups. *Educational and Psychological Measurement,* 1978, *38,* 437–443.

Dubin, J. A., Osburn, H., & Winick, D. M. Speed and practice: Effects on Negro and white test performances. *Journal of Applied Psychology,* 1969, *53*(1), 19–23.

Dugan, R. D. The industrial psychologist: Selection and equal employment opportunity. IV—Current problems in test performance of job applicants. *Personnel Psychology,* 1966, *19,* 18–24.

Dukes, P. E. *Effects of race of experimenter, self-concept and racial attitudes in the performance of black junior high school students.* Doctoral dissertation, The University of Michigan, 1975.

Duva, N. A. *Effects of asymptomatic lead poisoning on psychoneurological functioning of school-age urban children: A follow-up study.* Doctoral dissertation, Fordham University, 1977.

Dyer, P. J. Effects of test conditions on Negro-white differences in test scores. Doctoral dissertation, Columbia University, 1970. *Dissertation Abstracts International,* 1971, *31,* 5685 B. (Order No. 71–6166).

Emanuel, J. M. *The intelligence, achievement, and progress scores of children who attended summer Head Start programs in 1967, 1968, and 1969.* Doctoral dissertation, University of Alabama, 1970.

Emmons, C. A. *A comparison of selected gross-motor activities of the Getman-Kane and the Kephart perceptual motor training programs and their effects upon certain readiness skills of first-grade Negro children.* Doctoral dissertation, The Ohio State University, 1968.

Epps, E. G., Perry, A., Katz, I., & Runyon, E. Effect of race of comparison referent and motives on Negro cognitive performance. *Journal of Educational Psychology,* 1971, *62*(3), 201–208.

Equal Employment Opportunity Commission. *Guidelines on employment testing procedures.* Washington, D.C., 1966.

Evans, C. L. *The immediate effects of classroom integration on the academic progress, self-concept, and racial attitude of Negro elementary children.* Doctoral dissertation, North Texas State University, 1969.

Fagan, J., Broughton, E., Allen, M., Clark, B., & Emerson, P. Comparison of the Binet and WPPSI with lower-class five-year-olds. *Journal of Consulting and Clinical Psychology,* 1969, *33*(5), 607–609.

Farnham-Diggory, S. Cognitive synthesis in Negro and white children. *Monographs of the Society for Research in Child Development,* 1970, *35*(2), 1–84.

Farver, A. S., Sedlacek, W. E., & Brooks, G. C. Longitudinal predictions of university grades for blacks and whites. *Measurement and Evaluation in Guidance,* 1975, January, *7*(4), 243–250.

Fisher, G. The performance of male prisoners on the Marlowe-Crowne Social Desirability Scale: II. Differences as a function of race and crime. *Journal of Clinical Psychology,* 1967, *23,* 473–475.

Flanagan, J., & Lewis, G. Comparison of Negro and white lower class men on the General Aptitude Test Battery and the Minnesota Multiphasic Personality Inventory. *Journal of Social Psychology,* 1969, *78,* 289–291.

Flick, G. L. Sinistrality revisited: A perceptual-motor approach. *Child Development,* 1966, *37,* 613–622.

France, K. Effects of "white" and "black" examiner voices on IQ scores of children. *Developmental Psychology,* 1973, *8,* 144.

Fredrickson, L. C. Measure Intelligence: Species specific? Perhaps; Race Specific? Perhaps not. *Journal of Genetic Psychology,* 1977, *130,* 95–104.

French, R. L. The Motorola Case. *The Industrial Psychologist,* 1965, *2,* 29–50.

Frerichs, A. H. Relationships of self-esteem of the disadvantaged to school success. *Journal of Negro Education,* 1971, *40,* 117–120.

Gael, S., Grant, D. L., & Ritchie, R. J. Employment test validity for minority and nonminority telephone operators. *Journal of Applied Psychology,* 1975, August, *60*(4), 411–419. (a)

Gael, S., Grant, D. L., & Ritchie, R. J. Employment test validity for minority and nonminority clerks with work sample criteria. *Journal of Applied Psychology,* 1975, August, *60*(4), 420–426. (b)

Garrett, H. E. Klineberg's chapter on race and psychology: A review. *The Mankind Quarterly,* 1960, *1*(1), 3–10.

Garrett, H. E. The relative intelligence of whites and Negroes. *The Mankind Quarterly,* 1967, *8,* 64–79.

Gay, C. J. *Academic achievement and intelligence among Negro eighth grade students as a function of the self concept.* Doctoral dissertation, North Texas State University, 1966.

Geber, M., & Dean, R. F. A. Gesell tests on African children. *Pediatrics,* 1957, *20,* 1055–1065.

Georgi, N. J. *The relationship of self-concept in high school Negro students in Muncie, Indiana to intelligence, achievement, and grade point average.* Doctoral dissertation, Ball State University, 1971.

Gerstein, A. I., Brodzinsky, D. M., & Reiskind, N. Perceptual integration on the Rorschach as an indicator of cognitive capacity: A developmental study of racial differences in a clinic population. *Journal of Consulting and Clinical Psychology,* 1976, *44*(5), 760–765.

Gesell, A., & Ilg, F. Infant and child in the culture of today. New York: Harper, 1943.

Goffeney, B., Henderson, N. B., & Butler, B. V. Negro-white, male-female eight-month developmental scores compared with seven-year WISC and Bender test scores. *Child Development,* 1971, *42,* 595–604.

Golden, M., & Birns, B. Social class and cognitive development in infancy. *Merrill-Palmer Quarterly,* 1968, *14,* 139–149.

Golden, M., Birns, B., Bridger, W., & Moss, A. Social-class differentiation in cognitive development among black preschool children. *Child Development,* 1971, *42,* 36–45.

Goldfarb, J., Basen, J. A., & Kersey, J. Intelligence of pregnant indigent Negro adolescents assessed by the Quick Test. *Psychological Reports,* 1973, *32,* 539–542.

Goldman, R. D., & Hardig, L. K. The WISC may not be a valid predictor of school performance for primary-grade minority children. *American Journal of Mental Deficiency,* 1976, *80*(6), 583–587.

Goldsmith, A. F. The effects of verbal incentive, race, and sex of examiner on digit-symbol performance of Negro males and females. Doctoral dissertation, The City University of New York, 1969. *Dissertation Abstracts International,* 1970, *30,* 4370 B. (University Microfilms No. 69–19,041).

Goldstein, H. S., & Peck, R. Cognitive functions in Negro and white children in a child guidance clinic. *Psychological Reports,* 1971, *28,* 379–384.

Goodenough, F. *Measurement of intelligence by drawings.* New York: Harcourt, Brace and World, 1926.

Gordon, M. E., Arvey, R. D., Daffron, W. C., & Umberger, D. L. Racial differences in the impact of mathematics training at a manpower development program. *Journal of Applied Psychology,* 1974, *59,* 253–258.

Gordon, M. T. A different view of the IQ-achievement gap. *Sociology of Education,* 1976, *49,* 4–11.

Gould, L. J., & Klein, E. B. Performance of black and white adolescents on intellectual and attitudinal measures as a function of race of tester. *Journal of Consulting and Clinical Psychology,* 1971, *37*(2), 195–200.

Gray, S. W., & Klaus, R. A. An experimental preschool program for culturally deprived children. *Child Development,* 1965, *36,* 887–898.

Gray, S. W., & Klaus, R. A. The early training project: A seventh-year report. *Child Development,* 1970, *41,* 909–924.

Green, R. F. On the correlation between IQ and amount of "white" blood. Proceedings, 80th Annual Convention, APA, 1972, 285–286.

Green, R. L., & Morgan, R. F. The effects of resumed schooling on the measured intelligence of Prince Edward County's black children. *Journal of Negro Education,* 1969, *38,* 147–155.

Greene, J. E. A comparison of certain characteristics of white and Negro teachers in a large southeastern school system. *Journal of Social Psychology,* 1962, *58,* 383–391.

Greenwald, A. G. Consequences of prejudice against the null hypothesis. *Psychological Bulletin,* 1975, *82,* 1–20.

Guilford, J. P. *Personality.* New York: McGraw-Hill, 1959.

Guinagh, B. J. An experimental study of basic learning ability and intelligence in low socioeconomic-status children. *Child Development,* 1971 *42,* 27–36.

Hagen, J. W. The effect of distraction on selective attention. *Child Development,* 1967, *38,* 685–694.

Hall, V. C., Huppertz, J. W., & Levi, A. Attention and achievement exhibited by middle- and lower-class black and white elementary school boys. *Journal of Educational Psychology,* 1977, *69,* 115–120.

Hall, W. S., Reder, S., & Cole, M. Story recall in young black and white children: Effects of racial group membership, race of experimenter, and dialect. *Developmental Psychology,* 1975, *11,* 628–634.

Halpin, G., Halpin, G., & Torrance, E. P. Effects of sex, race, and age on creative thinking abilities of blind children. *Perceptual and Motor Skills,* 1973, *37,* 389–390.

Harris, A. J., & Lovinger, R. J. Longitudinal measures of the intelligence of disadvantaged Negro adolescents. *The School Review,* 1968, *76*(1), 60–66.

Harris, G. R. *A study of the academic achievement of selected Negro and white fifth-grade pupils when educational ability is held constant.* Doctoral dissertation, The University of North Carolina at Chapel Hill, 1967.

Harris, H. *The development of moral attitudes in white and Negro boys.* Doctoral dissertation, Columbia University, 1967.

Hatch, G. L., & Covin, T. M. Comparability of WISC and Peabody IQs of young children from three heterogeneous groups. *Psychological Reports,* 1977, *40,* 1345–1346.

Hawkes, T. H., & Furst, N. F. Race, socio-economic situation, achievement, IQ, and teacher ratings of students' behavior as factors relating to anxiety in upper elementary school children. *Sociology of Education,* 1971, *44,* 333–350.

Hawkes, T. H., & Koff, R. H. Differences in anxiety of private school and inner city public elementary school children. *Psychology in the Schools,* 1970, July, *7,* 250–259.

Hechinger, F. Saturday Review/World, February 9, 1974, p. 65.

Heilburn, A. B., & Jordan, B. T. Vocational rehabilitation of the socially disadvantaged: Demographic and intellectual correlates of outcome. *Personnel and Guidance Journal,* 1968, *47,* 213–217.

Henderson, N. B., Butler, B. V., & Goffeney, B. Effectiveness of the WISC and Bender-Gestalt Test in predicting arithmetic and reading achievement for white and nonwhite children. *Journal of Clinical Psychology,* 1969, *25,* 268–271.

Henderson, N. B., Fay, W. H., Lindemann, S. J., & Clarkson, Q. D. Will the IQ test ban decrease the effectiveness of reading prediction? *Journal of Educational Psychology,* 1973, *65*(3), 345–355.

Hennessy, J. J., & Merrifield, P. R. A comparison of the factor structures of mental abilities in four ethnic groups. *Journal of Educational Psychology,* 1976, *68*(6), 754–759.

Henning, J. J., & Levy, R. H. Verbal-Performance IQ differences of white and Negro delinquents on the WISC and WAIS. *Journal of Clinical Psychology,* 1967, *23,* 164–168.

Herskovitz, F. S. *The effects of an educational-vocational rehabilitation program upon the self-concepts of disadvantaged youth.* Doctoral dissertation, University of Pennsylvania, 1969.

Herzog, E., Newcomb, C., & Cisin, I. H. But some are more poor than others: SES differences in a preschool program. *American Journal of Orthopsychiatry,* 1972, *42*(1), 4–22.

Hills, J. R. Prediction of college grades for all public colleges of a state. *Journal of Educational Measurement,* 1964, *1*(2), 155–159.

Hills, J. R., & Gladney, M. B. Predicting grades from below chance test scores. *Journal of Educational Measurement,* 1968, Spring, *5*(1), 45–53.

Hills, J. R., & Stanley, J. C. Easier test improves prediction of black students' college grades. *Journal of Negro Education,* 1970, *39,* 320–324.

Holowinsky, I. Z., & Pascale, P. J. Performance on selected WISC subtests of subjects referred for psychological evaluation because of educational difficulties. *Journal of Special Education,* 1972, *6*(3), 231–235.

Howell Jr., G. C. *An investigation of response time in computerized psychological tests.* Doctoral dissertation, Georgia State University, 1977.

Hughes, R. B., & Lessler, K. A comparison of WISC and Peabody scores of Negro and white rural school children. *American Journal of Mental Deficiency,* 1965, *69*(6), 877–880.

Hutson, B. A. M. *Conservation and the comprehension of syntax in economically disadvantaged seven-year-old Negro children.* Doctoral dissertation, The University of Florida, 1973.

Hutton, J. B. *Relationships between preschool screening test data and first grade academic performance for Head Start children.* Doctoral dissertation, University of Houston, 1970.

Ilardi, R. L. *Family disorganization and intelligence in Negro pre-school children.* Doctoral dissertation, The University of Tennessee, 1966.

Ilg, F. L., & Ames, L. B. *School readiness: Behavior tests used at the Gesell Institute.* New York: Harper and Row, 1964.

Isaac, B. K. Perceptual-motor development of first graders as related to class, race, intelligence, visual discrimination, and motivation. *Journal of School Psychology,* 1973, *11*(1), 47–56.

Jackson, A. M. *Differential characteristics of reasoning ability in Negroes and whites.* Doctoral dissertation, Colorado State University, 1967.

James, D. H. *The effect of desegregation on the self-concept of Negro high school students.* Doctoral dissertation, University of Southern Mississippi, 1970.

Jensen, A. R. How much can we boost IQ and scholastic achievement? *Harvard Educational Review,* 1969. (a)

Jensen, A. R. Reducing the heredity-environment uncertainty. *Harvard Educational Review,* 1969, *39,* 449–483. (b)

Jensen, A. R. Do schools cheat minority children? *Educational Research,* 1971, *14,* 3–28.

Jensen, A. R. *Educability and group differences.* New York: Harper and Row, Publishers, 1973. (a)

Jensen, A. R. Level I and Level II abilities in three ethnic groups. *American Educational Research Journal,* 1973, *10*(4), 263–276. (b)

Jensen, A. R. Cumulative deficit: A testable hypothesis? *Developmental Psychology,* 1974, *10*(6), 996–1019. (a)

Jensen, A. R. The effects of race of examiner on the mental test scores of white and black pupils. *Journal of Educational Measurement,* 1974, *11,* 1–14. (b)

Jensen, A. R. Ethnicity and scholastic achievement. *Psychological Reports,* 1974, *34,* 659–668. (c)

Jensen, A. R. How biased are culture-loaded tests? *Genetic Psychological Monographs,* 1974, *90,* 185–244. (d)

Jensen, A. R. Interaction of Level I and Level II abilities with race and socioeconomic status. *Journal of Educational Psychology,* 1974, *66*(1), 99–111. (e)

Jensen, A. R. An examination of culture bias in the Wonderlic Personnel Test. *Intelligence,* 1977, *1,* 51–64 (a)

Jensen, A. R. Cumulative deficit in IQ of blacks in the rural south. *Developmental Psychology,* 1977, *13*(3), 184–191. (b)

Jensen, A. R. *Bias in mental testing.* New York: The Free Press, 1980.

Jensen, A. R., & Figueroa, R. A. Forward and backward digit span interaction with race and IQ: Prediction from Jensen's theory. *Journal of Educational Psychology,* 1975, *67,* 882–893.

Jensen, A. R., & Frederiksen, J. Free recall of categorized and uncategorized lists: A test of the Jensen hypothesis. *Journal of Educational Psychology,* 1973, *65*(3), 304–312.

John, V. P. The intellectual development of slum children: Some preliminary findings. *American Journal of Orthopsychiatry,* 1963, *33,* 813–822.

Johnson, D. F., & Mihal, W. L. Performance of blacks and whites in computerized versus manual testing environments. *American Psychologist,* 1973, August, *28,* 694–699.

Johnson, G. A. *A study of the relative academic success of Negro junior college graduates who transferred to Negro senior colleges in Mississippi in 1964.* Doctoral dissertation, Mississippi State University, 1970.

Johnson, J. C., & Jacobson, M. D. Current trends in Negro education and shorter papers. Section A: Operation Summer-Thrust: A study of the conceptual and verbal development of the culturally and educationally disadvantaged primary grade pupil. *Journal of Negro Education,* 1970, *39,* 171–176.

Kassinove, H., Rosenberg, E., & Trudeau, P. Cross validation of the environmental participation index in a group of economically deprived high school students. *Journal of Clinical Psychology,* 1970, *26,* 373–376.

Katz, I., Henchy, T., & Allen, H. Effects of race of tester, approval-disapproval, and need on Negro children's learning. *Journal of Personality and Social Psychology,* 1968, *8,* 38–42.

Katz, I., Roberts, S. O., & Robinson, J. M. Effects of task difficulty, race of administrator, and instructions on digit-symbol performance of Negroes. *Journal of Personality and Social Psychology,* 1965, *2*(1), 53–59.

Kaufman, A. S. Comparison of the performance of matched groups of black children and white children on the Wechsler Preschool and Primary Scale of Intelligence. *Journal of Consulting and Clinical Psychology,* 1973, *41*(2), 186–191.

Kaufman, A. S., & Kaufman, N. L. Black-white differences at ages 2½–8½ on the McCarthy Scales of Children's Abilities. *Journal of School Psychology,* 1973, *11*(3), 196–206.

Kazelskis, R., Jenkins, J. D., & Lingle, R. K. Two alternative definitions of creativity and their relationships with intelligence. *Journal of Experimental Education,* 1972, *41*(1), 58–62.

Kean, G. G. *A comparative study of Negro and white homeless men.* Doctoral dissertation, Yeshiva University, 1965.

Kennedy, W. A. *A follow-up normative study of Negro intelligence and achievement.* Tallahassee, FL: The Florida State University, 1965.

Kennedy, W. A., Van De Riet, V., and White, J. C. The standardization of the 1960 Revision of the Stanford-Binet Intelligence Scale on Negro elementary school children in the southeastern United States. Tallahassee: Florida State University, 1961.

Kennedy, W. A., Van De Riet, V., and White, J. C. A normative sample of intelligence and achievement of Negro elementary school children in the southeastern United States. *Monographs of the Society for Research in Child Development,* 1963, *28*(6).

Kennedy, W. A., & Vega, M. Negro children's performance of a discrimination task as a function of examiner race and verbal incentive. *Journal of Personality and Social Psychology,* 1965, *2,* 839–843.

Kinnie, E. J., & Sternlof, R. E. The influence of nonintellective factors on the IQ scores of middle- and lower-class children. *Child Development,* 1971, *42,* 1989–1995.

Kirkpatrick, J. J., Ewen, R. B., Barrett, R. S., & Katzell, R. A. Differential selection among applicants from different socioeconomic or ethnic backgrounds. Final Report to the Ford Foundation, May, 1967.

Klaus, R. A., & Gray, S. W. The early training project for disadvantaged children: A report after five years. *Monographs of the Society for Research in Child Development,* 1968, *33,* (4, Serial No. 120).

Klein, R. S. *A comparative study of the academic achievement of Negro 10th grade high school students attending segregated and recently integrated schools in a metropolitan area of the south.* Doctoral dissertation, University of South Carolina, 1967.

Klineberg, O. *Negro intelligence and selective migration.* New York: Columbia University Press, 1935.

Klineberg, O. (Ed.) *Characteristics of the American Negro.* New York: Harper, 1944.

Knowles, R. T., & Shah, G. B. Culture bias in testing: An exploration. *Journal of Social Psychology,* 1969, *77,* 285–286.

Koppitz, E. M. *The Bender-Gestalt test for young children.* New York: Grune and Stratton, 1964.

Kresheck, J. D., & Nicolosi, L. A comparison of black and white children's scores on the Peabody Picture Vocabulary Test. *Language, Speech, and Hearing Services in the Schools,* 1973, *4,* 37–40.

Lane, E. A. Childhood characteristics of black college graduates reared in poverty. *Developmental Psychology,* 1973, *8*(1), 42–45.

Laryea, E. B. *Race, self-concept, and achievement.* Doctoral dissertation, Columbia University, 1972.

Laskowitz, D. Wechsler-Bellevue performance of adolescent heroin addicts. *Journal of Psychological Studies,* 1962, *13*(1), 49–59.

Leahy, A. M. Nature-nurture and intelligence. *Genetic Psychology Monographs,* 1935, *17,* 237–307.

Lesser, G. S., Fifer, G., & Clark, D. H. Mental abilities of children from different social classes and culture groups. *Monographs of the Society for Research in Child Development* 1965, *30*(4), (Child Development Series #102), 1–115.

Lessing, E. E. Racial differences in indices of ego function relevant to academic achievement. *Journal of Genetic Psychology,* 1969, *115,* 153–167.

Leventhal, D. S., & Stedman, D. J. A factor analytic study of the Illinois Test of Psycholinguistic Abilities. *Journal of Clinical Psychology,* 1970, *26*(4), 473–477.

Levi, M., & Seborg, M. The study of I.Q. scores on verbal vs. non-verbal tests and vs. academic achievement among women drug addicts from different racial and ethnic groups. *The International Journal of the Addictions,* 1972, *7*(3), 581–584.

Levi, M., Tanner, P., Wirth, C., Lawson, R., & Sheetz, R. The study of intellectual ability and scholastic achievement of institutionalized men drug addicts belonging to three different racial-ethnic groups. *International Journal of the Addictions,* 1977, *12*(4), 451–457.

Levine, B. L. *Psychometric and demographic comparisons of Negro and white delinquents.* Doctoral dissertation, Illinois Institute of Technology, 1969.

Levinsohn, J., Lewis, L., Riccobono, J. A., & Moore, R. P. *National longitudinal study of the high school class of 1972; Base year, first and second follow-up; Data file user's manual.* Prepared for the National Center for Education Statistics, U.S. Department of Health, Education, and Welfare, by Center for Educational Research and Evaluation, Research Triangle Park, NC, 1976.

Levinson, B. M. A comparative study of northern and southern Negro homeless men. *Journal of Negro Education,* 1966, *35,* 144–150.

Levinson, F. V. D. K. *Early identification of educationally high risk and high potential pupils: Influences of sex and socio-cultural status on screening techniques.* Doctoral dissertation, University of California, Los Angeles, 1976.

Little, W. B., Kenny, C. T., & Middleton, M. H. Differences in intelligence among low socioeconomic class Negro children as a function of sex, age, and educational level of parents, and home stability. *Journal of Genetic Psychology,* 1973, *123,* 241–250.

Loehlin, J. C., Vandenberg, S. G., & Osborne, R. T. Blood group genes and Negro-white ability differences. *Behavior Genetics,* 1973, *3*(3), 263–270.

Long, H. B. Relationships of selected personal and social variables in conforming judgment. *Journal of Social Psychology,* 1970, *81,* 177–182.

Long, M. L. *The influence of sex, race, and type of pre-school experience on scores on the McCarthy Scales of Children's Abilities.* Doctoral dissertation, The University of Georgia, 1976.

Long, P. A., & Anthony, J. J. The measurement of mental retardation by a culture-specific test. *Psychology in the Schools,* 1974, *11,* 310–312.

Longstreth, L. E. A comment on "Race, IQ, and the middle class" by Trotman: Rampant false conclusions. *Journal of Educational Psychology,* 1978, *70*(4), 469–472. (a)

Longstreth, L. E. Level I-Level II abilities as they affect performance of three races in the college classroom. *Journal of Educational Psychology,* 1978, *70*(3), 289–297. (b)

Lopez, F. M. Current problems in test performance of job applicants. *Personnel Psychology,* 1966, *19,* 10–18.

Lorge, I., & Thorndike, R. A. *The Lorge-Thorndike Intelligence Tests.* New York: Houghton Mifflin, 1954.

Lowe, J. D., & Karnes, F. A. A comparison of scores on the WISC-R and Lorge-Thorndike Intelligence Test for disadvantaged black elementary school children. *Southern Journal of Educational Research,* 1976, *10,* 152–154.

Lunemann, A. The correctional validity of IQ as a function of ethnicity and desegregation. *Journal of School Psychology,* 1974, *12*(4), 263–268.

Maccoby, E. E., & Jacklin, C. N. *The psychology of sex differences.* Stanford, CA: Stanford University Press, 1974.

Mac Isaac, D. S. *Learning and behavioral functioning of low income, black preschoolers with asymptomatic lead poisoning.* Doctoral dissertation, Fordham University, 1974.

Mandler, G., & Sarason, S. B. A study of anxiety and learning. *Journal of Abnormal and Social Psychology,* 1952, *47,* 166–173.

Manning, E. J. *Intelligence and reading achievement of black disadvantaged tenth grade students.* Doctoral dissertation, The University of Oklahoma, 1977.

Manning, W. H. U.S. House of Representatives, subcommittee on Civil Service. Statement submitted by Educational Testing Service, Princeton, N.J. in a hearing on May 15, 1979. Winton H. Manning, Senior Vice-President of ETS.

Marmorale, A. M., & Brown, F. Bender-Gestalt performance of Puerto Rican, white, and Negro children. *Journal of Clinical Psychology,* 1977, *33*(1), 224–228.

Marsh, L. K. *Self-esteem, achievement responsibility, and reading achievement of lower-class black, white, and Hispanic seventh-grade boys.* Doctoral dissertation, New York University, 1974.

Marshall, M. S., & Bentler, P. M. IQ increases of disadvantaged minority-group children following innovative enrichment program. *Psychological Reports,* 1971, *29,* 805–806.

Marwit, S., & Neumann, G. Black and white children's comprehension of standard and nonstandard English passages. *Journal of Educational Psychology,* 1974, *66,* 329–332.

Matarazzo, J. D., & Wiens, A. N. Black Intelligence Test of Cultural Homogeneity and Wechsler Adult Intelligence Scale scores of black and white police applicants. *Journal of Applied Psychology,* 1977, *62,* 57–63.

Mathis, H. *Environmental participation index manual.* Washington, D.C.: Psychometric Studies, 1967.

Mathis, H. I. Relating environmental factors to aptitude and race. *Journal of Counseling Psychology,* 1968, *15*(6), 563–568.

Matzen, S. P. *The relationship between racial composition and scholastic achieve-*

ment in elementary school classrooms. Doctoral dissertation, Stanford University, 1965.

McAdoo, H. A. P. *Racial attitudes and self concepts of black preschool children.* Doctoral dissertation, The University of Michigan, 1970.

McCandless, B. R., Persons, W. S., & Roberts, A. Perceived opportunity, delinquency, race, and body build among delinquent youth. *Journal of Consulting and Clinical Psychology,* 1972, *38,* 281–287.

McCarthy, D. *Manual of the McCarthy Scales of Children's Abilities.* New York: The Psychological Corporation, 1972.

McClary, G. O. *Cognitive and affective responses by Negro and white children to pictorial stimuli.* Doctoral dissertation, The George Washington University, 1969.

McClelland, L. Effects of interviewer-respondent race interactions on household interview measures of motivation and intelligence. *Journal of Personality and Social Psychology,* 1974, *29*(3), 392–397.

McCormick, C. C., Schnobrich, J., & Footlik, S. W. IES Arrow-Dot performance in different adolescent populations. *Perceptual and Motor Skills,* 1966, *22,* 507–510.

McDaniel, E. L. Final report of Head Start evaluation and research: 1966–67. Section VIII: Relationships between self-concept and specific variables in a low-income culturally different population. ERIC Report #019124, 1967.

McGurk, F. C. J. Race differences—twenty years later. *Homo,* 1975, *26,* 219–239.

McKelpin, J. P. Some implications of the intellectual characteristics of freshmen entering a liberal arts college. *Journal of Educational Measurement,* 1965, *2,* 161–166.

McNamara, J. R., Porterfield, C. L., & Miller, L. E. The relationship of the Wechsler Preschool and Primary Scale of Intelligence with the Coloured Progressive Matrices (1956) and the Bender Gestalt Test. *Journal of Clinical Psychology,* 1969, *25,* 65–68.

Meeker, M., & Meeker, R. Strategies for assessing intellectual patterns in black, Anglo, and Mexican-American boys—or any other children—and implications for education. *Journal of School Psychology,* 1973, *11*(4), 341–350.

Mercer, J. R., & Smith, J. M. Subtest estimates of the WISC Full Scale IQs for children. Washington: U.S. Government Printing Office, 1972

Miele, F. Cultural bias in the WISC. *Intelligence,* 1979, *3,* 149–164.

Milgram, N. A. IQ constancy in disadvantaged Negro children. *Psychological Reports,* 1971, *29,* 319–326.

Milgram, N. A., & Ozer, M. N. Peabody Picture Vocabulary Test scores of preschool children. *Psychological Reports,* 1967, *20,* 779–784.

Miller, K. S., & Dregor, R. M. *Comparative studies of blacks and whites in the United States.* New York: Seminar Press, 1973.

Miller, M. D. *Patterns of relationships of fluid and crystallized mental abilities to achievement in different ethnic groups.* Doctoral dissertation, University of Houston, 1972.

Misa, K. F. *Cognitive, personality, and familial correlates of children's occupational preferences.* Doctoral dissertation, St. John's University, 1966.

Mitchell, N. B., & Pollack, R. H. Block design performance as a function of hue and race. *Journal of Experimental Child Psychology*, 1974, *17*, 377–382.

Moore, C. L. Racial preference and intelligence. *Journal of Psychology*, 1978, *100*, 39–43.

Moore, C. L., & Retish, P. M. Effect of the examiner's race on black children's Wechsler Preschool and Primary Scale of Intelligence IQ. *Developmental Psychology*, 1974, *10*(5), 672–676.

Moorehead, N. F. *The effects of school integration on intelligence test scores of Negro children*. Doctoral dissertation, Mississippi State University, 1972.

Morse, R. J. Self-concept of ability and school achievement of eighth grade students. Master's thesis, Michigan State University, 1963.

Moynihan, D. P. The Negro family: The case for national action, Office of Policy Planning and Research, United States Department of Labor, Washington, D.C., 1965.

Munday, L. Predicting college grades in predominantly Negro colleges. *Journal of Educational Measurement*, 1965, December, *2*(2), 157–160.

Murray, M. E., Waites, L., Veldman, D. J., & Heatly, M. D. Ethnic group differences between WISC and WAIS scores in delinquent boys. *Journal of Experimental Education*, 1973, *42*(2), 68–72.

Muzekari, L. H. Relationships between the Goodenough DAM and Stanford-Binet on Negro and white public school children. *Journal of Clinical Psychology*, 1967, *23*, 86–87.

Myrianthopoulos, N. C., & French, K. S. An application of the U.S. Bureau of the Census socioeconomic index to a large diversified patient population. *Social Science and Medicine*, 1968, *2*, 283–299.

Nalven, F. B., Hofmann, L. J., & Bierbryer, B. The effects of subjects' age, sex, race, and socioeconomnic status on psychologists' estimates of "True IQ" from WISC scores. *Journal of Clinical Psychology*, 1969, *25*, 271–274.

Neal, A. W. Analysis of responses to items on the Peabody Picture Vocabulary Test according to race and sex. *Journal of Educational Research*, 1975–76, *69*, 265–267.

Needham, W. E. *Intellectual, personality, and biographical characteristics of southern Negro and white college students*. Doctoral dissertation, University of Utah, 1966.

Nichols, P. L., & Anderson, V. E. Intellectual performance, race, and socioeconomic status. *Social Biology*, 1973, *20*(4), 367–374.

Nicholson, C. L. Correlations between the Quick Test and the Wechsler Intelligence Scale for Children-Revised. *Psychological Reports*, 1977, *40*, 523–526.

Normative Data Manual Research Bulletin 2-58. Distribution of 1957 entering freshmen on pre-admission indices. University System of Georgia. Office of Testing and Guidance. Regents, University System of Georgia. 244 Washington St. S.W., Atlanta, GA, June, 1958.

Oakland (Calif.) Public Schools, 1966–67 state test results. (Report #3, Oakland Public Schools, 1967–68, Oakland, California.)

Oakland, T. D., King, J. D., White, L. A., & Eckman, R. A comparison of performance on the WPPSI, WISC, and SB with preschool children: Companion studies. *Journal of School Psychology*, 1971, *9*(2), 144–149.

O'Leary, B. S. *Learning measures as predictors of task performance in two ethnic groups.* Doctoral dissertation, University of Maryland, 1972.

Olivier, K., & Barclay, A. Stanford-Binet and Goodenough-Harris test performances of Head Start children. *Psychological Reports,* 1967, *20*(3), 1175–1179.

Olshin, D. *The relationship of race and social class to intelligence and reading achievement at grades one and five.* Doctoral dissertation, Temple University, 1971.

Osborne, R. T. WISC factor structure for normal Negro pre-school children. *Psychological Reports,* 1964, *15*, 543–548.

Osborne, R. T. Stability of factor structure of the WISC for normal Negro children from pre-school level to first grade. *Psychological Reports,* 1966, *18*, 655–664.

Osborne, R. T. Population pollution. *The Journal of Psychology,* 1970, *76*, 187–191.

Osborne, R. T. Saturday Review/World. April 4, 1974, 8–12.

Osborne, R. T. Fertility, IQ, and school achievement. *Psychological Reports,* 1975, *37*, 1067–1073.

Osborne, R. T. Race and sex differences in heritability of mental test performance: A study of Negroid and Caucasoid twins. In *Human Variation,* Osborne, R. T., Noble, C. E., & Weyl, N. (Eds.), New York: Academic Press, 1978.

Osborne, R. T. *Twins: Black and white.* Athens: Foundation for Human Understanding, 1980.

Osborne, R. T., & Gregor, A. J. Racial differences in inheritance ratios for tests of spatial ability. Paper prepared for presentation at Instituto Internacional de Sociologia, XXII Congreso, Madrid, October 23–28, 1967.

Osborne, R. T., & Suddick, D. E. Blood type gene frequency and mental ability. *Psychological Reports,* 1971, *29*, 1243–1249.

Pandey, R. E. Intellectual characteristics of successful, dropout, and probationary black and white university students. *Psychological Reports,* 1974, *34*, 951–953.

Pavlos, A. J. Sex differences among rural Negro children on the Wechsler Intelligence Scale for Children. *West Virginia Academy of Science,* 1961, *33*, 109–114.

Pelosi, J. W. *A study of the effects of examiner race, sex, and style on test responses of Negro examinees.* Doctoral dissertation, Syracuse University, 1968.

Pentecoste, J. C., & Lowe, W. F. The Quick Test as a predictive instrument for college success. *Psychological Reports,* 1977, *41*, 759–762.

Perney, L. R., Hyde, E. M., Machock, B. J. Black intelligence—A re-evaluation. *Journal of Negro Education,* 1977, *46*(4), 450–455.

Pfeifer, C., & Sedlacek, W. The validity of academic predictors for black and white students at a predominantly white university. *Journal of Educational Measurement,* 1971, Winter, *8*(4), 253–261.

Pfeifer, C. M. Relationship between scholastic aptitude, perception of university climate, and college success for black and white students. *Journal of Applied Psychology,* 1976, *61*(3), 341–347.

Pfeifer Jr., C. M. *Academic ability and university climate in biracial academic prediction.* Doctoral dissertation, University of Maryland, 1972.

Phillips, J. *Performance of father-present and father-absent southern Negro boys on a simple operant task as a function of the race and sex of the experimenter and the type of social reinforcement.* Doctoral dissertation, University of Minnesota, 1966.

Powers, J. M., Drane, H. T., Close, B. L., Noonan, M. P., Wines, A. M., & Marshall, J. C. A research note on the self-perception of youth. *American Educational Research Journal,* 1971 *8*(4), 665–670.

Pryzwansky, W. B., Nicholson, C. L., & Uhl, N. P. The influence of examiner race on the cognitive functioning of urban and rural children of different races. *Journal of School Psychology,* 1974, *12*, 2–7.

Quay, L. C. Language dialect, reinforcement, and the intelligence-test performance of Negro children. *Child Development,* 1971, *42*, 5–15.

Quay, L. C. Negro dialect and Binet performance in severely disadvantaged black four-year olds. *Child Development,* 1972, *43*, 245–250.

Quay, L. C. Language dialect, age, and intelligence-test performance in disadvantaged black children. *Child Development,* 1974, *45*, 463–468.

Quay, L. C. Reinforcement and Binet performance in disadvantaged children. *Journal of Educational Psychology,* 1975, *67*(1), 132–135.

Raggio, D. J. *Effect of test taking experience simulation on the scores of black, disadvantaged and white, non-disadvantaged children on selected subtests of the WISC performance scale.* Doctoral dissertation, Mississippi State University, 1974.

Ratusnik, D. L., & Koenigsknecht, R. A. Normative study of the Goodenough Drawing Test and the Columbia Mental Maturity Scale in a metropolitan setting. *Perceptual and Motor Skills,* 1975, *40*, 835–838.

Ratusnik, D. L., & Koenigsknecht, R. A. Biracial testing: the question of clinicians' influence on children's test performance. *Language, Speech, and Hearing Services in Schools,* 1977, *8*, 5–14.

Raven, J. C. *Progressive matrices.* London: H. K. Lewis, 1956.

Ream, J. H. III. Evaluation of intelligence in youthful offenders: The Kahn intelligence tests. *Perceptual and Motor Skills,* 1978, *46*, 835–838.

Reinemann, J. O. The truant before the court. *Federal Probation,* 1948, *12*(3), 8–12.

Resnick, M. B. *Language ability and intellectual and behavioral functioning in economically disadvantaged children.* Doctoral dissertation, University of Florida, 1972.

Resnick, R. J., & Entin, A. D. Is an abbreviated form of the WISC valid for Afro-American children? *Journal of Consulting and Clinical Psychology,* 1971, *36*(1), 97–99.

Rieber, M., & Womack, M. The intelligence of preschool children as related to ethnic and demographic variables. *Exceptional Children,* 1968, *34,* 609–614.

Roach, R. E., & Rosecrans, C. J. Intelligence test performance of black children with high frequency hearing loss. *Journal of Auditory Research,* 1971, *11,* 136–139.

Roberts, J. *Intellectual development of children by demographic and socioeco-*

nomic factors. DHEW Publication No. 72–1012. Washington, D.C.: Government Printing Office, 1971.

Roberts, S. O., Horton, C. P., & Roberts, B. T. SAT versus GRE performance of Negro American college students. *Proceedings, 77th Annual Convention, APA,* 1969, *4,* 177–178.

Robertson, W. J. *The effects of junior high school segregation experience on the achievement, behavior and academic motivation of integrated tenth grade high school students.* Doctoral dissertation, The University of Michigan, 1967.

Robins, L. N., Jones, R. S., & Murphy, G. E. School milieu and school problems of Negro boys. *Social Problems,* 1966, *13*(4), 428–435.

Rochester, D. E., & Bodwell, A. Beta-WAIS comparisons for illiterate and indigent male and female Negroes. *Measurement and Evaluation in Guidance,* 1970, *3*(3), 164–168.

Rohwer, W. D., Ammon, M. S., Suzuki, N., & Levin, J. R. Population differences and learning proficiency. *Journal of Educational Psychology,* 1971, *62*(1), 1–14.

Rohwer Jr., W. D. Learning, race, and school success. *Review of Educational Research,* 1971, *41,* 191–210.

Rosenfeld, M., & Hilton, T. L. Negro-white differences in adolescent educational growth. *Research Bulletin,* Educational Testing Service, Princeton, N.J., September, 1969.

Ruda, E., & Albright, L. E. Racial differences on selection instruments related to subsequent job performance. *Personnel Psychology,* 1968, *21,* 31–41.

Ryan, J. S. *Early identification of intellectually superior black children.* Doctoral dissertation, The University of Michigan, 1975.

Ryan, L. E. *An investigation of the relationship between the scores earned by selected Negro and white children on the Wechsler Intelligence Scale for Children and the Wide Range Achievement Test.* Doctoral dissertation, Mississippi State University, 1973.

Rystrom, R. C. Testing Negro-standard English dialect differences. *Reading Research Quarterly,* 1969, *4,* 500–511.

Samuel, W. Observed IQ as a function of test atmosphere, tester expectation, and race of tester: A replication for female subjects. *Journal of Educational Psychology,* 1977, *69,* 593–604.

Samuel, W., Soto, D., Parks, M., Ngissah, P., & Jones, B. Motivation, race, social class, and IQ. *Journal of Educational Psychology,* 1976, *68*(3), 273–285.

Sandy, C. A. *The effects of material reward, sex, race, and socioeconomic strata on the Pintner-Cunningham Primary Test scores of kindergarten students.* Doctoral dissertation, University of Virginia, 1970.

Satz, P., & Mogel, S. An abbreviation of the WAIS for clinical use. *Journal of Clinical Psychology,* 1962, *18,* 77–79.

Savage, J. E. Testers' influence on children's intellectual performance. Doctoral dissertation, Northwestern University, 1971. *Dissertation Abstracts International,* 1972, *32,* 4429 A. (Order No. 72–7839)

Savage Jr., J. E., & Bowers, N. D. *Testers' influence on children's intellectual performance.* Washington, D.C.: U.S. Office of Education, 1972. (ERIC microfiche no. 064 329)

Scarr, S., & Weinberg, R. A. IQ test performance of black children adopted by white families. *American Psychologist,* 1976, *31,* 726–739.

Schneider, F. W. *Differences between Negro and white school children in conforming behavior.* Ann Arbor, Mich.: University Microfilms, Inc., 1968.

Scott, R. First to ninth grade IQ changes of northern Negro students. *Psychology in the Schools,* 1966, *3*(2), 159–160.

Scott, R. Social class, race, seriating and reading readiness: A study of their relationship at the kindergarten level. *Journal of Genetic Psychology,* 1969, *115,* 87–96.

Scott, R. Home Start: Family-centered preschool enrichment for black and white children. *Psychology in the Schools,* 1973, *10*(2), 140–146.

Scott, R. Home Start: Follow-up assignment of a family-centered preschool enrichment program. *Psychology in the Schools,* 1974, *11,* 147–149.

Scott, R. *Iowa Test of Preschool Development.* Cedar Falls, Iowa: Go Mo Industries, 1975.

Scott, R. Home Start: Third-grade follow-up assessment of a family-centered preschool enrichment program. *Psychology in the Schools,* 1976, *13,* 435–438.

Scott, R., Hartson, J., & Cunningham, M. Race of examiner as a variable in test attainments of preschool children. *Perceptual and Motor Skills,* 1976, *42,* 1167–1173.

Scott, R., & Sinclair, D. Ethnic-related cognitive profiles of black and white pre-school children. *Homo,* 1977, *28,* 116–120.

Seidel, H. E., Barkley, M. J., & Stith, D. Evaluation of a program for project Head Start. *Journal of Genetic Psychology,* 1967, *110,* 185–197.

Sekyra, F. III, & Arnoult, J. F. III. Negro intellectual assessment with three instruments contrasting Caucasian and Negro norms. *Journal of Learning Disabilities,* 1968, *1*(10), 564–569.

Semler, I. J., & Iscoe, I. Comparative and developmental study of the learning abilities of Negro and white children under four conditions. *Journal of Educational Psychology,* 1963, *54,* 38–44.

Semler, I. J., & Iscoe, I. Structure of intelligence in Negro and white children. *Journal of Educational Psychology,* 1966, *57*(6), 326–336.

Sewell, T. E. A comparison of the WPPSI and Stanford-Binet Intelligence Scale (1972) among lower SES black children. *Psychology in the Schools,* 1977, *14*(2), 158–161.

Sewell, T. E., & Severson, R. A. Intelligence and achievement in first-grade black children. *Journal of Consulting and Clinical Psychology,* 1975, *43*(1), 112.

Sherwood, J. J., & Nataupsky, M. Predicting the conclusions of Negro-white intelligence research from biographical characteristics of the investigator. *Journal of Personality and Social Psychology,* 1968, *8,* 53–58.

Shockley, W. Population pollution—the unmentionable threat to human resources. Presented at the Eighth Annual Air Capital Management Conference, Broadview Hotel, Wichita, Kansas, February, 1970.

Shockley, W. Dysgenics, geneticity, raceology. *Phi Delta Kappan,* January, 1972, 297–307.

Shuey, A. M. *The testing of Negro intelligence* (2nd Ed.). New York: Social Science Press, 1966.

Sigel, I. E., & Perry, C. Psycholinguistic diversity among "culturally deprived" children. *American Journal of Orthopsychiatry,* 1968, *38*(1), 122–126.

Silverstein, A. B. Factor structure of the Wechsler Intelligence Scale for Children for three ethnic groups. *Journal of Educational Psychology,* 1973, *65*(3), 408–410.

Simpson, R. L. Study of the comparability of the WISC and the WAIS. *Journal of Consulting and Clinical Psychology,* 1970, *34*(2), 156–158.

Sitkei, E. G., & Meyers, C. E. Comparative structure of intellect in middle- and lower-class four-year-olds of two ethnic groups. *Developmental Psychology,* 1969, *1,* 592–604.

Smith, A. L., Hays, J. R., & Solway, K. S. Comparison of the WISC-R and Culture Fair Intelligence Test in a juvenile delinquent population. *Journal of Psychology,* 1977, *97,* 179–182.

Smith, H. W., & May, W. T. Individual differences among inexperienced psychological examiners. *Psychological Reports,* 1967, *20,* 759–762.

Smith, M. S., & Bissell, J. S. Report analysis: The impact of Head Start. *Harvard Educational Review,* 1970, *40,* 51–104.

Smith, T. A., & Caldwell, M. B. Intellectual differences in Negro and white mental defectives. *Psychological Reports,* 1969, *25,* 559–565.

Smith, W. R. B. *The relationship between self-concept of academic ability, locus of control of the environment, and academic achievement of black students specially admitted to the University of Pittsburgh.* Doctoral dissertation, University of Pittsburgh, 1972.

Solkoff, N. Race of experimenter as a variable in research with children. *Developmental Psychology,* 1972, *7,* 70–75.

Solkoff, N. Race of examiner and performance on the Wechsler Intelligence Scale for Children: A replication. *Perceptual and Motor Skills,* 1974, *39,* 1063–1066.

Solomon, D. The generality of children's achievement-related behavior. *Journal of Genetic Psychology,* 1969, *114,* 109–125.

Solomon, D., Scheinfeld, D. R., Hirsch, J. G., & Jackson, J. C. Early grade school performance of inner city Negro high school high achievers, low achievers, and dropouts. *Developmental Psychology,* 1971, *4*(3), 482.

Soltz, W. H. *Comparative study of Negro-white differences on the MMPI and PAS.* Doctoral dissertation, University of Missouri, 1970.

Southern, M. L., & Plant, W. T. Differential cognitive development within and between racial and ethnic groups of disadvantaged preschool and kindergarten children. *Journal of Genetic Psychology,* 1971, *119*(2), 259–266.

Stanley, J. C., & Porter, A. C. Correlation of scholastic aptitude test score with college grades for Negroes vs. whites. *Journal of Educational Measurement,* Winter, 1967, *4*(4), 199–218.

Starkman, S., Butkovich, C., & Murray, T. The relationship among measures of cognitive development, learning proficiency; academic achievement, and

IQ for seventh grade, low socioeconomic status black males. *Journal of Experimental Education*, 1976, *45*, 52–56.

Starnes, T. A. *An analysis of the academic achievement of Negro students in the predominantly white schools of a selected Florida county.* Doctoral dissertation, University of Southern Mississippi, 1968.

Stephenson, B. L., & Gay, W. O. Psycholinguistic abilities of black and white children from four SES levels. *Exceptional Children*, 1972, *38*, 705–709.

Sternberg, R. I. *The relation between total and partial IQ's on the 1960 Stanford-Binet: A cross-ethnic comparison.* Doctoral dissertation, California School of Professional Psychology, Fresno, 1976.

Sternlof, R. E., Parker, H. J., & McCoy, J. F. Relationships between the Goodenough DAM Test and the Columbia Mental Maturity Test for Negro and white Headstart children. *Perceptual and Motor Skills*, 1968, *27*, 424–426.

Strauch, A. B. *An investigation into the sex × race × ability interaction.* Doctoral dissertation, The Pennsylvania State University, 1975.

Summerford, J. D. *Study of the basic concepts of disadvantaged kindergarten children in artificial and naturalistic contexts.* Doctoral dissertation, University of Georgia, 1977.

Sweet, R. C. *Variations in the intelligence test performance of lower-class children as a function of feedback or monetary reinforcement.* Doctoral dissertation, The University of Wisconsin, 1969.

The System Summary. A publication of the University System of Georgia. Vol. 13, No. 9, September, 1977, page 20.

Takacs, C. P. *Comparison of mental abilities between lower socioeconomic status five-year-old Negro and white children on individual intelligence measures.* Doctoral dissertation, Kent State University, 1971.

Tate, D. T. *A study of the relationship of socio-economic status and intelligence and achievement scores of white and Negro groups.* Doctoral dissertation, Oklahoma State University, 1967.

Tatham, C. B., & Tatham, E. L. Academic predictors for black students. *Educational and Psychological Measurement*, 1974, *34*, 371–374.

Taylor, D. R. *A longitudinal comparison of intellectual development of black and white students from segregated to desegregated settings.* Doctoral dissertation, University of South Florida, 1974.

Temp, G. Validity of the SAT for blacks and whites in thirteen integrated institutions. *Journal of Educational Measurement*, Winter, 1971, *8*(4), 245–251.

Thorne, J. H. *An analysis of the WISC and ITPA and their relationships to school achievement, socioeconomic status, and ethnicity.* Doctoral dissertation, University of Houston, 1974.

Thumin, F., & Goldman, S. Comparative test performance of Negro and white job applicants. *Journal of Clinical Psychology*, 1968, 455–457.

Tillery, W. L. *A comparison of the Pictorial Test of Intelligence* (PTI) *and Stanford-Binet* (S-B) *with disadvantaged children.* Doctoral dissertation, The Pennsylvania State University, 1972.

Trotman, F. K. *Race, IQ, and the middle-class.* Doctoral dissertation, Columbia University, 1976.

Trotman, F. K. Race, IQ, and the middle class. *Journal of Educational Psychology,* 1977, *69*(3), 266–273.

Trotman, F. K. Race, IQ, and rampant misrepresentations: A reply. *Journal of Educational Psychology,* 1978, *70*(4), 478–481.

Tufano, L. G. *The effect of effort and performance reinforcement of WISC-R IQ scores of black and white EMR boys.* Doctoral dissertation, University of Georgia, 1975.

Tulkin, S. R. Race, class, family, and school achievement. *Journal of Personality and Social Psychology,* 1968, *9*(1), 31–37.

Tulkin, S. R., & Newbrough, J. R. Social class, race, and sex differences on the Raven (1956) Standard Progressive Matrices. *Journal of Consulting and Clinical Psychology,* 1968, *32*(4), 400–406.

Turner, C. Effects of race of tester and need for approval on children's learning. *Journal of Educational Psychology,* 1971, *62,* 240–244.

Tyler, L. E. *The psychology of human differences* (3rd Ed.). New York: Appleton-Century-Crofts, 1965.

Vance, H., & Engin, A. Analysis of cognitive abilities of black children's performance on WISC-R. *Journal of Clinical Psychology,* 1978, *34*(2), 452–456.

Vandenberg, S. G. *A twin study of spatial ability.* Research report from the Louisville Twin Study, Child Development Unit, Department of Pediatrics, University of Louisville School of Medicine, Report No. 26, April, 1967.

Vane, J. R., Weitzman, J., & Applebaum, A. P. Performance of Negro and white children and problem and nonproblem children on the Stanford Binet Scale. *Journal of Clinical Psychology,* 1966, *22,* 431–435.

Vega, M. *The performance of Negro children on an oddity discrimination task as a function of the race of the examiner and the type of verbal incentive used by the examiner.* Doctoral dissertation, The Florida State University, 1964.

Walsh, J. F., D'Angelo, R., & Lomangino, L. Performance of Negro and Puerto Rican Head Start Children on the Vane Kindergarten Test. *Psychology in the Schools,* 1971, *8,* 357–358.

Warden, P. G., & Prawat, R. S. Convergent and divergent thinking in black and white children of high and low socioeconomic status. *Psychological Reports,* 1975, *36,* 715–718.

Wargo, M. J., Campeau, P. L., and Talmadge, G. K. Further examination of exemplary programs for educating disadvantaged children. Study #5: Mother-child home program, Freeport, N.Y. American Institute for Research in the Behavioral Sciences, 1971, 122–136. (ERIC Report #055128)

Wargo, M. J., Campeau, P. L., and Talmadge, G. K. Further examination of exemplary programs for educating disadvantaged children. Study #6: Project breakthrough. American Institute for Research in the Behavioral Sciences, 1971, 143–152. (ERIC Report #055128)

Warner, W., Meeker, M., & Eells, K. *Social class in America.* Chicago: Science Research Associates, 1949.

Weaver, S. J., & Weaver, A. Psycholinguistic abilities of culturally deprived Negro children. *American Journal of Mental Deficiency,* 1967, *72*(2), 190–197.

Wechsler, D. *Manual for the Wechsler Adult Intelligence Scale.* New York: Psychological Corporation, 1955.

Wellborn, E. S. A study of the effect of examiner race on individual intelligence test scores of black and white children. Doctoral dissertation, The University of Florida, 1972. *Dissertation Abstracts International,* 1973, *34,* 195 A. (Order No. 73-15, 555)

Wellborn, E. S., Reid, W. R., & Reichard, G. L. Effect of examiner race on test scores of black and white children. *Education and Training of the Mentally Retarded,* 1973, *8,* 194–196.

Wenk, E. A., Rozynko, V. V., Sarbin, T. R., & Robinson, J. O. The effect of incentives upon aptitude scores of white and Negro inmates. *Journal of Research in Crime and Delinquency,* 1971, *8,* 53–64.

Westinghouse Learning Corporation, Ohio University, 1969. The impact of Head Start, an evaluation of the effects of Head Start on children's cognitive and affective development: Volume 1, Text and Appendices A–E.

Whipple, D. W. *A study of the relationships among ethnic-social class, intelligence, achievement motivation and delay of gratification.* Doctoral dissertation, New York University, 1972.

Whiteman, M., & Peisach, E. Perceptual and sensorimotor supports for conservation tasks. *Developmental Psychology,* 1970, *2*(2), 247–256.

Wild, C. L. A summary of data collected from graduate examinations test-takers during 1978–79, March, 1980, Data Summary Report #4. Educational Testing Service, Princeton, N.J.

Willard, L. S. A comparison of culture fair test scores with group and individual intelligence test scores of disadvantaged Negro children. *Journal of Learning Disabilities,* 1968, *1*(10), 584–589.

Willerman, L., Naylor, A. F., & Myrianthopoulos, N. C. Intellectual development of children from interracial matings. *Science,* 1970, *170*(3964), 1329–1331.

Williams, D. E. *Self-concept and verbal mental ability in Negro pre-school children.* Doctoral dissertation, St. John's University, 1968.

Wilson, A. B., Jensen, A. R., & Elliott, D. L. Education of disadvantaged children in California. Unpublished monograph, 1966, 52 pages.

Winokur, D. J. *The effects of verbal reinforcement combinations and color of examiner on shifts in concept formation.* Doctoral dissertation, The Florida State University, 1964.

Winter, G. D. *Intelligence, interest, and personality characteristics of a selected group of students: A description and comparison of white and Negro students in a vocational rehabilitation administration program in Bassick and Harding high schools, Bridgeport, Connecticut.* Doctoral dissertation, Columbia University, 1967.

Wolf, R. The measurement of environments. In A. Anastasi (Ed.), *Testing problems in perspective.* New York: American Council on Education, 1964.

Wolfe, B. E. *A comparison of the impact of two kindergarten programs on the creative performance of disadvantaged Negro children.* Doctoral dissertation, University of Florida, 1970.

Wolff, J. L. Utility of socioeconomic status as a control in racial comparisons of IQ. *Journal of Educational Psychology,* 1978, *70*(4), 473–477.

Woodall, F. E. *Relationships between social adaptability and below average intelligence test performance for black and white elementary school children.* Doctoral dissertation, University of Georgia, 1975.

Worthington, C. F. *An analysis of WISC-R score patterns of black adolescent male delinquents.* Doctoral dissertation, University of Georgia, 1977.

Wyatt, M. A. *A study of the interaction between personality traits, IQ, and achievement in Negro and white fourth grade children.* Doctoral dissertation, University of Kentucky, 1972.

Wysocki, B. A., & Cankardas, A. A new estimate of Polish intelligence. *Journal of Educational Psychology,* 1957, *48,* 525–533.

Wysocki, B. A., & Wysocki, A. C. Cultural differences as reflected in Wechsler-Bellevue Intelligence (WBII) Test. *Psychological Reports,* 1969, *25,* 95–101.

Yando, R., Seitz, V., & Zigler, E. *Intellectual and personality characteristics of children: Social-class and ethnic-group differences.* Hillsdale, N.J.: Lawrence Erlbaum & Associates, 1979.

Yando, R., Zigler, E., & Gates, M. The influence of Negro and white teachers rated as effective or noneffective on the performance of Negro and white lower-class children. *Developmental Psychology,* 1971, *5,* 290–299.

Yater, A. C., Boyd, M., & Barclay, A. A comparative study of WPPSI and WISC performances of disadvantaged children. *Journal of Clinical Psychology,* 1975, *31,* 78–80.

Yates, L. G. *Comparative intelligence of Negro and white children from a rural-southern culture.* Doctoral dissertation, The University of North Carolina at Chapel Hill, 1967.

Yawkey, T. D., & Jantz, R. K. Differential effects of intelligence, race, SES, and sex variables on arithmetic achievement test performance. *Journal of Instructional Psychology,* 1974, *1*(2), 2–10.

Yen, S. M. Y. *A comparative study of test variability with Peabody Picture Vocabulary Test, Goodenough's Draw-A-Man Test, and Stanford-Binet Intelligence Scale as intellectual measurement with a group of urban low socio-economic status pre-school pupils.* Doctoral dissertation, Catholic University of America, 1969.

Yerkes, R. M. (Ed.) Psychological examining in the U.S. Army. *Memoirs of the National Academy of Sciences,* 1921, *15.*

Zagarow, H. W. *The prediction of academic success for black and white college students.* Doctoral dissertation, The University of Connecticut, 1973.

Annotated Bibliography

Since 1966, scores of important theoretical, speculative and conjectural articles and books have been published on the testing of Negro intelligence. Such articles which do not report new test findings may not have been reviewed in Volume 2 and thus may not be called to the attention of the reader. In this section significant theoretical contributions, reflecting both environmental and hereditary explanations for black-white mental test score differences, are brought together in an Annotated Bibliography. Entries cited in this section are not cited in the overall subject and author indexes unless they also happen to appear in the body of the text.

Adams, J., & Ward, R. H. Admixture studies and the detection of selection. *Science,* 1973, *180,* 1137–1142.
> Data analyses of admixture studies give little evidence of natural selection operating in U.S. black populations. Summary.

Alker, H. A., & Closson, M. B. Admission standards, the perceived legitimacy of grading and black student protests. *Cornell Journal of Social Relations,* 1973, *8,* 219–233.
> This study falsifies the claim that black students, who fail to meet traditional admissions standards but are nonetheless admitted to college, subsequently become politically active. On the contrary, it is students with exceptional talent for college work, as identified by SAT verbal aptitude scores, who, if they receive lower grades, become politically active. Several interpretations of this result, including status inconsistency and institutional racism, are discussed. Abstract.

Allen, G., & Pettigrew, K. D. Heritability of IQ by social class: Evidence inconclusive. *Science,* 1973, *182,* 1042–1044.

American Psychologist special issue, Psychology and children: Current research and practice, 1979, *34*(10).

Andor, L. E. *Aptitudes and abilities of the black man in Africa 1784–1963.* Johannesburg: South African Council for Scientific and Industrial Research, 1966.

An annotated bibliography compiled by L. E. Andor with an introduction by W. Hudson.

Angoff, W. H., & Ford, S. F. Item-race interaction on a test of scholastic aptitude. *Journal of Educational Measurement,* 1973, *10*(2), 95–106.

Several samples of black and white students were drawn from the 1970 PSAT administration in Georgia and studied for item × race interaction on both the verbal and mathematical sections of the test. When subsamples of candidates were drawn from their respective racial groups, matched on mathematical for the study of verbal items and matched on verbal for the study of mathematical items, there was an observable decrease in the size of the item × race interaction, suggesting that one factor contributing to that interaction was simply the difference in performance levels on the test shown by the two races. Abstract.

Armor, D. J. The evidence on busing. *The Public Interest,* 1972 (Summer), No. 28, 90–126.

The available evidence on busing, then, seems to lead to two clear policy conclusions. One is that massive mandatory busing for purposes of improving student achievement and interracial harmony is not effective and should not be adopted at this time. The other is that *voluntary* integration programs such as METCO, ABC, or Project Concern should be continued and positively encouraged by substantial federal and state grants. Summary.

Armstrong, C. P. Psychodiagnosis, prognosis, school desegregation and delinquency. *The Mankind Quarterly,* 1964, *V*(2), 1–18.

There is no evidence of "pathogenicity" to Negro children from segregated schools, but rather of "pathogenicity" from desegregated schools as shown by truancy, nervous habits, home deserting and juvenile delinquency. Summary.

Ashline, N. F., Pezzullo, T. R., & Norris, C. I. *Education, inequality, and national policy.* Lexington, Massachusetts: D. C. Heath and Company, 1976.

Attah, E. B. Racial aspects of zero population growth. *Science,* 1973, *180,* 1143–1152.

. . . this article is concerned with the consequences of different rates of approach to zero growth. Specifically, what would be the effects of different rates on the short- and long-term growth of the respective segments of the population? How long would it take the population to stabilize, and how much would the population have increased by then? What intermediate trends would appear in the proportion of nonwhites in the population, and what would be the relative sizes of the white and nonwhite segments in the long run? Summary.

Bachman, J. G., Kahn, R. L., Mednick, M. T., Davidson, T. N., & Johnston, L. D. *Youth in transition* (vol. I): *Blueprint for a longitudinal study of adolescent boys.* Ann Arbor, Michigan: Braun-Brumfield, Inc., 1967.

Bachman, J. G. *Youth in transition* (vol. II): *The impact of family background and intelligence on tenth-grade boys.* Ann Arbor, Michigan: Braun-Brumfield, Inc., 1970.

Our conclusions about racial differences are limited, as we said they would be. And we have specifically avoided any firm conclusions about the causes of these differences. In spite of these uncertainties, and in spite of the sampling limitations acknowledged earlier, we feel that the data on test scores and race add evidence to the view that so-called "racial differences" are primarily—if not exclusively—differences in cultural and educational opportunities. Summary.

Baker, J. R. *Race*. New York: Oxford University Press, 1974.

In summary, then, this is an outstanding book which should be read by anyone who wants to know what science has to say about race, and who may wish to cogitate about the problems which are raised in our society by the problem of race. Baker explicitly denies concern in his book with practical problems; it is left to the reader to ponder the practical consequences of the facts revealed. This is as it should be; we have to take our facts from zoologists, anthropometrists, psychologists, and other scientists concerned with the problem of race, but it is we, as citizens, not they, as scientists, who have to resolve the political, ethical and moral problems which are raised by these stubborn facts. They will not go away because we refuse to pay attention; nor will measures taken on grounds of compassion, rather than fact, resolve the problems. Many will blame Baker, as they blamed Jensen, for pointing out unwelcome facts; but these facts are not of their making. We may regret that nature produced man in such genetic diversity, but it is idle to blame the messenger for the message; let us rather try to draw wise conclusions from the uncompromising facts here outlined. Review by H. J. Eysenck in *Books and Bookmen, 19,* March, 1974.

Bane, M. J., & Jencks, C. The schools and equal opportunity. *Saturday Review of Education,* September 16, 1972, 37–42.

Quality education will reduce socioeconomic inequality, the reformers claim. This is a delusion. Schools have few long-term effects on the later "success" of those who attend them. An advance report by the authors of the forthcoming study *Inequality: A Reassessment of the Effect of Family and Schooling in America.* Summary.

Banfield, E. C. *The unheavenly city revisited.* Boston: Little, Brown and Company, 1974.

Because the book has proved to be so controversial and because it is being used in a wide variety of college courses, I have cited many more authorities, and a much wider range of them, than I did before. I make no pretense of "covering" the literature, however, because this is not intended to be that kind of book and because I take up so many matters in it. This is an essay—as I said in the preface to the original version, "an attempt by a social scientist to think about the problems of the city in the light of scholarly findings." Summary.

Bart, W. H., & Lele, K. *Defusing the intelligence × race debate: Comparison of intelligence item hierarchies for two races.* Paper presented at the Annual Meeting of the American Educational Research Association (61st, New York, NY, April 4–8, 1977).

Bartlett, D. P., Newbrough, J. R., & Tulkin, S. R. Raven Progressive Matrices:

An item and set analysis of subjects grouped by race, sex, and social class. *Journal of Consulting and Clinical Psychology,* 1972, *38,* 154.

Baughman, E. E. & Dahlstrom, W. G. *Negro and White Children.* New York: Academic Press, 1968.

> Here, then, are unwelcome facts, about race differences that we are bound to evaluate on a dimension of better or worse, superiority or inferiority, differences that a democratic society must be committed to try to reduce by the intelligent extension of opportunity. Here are more helpful facts, about correlates of these differences, which suggest directions in which remedy may be sought. Here is a fine example of basic research on a socially important topic that deploys quite modest resources in ways that subsequent research can confidently build on. Here is a study of children in the rural South that has much broader relevance. Review by M. Brewster Smith in *Science,* January 31, 1969, *163,* 461–462.

Baughman, E. E. *Black Americans; a psychological analysis.* New York: Academic Press, 1971.

> While the strength of this book lies with the author's insistence on confronting theoretical controversies with empirical data, its major weakness is in the exclusion of much significant research on blacks and whites. Three chapters on the affective states of blacks—'Self Esteem,' 'Rage and Aggression,' and 'Psychopathology'—makes little use of the extensive research literature on alienation, anomie, alcoholism, suicide and homocide, and mental illness. . . . Baughman's suggestions regarding education . . . are most disturbing. After arguing that integration of public schools has demoralizing effects on black children who must compete with the better-prepared white children, he suggests that it might be better to integrate schools beginning at the first grade and proceed in a 'grade-per-year' desegregation plan. . . . This book, despite its good intentions, may arouse suspicion and hostility in its black readers. Review by W. L. Yancey in *Am J. Soc.* 78:450, S '72 (taken from *Book Review Digest,* 1972).

Bayh, B. *Our nation's schools—a report card: "A" in school violence and vandalism.* Preliminary report of the subcommittee to investigate juvenile delinquency, based on investigations, 1971–1975. Printed for the use of the Committee on the Judiciary, Washington: U.S. Government Printing Office, 1975.

Bereiter, C. The future of individual differences. *Harvard Educational Review,* 1969, *39*(2), 310–318.

Bersoff, D. N. P. v. Riles: Legal perspective. *School Psychology Review, 1980,* 9(2), 112–122.

Bethell, T. Burning Darwin to save Marx. *Harper's,* 1978 (December), 31–38; 91–92.

> It is evident, surely, that the Age of Egalitarianism in which we really do live is in little danger of being supplanted. It becomes more secure with every passing day: we have *more and more* equality, although the idea of "more equality" obviously becomes contradictory at some point. But the idea of equality is now obligatory: it is settled and

certain, fixed in the firmament of opinion. To resist it ever so slightly is to invite the label *fascist*. In fact, we live not so much in the Egalitarian Age as in the Age of Compulsory Equality. Summary.

Biesheuvel, S. An examination of Jensen's theory concerning educability, heritability and population differences. *Psychologia Africana*, 1972, *14*, 87–94.

Block, N. J., & Dworkin, G. (Eds.) *The IQ controversy*. New York: Pantheon Books, 1976.

. . . the publication of Block's and Dworkin's *The IQ Controversy* is particularly timely and valuable. It is in the genre known as a "reader," that is to say it gives us a conspectus of prevailing opinions in the words of those who hold them . . .

A special strength of their book—and one that enormously enhances its value for college reading—is their generous allocation of space to such real professionals as Richard Lewontin and John Thoday, with a passing quotation from Michael Lerner.

Review by P. B. Medawar in *The New York Review*, February 3, 1977.

Bodmer, W. F., & Cavalli-Sforza, L. L. Intelligence and Race. *Scientific American*, 1970, *223*(4), 19–29.

Our aim in this article is to review, mainly for the nongeneticist, the meaning of race and I.Q. and the approaches to determining the extent to which I.Q. is inherited. Such a review can act as a basis for the objective assessment of the evidence for a genetic component in race and class I.Q. differences. Summary.

Bowen, W. G. Admissions and the relevance of race. *Educational Record*, 1977 (Fall), 333–348.

Brace, C. L., Gamble, G. R., & Bond, J. T. (Eds.) *Race and intelligence*. Washington, DC: American Anthropological Association, 1971.

Viewed from a humanitarian perspective, it would substantially improve the lot of mankind if the energy currently being devoted to the dubious demonstration of innate human unworth were rechannelled to the task of removing the non-innate but very real social inequities that cripple the lives of the very people for whom Jensen professes such concern. Summary.

Broman, S. H., Nichols, P. L., & Kennedy, W. A. *Preschool IQ: Prenatal & early developmental correlates*. Hillsdale, New Jersey: Lawrence Erlbaum Associates, 1975.

The sample of 12,210 white children had a mean IQ of 104.5 with a standard deviation of 16.7. The mean IQ in the sample of 14,550 Negro children was 91.3 with a standard deviation of 14.0. This difference of 13 points is similar to that found in most comparative studies of intellectual performance of Negroes and whites in the United States (Kennedy et al., 1963; Shuey, 1966; Dreger & Miller, 1968). Within socioeconomic status and sex subgroups, the IQ differences ranged from about 8 points in the lowest socioeconomic level to 13 points in the highest. Summary.

Brown, W. W., & Reynolds, M. O. A model of IQ, occupation, and earnings. *The American Economic Review*, December 1975, *65*(5), 1002–1007.

Brozek, J. Nutrition, malnutrition, and behavior. *Annual Review of Psychology,* 1978, *29,* 157–177.

Burket, G. R. PROJECT TALENT *Identification, Development, and Utilization of Human Talents: Selected pupil and school characteristics in relation to percentage of Negroes in school enrollment.* Washington, DC: Project TALENT Office, University of Pittsburgh, 1963.

> *Aptitude and Achievement.* Consider first the means of the nineteen selected Pr⌐ject TALENT tests that are shown in Tables 1–14. The most obvious trend is the tendency for the mean scores to decrease as the per cent of Negroes in school enrollment increases. The trend affects tests of nonverbal abilities (e.g., test 4, Abstract Reasoning) to about the same extent as tests of verbal abilities (e.g., test 2, Reading Comprehension). It cuts across geographical areas, appearing with almost the same strength in the four Office of Education areas sampled: the Mideast, the Great Lakes area, the Southeast, and the Southwest. Summary.

Burt, C. Inheritance of general intelligence. *American Psychologist,* 1972, *27,* 175–190.

> *Inheritance of General Intelligence* was Cyril Burt's acceptance speech of the E. L. Thorndike award from the American Psychological Association. He concluded what was to be his last formal paper with these remarks:
>
>> Thus, notwithstanding the provisional nature of the results here recorded, I think one claim can now safely be advanced. The recent cry that "the old issue of nature and nurture is out of date" is itself outdated. Modern genetics, besides its many profitable applications to agriculture and stock-breeding, has already made valuable contributions to human physiology, pathology, and medicine; it will assuredly prove yet more informative and fruitful in the field of psychology. (p. 189)
>
> After a short illness Burt died on October 10, 1971.
>
> See also in this section:
>
> Cronbach, L. J. Hearnshaw on Burt. *Science,* 1979, *206,* 192–194.
>
> Dorfman, D. D. The Cyril Burt question: New findings. *Science,* 1978, *201*(4362), 1177–1186.
>
> Dorfman, D. D. Burt's tables. *Science,* 1979, *204,* 246–254.
>
> Eysenck, H. J. The case of Sir Cyril Burt. *Encounter,* 1977, *48,* 19–24.
>
> Gillie, O. Burt's missing ladies. *Science,* 1979, *204,* 1035–1039.
>
> Hearnshaw, L. S. *Cyril Burt, Psychologist.* Ithaca, NY: Cornell University Press, 1979.
>
> Rubin, D. B. Burt's tables. *Science,* 1979, *204,* 245–246.
>
> Stigler, S. M. Burt's tables. *Science,* 1979, *204,* 242–245.

Buss, A. R. Regression, heritability, and race differences in IQ. *Developmental Psychology,* 1975, *11*(1), 105.

Carothers, J. C. *The mind of man in Africa.* London: The Garden City Press Limited, 1972.

> The book is concerned essentially with the mentality of man indigenous

to sub-Saharan Africa, both in regard to those aspects that are seen as ordinary or normal, and those that are seen as strange or disturbed, by the societies in which he lives. It is thus also and inevitably concerned with the parts that may have been played in his mental development by hereditary and by environmental factors. I have therefore attempted to present the reader with all those data in both these fields that, derived from the New World as well as from Africa, seem most relevant to this theme. Summary.

Chase, A. *The legacy of Malthus: The social costs of the new scientific racism.* New York: Alfred A. Knopf, 1977.

With the uncanniness of the drug agent's dog sniffing traces of marijuana among passengers' baggage, Chase detects and enthusiastically exposes every whiff of racism (most of them real, some imagined) among American scientists and writers. . . . Total public health, total health to every individual, is, in his belief, the single most important key to human betterment. He judges all ideas and theories from this singleminded perspective. There is no 'population problem,' only 'a sociobiological problem called poverty.' Of the literally thousands of writers' ideas Chase examines, few emerge unscathed, few escape his ridicule. Chase's work is logical, well researched and documented, yet, in the end, a 'single cause' hortatory explanation of most of society's problems. His is a valuable perspective that should be of wide use as a holding for both undergraduate and graduate libraries. *Choice,* Jl/ Ag '77, 14: 748, in *Book Review Digest,* 1977.

Clarizio, H. F., Craig, R. C., & Mehrens, W. A. (eds.) *Contemporary issues in educational psychology* (2nd edition). Boston: Allyn and Bacon, Inc., 1974.

In short, the book is grounded in a very traditional view of the field of Educational Psychology, and the issues reflect a survey of controversies in the field, rather than an analysis of its fundamental questions. Review by Karen K. Block in *Contemporary Psychology,* 1975, *20* (10), 787–788.

Clark, K. *Pathos of Power.* Harper & Row, 1974.

Clark is pleased to tender, once again, some things useful for the public to hear, and he is willing to lay them out with a full hand, with none of those petty reservations that may be the mark of a small nature. . . . The occasions for these papers are often public and ceremonial—e.g., Clark's receipt of an honorary degree, his inauguration as president of the American Psychological Association. They are moments when a tremor of style is expected and one might feel freer to speak in a more personal vein, without footnotes or shadings. One need not feel any special strain on these occasions to render a perfect justice to those with whom one disagrees—for Clark, men like Daniel P. Moynihan, Edward Banfield, Christopher Jencks, David Armor, Daniel Bell, and Nathan Glazer—and so Clark strikes out then in rather unmeasured assaults on what he calls a "new breed of social science mercenaries." Review by Hadley Arkes in "The Problem of Kenneth Clark" in *Commentary,* November, 1974, 37–46.

* *Pathos of Power,* Harper & Row, 179 pp., $7.95.

Cleary, T. A., Humphreys, L. G., Kendrick, S. A., & Wesman, A. Educational uses of tests with disadvantaged students. *American Psychologist,* 1975 (January), 15–41.

> A report prepared at the request of the American Psychological Association's Board of Scientific Affairs. It was published in the hope that it would stimulate discussion of the important issues involved. Summary.

Coleman, J. The concept of equality of educational opportunity. *Harvard Educational Review,* 1968, *38*(1), 7–22.

> Although there is wide agreement in the United States that our society accepts and supports the fundamental value of equal opportunity, when it comes to areas of specific application there is considerable disagreement over its meaning. In this article, the author traces the evolutionary shifts in interpretation of the concept of equality of educational opportunity, not only putting into perspective the different views which form the basis for disagreement today but also indicating how the current direction of change may influence the interpretation of this concept in the future. Abstract.

Coleman, J. S. *Equality of educational opportunity.* Washington, DC: U.S. Government Printing Office, 1966.

> . . . It is obvious that this is not a good study of the effects of education on minority-group performance; it is just the best that has ever been done. Moreover, it provides the best evidence available concerning the differential effects—or rather the lack of such effects—of schools. AAAS members may find it hard to believe that the $28-billion-a-year public education industry has not produced abundant evidence to show the differential effects of different kinds of schools, but it has not. That students learn more in "good" schools than in "poor" schools has long been accepted as a self-evident fact not requiring verification. Thus, the finding that schools with widely varying characteristics differ very little in their effects is literally of revolutionary significance. Review by R. C. Nichols in *Science,* December 9, 1966, *154,* 1312–1314.

Coleman J. S. Busing backfired. *The National Observer,* June 7, 1975.

Colman, A. M. 'Scientific' racism and the evidence on race and intelligence. *Race,* 1972, *14,* 137–153.

> In conclusion, a word of explanation is necessary for the use of the phrase 'scientific racism' in the title of this paper. I do not for one moment believe that Jensen and Eysenck, like so many previous adherents to the geneticist doctrine, are racists in the crude sense of viewing American blacks with hatred or wishing to oppress them. Eysenck, for example, is anxious to explain that such sentiments do not necessarily flow from his 'scientific' beliefs. Summary.

Condas, J. Personal reflections on the Larry P. trial and its aftermath. *School Psychology Review,* 1980, *9*(2), 154–158.

Conklin, K. R. Why compensatory schooling seems to make "no difference." *Journal of Education,* 1974, *156,* 34–42.

Crew, L. The new alchemy. *College English,* 1977, *38*(7), 707–711.

. . . I question the wisdom of thus legislating linguistic conformity. That very conformity makes it very likely that we will not discover and nurture the hundreds of otherwise very talented minority students who happen to have minimal facility with a linguistic skill we never require of the majority, viz., the ability to master an alien dialect as a condition of being taken seriously. Summary.

Cronbach, L. J. Heredity, environment, and educational policy. *Harvard Educational Review,* 1969, *39*(2), 338–347.

Cronbach, L. J. Five decades of public controversy over mental testing. *American Psychologist,* 1975 (January), 1–14.

An article prepared for an American Academy of Arts and Sciences study entitled "Social Science Controversies and Public Policy Decisions."

Cronbach, L. J. Hearnshaw on Burt. *Science,* 1979, *206*, 192–194.

Cronin, J., Daniels, N., Hurley, A., Kroch, A., & Webber, R. Race, class, and intelligence: A critical look at the IQ controversy. *International Journal of Mental Health,* 1975, *3*(4), 46–132.

Jensen's attack on blacks thus provides a rationale with which to undercut any and all reforms. Typically, an ideology whose main thrust is racist also contains ideas that hurt everyone—hence the crucial importance of destroying "Jensenism." Summary.

Darlington, C. D. The genetics of society. In A. J. Gregor (Ed.), *A Symposium on Race: An Inter-disciplinary approach.* Honolulu, Hawaii U. P., 1963.

Darlington, C. D. *The evolution of man and society.* New York: Simon and Schuster, 1969.

Darlington, C. D., F. R. S. *The little universe of man.* London: George Allen & Unwin, 1978.

Davis, B. D., & Flaherty, P. (Eds.) *Human diversity: Its causes and social significance.* Cambridge, MA: Ballinger Publishing Company, 1976.

Defense Race Relations Institute Library Bibliography, compiled by library division, Patrick Air Force Base, Florida, 1973.

Department of Educational Accountability *Annual Test Report,* 1977–78. Montgomery County Public Schools, Rockville, MD: December, 1978.

The breakdown of the test results by racial/ethnic category generally indicated that Asian students scored the highest, followed in order by White, Hispanic, and Black students. This was true for most of the CAT, ITBS, TAP, and MFRT results. The major exception was for Asian students in Grade 11 on the MFRT. They scored below Whites and at roughly the same level as Hispanics. This general trend has also been found on the tests administered nationwide by the National Assessment of Educational Progress (NAEP) for Whites, Hispanics, and Blacks. All groups performed better than their counterparts in most school districts around the country. Summary.

Deutsch, M., Katz, I., & Jensen, A. R. (Eds.) *Social class, race, and psychological development.* New York: Holt, Rinehart and Winston, 1968.

This is a book that "seeks to clarify the present state of knowledge about social and biological influences on intellectual development." It fails in its objective primarily because 10 of its 11 chapters either ignore biological influences or dismiss them with rather fatuous argumentation. This is done in spite of the fact that the family, twin, and adoption studies to date show environmental differences, as they exist and are measured today, accounting for only 10 to 30 per cent of the variance in IQ test scores. Review by J. M. Horn in *Contemporary Psychology*, 1973, *18*(5), 232–234.

Deutsch, M. Happenings on the way back to the forum. *Harvard Educational Review*, 1969, *39*(3), 523–557.

District of Columbia. *Investigation and study of the public school system* (Union calender No. 812, 91st Congress, 2d session, House Report No. 91–1681). Washington, DC: U.S. Government Printing Office, 1970.

Dobzhansky, T. Race and science: A symposium on diversity and equality. *The Columbia University Forum*, 1967, *10*(1), 5–6.

Dobzhansky, T. Differences are not deficits. *Psychology Today*, 1973 (December), 97–101.
    A distinguished geneticist pores over the evidence for the heritability of intelligence, finds it ambiguous, and is not convinced by Jensen's argument. Abstract.

Dorfman, D. D. The Cyril Burt question: New findings. *Science*, 1978, *201*(4362), 1177–1186.

Dorfman, D. D. Burt's tables. *Science*, 1979, *204*, 246–254.

Dreger, R. M., & Miller, K. S. Comparative psychological studies of Negroes and whites in the United States. *Psychological Bulletin*, 1968, *70*, 1–58.
    This is a review of psychological studies concerning Negroes and whites in the United States for the most part from 1959 through 1965. The topics covered include: the physical substrata of psychological and psychosocial functions, physical and motor development, psychophysical functions, intellectual functions, educational and occupational attainment and aspirations, temperament, social perceptions and attitudes, mental illness, crime and delinquency, family organization. Abstract.

Dupuy, H. J., & Gruvaeus, G. *The construction and utility of three indexes of intellectual achievement.* (Vital and health statistics: Series 2, Data evaluation and methods research; no. 74); DHEW Publication No. (HRA) 78–1348. Hyattsville, Maryland: U.S. Department of Health, Education, and Welfare, September, 1977.

Eaves, L. J., & Jinks, J. L. Insignificance of evidence for differences in heritability of IQ between races and social classes. *Nature*, 1972, *240*(5376), 84–88.

Eaves, L. J. Inferring the causes of human variation. *The Journal of the Royal Statistical Society*, Series A (General), 1977, *140*, Part 3, 324–355.

Educational Testing Service. Are aptitude tests unfair to Negroes? ETS investigates two kinds of "bias." *ETS Developments*, 1966, *14*(1), 1; 4.

Eells, K., Davis, A., Havighurst, R. J., Herrick, V. E., & Tyler, R. W. *Intelligence and cultural differences: A study of cultural learning and problem-solving.* Chicago: The University of Chicago Press, 1951.

Ehrlich, P. R., & Feldman, S. S. *The race bomb: Skin color, prejudice, and intelligence.* Quadrangle/The New York Times Book Company, 1977.
    In the first six chapters, the whole race-IQ debate is revealed as a scientifically useless discussion. Since there are no biological races to

begin with, the question of the inferiority or superiority of a race is meaningless. IQ itself is a measure of limited significance; there is no sign that ability to do well on IQ tests is largely inherited, and if it were largely inherited, this would tell us *nothing* about the cause of group differences. Furthermore, group differences in average IQ (regardless of how the groups are defined) are readily explained by the different environments to which members of different groups are exposed. The question of whether group differences are to any degree the result of genetic differences is both scientifically trivial and practically unanswerable. The persistence of the question is traceable primarily to a misunderstanding of genetics by a small group of scientists. Summary.

Ehrman, L., Omenn, G. S., & Caspari, E. (Eds.) *Genetics, environment, and behavior: Implications for educational policy.* New York: Academic Press, 1972.

Engelstad, D. S. The relation between family size, ordinal position and IQ in a sample of South Mississippi school children. *The Mankind Quarterly,* 1979, *19,* 193–213.

Erlenmeyer-Kimling, L., & Jarvik, L. F. Genetics and intelligence: A review. *Science,* 1963, *142*(3598), 1477–1478.

A survey of the literature of the past 50 years reveals remarkable consistency in the accumulated data relating mental functioning to genetic potentials. Intragroup resemblance in intellectual abilities increases in proportion to the degree of genetic relationship. Abstract.

Erlenmeyer-Kimling, L., & Stern, S. E. Heritability of IQ by social class: Evidence inconclusive. *Science,* 1973, *182,* 1044–1045.

Exhibit A: IQ trial, Plaintiffs take the stand. *APA Monitor,* December 1977, Vol. 8, No. 12, pp. 4–5.

Exhibit B: IQ trial, State witness testifies. *APA Monitor,* January 1978, Vol. 9, No. 1, pp. 15; 18.

Exhibit C: IQ trial, Defense experts testify. *APA Monitor,* April 1978, Vol. 9, No. 4, pp. 8–10.

Eysenck, H. J. *Race, intelligence and education.* London: Temple Smith, 1971.

Eysenck thinks that despite the genetically blurred outlines of the groups concerned (which he recognizes), and the uncertainties of what it is that IQ tests measure, and the differences in their social, medical, cultural and educational experience, it is important to study IQ differences between US whites and blacks. This is in order to estimate the contributions of genetic and environmental factors to the differences which have emerged. His book is largely a defense of Jensen's approach to this problem, a plea for further work in this and allied fields, and a claim that on the data so far available it looks highly probable that differences in gene frequencies are largely responsible for the IQ differentials found. Review. This book was also published in the United States as *The IQ argument: Race, intelligence and education,* New York: The Library Press, 1971.

Eysenck, H. J. *The inequality of man.* San Diego, California: EDITS Publishers, 1975.

Eysenck has written a generally inflammatory book clearly designed to tempt the lay reader into a pseudo-battle between Truth and Igno-rance. For the careful reader the battle fades out inconclusively. This book is an uncritical popularization of Jensen's ideas without the nuances and qualifiers that make much of Jensen's writing credible or at least responsible. It is a maddeningly inconsistent book filled with contradictory caution and in-caution; with hypotheses stated both as hypotheses and as conclusions; with both accurate and inaccurate statements on matters of fact. It is carelessly put together, with no index, few references, and long, inadequately cited quotes. Further-more, considering the gravity of Eysenck's theses, the book has an occasional jocularity of tone that is offensive. Review. Sandra Scarr-Salapatek, *Science, 174*(1223), December, 17, 1971.

Eysenck, H. J. National differences in personality as related to ABO blood group polymorphism. *Psychological Reports,* 1977, *41,* 1257–1258. (a)

Blood group polymorphisms of the ABO system are related to personal-ity differences, AB being more frequent among introverts, and the ratio A/B being higher among stable subjects. In view of the fact that Japanese are more introverted and more neurotic than British samples, it was predicted that Japanese, as compared with British, would have a higher proportion of AB carriers and a lower A/B ratio. Both predictions were confirmed by study of the established frequencies for blood groups in the two countries. Summary.

Eysenck, H. J. The case of Sir Cyril Burt. *Encounter,* 1977, *48,* 19–24. (b).

Feldman, M. W., & Lewontin, R. C. The heritability hangup: The role of variance analysis in human genetics is discussed. *Science,* 1975, *190*(4220), 1163–1168.

Fielder, W. R., Cohen, R. D., & Feeney, S. An attempt to replicate the teacher expectancy effect. *Psychological Reports,* 1971, *29,* 1223–1228.

Rosenthal suggests teachers' expectancies can influence pupil behavior as measured by gain in IQ. Following his design, 19% of 796 S's in 36 classes at 3 elementary schools were indentified to their teachers showing exceptional potential for intellectual gain, when in fact their names had been randomly selected. After one semester no trends could be drawn from analyses of grade level, sex, and minority group member-ship; nor was the "expectancy advantage" of the selected S's significant (p < .05). Summary.

Fogel, W. R., & Engerman, S. L. *Time on the cross: The economics of American-Negro slavery.* Boston: Little, Brown, & Company, 1974.

The book has raised issues that cut across the usual ideological lines. People concerned with giving blacks a "usable past" can't decide whether the book will give today's American blacks more to be proud of or will deprive them of conventional explanations for current prob-lems which rest partially on the assumption that slavery destroyed Negro family structure. Review by C. Holden in *Science,* December, 1974, *186,* 1004–1007.

Friedrichs, R. W. The impact of social factors upon scientific judgment: The "Jensen Thesis" as appraised by members of the American Psychological Association. *Journal of Negro Education,* 1973, *42,* 429–438.

Furby, L. Implications of within-group heritabilities for sources of between group differences: IQ and racial differences. *Developmental Psychology,* 1973, *9*(1), 28–37.

> In particular, our present knowledge of the relative shapes and heritabilities of the IQ distributions for blacks and whites suggests, but does not prove, that blacks and whites have similar genotypes for IQ but differ on IQ-determining environmental factors. Abstract.

Gage, N. L. I.Q. heritability, race differences, and educational research. *Phi Delta Kappan,* 1972 (January), 308–312.

> It is *not* that "compensatory education has been tried and it apparently has failed." Compensatory education needs more research and better-supported tryouts over a period of decades, not merely a single enthusiastic Presidential administration. Summary.

Garber, H., & Heber, R. *The Milwaukee Project: Early intervention as a technique to prevent mental retardation.* The University of Connecticut Technical Paper, National Leadership Institute, Teacher Education/Early Childhood, U.S. Department of Health, Education, & Welfare, March, 1973.

> Howard Garber and Rick Heber are professors at the University of Wisconsin. Their research specialities are learning disabilities. The Milwaukee Project is one of the most important longitudinal studies ever undertaken and it has yielded heartening results. For many poor children, early education of a nursery school variety can overcome mild ravages wrought by poverty. For others, however, those born into grinding poverty to mothers with severly limited maternal teaching skills, the usual preschool is too little and too late. Structured cognitive instruction must begin for these children in the cradle. The Milwaukee Project shows that the intellectual potentials of children don't have to be mangled by poverty and ignorance of parents. Cradle Schools can become an effective intervention mechanism to save them from this fate. The Milwaukee Project will be replicated widely as community agencies focus more clearly on specific needs for the intervention to prevent school failure. Abstract.

Garrett, H. E. Klineberg's chapter on race and psychology: A review. *Mankind Quarterly,* 1960, *1*(1), 3–10.

Gates, R. R. Studies of interracial crossing: The nature and inheritance of skin color. *International Anthropological and Linguistic Review,* 1953, *1*(4), 254–268.

Gentry, W. R. *The Ertl index and IQ: A validity study.* Unpublished Master's thesis, The University of Georgia, 1974.

> The Ertl hypothesis that the latency of the visual evoked response is significantly related to psychometric intelligence is not supported in this study. The correlations between the CNEA scores and IQ were all at chance level, with the exception of one significant positive correlation which was in the opposite direction from that predicted by Ertl. It was also shown that there were no significant differences between the CNEA scores for the two groups. That is, the normal and retarded students differed by fifty points in IQ but did not differ in their response time to a light stimulus. Summary.

Gillie, O. Burt's missing ladies. *Science,* 1979, *204,* 1035–1039.

Glass, D. C. (Ed.) *Genetics.* Second of a series on Biology and Behavior. Proceedings of a conference under the auspices of Russell Sage Foundation, the Social Science Research Council, and the Rockefeller University. New York: The Rockefeller University Press and Russell Sage Foundation, 1968.

Goldberger, A. S., & Lewontin, R. C. *Jensen's twin fantasy.* Washington, DC: U.S. Department of Health, Education, and Welfare; National Science Foundation, March, 1976.

>It should now be clear that the twin method cannot be used to extract meaningful estimates of the variances, and covariance, of the genetic and environmental components of human intelligence. Any plausible model for the resemblance between the twins will have so many more unknown parameters than observations that the task is futile. Summary.

Goldberger, A. S. Jensen on Burks. *Educational Psychologist,* 1976, *12*(1), 64–78.

>We critically examine the portions of Arthur Jensen's books that concern Barbara Burks' 1928 study of adoptive families. Jensen cites the low correlations of children's IQs with measures of home environment as evidence that environment plays only a minor role in the determination of intelligence. We find that Burks' sample was highly selective, that her environmental measures were limited, and that Jensen has misrepresented the content and implications of her study. Abstract.

Goldman, R. D. Hidden opportunities in the prediction of college grades for different subgroups. *Journal of Educational Measurement,* 1973, *10*(3), 205–210.

Goldstein, J. A critique of 'unequal educational opportunity.' *Educational Psychologist,* 1978, *12*(3), 332–344.

Gordon, C. *Looking ahead: Self-conceptions, race and family as determinants of adolescent orientation to achievement.* Washington, DC: American Sociological Association (for the Arnold M. and Caroline Rose Monograph Series), 1968.

Gordon, E. W., & Wilkerson, D. A. *Compensatory education for the disadvantaged; Programs and practices: Preschool through college.* New York: College Entrance Examination Board, 1966.

Gordon, R. A. Crime and cognition: An evolutionary perspective. *Proceedings of the 11 International Symposium on Criminology* held in the Oscar Freire Institute, August 7th, 1975.

>The diffusion of the human species over the planet prior to and during what might be called "the abstract reasoning revolution" virtually guaranteed separations and isolations that would produce stragglers during the crucial transition phase. Critics of the hypothesis of genetic differences in IQ between groups overlook the fact that a one or two standard deviation difference is not large on the scale of nature, although it may loom large on the scale of human affairs. Thus, there seems to be an aspect of inevitability to the theory I have set forth, concerning the present criminal crisis in urban communities. This aspect should not be surprising, for there are ample precedents in the

study of biological populations for self-initiated critical phases. Summary.

Gordon, R. A., & Rudert, E. E. Bad news concerning IQ tests. *Sociology of Education,* 1979, *52*(3), 174–190.

In concurrence with previous studies, no indications of racial bias in IQ tests were found. This evidence could be nullified only by assuming that explicit selection on IQ scores occurs throughout our status attainment models. . . . Since the use of IQ tests for selection purposes is typically a matter of public record, such an assumption seems highly unrealistic. The ultimate significance of the failure to find bias in IQ tests will depend on how easily changed IQ eventually proves to be, on a proper understanding of the magnitude of group differences, on assessments of the importance of IQ in determining other outcomes, and on the social importance of the outcomes so determined. Summary.

Gould, S. J. Morton's ranking of races by cranial capacity: Unconscious manipulation of data may be a scientific norm. *Science,* 1978, *200,* 503–509.

Samuel George Morton, self-styled objective empiricist, amassed the world's largest pre-Darwinian collection of human skulls. He measured their capacity and produced the results anticipated in an age when few Caucasians doubted their innate superiority: whites above Indians, blacks at the bottom. Morton published all his raw data, and it is shown here that his summary tables are based on a patchwork of apparently unconscious finagling. When his data are properly reinterpreted, all races have approximately equal capacities. Unconscious or dimly perceived finagling is probably endemic in science, since scientists are human beings rooted in cultural contexts, not automatons directed toward external truth. Summary.

Greenberger, E., & Marini, M. M. *Black-white differences in psychological maturity: A further analysis.* Center for Social Organization of Schools, Report No. 136, September, 1972. Baltimore, MD: The Johns Hopkins University.

Gunnings, T. S. Response to critics of Robert L. Williams. *Counseling Psychologist,* 1971, *2,* 73–77.

Guy, D. P. Issues in the unbiased assessment of intelligence. *School Psychology Digest,* 1977, *6,* 14–23.

Hall, V. C., & Turner, R. R. The validity of the "different language explanation" for poor scholastic performance by black students. *Review of Educational Research,* 1974, *44,* 69–81.

From the evidence they have gathered, the present researchers believe that it would serve no useful purpose to teach English as a second language to speakers of NNE if the goal is improved comprehension of SE. The black child has a great deal of contact with SE on radio and television and with people outside his family and neighborhood. If these contacts are not sufficient, then increased contact without formal education may be the most beneficial treatment (e.g., integration). Integration itself needs to be more carefully studied so that the additional benefits of several cultures learning from each other can be attained. The present authors know of no research or demonstration project directed toward maximizing the effects of integration. Finally, the authors are convinced that more effort should be directed toward studying universals of cognitive development rather than toward relatively superficial performance differences such as spoken dialects. Summary.

Harwood, J. The race-intelligence controversy: A sociological approach, I-Professional factors. *Social Studies of Science,* 1976, *6,* 369–394.

To understand why science develops as it does . . . what one must understand . . . is the manner in which a particular set of shared values interacts with the particular experiences shared by a community of specialists to ensure that most members of the group will ultimately find one set of arguments rather than another decisive . . . The debate about race and intelligence only begins to make sense when it is seen as one internal to academic life; between two groups of men who differ in personality, in academic background, and in political and social allegiance. Abstract.

Harwood, J. The race-intelligence controversy: A sociological approach, II-'External' factors. *Social Studies of Science,* 1977, *7,* 1–30.

Hébert, J-P. *Race et intelligence.* Paris: Copernic, 1977.

"Jean-Pierre Hébert," according to the information supplied by the publishers, is a pseudonym for four researchers who are known for their scientific work—two geneticists, one ethnologist, and one specialist in psychometric problems. They state that they have chosen anonymous publication so that criticism and discussion of the book might be based on the issues themselves and to avoid polemics involving individual people. Review by O. E. Favreau in *Contemporary Psychology,* 1979, *24*(1), 23–24.

Herrnstein, R. I.Q. *The Atlantic Monthly,* 1971, *228*(3), 43–64.

. . . The main significance of intelligence testing is what it says about a society built around human inequalities. The message is so clear that it can be made in the form of a syllogism:

    1. If differences in mental abilities are inherited, and

    2. If success requires those abilities, and

    3. If earnings and prestige depend on success,

    4. Then social standing (which reflects earnings and prestige) will be based to some extent on inherited differences among people.

Summary.

Herrnstein, R. J. *I.Q. in the meritocracy.* Boston: Little, Brown, & Company, 1973.

In the barrage of criticisms directed against Herrnstein, it is most noteworthy that no substantive counter evidence to his argument has yet come forth. Thus Herrnstein's opposition in the debate has raged on ideological rather than on scientific grounds. Herrnstein states: "One can search the scientific literature from one end to the other . . . and find no significant empirical challenge to the sizeable genetic contribution to scores on intelligence tests." In five engrossing chapters, he reviews the history of mental testing, the current theory and research on the meaning and nature of intelligence, its significance for educational and occupational attainments, the roles of genetic and environmental factors in the causation of individual differences in mental ability, and finally, in "The Specter of Meritocracy," his interpretation of the social implications of all this. As a specialist myself in this aspect of psychology, I can attest that these chapters provide the most up-to-date, accurate, and balanced nontechnical account of the mainstream theories and research on intelligence that can be found in print today. Both for nonspecialists and students of the behavioral sciences who want an overview of what's what about IQ, this is the book to read. Review. Jensen, A. R., *Chicago Tribune,* June 24, 1973.

Hirsch, J. Behavior-genetic, or "experimental," analysis: The challenge of science versus the lure of technology. *American Psychologist,* 1967, *22*(2), 118–130.

Hirsch, J. Behavior-genetic analysis and the study of man. *Science and the Concept of Race,* Columbia University Press, 1968, pp. 37–48.

I shall examine here some of the fallacies that have led to the widespread and long persisting *mis*use of the race concept. It is my intention to show that the notorious nature-nurture or heredity-environment question is, in fact, a pseudo question—a question that is being resolved neither in favor of the position which asserts a racial hierarchy nor of that which asserts absolute bisocial uniformity. Summary.

Hirsch, J. *Jensenism: The bankruptcy of "Science" without scholarship.* Unpublished manuscript, University of Illinois at Urbana-Champaign. Research support by Grant No. US PH MH 10715–09, awarded by the National Institute of Mental Health, DHEW.

Horn, J. N. The IQ myth revisited. *Texas Psychologist,* 1975, *27*(2), 19–21.

On April 22, 1975, CBS presented an hour-long program, "The IQ Myth," which argued that intelligence as currently measured has no genetic basis and that IQ tests present a social danger. The following letter addressed to Dan Rather, the program commentator, presented the other side of the issue. It is reprinted below with the permission of Dr. Joseph Horn—TP Editor. All in all Mr. Rather, I believe your program can be quite accurately characterized as biased in the extreme and designed to foist on the American public the notion that IQ testing today is a menace to society. I believe if you or your staff will do some further research you will agree that the program as originally presented was so in error as to require correction. In the final analysis, the confidence that the public has in the news media rests in the conviction that journalists, if given the evidence, will change their minds and do everything in their power to rectify their mistakes. Summary.

Houts, P. L. (Ed.) *The myth of measurability.* New York: Hart Publishing Company, 1977.

Sponsored by The National Association of Elementary School Principals with support from the Ford Foundation.

Hudson, L. Intelligence, race, and the selection of data. *Race,* 1971, *12*(3), 283–292.

Humphreys, L. G., & Dachler, H. P. Jensen's theory of intelligence. *Journal of Educational Psychology,* 1969, *60*(6), 419–426.

Criterion groups were formed in accordance with Jensen's designs. In contrast to his findings, both IQ and socioeconomic status (SES) are positively correlated with rote-memory scores, and there is little interaction. Also, correlations between rote memory measures and other intellectual variables show very little variability around very modest levels of correlations in the four criterion groups. Abstract.

Humphreys, L. G. Statistical definitions of test validity for minority groups. *Journal of Applied Psychology,* 1973, *58*(1), 1–4.

This study considers the problem of deciding when a selection test is invalid for members of a minority group. There is both a strong empirical and theoretical basis for rejecting the choice zero correlation between test and criterion as an appropriate null hypothesis. This choice, for one thing, typically requires that the population value of the correlation be higher in the minority group than in the majority group. Recommended instead is the direct comparison of correlations in minority and majority samples. Only in the event that the minority correlation is significantly lower and the confidence limits around that correlation include no useful levels of the relationship should the correlation be considered essentially zero. Abstract.

Hunt, J. McV. Has compensatory education failed? Has it been attempted? *Harvard Educational Review,* 1969, *39*(2), 278–300.

Ingle, D. J. Possible genetic bases of social problems: A reply to Ashley Montagu. *Midway,* 1970 (Winter), 105–121.

Jencks, C., Smith, M., Acland, H., Bane, M. J., Cohen, D., Gintis, H., Heyns, B., & Michelson, S. *Inequality: A reassessment of the effect of family and schooling in America.* New York: Basic Books, 1972.

The most striking finding is that, no matter how schools are assessed, *which* school a child goes to has a negligible effect on success, however measured. Schools may be integrated or segregated, expensive or cheap, with rich students or poor students, or merely ranked by degree of success, but differences between them make very little difference to students' success. The idea that schools make a big difference is a statistical illusion. Schools whose students have high IQ or achievement scores, or that have high percentages of students going on to college, do so almost entirely because the students in them *come* to school with high scores and with family backgrounds that lead to college. Review by A. L. Stinchcombe in *Science,* November, 1972, *122,* 603–604.

Jencks, C., & Brown, M. The effects of desegregation on student achievement: Some new evidence from the equality of educational opportunity survey. *Sociology of Education,* 1975, *48,* 126–140.

Reanalysis of the 1966 Equality of Educational Opportunity Survey, using a quasi-longitudinal design, suggests that the test performance of students in 51–75 percent white schools improved relative to national norms between first and sixth grade. Both black and white students in such schools showed improvement. Black students' performance relative to national norms seemed to decline slightly if they were in 76–100 percent white schools and seemed to remain constant if they

were in 0–50 percent white schools. The racial composition of high
school did not appear to have had any appreciable effect on either
black or white students' test scores between ninth and twelfth grades.
Abstract.

Jencks, C. *Who gets ahead? The determinants of economic success in America.*
New York: Basic Books, Inc., 1979.

Who Get Ahead? is a descriptive account of the determinants of economic success in America. Derived from a contract report by Harvard's
Center for the Study of Public Policy to the National Institute of
Education and the Department of Labor, the book summarizes the
efforts of Christopher Jencks and 11 colleagues to provide a thorough
analysis of available data on the relationships among the family characteristics, academic ability, personality, and educational, occupational,
and economic achievement of American men. Review by R. D. Mare
in *Science,* May 16, 1980, *208,* 707–709.

Jensen, A. R. Cumulative deficit in compensatory education. *Journal of School
Psychology,* 1966, *4,* 37–47.

The term *cumulative deficit* has become part of the specialized vocabulary associated with the concept of "cultural deprivation." The purpose
of this article is to delineate the meaning of the term *cumulative deficit,*
to distinguish it from other, related terms, and to outline briefly some
hypothesis concerning its psychological basis. Abstract.

Jensen, A. R. Social class, race, and genetics: Implications for education. *American Educational Research Journal,* 1968, *5*(1), 1–42. (a)

In our efforts to improve education we should not lose sight of the
focal point of our concern—the individual child. This means the biological as well as the social individual, for man's intelligence and educability are the products of biological evolution as well as of individual
experience. Not to recognize the biological basis of educability is to
harmfully restrict our eventual understanding and possible control of
the major sources of diversity in human capacities and potentialities.
Summary.

Jensen, A. R. Patterns of mental ability and socioeconomic status. *Proceedings
of the National Academy of Sciences,* 1968, *60*(4), 1330–1337. (b).

Children who are above the general average on Level I abilities but
below the average on Level II performance usually appear bright and
capable of normal learning and achievement in many situations, although they have inordinate difficulties in school work under the traditional methods of instruction. Many such children who are classed
as mentally retarded in school later become socially and economically
adequate persons when they leave the academic situation. On the other
hand, children who are below average on Level I, and consequently
on Level II as well, appear to be much more handicapped in the
world of work. One shortcoming of traditional IQ tests is that they
make both types of children look much alike. Tests that reliably assess
both Level I and Level II are needed in schools, personnel work,
and the armed forces. Equally important is the discovery or invention
of instructional methods that engage Level I more fully and provide

thereby a means of improving the educational attainments of many of the children now called culturally disadvantaged. Summary.

Jensen, A. R. Reducing the heredity-environment uncertainty: A reply. *Harvard Educational Review,* 1969, *39*(3), 449–483. (a)

Jensen, A. R. How much can we boast IQ? *Harvard Educational Review,* 1969, *39*(1), 1–123. (b)

Jensen, A. R. The Jensen thesis: Three comments (I. Race and the genetics of intelligence: A reply to Lewontin.) *Bulletin of the Atomic Scientists,* 1970, *26*(5), 17–23. (a).

Jensen, A. R. The heritability of intelligence. *Engineering and Science,* 1970, *33*(6), 1–4. (b)

So the conclusion we come to—which is certainly valid at least in the white European and North American populations in which the research was conducted—is this: In accounting for the causes of the differences among persons in IQ, the genes outweigh the effects of environment by 2 to 1. As environmental conditions are improved and made more alike for all persons in the society, the average intelligence level of the population will be somewhat increased, and the IQ differences among persons will be slightly reduced. But of course the differences that remain will inevitably be due even more to genetic factors. Summary.

Jensen, A. R. IQ's of identical twins reared apart. *Behavior Genetics,* 1970, 1, 133–148. (c)

Analysis of the data from the four major studies of the intelligence of MZ twins reared apart, totaling 122 twin pairs, leads to conclusions not found in the original studies or in previous reviews of them. A statistical test of the absolute difference between the separated twins' IQ's indicates that there are no significant differences among the twin samples in the four studies. All of them can be viewed as samples from the same population and can therefore be pooled for more detailed and powerful statistical treatment. Summary.

Jensen, A. R. The IQ controversy: A reply to Layzer. *Cognition,* 1972, *1*(4), 427–452. (a)

Jensen, A. R. Educability, hereditary transmission and differences between populations. *Revue de Psychologie Appliquee,* 1972, *22*(1), 21–34. (b)

Jensen, A. R. The case for I.Q. tests: Reply to McClelland. *The Humanist,* 1972 (Jan./Feb.), 14. (c)

Jensen, A. R. Genetics and education: A second look. *New Scientist,* 1972 (Oct. 12), 96–98. (d).

Academic aptitudes and special talents should be cultivated wherever they are found, and a wise society will take all possible measures to ensure this to the greatest possible extent. At the same time, those who are poor in the traditional academic aptitudes cannot be left by the wayside. Suitable means and goals must be found for making their years of schooling rewarding for them, if not in the usual academic sense, then in ways that can better their chances for socially useful and self-fulfilling roles as adults. Summary.

Jensen, A. R. *Genetics and education.* New York: Harper, 1972. (e)

The Jensen controversy has had a significant impact on scientific thinking about individual differences in ability, and the 1969 *HER* article
is still the best available statement of Jensen's position. This article
is certainly required reading for all serious students on individual differences, and it is basic to the understanding of the continuing controversy
as it unfolds. Review by R. C. Nichols, *Educational Studies,* 1974,
Vol. 5, Nos. 1/2, pp. 35–38.

Jensen, A. Race, intelligence and genetics: The differences are real. *Psychology Today,* 1973, *7*(7), 80–86. (a)

Jensen, A. R. Personality and scholastic achievement in three ethnic groups.
The British Journal of Educational Psychology, 1973, *43*(Part 2), 115–125.
(b)

Scores on the Junior Eysenck Personality Inventory of some 2,000
white, Negro, and Mexican-American school children, ages 9 to 13,
were examined in relation to measures of intelligence and home environment as predictors of scholastic achievement. Summary.

Jensen, A. R. *Educability & group differences.* New York: Harper & Row,
1973. (c)

In sum, the case erected by Jensen for the proposition that a substantial
genetic component exists in the IQ difference between the black and
the white population is neither frivolous nor compelling. The opposing
view, that no such genetic component exists, has long been popular
among social scientists and educators. But popularity is not corroboration. Jensen has demonstrated that the genetic hypothesis is a viable
one and that it must be considered seriously. Review by Carter Denni-
ston in *Science,* 1975 (Jan. 17), Vol. *187,* pp. 161–162.

Jensen, A. R. *Mental tests not culture-biased for blacks.* National Academy of
Sciences, Autumn Meeting, Washington, DC, 1973. (d)

Jensen concluded from his research on culture bias in mental tests
that the well-known average IQ difference of about 15 points between
whites and blacks, whatever its cause, will have to be explained in
terms of factors other than culture biased tests. Summary.

Jensen, A. R. *Educational differences.* London: Methuen & Company, Ltd.,
1973. (e)

Apart from the preface, a marvellously cogent piece of grumbling
about the unwarranted disfavor that the extreme hereditarians and
environmentalists-on-the-rebound have managed between them to heap
upon the genetic theory of intelligence, the best reading is provided
by some 40 pages entitled, "Can we and should we measure and study
race differences?" That, after all, is where Professor Jensen got himself
into political hot water, by arguing both that we can and that we
should. Review from *Economist,* 1973 (December 8), 249:119.

Jensen, A. R. How biased are culture-loaded tests? *Genetic Psychology Monographs,* 1974, *90,* 185–244. (a)

The culture-loaded Peabody Picture Vocabulary Test (PPVT) and the
culture-reduced Raven's Progressive Matrices (Colored and Standard
forms) were examined and compared in terms of various internal criteria of culture bias in large representative samples of white, Negro,

and Mexican-American school children, from kindergarten through the 8th grade, in three California school districts. On both the PPVT and the Raven the three ethnic groups, which show large mean differences, show very little difference in the rank order of item difficulties, the relative difficulty of adjacent items, the loadings of items on the first principal component, and the choice of distractors for incorrect responses. Abstract.

Jensen, A. R. *Race and mental ability.* Paper presented at a Symposium of the Institute of Biology on "Racial Variation in Man." Royal Geographical Society, London, September 19 and 20, 1974. (b)

In terms of what is already known about human evolution, about a host of other kinds of genetic racial differences, about the relative contributions of the constancy (relative to the variability within groups) of White-Negro differences in IQ and a wide variety of other indices of cognitive development from childhood to maturity, it appears highly probable that genetic factors are involved to a substantial degree in the lower average IQ of American Negroes. So far, I have not seen a serious attempt to adduce evidence, or comprehensive argumentation based thereon, to the effect that this hypothesis is either improbable or scientifically unwarranted. Summary.

Jensen, A. R. *Test bias and construct validity.* Invited address presented at the 83rd Annual Convention of the American Psychological Association in Chicago, September, 1975.

The large general factor measured by our standard tests of intelligence is clearly the same factor in blacks as in whites. The hypothesis that this general factor is a capacity for cognitive complexity, conscious mental manipulation and transformation of stimulus inputs, has led to predictions that are borne out empirically at a high level of significance. Neither science nor the cause of social justice is served by denying these findings. As researchers our response is to question, analytically criticize, replicate results, determine their limits as to other mental tests and populations, seek the causes of test scores variance, pit alternative theories against one another—and openly renounce those hypotheses that objective evidence repeatedly disproves. Summary.

Jensen, A. R. Twins' IQs: A reply to Schwartz and Schwartz. *Behavior Genetics,* 1976, *6*(3), 369–371. (a)

Jensen, A. R. Heritability of IQ. *Science,* 1976 (October 1), *194,* 6; 8. (b)

Finally, the evidence for the substantial heritability of IQ does not depend upon complex analyses in quantitative genetics. The fact that genetic factors are strongly involved in individual differences in IQ is firmly established by numerous studies of adopted children, whose IQ's are much less correlated with the IQ's of their adoptive parents (and with assessments of their adoptive environments) than with assessments of their biological parents, with whom they have had no postnatal relationship, and by studies showing that identical twins reared apart are more similar in IQ than fraternal twins reared together. Summary.

Jensen, A. R. g: Outmoded theory or unconquered frontier? *Creative Science & Technology,* 1979, *II*(3), 16–29.

Intelligence is not an entity, but a theoretical construct. If there is a more important construct in all of psychology, I cannot imagine what it is. The construct of intelligence is obviously and immensely important—to individuals and to the whole society—educationally, and occupationally, without doubt; and also, I daresay, for the general quality of human life. Its scientific importance goes without saying, for it is only through scientific study that we may gain a better understanding of this most important psychological construct. Summary.

Jensen, A. R. *Bias in mental testing.* New York: The Free Press, 1980.

Jensen's findings clearly have horrendous implications. Indeed they come close to saying that blacks are a natural and permanent underclass—an idea so shocking that the book is likely to spark the most explosive debate yet over race and IQ. While his critics will not have their shots until his book is published, their job, according to Jensen, is simple enough: disprove the evidence or learn to live with it. But he is confident that his evidence will stand. "I think I have shown that the black-white differences are real, not artifacts of the test system," he says. Review in *Time,* September 24, 1979, 49.

Jensen, A. R. *The current status of the IQ controversy.* Unpublished manuscript.

This article is based on lectures given by the author at the Universities of Adelaide, La Trobe, Melbourne, and Sydney, in Australia during September-October 1977. The lectures were cancelled by the authorities in three other Australian universities because of threatened demonstrations against the author's appearance on their campuses. Summary.

Jensen, A. R., & Osborne, R. T. Forward and backward digit span interaction with race and IQ: A longitudinal developmental comparison. Unpublished manuscript.

Longitudinal data on forward and backward digit span (FDS and BDS) obtained at five age levels between 6 and 13 years in samples of white and black children, along with WISC data from four age levels, were used to test the following hypotheses relevant to Jensen's Level I-Level II theory of abilities: (a) FDS and BDS involve different factors of cognitive ability, (b) BDS is more g loaded than FDS, (c) whites and blacks show a larger average difference in BDS than FDS, (d) the difference between FDS and BDS decreases with increasing age (or mental maturity), and (e) whites and blacks of the same WISC mental age do not differ in either FDS or BDS. All of these hypotheses are born out in general by the data, although not always consistently at every age level. Abstract.

Jorgensen, C. C. IQ tests and their educational supporters *Journal of Social Issues,* 1973, *29*(1), 33–40.

This article examines the validity of present IQ tests for measuring the intelligence of black Americans. It is concluded that such tests have little validity, and the issue facing contemporary psychologists is why the discipline should continue to condone their use in black communities. Abstract.

Joseph, A. *Intelligence, IQ and race—When, how and why they become associated.* San Francisco: R & E Research Associates, Inc., 1977.

Kagan, J. S. Inadequate evidence and illogical conclusions. *Harvard Educational Review,* 1969, *39*(2), 274–277.

Kamin, L. J. *The science and politics of I.Q.* Potomac, MD: Erlbaum, 1974. The author of this book steps squarely into the controversy over the heritability of IQ, motivated at least as much by the political implications of the questions as by its scientific interest. His position is that those who interpret the evidence as indicating that individual differences in IQ are largely inherited are "fundamentally incorrect." Secondarily, he wishes to counteract the effects of hereditarians upon policy makers, largely by impugning the evidence upon which their case rests. Review by D. N. Jackson in *Science,* 1975 (Sept. 26), Vol. *189,* pp. 1077–1080.

Kamin, L. J. Social and legal consequences of I.Q. tests as classification instruments: Some warnings from our past. *Journal of School Psychology,* 1975, *13*(4), 317–323. Social science instruments are not neutral. The concepts they are imbedded in, the aspects of reality they enable us to see, all have social and political consequences. That school psychologists need to pay close attention to the sociopolitical implications of their assessment instruments is illustrated through the woeful history of the use and misuse of the concept of intelligence in the United States during the first third of this century. Summary.

Kamin, L. J. A reply to Munsinger. *Behavior Genetics,* 1977, *7*(5), 411–412.

Kamin, L. J. A positive interpretation of apparent "cumulative deficit." *Developmental Psychology,* 1978, *14,* 195–196. Two recent studies by Jensen suggest that a cumulative deficit in IQ occurs in socioeconomically deprived black children. The child's IQ is thought to deteriorate progressively with age. The two studies, however, are cross-sectional in design. They might thus be interpreted as indicating that social and educational changes have facilitated IQ development in recently born black children. There are data which demonstrate that young black children have higher IQs than their older siblings, holding constant the age at testing. Abstract.

Kaplan, A. R. (Ed.) *Human behavior genetics.* Springfield, IL: Charles C Thomas Publishers, 1976. No two humans are exactly alike constitutionally. Their perceptions as well as their reactions to the same objective experiences are different. Individual human differences are subject to constant modification by the effects of environmental variables. These effects are modulated by the individuals' constitutional characteristics, which are the products of dynamic interactions between biological and psychosocial variables. Dichotomies between psychosocial and biological aspects of human behavior development are artificial. The discipline of human behavior genetics is involved with explorations and interpretations of the biological and psychosocial variables in an integrated context. Abstract.

Karlsson, J. L. *Inheritance of creative intelligence.* Chicago: Nelson-Hall, Inc., 1978.

Genetic studies of abnormalties and physical disorders are fairly common. Diabetes mellitus, alcoholic tendencies, schizophrenia, epilepsy, myopia, and hypertension are all thought to have a genetic basis. Yet, studies of how these disorders correlate with highly desirable personality traits have been relatively undeveloped. Dr. Jon Karlsson, an eminent geneticist, explores this territory in his study of giftedness and heredity. Abstract.

Katz, I. Some motivational determinants of racial differences in intellectual achievement. *Journal International de Psychologie,* 1967, *2*(1), 1–12.

This paper will examine the academic achievement of Negro students from the standpoint of some general concepts of motivational processes underlying the development of intellectual achievement behavior. Abstract.

Kaufman, A. S., & Dicuio, R. F. Separate factor analyses of the McCarthy Scales for groups of black and white children. *Journal of School Psychology,* 1975, *13*(1), 10–18.

The picture is one of consistency, and these findings have definite theoretical and practical implications. Of primary importance is the fact that when the MSCA is administered to a black or white child, the examiner can feel secure that the Scale Indexes thus obtained correspond fairly closely to the theoretical abilities underlying the tasks in the battery. Summary.

King, J. C. *The biology of race.* New York: Harcourt Brace Jovanovich, Inc., 1971.

Culture plays the major role in determining how human beings judge and react to one another. It is culture, not genotype, that leads one population to attempt to kill off another which it considers racially different. The purpose of this book has been to show that in spite of all their differences . . . human beings constitute one species whose most precious asset is, in fact, their diversity. Summary.

Kuttner, R. E. (Ed.) *Race and modern science: A collection of essays by Biologists, Anthropologists, Sociologists and Psychologists.* New York: Social Science Press, 1967.

For the solution of the problem of different races living together in mutual helpfulness and respect, we need, in addition to good will, relevant information and sound objective thinking. This book is a storehouse of the former and it should stimulate the latter. Its objectivity and dispassionate treatment of problems associated with race should discourage prejudice on the one hand and wishful thinking on the other, and encourage serious efforts to learn the facts and to use them wisely. Review by Charles C. Josey.

Langerton, E. P. *The busing coverup.* Cape Canaveral, FL: Howard Allen Enterprises, Inc., 1975.

Larry P. v. Riles, Civil Action No. 71–2270 (Northern District of California, 1971).

See also in this section:

Exhibit A: IQ trial, Plaintiffs take the stand. *APA Monitor,* December 1977, Vol. 8, No. 12, pp. 4–5.

Exhibit B: IQ trial, State witness testifies. *APA Monitor,* January, 1978, Vol. 9, No. 1, pp. 15; 18.

Exhibit C: IQ trial, Defense experts testify. *APA Monitor,* April 1978, Vol. 9. No. 4, pp. 8–10.

Bersoff, D. N. P. v. Riles: Legal perspective. *School Psychology Review,* 1980, *9*(2), 112–122.

Condas, J. Personal reflections on the Larry P. trial and its aftermath. *School Psychology Review,* 1980, *9*(2), 154–158.

MacMillan, D. L., & Meyers, C. E. Larry P: An educational interpretation. *School Psychology Review,* 1980, *9*(2), 136–148.

Madden, P. B. Intelligence test on trial. *School Psychology Review,* 1980, *9*(2), 149–153.

Reschly, D. J. Psychological evidence in the *Larry P.* opinion: A case of right problem—wrong solution. *School Psychology Review,* 1980, *9*(2), 123–135.

Lawler, J. M. *IQ, heritability, and racism.* New York: International Publishers, 1978.

Let me conclude then, by strongly recommending the book to my educational colleagues since it provides the best available critique of the theory and method of IQ testing. It also demonstrates clearly the value of a developed philosophical perspective for dealing creatively with an educational issue and thus is an example of cross-disciplinary work which is much needed in the field of education. Finally, *IQ, Heritability and Racism* proves, for those that need it proved, that a Marxist analysis can powerfully illuminate this critical educational issue. Foreword by Roger R. Woock.

Layzer, D. Heritability analyses of IQ scores: Science or Numerology? *Science,* 1974, *183,* 1259–1266.

Under prevailing social conditions, no valid inferences can be drawn from IQ data concerning systematic genetic differences among races or socioeconomic groups. Research along present lines directed toward this end—whatever its ethical status—is scientifically worthless. Summary.

Lerner, B. The war on testing: David, Goliath & Gallup. *The Public Interest,* 1980 (Summer), No. 60, 119–147.

Lerner, I. M. *Heredity, evolution, and society.* San Francisco: W. H. Freeman and Company, 1968.

Lesser, G. S. Problems in the analysis of patterns of abilities: A reply. *Child Development,* 1973, *44,* 19–20.

Lewontin, R. C. Race and intelligence. *Bulletin of the Atomic Scientists,* 1970, *26,* 2–8.

In this article, Richard C. Lewontin, professor of biology at the University of Chicago, dissects the Jensen paper which precipitated the growing controversy last year. Professor Lewontin's conclusion: Jensen is wrong! Summary.

Loehlin, J. C., Vandenberg, S. G., & Osborne, R. T. Blood group genes and Negro-white ability differences. *Behavior Genetics,* 1973, *3*(3), 263–270.

Data on samples of 40 and 44 Negro adolescents from two twin studies were used to test Shockley's hypothesis that blood group genes more characteristic of European than African populations would tend to be associated with good performance on cognitive tests within the U.S. Negro population. This was not found to be the case. This result may not, however, be a very strong test of the genetic basis of the between-group IQ difference, because of independent assortment of blood group and ability genes over a number of generations among U.S. Negroes. Abstract.

Loehlin, J. C., Lindzey, G., & Spuhler, J. N. *Race differences in intelligence.* San Francisco: Freeman, 1975.

This book is the most comprehensive, critical, and balanced review of the race-IQ issue ever to be published. Meticulously written by three cautious, qualified scholars with backgrounds in psychology and anthropology, it should help reduce the fervor that the controversy has generated in recent years and help move the central question it addresses out of politics and back to science where it belongs. The book could be misread, misinterpreted, and misquoted, given the inconclusiveness of the available evidence, but only if readers insist upon using it mischievously to continue the holy war between hereditarians and nonhereditarians. Review by B. K. Eckland in *Science,* Vol. 190, 1975 (November, 21), pp. 775–778.

MacMillan, D. L., & Meyers, C. E. Larry P: An educational interpretation. *School Psychology Review,* 1980, *9*(2), 136–148.

Madden, P. B. Intelligence test on trial. *School Psychology Review,* 1980, *9*(2), 149–153.

McClelland, D. C. I.Q. tests and assessing competence. *The Humanist,* 1972, *32,* 9–12.

McGurk, F. C. J. Race differences—twenty years later. *Homo,* 1975, *26,* 219–239.

The Negro of today bears the same relationship to the contemporary white as did the Negro of the World War I era to the white at that time. Socioeconomic changes have not resulted in a higher relative intellectual status for the Negro. Summary.

Mercer, J. R. IQ: The lethal lable. *Psychology Today,* 1972 (September) 44–47; 95–97.

Miele, F., & Osborne, R. T. Racial differences in heritability ratios for verbal ability. *Homo,* 1973, *24,* 35–39.

Milkman, R. A simple exposition of Jensen's error. *Journal of Educational Statistics,* 1978, *3*(3), 203–208.

Miller, K. S., & Dreger, R. M. (Eds.) *Comparative studies of blacks and whites in the United States.* New York: Seminar Press, Inc., 1973.

As a comprehensive review of black-white comparisons which successfully avoids the twin traps of propaganda and "value-free objectivity," this volume will constitute a lasting reference work. It will be indispensable to researchers, students, and public servants in the areas of race, race relations, and urban studies, and will also be useful and enlightening to concerned citizens. Summary.

Miller, L. P. (Ed.) *The testing of black students: A symposium.* Englewood Cliffs, NJ: Prentice-Hall, Inc., 1974.

Montagu, A. (Ed.) *Race and IQ.* New York: Oxford University Press, 1975.

Some fourteen reprints of articles which previously appeared in various popular and scientific journals are contained in this book; as well as an introduction by Ashley Montagu who is by profession an anthropologist. We are told on the blurb that he first attacked the term 'race' as a usuable concept over thirty years ago in his classic *Man's Most Dangerous Myth,* and that he here debunks the term 'IQ' and takes on all those—including Arthur Jensen, William Shockley, R. J. Herrnstein and H. J. Eysenck—who claim to have found a link between the two. We are further told that parents, educators, psychologists, lawmakers, and anyone interested in this difficult and controversial subject upon which so much social and political action must be based will find this book of fundamental interest. This is not a view with which I can concur. The assiduous reader will find little here to clarify his understanding of the substantive issues, but much to enlighten him on the ways in which polemics in this field are conducted nowadays. Review by H. J. Eysenck.

Moore, C. L. Racial preference and intelligence. *The Journal of Psychology,* 1978, *100*(1), 39–43.

Moore, R. S. Racism in science and society. *Patterns of Prejudice,* 1975, *9*(6), 5–9.

Moynihan, D. P. Sources of resistance to the Coleman report. *Harvard Educational Review,* 1968, *38*(1), 23–35.

Munsinger, H. A reply to Kamin. *Behavior Genetics,* 1977, *7*(5), 407–409.

Myers, H. F., Rana, P. G., & Harris, M. *Black child development in America 1927–1977: An annotated bibliography.* Westport, Connecticut: Greenwood Press, 1979.

Newby, I. A. *Challenge to the court: Social scientists and the defense of segregation, 1954–1966* (Revised edition). Baton Rouge, Louisiana: Louisiana State University Press, 1969.

This book, a scurrilous work which at no time should have been honored with print, was reviewed by me in NATIONAL REVIEW (Feb. 13, 1968) at the time of its first appearance. Louisiana State University Press has now taken the step of issuing a "revised edition." Actually, the original plates were re-used; the revision consists solely of appended short statements of defense by some of those writers who were victimized by Newby's original charge of "scientific racism"—A. James Gregor, Frank C. J. McGurk, R. T. Osborne, Wesley Critz George, Carleton Putnam, Nathaniel Weyl and Ernest van den Haag. A final reply by Newby closes the present volume. Review in *National Review,* September 9, 1969, *21*(35), 915–917.

Nichols, R. C. Policy implications of the IQ controversy. In L. S. Shulman (Eds.), *Review of research in education* (Vol. 6). Itasca, Illinois: Peacock, 1979.

The IQ controversy appears to be the result of the presumed implications of the heritability of intelligence for the distribution of educational resources. Since the heritability has been demonstrated to be neither 0.0 nor 1.0, the policy implications do not follow directly from the empirical results but depend instead on various political values. Additional research arising out of the controversy suggests that the initial assumption that the distribution of educational resources will have important effects on broader social problems is not correct. Summary.

Nichols, R. C., & Otterbein, C. S. Multivariate analysis of twin data: Some methods and findings. In *Improved Methods for Family Analysis of Educational Data*. Symposium presented at the meeting of the American Educational Research Association, San Francisco, California, April, 11, 1979.

Osborne, R. H. *The biological and social meaning of race*. San Francisco: W. H. Freeman and Company, 1971.

In terms understandable to the layman, thirteen distinguished scientists discuss the current state of knowledge about race. While treating this complex subject within the context of population concepts and the science of genetics, they emphasize social factors. Summary.

Osborne, R. T., & Miele, F. Racial differences in environmental influences on numerical ability as determined by heritability estimates. *Perceptual and Motor Skills*, 1969, *28*, 535–538.

Osborne, R. T. Unequal educational opportunity. *Psychological Reports*, 1973, *33*, 412. (a)

From the tabled results it is clear that in Georgia, school expenditure does not have a notable positive effect on school achievement. On the contrary, the relationship between expenditure per child and achievement is significantly negative. Also negative are the rs between percent non-white population and IQ and achievement. However, the relationship between expenditure per child and non-white population percentage is positive and significant. Summary.

Osborne, R. T. Fertility ratio: Its relationship to mental ability, school achievement, and race. *The Journal of Psychology*, 1973, *84*, 159–164. (b)

Osborne, R. T., Noble, C. E., & Weyl, N. (Eds.) *Human variation: The biopsychology of age, race, and sex*. New York: Academic Press, 1978.

In the spectrum of recent books dealing with race and sex differences, this one, while its chapters vary, on the whole falls clearly toward the hereditarian side. I need not, therefore, waste time peddling it to psychologists of that persuasion—they will doubtless read it in any case, nodding approval as they go. Rather, let me urge the dedicated environmentalists to take a look at it. Some of its chapters won't give them too much trouble, but some ought to shake them up a little. And the shaking up of fixed ideas may well be what is most needed these days in this difficult and controversial area. Review in *Contemporary Psychology*, 1979, *24*(7), 571.

Page, E. B. How we *all* failed in performance contracting. *Educational Psychologist*, 1972, *9*, 40–42. (a)

Page, E. B. Miracle in Milwaukee: Raising the IQ. *Educational Researcher*, 1972, *1*(10), 8–16. (b)

The Milwaukee Project, then, is here viewed as deficient on three counts: biased selection of treatment groups; contamination of criterion tests; and failure to specify the treatments. Any one of these would largely invalidate a study. Together, they destroy it. Further serious questions have emerged about the availability of technical information for the scientific community. Yet the Milwaukee Project may be one of the most widely publicized studies in educational history. Its "results" are known to millions. And it may exert an influence over national policy. Summary.

Peterson Jr., D. A. The effects of sickle-cell disease on black IQ and educational accomplishment: Support for Montagu and "Sociogenic Brain Damage". *American Anthropologist*, 1974, *76*, 39–42.

Portes, A., & Wilson, K. L. Black-white differences in educational attainment. *American Sociological Review*, 1976, *41*, 414–431.

Main and interactive effects of racial differences in educational attainment are examined on the basis of a recent longitudinal sample of the U.S. high school population. Availability of appropriate measures permits comparison between "comprehensive" models of the attainment sequence between blacks and whites. In agreement with past results, it is found that blacks have higher educational attainment than whites of similar parental status and ability. This additive race effect disappears, however, when the full set of intervening variables is considered. Abstract.

Possony, S. T. UNESCO and race: A study in intellectual oppression. *Mankind Quarterly*, 1968, *8*, 115–146.

Prejudice and pride: The Brown decision after twenty-five years May 17, 1954-May 17, 1979. Report from the National Academy of Education.

This report was developed pursuant to a request from Dr. Mary F. Berry, Assistant Secretary for Education, Department of Health, Education, and Welfare. The request to the Academy was to identify distinguished authorities on the sociology, law, and politics of the Brown decision—authorities who would represent an informed spectrum of opinion, and who would serve as Panel Contributors to a thoughtful Academy report commemorating the twenty-fifth anniversary of the Brown decision. Preface.

Racial isolation in the public schools (Vol. 1). A report of the U.S. Commission on Civil Rights. Washington, DC: U.S. Government Printing Office, 1967.

Reed, T. E. Caucasian genes in American Negroes. *Science*, 1969, *165*, 762–767.

Published estimates of the proportion, in American Negroes, of genes which are of Caucasian origin are critically reviewed. The criteria for estimating this proportion (M) are discussed, and it is argued that all estimates published to date have either deficiencies pertaining to the African-gene-frequency data used or statistical inaccuracies, or both. Other sources of error may also exist. Summary

Reschly, D. J. Psychological evidence in the *Larry P.* opinion: A case of right problem—wrong solution. *School Psychology Review*, 1980, *9*(2), 123–135.

Rice, B. Race, intelligence and genetics: The high cost of thinking the unthinkable. *Psychology Today*, 1973, *7*(7), 89–93.

Rist, R. C. (Ed.) *Desegregated schools: Appraisals of an American experiment.* New York: Academic Press, 1979.

Rosenthal, R., & Jacobson, L. *Pygmalion in the classroom.* New York: Holt, Rinehart and Winston, 1968.

In conclusion, then, the indications are that the basic data upon which this structure has been raised are so untrustworthy that any conclusions based upon them must be suspect. The conclusions may be correct, but if so it must be considered a fortunate coincidence. Review by R. L. Thorndike in *American Educational Research Journal,* Vol. 5, No. 4, November 1968, pp. 708–711.

Roslansky, J. D. (Ed.) *Genetics and the future of man.* Amsterdam: North-Holland Publishing Company, 1966.

Rubin, D. B. Burt's tables. *Science,* 1979, *204,* 245–246.

St. John, N. H. De facto segregation and interracial association in high school. *Sociology of Education,* 1964, *37,* 326–344.

Samuda, R. J. Racial discrimination through mental testing: A social critic's point of view. *IRCD Bulletin,* 1973, No. 42, 1–16.

Samuda, R. J. *Psychological testing of American minorities: Issues and consequences.* New York: Dodd, Mead & Company, 1975.

In essence, this book deals more with social justice than with psychometrics. It is intended to signify and delineate in summary form the important ways in which psychological testing can and does impede the parity of American minorities and deny them access to and participation in the goods of the society. Preface by the author.

Sarason, S. B. Jewishness, blackishness, and the nature-nurture controversy. *American Psychologist,* 1973, Vol. 28, 962–971.

This article was an invited address presented at the annual meeting of the American Association of Mental Deficiency, Atlanta, Georgia, May 30, 1973.

Sattler, J. M. *Assessment of children's intelligence.* Philadelphia: W. B. Saunders Company, 1974.

The underlying assumption of the text is that individually administered intelligence tests, such as the Stanford-Binet, the WISC, and the WPPSI, have much more to offer than just an "IQ." It would be a waste of valuable time if the psychologist's only goal were to produce an IQ. There are many well standardized instruments in the field of psychology and education that, under appropriate conditions, provide valid measures of intelligence. However, a thorough analysis of a child's performance on the Stanford-Binet, the WISC, or the WPPSI permits the examiner to gain an understanding of certain cognitive and conative features that no paper-and-pencil, group-administered test can provide. Summary.

Sattler, J. M., & Kuncik, T. M. Ethnicity, socioeconomic status, and pattern of WISC scores as variables that affect psychologists' estimates of "effective intelligence." *Journal of Clinical Psychology,* 1976, *32*(2), 362–366.

Scarr-Salapatek, S. Race, social class, and IQ. *Science,* 1971, *174*(4016), 1285–1295.

Scarr-Salapatek, S. Heritability of IQ by social class: Evidence inconclusive. *Science,* 1973, *182,* 1042–1047.

Schmidt, F. L., Berner, J. G., & Hunter, J. E. Racial differences in validity of employment tests: Reality or illusion? *Journal of Applied Psychology,* 1973, *58*(1), 5–9.

It was concluded that psychologists concerned with the applicability of employment tests to minority groups should direct their future efforts to the study and determination of test fairness rather than to the pseudo-problem of racial differences in test validity. Abstract.

Schoenfeld, W. N. Notes on a bit of psychological nonsense: "Race differences in intelligence." *International Journal of Mental Health,* 1975, *3*(4), 27–45.

When I try to summarize what I have been saying, it all seems to me to reduce to the simple statement that the idea of "race differences in intelligence" is nonsense—nonsense in the framing of the question, nonsense in the populations tested, nonsense in the instrument used, nonsense in the "intelligence" that is postulated. Summary.

Senna, C. (Ed.) *The fallacy of I.Q.* New York: The Third Press, 1973.

The book's title itself is a dead give away to what the reader can expect of the contents. This slim volume presents the efforts of six writers who in various ways pooh-pooh the I.Q. Most of the selections have been previously published separately, but it is probably useful and instructive to see them all together. Review by A. R. Jensen.

Sharp, E. *The IQ cult.* New York: Coward, McCann, & Geoghegan, 1972.

To sum up, IQ tests were oversold in the beginning and capabilities were attributed to them that they never had. For years they held undisputed sway in the schools—an article of faith second only to the Pledge of Allegiance. In the 1960's their power started to wane, and attention has turned to other approaches where, in some cases, experimentation has been quietly going on for a long time. Summary.

Sherwood, J. J., & Nataupsky, M. Predicting the conclusions of Negro-white intelligence research from biographical characteristics of the investigator. *Journal of Personality and Social Psychology,* 1968, *8*(1), 53–58.

Seven biographical items were found to be significant predictors of category of research conclusions: age when research was published; birth order; whether grandparents were American or foreign born; level of mother's education; level of father's education; rural or urban childhood; and undergraduate standing. Summary.

Shockley, W. Models, mathematics, and the moral obligation to diagnose the origin of Negro IQ deficits. *Review of Educational Research,* 1971, *41*(4), 369–377. (a)

Shockley, W. Negro IQ deficit: Failure of a "malicious coincidence" model warrants new research proposals. *Review of Educational Research,* 1971, *41*(3), 227–248. (b)

Shockley, W. Dysgenics, geneticity, raceology: A challenge to the intellectual responsibility of educators. *Phi Delta Kappan,* 1972, 297–307.

Smith, M. S., & Bissell, J. S. Report analysis: The impact of Head Start. *Harvard Educational Review,* 1970, *40*(1), 51–104.

The Westinghouse-Ohio national evaluation of Head Start evoked criticism from both social scientists and statisticians when it was issued last Spring. The authors present a history of Head Start and of the national evaluation. They raise serious questions about the sampling procedures used in the study, and they present the results of a re-analysis which suggest that some full-year Head Start centers were effective, particularly those with black children in urban areas. Policy implications discussed by the authors focus on the relationship between program evaluation and public policy. Summary.

Sowell, T. (Ed.) *Essays and data on American ethnic groups.* Washington, DC: The Urban Institute, 1978.

This volume is one of the products of a study of American ethnic groups that was conducted at The Urban Institute from 1972 to 1975 under the direction of Thomas Sowell. Of the dozen or so groups that were examined, six were selected for special emphasis here: those with black, Chinese, Japanese, Irish, Italian, or Jewish background. While the social and economic evolution of each of these groups is unique, they also hold some characteristics in common: they are all minorities, they share many aspects of the immigrant experience, although only blacks suffered the burden of slavery; and all have faced exceptional barriers and experienced frustration in achieving economic and social mobility. Preface by William Gorham.

Spuhler, J. N. (Ed.) *Genetic diversity and human behavior.* Chicago: Aldine Publishing Company, 1967.

The book first provides descriptions and analyses of behavior that include studies of the proper description of behavioral phenotypes, their classification and appropriate analysis, their inheritance mechanisms and development, and their function, particularly with respect to social organization. Next, polygenic inheritance is treated, and methods that may be used to analyze polygenic systems are discussed, including multivariate analysis and the use of human isolates. Finally, behavior is considered from an evolutionary point of view, by two main classical methods of phylogenic investigations—comparative study of related organisms and the study of prehuman and early human remains by paleontological and archaeological methods—as well as by more modern methods using gene frequencies in populations. Summary.

Stanley, J. C. Predicting college success of the educationally disadvantaged. *Science,* 1971, *171,* 640–647.

Test scores predict the college grades of educationally disadvantaged students at least as well as they do those of the advantaged. High school grades considerably augment the prediction for both groups. Regardless of socioeconomic level, students who are predicted to earn quite low grades within a particular college will tend to have academic difficulties if enrolled in it. Summary.

Starr, B. J., Greenberger, E., Seidler, A. J., Marini, M. M., Sorensen, A. B., Campbell, P., & O'Connor, J. *Black-white differences in psychosocial maturity.* The Johns Hopkins University Center for Social Organization of Schools: March, 1972, Report No. 127.

Stephan, W. G. School desegregation: An evaluation of predictions made in Brown v. Board of Education. *Psychological Bulletin,* 1978, *85*(2), 217–238.

Hypotheses concerning the effects of desegregation on prejudice, self-esteem, and achievement were derived from testimony given by social scientists in *Brown v. Board of Education.* On the basis of a review of the evidence concerning these hypotheses, it is tentatively concluded that (a) desegregation generally does not reduce the prejudices of whites toward blacks, (b) the self-esteem of blacks rarely increases in desegregated schools, (c) the achievement level of blacks sometimes increases and rarely decreases in desegregated schools, and (d) desegregation leads to increases in black prejudice toward whites about as frequently as it leads to decreases. These conclusions should be regarded as tentative because (a) most of the studies have investigated only the short-term effects of desegregation, (b) the extent and type of desegregation varied greatly from study to study, (c) the studies were done in different regions with children who differed in age, (d) the studies often employed noncomparable measures of each variable, and (e) social class and IQ were typically not included as control variables. Abstract.

Sternberg, R. J., & Detterman, D. K. (Eds.) *Human Intelligence: Perspectives on its theory and measurement.* Norwood, NJ: Ablex, 1979.

Stigler, S. M. Burt's tables. *Science,* 1979, *204,* 242–245.

Stinchcombe, A. L. Environment: The cumulation of events. *Harvard Educational Review,* 1969, *39*(3), 511–522.

Tavris, C. After the baby boom . . . The end of the IQ slump. *Psychology Today,* 1976 (April), 69–74.

The brightest and best of our students have shown an average drop in SAT scores over the last 12 years. Educators blame television, permissiveness and each other's teaching methods. Now, a meticulous researcher predicts that the IQ slump will be over around 1980, and the IQ boom will be just ahead. The reason: today's low scores are preceded by children born close together in large families. Abstract.

Test scores and family income: A response to charges in the Nader/Nairn report on ETS. Princeton, NJ: Educational Testing Service, February, 1980.

Test use and validity: A response to charges in the Nader/Nairn report on ETS. Princeton, NJ: Educational Testing Service, February, 1980.

Thomas, C. L., & Stanley, J. C. Effectiveness of high school grades for predicting college grades of black students: A review and discussion. *Journal of Educational Measurement,* 1969, *6*(4), 203–215.

Our findings suggest that . . . academic aptitude and achievement-test scores are often (relative to high school grades) better predictors of college grades for blacks than they are for whites. The best forecasts are made, however, when *both* test scores and high school grades are used optimally to predict college grades. Summary.

Tindall, G. On cant, fashion & conformity. *Encounter,* 1977, *48*(6), 66–71.

Tobias, P. V. Brain-size, grey matter and race—Fact or fiction? *American Journal of Physical Anthropology,* 1970, *32,* 3–25.

From my little venture into the study of the brain, I have emerged with the conviction that vast claims have been based on insubstantial evidence. I conclude that there is no acceptable evidence for such structural differences in the brains of these two racial groups; and certainly nothing which provides a satisfactory anatomical basis for explaining any difference in I.Q. or in other mental and performance tests, in temperament or in behaviour. Summary.

Tobias, P. V. I.Q. and the nature-nurture controversy. *Journal of Behavioural Science,* 1974, *2*(1), 5–24.

Vandenberg, S. G. (Ed.) *Progress in human behavior genetics: Recent reports on genetic syndromes, twin studies, and statistical advances.* Baltimore: The Johns Hopkins Press, 1968.

> The papers in this volume represent the full spectrum of activities in human behavior genetics and will be of interest to psychologists, psychiatrists, and geneticists. Summary.

Watley, D. J. Black brainpower: Characteristics of bright black youth. In D. Gottleib (ed.), *Youth in contemporary society.* Beverly Hills, CA: Sage Publications, Inc., 1973.

Wienke, R. Are there racial differences in educability? *Journal of Human Relations,* 1970, *18,* 1190–1203.

> It is disappointing to be unable to make any definitive conclusions with respect to intelligence and test scores. This is an area which deserves the most careful attention. The work presented to this point suggests that intelligence tests no longer have the predictive validity they once had with respect to school achievement. If this is so, and it requires immediate and definitive research, then it will be necessary to re-examine the concept of the intelligence test. Summary.

Willerman, L., & Turner, R. G. (Eds.) *Readings about individual and group differences.* San Francisco: W. H. Freeman and Company, 1979.

Williams, R. L. Abuses and misuses in testing black children. *The Counseling Psychologist,* 1971, *2,* 62–72. (a)

> The single, most salient conclusion is that traditional ability tests do systematically and consistently lead to assigning of improper and false labels on Black children, and consequently to dehumanization and Black intellectual genocide. This conclusion is neither new nor is it surprising. The information has been known for many years. It was not until the Association of Black Psychologists generated some heat in this area by calling a moratorium on the testing of Black people, however, that the *real* issues began to surface. Summary.

Williams, R. L. On black intelligence. *Washington University Magazine,* 1971, *41*(3), 34–37. (b)

> In this article, based on his address presented as part of the University's inaugural series for new professors, Dr. Williams points out that "it is seriously questioned today whether traditional ability tests may serve as valid measures of Black intelligence." Since standard I.Q. tests are "biased in favor of middle class whites," he maintains, appropriate measuring instruments and educational models for Black children must be developed. Abstract.

Williams, R. L. *The BITCH-100: A culture-specific test.* Paper presented at the American Psychological Association, Honolulu, Hawaii, September, 1972.

Wilson, E. O. *Sociobiology: The new synthesis.* Cambridge, MA: The Belknap Press of Harvard University Press, 1975.

> . . . Sociobiology, a new and highly controversial scientific discipline that seeks to establish that social behavior—human as well as animal—has a biological basis. Its most striking tenet: human behavior is geneti-

cally based, the result of millions of years of evolution. Some sociobiologists go so far as to suggest that there may be human genes for such behavior as conformism, homosexuality and spite. Carried to an extreme, sociobiology holds that all forms of life exist solely to serve the purposes of DNA, the coded master molecule that determines the nature of all organisms and is the stuff of genes. Review in *Time*, August 1, 1977, 54–63.

Wilson, E. O. *On human nature.* Cambridge, MA: Harvard University Press, 1978.

Wilson presents a philosophy that cuts across the usual categories of conservative, liberal, or radical thought. In systematically applying the modern theory of natural selection to human society, he arrives at conclusions far removed from the social Darwinist legacy of the last century. Sociobiological theory, he shows, is compatible with a broadly humane and egalitarian outlook. Human diversity is to be treasured, not merely tolerated, he argues. Discrimination against ethnic groups, homosexuals, and women is based on a complete misunderstanding of biological fact. Summary.

Wonderlic, E. F. & Associates, Inc. Wonderlic Personnel Test. *Negro norms: A study of 38,452 job applicants for affirmative action programs.* Northfield, IL: E. F. Wonderlic & Associates, Inc., 1972.

This summary of statistical data is a cooperative research effort to present under current conditions, the standardization of the Wonderlic Personnel Test for Negro Job Applicants. While adding substantially to our knowledge, this project confirms the normal distribution findings of the 1950 study of 36,864 applicants as well as the 1960–61 Performance Norms Study of 53,864 job applicants with a much larger sample utilizing modern computer technology. Summary.

Author Index

Abercrombie, D. H., 179, 185
Aberdeen, F. D., 200
Abramson, T., 31, 170
Adams, H. B., 39
Adams, J., 150
Adesso, V. J., 111
Albright, L. E., 135, 138
Alcorn, C. L., 151
Alexander, T., 7, 24
Ali, F., 5, 9, 27
Allen, H., 183
Allen, M., 5, 10, 19, 27
Alley, G. R., 151
Ames, L. B., 31, 32, 178
Ammons, C. H., 134, 154
Ammons, M. S., 77
Ammons, R. B., 134, 154
Anastasi, A., 51
Anderson, H. E., 152
Anderson, V. E., 70
Angoff, W. H., 100
Applebaum, A. P., 88
Arnoult, J. F., 81
Arnoult, J. R., 200
Arvey, R. D., 130
Asbury, C. A., 32
Atchison, C. O., 109
August, J., 31

Bachman, J. G., 101
Backman, M. E., 101
Baker, E. A., 32
Baratz, S., 182
Barclay, A., 5, 10, 15, 19, 23, 24, 26, 27, 94
Barkley, M. J., 18, 26
Barnebey, N. S., 33, 175
Barr, A. J., 256
Barrett, R. S., 131
Bartlett, D. P., 33
Bartlett, E. J., 167
Basen, J. A., 153
Baughman, E. E., 33
Belden, B. R., 102

Benson, A. L., 110
Bentler, P. M., 13, 26
Berendes, H. W., 70
Berke, N. D., 201
Bernal Jr., E. M., 201
Bienvenu Sr., M. J., 202
Bierbryer, B., 156
Birns, B., 5, 6, 24, 28, 291
Bissell, J. S., 37, 92
Blair, G. E., 202
Blatt, B., 6, 25
Blue, C. M., 153
Bodwell, A., 135
Boehm, V. R., 126, 132, 138
Boney, J. D., 101, 202
Bonner, M. W., 102
Boone, J. A., 111
Borgen, F. H., 111
Bowers, J., 112
Bowers, N. D., 175
Bowles, F. L., 203
Boyd, M., 23, 24, 94
Bradley Jr., N. E., 203
Bradley, R. H., 7, 27
Breland, H. M., 279, 282, 285, 287–289
Bridger, W., 6, 24, 28
Bridgette, R. E., 204
Brodzinsky, D. M., 43
Brooks, G. C., 116
Broughton, E., 5, 10, 19, 27
Brown, F., 66
Burke, B. P., 204
Burks, B. S., 79
Burnes, D. K. S., 205
Burnes, K., 35
Busse, T. V., 7, 24
Butkovich, C., 84
Butler, B. V., 43, 44, 49

Caldwell, B. M., 7, 27
Caldwell, M. B., 35, 36, 156, 161, 162
Cameron, H. K., 112
Campeau, P. L., 21, 22, 26

Cankardas, A., 137
Cardall, C., 102
Carlson, J. S., 42
Carpenter, F. A., 205
Carringer, D., 161, 162, 185
Carroll, I. V., 206
Carver, R. P., 36
Carwise, J. L., 206
Cawley, J. F., 8, 26
Centra, J., 112
Cerbus, G., 36
Chovan, W. L., 8, 24
Christensen, L., 139
Cicirelli, V. G., 36, 37, 92
Cisin, I. H., 50
Clark, B., 5, 10, 19, 27
Clark, D. H., 63
Clark, K., 14, 25
Clark, M., 14, 25
Clarkson, Q. D., 49
Cleary, T. A., 102, 113
Clegg, S. J., 153
Close, B. L., 104
Coffman, W. E., 102
Cohen, J., 159
Cole, M., 167
Cole, N. S., 37
Cole, S., 127
Coleman, J. S., 37, 97
Collins, Sister M. A., 207
Condit, J. E., 140
Conner, C., 127
Cook, C., 152
Cooper, G. D., 39
Cooper, W., 37, 92
Costello, J., 5, 8, 9, 27, 168
Covin, T. M., 11, 27, 41, 153
Crain, R. L., 253
Crandall, V. C., 183
Crown, P. J., 207
Cunningham, M., 162

Daffron, W. C., 130
Dahlstrom, W. G., 33
D'Angelo, R., 9, 21, 24, 27
Darlington, R. B., 41, 98, 292
Daston, P. G., 39
Datta, L., 41
Davis, J., 115, 122
Davis, M., 41
Davis, S. C., 114
Deitz, S., 127
DeNeufville, R., 127

Denmark, F. L., 10, 26
Deutch, J. A., 208
Dickie, J., 9, 27
Diener, R. G., 140
Dill, J. R., 169, 208
Dillon, R., 42
Drane, H. T., 104
Dregor, R. M., 110
Dubin, J. A., 103
Dugan, R. D., 115
Dukes, P. E., 209
Duva, N. A., 209
Dyer, P. J., 171

Eckman, R., 15, 27
Eells, K., 169, 180
Elardo, R., 7, 27
Elliott, D. L., 107
Emanuel, J. M., 210
Emerson, P., 5, 10, 19, 27
Emmons, C. A., 210
Engin, A., 88
Entin, A. D., 105
Epps, E. G., 116
Evans, C. L., 211
Evans, J. W., 36, 92
Ewen, R. B., 131

Fagan, J., 5, 10, 19, 27
Farnham-Diggory, S., 42
Farver, A. S., 116
Fay, W. H., 49
Fifer, G., 63
Figueroa, R. A., 57, 60, 97
Fisher, G., 140
Flanagan, J., 141, 148
Flick, G. L., 10, 24
Footlik, S. W., 155
Ford, S. F., 100
Fowler, W. R., 37
France, K., 175, 181
Frederickson, L. C., 11, 25
Frederikson, J., 58
French, K. S., 43
French, R. L., 131
Frerichs, A. H., 43
Furst, N. F., 48

Gael, S., 124, 128, 129, 132, 138
Garfunkel, F., 6, 25
Garrett, H. E., 129, 263
Gates, M., 172
Gay, C. J., 211

Gay, W. O., 85
Georgi, N. J., 212
Gerstein, A. I., 43
Gesell, A., 130
Gladney, M. B., 117
Goffeney, B., 43, 44, 49
Golden, M., 5, 6, 24, 28, 291
Goldfarb, J., 153
Goldman, R. D., 44
Goldman, S., 136
Goldsmith, A. F., 168
Goldstein, H. S., 44
Goodenough, F., 180
Goodnight, J. H., 256
Gordon, M. E., 130
Gordon, M. T., 44
Gould, L. J., 45, 171, 181
Granger, R., 37, 92
Grant, D. L., 128, 129
Gray, S. W., 22, 23, 41, 45, 46, 292
Green, R. F., 154
Green, R. L., 46
Greene, J. E., 130
Greenwald, A. G., 160
Gregor, A. J., 72–74
Guilford, J. P., 216
Guinagh, B. J., 46
Gutride, M., 7, 24
Guttentag, M., 10, 26

Hagen, J. W., 134
Hall, V. C., 47
Hall, W. S., 167
Halpin, G., 48
Harris, A. J., 48
Harris, G. R., 212
Harris, H., 213
Hartig, L. K., 44
Hartson, J., 162
Hatch, G. L., 11, 27, 41
Hathaway, M. L., 8, 24
Hawkes, T. H., 48
Hays, J. R., 147
Heatly, M. D., 145
Hechinger, F., 279
Heilbrun, A. B., 130
Helwig, J. T., 256
Henchy, T., 183
Henderson, N. B., 43, 44, 49
Hennessy, J. J., 103
Henning, J. J., 142
Herskovitz, F. S., 213
Herzog, E., 50

Hills, J. R., 117, 118
Hilton, T. L., 78, 102
Hirsch, J. G., 107
Hofmann, L. J., 156
Holowinsky, I. Z., 50
Holthouse, N., 37, 92
Horton, C. P., 121
Howell Jr., G. C., 213
Hughes, R. B., 50
Huppertz, J. W., 47
Hutson, B. A. M., 214
Hutton, J. B., 214
Hyde, E. M., 75

Ilardi, R. L., 215
Ilg, F. L., 32, 178
Isaac, B. K., 51
Iscoe, I., 82

Jacklin, C. N., 258
Jackson, A. M., 215
Jackson, J. C., 107
Jacobson, M. D., 60
James, D. H., 216
Jantz, R. K., 95
Jenkins, J. D., 104
Jensen, A. R., 46, 52–59, 107, 131, 132, 136, 138, 141, 158–160, 167, 177, 179, 181, 188, 192, 255, 259
John, V. P., 59
Johnson, D. F., 59
Johnson, G. A., 217
Johnson, J. C., 60
Jones, B., 105, 163
Jones, R. S., 77
Jordan, B. T., 130

Karnes, F. A., 65
Kassinove, H., 104
Katz, I., 116, 182, 183
Katzell, R. A., 131
Kaufman, A. S., 11, 25, 61
Kazelskis, R., 104
Kean, G. G., 217
Kennedy, W. A., 61, 81, 88, 97, 181, 291, 292
Kenny, C. T., 64
Kern, F. E., 152
Kersey, J., 153
King, J. D., 15, 27
Kinnie, E. J., 12, 25
Kirkpatrick, J. J., 131, 138
Klaus, R. A., 22, 23, 41, 45, 46, 292
Klein, E. B., 45

Klein, E. R., 171, 181
Klein, R. S., 218
Klineberg, O., 263
Knight, D., 35, 161, 162
Knowles, R. T., 62
Koenigsknecht, R. A., 16, 20, 27, 180, 185
Koff, R. H., 48
Koppitz, E. M., 66
Kresheck, J. D., 63

Lane, E. A., 118
Laryea, E. B., 218
Laskowitz, D., 142
Lawson, R., 143
Lazar, I., 41, 98
Leahy, A. M., 79
Lesser, G. S., 63
Lessing, E. E., 64
Lessler, K., 50
Leunes, A., 139
Leventhal, D. S., 12, 28
Levi, A., 47
Levi, M., 143, 148
Levin, J. R., 77
Levine, B. L., 219
Levinsohn, J., 249–250
Levinson, B. M., 132
Levinson, F. V. D. K., 219
Levy, R. H., 142
Lewandowski, D. G., 140
Lewis, G., 141, 148
Lewis, L., 249
Lindemann, S. J., 49
Lingle, R. K., 104
Linn, R., 112
Little, W. B., 64
Loeb, J. W., 114
Loehlin, J. C., 65
Lomangino, L., 9, 21, 24, 27
Long, H. B., 144
Long, M. L., 220
Long, P. A., 155
Longstreth, L. E., 86, 119
Lopez, F. M., 132, 138
Lorge, I., 134
Lovinger, R. J., 48
Lowe, J. D., 65
Lowe, W. F., 120
Lunemann, A., 65

Maccoby, E. E., 258
Machock, B. J., 75
Mac Isaac, D. S., 220

Mahard, R. E., 253
Mandler, G., 183
Manning, E. J., 221
Manning, W. H., 280, 288
Marmorale, A. M., 66
Maroney, R. J., 140
Marsh, L. K., 221
Marshall, J. C., 104
Marshall, M. S., 13, 26
Marwit, S., 176, 181, 188
Matarazzo, J. D., 133
Mathis, H., 104
Mathis, H. I., 134
Matzen, S. P., 222
May, W. T., 167
McAdoo, H. A. P., 222
McCandless, B. R., 145
McCarthy, D., 61
McClary, G. O., 223
McClelland, L., 134
McCormick, C. C., 155
McCoy, J. F., 16, 20, 24
McDaniel, E. L., 67
McGurk, F. C. J., 29, 76, 108, 110, 192, 291–293
McIntosh, E. I., 150
McKelpin, J. P., 119
McNamara, J. R., 13, 27
Meeker, M., 67, 169, 180
Mercer, J. R., 83
Merrifield, P. R., 103
Meyers, C. E., 19, 25
Middleton, M. H., 64
Miele, F., 68
Mihal, W. L., 59
Milgram, N. A., 13, 26
Miller, K. S., 110
Miller, L. E., 13, 27
Miller, M. D., 223
Misa, K. F., 224
Mitchell, N. B., 68
Mogel, S., 105
Moore, C. L., 14, 25, 28, 169, 170, 185
Moore, R. P., 249
Moorehead, N. F., 224
Morgan, R. F., 46
Morse, R. J., 69
Moss, A., 6, 24, 28
Moynihan, D. P., 130
Munday, L., 119
Murphy, G. E., 77
Murray, H. W., 41, 98
Murray, M. E., 145

Murray, T., 84
Muzekari, L. H., 69
Myrianthopoulos, N. C., 23, 25, 43

Nalven, F. B., 156
Nataupsky, M., 184
Naylor, A. F., 23, 25
Neal, A. W., 70
Needham, W. E., 225
Neumann, G., 176, 181, 188
Newbrough, J. R., 33, 87
Newcomb, C., 50
Ngissah, P., 105, 163
Nichols, P. L., 70
Nicholson, C. L., 71, 151, 177
Nicolosi, L., 63
Noonan, M. P., 104

Oakland, T. D., 15, 27
O'Leary, B. S., 226
Olivier, K., 15, 26
Olshin, D., 226
Osborne, R. T., 16, 28, 65, 71–74, 97, 192, 280
Osburn, H., 103
Owen, D. R., 32
Ozer, M. N., 13, 26
Oziel, L. J., 36

Pandey, R. E., 120
Parker, H. J., 16, 20, 24
Parks, M., 105, 163
Parry, M., 117
Pascale, P. J., 50
Pavlos, A. J., 74
Peck, R., 44
Peisach, E., 23, 24, 92
Pelosi, J. W., 167, 227
Pentecoste, J. C., 120
Perney, L. R., 75
Perry, A., 116
Perry, C., 19, 24
Persons, W. S., 145
Pfeifer, C., 121
Pfeifer, C. M., 120
Pfeifer Jr., C. M., 227
Phillips, J., 228
Plant, W. T., 20, 25
Pollack, R. H., 68
Porter, A. C., 118, 122
Porterfield, C. L., 13, 27
Powell, L. S., 7, 24
Powers, J. M., 104
Prawat, R. S., 89

Pryzwansky, W. B., 177
Purkey, W., 127

Quay, L. C., 16, 28, 75, 76, 166, 167

Raggio, D. J., 229
Ratusnik, D. L., 16, 20, 27, 180, 185
Raven, J. C., 134
Ream, J. H. III, 146
Reder, S., 167
Ree, M., 7, 24
Reichard, C. L., 176
Reichard, G. L., 89
Reid, W. R., 89, 176
Reinemann, J. O., 146
Reiskind, N., 43
Report of Oakland (Calif.) Public Schools, 1966–
    67 State test results, 71
Resnick, M. B., 229
Resnick, R. J., 105
Retish, P. M., 14, 28, 169, 170, 185
Riccobono, J. A., 249
Rieber, M., 17, 26
Ritchie, R. J., 128, 129
Roach, R. E., 76
Roberts, A., 145
Roberts, B. T., 121
Roberts, J., 77
Roberts, S. O., 121, 182, 183
Robertson, W. J., 230
Robins, L. N., 77
Robinson, J. M., 182, 183
Robinson, L. F., 114
Robison, J. O., 147
Rochester, D. E., 135
Rohwer Jr., W. D., 77, 89
Rosecrans, C. J., 76
Rosenberg, E., 104
Rosenfeld, M., 78
Royce, J. M., 41, 98
Rozynko, V. V., 147
Ruda, E., 135, 138
Runyon, E., 116
Ryan, J. S., 230
Ryan, L. E., 231
Rystrom, R. C., 153

Saccuzzo, D. P., 140
Sall, J. P., 256
Samuel, W., 105, 163–166
Sandy, C. A., 231
Sarason, S. B., 183
Sarbin, T. R., 147

Satz, P., 105
Savage, J. E., 175, 181
Scarr, S., 7, 27, 79
Schaefer, E., 41
Scheinfeld, D. R., 107
Schemmel, D., 37, 92
Schiller, J. S., 36, 92
Schneider, F. W., 79
Schnobrich, J., 155
Scott, R., 17, 18, 25, 26, 80, 81, 162, 166, 185, 292
Seborg, M., 143, 148
Sedlacek, W., 121
Sedlacek, W. E., 116
Seidel, H. E., 18, 26
Seitz, V., 93
Sekyra, F., 81
Semler, I. J., 82
Severson, R. A., 82
Sewell, T. E., 5, 10, 18, 27, 82
Shah, G. B., 62
Sheetz, R., 143
Sherwood, J. J., 184
Shockley, W., 65
Shockley, W. B., 72
Shuey, A. M., 82, 108, 110, 181, 192, 259, 291–293
Sigel, I. E., 19, 24
Silverstein, A. B., 83
Simpson, R. L., 106
Sinclair, D., 18, 26
Sitkei, E. G., 19, 25
Smith, A. L., 147
Smith, H. W., 167
Smith, J. M., 83
Smith, M. S., 37, 92
Smith, T. A., 36, 156
Smith, W. R. B., 232
Snider, B., 151
Snipper, A. S., 41, 98
Solkoff, N., 83, 173–175, 181, 185
Solomon, D., 84, 107
Soltz, W. H., 233
Solway, K. S., 147
Soto, D., 105, 163
Southern, M. L., 20, 25
Stanley, J. C., 118, 122
Starkman, S., 84
Starnes, T. A., 233
Stedman, D. J., 12, 28
Stephenson, B. L., 85
Sternberg, R. I., 234
Sternlof, R. E., 12, 16, 20, 24, 25

Stith, D., 18, 26
Strauch, A. B., 234
Suddick, D. E., 72, 74
Summerford, J. D., 235
Suzuki, N., 77
Sweet, R. C., 236

Takacs, C. P., 237
Talmadge, G. K., 21, 22, 26
Tanner, P., 143
Tate, D. T., 238
Tatham, C. B., 122
Tatham, E. L., 122
Taylor, D. R., 238
Temp, G., 115, 122
Thorndike, R. A., 134
Thorne, J. H., 239
Thumin, F., 136
Tillery, W. L., 239
Torrance, E. P., 48
Trotman, F. K., 85, 86, 97, 240
Trudeau, P., 104
Tufano, L. G., 240
Tulkin, S. R., 33, 86, 87
Turner, C., 169, 170, 185
Tyler, L. E., 259

Uhl, N. P., 177
Umberger, D. L., 130

Vance, H., 88
Vandenberg, S. G., 65, 72
Van De Riet, V., 61, 81, 88, 292
Vane, J. R., 88
Vega, M., 181, 241
Veldman, D. J., 145
Vergason, G. A., 153

Waites, L., 145
Walsh, J., 9, 27
Walsh, J. F., 21, 24
Warden, P. G., 89
Wargo, M. J., 21, 22, 26, 291
Warner, W., 169, 180
Weade, B. L., 150
Weaver, A., 22, 24
Weaver, S. J., 22, 24
Wechsler, D., 134
Weinberg, R., 7, 27
Weinberg, R. A., 79
Weitzman, J., 88
Wellborn, E. S., 89, 176
Wenk, E. A., 147

Westinghouse Learning Corporation, Ohio
    University, 1969., 37, 90
Whipple, D. W., 241
White, J. C., 61, 81, 88, 292
White, L. A., 15, 27
White, W. F., 153
Whiteman, M., 23, 24, 92
Wiens, A. N., 133
Wild, C. L., 109, 122
Wilkerson, D., 139
Willard, L. S., 92
Willerman, L., 23, 25
Williams, D. E., 242
Williams, R., 127
Wilson, A. B., 107
Wilson, C. S., 161, 162, 185
Wines, A. M., 104
Winick, D. M., 103
Winokur, D. J., 243
Winter, G. D., 243
Wirth, C., 143

Wolf, R., 85
Wolfe, B. E., 244
Wolff, J. L., 86
Womack, M., 17, 26
Woodall, F. E., 245
Worthington, C. F., 245
Wyatt, M. A., 246
Wysocki, A. C., 136
Wysocki, B. A., 136, 137

Yando, R., 93, 172
Yater, A., 5, 10, 19, 27
Yater, A. C., 23, 24, 94
Yates, L. G., 246
Yawkey, T. D., 95
Yen, S. M. Y., 247
Yerkes, R. M., 108, 263, 276, 291–293
York, M. W., 39

Zagarow, H. W., 248
Zigler, E., 93, 172

Subject Index

A

ABC Inventory to Determine Kindergarten and School Readiness, 219

Academic achievement
in children from intact and broken families, 207
with educational ability held constant, 212
as effected by
integration, 211
race, 218–219
segregation, 218, 230
factorial nature of, 84
as a function of self-concept, 211–212
interaction of with personality and IQ, 246
of Negro college students, 217
of Negroes in predominately white schools, 233–234
nonintellectual correlates of, 112
normative study of Negro, 61–62
prediction of, 82–83, 101–102, 111–112, 116–117, 203–204, 248
relationship of to
anxiety, 48–49
cognitive development and IQ, 84–85
ego functions, 202
mental abilities, 223–224
race, 77
self-concept, 212, 232
self-esteem, 43
socio-economic status and intelligence, 238
sociological factors related to, 32

Academic growth, comparison of in Negro and white colleges, 112–113

Academic Promise Tests, 92, 93

Achievement motivation, 241–242

Adopted blacks, effects of white families on, 79

Adults not in college, 126–138

Afro-American children, validity of WISC for, 105

Age, effects of on "True IQ," 156

American College Test, 109, 114, 115, 119, 120, 125, 198, 203, 204, 217, 238, 255, 256, 259, 261, 264, 269, 271, 293

American Council on Education Psychological Examination, 109, 110

American Negro, characteristics of, 263

Ammons Full-Range Picture Vocabulary Test, 39

Anxiety
effects of integration on, 202
relationship of to
achievement, socio-economic status, IQ, and race, 48–49
intellectual and non-intellectual factors, 109

Aptitude, as related to environmental factors, 134

Arithmetic achievement
effects of intelligence, race, SES, and sex on, 95
prediction of for white and non-white children, 49

Armed Forces Qualifications Test, 127, 128, 137, 138, 294

Army Alpha, 143, 144, 148, 263, 264

Army Beta, 39, 263

Army General Classification Test, 143, 263

Arrow-Dot Test, 155, 156

Attitudes
moral, 213
toward education, 206–207

Aural Aptitude Test, 36

B

Bayley Scales of Infant Development, 43, 44, 229, 230

Bell System Qualification Test I, 137, 294

Bender-Gestalt Test, 13, 27, 36, 43, 44, 49, 51, 66, 96, 219

Benton Visual Retention Scale, 151

Bias in testing, 55, 62–63, 68, 94–95, 102–103, 113–114, 115

Black Intelligence Test, 109, 111, 125

Black Intelligence Test of Cultural Homogeneity, 133, 134, 137, 155, 294

Block design performance, as a function of hue and race, 68–69

Blood group genes and ability differences, 65

Blood, "white," correlation between IQ and amount of, 154

Boehm Test of Basic Concepts, 236, 237

Brain damage, effects of in Progressive Matrices, 152–153

C

California Achievement Tests, 62, 84, 130, 143

California Capacity Questionnaire, 144

California Reading Test, 176

California Short-Form Test of Mental Maturity, 205, 206, 211

California Test of Mental Maturity, 35, 48, 56, 67, 68, 69, 71, 80, 84, 96, 102, 161, 202, 203, 217, 222, 233, 241

Cattell Culture Fair Intelligence Test, 48, 92, 93, 147, 168, 202, 210, 224, 227, 230

Cattell Infant Intelligence Scale, 6, 21, 22

Chicago Non-Verbal Examination, 18, 46

Clark's Doll Test, 14

Cognitive abilities of black children, 88

Cognitive Abilities Test, 72, 119

Cognitive capacity, racial differences in, 43

Cognitive development
  effects of Head Start on, 90–91
  of preschool children, 7–8
  relationship of to academic achievement and IQ, 84–85
  and social class, 5–6
  social class differentiation in, 6

Cognitive functioning, effects of examiner's race on, 177

Cognitive performance, effects of race of comparison referent upon, 116

Cognitive synthesis, racial differences in, 42–43

College admissions, 277–289

College freshmen, intellectual characteristics of, 119

College grades, prediction of, 117–118

College graduates, black, 118–119

College students, 109–125, 225
  intellectual, personality, and biographical characteristics of, 225

College success, relationship of to scholastic aptitude, 118, 120

Columbia Mental Maturity Scale, 16, 20, 21, 24, 27, 81, 82

Comprehensive Tests of Basic Skills, 144

Computerized testing, 59–60, 213–214

Concept formation, effects of verbal reinforcement and color of examiner on, 243

Concept learning, 201–202

Conforming behavior, racial differences in, 79–80

Conforming judgment, relationship to personal and social variables, 144–145

Conservation, Piaget's Principle of, 23, 92

Convergent and divergent thinking by SES and race, 89

Cooperative Reading Comprehension Test, 112

Creative thinking abilities of blind children, 48

Creativity
  definitions of, 104
  of disadvantaged children, 244
  relationship of
    to intelligence, 104, 204–205
    to self-concept, 204–205

Cultural differences
  in the measurement of intelligence, 8
  in WB II test scores, 136–137

Culturally deprived children
  conceptual and verbal development of, 60–61
  echoic responses of, 153
  psycholinguistic abilities of, 22–23
  psycholinguistic diversity among, 19

Culture-specific test, measurement of mental retardation by, 155

Cumulative deficit in IQ, 53, 56–57

D

Davis-Eells Test of General Intelligence, 201

Deaf children, assessment of intelligence of, see also Hearing loss, 153

Delinquents, 139–149
  comparison of intelligence test scores for, 147
  efficiency of PPVT in estimating WISC scores of, 140
  ethnic group differences in, 145–146
  intelligence test score patterns of, 245–246
  Negro and white, 219
  Verbal-Performance IQ differences of, 142

Desegregation,
  adjustment to, 200
  correctional validity of IQ as a function of, 65–66
  effects of on self-concept, 216–217

Detroit Tests of Learning Aptitude, 8

Developmental scores, racial and sex differences in, 43–44

Deviation Social Quotient, 150

Dialect
  effects of
    on IQ scores, 75–76
    on story recall, 167
  as related to intelligence test performance, 166
  use of in administering tests, 16, 207–208
Differential Aptitude Tests, 45, 102, 107, 108, 132, 171, 172
Digit span, interaction with IQ and race, 57–58
Digit Span Test, 47, 134, 157
Digit-symbol performance
  effects of race of examiner on, 168, 182
  effects of sex of examiner on, 168
Disadvantaged children, 43, 45–46
  basic concepts of, 235–236
  cognitive development of, 20
  comparison of culture fair test scores with other test scores, 92–93
  comparison of two intelligence tests with, 239–240
  conservation and comprehension of syntax in, 214
  determinants of school behavior of, 6–7
  effects of
    dialects on IQ scores of, 75–76
    examiner characteristics on test performance of, 8–9
    test taking experience simulation on scores of, 229
  impact of kindergarten programs on creative performance of, 244
  intelligence and reading achievement of, 221
  intelligence test performance of, 23, 65
  IQ constancy of, 13
  IQ increases of, 13
  IQs of, 9
  language ability and intellectual and behavioral functioning in, 229–230
  pattern analysis of WISC scores of, 37
  performance of, 37
  programs for educating, 21–22
  reinforcement and intelligence test performance in, 76
  reliability and validity of PPVT scores of, 9
  self-concepts of, 213
  sociological characteristics of, 107
  use of dialect with, 16
  vocational rehabilitation of, 130–131
Divergent and convergent thinking by SES and race, 89
Drawing A Man, 13, 15, 16, 20, 21, 26, 27, 49, 62, 69, 70, 77, 221, 222, 247, 248

Drawings, measurement of intelligence by, 180
Drug addicts
  intellectual ability and scholastic achievement of, 143–144

E

Educational difficulties, psychological evaluation for, 50
Educational opportunity, equality of, 37–39
Educational Quality Assessment, 235
Edwards Social Desirability Scale, 171
Ego functions, relationship to academic achievement, 202
Employee Aptitude Survey, 103
Employment opportunity, 115–116
Employment testing, 131–132
  validity of, 126, 128–129
EMR boys, effect of reinforcement on IQ scores of, 240–241
English, standard and non-standard, 176–177
Environment, effects of on human development, 101
Environmental factors as related to race and aptitude, 134
Environmental Participation Index, 104, 134
Ethnic backgrounds
  differential selection among applicants from, 131–132
  in mentally retarded children, 150–151
Ethnic differences, see also race differences
  in cognitive profiles, 18
  in competence, 42
  in delinquent boys, 145–146
  in factor structure of WISC, 83
  in intellectual and personality characteristics, 93–94
  in intelligence of preschool children, 17
  in mental ability and achievement, 103
  in patterns of mental abilities, 101
  in relationship
    between total and partial IQ's, 234
    of mental abilities to achievement, 223–224
  in structure of intellect, 19–20, 103
  in task performance, 226
Ethnicity
  correctional validity of IQ as a function of, 65–66
  relationship of to school achievement, intelligence, and socioeconomic status, 239
  and scholastic achievement, 54–55
Ethnic-social class, relationship of to intelligence and achievement motivation, 241–242
Examiners, differences among, 167

Examiner's race, 14, 54, 158–188
    effects of on
        anxiety, 182–183
        attitude, 45
        children's learning, 169
        cognitive functioning, 177
        creativity, 208–209
        learning, 183–184
        observed IQ, 165
        shifts in concept formation, 243
        story recall, 167
        test attainments, 162–163
        test performance, 8–9, 14–15, 31, 33, 35–
            36, 54, 83–84, 90–91, 161–162, 168,
            175–176, 179–182, 207–208, 209, 227,
            228–229, 241
    as a function of children's performance, 179–
        180, 241
    as related to
        intelligence test scores, 83–84
        performance on a simple operant task, 228–
            229
Examiner's sex, effects of on
    digit-symbol performance, 168
    performance on a simple operant task, 228–
        229

F

Factor structure of WISC, 16, 71, 83
Factor structures of mental abilities, 103
Family disorganization and intelligence, 215
Father-present, father-absent boys, performance
    of, 228–229
Fertility, relationship of IQ and school achieve-
    ment to, 72
Figure Copying Test, 52, 54, 178, 179
French's Wide Range Arithmetic Test, 226
French's Wide Range Vocabulary Test, 226

G

General Aptitude Test Battery, 101, 134, 141,
    143, 147, 148
Gesell Developmental Schedules, 208
Goodenough Drawing Test, 180
Goodenough-Harris Drawing Test, 231
Graduate Record Examination Aptitude Test,
    109, 112, 113, 121, 122, 123, 125, 293
Guilford-Martin Personnel Inventory, 136
Guilford's Five Tests of Divergent-Convergent
    Thinking, 89, 216
Guilford-Zimmerman Aptitude Survey, 120,
    225

H

Head Start Children, 7–8, 20–21
    IQ's of, 9–10
    performance of Puerto Rican and Negro, 21
    prediction of first grade success of, 214–
        215
    reading achievement of, 205–206
    test performance of, 15–16
Head Start Programs, 5–18, 20–21, 25–26, 210
    effects of on children's cognitive and affective
        development, 90–91
    evaluation of, 17, 18
    impact of, 36–37
    and later school competence, 41
Hearing loss, intelligence test performance of
    children with, see also Deaf children, 76
Henmon-Nelson Test of Mental Ability, 85, 199,
    221, 238
Heritability of mental test performance, race and
    sex differences in, 72–73
Heritability of spatial ability, race differences in,
    73–74
Heroin addicts, intelligence test performance of,
    142–143
High school students, 100–108
Hispanic children, reading achievement and self-
    esteem of, 221–222
Home stability as related to intelligence, 64–
    65
Homeless men
    comparison of Negro and white, 217–218
    regional differences in, 132
Hunter College Aptitude Scale for Gifted Chil-
    dren, 63

I

Illinois Test of Psycholinguistic Abilities, 7, 8,
    9, 12, 13, 19, 20, 22, 23, 28, 29, 37, 45,
    46, 49, 85, 90, 91, 92, 98, 152, 167, 191,
    200, 239
Illiteracy, adult Negro, 135, 201
Incentives, effects of upon aptitude scores, 147–
    148
Inmates, 139–140, 147–148
Intact and broken families, school related varia-
    bles in children from, 207
Integration, effects of on
    black college attendance, 253
    intellectual development, 238–239
    intelligence test scores, 224–225

racial attitude, academic progress and self-concept, 211
self-concept and anxiety, 202
Intellect, ethnic differences in structure of, 19–20
Intellectual ability
  of college students, 225
  of drug addicts, 143–144
  of patients on a Negro admission ward, 127
  by social class and ethnic group, 93–94
Intellectual development
  of children from interracial matings, 23
  effect of integration on, 238–239
  relationship of to socio-economic factors, 76–77
  of slum children, 59
Intellectual measurement of preschool children, 247–248
Intellectual performance, as related to race and SES, 70–71
Intellectual structure of southern Negroes, 36
Intellectually superior black children, identification of, 230–231
Intelligence
  of children from intact and broken families, 207
  of disadvantaged students, 221
  effects of on arithmetic achievement, 95
  and family disorganization, 215
  as a function of self-concept, 211–212
  in low SES children, 46–47
  measurement of by drawings, 180
  normative study of Negro, 61–62
  of offenders, 146
  of pregnant indigent adolescents, 153–154
  racial differences in, 243–244
  and racial preference, 14
  as related to perceptual-motor development, 51
  relationship of to
    achievement and socio-economic status, 238
    creativity, 104, 204–205
    ethnic-social class and achievement motivation, 241–242
    non-intellective factors, 205
    race and social class, 226–227
    self-concept, 204–205, 212
  and selective migration, 263
  structure of, 82
  of whites and Negroes, 129–130
Intelligence test performance
  changes in of special education students, 203
  of children with hearing loss, 76

of disadvantaged children, 75–76, 92–93
effects of
  examiner's race on, 90–91
  integration on, 224–225
  as a function of feedback or monetary reinforcement, 236–237
  as related to language dialect, 166
  relationship of to
    school achievement, socio-economic status, and ethnicity, 239
    social adaptability, 245
Interaction and compensatory education, 10, 97–99
Inter-American Test of General Ability: Picture Vocabulary, 37, 38
Interracial matings, intellectual development of children from, 23
Iowa Test of Pre-school Development, 18, 162, 163
Iowa Tests of Basic Skills, 72, 81, 87, 95, 241
IQ
  boosting, 141
  changes in northern children, 80
  constancy in disadvantaged children, 13
  correlation of with amount of "white" blood, 154
  effects of
    non-intellective factors on, 12
    race of examiner on, 165
    reinforcement on, 240–241
  and family size, 71–72
  interaction of with
    achievement and personality traits, 246
    race and digit span, 57–58
  as a predictor of academic progress, 82–83
  relationship of to
    anxiety, 48–49
    cognitive development and academic achievement, 84–85
    fertility and school achievement, 72
    race, 85–86, 105–106
    self-concept, 67
    social class, 105–106
  scores
    of children of educators and non-educators, 206
    of women drug addicts, 143
  stability of, 34, 48
  Verbal-Performance differences, 142
IQ-achievement gap, 44–45

J

Jensen's hypothesis, a test of, 58–59

Job applicants, test performance of, 132–133, 136
Jr.-Sr. High School Personality Questionnaire, 202
Junior Eysenck Personality Inventory, 54

K

Kahn Intelligence Test, 8, 146
Kindergarten attendance, effects of on IQ, 34–35
Kuhlmann-Anderson Intelligence Tests, 48, 75, 80, 118, 156, 211
Kuhlmann-Finch Tests, 151

L

Lead poisoning
    effects of on psychoneurological functioning, 209–210
    functioning of children with, 220
Learning ability in low SES children, 46–47
Leiter Adult Intelligence Scale, 201
Leiter International Performance Scale, 9, 10, 27, 153, 229, 231
Letters Sets Test, 201
Lincoln-Oseretsky Motor Development Scale, 151, 152
Listening-Attention Test, 54, 178, 179
Lorge-Thorndike Intelligence Tests, 33, 48, 52, 53, 54, 56, 59, 65, 66, 71, 84, 87, 88, 95, 96, 104, 134, 169, 178, 179, 200, 209, 212, 218, 219, 223, 241, 246, 292
Low achievers, IQ's of, 41

M

Marianne Frostig Developmental Test of Visual Perception, 151
Marlowe-Crown Social Desirability Scale, 141, 171, 183
Mathematics training, racial differences in impact of, 130
McCarthy General Cognitive Indexes, 61
McCarthy Scales of Children's Abilities, 61, 220
Memory for Numbers, 52, 56, 178, 179
Mental ability
    and blood type genes, 74
    differences and blood group genes, 65
    interaction of
        with race and sex, 234–235
        with race and socio-economic status, 55–56
    racial differences in, 237–238
    as related to self-concept, 242–243

relationship of to achievement, 223–224
    by social class and culture group, 63–64
Mental defectives, racial differences in intelligence of, 156–157
Mental retardates, perceptual motor performance of, 151–152
Mental retardation, measurement of by a culture-specific test, 155
Mental test scores
    effects of race of examiner on, 54
    relationship of to social status and home environment, 7
Mentally retarded children, 150–151
    classification of, 39, 41
    race and sex differences in IQ of, 106–107
Merrill-Palmer Developmental Test, 237
Metropolitan Achievement Tests, 85, 91, 202, 221, 228, 240
Metropolitan Readiness Test, 91, 92, 211
Metropolitan Reading Readiness Test, 17, 205, 223
Mexican-Americans
    concept learning among, 201–202
    strategies for assessing intellectual patterns in, 67–68
Michigan M-Scales, 112
Migration and Negro intelligence, 263

N

National College Freshman Testing, 110
National longitudinal study, 249–276
National Longitudinal Study Test Battery, 254, 258, 259, 261, 264, 265, 269, 271
National Merit Scholarship Qualifying Test, 111, 112
National Teacher Examinations, 38, 109, 110, 111, 130
Nature-nurture controversy, 11
Non-intellective factors, relationship of to measured intelligence, 205
Non-intellectual correlates of academic achievement, 112

O

Occupational preferences, cognitive, personality, and familial correlates of, 224
Offenders, intelligence of, 146
Otis Alpha, 48
Otis Gamma Tests of Mental Abilities, 216, 230
Otis-Lennon Mental Ability Test, 85, 198, 238, 240
Otis Quick-Scoring Mental Ability Test, 139, 140, 204, 212, 216, 218, 228

Otis Quick-Scoring Mental Ability Test, Beta Test, 48, 211, 216, 224

P

Paternal deprivation, effects of upon Negro boys, 208
Peabody Picture Vocabulary Test, 5, 7, 8, 9, 11, 13, 14, 17, 19, 21, 22, 26, 27, 29, 31, 32, 33, 45, 46, 47, 48, 50, 51, 55, 59, 60, 61, 63, 70, 78, 85, 95, 102, 140, 153, 168, 170, 171, 172, 173, 175, 176, 188, 190, 219, 220, 222, 223, 229, 247, 248, 291
Perceptual development of preschool children, 7–8
Perceptual motor performance of mental retardates, 151–152
Perceptual motor training, effects of upon readiness skills, 210–211
Personality
  characteristics
    of college students, 225
    racial differences in, 243–244
  of children from intact and broken families, 207
  correlates of occupational preferences, 224
  measures, prediction of intellectual performance from, 6
  Negro-white differences in integrated classrooms, 32–33
  traits, interaction of with achievement and IQ, 246
Personality Assessment System, 233
Personality Rating Scale, 6
Pictorial stimuli, cognitive and affective responses to, 223
Pictorial Test of Intelligence, 196, 239, 240
Picture Order Test, 134
Pintner-Cunningham Primary Test, 48, 231
Pintner General Abilities Test, 48, 207
Police applicants, intelligence test scores of, 133–134
Porteus Maze Test, 10, 39
Prediction
  of academic achievement, 44, 101–102, 122, 248
  of college success, 113–114, 117–118, 119–120, 121, 227–228
  of high school achievement, 107
  of intellectual performance, 6
  of Negro-white intelligence research, 184
Preliminary Scholastic Aptitude Test, 100, 101, 102, 103
Preschool children, 5–30

Preschool enrichment programs, 80–81
Preschool experience, influence of on ability scores, 220
Preschool programs, impact of on creativity, 244
Primary Mental Abilities, 32, 34, 35, 73, 80, 81, 96, 198, 211, 213, 214, 246
Programmer Aptitude Test, 109, 116
Project Talent Test of Cognitive Ability, 235
Psycholinguistic abilities, 200–201
  differences among culturally deprived children, 19, 22–23
  by socio-economic status, 85
Psychoneurological functioning, effects of lead poisoning on, 209–210
Puerto Rican children, performance of, 21, 61–62
Purdue Pegboard, 168
Purdue Perceptual-Motor Survey, 151

Q

Quick Test, 71, 101, 120, 134, 140, 154

R

Race
  analysis of Raven Progressive Matrices by, 33
  block design performance as a function of, 68–69
  effects of
    on ability scores, 220, 231–232
    on arithmetic achievement, 95
    on creative thinking abilities, 48
    on Progressive Matrices scores, 152–153
    on self-concept and achievement, 218–219
    on story recall, 167
    on "True IQ," 156
  interaction with
    interviewer and respondent, 134–135
    IQ and digit span, 57–58
    mental abilities and socio-economic status, 55–56
    sex and ability, 234–235
  relationship of to
    anxiety, 48–49
    environmental factors, 134
    intelligence, 70, 71, 85–86, 105–106, 226–227
    motivation, 105–106
    perceptual-motor development, 51
    reading achievement, 17, 226–227
    scholastic achievement, 77, 222
    social class, 17, 105–106
    socio-economic status, 70–71

Race differences, *see also* ethnic differences
  in ability as related to blood group genes, 65
  in Bender-Gestalt performance, 61–62
  in black intelligence test scores, 111
  in characteristics of teachers, 130
  in cognitive capacity, 43
  in cognitive development of disadvantaged children, 20
  in cognitive synthesis, 42–43
  in college students, 114–115, 119, 120
  in computerized testing, 59–60
  in conforming behavior, 79–80
  in convergent and divergent thinking, 89
  in correlation of scholastic apptitude test scores with college grades, 118
  in delinquents, 219
  in developmental scores, 43–44
  in educational growth and aptitude, 78–79
  in the effects of speed and practice on performance, 103
  in the effects of test conditions, 171
  in ego function relevant to academic achievement, 64
  in heritability of mental test performance, 72–73
  in heritability of spatial ability, 73–74
  in homeless men, 217–218
  in impact of mathematics training, 130
  in intellectual ability and achievement of drug addicts, 143–144
  in intellectual assessment, 81–82
  in intelligence test scores, 11, 61, 63, 69–70, 75, 86–87, 88–89, 96, 99, 129–130, 246–247
    and achievement, 231
    of mental defectives, 156–157
    and personality, 243–244
    of rural children, 50–51
  in learning abilities, 82
  in mental abilities, 33–34, 52–53, 237–238
  in MMPI and PAS scores, 233
  in perceptual motor performance, 151–152
  in performance as a function of race of examiner, 179–180
  in personality, 32–33
  in prediction of college success, 227–228
  on Raven Progressive Matrices, 87–88
  in reasoning ability, 215–216
  in Rorschach responses, 31–32
  on selection instruments, 135
  in social desirability, 140–141
  in structure of intelligence, 82
  in students in a vocational rehabilitation program, 243–244
  in teacher expectation, 127
  in test performance of job applicants, 136
  in test scores of teachers, 110–111
  in validity of employment and training selection, 126
  in validity of SAT, 115
  in WISC scores, 35
  in WPPSI scores, 11–12
Race of examiner, *see* Examiner's race
Race-item interaction on scholastic aptitude, 100–101
Racial attitudes
  effects of integration on, 211
  effects of on performance, 209
  of preschool children, 222–223
Racial preference and intelligence, 14
Raven's Coloured Progressive Matrices, 18, 47, 48, 52, 55, 78, 82, 152
Raven's Progressive Matrices, 13, 27, 33, 47, 52, 54, 87, 88, 96, 101, 134, 143, 144, 151
Readiness skills, 210–211
Reading Achievement
  of adult Negro illiterates, 201
  cognitive correlates of, 32
  comparison of Head Start and Non-Head Start children, 205–206
  of disadvantaged students, 221
  of lower-class children, 221–222
  prediction of, 49–50
  relationship to race and social class, 226–227
Reasoning ability, race difference in, 215–216
Reinforcement
  effects of on IQ scores of EMR boys, 240–241
  effects of on shifts in concept formation, 243
Reliability and validity, 96–97
Revised Beta Examination, 135, 137, 143, 219
Rystrom Dialect Test, 153

S

Sarason Test Anxiety Scale, 83, 173
SAS, user's guide to, 256
Scholastic achievement
  of drug addicts, 143–144
  and ethnicity, 54–55, 239
  relationship of to
    fertility, 72
    IQ, 72, 239
    racial composition, 222
    self-concept, 69
    socio-economic status, 239

Scholastic aptitude
  item-race interaction, 100–101
  relationship of to college success, 118, 120
Scholastic Aptitude Test, 102, 109, 112, 113, 114,
    115, 117, 118, 119, 120, 121, 122, 125, 198,
    217, 227, 228, 232, 248, 255, 256, 258, 259,
    261, 264, 271, 293, 296
School and College Ability Tests, 36, 37, 59,
    60, 78, 79, 96, 112, 118
School children, 31–99
School problems of Negro boys, 77
Screening Test of Academic Readiness, 214
Segregation, effects of, 32, 102, 113, 200, 202,
    204–205, 211, 216, 218, 222, 224–225, 230,
    233–234, 238–239
Self-concepts
  of ability and school achievement, 69
  in a low-income population, 67
  of preschool children, 222–223
  as related to
    academic achievement, 211–212, 232
    creativity, 204–205
    desegregation, 216–217
    educational-vocational rehabilitation, 213
    integration, 202, 211
    intelligence, 204–205, 212, 242–243
    performance, 209
    race, 218–219
Self-esteem
  of lower class children, 221–222
  relationship of to school success, 43
  of southern adolescents, 204
Sequential Tests of Educational Progress, 36, 78,
    79, 191, 203
Sex
  analysis of Raven Progressive Matrices by, 33
  effects of on
    ability scores, 220
    arithmetic achievement, 95
    creative thinking abilities, 48
    performance, 161–162
    Progressive Matrices scores, 152–153
    test responses, 70, 227, 231–232
    "True IQ," 156
  interaction with race and ability, 234–235
Sex differences
  in heritability of mental test performance, 72–
    73
  in high risk and high potential pupils, 219–
    220
  in illiterate and indigent Negroes, 135
  in intelligence test scores, 64–65, 74–75
  in patterns of mental abilities, 101

the psychology of, 258
  on Raven Progressive Matrices, 87–88
Shah's Nonverbal Group Test, 62, 63
Short Employment Tests, 136
Slosson Intelligence Test, 31, 32, 151, 177, 214
Slum children, intellectual development of, 59
Social adaptability, 245
Social class
  in America, 169
  analysis of Raven Progressive Matrices by, 33
  relationship of to
    intelligence test scores, 105–106, 226–227
    motivation, 105–106
    race, 17, 105–106
    reading achievement, 226–227
    reading readiness, 17
Social class differences
  in cognitive development, 5–6
  in intellectual characteristics, 93–94
  in mental abilities, 63–64
  in personality characteristics, 93–94
  on Raven Progressive Matrices, 87–88
Social desirability, as a function of crime and
    race, 140–141
Socio-economic status
  achievement by, 47–48
  differences
    in patterns of mental abilities, 101
    in a preschool program, 50
  differential selection among applicants, 131–
    132
  effects of on
    arithmetic achievement, 95
    high risk and high potential pupils, 219–
      220
    performance, 161–162
    test scores, 231–232
    "True IQ," 156
  interaction of with mental abilities and race,
    55–56
  psycholinguistic abilities by, 85
  relationship of to
    achievement, 238, 239
    anxiety, 48–49
    convergent and divergent thinking, 89
    ethnicity, 239
    home environment, 7
    intelligence, 70–71, 75, 76–77, 86–87, 97,
      238, 239
    learning proficiency, 77–78
    mental test performance, 7
    race, 70–71
    WISC scores, 35

Spatial ability, heritability of, 73–74
Spatial Relations Test, 201
Speed and Persistence Test, 54, 178, 179
Sprigle School Readiness Screening Test, 214, 219
SRA Non-Verbal Test, 219
SRA Primary Mental Abilities, 207
SRA Tests of Educational Ability, 212
Stanford Achievement Test-Reading, 54, 65, 66, 71, 75, 82, 91, 92, 93, 96, 205, 219, 246
Stanford Binet Intelligence Scale, Forms L and M, 5, 7, 8, 9, 10, 11, 13, 14, 15, 16, 18, 19, 21, 22, 23, 26, 27, 29, 33, 34, 35, 45, 46, 48, 50, 62, 64, 67, 69, 70, 75, 76, 79, 81, 82, 88, 89, 92, 95, 96, 97, 161, 166, 168, 196, 198, 208, 215, 229, 230, 231, 244, 247, 248, 291, 292
Stanford-Binet Intelligence Scale (L-M), 69, 70, 167, 200, 219, 221, 234, 239, 240, 246

T

Teacher attitudes, 41–42
Teacher expectation, based on race of student, 127
Teacher's race and effectiveness, 172–173
Teachers, test scores of, 110–111
Terman-McNemar Test of Mental Ability, 118
Test Anxiety Questionnaire, 183
Test bias, see Bias in testing
Test of Academic Aptitude (Short Form), 218
Tests of Academic Progress, 71, 72
Torrance Tests of Creative Thinking, 48, 169, 209
Truants, 146–147

U

U-Scale, 242

V

Van Alstyne Picture Vocabulary Test, 242
Vane Kindergarten Test, 9, 21
Vineland Social Maturity Scale, 7, 20, 21, 22, 150
Vocational rehabilitation, 243–244
    effects of on self-concepts, 213
    of the socially disadvantaged, 130–131

W

Wallin Pegboard B, 10
Wechsler Adult Intelligence Scale, 79, 102, 104, 106, 107, 132, 133, 134, 135, 137, 138, 140, 142, 143, 145, 146, 150, 151, 154, 168, 201, 213, 217, 227, 233, 243, 244, 294
Wechsler-Bellevue Intelligence Scale—Form I, 136, 137, 142
Wechsler Intelligence Scale for Children, 11, 15, 16, 23, 27, 28, 31, 32, 33, 35, 36, 37, 39, 43, 44, 45, 49, 50, 51, 59, 63, 65, 68, 70, 71, 74, 75, 76, 77, 79, 81, 82, 83, 89, 90, 93, 94, 95, 104, 105, 106, 107, 140, 142, 145, 146, 151, 153, 155, 156, 157, 164, 165, 173, 174, 175, 176, 188, 195, 196, 200, 203, 205, 208, 214, 219, 225, 226, 227, 229, 231, 236, 237, 239, 258, 277–289, 292
Wechsler Intelligence Scale for Children—Revised, 41, 57, 65, 71, 88, 95, 147, 194, 210, 235, 240, 241, 245
Wechsler Preschool and Primary Scale of Intelligence, 5, 8, 10, 11, 12, 13, 14, 15, 19, 20, 23, 27, 29, 61, 94, 95, 169, 170, 191, 207, 210, 219, 220, 226, 227, 291
Wide Range Achievement Test, 49, 84, 231, 239, 240
Wonderlic Personnel Test, 131, 135, 136, 137, 138, 143, 226, 294